But to *Adam* in what sort
Shall I appeer? shall I to him make known
As yet my change, and give him to partake
Full happiness with mee, or rather not,
But keep the odds of Knowledge in my power
Without Copartner? so to add what wants
In Femal Sex, the more to draw his Love,
And render me more equal, and perhaps,
A thing not undesireable, somtime
Superior: for inferior who is free?

Milton, *Paradise Lost*, Book ix

★ ★ ★ ★ ★

·J. R. POLE·

The Pursuit of Equality
in American History

★ ★ ★ ★ ★

REVISED EDITION

University of California Press

BERKELEY · LOS ANGELES · OXFORD

University of California Press
Berkeley and Los Angeles, California

University of California Press, Ltd.
Oxford, England

First Edition © 1978
First Paperback Printing 1979
Second Cloth Printing 1979
Second Edition Revised and Expanded © 1993 by
The Regents of the University of California

Originally presented as the Jefferson Memorial Lectures at Berkeley

Library of Congress Cataloging-in-Publication Data

Pole, J. R. (Jack Richon)
The pursuit of equality in American history / J. R. Pole.—2nd rev.
and expanded ed.
p.   cm.
"Originally presented as the Jefferson memorial lectures at Berkeley."
"A Centennial Book"—P.
Includes bibliographical references and index.
ISBN 0-520-07987-6 (alk. paper)
1. Equality before the law—United States—History.
2. Civil rights—United States—History.
3. United States—Constitutional history.   I. Title.
KF4764.P64   1993
342.73'085—dc20
[347.30285]   92-12928
CIP

Printed in the United States of America

9 8 7 6 5 4 3 2 1

The paper used in this publication meets the minimum requirements
of American National Standard for Information
Sciences—Permanence of Paper for Printed Library Materials,
ANSI Z39.48-1984. ♾

To the memory of
Richard Hofstadter

Contents

Preface

"A new nation, conceived in liberty and dedicated to the proposition that all men are created equal." Lincoln's words are a masterly fusion of the two central commitments of the American republic to its individual citizens and inhabitants. If people under American jurisdiction are equal in their rights, they cannot in the nature of things have unequal rights to other goods such as liberty or property. The idea of equality begins with a logical as well as a moral primacy in the nation's life. An egalitarian sense of social purpose has been allied to the moral status of equality of individual rights as a justification for the existence of the nation throughout the national life of the United States.

This primacy, however, has never amounted to exclusive possession. A study of the history of the idea of equality would claim too much for itself if it purported to be a complete account of American political and social thought, and I do not make that claim for this heavily revised version of *The Pursuit of Equality in American History*. Other concepts and convictions, giving priority to hierarchies of social, economic, or ethnic status, have always commanded their share of public consent. The idea of equality, however defined, has had to contend with these rivals for its claim on public policy as well as for private intercourse. These variant views are not mere aberrations from the American mainstream; the history of American social and political thought cannot be understood as the enactment of a single liberal or equalizing principle. Many Americans have positively rejected ideas of equality, and those who did the

rejecting have often made the rules by which the others had to live. Their views are encountered at frequent intervals in these pages; if they were not, indeed, the story of the struggle for equality would hardly need to be told. What can be claimed for the principle of equality is that it *engages* with these rival ideas and alternative preferences at crucial turnings in American public life. Although a history of the pursuit of equality may not amount to a complete history of American political thought, it is indispensable to an understanding of that history.

The specific contexts of demands for equality have thus been determined by a variety of challenges and circumstances both local and historical, which have taken the form either of anti-egalitarian social power or of divisions of interest among the categories of equality, which are explained in the analysis to follow. Thanks in no small part to the inspiration of Quentin Skinner, historians have become sensitive to the need to appreciate the ambience of historical context if they are to understand the precise historical meanings of political ideas; and this thesis has even broader connotations when those ideas have social and moral, and sometimes religious or scientific, elements which themselves condition the application of the ideas. Theories and convictions about equality take as their subject human nature in its various historical contexts. But this is not to assert that a particular historical context, say the period of the American or French revolutions, or that of Jacksonian democracy of the Civil War and Reconstruction, or of the civil rights struggle of the mid-twentieth century, can be conceived of and studied as though it were a self-sufficient historical entity. Every historical context is itself a complex phenomenon, which in the nature of the case has been historically arrived at; the deeds and the rhetoric of the past enter into and become part of the future.

In writing the original version of this book I was conscious of the need to keep in mind the subtle ways in which distinct contexts revealed their own shades of emphasis, sometimes leading to divergent meanings, in the concept of equality. In this extended revision, I have, I think, placed more emphasis on the not-less-subtle ways in which the ideas of the past in each of its phases have contributed to shaping a later present. Every specific instance of a historical context contributes to the shape and character of its successors.

A particular point needs to be made here about the specifically American aspect of this book's theme. A distinctive feature of the

American context arises from the federal structure of the national system of government. Even the branches of the central government, legislative, executive, and judicial, with structural differences between the legislative houses, have a kind of federalism in their relations to each other; beyond the federal government, the quasi-independence of the states stood for something like a century and a half as a semi-sacred barrier against the enforcement of uniform central policies. The problem was at its most intractable between the Reconstruction period that followed the Civil War and, roughly speaking, the renewed empowerment of federal government that accompanied the New Deal. This was a long period—for many, a lifetime. So long as the maintenance of this federal structure remained an object more sacred than that of securing the equal rights of individuals under the same Constitution, equality, even defined in its most elemental form as equality of rights, faced a formidable enemy from within the ranks of the governmental structure. Non-Americans have often found this hard to reconcile with the professed national commitment to equality as a constitutional principle. Americans have differed on the question depending on points of view, but have often appeared to remain satisfied with the federal solution, so long as their own particular oxen were not being gored.

However that may be, the federal principle as historically enforced suggests certain limits to the generalization of American experience. Much of the argument and analysis of this book has significant bearing on the experience of other countries which, in general terms, have an interest in egalitarian principles; there is no reason not to suppose that the categorical analysis which informs this book would prove its relevance in Europe, which has its own Charter of Human Rights—and, indeed, its own version of federalism. But historically at least, the American federal system has made the United States a special case. It seems unlikely that any other nation whose constitution was "the supreme law of the land" would have been determined to preserve its governmental structure at the cost of national policies to the extent of preventing the latter from being carried into effect for the benefit of its citizens.

When the demand for equality is explored to its historical depths, the analysis reveals the core of the peculiarly intense individualism that has characterized American life. (This is why Alexis de Tocqueville's preoccupation with equality in America demanded of him an equally profound analysis of individualism—a concept derived from France and whose

implications, for Tocquevillle, were not confined to America.) In more than one sense all this represents the American form of a general characteristic in societies that have come to be considered under the rubric of *modern*. Twenty or so years after the English appearance in 1840 of Tocqueville's book on America, a salient aspect of the individualist principle was reflected in Sir Henry Maine's celebrated remark, which has a strong claim to be considered one of the most-often-quoted sentences of its age, that "the movement of progressive societies has hitherto been a movement *from Status to Contract*."[1]

The definition, of course, has a circular tendency, since it is the movement from status to contract that defines societies as "progressive." The American contribution to this development had been particularly positive; status was formally abolished, and contract installed as a governing principle in the Constitution itself. The justice of this principle was founded on the assumed equality of contracting parties; even the state was believed to owe both its origins and its right to exist to somewhat analogous contractual agreements. The rapid expansion of the market economy soon translated equality in moral and contractual rights into equality of opportunity. This concept, one of the richest in the varied lexicon of equalities, proved to be a fountain of new possibilities. Opportunity, however, for what?

Opportunity for individual economic advancement was often offered as an end in itself. But self-advancement was a mere first step in the endless voyage of self-discovery. The American pursuit was only, perhaps, the American way of doing what others were doing—and had long been doing—in the varied contexts of their own cultures; but it was from asserted equalities of rights that Americans made their own progress to the assertion of a right to self-discovery and self-fulfillment. The Declaration of Independence itself authorized this pursuit, but it was to lead further than Jefferson or his generation would have imagined. Self-fulfillment, however, depended all too often on the will of others. For fairly obvious psychological reasons, it was attainable only for those who enjoyed the satisfactions of a modicum of self-respect. This crucial ingredient of an individual's psychology in an individualistic society was itself influenced, in some situations determined, by a host of surrounding

1. Sir Henry James Sumner Maine, *Ancient Law* (1861; Everyman ed., London, 1931), 100.

circumstances. When equality became a matter of public policy, it was gradually perceived as a fact of unavoidable import that some of these circumstances lay within the control or at the disposal of government. Equality of esteem, a distinctive class in the list of categories which were proposed in the original version of this work, was proved by experience to be a conditioning factor for the fulfillment of those individual satisfactions that seemed implicit in the American promise. I believe that this revision has more fully explored the processes by which the concept of equality of rights led by subtle courses to the demand for an equality of claims to self-respect. This subject has its own rich and extensive literature, and one consequence of this, for the present version of this book, has been that the problems of the social psychology and moral philosophy surrounding these questions have been brought into the argument.

This revision, however, has retained the original analysis of equality into separate categories, for the excellent reason that the analysis has stood the test of time. But by exploring their logical relationships and historical development in greater depth, many passages of this revision have, I hope, imparted a virtually new value to the history itself. Since the book was written, political demands for equality for new "class" categories have been put forth, such as for the disabled, the elderly, and indeed, for the ugly, with associated political demands. They do not find a place here. William of Ockham laid down that essentials should not be multiplied, a view by which I hope I have been influenced. On reflection, these additional classes appear to add nothing of substance to the individual rights and claims that find their place in the original list.

I have, however, taken advantage of this revision to suggest that in addition to the formal categories already referred to, equality may be considered as a metaphor. I have also have tested some of the limits of the idea which I called *interchangeability*. That notion was originally introduced on the assumption that women were in principle interchangeable with men. But that assumption has itself proved to be one of the sources of division among American women pressing for a more satisfactory place in society and a more substantial affirmation of their rights and of their sense of identity; a completely rewritten chapter on the subject explores the lines of tension between the rights-centered and the collectivist standpoints within the women's movement. The concept of interchangeability has proved its use both in historical analysis and the explorations of the aims and values of the women's movement. But it has

its deceptions, both for history and for policy. Interchangeability of *abilities* among individuals of opposite sexes, or of differing ethnic backgrounds, does not necessarily imply that their *motivations* are interchangeable. Neither women nor men can be required to *want* to do everything that the other sex want to do, nor to be what the other sex (or most of them) want to be. Freedom of choice on an equal basis cannot impose on individuals an obligation to select any particular choice.

It is a fairly commonplace observation that the historical American preoccupation with rights has not been accompanied by any comparable emphasis on obligations or duties. If people are equal in their rights, as claimed from the state, are they not equal in their duties owed to the state? The question has not been prominent in the numerous expositions of theories of rights. The classic Marxist moral formula called for each to give according to his ability that each might receive according to his need. (The masculine formulation in no way excludes females from the governance of this principle.) The original formula clearly implied that people had *differing* needs. But even in Marxist societies, no clear standard has been established for determining how and by what principles the needs of individuals were authorized to differ from each other. American makers of policy began to direct their attentions to the problem of defining not equal needs, but *minimum* needs, when the whole country was blasted by the Great Depression; the corollary of maximum needs never attracted much scrutiny. Except for some limited explorations into socialism, the idea of equality of obligation is a largely unwritten chapter in American thought, consisting at best of drafts and notes rather than continuous prose.

Historical silence leaves few records for research. The historian, along with the philosopher and the political scientist, is left to speculate. It is not difficult to see that in their preoccupation with individualist motives and individualist justifications, Americans have preferred to stress positive gratification than the seemingly more negative characteristics of social obligations. The historical formulation of the American doctrine of equal rights reinforced this preference, since the American concept of equal rights was codified at a period when most of the threats to those rights appeared to come from too-powerful and overbearing government; rights, so formulated, were in essence defenses against abuses of power by those in authority. This, however, introduced a paradox in the very nature of the American commitment: political authority was sup-

posed to be exercised only by governments resting on a majority of equal votes. Equal rights in one sphere might be threatened by the will of a majority of similarly equal rights when exercised politically. Problems arising from this kind of self-contradiction could not be resolved by recourse to first principles or to any automatic internal mechanism; nor does it seem that permanent and definitive solutions could be expected by reference to the solution of any one problem.

These difficulties did not in themselves explain American reluctance to develop a theory of the equality of political duties. But from the beginnings of the republic, economic prospects beckoned to reward enterprise and effort. When the state existed to confer protection and to reward aspiration, and when in fact it made exceptionally few demands on the individual, the idea of the individual's duty towards the state was a consideration of minimal significance. In American history, equal rights meant equal claims rather than equal obligations.

This principle was an essentially individualist principle. It has often been felt to be in competition with the aims and needs of collectivities, whether they were represented in the form of organized labor, of religious, racial, or ethnic groups, or of organized women. This book is a study in history, not a work of advocacy, still less a tract; but it is written in the conviction that a certain consonance exists between the American Constitution's regard for the rights of individuals and a much older and broader Western tradition which has particular regard for the integrity of the individual's experience and conscience. The primacy of the individualist principle, however, is a matter of history; it is not a law of nature, and it does nothing to diminish the force of collective sentiments or the efficacy of collective action. To the historian falls the task of recording and analyzing the nature of the internal conflicts that arose when these collectivities went so far as to claim to predominate over, even to supersede, the claim to individual rights as a moral foundation for political action. Whatever may be the reader's convictions, the author feels entitled to assert that no intelligent conclusions on the merits of these intense and often bitter controversies can be formed without an appreciation of their historical provenance.

It is clear, when one reviews the immense wealth of literature on various aspects of equality that has appeared since this book was published in its original version in 1978, that this revision literally could not have been written at an earlier date. While the author may claim that

much of the original version anticipated these developments, it is also true that much of the information and some of the most fascinating contributions to the debates on equality were not then available. It is equally true that this revision, which has been the work of several years, could not have come to light without the advice and comment I have received from a variety of scholars. My intellectual debts are numerous. Robert Lane, whatever he may think of the outcome, has always made his sagacious judgment available, and the text will show the importance of his friendly habit of transmitting his views in offprints of his essays. William Nelson, John Philip Reid, Eban Moglen, and members of the New York University Law School Legal History Colloquium were detailed and rigorous (in certain cases, explosive) in their comments. Substantial portions of the work were accomplished while, at Professor Nelson's invitation, I held a Goleib Fellowship at NYU Law School, and later during my tenure as a Senior Research Fellowship at the Center for the Study of American Culture at the College of William and Mary. Daniel W. Howe closely read most of the earlier half of the manuscript, while Michael Les Benedict gave me the benefit of a rigorous scrutiny of the passages dealing with the post-Reconstruction and Progressive periods. Other chapters have been read by Joyce Appleby, Eric Barendt, John Zvesper, and Elizabeth McCaughey. I owe a particular debt to Eric Foner for reviewing the entire manuscript. I would also like to thank Rebecca Starr and Marie-Madeleine Dunning for checking my references, while acknowledging my own responsibility for any errors that may have survived.

It would no doubt be possible to write as many different accounts of the history of the idea of equality as there are people who are interested in the subject; apart from the ordinary grounds of scholarly dispute, the issues are inherently political, and are subject to the heat of ideological passions. There would have been no way to unify all the points of view I have consulted. It may, for this reason, be more than ordinarily pertinent to exempt my generous and disinterested readers from complicity in my analysis or conclusions. I should add, by way of chronological explanation, that I have aimed so far as possible to conclude this narrative and analysis in the early 1980s. This has not always been consistently maintained, particularly with reference to the issues of religion, but in principle I preferred to avoid entering into a commentary on debates and events which are still current at the time of writing, and

promise to be at issue for an indefinite future. Those, too, will take their turn in history, and there is much in this record that flows directly into current debates. The present cannot steer or direct itself without understanding and coming to terms with the past, but historical judgment almost always gains from the perspective to be got from distance in time.

J. R. P.
Oxford
25 June 1992

Chapter One

The Idea of Equality
in a Hostile World

Not only were the people of Britain's North American colonies the first subjects of any of Europe's colonial empires to gain their independence from the Old World, but they were the first of any nation to base their national existence on an abstract moral principle. The principle that all men are created equal was inseparably woven into the moral foundation on which the Continental Congress justified the colonies' rebellion against the crown and the existence of the United States as an independent nation. The people who made these claims against British sovereignty did so in a collective capacity; the time had come, said the Declaration of Independence, for one people to separate itself from another. Yet the men who claimed this collective right to equality were animated by individualistic motives and sustained by an individualistic philosophy. By the same act they staked their claims as free individuals, equal in their freedom, equal in their rights and equal in the claims that those rights gave them against whatever government they lived under. This was a principle which they and their heirs would carry with them under new governments made at home.

Moreover, the truths which supported these claims were held to be "self-evident." Although the concept of self-evidence is by no means self-explanatory and had a long history dating at least from Thomas Aquinas, its overt rhetorical sense in the immediate, popular context of an appeal to "the opinion of mankind"—which meant American opinion

before any other—was plainly egalitarian. The force of these truths was equally accessible to everyone with the faculty of reason.[1]

Reason was held in high regard in the Enlightenment, in America no less than in Europe. But reason itself is not exactly a motive; the idea of equality owed much of its political power to forces that lay deeper than any possible articulation of abstract ideas. Long before the Declaration of Independence unified these forces, ideas of equality, less clearly expressed but no less passionately felt, had been serving as the vehicle for pent-up feelings of deprivation, resentment and social indignation. Ideas and ideals of equality have had more dynamic force in America than in any other major nation, and for this very reason, American history, more than that of any other nation, was destined to prove that equality could not be reduced to a single, indivisible concept, and still less to a principle that could hold together and guide the whole nation in all its manifold elements; and this was due to the earnestness of the commitment. Since the founding of the republic, equality as an idea, or as a metaphor, has owed much of its power of evolutionary survival to a proven ability to adapt itself to different interests in whose service it has assumed different meanings. A historical study of equality in America—and the same would be true elsewhere—is therefore inevitably in part a study in the history of language and meaning.

This should not be taken to mean that the study of equality is nothing more than another means of approach to the conflicts and disunities of American history. It is better taken as a means of understanding the republic through its own metaphorical language. For the very fact that the language is embedded in the organic laws of the United States and is indispensable to any formulation of its moral code has meant that Americans—to a greater extent than other peoples—have had to address themselves to the same texts, which were and remain accessible

---

1. According to one old philosophical tradition, a truth may be self-evident to some but not to others; Aquinas held that the intelligence of the perceiving mind affects the self-evidence of the thing perceived; but this of course does not mean that different *interpretations* of it are permissible, only that some minds can see the truth and that others cannot. Morton White, *The Philosophy of the American Revolution* (New York, 1978), 6–7. White observes that American revolutionaries could sanction various forms of elitism, which some of them certainly did; but there is no surviving evidence that these philosophical refinements entered into the discussions of the Continental Congress, and we may add that if they had, they would have undoubtedly impaired the moral appeal that the Declaration was expected to exert.

(though not perhaps self-evident) to all. The necessity to extract some intelligible meaning from the language of equality has caused Americans on different sides to address themselves to the same problems, addressing each other in a common dialogue, and frequently reaching variant conclusions in nuances of the same language.

Rhetoric should never be underestimated as a force in human affairs. It helps people to stake out their beliefs and gives them the courage to claim their rights. It has been primarily in circumstances of social ferment, or the threat of it, that ideas of equality have been able to stamp a lasting imprint on social institutions, but in more stable times that imprint has often survived to determine the cast of mind in which men and women confronted their future. In the pages that follow, the evocation of equality, its possible rival meanings, and the emotions behind them will necessarily appear principally in connection with familiar periods of upheaval, which have brought discontents to the surface and have sometimes reshaped the contours of society. The American Revolution in all its aspects constituted an upheaval which was also a point of departure and reference for all subsequent definitions of equality; it was a major event in the ideology and rhetoric of world history. America thenceforth became an example and bore a responsibility from which even isolationism could not entirely shield it. The religious revivals later called the Great Awakening had earlier begun to redefine the boundaries of sectarian relationships and laid foundations for a positive doctrine of religious equality, a process assisted by the application to public policy of philosophical principles that sprang less from religion itself than from Enlightenment ideas about religion.

If social and economic opportunities were not equally distributed in the early republic, they were numerous and geographically widespread. In certain areas, as we shall see later, these conditions not only took the edge off social discontent but satisfied a large proportion of politically capable voters that the material conditions and social comfort they possessed amounted to what they meant by "equality." In such circumstances, equality meant politically conservative resistance to change; that same conservatism could also mean resistance to opening the means to similar satisfaction to other classes or other races. At the most extreme, this meant that the fulfillment of the aspirations of one class was achieved at the cost of the dispossession of others; at the least, the exposure of this contradiction in the meaning of an apparently common

use of language reveals the limits of applied ideology. But the advance of inequalities that marked the rapid development of an industrial economy gave rise to new protests; and Andrew Jackson's egalitarian rhetoric and hostility to the Bank of the United States did little to check the real process of uneven redistribution that was taking place in Jacksonian America and in succeeding years. Yet for white Americans—and for them only—Jackson signaled conspicuous public recognition of the concept of equality of opportunity, which was soon to enter into the conventions of campaign rhetoric.

Upheavals are the moments of history when issues become most sharply identified. But it would be a mistake to concentrate on them as though they were devoid of historical context. The currents of dissatisfaction must run deep before a political upheaval turns into a moment of redefinition. Undoubtedly the Civil War and its aftermath brought about a redefinition of equality, though the underlying principles had already received constitutional sanction. The promise of "due process of law" incorporated in the Fifth Amendment in 1791 adopted the principle of equality before the law, at least in the narrow sense that in a society already professing republican principles, social privilege was theoretically banished from the courtroom. But in its early manifestations this was a protective doctrine, assuring procedural regularities rather than interventionist policies. This doctrine of protection against government intrusion, moreover, only served to emphasize the most abrasive contradiction in the American science of government; for the property rights protected included the right to own Negro slaves. Where the supposedly equal right of all men to their personal liberty conflicted with the equal right of all slave owners to their property in slaves, it was the latter which triumphed. In the most bitter of all acid tests, even the elements within the Jeffersonian trinity were found not to be equal among themselves, for the right of some men to pursue happiness through property trumped the right of others to liberty—and *their* right to pursue happiness, too.

What the Civil War and Reconstruction years achieved was to raise the question of whether equality before the law ought not for the future to call for governmental intervention rather than mere passive defense. Reconstruction did not succeed in resolving these problems in the lifetime of those who fought its battles; for a generation or more, egalitarians of race lost their grip on American development, even while other

issues took precedence in the name of equality of opportunity. Yet the idea of a national commitment that included all Americans, regardless of race or class or religion, and regardless eventually of sex, refused to die, because the unprivileged sections of the American community refused to accept defeat and were able to fight back with the rhetoric of egalitarian principles implanted so deeply in American ideology and in the Constitution itself. One of the most remarkable features of the period that began early in the twentieth century but gained impetus with the Depression, through the New Deal and more particularly out of the Second World War, was a prolonged insistence on equality as the central objective of social policy. The aim was to be achieved by varying combinations of education, exhortation, legislation, and constitutional law. Earlier phases had never lasted more than two or three presidential terms at most, but the war was swiftly followed by a new and prolonged threat to America's moral assurance and physical stability—Korea and the Cold War. To these external factors were added a civil rights movement of exceptional vitality, leadership, and social depth, and a Supreme Court possessed of an exceptional conviction as to the social obligations of the law.

The idea of equality, in its varying manifestations, had thus revealed since the nation's founding hours a tenacity which afforded a peculiar glamor to American claims and pretensions, and some justification to the offer, or threat, of social justice which America had always claimed to hold out to the common people in face of the empires, monarchies, priesthoods, social hierarchies, and all their attendant prejudices, of the Old World. The offer was open to white people only. The accessibility of the land to the multitudes from Europe and the multiplying masses of their descendants was a disaster for America's earlier native populations; neither African American slaves nor their free descendants were invited to share the benefits; Orientals in due course were either excluded or circumscribed. Constitutional logic followed the distribution of social and economic power—or was brusquely thrust aside. But constitutional logic nevertheless had a certain internal structure which could be put to effective use when subterranean shifts occurred in the society which it served.

The tenacity of American egalitarian principles and their ability to rebound under new circumstances owed a great deal to the historical structure of American institutions and to the constitutional origins of the

nation; similarly, the idea owed much of its vitality to the fact that equality had entered into the language of justice. Egalitarian movements of course consisted of vast social classes, but these classes were made up of individuals, and it was to individuals, without regard for their social definition, that the Constitution itself offered justice in the form of equal protection. Equal protection meant protection for legally equal individuals; the American Constitution and the ideology which informed it were grounded in a historically unusual insistence on the political primacy of the individual citizen. When dissatisfied individuals used the political or legal process to remind American governments of this obligation they did not always succeed in their aims, but they had the satisfaction, however remote, of warning the government that its entire right to govern was founded on this commitment. The concept of equality had achieved an unprecedented maturity in America by the time of the making of the Constitution. But it arose from a movement with ancient antecedents.

Philosophical Antecedents and Ancient Examples

Although ideas of equality resonated in the mythological founding of cities, they did not form a stable component of the ancient world's political, economic, or even philosophical life. When in fifth-century Athens the Sophists argued against all prevailing thought that men were equal in sharing the faculty of reason, they were thinking for the sake of thinking rather than responding to social discontent.[2] But the thought had a way of getting caught up in later movements. To say that all men—the notion was not extended to women—shared the faculty of reason was not necessarily to maintain that all shared it in an equal degree; the importance of the Sophists' observation was that it asserted a common humanity made explicit through a common faculty. It meant that men owed one another whatever was required of reasonableness, and it was egalitarian because it cut across the more conventional belief that differing endowments of reason, as also of virtue and other qualities, constituted precisely the differences that distinguished those who were to rule and those whose whole duty was to obey. Aristotle on the other hand was sure that all men possessed reason but thought that the

2. I am indebted to Professor George Forrest for comment on these matters.

distinguishing mark of slaves was that they possessed only so much of the power of reason as would enable them to understand their masters, without being able to reason for themselves; he concluded that manual workers ought not to participate in government because their lives denied them the opportunity to cultivate the qualities essential to wisdom.[3]

The truth that all men were capable of virtue and of experiencing happiness was perceived by Stoics and Epicureans as a kind of equality, but these opinions were rare and were maintained against the general current of the age or as philosophical generalities with little meaning for either governments or private authorities. None challenged the right of the naturally superior to rule the naturally inferior. Such assumptions were hardly questioned until the early Renaissance produced in the writings of Marsilius of Padua and Nicholas of Cusa an idea of equality which maintained, not that people were by nature equally endowed, but that all could and should in some way take their parts in law and government, through elections and councils, to the extent of their capacities. But these views could be upheld with any claim to plausibility only if one also claimed that the ignorant should consent to the rule of the wise.[4]

The concept of a republic, both as it was expounded in the writings of Machiavelli and in the historically modified forms in which it was received by the American republicans of the eighteenth century, owed more to certain familiar examples from Greece and Rome than to the ratiocinations even of their more celebrated philosophers. Sparta was believed to have been founded by Lycurgus on the basis of an egalitarian division of land and duties. Its simple but demanding way of life formed one of the prototypes of the values and mores that republics had to maintain if they were to survive.[5] In the political world that Aristotle

3. Aristotle, *Politics*, VII, ix, 1; I, v, 8. Trans. T. A. Sinclair, rev. Trevor J. Saunders (Harmondsworth, 1983). Plato, in the *Phaedo*, maintains that all equal things share in the *essence* of equality—which contributes little to its political necessity.

4. Sanford A. Lakoff, *Equality in Political Philosophy* (Cambridge, Mass., 1964), 12–59.

5. Americans knew the ancient world through the English translations of Plutarch's *Lives of the Noble Grecians and Romans*. Ancient history was also accessible in Montesquieu's *Spirit of the Laws*, published in 1748 and widely read in the colonies. The attractions of the Spartan way of life were not greatly appreciated by Alexander Hamilton, who described that city as "little better than a well regulated camp." *Federalist* 6, in Jacob E. Cooke, ed., *The Federalist* (Middletown, Conn., 1961).

surveyed from Athens some three and a half centuries before Christ, claims of equality had long caused civic dissension and instability; these threats, combined with Aristotle's concern for the principles of justice in civil society, justified a central place in his analysis of politics. The aim of the state was justice. "All men believe that justice means equality in some sense, and they are in limited agreement with the philosophy of justice which I explained in my *Ethics:* they hold that justice is some entity which is relevant to persons, and that equality must be equal for equals." The important thing was to compare like with like, and the essence of the problem—"for which we need political philosophy"— was to find those things to which the principle of equality was appropriate. [6] Democracy, Aristotle explained, "arose from the idea that those who are equal in one respect are equal absolutely." [7] Although Aristotle was acutely aware of the pressure exerted by the seafaring classes, particularly the rowers of the Athenian navy, and of seaport populations, on demands for democracy, he believed they should form no part of the political state; his real faith was that an agricultural people "with no great abundance of possessions" was best adapted for democracy, and he approved laws which prohibited the acquisition of lands beyond prescribed amounts. [8] Throughout this analysis he insisted on the dangers to social stability that arose from grievances inflicted by injustice in forms perceived as inequalities; and outraged feelings of honor seem to have been just as emotive as economic discontents. There were various forms of government that could achieve stability, but the best and safest government was the kind in which justice itself gave assurance of stability; and justice, as we have seen, always required that people be satisfied by equal treatment. The argument was richly informed by the social psychology of dispossession; but Aristotle did not translate these sentiments into those assertions of *rights* which have played such a formative part in the thoughts of Anglo-American constitutional thinkers. [9]

Aristotle drew from a wide range of historical examples. But it was the Roman Republic that provided republican thinkers from the Renais-

6. *Politics,* III, xii.
7. Ibid., V, i.
8. Ibid., VI, iv; VII, vi.
9. Ibid., III, ix, x, xi, xii; V, i.

sance onward with the most exemplary case of an attempt to legislate for some sort of landowners' equality in the celebrated Agrarian Law of Tiberius Gracchus. Unfortunately, however, this ambitious attempt to check the acquisition of great private estates carries an ambiguous legacy for those who would teach from republican examples. It was clearly consistent with the principles of equality and simplicity which were so generally held to be at the foundation of republican values, and it reappeared as the cardinal principle of James Harrington's *Oceana*, originally published in 1656, which transmitted some of the central values of the English Commonwealth to successive generations in England and America. Yet the Gracchian experiment had disastrously failed, exciting the wrath of all-too-powerful patricians; Machiavelli, who repeatedly emphasized the virtues of republican poverty and its attendant simplicity, blamed the Gracchian law for ruining the republic.[10] The landowners, speculators, and merchants who dominated the formative phases of the American Republic were not likely to endanger their ambitions with an agrarian law of their own making.

Americans educated in the whig tradition shared with their British contemporaries a veneration for Cicero, who was affectionately known as "Tully" from his middle name, Tullius. Latter-day libertarians could derive inspiration from Cicero's passionate defense of the Roman Republic in its last days. Cicero, who described the state as "an association of citizens united by law," claimed that equality of rights was "part of the law." He asked rhetorically by what principle of right an association of citizens could be held together when the status of these citizens was not equal. To say this was not to say that all men could be equal in property or natural capacity; the equality that ought to be enjoyed by all who were citizens of the same commonwealth was an equality of rights in their mutual relations.[11]

This principle was to have a profound continuity, and capacity for revival, in the traditions of republican political thought; it was compatible, given allowances for different historical traditions and a considerable extension in the circumference of concern, with the view of such American political philosophers as Ronald Dworkin and Michael Walzer in the

10. *Discourses*, I, xxxvii; I, iii; III, i; xxv.

11. Cicero, *On the Commonwealth*, XXXII, trans. George Holland Sabine and Stanley Barney Smith (rpr., Indianapolis, 1976), 136–37.

late twentieth century that government owed it to all persons under its authority to treat them with equal *respect*. [12]

Ably supported by Tacitus and Sallust, Cicero had expounded views of law and liberty which merged convincingly with the English tradition. But these sources were wholly secular. When American colonists expounded the law, on the other hand, they frequently invoked their religious provenance. The Ten Commandments had made no distinctions of rank or person. The first monotheistic religion instructed its followers of the threat of God's equal justice with at least as much credibility as of the assurance of his equal love. Nor did the Old Testament offer much prospect of alleviation from this formidable aegis by way of separation of church and state.

And then, in the teachings and sufferings of Jesus, there appeared among the Jewish people of the early Roman Empire a different perspective from that of political theory, and one not generally represented among the founders of republican ideology. A distinction was first suggested between the things that were Caesar's—the secular power—and the things that were God's. Particularly as expounded by Paul, these doctrines informed the mind of Christendom, East and West, that terrestrial inequalities would have no influence on the final judgment. But there was something subversive about this doctrine. It taught humble men and women that certain spiritual values were of greater significance than any worldly power, and there would always thenceforth be some who would defy worldly powers in the name of those values. But the Church could not afford such humility. When, from the time of Constantine, it became a secular power in its own right, its leaders probably acquired more expertise in the crafts of politics and war than they taught by way of spirituality. For the Christian prince, the obvious tactic was to co-opt the Church as an arm of government; only at rare moments in Western history has the egalitarian principle at the heart of Christianity entered more than briefly into the calculations of Christian statesmen. Christianity, however, placed on every individual Christian a considerable burden of responsibility for his or her own salvation, a doctrine which some Christian sects could later carry to the poor and dispossessed with disconcerting consequences for whatever powers at particular times were, in the Apostle's words, "the powers that be." The political mean-

12. These writers are discussed in Chapter 14.

ings of these doctrines have never entirely ceased to disturb the composure of ecclesiastical authorities and their secular allies.

The wisdom of the ancient world and the spirituality of the Christian religion sprinkled through many channels into the education of the generations who settled North America and founded its various states. Less than a century before the planting of the English colonies, the Christian church itself underwent a schismatic convulsion which had profound consequences for ideas of equality. In principle, the Protestants removed the mystery from the priesthood and—with the indispensable assistance of the invention of printing—made the Bible accessible to every churchgoer. In practice this more usually meant making it available to heads of families: it is risky to generalize the democratic process. Similar reservations immediately apply to the social consequences of printing, which governments almost invariably claimed the power to control. But to be left with the Protestant spirit, in an age of increasing commercial and intellectual enterprise, is far from being left empty-handed. Scripture was made accessible as a matter of principle, and lay persons could themselves read and meditate on the texts their ministers expounded. A remarkably similar revolt against the mystery of the ministry was to occur in America beginning in the 1730s: like the Reformation, the Great Awakening was a revolt against authority, but its course was much easier than that of the early Protestants because it all took place within the aegis of the Protestant religion, so that the rebels could seize weapons from the armory of the established clergy.

During the early generations of American settlement, theories of equality, or about equality, could be extracted from a variety of sources. One of the most powerful was Hugo Grotius's *Introduction to the Jurisprudence of Holland*, published in 1619–20, which argued for a connection between rights and the laws of nature. The law of nature did not decree protection for universal and inalienable rights, which had not yet appeared in political thought; it did decree respect for the obligation of contract, and "sociability," the essential condition of human life, similarly entailed respect for the rights of individuals. [13] Rights were ineffective without law. But English law had always recognized an array of legally specified rights, of which the authoritative English source rediscovered

13. Richard Tuck, *Natural Rights Theories, their Origin and Development* (Cambridge, 1981 [?]), 68; 90–94; 127.

and celebrated by the common lawyers and parliamentarians of the early seventeenth century was no other than Magna Carta. The fermenting world of commerce might have little time for abstractions, but it attached importance to those rights that were to be found in contracts sustained by the common law of England. None of this carried doctrines of universal rights or universal equality; what was implied, however, amounted to certain specified *equalities,* and in this sense all the free men of England were supposed to enjoy certain fundamental protections under the aegis of Magna Carta. [14]

It would be extravagant to maintain from this that either King John and his rebellious barons in 1215 or the common lawyers some four hundred years later intended to lend their names to ideas of equality. But the outbreak of civil war in the 1640s suddenly unstopped a spate of social discontent, of religious passion and clamorous demands for political attention, which had no precedent in English history. In an early pamphlet, John Lilburne asserted that the "only and sole legislative law-making power *is originally inherent in the people, and derivatively in their Commissions chosen by themselves by common consent, and no other. In which the poorest he that lives hath as true a right to give a vote, as the richest and greatest."* [15] The Puritan imperatives behind this thinking would have been well understood by Lilburne's contemporary, Roger Williams, over the sea in Rhode Island. John Wildman demanded elections to Parliament in which "all free-born men at the age of twenty-one years and upwards be the electors"—excepting those who by delinquency had deprived themselves of their freedom. [16] But the Levellers were by no means of one view, and the more democratic assertions proved difficult to sustain in detail, principally because the Levellers in general shared the prevailing belief that a free individual must be independent of the will of any man. Maximilian Petty was thus not inconsistent when he said at one point, "We judge that all inhabitants that have

14. The most frequently invoked is in clause 39: "No free man shall be taken, imprisoned, disseised, outlawed, banished, or in any way destroyed, nor will We proceed against or prosecute him, except by the lawful judgment of his peers and by the law of the land." And clause 40: "To no one will We sell, to none will We deny or delay, right or justice."

15. John Lilburne, *The Charters of London,* quoted by C. B. Macpherson, *The Political Theory of Possessive Individualism* (Oxford, 1962), 3–4.

16. John Wildman, "The Case of the Army Truly Stated," in A. S. P. Woodhouse, ed., *Puritanism and Liberty* (Chicago, 1951), 433.

not lost their birthright should have an equal voice in elections" but later admitted that "apprentices, or servants, or those that take alms" should be excluded because "they depend upon the will of other men and should be afraid to displease them. For servants and apprentices, they are included in their masters." [17]

General Henry Ireton, speaking for the army command, returned again and again to the interests of property: "I think," he declared, "that no person hath a right to interest or share in the disposing of the affairs of the kingdom, and in determining and choosing those that shall determine what laws we shall be ruled by here—no person hath a right to this, that hath not a permanent fixed interest in this kingdom"—an expression echoed by George Mason when he wrote the Virginia Declaration of Rights some century and a quarter later. [18] But true Levellers could not agree to define the purposes of the state by the protection of property. "The chief end of this government," said Major William Rainborough, "is to preserve the persons as well as the estates, and if any law shall take hold of my person it is more dear than my estate." [19]

These were the voices of a small minority heard at a rare moment of political opportunity. But theirs was not the only sense in which equality could be understood. The egalitarianism of the Levellers' great contemporary, Thomas Hobbes, was that of total submission. All subjects of the Leviathan were subject equally to its laws and equally powerless; for this was the only way for humanity to extricate itself in safety from the terrible war of all against all that was its natural condition. Yet the struggles and intense theological embroilments of the seventeenth century also gave rise to a weariness of dogmatism and with it a new, more indulgent mood characterized by the increasingly affectionate Latitudinarian interest in—and optimism about—human nature.

This new philosophy of benevolence, which profoundly influenced the third Earl of Shaftesbury and the Scottish philosopher Francis Hutcheson (Adam Smith's teacher) contained the seeds of a more systematic theory of equality. [20] John Locke had taught Shaftesbury's grandfather,

---

17. Woodhouse, ibid., 53, 83.

18. Ibid., 57; W. W. Hening, *Statutes of Virginia*, II, 280.

19. Woodhouse, ibid., 67.

20. Benevolence quite rapidly came to be so widely received that Alexander Pope was able to adopt it as a theme of his vastly popular poem, *An Essay on Man*, which was composed in the early 1730s in one of the poet's own rather rare benevolent periods. For

the first Earl, that in the state of nature that had preceded the organization of civil society, people had a natural *right* to property but they had no means of protecting these rights. The purpose of civil law was to incorporate natural rights, but it could never supersede them. This was a different view from that of Hobbes, who held that natural and civil law occupied the same moral space.[21] For Locke and his disciples the function of civil law was to give security to already existing natural rights. Just government could come into existence only by the consent of those who voluntarily entered into it and lived under it for the protection of rights already recognized by natural law.

Two distinct themes of great future significance were implicit in these views. One is sometimes called "voluntarism" because it founded the state on personal motive and independent action; in the eighteenth and early nineteenth centuries, with the emergence of laissez-faire in political economy and the development of theories of competitive free enterprise, this doctrine would broaden into a general attitude concerning the relationship of society to its members and thence into a view of the obligations of government. French political thinkers articulated the concept of "individualism" to describe this new principle, which, though it soon came to be recognized as the motivating force of entrepreneurial economics was used for many years as a term of condemnation; it is no doubt of some significance that it gained its earliest favorable connotation in the United States.[22]

The second of these themes was that of equality. For if people had voluntarily decided to enter into a compact to form a civil society, then at least to the extent of being signatories to the agreement, they were equals; each would have been equally free *not* to enter. These individual people with their equal wills had each a similar interest in securing their properties; and the fact that the amounts of property could differ made

---

an excellent discussion of the process, in the context of the origins of anti-slavery thought, see David Brion Davis, *The Problem of Slavery in Western Culture* (Ithaca, 1966), 348–64.

21. *Leviathan*, I, ch. 15.

22. Koenrad W. Swart, "Individualism in the mid-Nineteenth Century (1826–1860)," *Journal of the History of Ideas* XXIII (1962): 77–90; Yehoshua Arieli, *Individualism and Nationalism in American Ideology* (Cambridge, Mass., 1964), 225–31; J. R. Pole, "American Individualism and the Promise of Progress," an inaugural lecture, University of Oxford, 1980.

no difference to the equality of wills, because each had to be motivated by an equal interest in his *own* property.

In Locke's thought this approach was fortified by the belief that God had given the world to men in common, and that no one was entitled to possess more than he could actually use for himself and his family. The difficulties of reconciling this position with Locke's attributed plans for a hierarchical distribution of land, rank, and political power in Carolina for the use of his patron Shaftesbury are well known to students of his thought; they can be resolved to the extent that these conditions were believed to give settlers the opportunity for the degree of material independence that made men fit for freedom.[23] Although Locke did not believe that all persons were equal in native abilities, there was a sense in which his epistemology contained both a marked individualism and a latent egalitarianism; for if each individual's mind began life as a tabula rasa, a blank sheet on which life was to imprint experience, were not these blank minds in some sense equal at their beginnings?[24]

The radical streak in Locke's thinking had subversive implications for the social and political order of his time.[25] The increasing influence of his political thought in the American colonies especially after about the middle years of the eighteenth century gave considerable moral legitimation to the doctrines which became precepts for Thomas Jefferson. In the Declaration of Independence, where Locke's "Life, liberty and estate" became "Life, liberty, and the pursuit of happiness," the whole position rested on the foundation of natural equality in human rights.[26]

23. M. Eugene Sirmans, *Colonial South Carolina: A Political History, 1663–1763* (Chapel Hill, N.C., 1966), 8–9, takes the view that the weight of the argument in the question of Locke's collaboration with Ashley (later Lord Shaftesbury) indicates that the ideas were mainly Ashley's.

24. John Locke, *Essay Concerning Human Understanding*, ed. A. S. Pringle-Pattison (Oxford, 1934), II, ch. xxvii. There may be an escape from this difficulty by way of the view, which Locke does not appear to have considered, that even in their blank states, human minds were different and unequal in their natural powers to interpret experience.

25. Julian H. Franklin, *John Locke and the Theory of Sovereignty* (Cambridge, 1978), esp. chs. 3 and 4. Locke's commitment to, and involvement in, radical politics, and their relationship to his political thought, are explored in Richard Ashcraft, *Revolutionary Politics and Locke's Two Treatises of Government* (Princeton, 1986).

26. By 1753, when William Livingston of New York and his associates were writing the essays published as *The Independent Reflector*, he was already "the renowned Mr. LOCKE." Soon after, he is "the celebrated Mr. LOCKE." Milton M. Klein, ed., *The Independent Reflector* (Cambridge, Mass., 1963), 173, 406. James Otis asserted the value of Locke's

For Locke the postulates of the condition of natural equality of rights were at least in a residual sense more theological than for Jefferson. Locke's views descended from the Calvinistic doctrine of the calling, which was a summons from God, but a summons which it was each adult individual's duty to interpret for himself (or herself).[27] But Locke was writing on civil government, not ecclesiastical; the rights he affirmed must by an inevitable logic contain the principles of equality which made them good for individuals consenting to live under civil government.

All this appears to give the idea of human equality an encouraging warrant of moral, intellectual and theological respectability. But these ideas had to fight for their survival in a predominantly hostile world, where massive inequalities of power were arranged to correspond with commensurate inequalities of property, and in which the moral principle of equality suffered the fate of being incorporated into this very structure of power. Alexander Pope stated the case with characteristic felicity in perhaps his most widely read poem:

> Order is Heavn's first law, and this confest,
> Some are, and must be, greater than the rest,
> More rich, more wise; but who infers from hence
> That such are happier, shocks all common sense.
> Heaven to mankind impartial we confess,
> If all are equal in their happiness:
> But mutual wants this happiness increase;
> All nature's difference keeps all nature's peace.[28]

Material inequalities, linked to the structure of political power, were justified on the ground that they promoted an equality of happiness, a

---

contribution over that of "a *few* of other nations" with a meaningful reference to "our *English* writers" in *The Rights of the British Colonies Asserted and Proved*, in Bernard Bailyn, ed., *Pamphlets of the American Revolution*, vol. 1 (1750–1765) (Cambridge, Mass., 1965), 436–37. Jefferson, who regarded Bacon, Newton, and Locke as the guiding spirits of modern civilization, described Locke's little book on government as "perfect as far as it goes." Nathan Schachner, *Thomas Jefferson: A Biography* (New York, 1957), 391. Locke's influence on both American and British thought in the eighteenth century is explored by Isaac Kramnick, *Republicanism and Bourgeois Radicalism: Political Ideology in Late Eighteenth Century England and America* (Ithaca, N.Y., 1990).

27. John Dunn, *The Political Thought of John Locke* (Cambridge, 1969), 223.

28. *Essay on Man*, IV, 49–56. The poem appeared in two parts in 1733 and 1734. It will be noted that the idea that happiness was the object of the social order was already familiar. Pope was anything but an original thinker, and the neat balance of his harmonious pentameters and pungent couplets reinforced almost to the point of parody the central doctrine of order contained in the lines.

theory that could hardly have appeased social envy or fed the hungry. But it hinted at a need to explain the social order on the principle that each individual's needs were to be given equal consideration, a theme capable of development in the hands of political reformers. Arthur O. Lovejoy, who employed this passage to emphasize the theme of hierarchy in his magnificent exposition of the Great Chain of Being, undervalued this point when he broke off the quotation in the middle of the third line.[29]

According to the cosmology of the Great Chain, which dominated much Western thought at least from the fifteenth century until it ran to ground in the egalitarian indignation of the Enlightenment, the human race was only one link in the Great Chain which bound the whole order of the universe from God downward in a series of interdependent gradations. It was a concept of superb aesthetic harmony which enabled people to think about the cosmic order with greater comfort, and moreover with greater clarity and certainty, than they have been able to do under the auspices of General Relativity. By a powerful analogy it also provided an explanation for the necessity of rank and authority in the kingdoms of the world. Mankind was believed to occupy a special position in the Chain, halfway between the angels and the beasts, incorporating some of the qualities of each but actually superior to the angels in the power of reason. This imagery stenciled in people's minds a picture which reflected the existing structure of political authority, with power descending from the king and his court through different ranks marked off from one another by birthright and title.[30]

God created nothing in vain. The universe had been constructed on the principle of plenitude, by which everything in existence had its use to the whole and everything that could be of use to the whole must already be in existence, a state of affairs that left no justification for dissatisfaction and no room for improvement. It was the principle of plenitude that satisfied Jefferson that if dinosaurs had once existed on earth, as proved by the finding of their bones, they must exist somewhere still, if only they could be found.[31] The point is of interest because it is an example of that common phenomenon, the co-existence of

29. Arthur O. Lovejoy, *The Great Chain of Being* (Cambridge, Mass., 1948), 206.

30. A classical exposition of the theory will be found in E. M. W. Tillyard, *The Elizabethan World Picture* (London, 1938).

31. Daniel Boorstin, *The Lost World of Thomas Jefferson* (New York, 1948), 41.

archaic and newer ideas in the same intellectual structure. Yet by virtue of its very completeness, the theory had in the most obvious sense nowhere to go. It could answer no new questions except by positing subdivisions of its own orders, and when early geological discoveries began to indicate that some parts of the world were older than others, the Great Chain of Being was doomed; it constituted a perfect example of an exhausted scientific paradigm.

This cosmic picture had in truth never been linked with the order of human affairs by any strictly logical connection. It was no more than an analogy. It did not follow from the Great Chain of Being, of which mankind was one sector, that an identical chain must connect the creatures *within* that sector; it would have been just as logical to think of all men as equals within their allotted space. The analogy with divine authority would have had little force if it had not served the interests of the secular powers, who were also able to summon the Pauline doctrine that secular power was vested with divine authority. (Among the preachers of printed election sermons in colonial New England there was probably no more popular text than Romans 13: "The powers that be are ordained of God.") There was no one of equal weight to confute these views emanating from the oracles of church and state, no less from New England magistrates and divines than from those of the Old World. Except in the most abstract moral sense, ideas of earthly equality thus had few friends in the hard world of political authority or distribution of wealth; such ideas were subversive of almost all the received precepts of order on which these institutions depended for their survival. It was not for nothing that the early Christians were regarded as a threat to the existing order or that when in time the Church came to terms with the state it coined the word *hierarchy* to describe the ecclesiastical structure of degree and authority which in important ways reflected those of the secular power.

When great inequalities in society were seen and felt as great injustices, equality became a program of action. But its social force derived from a moral intuition rather than a doctrine.[32] In America as anywhere

---

32. "Intuitive dissatisfaction is an essential resource in political theory. It can tell us that something is wrong, without necessarily telling us how to fix it." Thomas Nagel, "Equality and Partiality," The John Locke Lectures at the University of Oxford, March, 1990, 1–9. I am much indebted to Professor Nagel for letting me see his draft of these lectures.

else in the world, it proved exceptionally difficult to convert this intuition into a credible rationale for a new social order. On such questions as how civil society was to be organized, how it should meet the needs of supply and demand, or how it might provide military defense or organize systems of justice and administration, equality, as an ideal, suffered from an inherent weakness; it had very few suggestions to offer that could challenge the authority of the existing structures of moral, theological and economic power. If ideas of equality were to survive or make progress, their proponents had to prove themselves equal to two intellectual tasks: they had to convince their contemporaries that these existing orders, derived from an ever more distant feudal past, were either unjust or inefficient or both, and they had to proceed from this to argue that equality was compatible with effective economic and political institutions. It may be doubted whether this latter argument has ever fully succeeded.

Chapter Two

In the American Environment:
Emergence of a Self-Evident Truth

Unusual Opportunities—Unequal Results

For reformist thinkers of eighteenth-century Europe, whatever their faith in the ultimate triumph of reason, the practical prospects appeared bleak. The masses of the people, whether rural or urban, were held in subordination by crippling taxation, deprivation of the meanest judicial rights, and a total lack of direct political power. When the French *philosophes* confronted the problems of social justice in this context, the demand for equality of burdens and duties, supported by the necessary ligaments of equality before the law, came to light as the elemental demand of social justice. In these circumstances the demand for equality emerged not as an articulated or detailed theory of government but as a cry of outrage, corresponding exactly to Giovanni Sartori's description of it as a "protest ideal." [1] But social resentment did not have the power to convert it into a clearly defined political objective. The *philosophes* were in general prepared to strengthen the monarchy as the only agency capable of reducing the nobility and the Church. The French monarchy, never able to nerve itself to the task, eventually disappeared in the avalanche which buried not only the orders, ranks, privileges, and abuses of the ancien régime, but also much of its progress, humanity, and promise.

1. Giovanni Sartori, *Democratic Theory* (New York, 1965), 325–26.

In Britain's American colonies the social situation was profoundly different. No single hierarchy unified the vast semi-circle of possessions reaching down from the continent to the lucrative Caribbean islands, whose many climates, economies, and governments could not be said to sustain a single social structure. The great molding and unifying force of the monarchy itself was present in name and authority but correspondingly conspicuous by its absence from colonial soil and assembly politics. Colonial societies had their distinctive characters, and each was held together by sanctions which included the power of property together with a traditional deference for visible authority and social status. Ambitious men, if they had an advantageous beginning or a stroke of good fortune, were rather more likely to find opportunities for improvement in colonial society, which offered fewer heights to scale than that of Britain or elsewhere in Europe, but probably more paths of access to those heights that were in view.

But ambition for personal advancement is not an inherently egalitarian motive. The great landlords of the Connecticut River valley, of the Hudson valley, of northern New Jersey, of the Chesapeake Bay, and of South Carolina owed their vast wealth and consequent social influence and political power to a variety of factors, among which inheritance often played a significant part, but there was little in their styles of life to acknowledge much obligation to the principles of equality. It is true that both they and the great merchants who dominated the politics of the seaport cities occasionally permitted themselves the luxury of more democratic sentiments than were often heard from their British contemporaries, a tendency which gained marked impetus under the stresses of the domestic political scene during the Revolution. Twenty years before independence the Philadelphia Presbyterian leader Francis Allison hinted at a wider social vision when he told his congregation of his hope for "equal laws, equally executed," for all were entitled to protection, to reap the benefit of honest industry, with equal access to public honors and places of profit and trust according to their abilities and qualifications to serve the public; equal rights and privileges went with equal burdens. [2] But this sort of general social criticism was still rare. There existed virtually no such concept as that of redistribution of wealth in the name

2. Francis Allison MSS, Presbyterian Historical Society, Philadelphia; sermons, folder 5, V; 1756.

of social justice; even slavery was only beginning to be questioned, and then for the most part in Pennsylvania, where its abolition would make little economic difference.

Not that society enjoyed a state of profound and harmonious peace; land riots in New York in the 1760s were at least in part a response to population pressures that could threaten the security of some of the more extended—and unutilized—of these landed properties. But significantly these disorders were treated by the provincial authorities as matters of law and order, not of issues for the political agenda. The magisterial classes might be men of well-authenticated commonwealth principles, particularly when it came to relations with Britain, but in their own domains they were not required to have a program of social reform.

With some exceptions, the same could be said of the dissident elements in these societies. The sporadic outbreaks of discontent that occurred in both countryside and cities following the stresses and costs of the mid-century wars were impelled by indignation but not sustained by theory; there was, on the whole, very little by way of systematic political analysis pointing in the direction of a radically egalitarian reorganization of society. Even the better organized Regulators of North and South Carolina, the former of whom could mount a pitched battle against government troops, suffered ultimately from the same kind of weakness. Their sufferings from exploitation, banditry, and misgovernment were bitter, and their remedies extreme. These conditions drove the Regulators of North Carolina somewhat closer to a social theory than was usual among their contemporaries. These reformers-in-arms related their condition directly to failures in the political and judicial system. Significantly, for their grievances were purely internal and had nothing to do with colonial grievances against Britain, the North Carolina Regulators cited as the basic cause of their discontent "the unequal chances the poor and the weak have in contentions with the rich and the powerful."[3] But despite their tough resistance, they were broken in battle, and their defeat was followed by executions; like other dissidents elsewhere, they lacked the political ingredients that reform movements would need to carry their aims. Elsewhere, grievances against landlords in rural areas

---

3. Marvin L. Michael Kay, "The North Carolina Regulation, 1766–1776: A Class Conflict," in Alfred F. Young, ed., *The American Revolution: Explorations in the History of American Radicalism* (De Kalb, Ill., 1976), 88.

and against government that was felt to favor the rich were none the less serious for being vocal more often than violent. But dissidents everywhere suffered from similar disadvantages. They had no general power base in the country, little capacity for political organization, and hardly even a coherent ideology.

This lack of coherence was not far below the surface of political unity even in Pennsylvania, where radical ideals fused with political organization more effectively than anywhere else in the revolutionary colonies. The issue reflected a tension between those who wanted to put the primary emphasis of their republican philosophy on individual rights and those who emphasized the primary interests of the community. Ultimately, no doubt, there could be no individual rights without a community in which to exercise them, and no valid republican community without an effective defense of individual rights. But in circumstances where private interests, whether religious, economic, or political, were clashing with community demands for economic control and political conformity, the differences could quickly run to extremes. During the war that soon followed, Benjamin Rush, who had good radical credentials, pursued the line of individual rights, while the no less radical Christopher Marshall insisted that society had needs to which private self-interest must be subordinate. The precise meaning of republicanism, as Eric Foner has remarked, remained to be worked out;[4] but it would have been optimistic, if not partisan, to have claimed that any one precise meaning would ever be a matter of agreement.

For similar reasons, it would have been foolhardy rather than prophetic to have looked forward from some notional point in the middle of the century to foresee the proclamation of the ideal of natural rights equality as the general principle of the American people. Yet that is what happened in the American Revolution. And the flag was inscribed and unfurled by the privileged leaders of an unequal society. History may have taken this leadership by surprise, but when its more articulate members looked back at what they had done, they could discern a logic in it all that was hidden from the ordinary practitioners of colonial politics.

In the course of some century and a half of development, in America as elsewhere, unequal opportunities had led to unequal results. But the

4. Eric Foner, *Tom Paine and Revolutionary America* (London, 1976), 119–20.

experiences of American settlement and growth could not ratify these results with the sanction of ancient privilege; a colonial gentleman's education contained a portion of republican principles, which blended more harmoniously with his experience of both social and political life than could have been the case in England. The small landowner and artisan entertained no extended views of a new social order. What they wanted was not real equality so much as space, some security, and a conviction of personal independence; the larger landowner, who already possessed these advantages, would be more likely to seek assurance that his position was a reflection of his true worth. Even privilege had in some degree to be earned. It is in this light that demands for and assertions of equality are best understood, and given this understanding and the disorders of a revolutionary political situation, these demands and assertions rapidly became a powerful moral and social force.

George Mason, one of the biggest land and slave owners in northern Virginia, and one who had imbibed the purest republican principles, made an illuminating contribution to the mystique of American equality with some remarks, seemingly written in April 1775, on annual elections in the Fairfax Independent Company, a militia company whose training had become a matter of more than mere formal display with the menacing news of conflict in the Northeast. The fact that both the members and officers of this company were elected was a cause for republican satisfaction. "Upon this generous and public-spirited plan," Mason observed, "gentlemen of the first fortune and character among us have become members of the Fairfax Independent Company, have submitted to stand in the ranks of common soldiers, and pay due obedience to officers of their own choice." The company was in fact limited to one hundred members. It had been formed at a meeting of "a Number of Gentlemen and Freeholders of Fairfax County" with Mason himself in the chair; these gentlemen do not seem to have subjected themselves to much risk of having to take orders from their social inferiors. The principle which Mason upheld was that of taking orders from one's equals, but his style clearly reveals that taking orders from anyone at all was a new idea for Virginia gentlemen. Mason's memorandum contains the famous statement, "We came equals into this world, and equals we shall go out of it," which reverberates with an echo from Ecclesiastes but does not preclude inequalities between these two salient events. There is no occasion to doubt Mason's sincerity. His principles throughout his

life were consistently republican and illustrate the pride of a republican aristocrat.[5]

The self-assurance of the colonial upper classes was almost everywhere sustained by an equally assured grip on the institutions of political, legal, and economic power. They held dominant positions on legislative committees, served as judges and magistrates, formed bar associations, were well placed to adapt their plantations to changes in soil productivity or their businesses to market pressures; their credit enabled them to borrow both for expansion and for self-protection. They were coming increasingly in the mid-eighteenth century to adopt lifestyles of conspicuous social distinction.

Privilege and Protest

Allowing for inevitable difficulties facing a developing economy interrupted by wars, shortages of currency, inconsistent capitalization, and very wide differences in such matters as soil fertility, the colonies were doing well compared with other sectors of the Atlantic world. By restricting the comparison to the free population, it can be shown that the colonial wealth shortly before the Revolution compared not unfavorably per capita with that of Great Britain. The upward trend in price levels and the exceptionally high rate of population increase, which doubled approximately every twenty-five years, strongly suggest that colonists in general had some confidence in the future.[6] Within and among the colonies, however, the distributions of wealth were conspicuously uneven. One way of putting the statistics together suggests that greater inequalities of wealth existed in New England than in the southern colonies, but it is unrealistic to exclude the unfree population from southern statistics because the slaves, while minimal consumers, produced the wealth on which their masters grew rich. The middle colonies emerge from these comparisons with a somewhat more even spread of wealth than either their northeastern or southern neighbors.

A boom stimulated by the Seven Years War collapsed soon after 1763

5. Robert A. Rutland, ed., *The Papers of George Mason, 1725–1792* (Chapel Hill, 1970) 1:229.

6. Alice Hanson Jones, *Wealth of a Nation to Be: The American Colonies on the Eve of the Revolution* (New York, 1980), 183–85, 300; John J. McCusker and Russell R. Menard, *The Economy of British America, 1607–1789* (Chapel Hill, N.C., 1985), 66–67.

into a general depression, accentuated by currency restrictions imposed from Britain. Many Philadelphia workers of different kinds experienced a drop in earning power amounting to thirty percent in the period leading to the outbreak of the Revolution.[7] Poor relief became a major concern of city government in Boston and Philadelphia.[8] Although these difficulties were neither universal nor consistently prevalent, they indicated that prosperity could certainly not be taken for granted, that it was not evenly shared—or distributed according to deserts; and they also reminded colonists that some of the factors on which they depended were controlled by a British government in which they had no official voice. Moreover, many colonial inhabitants could well have been aware of signs suggesting that inequalities of income were increasing, if not dramatically, then gradually but visibly over time.[9]

Conspicuous consumption may represent nothing more provocative than the difference between two different ideas of good taste. But colonial conditions often threw people together in relatively informal settings where conspicuous differences could be highly provocative. "Is not half the property in the city of Philadelphia owned by men who wear LEATHERN APRONS?" a writer in one of the city papers demanded rhetorically. And, still more meaningfully, "Does not the other half belong to men whose fathers and grandfathers wore LEATHERN APRONS?"[10]

Conspicuous underconsumption could be even more offensive than ostentation. In the Hudson valley, great areas of privately owned land lay vacant while the increasingly crowded population of western Massachusetts, seeking space to the west, was spilling over into and occupying these unused estates of the New York patroons. Disorders flared up in the 1750s, to be renewed by the tenant-landlord riots of 1766.[11] All this did not amount to a radically egalitarian upsurge of agrarian revolt. These squatters only wanted room for themselves. What they resented as a natural injustice was the engrossment of the natural resources of a

7. Gary B. Nash, *The Urban Crucible: Social Change, Political Consciousness and the Origins of the American Revolution* (Cambridge, Mass., 1979), 233.

8. Ibid., 253–54.

9. McCusker and Menard, *Economy of British America*, 59.

10. *Pennsylvania Packet*, 18 March 1776.

11. For analysis of these discontents, which digs behind the conventional categories, see Patricia U. Bonomi, *A Factious People: Politics and Society in Colonial New York* (New York, 1971), 211–23.

vast hinterland on the basis of land titles granted in previous generations. Their sentiments were probably best articulated by a recently
arrived Irish radical, Dr. Thomas Young, who saw what was happening
and took their side. "The Earth is the Lords, and the fullness thereof," he
wrote in a polemical pamphlet, "but N. York Gentlemen, have for about
a Century pretty strongly disputed his Title and seem resolved that
neither he nor his Creatures shall have any share in the premises unless
on the terms of being their servants forever." [12] Young, perhaps slightly
more given to speculation than most of the dissidents, also observed that
God was a republican and "no *respecter of persons,* ceremonies or modes
of worship." [13] On these terms it was only too clear that the patroons
and other great men of New York were not republicans, a point that
even in 1766 was evidently held against them.

The fullest and most articulate development of this strand of radical
thinking occurred in Pennsylvania, where the imperial crisis gave the
Philadelphia radicals an unwonted opportunity to seize the political
initiative. One mainspring of this impulse undoubtedly came from the
militia, an active and conspicuous force with the advancing threat of a
military outcome to the quarrel with Britain. James Cannon, one of the
leading Philadelphia radicals, drafted a broadside which, as coming from
the Committee of Privates, was addressed to all military associators. This
statement attributed "the happiness of America" to the absence of all
rank "above that of freemen." (This would not have been an accurate
depiction of New England, where the designation of "esquire" was
coveted and proclaimed.) "Over-grown rich men" were not to be trusted
because they were too apt to frame those social distinctions from which
they could expect to benefit." It is, however, significant of the difficulties
which radicals encountered even in Pennsylvania that when the time
came to draw up a bill of rights, the state convention rejected a clause
denouncing "an enormous Proportion of Property vested in a few Individuals." This was the Pennsylvania radicals' closest approach to an
agrarian law on Harringtonian lines. [14] Equality of rights was neither
expected nor intended to result in an equality of goods. The religious

12. Pauline Maier, *The Old Revolutionaries: Political Lives in the Age of Samuel Adams*
(New York, 1980), 119.
13. Ibid., 126. Emphasis in original.
14. Eric Foner, *Tom Paine,* 129, 133.

revivals dating from the late 1730s, followed by long periods of war, which inflicted heavy strains and losses on the affected regions, had disruptive effects on many widely dispersed communities. Both visitors and domestic observers noticed a social atmosphere that was disturbed by an insubordinate spirit. The Stamp Act crisis made matters worse by arousing the mobs in overt attacks on property. "A Spirit of Levillism Seems to go Through the Country," as Thomas Cushing wrote anxiously to Thomas Hutchinson, Lieutenant Governor of Massachusetts, "and very little distinction between the highest and the lowest in Office." [15] Six years later a young English visitor in Maryland reported that "an idea of equality seems generally to prevail, and the inferior order of people pay little but external respect to those who occupy superior stations." [16] In the same year an Anglican cleric, the Reverend Jacob Duché, told his parishioners in a sermon in Philadelphia that "the poorest labourer upon the shore of the Delaware thinks himself entitled to deliver his opinions in matters of religion and politics with as much freedom as the gentleman and the scholar." Duché was not talking about equality of wealth so much as equality of expectations. We shall need to bear this distinction in mind, because it hints at the category which emerged in full force in the nineteenth century as Equality of Opportunity. "Indeed," he went on, "there is less distinction between the citizens of Philadelphia, than among those of any civilized city in the world. Riches give none. For every man expects one day to be on a footing with his wealthiest neighbor." [17] These roseate views would not have given much comfort to the artisans, small traders, and day laborers, not to mention the considerable numbers of indentured servants and the small number of slaves who were left out of account. "A poor man has rarely the honor of speaking to a gentleman on any terms, and never with any familiarity but for a few weeks before the election," was an anonymous sarcastic complaint that cut closer to the bone; "how many poor men, common men and mechanics, have been made happy within this fortnight by a shake of the hand, a pleasing smile, and a little familiar chat

15. Cushing to Hutchinson, 15 December 1766, in Hutchinson Letterbooks transcripts, Massachusetts Historical Society, xxv, 119.

16. William Eddis, *Letters from America*, ed. Aubrey C. Land (Cambridge, Mass., 1969), 65.

17. Daniel J. Boorstin, *The Americans: The Colonial Experience* (Harmondsworth, 1965), 349.

with gentlemen who have not these seven years past condescended to look at them. Blessed state that brings all so nearly on a level! In a word, electioneering and aristocratical pride are incompatible." [18] The bitterness of this expression is that of a man who feels deprived of legitimate consideration; in its own way it is evidence of a new demand for equal recognition. Here we encounter an early expression of the desire for Equality of Esteem.

Even in distant and comfortable Virginia the newly rising sect of Separate Baptists was spreading a disturbing spirit of informality and brotherhood which carried an implicit challenge to the established dignities of church and state. The Baptists did not preach political equality, but they exalted a fellowship of the emotions which went so far as to include blacks and even slaves. [19]

Collective Self-Esteem and Personal Independence: The Emergence of Political Identity

American national consciousness was born out of a struggle for equality. From the death of George II in 1760, almost every act of British policy served in some way to impress on Americans that they were deemed to be unequal in legal rights and political status within the British Empire and under the British Parliament. This inequality before the law was refracted in American emotions in a form in which it was most deeply resented—inequality in esteem.

The king's death itself opened the way for the first significant demonstration of these inequalities. All things done in the king's name, including parliamentary sessions and writs issued, came to an end six months after the end of his life. Massachusetts merchants strongly objected to a form of writ, issued by the Superior Court and called a writ of assistance, which authorized customs officers to call for public assistance when entering warehouses, stores, and even private homes in search of illicit goods; the sweeping powers conferred by writs of assistance differed very little if at all from those of the general warrants sometimes issued for similar reasons in Britain. When the old writs expired the

18. *Pennsylvania Evening Post*, 27 April 1776.
19. Rhys Isaac, *The Transformation of Virginia, 1740–1790* (Chapel Hill, N.C., 1983), ch. 8.

authorities would have to issue new ones. The Boston merchants seized this opportunity, briefing James Otis and Oxenbridge Thacher to challenge the legality of the writs in the Superior Court of the Province. Otis, taking his argument in part from an article in the London *Gentlemen's Magazine*, made a fiery speech claiming that acts against the constitution were void and that officers in the plantations were under the same limitations as at home. [20] This latter point was not lost on Americans when cases based on similar principles reaching the common law courts in London were found to have strikingly dissimilar outcomes.

The salient case was *Wilkes v. Wood*, the first of the General Warrants cases, which arose out of a search of the premises of John Wilkes, Member of Parliament, on a general warrant. Wilkes, as editor of a paper called *The North Briton*, [21] had alleged that the King's speech from the throne had been written by his former tutor, the Earl of Bute, an allegation which the Secretary of State, George Dunk, Earl of Halifax, considered a seditious libel. Halifax sent his agent Robert Wood to arrest Wilkes, ransack his house, carry away his papers, and arrest even his printers. Within a fortnight Wilkes, claiming privilege as a Member of Parliament, appeared to sue for damages in the Court of Common Pleas. The Chief Justice of the Common Pleas—Sir Charles Pratt, an old-fashioned whig and a friend of Pitt—found in Wilkes's favor on the point of privilege without resolving the legality of general warrants, but the outcome was proclaimed as a vindication of the liberties of the subject against an abuse of powers on the part of agents of the state.

Pratt, soon elevated to the peerage in the name by which he is known to history as Lord Chief Justice Camden, owed his status as a hero of civil liberty more to his ruling in the ensuing and allied case of *Entick v. Carrington*. [22] General warrants were now declared illegal for the reason, very significant from the colonial point of view, that they conferred powers unknown to common law. Even the much more conservative

20. Lyman H. Butterfield, ed., *The Adams Papers: Diary and Autobiography of John Adams* (Cambridge, Mass., 1961) 1:211–12; Nelson B. Lasson, *The History and Development of the Fourth Amendment* (Baltimore, 1937), 55–57.

21. The title was a sarcastic reference to the alleged Scottish influence on the crown.

22. T. B. Howell, *A Complete Collection of State Trials* (London, 1816), XIX, 1159 ff.; Sir Charles Grant Robertson, *Select Statutes, Cases and Documents* (London, 1947), 455; J. Steven Watson, *The Reign of George III, 1760–1815* (Oxford, 1960), 98–101; John Brewer, *Party Ideology and Popular Politics at the Accession of George III* (Cambridge, 1960), 220.

Lord Mansfield, who presided over the King's Bench, agreed with Camden about the illegality of general warrants.[23] These cases were closely followed in the colonies, where Camden's stature was enhanced by his rousing defense of colonial liberties in the debate over the Declaratory Act in 1766. Colonial newspapers carried frequent favorable references to his conduct and principles, and American gratitude to an English whig judge is still recorded in the names of towns and counties along the east coast.[24]

These decisions had important implications for the colonies. When the House of Commons followed the courts by declaring general warrants illegal, it excepted such cases as Parliament might provide for by statute, a loophole of which it soon took advantage. In 1767 Parliament passed the Townshend Act, not only imposing a new round of tariffs on imports into the colonies but formally legalizing writs of assistance in America and designating the superior court of each province as the issuing authority.[25] Nothing could have more forcibly demonstrated to Americans that they did not share as equals in the rights and privileges which protected the liberties and properties of Englishmen at home.[26] The invidious distinction between the English at home and the British in America in respect of these rights was a theme of John Dickinson's *Letters from a Farmer in Pennsylvania*, probably the most influential publication on colonial rights to appear before 1776.[27]

The Townshend Act caused acute difficulties for American judges. If,

23. Mansfield went as far as to say that general warrants would be illegal even in spite of resolutions of Parliament, though it is a moot point whether his opinion would have yielded to statute; many American judges ignored this distinction in order to deny the legality of the writs. They thereby contributed in practice to the development of the American doctrine of constitutional, or in this case common law, supremacy. Grant Robertson, *Select Statutes*, 454–55.

24. Newspapers in which these events were relayed to the American public included *The Connecticut Courant, The New York Gazette, The New York Mercury, The Boston Gazette, The South Carolina Gazette,* and several versions of *The Virginia Gazette,* to name only a few.

25. The draftsmen who drew up this provision had the awkward task of concealing the possibility that search warrants used by colonial customs officers might have been illegal in the past; they therefore described the act's purpose as that of removing any doubts that might exist on the question. M. H. Smith, *The Writs of Assistance Case* (Berkeley and Los Angeles, 1978), 453–55.

26. Lasson, *Fourth Amendment*, 65 n. 50.

27. As, for example, in Purdie and Dixon's *Virginia Gazette*, 10 March 1768. The essay in question is no. IX of the series.

as Otis held, the common law would control statute, then the law itself was doubtful—but so, unfortunately, might be the future of an American judge who defied an act of Parliament. Yet American judges, with a few exceptions, faced these problems with consistency and determination and in most cases after searching their consciences and their legal principles concluded by refusing authority for the writs. "Though my duty and my inclination would lead me to do everything to promote the King's service, yet I conceive that I am not warranted by Law to issue any such Warrant," wrote Chief Justice William Allen of Pennsylvania to John Swift, collector of the port of Philadelphia, an opinion which gains weight from the fact that Allen later remained loyal to the crown. [28]

From an early stage in the controversies aroused by parliamentary taxation of the colonies, there were colonial spokesmen who held that even the British constitution was inferior to the authority of natural law. But this was not the crux of the argument. Americans stood generally on the British constitution and common law, which embodied all the sanctions required by just government, owing their validity to the belief that they actually protected and enforced the rights derived from the laws of nature. What was really natural about Americans' rights was that they belonged to Americans because they belonged to all true-born or "natural born" Englishmen; and this assertion claimed all that was needed about equality. The connection was most clearly explained by the learned Virginia lawyer Richard Bland: "I am speaking of the *rights* of a people: *rights* imply *equality*, in the instances to which they belong. ... By what right is it, that parliament can exercise such power over the colonies, who have as natural a right to the privileges and liberties of Englishmen, as if they were actually resident within the Kingdom?" [29]

Colonial arguments were almost always armored by legal reasoning. But colonial feelings were driven by forces more urgent than the logic of the law, and none was more powerful than injured self-esteem. This latter sentiment was both personal and collective, and no American felt or exemplified it more deeply than George Washington, whose distinguished service as a militia officer during the French and Indian War was

28. O. M. Dickerson, "Writs of Assistance as a Cause of the American Revolution," in Richard B. Morris, ed., *The Era of the American Revolution* (New York, 1939; rpr., 1965), 40–75.

29. Richard Bland, *An Enquiry into the Rights of the British Colonies* (Williamsburg, 1769). The emphasis is in the original.

soured by his disappointed desire for a king's commission and his acute resentment at inferiority of rank. It had been suggested by the governor that he might bear the rank of a militia colonel, but with only the pay and powers of a captain, in which case, he painfully observed, "Every Captain bearing the King's Commission, every half-pay Officer, or other, appearing with such a commission would rank before me."[30] In the future commander of the continental armies, the symbolic importance of this sentiment could hardly be overrated. Many years later, after the first Continental Congress had already dispersed, the Tory Daniel Leonard put his finger on the point in more general terms: "The Whigs flattered the people with the idea of independence," he said; "the tories plan supposed a degree of subordination, which is rather a humiliating idea."[31]

In a very true sense, the American whigs were right. Since the crown had determined by proclamation in 1763 the limit of colonial settlement to the westward, British policies whether royal or parliamentary had introduced a series of new intrusions into colonial affairs. The Revenue (or Sugar) Act of 1764 placed British customs officers on colonial soil, where their duties infringed constantly on cherished local practices. The measures that followed in an unsteady succession—the Stamp Act, the Declaratory Act with its assertion of the right of Parliament to legislate for the colonies "in all cases whatsoever," the Townshend tariffs, Parliament's threat to suspend the New York Assembly, the tea duty and eventually the so-called "Intolerable Acts" of 1774—all had the same effect: they conspicuously instructed Americans to regard themselves as inferiors, both personally vis-à-vis British officials and publicly in the ultimate control of policies which affected their fate. The word *equality* itself made comparatively few explicit appearances in the language of American protest, but the emotions aroused by inequality were present everywhere.

When Thomas Jefferson assumed the task of drafting Virginia's instructions to its delegation to the Continental Congress in September 1774, he drew together the individual and public aspects of the problem

---

30. Bernhard Knollenberg, *George Washington: The Virginia Period, 1732–1775* (Durham, N.C., 1964), 25.

31. Massachusettensis, 19 December 1774, in Bernard Mason, ed., *The American Colonial Crisis* (New York, 1972), 12.

with that felicity of expression which was soon to earn even higher literary responsibilities. "Can any reason be assigned," he asked, "why 160,000 electors in the island of Great Britain should give law to four millions in the states of America, every individual of whom is equal to every individual of them, in virtue, in understanding, and in bodily strength?"[32]

Less than two years later the rhetorical question turned to a passionate affirmation. Jefferson's original or Rough Draft for the Declaration of Independence began by asserting that, "We hold these truths to be sacred and undeniable, that all men are created equal and independent; that from that equal creation they derive rights equal and inalienable."[33] Equality of rights was now identified as the condition of an equal creation; and this conclusion was in no way modified by the more famous and rhetorically more powerful words of the Declaration of Independence, where the truths became "self-evident" and the rights in which men were equal flowed directly from the will of the creator. If one accepted the premise, there was no arguing with the inference; if one did not accept the premise, one was inaccessible to the self-evident.

The political aims of the Declaration of Independence were collective. The time had come for *one people* to assume its equal station in the world among other nations. But the philosophical premise of this collective equality was inseparable from the belief in the moral equality of individuals. Thomas Paine's powerful attack on the hereditary claims of the monarchy carried the same implications. "Mankind being originally equals in the order of creation, the equality could only be destroyed by some subsequent circumstance." The target of Paine's rhetoric was soon disclosed—"the distinction between KINGS and SUBJECTS" which, unlike that between male and female, could not be naturally accounted for.[34] Even John Adams, who disliked Paine's style, deeply resented his irreligion, and feared the democratizing consequences of his rhetoric, could only agree with the basic tenet that no man was born with a right to rule over others.

Adams's own first publication, *A Dissertation on the Canon and Feudal Law*, which appeared in 1765, was directly addressed to these questions.

---

32. Julian P. Boyd, ed., *The Papers of Thomas Jefferson* (Princeton, 1951–) 1:423.
33. Ibid., 423–28.
34. Philip S. Foner, ed., *The Complete Writings of Thomas Paine* (New York, 1945) 1:9.

He denounced "feudal" dignities as an affront to the true dignity of human nature and bitterly attacked "all that dark ribaldry of heredity, indefeasible right,—the Lord's anointed,—the divine, miraculous original of Government, with which the priesthood has enveloped the feudal monarch in clouds and mysteries, from which they have deduced the most mischievous of all doctrines, that of passive obedience and non-resistance."[35] Years later, when he was serving as American commissioner in France during the War of Independence, Adams received a missive apparently emanating from no less a source than George III himself which held out the offer of ennoblement to leading Americans in a restored allegiance to the crown. Adams's response was true to his most fundamentally American convictions. "An aristocracy of American peers!" he exclaimed in his autobiography: "hereditary peers I suppose were meant, but whether hereditary or for Life, nothing could be more abhorrent to the general Sense of America at that time, which was for making every Magistrate and every Legislator eligible and that annually at least."[36]

These sentiments expressed the truths which American whigs understood and believed in as they rallied their resistance to Britain. Those states that adopted declarations of rights as preambles to their new constitutions used the occasion to affirm the egalitarian basis on which the authority of the new government was held to rest. The first was "that all men are by nature equally free and independent, and have certain inherent rights, of which, when they enter into a state of society, they cannot by any compact deprive or divest their posterity," in the words of Virginia as drafted by George Mason of the Fairfax Independent Company; these rights included "the enjoyment of life and liberty, with the means of acquiring and possessing property, and pursuing and obtaining happiness and safety." Some five months later Pennsylvania adopted the same language. When Massachusetts, after a long process of deliberation in its town meetings, adopted its own constitution in 1780, the first article of its Declaration of Rights began with almost identical words: "All men are born free and equal, and have certain natural, essential, and unalienable rights."[37]

35. Charles Francis Adams, ed., *The Works of John Adams* (Boston, 1850) 9:375–78.
36. Butterfield, *Adams Papers* 4:149–52.
37. J. R. Pole, ed., *The Revolution in America, 1754–1788: Documents of the Internal Development of America in the Revolutionary Era* (London, 1970), 519, 530–31, 480.

The Declaration of Independence took its place in this context as the unifying expression of a common sentiment. So far as might be possible where a collectivity of states claiming independent sovereignty could be considered a nation, it amounted to a national commitment. Jefferson said half a century later that he had aimed to express "the common sense of the subject."[38] But certainly it was not the only philosophically available common sense. More than a quarter-century had passed since the publication of Montesquieu's *Spirit of the Laws*, possibly the most influential work of political science known to Jefferson's generation. Montesquieu had taken to previously unknown lengths a profound cultural relativism, from which he derived a moral relativism in which laws and moral codes were related to the climates and customs of different civilizations. Alternatives to Jefferson's universalism were thus certainly open to discussion; they would be more widely absorbed within the next few years; indeed, cultural relativism would soon revive in the United States with the advance into political prominence of the increasingly ominous division between North and South. The moral universality of Jefferson's "self-evident" truths captured the imagination in 1776 because it expressed the passions of a morally inspired revolt. It caught the mood of independence before political responsibility had been translated into the more tortuous complexities of self-government. The timing for such a universal declaration was right; perhaps it was the only timing that was historically possible.

When the Declaration as proclaimed by the Continental Congress told the world that the truths on which the Americans based their revolt were "self-evident" it told the people that these were things they could see for themselves. There was a close analogy with Protestant theology and especially with Calvinism, with which many Americans were familiar in one form or another. Calvinist religious instructors taught that each individual bore throughout his or her life a primary responsibility to God; and in much the same way, the Declaration of Independence taught people that each of them bore a responsibility to government. This may not at first have been much more than a symbolic statement, but the fact was that Americans were at that moment taking the burden of government upon their own shoulders. And the burdens were heavy. Liberty for the Puritans had never been meant liberty for the hedonistic pursuit

---

38. Carl L. Becker, *The Declaration of Independence* (1922; rpr., New York, 1959), 25.

of one's own earth-bound aims or material gain. "The pursuit of happiness" was not a phrase that would have occurred to New England's founding generations, or of which they would have approved. Liberty for them meant liberty to serve Christ. But when human happiness had been promoted to a place not only of profit but of honor in men's values, then it fell to the human race to determine those values.

The consequential responsibilities were plain. Every individual had an equal share in determining those values, following from his equal right to liberty and to happiness. It was not in their abilities or characters but in their rights that men were equal. On the basis of this principle, men depended for their rights on their individuality as men, not on hereditary privileges, not on family or social status, not on race or even religion. Whether the same principle would as naturally extend to women was a question not yet on anyone's political agenda. If, as was almost universally believed, women were by their *nature* different from men, then although they might have equal rights, these would be rights to different social goods. When in later generations radical feminist spokeswomen claimed that the rights of women were exactly identical to those of men, they could not win the argument by quoting the Declaration of Independence and substituting their own sex for men's. They had in effect to carry conviction in the claim that women were virtually *interchangeable* with men in all the activities of economic and political life. The case was capable of proof, but it did not fall into the category of self-evident truths.

The Declaration of Independence proclaimed a universalist egalitarian rhetoric as the standard of a highly differentiated social order. It could not determine the future of that order, and its language could never be translated into specific institutions. What it could do in the hands of social reformers was to serve as a kind of moral prompter, a reference text for self-evaluation, and it may be partly for this reason that Americans seem to have often felt required to judge themselves by abstract moral standards which seem impossible to satisfy. Considered as moral philosophy the Declaration of Independence is not invulnerable; but it was not addressed to an academic seminar. It was a highly charged political proclamation addressed to the opinion of mankind, its egalitarian universalism was the only sense which all could understand, and that was the light that it handed to future generations.

Chapter Three

The Articulation of Equality
in the New Republic

An outraged sense of equality was the moral impulse of the American Revolution. The Revolution in its turn, brought by the Constitution and the Bill of Rights to a completion which had not been anticipated in its origin, proved to be the agency by which equality was placed in the center of the American nation's public morality. But outraged feelings do not always yield clear thinking, and even the most articulate of the colonists might have had difficulty in finding the language to define the issues in terms of the indignation aroused by the experience of being denied that equality of esteem to which as British subjects they felt fully entitled. Yet that was what lay at the heart of their protest. For American politics, however, the consequences were far from clear. Americans were certainly not going for the future to confer equal esteem on one another on the basis of nothing more solid than a revolutionary ideal; but when men and women for whatever reason were denied esteem, they could turn in the last resort to a principle that was inseparable from the Republic because it was involved in its moral foundations.

Another principle, more easily defined and more clearly understood, was that of equality before the law, one of the fundamental ideals of the Enlightenment in Europe. The common law of England, which had been received in the colonies since the early years of the eighteenth century, did not in fact incorporate a complete equality among the crown's subjects; the principle of benefit of clergy, by which any person who could make some sort of claim to be able to read and write stood a good

chance of having a serious sentence commuted, could hardly be considered egalitarian, though it saved the lives of innumerable men and women, including slaves. But the common law had vindicated the rights of Englishmen in the general warrants cases, as colonists well knew, and in any case the colonists claimed the protection of the common law on an equal footing with the inhabitants of the British Isles. These principles would not always be honored in American law, but they would be present in the language of debate.

Equality and the Language of Political Relations

The full meaning of a revolution based on these principles took some time to absorb. But it was clear from the beginning that no form of American government could derive its authority from hereditary right—with the understood exceptions in the historical context of the right of whites to rule blacks and of men to rule over women. The British had traditionally used two forms of language when asserting their authority in the colonies. The more formal of these, parliamentary sovereignty, had its most unequivocal expression in the Declaratory Act of 1766, which made no claim to give new law but instead declared the existing constitutional right of Parliament to legislate for the colonies "in all cases whatsoever."[1] The more informal but perhaps more pervasive language was that of paternalism. Even William Pitt, Earl of Chatham, one of the Americans' most celebrated friends in Parliament, had said in connection with the Townshend duties that "in all laws relating to trade and navigation especially, this is the mother country, they are the children; they must obey and we prescribe."[2]

Charles Townshend had made elaborate use of this imagery. He described the Americans as "children planted by our care, nourished up by our indulgence . . . and protected by our arms." But the most acute British critics of ministerial policies exposed the self-induced illusions of

1. *Statutes of the Realm,* 6 Geo. III c. 12.
2. Charles Ritcheson, *British Politics and the American Revolution* (Norman, Okla., 1954), 138. As a matter of fact, this position was consistent with his views on the Stamp Act. Taking the colonists' money out of their pockets without their consent was about the only thing Parliament could *not* legitimately do, a standpoint with which the colonists could not live for long. I. R. Christie, *Crisis of Empire: Great Britain and the American Colonies 1754–1783* (London, 1966), 62.

this spuriously protective posture. "They planted by your care?" retorted Isaac Barré; "No! Your oppression planted them in America. . . . They nourished up by your indulgence? They grew up by your neglect of them. . . . They protected by your arms? They have nobly taken up arms in your defence."[3] A few months before independence was declared in Philadelphia, Dr. Richard Price, the English Presbyterian minister and radical political economist who was a much better friend of the Americans than Chatham, attacked the same illusion in an essay which analyzed the controversy in terms of political justice: " 'But we are the PARENT STATE,' " he quoted, with reference to the prevailing moral sentiment; "These are the magic words which have fascinated and misled us." And he proceeded to point out that if one took the parental analogy at its word, since children have a habit of growing up, Britain should have gradually relaxed its authority. But the concept itself was false. "No wonder then, that they have turned upon us and obliged us to remember, that they are not children."[4]

American Tories found it quite natural to use the same language. We have noticed Daniel Leonard's willing acceptance of "a degree of subordination"—admittedly "rather a humiliating idea." The Reverend Samuel Seabury, addressing the merchants of New York in 1774, referred to "this unnatural and unhappy contention between our parent country and us"—the unnaturalness itself being in the character of a child's ingratitude to its parents. The Boston Tory Peter Oliver could not have been improved on by his British ministerial contemporaries: Massachusetts was a colony "nursed, in its infancy, with the most tender care and attention; which has been indulged with every gratification that the most forward child could wish for" and which had been treated with liberality and repeatedly saved from destruction. Once again, its rebellion, recalling that of an ungrateful child, was "unnatural."[5]

3. Christie, *Crisis of Empire*, 52–53.
4. "Observations on the Nature of Civil Liberty, the Principles of Government, and the Justice and Policy of the War with America," in Bernard Peach, ed., *Richard Price and the Ethical Foundations of the American Revolution* (Durham, N.C., 1979), 84. Edwin G. Burrows and Michael Wallace, "The American Revolution: The Ideology and Psychology of National Liberation," *Perspectives in American History* 6 (1972): 241, 248.
5. Quotations from Samuel Seabury, *The Congress Canvassed* (New York, 1774); "Peter Oliver's Origin and Progress of the American Rebellion: A Tory View," in Morton and Penn Borden, eds., *The American Tory* (Englewood Cliffs, N.J., 1972), 16, 24–25.

Such language would clearly have been wholly inappropriate in the context of the social and political relationships that followed independence. At both the interstate level of the Continental Congress and that of the new state legislatures, the American system depended for its authority on one or another form of election, while locally elected committees corresponded with the assemblies and officiated throughout the communities. Paternalistic relations might still prevail in many family lives, especially on the larger plantations, but there was no rationale by which the language of these relations could be transferred to those of public life and political authority.

When Americans looked around them and observed the life lived by themselves and their families, what they saw was a society formed of the intricate network of families and communities. But when they *theorized* about government, they spoke as though they perceived something quite different: a political society founded by the rational intent of independent individuals, or in the terminology of prevailing psychological theory, on acts which combined the faculties of reason and will. This formula for explaining the origins of political society appeared in the declarations of rights adopted by Virginia and Massachusetts, and everywhere it was assumed by men who addressed themselves to public affairs that individuals formed governments to protect their rights.[6]

The philosophical credentials of this position derived from Locke's *Second Treatise*, which was seldom referred to in the debates over American constitutions either state or federal but whose intellectual presence had entered into the fibers of American political thought. The voluntary arrangements which had initiated government were by definition contractual; a mature legal principle, well known and fully respected in the world of commerce, had been adapted into politics. Nor was this a momentary fashion. When early in the nineteenth century the Virginia lawyer St. George Tucker composed an American edition of Blackstone's *Commentaries on the Laws of England*, a book which even before the

---

6. Samuel Eliot Morison, *Sources and Documents Illustrating the American Revolution, 1764–1788* (Oxford, 1923–1962), 149; J.R. Pole, ed., *The Revolution in America, 1754–1788* (London, 1970), 479; George Washington to the President of Congress, 17 Sept. 1787, in Winton U. Solberg, ed., *The Federal Convention and the Formation of the Union of the American States* (Indianapolis, 1958), 363–64. For an exposition of current psychological theory and its significance for social order, see Daniel W. Howe, "The Political Psychology of *The Federalist*," *William and Mary Quarterly* 64 (July 1987): 3.

Revolution had become a best-seller on the American market, he explained in Lockeian terms the founding processes of American government: "The world, for the first time since the annals of its inhabitants began, saw an original written compact formed by the free and deliberate voices of individuals disposed to unite in the same social bonds; thus exhibiting a political phenomenon unknown to former ages." [7]

Notwithstanding their distinguished lineage, these views did not correspond to any observable facts. In creating new governments Americans made strenuous efforts to maintain as much continuity with past institutions as was practically possible, even in the first instance calling new elections on the basis of the colonial election laws. The chaos of a renewed "state of nature" was what they bent their minds to avoiding. New political societies were formed not from a state of nature but from social custom and political practice. In the light of the realities of American life, both social and political, the popularity of the theory of political contract requires a more positive explanation than that it was merely available or convenient. It was *required*, for two morally persuasive reasons. In the first place it was essential to establish a new basis for the *legitimacy* of the new forms of government, and no basis could be more secure than the willed consent of free individuals; and in the second place, but logically co-existent with the first, as we have already seen, these free individual wills were and had to be *equal* wills. The new politics called for a new political language, but one with roots in a well-authenticated moral tradition which everyone could understand. The language of equality was the only legitimizing language to take the place of the discarded language of divine right monarchy and paternal or hereditary authority.

The language of the past did not say all that would need to be said about the complex of structures, societal, educational, and political, that would be required in the new political order that men hoped to build—and that some women also hoped to share in building. They had inherited a language in which the concepts of aristocracy and monarchy held an ambiguous place, honorable as symbolic of leadership and authority, yet resented as imperious, haughty, tyrannical and lacking in the legitimacy conferred by consent. The worst that could be said of a man or a

7. St. George Tucker, ed., *Blackstone's Commentaries* (Philadelphia, 1903), vol. 1, app. 4.

set of men was that they entertained monarchical aspirations or believed in the hereditary principle. In the early Federalist period, following the establishment of the national government in 1789, this charge was repeatedly thrown at John Adams, Alexander Hamilton (with some justification), even at George Washington, and at the Federalists in general. It was revived by opponents of Andrew Jackson, who derisively styled him King Andrew the First and depicted him in royal robes.[8] Yet there were those, John Adams and Alexander Hamilton among them, who doubted whether the monarchical inclinations of men could be expunged by a revolution.

Meanwhile in the early search for a republican language, the more benign attributes of aristocracy were discovered in the context of the Enlightenment's fundamental respect for the concept of "nature." If the Republic could tap the sources of its own "natural aristocracy"—what Jefferson in old age referred to as an "aristocracy of virtue and talent"— it could discover its own authentic form of leadership and save itself from the worst abuses of democracy.[9] Republicans kept the idea of aristocracy alive in the form of superior natural quality, native to the individual but to be nurtured for the public service. "Co-operating with nature in her natural œconomy," Jefferson wrote to one of nature's aristocrats, David Rittenhouse, in 1778, "we should dispose of and employ the geniuses of men according to their several orders and degrees"—from which men had unnaturally and therefore wrongly departed. The only aristocracy in the United States, according to the Constitutionalist pamphleteer Jonathan Jackson, was that of "experience and understanding." And he adopted this terminology to add, "What I shall aim at, will be to draw out this *natural aristocracy*, if it must be called so." If it must, it was because John Adams had so called it in his recent *Defence of the Constitutions of Government of the United States*, a work written while the author was on duty in Europe, published in 1786, and

8. Noble E. Cunningham, *The Jeffersonian Republicans: The Formation of Party Organization, 1789–1801* (Chapel Hill, 1957), 45, 98–99; and idem, *The Jeffersonian Republicans in Power: Party Operations, 1801–1809* (Chapel Hill, 1963), 10; Lance Banning, *The Jeffersonian Persuasion: Evolution of a Party Ideology* (Ithaca, N.Y., 1978), 238–45; Marvin Meyers, *The Jacksonian Persuasion: Politics and Belief* (Stanford, 1957) 5; J.W. Ward, *Andrew Jackson, Symbol for an Age* (New York, 1955).

9. Philip B. Kurland and Ralph Lerner, eds., *The Founders' Constitution* (Chicago, 1987) 1:525.

patriotically designed to defend the state constitutions against certain French republican criticisms.[10] Benjamin Rush, another of Jefferson's distinguished circle of Philadelphia associates, published a pamphlet in 1777 in which he agreed that the absence of "artificial distinctions of men into noblemen and commoners" only made way for the emergence of "natural distinctions of rank in Pennsylvania"—and natural distinctions were those based on "superior degrees of industry and capacity." Rush discerned new dangers in the inevitable political influence accruing to new forms of wealth. [11] The attraction of adapting this linguistic heritage to republican ideals gradually faded in the nineteenth century as politicians and commentators grew more comfortable and satisfied with the principles and language of democracy.

Interest Politics and the Beginnings of Political Equality

The Declaration of Independence encouraged Americans to commit their ideas of political justice to the belief that each individual possessed certain rights in which he stood independent of all other individuals. Government existed to bring about the best conditions for the preservation of these rights. But it did not follow that all had equal rights to participate in making laws—that would depend on qualifications appropriate to the needs of society, and men of influence generally agreed that the interests of society as a whole were safest in the hands of the owners of property. The corollary to this position of political privilege was that men of property should make it their business to ensure through just laws that worthy individuals would have the opportunity to acquire property. Some of the new states put these theories into official form in the declarations preceding their constitutions. The Address which the Massachusetts constitutional convention sent out to accompany its new constitution in 1780 justified the property qualifications for the suffrage—which were actually slightly higher than they had been under the crown—by explaining that those who were excluded could hope to earn enough to qualify; only the idle and profligate would be perma-

10. Ibid., 526–27, 543; Jonathan Jackson ["A Native of Boston"], *Thoughts on the Political Situation of the United States* (Worcester, 1788), 57.

11. Benjamin Rush, *Observations on the Present Government of Pennsylvania in Four Letters to the People of Pennsylvania* (Philadelphia, 1777), 9.

nently kept out. [12] We even have here a glimmering of the doctrine that would eventuate as equality of opportunity. In this case, economic opportunity is assumed to exist; a young man making good use of his opportunities would earn his right to political participation. In the Declaration of Rights—which appears to have had a more formal status as a statement of intent—the voluntarily associating individuals were immediately spoken of as "citizens," who seem on first sight to be interchangeable with the "inhabitants." But not all inhabitants enjoyed equally the advantages of citizenship; by common consent, citizenship was less than coextensive with the whole population, and citizens were always historically defined as persons invested with certain privileges. Opinions might differ as to the extent to which inhabitants of secondary status could aspire to qualify for citizenship, but for many in all the original states the promise of the Revolution could be fulfilled only by the progressive extension of the concept of citizenship. It was only with these limitations that the early constitution-makers could be said to have committed themselves to a theory of political equality.

It was, therefore, a theory of very limited scope—a foundation rather than a structure. Different convictions as to the obligations of government were buried in it from the beginning, and no clear original intent could be extracted. The Address and the Declaration contained, between them, many debatable propositions. From different convictions differing systems might have arisen. But the most effective steps towards the implementation of a politics of the political equality of individuals were taken for practical rather than theoretical reasons.

In view of the force generated by ideas and sentiments of equality it may even seem a little curious that no distinct theory of the political equality of individuals had appeared in colonial politics. It is true that colonial legislatures in the late stages of their existence received many petitions requesting extensions of representation from under-represented counties, and these looked in the direction of a broader participation; but even in Pennsylvania, which was soon to be seized by radicals, these petitions invariably based their claims as much on the

12. Pole, *Revolution in America*, 475. This document, which was drafted by Samuel Adams, is more collectivist in tone than the formalistic language of the Declaration of Rights. "The interest of society is common to all its members" (473), for example. Massachusetts's puritan heritage, which could never have been completely at home with the political economy of individualism, was safe in the hands of Samuel Adams.

property held and taxes paid by the community as on the numbers of inhabitants. [13] Equality, moreover, was often held to mean equality of towns or corporate units, not equality of persons, but even so defined it was hard to find any principle of equality in colonial electoral laws. The idea that political justice called for a system of rule by a majority of politically equal individuals was not inherent in early American ideas of the elements of republican government and was certainly not what Americans were fighting for in their struggle against Britain; the majority principle entered almost inadvertently into American political practice during the Revolution. The consequences were far-reaching, but the outcome was not in any primary sense due to the convictions of whig theorists who, had they been so minded, could have made more vigorous efforts in that direction in earlier years.

As is usual in cases of major political advance, the new principle got its strength from the fact that it served powerful existing interests. Wherever, as happened in Massachusetts between 1775 and 1780, in other states at different times, and in the wider arena of Federal government in 1787, strong concentrations of property were allied with the greatest concentrations of numbers, the interest of property had much to gain and little to fear from the introduction of majority rule. [14] To argue that true American whigs introduced majority rule as a matter of principle does less than justice to their demonstrated capacity for political realism. [15] But once their perception of political realities had enabled them to grasp this strand and weave it firmly into the new constitutional fabric, the formalistic element of voluntarism in whig theory was toughened and enlarged into a prominent theme of American political thought. [16] It was soon very easy and almost natural for Americans to believe that majority rule was a Revolution principle.

13. J.R. Pole, *Political Representation in England and the Origins of the American Republic* (London, 1966; Berkeley, 1971), 260–65.

14. Ibid., 169–249, 373–82, 538. These conclusions are confirmed in some subsequent studies, for example, Merrill Jensen, *The American Revolution within America* (New York, 1974), 66; Stephen E. Patterson, "The Roots of Massachusetts Federalism: Conservative Parties and Political Culture Before 1787," in Ronald Hoffman and Peter J. Albert, eds., *Sovereign States in an Age of Uncertainty* (Charlottesville, 1981).

15. As maintained by Gordon S. Wood, *The Creation of the American Republic* (Chapel Hill, 1969), 170–72.

16. In this connection, see Yehoshua Arieli, *Individualism and Nationalism in American Ideology* (Cambridge, Mass., 1964), 158–80.

The principle of the equality of political individuals, which translates into that of one man, one vote—and ultimately into one person, one vote—in approximately equal electoral divisions, was implicit in the Constitution of the United States, rather than being expressly declared by it. Except for certain listed prohibitions, like those on ex post facto laws and laws impairing the obligation of contracts, the Constitution does not declare its own underlying principles, and such a declaration was not called for in its context. Nor is it part of the purpose of the present argument to insist that the establishment of majority rule was one of the aims which brought the Constitution into existence. Some of the delegates had expressed their fears of majority rule, and the Constitution's elaborate internal structures were designed in no small part to contain the force of sheer majorities. But no alternative existed as a general rule; in the strongly expressed opinion of the nationalist leaders, it was the minimum unifying principle on which the constitutional machine could function. Even so, each state was to retain the right to regulate its own suffrage; it was generally agreed, at least among the classes who exercised political power—a power that could be exercised only through the electoral system itself—that before men had the right to vote they should have some sort of commitment to the wellbeing of a society based on the ownership of private property. But whatever these variations might be among the individual states, the evidence both of the debates and of the political context implies that electoral districts were expected to be approximately equal in numbers, although these numbers remained to be determined.[17] The Bostonian Jonathan Jackson, in a well-reasoned pamphlet reviewing American politics in 1788, asked, "Why should there ever be any other rule than numbers, by which to determine the proportion of a representative body, between different corporations and communities?" It was absurd that Virginia should have no greater voice than Delaware or Rhode Island.[18] Already, in the same

17. Both Madison and Wilson pleaded for "proportional representation" in *both* houses of the new Congress and used the term again in opposing equal representation of the states in the upper house. What they wanted was majority rule on a proportional basis. In a government which acted equally on its individual citizens, the only way to obtain this objective would be through approximately equal electoral districts, a point that may have seemed too obvious to detain the Convention. Max Farrand, ed., *The Records of the Federal Convention of 1787* (New Haven, 1911), (Madison) I, 36–37, etc.; (Wilson) I, 179, etc.

18. Jackson ["A Native of Boston"], *Thoughts*, 36, 33–34.

year as the drafting of the new Constitution, the moral logic of representation according to numbers was clear enough as a principle for the future to control the electoral system laid down by the great Northwest Ordinance of 1787.[19] Washington himself had strong views on the need to keep representatives in close touch with their constituents, and it was agreed that the number was not to exceed one representative for every thirty thousand inhabitants, the other proviso being that each state was to have at least one representative.[20] Slight variations might be tolerated for practical purposes, but the Constitution contained no internal rationale on which, once men had the vote, some men's votes could be given more weight than others. The same system was to apply to the electoral college, invented as an intermediary process for the election of the president and vice-president of the United States.

The exception to the basic principle of individual political equality might appear to have lain elsewhere—in the separate and equal representation of each state in the Senate. Since the states were then and have ever since been extremely unequal in population, this concession to the concept of state sovereignty necessarily qualified the representation of individuals in the federal Congress. But it cannot be argued from this that the system of state representation in the Senate introduced a rationale for any alternative basis of representation in the House, or in the lower houses of the state systems. Indeed, the massive inequalities reflected in the Senate gave all the more point to the majoritarian principle prevailing in the House. States were by definition political entities, but they were in no sense representative of anything other than their own citizens; they did not owe their existence to some felt need to represent any specified interests. The political survival of the states as elements in the federal system was not a basis from which it would be possible to conduct a reasoned argument for *other* forms of interest representation, such as those of regional, class, ethnic or economic groupings within the states. The leading nationalists in the Convention, who in addition to Madison included James Wilson, Rufus King, and Gouverneur Morris, wanted equality of political individuals because they wanted a direct relationship between the central government and its citizens scattered throughout the states. But republican principles by this time had also

19. *Journals of the Continental Congress* 32:334–43.
20. Farrand, *Convention of 1787*, II, 643–44; Constitution of the United States, Art. I, sec. 2.

begun to suggest that political equality was the only acceptable foundation for political justice; a community, after all, was only a collection of persons all of whom were deemed to be equal.

The new Constitution in fact cut clean through the lines surrounding the states to operate directly on every individual subject to its jurisdiction, which meant every individual within the boundaries of the Union. It had this power because it conferred on Congress and the President the power to make and sign laws which affected individuals directly and without regard for any protection conferred by state citizenship. Although the Constitution did not expressly define the concept of citizenship, both its language and its essential operation made every citizen of any state into a citizen of the United States; and the Constitution also made it the duty of the Congress to establish "a uniform rule of naturalization." [21]

It was clear to every participant in the debate over the powers of the proposed new federal government, both for and against, that it would operate directly on individuals. By the same token it was equally clear that the Constitution would regard these individuals as equals. Its terms expressly prohibited the granting of titles of nobility, [22] and could clearly not be made to justify other forms of privilege. The fact that the Constitution would act in this way was not in doubt; the heated debates over the powers of the federal government flared up precisely because these powers would detract from the integrity of the states as sovereign political bodies. Opponents of the Constitution made no contest of the fact that it would operate directly on individuals but vehemently objected precisely *because* it would cut through state boundaries in the process. [23] The concept of individual political equality had by this time made headway from the electoral systems adopted by the states' various forms of republican government, in some of which it was clearly defined; [24] but even at their clearest, state constitutions stopped at the boundaries of their own states. The Federal Constitution did more than

21. Ibid., Art. I, sec. 8.

22. Ibid., Art. I, sec. 9.

23. *The Federalist*, ed. Jacob E. Cooke (Middletown, 1961), nos. 15, 16; *Debates in the House of Representatives of South Carolina on the Ratification of the Proposed Constitution of the United States* (Charleston, 1789), 3–4; Cecelia M. Kenyon, ed., *The Antifederalists* (Indianapolis, 1966), 379; [William Findlay], *Address from an Officer* (Philadelphia, 1787), v, 3, 6. Many other comments to the same effect could be cited.

24. Massachusetts and Virginia have been discussed as prominent examples.

any other instrument to define political equality as a fundamental principle of American government.

Natural Law in the Crucible of Slavery

It was easier to agree with the proposition that a republican form of government—guaranteed by the Constitution to each state—should be molded to the needs of a republican society than to determine exactly what those forms should be or what those needs were. In the American context nothing was clearer or more generally understood than that republics were incompatible with rule based on hereditary privilege; all forms of inherited advantage were suspiciously tainted with un-American principles. It was precisely for this reason that opponents of banks and other chartered corporations constantly complained in the early years of the Republic and down through the Jacksonian era that these institutions threatened to create a new aristocracy whose illegitimate gains would be handed down to future generations. The pure foundations of the Republic were threatened by a new, insidious, and potent corruption.

Republican society could tolerate many variations on the theme of equality. But the Revolution raised for the first time as a major issue of public debate the question as to whether it could tolerate equality's absolute negation in the form of human slavery. Jefferson took advantage of his commission to draft the Declaration of Independence to express his feelings about the slave trade (a safer target than slavery itself, which existed in all the colonies), for which he laid the blame squarely, if not quite fairly, at the door of George III, thus exonerating his fellow-countrymen from any direct moral obliquity. He concluded by denouncing the British for inciting the enslaved Negroes to rise against their American masters, who emerged as the doubly injured victims of this complicated plot. Despite these foils and baffles, his language was too provocative for powerful interests in Congress, and the entire paragraph was excised. [25]

Many members of the revolutionary generation, however, and many of them in slave states, were inspired by the libertarian impulse and dismayed by the anomaly of slavery within their own societies. The

25. Julian P. Boyd, ed., *The Papers of Thomas Jefferson* (Princeton, 1951) 1:426–28.

word *slavery* was often used by the colonists in opposing the supposed British threat to their liberties; they felt they knew what it meant. Slavery was denounced as incompatible with the republican principles that Americans now sought to enact for themselves; Southern Methodists such as Francis Asbury, who became America's first Methodist bishop, and his colleague Thomas Coke, both in the Chesapeake area, circulated petitions denouncing slavery in the early 1780s and at a meeting held at Christmas, 1784, Methodist leaders banned slave owners from joining their society. These church leaders were abolitionists. But their sense of urgency was not universally shared by their sect in the South, and others, such as the Virginian Methodist minister Devereaux Jarrett (who owned twenty-four slaves), regarded this immediatism as dangerous; their gradualist approach to abolition left their own interests intact and did not threaten society with the social or economic consequences of sudden emancipation in the name of moral or religious law.[26]

The greatest contribution to slave liberation was made by the slaves themselves. Their opportunity arose from British incitements to desert their masters, accompanied by offers of liberation and protection. According to Jefferson's own calculation, no fewer than 30,000 slaves in Virginia fled during the British invasion of 1780, and similar proportions deserted in South Carolina. These were large numbers, enough to warn Americans that vast quantities of property were at risk for them in the enterprise of revolution.[27]

From an early phase, there were many American slave owners who found it impossible to live with their own consciences and own slaves at the same time. The large number of manumissions in the Chesapeake states help to explain the rapid rise of a free black population in the years following the War of Independence. The free black population of Maryland rose from 1,817 in 1755 to 8,000 in 1790 and nearly 20,000 by the end of the century; Virginia's census of 1782 revealed 1,800 free blacks, followed by 13,000 in 1800 and 20,000 a decade later.[28] The scale of

26. Gary B. Nash, *Race and Revolution* (Madison, 1990), 9–10, 12, 14–15, 18–19.

27. Ibid., 60. Nash describes the American Revolution as "the largest slave uprising in American history," 57. According to him, many escaped slaves joined the British or formed black militia units, often suffering heavy losses from wounds, disease, and malnutrition. Most of those who survived the war were evacuated by the British to Florida, Jamaica, or Nova Scotia.

28. Ibid., 18.

these operations would be enough to dispatch the idea that men are moved only by their own material interests. These personal manumissions were followed soon after the war by the birth of a cluster of abolition societies, which drew their inspiration from the republican belief in the natural liberty of the person, and their rhetoric from the Declaration of Independence. These societies worked as pressure groups to bring about gradual emancipation by state legislatures. The moral force at work here was primarily derived from the conviction, in which English law was reinforced by Enlightenment principles, that liberty was the natural condition of the human race; and the American Republic was itself founded on claims to natural liberty. To deny liberty was, of course, to deny the moral claim to equal rights; that denial might have serious implications for the character of the Republic itself. Thus, for example, Luther Martin, attorney general of Maryland, declared in 1788 that slavery was "inconsistent with the *genius of republicanism* and has a tendency to *destroy* those *principles* on which it is *supported, as it lessens the sense* of the *equal rights of mankind*, and habituated us to *tyranny* and *oppression*." [29] Black petitions for an end to slavery, and for equal treatment by the newly emancipated American society, show that their authors had well understood the universalist principles on which the master race based its claims to liberty. There is little sign, however, that they got a respectful hearing. [30]

White emancipationists of this era were prepared to accept the moral imperative of liberty for their fellow human beings without necessarily accepting—or even working through—its implications for equality in their own society. The libertarian impulse in fact revealed the limits of American society's ability to square itself with the precepts of equality. The principal proponents of emancipation were almost invariably unwilling to contemplate either legal or social equality for the freed slaves. They tended to be content with programs that would permit slavery an attenuated existence for the following generation; even Pennsylvania's emancipation laws would have made it possible, in theory, for children of slaves to gain their freedom only in 1848. St. George Tucker, in

29. Ibid., 19.
30. For examples of such petitions, see ibid., 167–201.

Virginia, would have spread emancipation over 100 years, would have planned to colonize the freedmen and women, and would never contemplate admitting them to the equal benefits of civil society.[31]

These programs of emancipation varied from state to state. But their general adoption of gradualism, even in so fundamental a matter as human liberty, has important theoretical implications. For if, in the language of the Declaration of Independence, which was America's collectively proclaimed philosophy, men's right to liberty (not to mention the right to pursue happiness) was natural and inalienable, it was also, by definition, not subject to negotiation. Yet it appeared from almost all the advocacy of emancipation that came from white sources that the fulfillment of the natural rights of African Americans could in fact be subject to prolonged delays and restrictions, to be determined entirely by the white population at its own discretion in ways compatible with its own comfort. St. George Tucker was keenly aware of the dilemma, which he attempted to overcome by arguing that absolute rights were not necessarily distributed equally and universally.[32] Abraham Lincoln told a later generation of Americans that the nation was "conceived in liberty, and dedicated to the proposition that all men are created equal." A proposition, according to Euclid (whom Lincoln had studied) was a statement that awaited demonstration. The nation's founding experience suggested that even the equal rights on which it based its existence were subject to historical contingency. The next two hundred years would also subject them to considerable refinement and redefinition.

Republican principles did not require that the same fate be allotted to all, but they did exert a powerful and pervasive influence on the courts, where legal principles required that every individual was to be received and treated with equal fairness. Nor was this merely a matter of formal procedure. The force of republican sentiments was revealed in the sympathetic attitude of the courts of Maryland and Virginia to slave claims for liberation on grounds, usually supported only by hearsay, of having

31. Ibid., 34, 46. Tucker's project is printed as an appendix to his edition of Blackstone's *Commentaries on the Laws of England.*
32. Nash, *Race and Revolution,* 151–52.

had free mothers or forebears. These judicial acts of emancipation died out toward the end of the century, at a time of increasing restrictions on the liberties of the rising population of free blacks. Doubts about slavery had never had a safe reception in the lower South, where the slave labor force was fully entrenched. Many of the more ambitious planters were looking southwestward to further expansion where their fortunes would depend on slavery. The 1790s also brought floods of refugees from the slave uprising in San Domingo. The climate was changing for the worse with regard to race, while in other respects it was opening to wider ideas of opportunity.[33]

Social Foundations of an Egalitarian Republic

Republican governments could clearly be adapted to different economies, different social forms, and possibly even to conflicting moral principles. But certain principles were held in common. In the American context, as we have seen again and again, nothing was clearer or more generally understood than that republican principles were incompatible with rule based on hereditary privilege. It was precisely for this reason that opponents of banks and other chartered corporations constantly complained in the early years of the Republic and down through the Jacksonian era that these institutions threatened to create a new aristocracy. Aristocracies, whether based on landed inheritance coupled with political privilege, or on commercial inheritances able to purchase legislative advantages, or still worse on unproductive paper money, were unfair, unequal, and by implication un-American.

Equality, which had always been a language of social and political protest, gained additional force from its sources in republican ideology. One of the earliest targets was the Bank of North America, founded in Philadelphia in 1781 at the instance of Robert Morris, partly with a view to funding the financial operations of the Continental Congress. It was the new republic's first bank, but it had been granted a charter by the Commonwealth of Pennsylvania as well as by the Congress, and it

33. Duncan J. MacLeod, *Slavery, Race and the American Revolution* (Cambridge, 1974), 21, 59, 99, 182; Robert McColley, *Slavery and Jeffersonian Virginia* (Urbana, 1964); Ira Berlin, *Slaves Without Masters: The Free Negro in the Antebellum South* (New York, 1974); Nash, *Race and Revolution*, ch. 2.

attracted the hostility of the radical or Constitutional party which had set up the Constitution of 1776. The contest was joined again in March 1786, in reaction to a recent success by the radicals, who had prevailed on the legislature to repeal the state charter. A petition signed by 624 inhabitants of Philadelphia noted that the anti-bank bill had been rushed through with indecent haste and given two readings on the same day. (The fact that assembly proceedings were now available to the public made this reference to legislative history possible, a striking example of the democratization of politics as a direct result of the Revolution.[34]) The defeat of a number of members in the ensuing elections suggested that the repeal was unpopular, the petitioners observed.

The former assembly had moved the repeal after receiving a set of anti-bank petitions, which had been referred to a committee with an instruction "to enquire whether the bank established at Philadelphia, be compatible with the public safety, and that equality which ought ever to prevail between the citizens of a republic, and to report thereon." The issue was joined on the most fundamental of grounds that could be chosen: the public safety, the ethical principles of the republic. But the committee had disappointed the radicals by reporting in favor of the bank, commenting that its supporters included "the most respectable citizens among us." This language drew from Mr. Smilie (later to appear as an Anti-Federalist) the caustic comment that the committee was "holding out an aristocratical idea. An honest man's the noblest work of God," he affirmed, and "a democratical government like ours, admits of no superiority. A virtuous man, be his situation what it may, is respectable. If we enquire what constitutes the respectability mentioned in the report, we shall probably find it riches. They have more money than their neighbours and are therefore more respectable."[35]

An anti-bank petition received by the present assembly produced an interesting and subtle variation on the republican theme of its predecessors. "The directors," it declared, "are enabled to give such preferences in trade, by advances of money to their particular favourites, when most needed, as to destroy that equality which ought to take place in a

34. For a general account of this development, see J.R. Pole, *The Gift of Government: Political Responsibility from the English Restoration to American Independence* (Athens, Ga., 1983), ch. 5.

35. Mathew Carey, ed., *Debates and Proceedings in the General Assembly of Pennsylvania on . . . the Charter of the Bank* (Philadelphia, 1786), 1–7, 17, 20–21.

commercial country." [36] Pennsylvania, then, was recognized by the anti-bank party as a commercial republic, but for that very reason ought to cling fast to the foundations of equality and eschew the kinds of favoritism which would permit the rise of a new aristocracy. This rhetoric was characteristic of a moral style that was to appear soon afterwards in Anti-Federalist attacks on the Constitution, after that in the opposition to Hamilton's banking and economic policies, and again in the Jacksonian war on the Second Bank of the United States. It was a moral style rather than social or political analysis; it stood on a moral typology of the republic rather than on an empirical examination of popular needs or economic events. An equally democratic and egalitarian alternative to this emotionally powerful but economically sterile opposition was in fact to prove more popular from the early years of the nineteenth century. The expansion of the facility of banking through the proliferation of banks throughout the country, until banks became the agencies of local growth, was a process accompanied by risks, fluctuations, and at times heavy costs, but it was this process that opened the developmental credit needed as much by small farmers and artisans as by wealthy merchants or land speculators.

The bank's enemies had a majority in the Pennsylvania legislature in 1786. [37] Yet the petition which argued for the principles of a "commercial country" had hinted at a significant shift of ground. For the equality "which ought to take place" was here an equality of access to the commercial activities of the country; we find here another hint of the forthcoming doctrine of equality of opportunity. Although this phrase had not yet appeared as a party slogan, the bank's friends in the assembly had already understood the underlying issue of the connection between economic development and individual opportunity. George Clymer pointed out that banks were encouraged in all the commercial nations of Europe; equating republicanism with liberty, he argued that the more republican a country was, the greater would be the success of its banks. The bank had an interest in general prosperity. A director of the Bank

36. Ibid., 15.

37. A resolution to repeal the act which had repealed the bank charter failed by twenty-eight to forty-one; the lists on either side were subscribed. It appears from expressions such as "We on this side" and "My worthy friend over the way" that the Pennsylvania members arranged themselves on opposite sides of the House, as in the House of Commons. Ibid., 132, 27.

of North America told the assembly that through its foreign stockhold-
ing, amounting to $360,000, the bank was bringing money into the
country, and he denied that the charter gave it a monopoly. Robert
Morris, in a cogent defense of the Bank's record, explained that its
operation was to supply a merchant who could then unload a shipful of
goods when he had the goods but not the cash. The profit rate of seven
and three-quarters to eight percent was not exorbitant. As for the fears
of influence, he could only observe that the bank had had the opportunity to create an influence since January 1782, but who had seen or felt
this influence? There was none in the legislature.[38]

The Bank of North America's enemies in Pennsylvania clearly
thought of themselves as the true bearers of the republican faith. They
appeared in different states in different guises but with the same principles wherever the local circumstances raised the issues of unfair privilege
against undeserved hardship or disadvantage. The contrast could be
more extreme in conditions of rural settlement, as the settlers who came
to Kentucky's first constitutional convention knew. Meeting at the beginning of 1785, they hoped to forestall the engrossment of the rich
lands that lay before them by resolving that "to grant any Person a
larger quantity of land that [sic] he designs Bona Fide to seat himself or
his Family on, is a greevance, Because it is subversive of the fundamental
principles of a free republican Government to allow any individual, or
Company or body of Men to possess such large tracts of Country in
their own right as may at a future day give them undue influence, and
because it opens a door to speculation by which innumerable evils may
ensue to the less opulent parts of the Inhabitants and therefor ought not
to be done in the future disposal of Lands in this District."[39]

This was good, sound, old-fashioned republican doctrine, with credentials running back to antiquity. When Madison said in the Philadelphia Convention about eighteen months later that no "agrarian attempts" had yet been made in this country he seems to have overlooked
this resolution to the near west of his own state; but when he added
immediately that "symptoms of a levelling spirit" had already given
notice "of the future danger," though he probably had his eye principally
on Shays's rebellion in Massachusetts, he left no doubt that he regarded

38. Ibid., 28, 29–30, 32, 44–58.
39. Pole, *Revolution in America*, 379–82.

the doctrine of equality with feelings in which intellectual approbation was mixed with social fears.[40] Equality, for Madison the ultimate source of justice, shone with a diffused light in which different features of the political landscape were refracted in variant colors; the abstract principle could never determine the justice of specific policies in particular cases. When Madison went on to recommend the creation of a second house of legislature whose members were to be distinguished for "wisdom & virtue" and should hold office, in his opinion, for nine years, he left hardly less room for doubt that virtue itself was inseparable from a primary regard for the permanent interests of property. Justice required protection of the exercise of equal rights, which at this stage of the argument simply meant unequal property; and the basic reason for having a republic was to protect the right to property, a principle that he by now regarded as the safest indication of the possession of virtue.

The general philosophical problem of the protection of minority interests—being the interests of equal individuals—in a society governed by majority rule had acquired sudden intensity in postwar America; by the time of the Philadelphia Convention, Madison had had the disagreeable advantage of watching the majority in action in Virginia, where he served as a legislator, but he also drew gloomy conclusions about human behavior from the rage for paper money in states other than his own. He explained the problem in clear if somewhat abstract terms in November 1787, when it came his turn to make his first contribution to *The Federalist*, which has an important bearing on the study of the role of equality in American political ideology.[41]

Equality makes its presence felt in this famous essay mainly by indirection. It is "the various and unequal distribution of property" that constitutes both the most common and most durable source of faction, with all its consequences in civil discord and personal insecurity. But the differences which caused these conflicts themselves immediately resulted from "different and unequal faculties of acquiring property." This remarkable statement reveals Madison's true preoccupation. The adverb *immediately* which he chose for emphasis assumes that *mediating* social institutions were absent. Yet Madison knew very well that the vast differences of property which any realistic observer could observe in the

---

40. Farrand, *Convention of 1787* 1:422–23.

41. Cooke, *Federalist* no. 10. See also his scathing remark about "the pestilent effects of paper money" in *Federalist* 44.

contemporary states, and more than most in his own Virginia, had arisen for a wide variety of causes; among these causes, differences of individual ability certainly played their part, but they could hardly be said to outweigh such social factors as inheritance. The rights of inheritance, however, did not result "immediately" from differences of faculty. They rested almost entirely on law and could be altered by law, as had recently happened with the abolition of both primogeniture and entail in Virginia, at the instigation of his friend Thomas Jefferson. Property was a civil institution which could not exist without the support of laws, and those laws would have on many occasions to *mediate* among rival interests, any of which might equally claim derivation from natural rights.

Madison was engaged in an intellectual struggle to conflate the *ability* to acquire property with the *right* to acquire property, setting up protections for the ability in the name of rights. In this cause he had said a few lines earlier that the rights themselves originated in the "diversity of faculties." No one would have disputed that men's faculties were diverse. But Madison might have had greater difficulty in explaining in what philosophical sense it could be maintained that the diversity was itself a *source* of rights. The rights in question were everywhere the same rights, held by different people of diverse faculties. And few would have contested the proposition that men had a natural right to the exercise of the faculties with which they were diversely endowed. Whether, as Madison wished to argue, they therefore had a natural right to all the "immediate" consequences of exercising these faculties was the critical question raised by this argument, and one that he preferred to answer by assumption rather than inquiry. [42]

Madison also took advantage of this essay to qualify the validity of the emerging principle of political equality, at least when exercised without restraints. The aim of the republic was to protect men's equal rights, now threatened by unrestrained majority rule; the essential safeguard lay in "the scheme of representation." Madison's overwhelming concern was to avert the "spectacles of turbulence and contention" that had always characterized pure democracies, a state of affairs resulting from "reducing mankind to a perfect equality in their political rights,"

---

42. Since this passage was written I have had the pleasure of consulting the closely similar analysis in Jennifer Nedelsky's excellent monograph, *Private Property and the Limits of American Constitutionalism: The Madisonian framework and Its Legacy* (Chicago, 1990), chs. 1 and 2.

and he wrote scornfully of "theoretic politicans" who had supposed that in these circumstances men would be "perfectly equalized and assimilated in their possessions, their opinions, and their passions." Each proposition could be stated in the language of equality. But equality was coming to be a disguised synonym for interests, and equality no longer appeared to provide resolutions for the tensions between them.

Madison's fears of majority rule were nicely matched by the Anti-Federalists, whose fears centered on the dangers of political aristocracy and economic privilege. George Mason, always a steadfast republican, objected to the "improper power of the Senate," which he believed would "destroy any balance in the government." The government would begin life as "a moderate aristocracy," after which it would become either a monarchy or "a corrupt oppressive aristocracy." These objections were based on what Mason perceived as a gross inequality in the distribution of effective political power, which would lead to unequal consequences of other sorts, all tending to do away with the egalitarian basis essential to a republic. Inequality was here seen as a direct source of other forms of injustice.

The economic anxieties of other Anti-Federalists were more explicit. An eloquent Massachusetts farmer, Amos Singletary, very clearly saw the danger that lawyers, men of learning, and moneyed men would get into power and manage the Constitution in their own interests; the New York merchant Melancton Smith, himself a man of some substance, spoke eloquently of the fears of "the poor and middling class" and illuminated the keenly felt social distinctions that divided the society of the aspiring republic. Speaking of those he called "the great," he explained that they considered themselves above the common people and entitled to more respect; they did not associate with them. "Being in the habit of profuse living," he said, "they will be profuse in the public expenses. They find no difficulty in paying their taxes, and therefore do not feel public burdens. Besides, if they govern, they will enjoy the emoluments of the government."[43] Anti-Federalists were certain that the social character and structure of the Republic were inseparable from its political forms.

For these reasons, the abuses they feared and anticipated threatened to subvert the entire basis of the Republic. Far from protecting the rights of individuals, or of local communities and unprotected interests like

43. Kenyon, *Antifederalists*, 1, 384–85.

those of the indebted farmers of Massachusetts, the Constitution established a framework in which Anti-Federalists believed they could see the very machinery by which the privileged classes would climb to new and unassailable power. They would run the government, and they would run the economy. Madison worked in close harmony with Alexander Hamilton through the winter and early summer of 1787–1788 in the composite personality of Publius while writing *The Federalist*. But when Hamilton in his new persona as Secretary of the Treasury pursued economic policies that seemed to justify the fears of the former Anti-Federalists by raising a new class based on money and manufactures, Madison's share of Publius marched off in a different direction. Equality suddenly emerged as an active principle justifying surprisingly interventionist proposals for social policy.

Writing in 1792 in *The National Gazette*, which had been founded to report the activities of the new federal government, Madison now suggested that legislative measures might be needed to establish "political equality for all." This move makes political equality, a principle he had wished to circumscribe both in the Convention and in *The Federalist*, into an active instrument of social and economic policy. His earlier stand had already shown that he was willing to adapt the pure principles of equality to superior social purposes, but circumstances had considerably changed. The new circumstances brought by Hamilton's programs prompted a reconsideration of the purposes that equality should be made to serve. Those purposes, he went on, might call for new laws to restrain "*unnecessary* opportunities from the few to increase the inequality of property by an immoderate, and especially unmerited, accumulation of riches." Still more: Madison, who had discerned some signs of leveling tendencies in 1787—though no agrarian movement—now actually advocated laws aimed silently to "reduce extreme wealth towards a state of mediocrity, and raise indigence towards a state of comfort."[44]

44. Gaillard Hunt, ed., *The Writings of James Madison* (New York, 1900–1910) 6:86, 87, 104–05, 106–23. The case could be made that Madison's views of 1787 and 1792 might be harmonized by arguing that legislative intervention was called for on grounds not inconsistent with the protection of the exercise of peoples' original faculties just in those cases where socially dangerous accumulations of wealth were *not* the results of the free exercise of equal rights. The legislative intervention envisaged by Madison and other early members of the Jeffersonian Republican party was to correct the results of previous legislative intervention, and this was basically the opposition view as Hamilton's program unfolded. But, as we have said, previous inequalities were also determined or sustained by law.

Madison was not proposing a state-regulated economy. But on lines wholly consistent with the most ancient principles of republican thought, he was taking his stand against those excessive accumulations of wealth, whether in land, commerce, or money, that placed undue power in the hands of the propertied classes, creating a new aristocracy which threatened the cherished independence of small landowners and ultimately undermined the stability of the state. His views were equally compatible with the advancing columns of laissez-faire economics, and he made a point that would remain an orthodoxy into the twentieth century when he argued that government should refrain from aiding one interest against another.

These fears were not trivial or groundless. Immense disparities of private or corporate wealth would grow up under the aegis of the Constitution. Corporate power would in the future have determinant effects on government policies both foreign and domestic. Although such corporate wealth was frequently amassed with the assistance of grants of various forms of government privilege such as tariffs, tax immunities, and bounties, it was persistently defended on the basis of the equal individual rights that Madison had expounded in *Federalist* 10; and this was in fact an exposition of widely held views. Within five years, Madison had come round to suggesting the radically alternative view that the very principle of equality had a primarily social rather than an individualist basis. He would have replied that if this was a criticism, the new analysis was called for in the defense of the individual rights of the classes who were threatened by the new plutocratic politics. Thus Madison's political thinking could provide the sources for alternative social policies when equality was invoked as the criterion of social justice in America.[45]

The Equalizing Principle of the Constitution

History was to show that the structure of the Constitution could yield differing practices and interpretations. In certain respects, however, the structure itself strongly implied certain principles, and this implication was nowhere stronger than in the principle that the votes of citizens

45. Michael Les Benedict, "Laissez-Faire and Liberty: A Re-Evaluation of the Meaning and Origins of Laissez-Faire Constitutionalism," *Law and History Review* 3:2 (1985).

were to have equal weight. The political thought surrounding the Constitution converged on this principle; nothing in the text led in any other direction. In this sense the Constitution may be said to have contained or embodied the values which it was intended to transmit, and other provisions pertained more explicitly to the expression of these implicit values.

The Constitution created the new and comprehensive class of United States citizens, all of them, as we have also seen, equal in their rights as citizens. It reinforced this principle in a clause, usually called the Comity Clause, which updated a similar clause of the Articles by providing that "The Citizens of each State shall be entitled to all the Privileges and Immunities of Citizens in the several States."[46] A citizen of Massachusetts traveling in South Carolina might not be a citizen *of* South Carolina, but while in that state he was entitled to all the privileges and immunities of its own citizens. There could be no other meaning; and laws passed by South Carolina in the early nineteenth century to restrict the liberty of sailors from northern states whose ships were docked in its ports were plainly unconstitutional.[47] The sailors in question, of course, were free Negroes, and it is central to the present argument that state laws restricting the privileges and immunities of citizens of the United States, or of other states, on grounds of racial or any other social designation were incompatible with the equality of rights protected by the basic text of the Constitution, and would not in principle have had to wait for the Fourteenth Amendment. In deference to state susceptibilities the Comity Clause has always been interpreted very narrowly by the Supreme Court; it has been held to mean only that a state may not discriminate in favor of its own citizens against others. The opportunity of converting the clause into an instrument of nationally enforced equality has been studiously neglected.[48]

46. U.S. Constitution, Art. IV, sec. 2.

47. Charles S. Sydnor, *The Development of Southern Sectionalism, 1819–1848* (Baton Rouge, 1948), 223.

48. The notion that a citizen carries with him through any state he may visit all the rights he may enjoy in his own state has been rejected: *Detroit v. Osborne*, 135 U.S. 492 (1890); *Dred Scott v. Sanford*, 19 Howard 393 (1857); *McKane v. Durston*, 153 U.S. 684 (1894). For discussion, see *The Constitution of the United States of America, Analysis and Interpretation*, Library of Congress, Legislative Reference Service (Washington, D.C., 1952), 686–92. The Articles of Confederation had attempted to achieve the aims of the Comity Clause in rather more diffuse language (Article IV), and it is not without interest

Another potential source of egalitarian principles derived from the text of the Constitution was the Guarantee Clause, which guarantees to each state "a republican form of government."[49] No one has ever been sure what this phrase means or was intended to mean; John Adams once reflected that he had never understood it—"and I believe no man ever will."[50] The Supreme Court was profoundly reluctant to use it as authority for entering into the relations between states and their citizens, and it proved an ineffective instrument for shaping constitutional policies. In the crisis of authority following the Civil War, Charles Sumner told the Senate that the clause was "like a sleeping giant. . . . There is no clause which gives to Congress such supreme power over the states as that clause." Sumner wanted to use it to underwrite political as well as civil rights in the former Confederate states, but William Pitt Fessenden did not see how it could be held to apply to them without extending it to the North—where Sumner himself was content to rely on the weaker implications of the Thirteenth Amendment, which had abolished slavery and its marks. When in 1875 a woman brought suit claiming her right to register as an elector, the Supreme Court dismissed her claim under the Fourteenth Amendment but considered it under the Guarantee Clause, though this procedure merely gave it the opportunity to foreclose discussion by observing that it was now too late to consider an argument on these grounds. (It might better have said too early.) Since 1867, when Radical Republicans briefly stirred it into use, the Guarantee Clause has never done more than stir in its untroubled sleep.[51]

---

that in 1785 the Senate of Massachusetts requested an opinion of the meaning of this clause from the Supreme Judicial Court. The Court rendered an opinion closely corresponding to the meaning of the clause under the Constitution, as interpreted above: "We are therefore of opinion that all persons who are or shall be naturalized by any State of the Union, from any class or denomination of aliens, are by the Confederation considered as entitled to all the privileges and immunities of free Citizens of the several States, and of course in this Commonwealth [of Massachusetts] whenever they shall come to reside within the same." Francis Dana papers, Massachusetts Historical Society, vol. 39: General and Supreme Judicial Court, 1785–1791.

49. Constitution, Art. IV, sec. 4.

50. William M. Wiecek, *The Guarantee Clause of the United States Constitution* (Ithaca, N.Y., 1972), 13–17.

51. Charles O. Lerche, Jr., "Constitutional Interpretations of the Guarantee Clause of a Republican Form of Government during Reconstruction," *Journal of Southern History* 15 (1944); Arthur E. Bonfield, "The Guarantee Clause of Article IV: A Study in Constitutional Disuetude," *Minnesota Law Review* 36 (1962): 546–47; *Congressional Globe*, 39th

Anti-Federalist fears, so rampant in the controversy over ratification, were considerably quieted by the Bill of Rights, adopted by the first Congress of the new Constitution. James Madison, who was deeply disappointed by important aspects of the Constitution of which he was credited with the paternity by later generations, approached the project of a Bill of Rights with disagreeably mixed feelings; he believed in the libertarian principles and recognized the political imperatives of responding to public opinion, not least in Virginia, where the Constitution had been adopted by a very narrow majority, but he felt extreme distaste for the political wrangles it would involve him in, mixed with skepticism as to whether it could achieve its objectives. He had seen the Virginia legislature ride roughshod over his own State's Bill of Rights and came to Congress with little faith in the efficacy of such restraints on legislative power. But there were cogent political reasons for proceeding, not the least being that it would undermine the Anti-Federalist pressure for another convention to revise the work of that of 1787.[52]

These amendments—which Madison originally intended as modifications of the existing phraseology of the Constitution rather than as the additions that they eventually became—were directed primarily against possible abuses of government power. In providing protection against such abuses as unreasonable searches and seizures—a direct descendant of Camden's *General Warrants* rulings—and enforced self-incrimination, and most of all in securing the citizen against deprivation of life, liberty, or property without due process of law, the amendments were explicit in reinforcing the status of American citizens as equals before the laws. There was no new principle at stake in these claims to protection, most of which derived ultimately from Magna Carta itself. (More novel principles were indeed affirmed in the right of peaceable assembly, the liberty of the press, and, of course, the separation of church and state.) But there are reasons for believing that most of the first ten amendments, specifically the second to the eighth, were intended to apply to the states as

Cong., 1st sess. (1866), 702–08; *Minor v. Heppersett*, 21 Wall. 262; Wiececk, *Guarantee Clause*, 292.

52. Leonard Levy, *Constitutional Opinions* (New York, 1986), ch. 5; defending his commitment to the Bill of Rights in later years, Madison explained that he had deferred to his constituents' obvious desire to have a bill added to the draft Constitution. Drew R. McCoy, *The Last of the Fathers: James Madison and the Republican Legacy* (Cambridge, 1989), 89.

well as to the federal government; it was only in 1833 that the Supreme Court ruled that they did not reach into the states. This decision rested on a reading of the language of the amendments that deferred to the prerogatives of the states on all matters not essential to federal power.[53] There were, of course, serious and principled differences of opinion on these matters, but the language of the amendments did not require these concessions.

The Constitution was designed for a plural society, or perhaps better for a plurality of societies, having diverse forms of government. But the republican character that was guaranteed to all of them, present and future, enshrined certain elemental equalities. American citizens were to be equals before the law; they were in general and with some reservations to be equals in the weight attached to their votes; the First Amendment made the federal government a neutral among religions. Nothing in the Constitution could be adduced to deny or depreciate these principles. But they could have no power to determine the courses of economic development or social formation that might grow strong by invoking other equalities. The restless force of equality of opportunity would test the resilience and probe the validity of its moral and intellectual sisters. Much would depend for the American future on whether these quarrels could be kept within the family.

53. The First Amendment is the only one to begin with an express restraint on Congress: "Congress shall make no law respecting an establishment of religion." The remainder are expressed in general negative terms, such as "No person shall be held to answer . . . ," which plainly means that *no* government, either federal or state, shall do whatever is prohibited. For fuller exposition of this point, see W.W. Crosskey, *Politics and the Constitution*, 2 vols. (Chicago, 1953) 2:1070; J.R. Pole, "The Individualist Foundations of American Constitutionalism," in Herman Belz, Ronald Hoffman, and Peter J. Albert, eds., *To Form a More Perfect Union: The Critical Ideas of the Constitution* (Charlottesville, 1992); *Barron v. The Mayor and City Council of Baltimore*, 7 Pet. 243, 8 L.Ed. 672 (1833).

Chapter Four

A Multiplicity of Sects

Long before Enlightenment *philosophes* had formulated a doctrine of the separation of church and state, Roger Williams had spoken of the wall placed by God to separate the garden of his church from contamination by the wilderness of the world.[1] Whether or not a church so protected could have saved the souls of worldly persons, experience had taught Williams that governments could never be trusted to serve the true interests of religion; any form of establishment, however intended, was likely to become oppressive. The only true policy was therefore to free religion from all danger of political interference.

This religious source of the idea of separation was almost opposite to that of the Enlightenment, whose inspiration was secular and whose main aim was to keep the church's hands off the state. In England, where the dilemma was thought to have been solved by an establishment in which the headship of both church and state were merged in the person of the monarch, dissenters and Roman Catholics found themselves separated from the church while they were included in the state, in which, however, they were often deprived of political privileges and civil protections. But after the Glorious Revolution, a policy of toleration supplemented by an attitude of accommodation blurred the more divisive edges of principle. In some of Britain's American colonies the

---

1. Mark De Wolfe Howe, *The Garden and the Wilderness: Religion and Government in American Constitutional History* (Chicago, 1965), 6–7.

Church of England was the officially established church. But in the absence of the symbolic or administrative weight of an American bishop, and increasingly adaptable to local conditions, it grew if anything even more relaxed in doctrine and temperate in practice than at home. Much the most formidable example of an oppressive and extortionate church was that of Rome, established through large parts of Europe and in the American colonies of Catholic powers such as Spain, France, and Portugal; and it was this establishment, especially in France, that excited the fierce anti-clericalism associated with the French Enlightenment and conspicuously shared by Thomas Jefferson. [2]

Jefferson and his contemporaries in the American Enlightenment hated religious persecution as cruel, impious, and irrational. Jefferson believed that the liberties of the people were a gift of God and that people must know and believe this to make their liberties secure. [3] It was not irreligion, but observation of the abuses of religion as a power in the state, that drove Jefferson to his convictions; and it was these convictions that he declared in 1803, when, as President of the United States (in a letter to the Baptists of Danbury, Connecticut) he affirmed that he contemplated "with sovereign reverence that act of the whole American people which declared that their legislature should make 'no law respecting an establishment of religion, or prohibiting the free exercise thereof,' thus building a wall of separation between Church and State." [4]

Jefferson, who was later to acquire more experience of walls when building the famous serpentine wall at the University of Virginia, was not seemingly aware of the ambiguities of his powerful but misleading metaphor. Neither was the Supreme Court, when adopting it nearly one hundred and fifty years later in a case arising from state action to repay the bus fares of children attending a Catholic parochial school, in which the justices addressed themselves to Jefferson's language in order to satisfy themselves of the meaning of the amendment. The belief that the wall of separation was there to protect government from the influence of religion just as surely as to protect religion from political persecution

---

2. Norman Hampson, "The Enlightenment in France," in Roy Porter and Mikulas Teich, eds., *The Enlightenment in National Context* (Cambridge, 1981), 46–48.

3. Thomas Jefferson, *Notes on the State of Virginia*, ed. William Peden (Chapel Hill, 1954), 163.

4. *Complete Works of Thomas Jefferson*, ed. H. A. Washington (Washington, 1854), VIII, 113.

was amplified in Mr. Justice Felix Frankfurter's words when he said that, "If nowhere else, in the relations between Church and State, good fences make good neighbors."[5]

Jefferson's metaphor, which eventually came to play a prominent part in the literature of the subject, seems to belong to the realm of visual imagery rather than analytical thinking. The First Amendment contains two clauses, referring first to "an establishment" of religion and then to its "free exercise." Much of the history of the subject since state aid to parochial schools was challenged in 1947 has run along the line of the implicit tension between these clauses, and it is doubtful whether any one metaphor would aptly fit both. Moreover, the metaphor did not play any decisive part in First Amendment adjudications before being called to mind in that case, and it is inappropriate to any of the relationships that have existed between religion and the state throughout the history of American society.[6]

The constitutional obligation to adjudicate, which is inseparable from the First Amendment, necessarily involves the courts, which are an arm of the state, in attempting to determine what beliefs are and what are not genuinely religious. And since sects or religious organizations are made up of individuals, adjudication has also involved the courts in deciding whether principles that apply to sects apply equally to individuals. While this task is undertaken with this question in mind, the courts feel obliged to offer a higher level of protection to the religious conscience than to the irreligious one. Finally, the haunting question that emerges from these discussions is that of whether the agnostic or irreligious conscience is not entitled to equal consideration with the religious one.[7]

5. Anson Phelps Stokes, *Church and State in the United States*, 3 vols. (New York, 1950) 2:520. Frankfurter's remark occurs in the closely related "released-time" case of *McCollum v. Board of Education*, 333 U.S. 203 (1948).

6. It may be noticed that these views reverse those expressed in J.R. Pole, *The Pursuit of Equality in American History* (Berkeley and Los Angeles, 1978), 60. The wall did not crumble, as there stated; it never existed.

7. Since the First Amendment prohibition refers to Congress, not the judiciary, the courts do not transgress when they adjudicate on these questions; in a sense, therefore, "the separation of church and state" is a misnomer for the American situation. What the courts have to do is to determine whether the legislative branch has transgressed, and the executive is presumably entitled to enter into the same questions when considering the constitutionality of legislation; these questions arise because Congress and the states constantly interact with religion—which it seems to be the overt intention of the First Amendment to avoid. As Chapter 5 will show, the development by American judges of

These arcane but unavoidable complexities were certainly not apparent to the minds of the eighteenth-century politicians and sectarians who struggled to extract some consistent position from the complexities of their own times. The story can best be understood in three phases. The first has tracings in the early antinomian controversies of the 1630s in Massachusetts Bay, leading to the expulsion of Anne Hutchinson and the migration of Roger Williams to Rhode Island. But the principles at stake and their political consequences took more permanent form a century or more later with the religious revivals of the 1740s, later known as the Great Awakening. This phase ends with the adoption of the First Amendment, handing on to the future both the constitutional doctrine of separation and the acceptance of the social character of American religious pluralism. In both the first and second phases, the doctrinal controversies and settlements were contained within a generally unquestioned Protestant aegis. But the second phase is marked by an entirely unanticipated development: the emergence in the second quarter of the nineteenth century of a positive challenge to this aegis, and therefore to the quality of religious pluralism, by a militant Roman Catholic church. These issues persisted fitfully, and were revived to overlap with a third phase, which can be discerned as emerging in the Second World War, when the state began to lose its power to inquire into the validity of claims to religious faith, to be eventually deprived of authority to distinguish between religious and irreligious moral convictions. The real meaning of state neutrality was placed under a course of profound re-examination, most notably by the moral crisis presented by the war in Vietnam.

Equality of religion could in principle subsist for centuries as a question to be determined between an established religion and dissenting sects, the latter of which in their own turn were rivals among themselves. In other words it could be considered as a question of group equality rather than of individual equality. At heart, however, it always involved problems of individual religious choice: an established church tried to predetermine this individual choice, while sects struggled to claim it for themselves. The history of the egalitarian principle must be sought in the

---

a common law doctrine of blasphemy strongly indicates a continuing interaction between public policy and religion. In these cases the judges seem to be making *law* in a manner prohibited to the legislature.

course and outcome of these fierce sectarian contests; they formed the context within which the individual will was obliged to operate in proving its claim to be an equal will exercising an equal conscience.

The Sectarian Struggle for Religious Liberty

It is difficult to adapt the conventional language of the separation of church and state to the religious polity of the early Puritans. They had emigrated from England to get away from an oppressive state, and in certain important respects they devoutly believed in separation; the Calvinist clergy of New England exercised none of the civil and disciplinary powers that fell as a matter of course to every level of the broad ecclesiastical hierarchy in England. Magistrates and ministers exercised different functions, and the clergy did not seek election to public office. Yet the very purpose of the state was to maintain the conditions in which the churches could perform their ministry, and this purpose was compatible with state-imposed taxes for the support of the clergy. Only church members were entitled to vote. In Connecticut, the early settlers incurred John Winthrop's disapproval by relying on clerical counsel in civil matters. Roger Williams, who advocated religious toleration for the sake of civil peace, thought his way through to the extreme view that no true church had existed since the rise of the papacy. It followed that the state could not rightly protect the untrue or imperfect churches men had set up; all must await the Second Coming of Christ, in fulfillment of prophesies in which all Christians believed. [8]

In the course of some two generations, the main body of the ministry in New England had to accommodate itself to a dilution in the religious fervor of the population. It was not that the religious people lost their religion, but rather that in a growing population there were more who did not share it, or shared it only in a diminished degree. A seriously decreasing proportion of inhabitants showed the necessary disposition to become church members, in spite of the fact that church membership was a necessary qualification for political privileges. As the children of nonmembers were for obvious reasons less likely to be presented or present themselves for membership, the situation grew more serious as

8. Edmund S. Morgan, ed., *Puritan Political Ideas, 1558–1794* (Indianapolis, 1965), XXV–XXXV, 222–23.

the population multiplied. To meet this incipient crisis and offer the hope of redemption to the children, the Half-Way Covenant was devised and first adopted in 1662, by which parents who were not professing Christians could present their children for baptism. It was not this theological compromise but King Philip's War in 1675 that revived the people's fears and with them the search for religious comfort; then they came flooding back into the churches. But the clergy could rebuild the bridge between church and community only by admitting compromises in the original covenant of grace and recognizing that unregenerate persons possessed capabilities that had previously been denied. A generally more secular frame of mind continued to pervade those affairs that were not the strict province of the church, and perhaps to define the limits of those that were. [9]

The Puritan ministry's historic grip on the community through the government was shattered when, after the Massachusetts and other relevant charters had been annulled, a consolidated Dominion of New England was established by the crown in 1686. One effect was to create a situation in which the churches were obliged to reach out into the community as they had been less willing to do before. In the process they were now willing to sacrifice some of their purity of doctrine, and this seems to have given some impetus to the adoption of half-way covenants in the congregations. [10] Another effect was that the idea of establishment was weakened. The Dominion itself fell with the Glorious Revolution in England. The new charter of Massachusetts, conferred by the crown in 1691, granted liberty of conscience to all except Roman Catholics but said nothing about any form of ecclesiastical constitution. A law passed by the legislature in its first session to re-establish the platform of church discipline was disallowed by the crown, and about thirty years later a royal instruction prevented progress in a legislative move to call a synod. [11] On the whole, the concept of religious equality

9. Robert G. Pope, "New England versus the New England Mind: The Myth of Declension," *Journal of Social History* 3:2 (Winter 1969–70).

10. Idem, *The Half-Way Covenant: Church Membership in Puritan New England* (Princeton, 1969), 274–76.

11. Thomas Hutchinson, *The History of the Province of Massachusetts-Bay* (London, 1768), ed. L.S. Mayo (Cambridge, Mass., 1936) 2:8–9. Richard R. Johnson, *Adjustment to Empire: The New England Colonies, 1675–1715* (Leicester, 1981), ch. 3, 209–41.

at the personal level had made more progress than was the case under the original charter and certainly more than had been intended by the forces who took the news of the revolution in England as a signal for the restoration of their former powers.

A renewal of religious concern proved to be compatible with a decrease in the clergy's influence on politics. The drift was countenanced, even encouraged, by many of the Congregational clergy of Massachusetts during the early eighteenth century. But in Connecticut, the adoption in 1708 of the Saybrook Platform, which brought that province closer to the Presbyterian churches of the middle colonies and marked what has been called a "parting of the ways" between the churches of Connecticut and Massachusetts, was implemented by legislative authority. [12] Connecticut, which was not a crown colony and whose old charter had survived the chaos, was thenceforth to have a more co-ordinated system under more explicit legislative authority. Massachusetts remained highly federal, with a system of independent congregations, each of which was allowed to levy taxes to support its local establishment. It was in Massachusetts that the Arminian tendency, which meant not merely a generally tolerant attitude to diversity but a positive rejection of the strict Calvinist doctrine of human depravity, appeared to be making the most congenial progress in civil society. To resist these teachings, Jonathan Edwards, minister of Northampton, appeared in his pulpit in 1734 to preach five sermons insisting on the doctrine of justification by grace alone. Edwards discerned heresy in the increasing willingness of the Congregational clergy to tolerate ideas of human capability in dealing with spiritual problems. There was no dearth of texts for the doctrine that all depended on the will and grace of God, making the presumption of human influence a form of heretical arrogance.

Edwards's singular power and intensity unsettled his audience. But the process was indirect, almost subterranean. In 1736 a remarkable revival of religion shook Northampton and neighboring towns, on Edwards's own account affecting "all sorts, sober and vicious, high and low, rich and poor, wise and unwise. It reached the most considerable

12. C.C. Goen, *Revivalism and Separatism in New England, 1740–1800* (New Haven, 1962), 3.

families and persons, to all appearance, as much as others."[13] A few more years were to pass before the English settlements were shaken, between 1740 and 1742, by the greatest spiritual upheaval in their history.

When the Calvinist clergy turned their attention to worldly affairs, they were apt to deprecate their accumulation of riches and draw the people's minds back to the primal rule and condition of equality among men. But the "Rule of Equity," which forbade envy of one's neighbor's goods or fortune, clearly permitted a basic acceptance of the ways in which the goods of this world happened to be distributed in civil society. Calvinists were not concerned with any program of social action or even of prescriptive social judgments; Edwards himself treated the distribution of worldly goods as a matter for contentment.[14] Calvinism had little to offer to those who resented the social status of their worldly superiors; a system which declared that some were elect and the rest were damned might disclaim all official knowledge of the exact distribution of these fates, but the clergy could comfort themselves that it was most unlikely that the teachers of the doctrine would prove to be among its victims. Meanwhile, they could entertain the idea of a relationship between spiritual and worldly attributes. The implications of Calvinist teaching had from its beginnings at least not been inconsistent with notions corresponding to hierarchy in the social order. As John Winthrop had himself said in a celebrated sermon, "In all times some must be rich and some poore, some highe and eminent in power and dignitie; others meane and in subieccon."[15] The apparently more relaxed mentality of the Half-Way Covenant was not particularly conducive to ideas of personal equality; it conferred advantages of the highest spiritual importance on the children of those who had once been baptized. The point could hardly have been put more clearly than by Increase Mather when he said in 1678 that "God hath seen meet to cast the line of Election so, as that it doth (though not wholly and only, yet) for the most part run through the loyns of

13. Jonathan Edwards, "A Narrative of Surprising Conversions" (1736) in *Select Works of Jonathan Edwards* (London, 1965) 1:19.

14. Alan Heimert, *Religion and the American Mind from the Great Awakening to the Revolution* (Cambridge, Mass., 1966), 304–08.

15. John Winthrop, "Modell of Christian Charity," *Winthrop Papers*, ed. A.B. Forbes, 5 vols. (Boston, 1929–47) 2:282.

godly parents." [16] The way of salvation ran through the genetics of privilege.

Neither the theological tendencies of the Half-Way Covenant nor the doctrines of its opponents suggested that equality of religious choice was a prominent issue when Jonathan Edwards became the first influential minister of his generation to attack the Half-Way Covenant and to insist on the immediacy of God's grace. But in one important sense, Edwards forced a possibly unintended shift in the balance; both emotionally and intellectually he made a powerful and sustained contribution to the sense of the importance of the individual. Other ministers maintained and diffused the same message. George Whitefield, who laid greater stress on God's love and grace than did some of his contemporaries, traveled so widely and became known for the same mission in so many provinces that he has been described as America's first "national" figure—a sobriquet which would ordinarily presuppose the existence of a nation. [17] The egalitarian implications of these teachings might depend on the thrust of an individual preacher; the passion of Edwards and his fellows was directed towards saving souls. While this meant that the social or political consequences, whatever they might be, were of secondary importance from the preacher's point of view, it also meant that men and women were being appealed to as beings capable of responsibility for their own lives, and almost, as many must have felt, for their own salvation. Edwards may not have wished to unpack the social implications of his theological message, but he could not stop others from going more directly to this point, and he could hardly prevent even his own audience from doing their own unpacking.

The new light struck where it would, without regard for social station. An intense preoccupation with one's own soul might teach the believer that all were equal in the sight of God, or at worst that all people shared a grim equality in depravity, but it did not require people to question or reform social institutions. The new light separated its beneficiaries from the old, unilluminated ministry and their congregations and called on the newly illuminated to form "separate" churches. But Separatism was never simply a religion of the disinherited, and in the Awakening, as

16. *Pray for the Rising Generation*, quoted by Edmund S. Morgan, *The Puritan Family*, (New York, 1966), 182–83.

17. H. Richard Niebuhr, *The Kingdom of God in America* (New York, 1956), 126.

noted by Edwards in the earlier phase, the evidence suggests that a fairly representative segment was swept by the movement.[18] Poor and humble adherents were balanced in proportions that seem to have related to the normal structure of the community by members of the most prominent local families.

There does not seem to be any evidence, however, that these religious convictions tended to align members of wealthy or prominent families with any sort of movement for social reform. The wealthier classes of Boston were inspired by Whitefield's preaching of God's grace but felt no such sympathy when James Davenport attacked their privileges along with the corruption of the established clergy. Although Davenport's inflammatory preaching aroused the tattered poor of Boston and caused a corresponding moment of alarm among the burghers and the magistracy (who had him declared non compos mentis), there was no apparent decline in the following of the city's clergy and no one seems to have claimed that either social structure or civic policy were affected by these manifestations.[19]

The Separates questioned established religious authority by the very nature of their faith. Nothing could make the matter plainer than the title of Gilbert Tennent's sermon of 1740, *The Danger of an Unconverted Ministry*.[20] Tennent had no socially subversive aims, but his message could not be devoid of social implications. The idea of a laity educated in religion had entered powerfully into the early appeal of Protestantism. But education had its own arcane hierarchy. It fell to the self-proclaimed New Light clergy to attack these bastions of a new privilege and assert that education and the higher learning, Hebrew, Greek, and Latin, established positions of spiritual authority closely linked with social esteem— none of these attributes, which were merely the products of formal schooling, could give a man the knowledge that came from the light

18. Goen, *Revivalism*, 188–91.

19. Gary B. Nash, *The Urban Crucible: Social Change, Political Consciousness and the Origins of the American Revolution* (Cambridge, Mass., 1979), 208–12. It is significant that Nash, who (on his own reckoning) takes Davenport more seriously than most historians have done, himself points out that the Boston clergy kept their flocks. Nash more than once finds "deference" crumbling but does not notice its tendency to resurrection. He rightly draws attention to the background of the currency crisis but does not show that any long-term social consequences resulted from these disorders or from Davenport's fiery intervention. Davenport's career of prominence was brief.

20. Printed in Richard L. Bushman, ed., *The Great Awakening: Documents on the Revival of Religion, 1740–1745* (New York, 1970), 87–93.

itself. The educated ministry had no authority to preach from their education. The Separates wanted to set up their own churches and naturally wanted to support their own ministers without being taxed to support those they had renounced. These demands followed entirely from their religious convictions and not from any intended criticism of the political order. But they had no need of colleges like Harvard and Yale and no respect for the prestige conferred by those institutions. Moreover, religious conviction could be a disturber of the peace, for those who had experienced conversion felt impelled to carry the message abroad to other neighborhoods. Many newly converted ministers felt that itinerancy was a duty of their conversion. It is easy to see that it was more than that; it must have been a means of expressing a certain restlessness in the quiet communities of New England. Itinerant ministers, however, threatened the tranquility of existing congregations in a manner which we have learnt to associate with "invasions of territory" and often met with bitter resistance. Itinerant evangelists who succeeded in attracting audiences against the will of the established minister—and the minister could hardly be expected to welcome the brotherly aid of an uninvited guest who made a point of being his superior in God's grace—naturally shook the standing of the clergy. The social order that sustained the established clergy could survive these incursions, but not without some conscious readjustments in its own internal relationships. Even within the old order, commitment required some sort of personal decision rather than the repetition of habit.

Nothing more emphatically demonstrated the Separates' rejection of established religion than their insistence on lay ordination, which to them was the necessary consequence of the fact that a man who had experienced divine truth was superior in religious knowledge even to a learned minister who had never known true conversion. The same was true of women. If the new light did not respect rank, it was soon clear that it did not practice sexual favoritism; what was true for men was true for women, and although women would wait more than two more centuries before becoming ministers, they took a much more conspicuous and influential part in the activities of Separatist congregations.[21] Edwards's own earliest observations were of the influence of pious—or

21. Anne Hutchinson, who was banished from Massachusetts in 1637 because she had taken it upon herself to preach on the authority of direct revelation from God, may in this context be considered a striking example of the exception that illustrates the rule.

reformed—young women on the moral conduct of their communities.

Separate churches were formed by new light congregations who could no longer agree to support orthodox ministers. But the laws extracted tax payments to support ministers of the established church: to that extent ecclesiastical establishment did survive in Massachusetts under the second charter as well as in Connecticut. Under laws dating from 1728 and 1729, Quakers and Baptists—or Anabaptists, as the latter were called—were formally exempt from these requirements. The earliest Separatist movement toward Baptism seems to have been a device for escaping "double taxation"—for orthodox ministers as well as their own. On its merits, however, the Baptist argument had the force of a consistent inner logic. If it was true that conversion depended on the light, and that only a person who had experienced true conversion could be properly baptized, then baptism without conversion was an empty ceremony, and infant baptism was a hollow and blasphemous practice. In August 1751 Isaac Backus, the young new light minister of Titicut in Massachusetts, who was to become the most powerful Baptist spokesman in the land, overcame three years of misgivings over these difficult questions and allowed himself to be immersed.[22] This was a departure from all the orthodoxies of his training that Jonathan Edwards was never able to make.

The new light community, meanwhile, was by its nature or by God's grace a closed and select community. Secure in their moral superiority to the learned ministry, the New Lights do not seem to have been led by God's grace toward an excessive humility or a more egalitarian view of their human or spiritual worth. "We believe," declared the Confession of the Mansfield Separates in 1745, "that we are of that Number who are Elected of GOD to eternal Life, and that Christ did live on Earth, die and live again for us in particular."[23] Among themselves they were entirely democratic and egalitarian; but their reasoning could have led just as well to a new kind of moral hierarchy as had that of the old Calvinists.

In one important sense, however, the revival, by shaking the old congregations until in many cases they split into separate churches, did

---

22. William G. McLoughlin, *Isaac Backus and the American Pietistic Tradition* (Boston, 1967), 58; William G. McLoughlin, ed., *Isaac Backus on Church, State and Calvinism: Pamphlets, 1754–1789* (Cambridge, Mass., 1968), 29.

23. Quoted in Goen, *Revivalism*, 151.

influence the old lights as well as the new. Wherever the revival spread, it forced ordinary people to question the authorities to which they had habitually deferred. And whatever the outcome, the process required people to make up their own minds. The very nature of the Pietist challenge detracted from the old clergy's power to command obedience on the basis of authority alone. But these effects in themselves might have receded within a couple of years if they had been left alone. The dispute began to get its political dimension when ministers, with support from town officers, fought—sometimes physically—to keep itinerants out, just as they invoked the law to enforce tax payments. Behind them, the General Court still maintained the old line of connection between spiritual and political authority.

The Awakening, like all great religious movements, had disturbing effects on the social order. But also in common with other revivals of religion, the spiritual effects of the Awakening ran out like a receding tide; the shore was marked and freshened by the incursion, but after two years of swirling floods, the main effort was spent. By 1744 the dejected clergy had no news to report.[24] Many later revivals occurred, but the devoted and hard-working itinerants of many sects knew human nature too well to expect the effects of their labors to survive without repeated visitations and ever-renewed exhortations.

At heart the Awakening represented a renewal, a rebirth, of the spiritual impulses that earlier, in northern and central Europe in the early sixteenth century, had forged the Protestant Reformation. But a movement whose aims were spiritual rather than social or—still less—political, and whose primary impulse faded some thirty years before the first Continental Congress, does not seem to stand forth as a strong candidate among the social or political influences leading to the American Revolution. Pietist doctrine concerned the salvation of souls; it was not a political theory. By teaching that each individual ought to have a personal relationship to God, and that this relationship was incomparably more important than those that belonged to the world, Pietism enhanced the self-esteem of its adherents and gave the humblest among them a sort of lifeline of spiritual escape from whatever troubles or oppressions they might suffer in the world. Among its adherents, the

24. Nathan O. Hatch, "The Origins of Civil Millennialism in America," *William and Mary Quarterly* 31:3 (July 1974), 414.

revival encouraged a new and intense spiritual intimacy to which rank and precedence were entirely irrelevant, but this intimacy did not spread itself beyond the beam of the new light. Although some Pietist preachers defied the secular authorities and provoked breaches of the peace, Pietism had no theological message that required its initiates to disregard such institutions as the courts, the legislatures, or the laws of property. If it were true, as many historians have maintained, that a linear connection developed from the religious revivals to the democratization of American society and the formation of a revolutionary national consciousness, it would be necessary to explain the effects of those revivals on the large proportion of Americans whom they left unmoved or even hostile. When the matter is put this way, it can hardly be said that arguments based on the social consequences of pietistic theology have established the connection. [25] The argument leaves too much unexplained; if those in sympathy numbered as much as half the population—which is only a guess—then as many stayed with the old faith, or with none. It was not the Baptists, still less the Quakers, who led the people in the direction of resistance to British policies; on the contrary, it was the established or "liberal" clergy who exhorted their congregations in defense of American liberties. In later years, Boston, the leading center of intellectual influence, shifted towards Unitarianism and Universalism, both of which had legitimate claims on American sentiment. The Pietists challenged the existing political order and sometimes broke the laws, not because Pietism was a social or political theory but because the law supported the social order in trying to suppress them. The law against itinerancy stood directly in their path. In their defiance, the Separates may well have drawn to their side some people who had private causes of discontent; old lights certainly felt threatened by a general spirit of rebelliousness which the limited police powers of the parish might have found hard to control. [26]

This is not to argue that there was no connection between theology and the emergence of more egalitarian views of society. But the experience of religious conversion meant different things in different societies.

---

25. A more detailed analysis of this question may be found in my *The Pursuit of Equality in American History* (1978), pp. 68–69 n. 18.

26. Richard L. Bushman, *From Puritan to Yankee: Character and Social Order in Connecticut, 1690–1765* (Cambridge, Mass., 1967), 235–37.

The example of the Quaker presence in North America provides a curious paradox in this connection. In their theology and in their internal relations among themselves, the Friends were among the most consciously egalitarian of sects; but they had no mission to reform social relationships that underlay their own political control, and the more prosperous members of their own later generations melted almost imperceptibly into the merchant gentry of Philadelphia—or, as in the case of the Penn family, became Anglicans. Yet it was the Quakers who, rich and poor, made one of the most internationally powerful and sustained attacks on slavery.[27]

Colonial societies, in fact, differed widely from one another in religion and in religious policy, responding in correspondingly different ways to the rise of Pietism. Pennsylvania, a scene of increasing religious diversity over which Quaker power was gradually losing its political grip, offered no resistance at all, and it is significant that historians have not generally attributed the rise of egalitarian or democratic feelings in Pennsylvania to the social effects of the Great Awakening. The point is a negative one, which helps to explain the more positive developments in New England and to a lesser extent in the South. Political oppression, maintained over long years of repeated distraints, imprisonments, and nagging persecutions forced the survivors of the Awakening to turn to politics, making them conscious that equality of religion must be taken up as a political cause, to be safeguarded by laws as well as by conscience.

The Development of the Baptist Case
for Separation of Church and State

Religious intolerance was nothing new in New England, where official policies were sharply out of keeping with the intentions of the English Act of Toleration. The Massachusetts Congregational churches had never had much taste for the compromises which formally exempted Quakers and Baptists; except in Rhode Island, the rulers of the New England provinces had no inclination to follow the British preference for co-existence of rival religions and a deprecation of persecution. After the

27. David Brion Davis, *The Problem of Slavery in Western Culture* (Ithaca, 1966), ch. 10, 483–93; Alan Tully, *William Penn's Legacy: Politics and Social Structure in Provincial Pennsylvania, 1726–1755* (Baltimore, 1977), 73–78.

fading of the Awakening, Separation went into an early (though not a complete) decline, partly because of painful internal differences over the theory of infant baptism but partly because the coercive measures employed by the State were very effective. Separates who refused to pay taxes assessed for the official clergy had their homes invaded and their goods seized for sale at auction, while they themselves were often thrown into jail. In Connecticut the town of Windham added a new story to its jail in 1753 to make room for expected new inmates.[28] In Massachusetts the General Court imposed new obstacles to Baptist exemptions. By a law of 1753, the procedures by which a Baptist could get an authorized certificate of his religious affiliation, as required for tax exemption, were tortuous, humiliating, and in many cases impossible to fulfill. Despite bitter protests this act was renewed in 1757 and survived until 1770; in Connecticut, legal disabilities were even more severe.[29]

It was these repressions that forced the Baptists to turn their attentions to politics and led Isaac Backus to reflect gravely on the possible consequences of placing all power over religious conscience in the hands of the State. The Massachusetts Baptists replied to the act of 1753 with a *Memorial and Remonstrance* drawn up the next year and presented to the General Court by a committee "on behalf of several societies of the people called Baptists." This pamphlet represented an important step in the clarification of Baptist attitudes to church and state as well as to the right relationship between churches. It warned the legislature that the act of 1753 was contrary to the laws of England—a serious line to take in Massachusetts, where legislative autonomy had always been regarded with exceptional jealousy. The Baptist committee not only hinted at their preference for Britain's broader tolerance but implied that oppressed colonial minorities might seek parliamentary or royal protection. They went on to assert their right to freedom from persecution equally with any religious group—a claim based at least nominally on the English Act of Toleration.

These were the beginnings of a political argument about equality, not a theological one. But the egalitarian practices which the Baptists are often said to have contributed to the character of American social assumptions were far from being the only kind that could be fairly drawn

28. Goen, *Revivalism*, 195.
29. Ibid., 269.

from Christian teaching. The liberal Calvinist minister Jonathan May-
hew—soon to be one of Backus's political opponents—explained another view, when he said in a sermon in 1754, quoting Luke 12:48, "It
is an established maxim of God's equal government that 'Unto whomso-
ever much is given, of him much shall be required.' "[30] Equality here
became a doctrine of service, but it made no pretense that men were
equally endowed, nor did it quarrel with the unquestionable distribution
of things. In this reading, equality is indistinguishable from such concepts
as fairness.

In face of the relentless application of the tax laws and of persecution
in some country towns, in 1767 twenty Baptist churches overcame their
scruples about entering into larger organizations and sent representatives to the Massachusetts town of Warren, where they began the
association bearing that name. The problem posed by the requirement
of certificates for tax exemption had taken an acute form in the recently
settled town of Ashfield, where an act of the legislature vested power
in the proprietors rather than in the inhabitants. Upon the nonpayment
of religious taxes by Baptists in the town, the proprietors used their
powers to sell at auction 398 acres of property owned by the Baptists,
valued at £363.13s., for a paltry £19.3s. Failing redress at home, the
grievance committee resolved to take the whole issue to the Lords of
Trade in London, in which they seem to have had some indirect assistance from Governor Hutchinson, who did not like Baptists but was
willing to see the General Assembly's authority called into question. The
outcome was that in July 1771 the crown disallowed the law objected
to by the grievance committee. The Baptists had been relieved in their
distress not by the General Assembly in which they were represented
but by the royal authority which presided over the whole Empire.[31] The
Baptists' struggle for religious liberty was prolonged into the period
when the General Assembly of Massachusetts became preoccupied with
the quarrel with Britain. But the advance of the conflict gave the Baptists
no cause for comfort when American liberties were taken under the
protection of the Congregationalist majority. It seemed far from certain

30. A.W. Plumstead, ed., *The Wall and the Garden: Selected Massachusetts Election
Sermons, 1670–1775* (Minneapolis, 1968), 298.
31. Isaac Backus, *Church History of New England from 1620 to 1804* (Philadelphia,
1804), 192–93; McLoughlin, *Backus on Church, State, and Calvinism*, 11–12; idem, *New
England Dissent, 1630–1833*, 2 vols. (Cambridge, Mass., 1971) 1: ch. 29, 531–46.

that Baptists or other religious minorities, who could now be truly classified as "dissenters," would have protection for their own religious rights if ever Massachusetts became an independent state.

The Baptists were taking obvious risks. The least lack of enthusiasm for the more popular notion of American liberties, the least suspicion of sympathy with Britain, exposed them to grave suspicions of treachery to the American cause in the rising struggle with crown and parliament. Yet the legislature persisted in renewing the tax laws, leaving the Baptists little choice but to show equal persistence in opposition. An incidental irony which did not escape Backus's notice was that the fee of fourpence local money or threepence sterling was the same as the tea tax which had provoked the Boston Tea Party![32] In 1773, in default of remedies, the grievance committee proposed to individual Baptists that they refuse to comply with the tax requirements—virtually civil disobedience. Although this plan was not translated into action by many churches, the discontent of so significant a faction had to be pondered by legislators as questions of loyalty became increasingly urgent.

Backus's arguments pointed directly towards the doctrine of the separation of church and state. In an important pamphlet, *An Appeal to the Public for Religious Liberty*, published to promote the campaign for civil disobedience, he explained that God had appointed two kinds of government, ecclesiastical and civil, and emphasized that "they ought not to be confounded together." It is clearly implicit that the free exercise of religion would stand to benefit from the separation of religion and government. In the matter of taxation and representation he was careful to observe that the Baptists agreed with their legislators; the question they raised was of a different order—whether their civil legislators could claim to be their representatives in religious affairs. "They [our opponents] often talk about *equality* in these affairs," Backus exclaimed in a revealing comment, "but where does it appear?"[33] The Baptist case for religious equality did not draw its strength from the Anglo-American Commonwealth tradition, however, nor did it rest on natural rights. Backus was satisfied with those granted in the charter. These distinctions were of considerable philosophical importance. Backus might have had difficulties in asserting the natural rights of a creature whose condition,

32. Backus, *Church History*, 192.
33. Ibid.

since the Fall, was one of fundamental moral depravity. He denounced the Congregationalists for using the word *equality* as an excuse for taxing Baptists to support Congregational ministers. But natural rights found their way into the argument by a different route, leading to a conclusion of surprising similarity to that of his whig opponents, when he described "equal liberty of conscience" as "that dearest of all rights"—a right given by God.[34] On the other hand, Backus could have no sympathy with philosophers who were prepared to talk of the laws of nature as though God himself were subject to them—as though he were in truth "nature's God." In terms of rights with which people were equally endowed, and which therefore imposed moral restraints on religious oppression, his reasoning led in the same direction as that of political Whigs or liberal clergy. Backus was getting the better of an argument in their own language.

The meeting of the Continental Congress in September 1774 gave the Massachusetts Baptists a new and more spectacular stage. Backus traveled to Philadelphia with two colleagues carrying a memorial from about twenty of their churches, giving a summary of the oppressions suffered under the tax law.[35] They presented the memorial at a meeting with the Massachusetts delegation on the evening of 14 October, when John Adams replied with a speech about the mildness of the Massachusetts arrangements for religious establishment. But the meeting does not seem to have been in private, and Israel Pemberton, an elderly and distinguished Philadelphia Quaker, intervened with a forthright speech about religious persecution in Massachusetts which Adams regarded as "quite rude." Adams told him that the people of Massachusetts were as religious and conscientious as the people of Pennsylvania, and their consciences dictated to them that it was their duty to support their existing laws—an assertion which must have seemed to the Baptists like a very special case of special pleading. Samuel Adams, another member of the Massachusetts team, who had been a member of the legislature when the particular matters complained of were debated, gave the meeting an account of those events which satisfied his colleagues that no oppression

34. Ibid., 338. In principle it seems difficult to see much difference for Baptists and the orthodox Calvinist clergy in the problem of natural rights in relation to man's fallen condition. It was perhaps mainly a question of what they preferred to emphasize.

35. McLoughlin, *New England Dissent* 1:558–60.

had occurred. But John Adams developed a strong suspicion that they were becoming entangled in a Quaker plot, to which the Massachusetts Baptists were lending themselves, to sow disunity in the American cause. The Boston lawyer Robert Treat Paine snarled at Backus that they were only contending against paying a little money, not about conscience; to which the Baptist minister replied with another affirmation of faith: "It is absolutely a point of conscience with me," he said, "for I cannot give in the certificates they require without implicitly acknowledging that power to man which I believe belongs to God." This declaration, together perhaps with the obvious dangers of disunity, seems to have made an impression; the meeting closed with assurances that the Massachusetts delegation would see what could be done for the Baptists' relief.[36] Backus was later able to claim that not one Baptist had been listed by the General Court among the 311 who were banned as traitors from returning to Massachusetts. Yet in spite of the assurances given at the Philadelphia meeting, independence did nothing to relieve the Baptists' anxieties; in 1777 the legislature passed a further tax exemption law, which still required Baptists to pay for exemption certificates to be issued by town clerks.[37]

When the legislature presented the towns with a new constitution in 1778, Backus renewed the attack with a powerful assertion that civil rulers could not represent Baptists in religious affairs. As to the fee for exemption certificates, he echoed the tones of colonial resistance to parliamentary taxation: "It is not the PENCE but the POWER that alarms us." Backus snatched his sharpest tactical weapon in this argument from the grasp of the liberal Congregational clergyman Charles Chauncy, who had forged it ten years earlier for use against an Anglican bishop in America. In that dispute, Chauncy had declared, "We are, in principle, against all civil establishments in religion," and concluded, "By the Gospel-charter all Christians are vested with precisely the same rights." Backus had only to quote these expressions to prove his opponents' divergence from their own principles.[38]

These struggles revealed significant differences of principle between

36. L.H. Butterfield, ed., *Diary and Autobiography of John Adams* (Cambridge, Mass., 1961) 2:152–54; Backus, *Church History*, 192–93; McLoughlin, *New England Dissent* 1:558–61.
37. Backus, *Church History*, 196.
38. McLoughlin, *Backus on Church, State and Calvinism*, 350–65.

Isaac Backus and his whig-republican contemporaries of the civic human-ist persuasion about the origins and necessity of government. The latter tended, with different degrees of emphasis and inclination, to regard government as a disagreeable phenomenon, though not all would have gone as far as Thomas Paine's assertion that it was "a badge of lost innocence." The concept of some sort of innocence, however, was ex-tremely important, for American whigs had accepted the idea of a state of nature in which rights already existed and held as an article of political faith that property belonged among those rights. These views and the disposition to regard them as fundamental had little in common with the thought of the Pietists, for whom heresy began when people forgot or denied original sin. Backus took a less sanguine view of any suppositious state of nature and recognized clearly that there could be no liberty worth having without government; the only alternatives to civil govern-ment were tyranny and licentiousness. The crucial need that was proved in these prolonged disputes was to break down not only religious monopolies but all vestiges of religious privilege.

The equality of religious conscience that Backus and the Baptists contended for was equality among Christians. These views were in no sense libertarian, nor were they motivated by considerations of toler-ance. They did not imply equality for fundamentally differing religions (and Catholicism was "fundamentally" different) or between religion and irreligion. What these arguments did, under different circumstances and in different times, was to resume the attack on the concept of religious establishment, which Roger Williams had opened from his own radical standpoint in early Massachusetts and William Penn had incorporated into the fundamentals of his plan for Pennsylvania some fifty years later. With the memorial which Backus took with him to Philadelphia in 1774, they constituted the early steps in America towards the solution of complete state neutrality which, for the Federal government, was nomi-nally implied in the First Amendment.

Principles of religious equality were more an incidental than an inten-tional product of these controversies. Despite the bitter conflicts be-tween political parties developing in the 1790s (and possibly to some extent because of them), many of the newer clergy felt increasingly impelled to define the character and purposes of the Republic in religious terms. Christianity was seen as the religion of a free republic and republi-can government as the only form suitable to the true principles of

Christianity. With this view, Backus's colleague John Leland, who did most of his mission work in Virginia, agreed, expressing religious sentiment in terms of political sympathies: "As far as church government on earth is the government of Christ," he said in a sermon in 1804, "it is of democratical genius." Its forms of government were congregational, and the spirit which ruled among the subjects of Christ's kingdom "greatly resemble the genius of a republic, and as greatly confronts the inequality and haughtiness of monarchies." [39]

The importance of this partly successful struggle lay in a clarification of the issues. Isaac Backus and his colleagues had forced their contemporaries to define the objects and terms of the relationship between church and government and had gone far to demonstrate that no form of establishment for one religion could be wholly compatible with equality for others. It was important, too, that Backus had defined the moral basis of the claim for equality of conscience, for that claim did not rest exclusively on the whig idea of social contract. The rights of religion were prior to those of society. (So, of course, were the rights of property in the civic humanist tradition, but there lay the difference.)

These distinctions emerged in the same period in Virginia. The Baptist Separates disturbed the spiritual tranquility of the Valley of Virginia during the late 1760s; small but settled Baptist communities were startled by these incursions; the Anglicans were often enraged. But the Baptists' claims on other peoples' souls and their own claims to recognition stopped far short of any interest in controlling the political system. In Virginia no more than in New England did they seek a new political order or a redistribution of worldly goods, and in this sense their contribution to the spread of ideas of equality was less than has sometimes been claimed for them; it was not in any case a contribution for which they wished to claim credit. Yet in spite of these reservations the Separates and more militant Baptists did challenge the social order. The

39. Edwin Scott Gaustad, "The Backus-Leland Tradition," in W.S. Hudson, ed., *Baptist Concepts of the Church* (Philadelphia, 1959), 123. Nathan O. Hatch, *The Sacred Cause of Liberty: Republican Thought and the Millennium in Revolutionary New England* (New Haven, 1977), 145, 146–59. As early as 1779 the Rev. James Dana described the ancient government of the Hebrews as "a confederate republic with JEHOVAH at the head." Anticipating Alexis de Tocqueville's expression, he went on to say that "equality of condition was provided for, and the means of corruption prevented" (159). Equality was no less important in this vision of the republic than in that of the civic humanist tradition.

equality of relationships and simplicity of dress and manner in their own communities contrasted sharply with the preoccupation with rank, etiquette, and formalities of style and procedure which did much to give the Virginian gentry its exalted tone.[40]

The formal privileges of the Anglican church were extensive, but they were exercised with little severity or determination. The main instrument at hand for restraining the excesses of the new invaders was a requirement that preachers obtain a license to preach only in specified places. Itinerancy defied this restriction even where the preachers might have been able to comply with the regulations. The noise made by the Separates seems to have been disproportionate to their numbers, which are difficult to estimate; the rapidity of growth was more alarming to the gentry than the actual numbers. The seven Separate Baptist churches recorded in 1769 had already become fifty-four by late 1774.[41] Their political influence, however, was associated with concentration of numbers, of particular value through the patronage they gained in the House of Burgesses.

Principles and Politics of Religious Toleration: The Enlightenment in Action

The intellectual heritage of Thomas Jefferson and James Madison was entirely different from that of the Baptists whose cause they adopted in the Virginia legislature. They believed in liberty of thought and conscience with a conviction as intense as the Baptists' belief in salvation. Although Jefferson and Madison acknowledged the existence of a Creator, and Madison had received a large theological component in his education at the College of New Jersey (Princeton), and although both perceived an ultimate connection between the reasons for religious belief and the reasons for liberty of conscience, it would nevertheless have been intellectually possible for them to hold that belief without faith in personal salvation. Both men were heavily in debt to Locke's *Letter on*

40. Rhys Isaac, *The Transformation of Virginia, 1740–1790* (Chapel Hill, 1982), 163–72.

41. Ibid., 12–13; 173. Also idem, "Evangelical Revolt: The Nature of the Baptists' Challenge to the Traditional Order in Virginia, 1765–1775," *William and Mary Quarterly* 31:3 (July, 1974), 346 n. 2; Wesley M. Gewehr, *The Great Awakening in Virginia, 1740–1790* (Durham, N.C., 1930), passim.

Toleration; but for them, toleration was never enough, and they preferred the stronger concept of religious liberty. The rationalist thinking of their age drew on a considerable heritage from the seventeenth century, which had gained enormous subsequent vitality from Newton's demonstration that the universe was co-ordinated by mechanical and rationally explicable laws. The works of European philosophers were easily compatible with the Anglican affiliations of many American leaders, especially those in the southern provinces and in New York, where their outlook was often tinged with a worldliness that sometimes passed over into deism. In America as in Britain such men—Jefferson was in this something of an exception—rarely became subject to the violent anticlericalism that affected French intellectuals after rising from similar philosophical sources. (The French had experience as well as philosophy to feed their indignation.) American Anglican consciences tended to take their color from the English attitude, and there was little to terrify them in the powers of their own established churches.

Jefferson's mind and temperament were in keeping with this intellectual background. He was far from irreligious; his deepest moral convictions would have been shattered by a denial of a religious explanation of the world. But his deism reflected an earnest rejection of dogma. He was horrified by both the cruelty and the sheer absurdity of religious persecution, for which he blamed the priesthood and of which he suspected New England. The truth—an abstract concept for which he had the most profound devotion—could never be discovered, nor could people be led to it, by coercion. "The legitimate powers of government extend to such acts only as are injurious to others," he declared in a famous passage. "But it does me no injury for my neighbor to say there are twenty gods, or no god. It neither picks my pocket nor breaks my leg." The only way to seek the truth, and the only way to convince others, was by reason and persuasion. "To make way for these, free enquiry must be indulged." [42]

Although it was widely held that some form of established or at least officially recognized religion was indispensable to social order, this conviction did not extend to the benefits of moral coercion, on which point Jefferson's skepticism was widely shared. One did not have to be a revivalist to see the fruitlessness of compulsion. In keeping with these

42. Peden, ed., *Notes on the State of Virginia,* 159–60.

views, the Virginia Declaration of Rights was drawn up to include a straightforward statement of the generally agreed latitudinarian principles of religious freedom: "That religion, or the duty we owe to our Creator, and the manner of discharging it, can be directed only by reason and conviction, not by force or violence; and therefore men are equally entitled to the free exercise of religion, according to the dictates of their conscience; and that it is the mutual duty of all to practice Christian forbearance, and love, and charity towards each other."[43]

This language, however, was compatible with more than one possible form of religious establishment. The one guiding condition was that of Christianity; in common with nearly all American states of the new Republic, Virginia expected not only Christianity, but its Protestant variety, to pervade all religious observance as fostered or recognized by the State. But both local and provincial government had long been in the hands of men who regarded the established church as a symbol of their own predominance. Jefferson's campaign to overturn the establishment of the Episcopal Church—as the Church of England was now called— therefore met with deeply entrenched and widespread opposition. The moderate but convinced Anglicans who dominated the legislature, led and rallied by Edmund Pendleton, put up a resistance which later caused Jefferson to reflect that the movement "brought on the severest contests that I have known."[44]

When Jefferson became governor of Virginia in 1779, the management of his bill for religious freedom passed into the hands of the younger Madison, who until that time had been personally little known to Jefferson. The struggle was prolonged over several years. Many sectarian interests could have been satisfied by a general act requiring taxation in support of religion while leaving individuals to decide which sect to support; in 1784 Patrick Henry helped to promote two legislative measures, one to give corporate status to the Episcopal Church and the other to assess and raise taxes for the support of all sects without discrimination. With Jefferson now serving as American minister in France, Madison undertook the task of parliamentary and public opposi-

43. J.R. Pole, ed., *The Revolution in America: Documents on the Internal Development of America in the Revolutionary Era, 1754–1788* (London, 1970), 521.

44. *Autobiography*, quoted in Bernard Mayo, *Jefferson Himself* (Charlottesville, 1942), 79.

tion. The incorporation bill, which gave the Episcopal clergy control of church property, was passed in December 1784; from the anti-establishment point of view, however, it was far more important to defeat the assessment bill, which would give support to religion in general, presumably meaning only to sects of the Protestant variety. The opposition to assessment was extremely widespread—an early petition carried ten thousand signatures—but its sources were various, and not wholly consistent. They included large numbers of Baptists whose thought traced a line from Roger Williams in desiring to keep the church free of the impurities of the state. The also numerous Presbyterians, less averse to some state connection, had moved gradually to a separationist position. Among these massive social forces, Madison's Enlightenment rationalism was the position of a comparatively small minority, and only one-fifth of all signatories to anti-assessment petitions actually put their names to his own historically celebrated *Memorial and Remonstrance*. [45] The success of the action, however, owed much to Madison's skill as a parliamentary tactician—particularly considering that he was overwhelmed by Patrick Henry as an orator. By the time the bill came up, the legislators had been impressed by the force, passion, and geographical distribution of the opponents of any form of assessment supported by the state. After the defeat of the assessment bill Madison was in a position to call up Jefferson's Bill for Establishing Religious Freedom, which passed into law in January 1786. Jefferson, now moving in French salon and court circles, had reason to boast of the achievement; it was one of the three things he caused to be engraved on his tombstone. [46]

The *Memorial and Remonstrance*, written by Madison in 1785, has often been regarded as the centerpiece of the campaign against the bill for religious assessments. The majority of Madison's fellow countrymen, however, were less moved by the reasonableness of the Enlightenment than by their own desire for religious independence. The significance of Madison's pamphlet is historic: it argues a case that survives the passions

45. Thomas E. Buckley, *Church and State in Revolutionary Virginia, 1776–1787* (Charlottesville, 1977), 25–26, 175, 176, 177. Merrill D. Petersen and Robert C. Vaughan, *The Virginia Statute for Religious Freedom: Its Evolution and Consequences in American History* (Cambridge, 1988) for comment on all these issues.

46. The tombstone, on the grounds of Monticello, here ranks as an original document. Elwyn A. Smith, *Religious Liberty in the United States: The Development of Church-State Thought Since the Revolutionary Era* (Philadelphia, 1972), 11–13.

of the hour, and it must be examined in some detail because it could be applied without alteration to a situation that arose in the middle of the twentieth century. This is not to say that its persuasive reasoning had no contemporary support, though it was endorsed in only thirteen of Virginia's more than fifty counties. There can be little reason to believe that it would have carried the day without the massive campaign of the various sects of dissenters. It fell to Madison to orchestrate this opposition, not to create it.

The *Memorial* is a striking example of Madison's craftsmanship in combining philosophical and political considerations into a single argument, in which he was soon to excel as a contributor to *The Federalist*, and as with the later document, the recourse to fundamental principles gives the *Memorial* a general character as a commentary on the meaning of religious freedom. Much of this carefully worded pamphlet was acceptable to the Baptists, who had played such an important part in fighting for sectarian autonomy, and formed a possibly decisive component of Madison's own constituents in Orange County. Madison's faith, reinforced by the theological studies in which he had steeped himself as a student at Princeton, disposed him to make a political principle of the precept that man's duty to God was prior to any duty he owed to the state. Any civil government was subordinate to that of God, which was why no man's right in religion could be abridged by the establishment of civil government. But Madison's position, as he developed it in the *Memorial*, was distinctly to the rationalist side of the Baptists. They held that no government could come between the individual and his conscience because the kind of knowledge with which the conscience worked was given by God and was not answerable to human government. Madison was close to this when he said that men owed their prior duty to God, but his concept of human judgment owed more to the idea of the autonomy of reason. The right to follow one's own religious convictions was inalienable "because the opinions of men, depending only on the evidence contemplated by their own minds, cannot follow the dictates of other men." This was a rationalist view of the effect of evidence in the formation of opinion, the key being reliance on *opinion* rather than *faith*. It was followed appropriately by a reference to man's duty to his Creator. Further down, Madison developed a lucid expression of the basically humanist rationality of the Enlightenment: "Whilst we assert for ourselves a freedom to embrace, to profess and to observe,

the Religion which we believe to be of divine origin, we cannot deny an equal freedom to those whose minds have not yielded to the evidence which has convinced us. If this freedom be abused, it is an offense against God, not against man." Madison *believed* the Christian religion to be of divine origin, but he believed it on the basis of evidence which, he was well aware, might fail to carry conviction with other reasonable minds. The divine and human elements were nicely balanced, and it would be hard to say which led the argument. Madison would not have seen a contradiction: each was incomplete without the other. It is more doubtful that he would have wanted to pursue these thoughts to purely secular conclusions. Nevertheless he had indicated a course which in the intellectual and social climate of the mid-twentieth century would lead further in that direction than he could have foreseen.

The *Memorial* carried conviction with the Virginia electorate on other and more political grounds. "Who does not see," Madison argued, "that the same authority which can establish Christianity, in exclusion to all other Religions, may establish with the same ease any particular sect of Christians, in exclusion to all other sects?" The assessment bill violated "that equality which ought to be the basis of every law"—a charge that could be supported by simply quoting the Virginia Declaration of Rights. The reasoning and rhetoric of Madison's appeal to public opinion ran straight back to Jefferson's in the Declaration of Independence. Equality in religion was "held by the same tenure with all our other rights. If we recur to its origin, it is equally the gift of nature." The equality which lay at the foundation of this claim for religious freedom was essentially a personal equality, for the individual's obligation to his or her own conscience preceded any obligation to a sectarian organization. Even so, the legislators of Virginia were less fully committed to a complete withdrawal from religious affairs than has sometimes been supposed. They ordained that Sunday was to be a day of rest and laid down serious penalties for sabbath-breaking; they assumed, in common with both the Evangelical and the more traditional sects, that the norms and values associated with Protestant Christianity would pervade the state in future ages. [47]

Madison was happily aware that religious freedom rested on other and firmer foundations than those supplied by arguments of finely spun

47. Buckley, *Church and State,* 181–82.

rationality. Individual states might retain their religious establishments, but no single establishment could be expected to dominate the nation. The Union was developing with a curiously mixed and uncommitted kind of religious pluralism. States differed widely in their policies; Connecticut retained its Congregational system until 1818, and when Massachusetts finally ended its residue of support for the Congregational churches in 1833, it was not on the strength of opposition to establishment but because the spread of Unitarianism was taking control of the churches away from the Congregationalists themselves.[48] In neither state did disestablishment draw its impetus directly from the revolution. But Madison had already seen that the variety of religious affiliations in the United States would be a safeguard against any national establishment of the European kind. Speaking on this theme in the Virginia ratifying convention in June 1788, he explained, "This freedom arises from the multiplicity of sects, which pervades America, and which is the best and only security for religious liberty in any country."[49] This was a variation of the theme he had explained in *The Federalist* 51, an extension of his argument in *Federalist* 10 that political freedom was secured by the existence of various independent interests operating within the same political system. "In a free government," he argued, "the security for civil rights must be the same as for religious rights. It consists in the one case in the multiplicity of interests and in the other, in the multiplicity of sects. The degree of security in both cases will depend on the number of interests and sects; and this may be presumed to depend on the extent of the country and the number of people comprehended under the same government."[50]

Many people who wanted safeguards for religion against the state, control of which might fall into unfriendly hands, were still willing to support provisions permitting the government to aid religious organizations, provided always that such aid was equally distributed. These differences caused prolonged debate during the drafting of the First Amendment to the Constitution. Madison, now a member of the House

48. Howe, *Garden and Wilderness*, 36; Stokes, *Church and State* 3:376–80.

49. Saul K. Padover, ed., *The Complete Madison: His Basic Writings* (New York, 1953), 306.

50. Jacob E. Cooke, ed., *The Federalist* (Middletown, Conn., 1961), 351–52. In the last sentence Madison is also answering the argument, derived from Montesquieu, that republican liberty can be maintained only in small areas of government.

of Representatives and the leading member of the committee drafting a bill of rights, wanted a specific safeguard for conscience. This moral autonomy of the individual was a basic ingredient of his idea of republican principles, but the chief difficulty was to frame a statement that committed the government to complete neutrality without seeming more hostile to religious sentiments than was true to the feelings of most members of Congress and also of the people they represented. In this lay the explanation of the ambiguity that has always lain coiled within the formal American doctrines of separation of church and state. Representative American spokesmen wished at heart for a system that would be neutral but hospitable to religion, as opposed to the alternative of a neutrality that would seem positively inhospitable. But even so mild a concept as hospitality might leave the irreligious conscience on an unequal footing. The dilemma has never yielded a completely satisfactory solution. The First Amendment section on religion stated briefly, but not with self-explanatory simplicity, that "Congress shall make no law respecting an establishment of religion, nor prohibiting the free exercise thereof." The reference to "conscience" had gone, no doubt to Madison's disappointment.[51] The language imposed a sweeping ban on federal intervention in religious activities; the interpretation of this language was to exercise the most refined ingenuity of lawyers and judges in later centuries.

As presidents of the United States, Jefferson and Madison both viewed their duties as calling for a strict application of the First Amendment. Jefferson refused to declare any national observances such as fasts or days of thanksgiving; Madison vetoed bills to incorporate the Protestant Episcopal Church in Federal territory and to reserve a parcel of land in the Mississippi Territory for the use of Baptist churches.[52] He condemned both measures as involving the federal government in the activities of religious bodies in a manner prohibited by the Constitution. The principle was clear: real religious freedom must also mean religious self-sufficiency, and state intervention to assist a church in any way was a denial of the self-sufficiency of that church and to that extent an encroachment on the basic neutrality, not only of the state toward the church—which was Madison's concern as President—but of the church

51. Smith, *Religious Liberty*, 45–47.
52. Padover, ed., *Complete Madison*, 307–08.

towards the state. For the most part, however, Americans found it difficult to reconcile this degree of constitutional purity with their real and far-reaching religious commitments. The constitutional history of the issue of separation was to be not only prolonged but intensely complicated. The First Amendment had inscribed the language through which the issue was to be judged. But Jefferson, who had not been a party to the framing of that Amendment, added further mysteries to the language of constitutional argument by erecting a metaphysical wall to keep church and state apart without admitting any possibility that it might ever be scaled from either side.

Chapter Five

Religion and Individual Conscience

No one is ever quite alone with his or her own conscience. The company kept on occasions of solitude frequently includes a heritage of religion and family, of teachers and familiar voices past and present, God being, for many, the closest of all. A minister of religion, a member of the family, a friend, can always argue with the individual conscience, simply adding to the voices that conscience hears; but the essential theme of the Enlightenment, as argued in America by Jefferson, Madison, and their contemporaries, was simply that the individual conscience cannot be coerced by either church or state. No government can tell the citizen what is true and what is false, least of all in matters pertaining to God, and no church can enforce its own doctrines through state law. But the full implications of this belief were difficult, especially for religious people who took it for granted that God always played a central part in human affairs.

With the drafting and adoption of the First Amendment to the American Constitution, most of those concerned were probably reasonably satisfied of three things: first, that the somewhat elliptical language of the section on religion went as far as practically possible in the direction of preventing the new federal government from having any sort of religious policy of its own; secondly, that the states were free to do as their own inhabitants thought fit; and thirdly, that these things had been achieved with a minimum of intrusion into the full and free exercise of religion by any religious sect. The fact that Madison as president had

to veto a bill to incorporate a church and another setting aside lands for churches in federal territory suggests that members of Congress were not unduly concerned about the express meaning of the amendment, but the extraordinary complexities that were to be experienced in the process of applying this language to cases of specific—often severe— conflict between different religions, and between the state and individuals, were wholly unanticipated both at the time of drafting and for a long time afterward.

The principle that had emerged from the conflicts of the eighteenth century was that of government neutrality toward rival sects, a posture which, at the personal level, also required neutrality toward the individual members of those sects. Ultimately, for reasons that were not to be fully unraveled for nearly two centuries, this would require some branch of government—the courts if not the legislature—to decide whether *every* individual conscience, religious or irreligious, was entitled to equal treatment under the Constitution. Long before that began to happen, the second phase of the development of equality in religion saw a transformation of the scene from which the First Amendment had emerged.[1] The rise of a militant Roman Catholic Church created a type and scale of sectarian conflict which no one had anticipated and for which no one was prepared. And even this only prepared the way for the emergence of a pluralism of religions which shattered the old and quiet assumption that America was a Protestant country.

The Protestant Aegis Challenged

George Washington's Farewell Address is not usually considered a religious statement, which makes his one reference to religion all the more instructive. Congratulating his fellow countrymen on their advantages, Washington told them, "with slight shades of differences, you have the same religion, manners, habits, and political principles."[2] The assumption was that the similarities in their religious beliefs disposed people toward agreement in matters affecting their more material interests. Happily free from the obsessions which had so often visited civil

1. As outlined at the beginning of Chapter 4.

2. James Richardson, comp., *Messages and Papers of the Presidents, 1789–1897* (Washington, D.C., 1896) 1:213–24.

and religious wars on the peoples of Europe, the people of the different states could settle such differences as arose among them peaceably within their existing institutions.

Washington's own state of Virginia had repealed its restrictive laws against Roman Catholics in 1785.[3] But his generation handed on to its successors the fundamental conviction that the American people were Protestant. Their broad lands and favorable circumstances gave room for minorities, on the implied condition that their practices held no threat to the republican character of the Union. But that character, a declared attribute of the Constitution itself, was permeated with Protestant assumptions about history and society. It is no exaggeration to say of some of the most prominent Americans of that generation, including Thomas Jefferson and Washington himself, that they were better Christians in their politics than in their religion.

The elemental Protestant Christianity to which Washington referred (his generation did not regard the differences between Protestants and Catholics as "slight shades of differences") was no merely sleeping force: it exerted its influence in the interpretation of the laws and was assumed on several occasions to have passed into that part of the common law which the United States had received from England. Early state reports contain plentiful instances of this assumption. In 1811 Chief Justice James Kent of New York punished an atheist for blasphemy against the Christian religion, laying it down that "the case assumes we are a Christian people, and the morality of the country is deeply engrafted upon Christianity, and not on the doctrines and worship of these imposters"—by which he alluded to Mahomet and the Grand Lama, who had somehow got into the exposition of the case. The reception through common law was confirmed by the Supreme Court in 1844, when the United States was again referred to as "a Christian nation." The basically religious character of the American people continued to inform the opinions of the Supreme Court, without express reference to Christianity, when it was held in 1892 that the laws affecting the labor of contracted immigrants could not exclude a minister of religion who had been summoned from abroad: "No purpose or action against religion can be imputed to any legislation," declared the Court, "because this is a religious people. This

3. W. W. Hening, *The Statutes at Large of Virginia, 1619–1792* (Richmond, 1809–1823) 12:120.

is historically true. From the discovery of this continent to the present hour, there is a single voice making this affirmation."[4] Such different foreign observers as Alexis de Tocqueville in the 1830s and James Bryce some half-century later regarded Christianity as a national though not an established religion.[5]

The pervasiveness of this assumption exerted a controlling effect on the interpretation of the First Amendment; if its national implications were secular, they were at a heavy discount against the principles attached to it by those who wanted to protect rather than curtail the interests of religion. The "free exercise" clause was at liberty to range into the territory of the "establishment" clause.[6] Until nearly the middle of the nineteenth century, moreover, the essence of American religion was a Protestantism whose reserves of strength and numbers were so immense that no rival seemed capable of challenging either the tenure of Protestant theology or the Protestant character of the flourishing sectarian diversity which burgeoned under the protection of the Constitution.

The nationalizing creed that grew alongside this elemental Protestantism was that of laissez-faire capitalism. While evangelical preachers might still occasionally lament the national obsession with material gain, popular religious teaching had little difficulty in reconciling the Sermon on the Mount with *The Wealth of Nations*. The spirit of individual economic enterprise, under the peculiar advantages of self-government and democracy, was celebrated by ministers of religion as well as by Fourth of July orators for its power to make America a beacon to less exemplary nations. The Reverend Lyman Beecher, perhaps the most prominent of the evangelical preachers of the Jacksonian era, urged in

4. Mark De Wolfe Howe, *The Garden and the Wilderness: Religion and Government in American Constitutional History* (Chicago, 1965), 28–29; Nathan O. Hatch, *The Sacred Cause of Liberty: Republican Thought and the Millennium in Revolutionary New England* (New Haven, 1977), passim, esp. ch. 4; *Church of the Holy Trinity v. United States*, 143 U.S. 457 (1892), where "this is a Christian nation" (471). The voice of Thomas Paine was presumably inaudible to the bench.

5. Alexis de Tocqueville, *De la Démocratie en Amérique* (1840), ed. J.-P. Mayer (Paris, 1961) 2:308–15; James Bryce, *The American Commonwealth*, 2 vols. (London and New York, 1891) 2:560, 570–99.

6. It may be convenient to remind the reader of the wording of this section: "The Congress shall make no law respecting an establishment of religion, or prohibiting the free exercise thereof."

this spirit that with the aid of education, America could do its duty to the world by extending the missionary combination of Protestantism and self-government. This revival of the Protestant style in libertarian rhetoric was not merely hortatory in purpose; it was prompted by the rising tide of the Catholic presence in the American Republic. Civil and religious liberty, which were linked as Protestant virtues, were the indispensable conditions of the millennium, which Beecher was firmly convinced was intended to begin in America. Americans had the duty of making their country ready for it. But this conflict was already putting new stress on the values associated with religious equality, and was perhaps even threatening a revaluation. Beecher did not deny Catholics the equal rights of all religious denominations, but he did insist that their children be subjected to the assimilative powers of America's common schools and republican institutions. The Roman Church must withdraw its claims to intervene in other countries' free institutions, and Catholics must accede to the fundamental republican principles of the rights of conscience and free inquiry.[7] These were basically individualist arguments, descended ultimately from the principles of the Reformation but more immediately from the precepts of the Enlightenment, and they rested on the equal rights of the religious consciences of free individuals.

The ministry's misgivings about human depravity seemed to be nicely balanced by their manifest satisfaction with the American combination of liberty, prosperity and Protestantism. Horace Bushnell, a young man in 1835, explained in a sermon that pure religion had to begin again at the beginning in a new world "and call up around it all its own proper institutions. And He who apportions all events to their times with sovereign wisdom had reserved such a world unknown . . . a vast continent of forests still in the wilderness of nature. . . . It was Protestantism in religion that produced republicanism in government."[8]

All the leading branches of Protestant theology in the growing republic placed intense emphasis on the worth of the individual. In the Universalist and Unitarian forms, an optimistic and positive view of human

7. Lyman Beecher, "A Plea for the West," in Daniel Walker Howe, ed., *The American Whigs: An Anthology* (New York, 1973), 133–47; Hatch, *Sacred Cause*, 170–71. This is an early use of the concept of assimilation.

8. Horace Bushnell, *Crisis of the Church* (Hartford, 1835), quoted in Elwyn A. Smith, *Religious Liberty in the United States: The Development of Church-State Thought Since the Revolutionary Era* (Philadelphia, 1972), 11–13.

achievements displaced the increasingly unacceptable Calvinist emphasis on depravity; where strict Calvinists still appeared to deprive their subjects of hope for salvation through their own efforts, the newer and more humanistic faiths gave them reasons for believing that they could contribute to their own salvation. Calvinism declined not only in such urbane milieux as Boston and New York but on the midwestern frontier, where hardworking men and women were determined to place their faith in more hopeful doctrines. [9]

There was little in these attitudes to offer moral resistance to the growth of private wealth. After the Mexican War and the Compromise of 1850, northern ministers of religion lent themselves with increasing passion to the moral crusade against slavery; once the issue had been opened, any faith that valued the individual could hardly do less, and the only cause for surprise or seeming to require explanation in the rise of the abolition movement is not that it should have happened, but that the northern churches should have hesitated so long before opening their fire. A few similar voices were raised against the morals and effects of the dominant preoccupation with acquisitive business enterprise. [10] But concern for individual worth reflected a kind of withdrawal from areas of public policy in which churches had often taken part in the past. During and for a generation after the Revolution it was a common complaint of the clergy that the virtues of simplicity of life and dedication to religion were getting lost in a welter of lust for private gain. But it was not until the later nineteenth century, when questions of the social accountability of wealth were raised once more, that the Protestant churches showed any appreciable concern over the moral implications of the economic system. With the rise of great corporations and vast accumulations of wealth, Protestantism adapted its role, which had been formed earlier in the mercantile era, as a sort of moral caretaker for the methods and consciences of businessmen. [11] But it was not out of keep-

9. W.W. Sweet, *Religion in the Development of American Culture, 1765–1840* (New York, 1952), 234–35, 210.

10. The best known was Emerson, notably in "Self-Reliance"; *Emerson's Complete Works: Essays* (Boston, 1883–93) 1:85–86. A clerical voice was that of the Presbyterian theologian and iron master, Stephen Colwell, *New Themes for the Protestant Clergy* (Philadelphia, 1851).

11. Sidney E. Mead, *The Lively Experiment: The Shaping of Christianity in America* (New York, 1963), 138–42.

ing with this spirit that the Reverend Henry Ward Beecher, probably the most celebrated cleric of his time, could declare in 1879 that "God intended the great to be great and the little to be little." [12]

Differences among Protestant sects were deep and often bitter. But all of them accepted a basic affinity between Protestantism and the republican ideals of the Constitution. A school of Connecticut theologians, all born in the eighteenth century, worked to adapt a belief in the divine authority of government to the conditions of popular sovereignty. The eldest, Timothy Dwight, President of Yale, was already an adult at the time of the Revolution; his pupil Lyman Beecher (1775–1863) practiced the belief that Christians ought to endeavor to influence events; and Nathaniel W. Taylor, born after the Revolution (though he did not live as long as Beecher), became Professor of Divinity at Yale, where he developed the argument, certainly heretical by earlier standards, that man was the author of his own sin and consequently responsible for his own salvation, a doctrine that displaced the efficacy of grace and came full circle with the power of works. [13] This self-conscious identification was no mere exuberance of the national spirit, however. Centuries of English and American history had taught Protestants to regard the Church of Rome as an inveterate enemy. Many of the revolutionary state constitutions specified the Protestant branch of Christianity when prescribing qualifications for political office, and in Massachusetts, the omission of this provision from the listed qualifications for the governorship generated more objections from the towns than any other aspect of the Constitution of 1780. [14]

When Catholic immigrants from Ireland and Germany began to establish conspicuous and growing footholds in the early nineteenth century, Protestants almost everywhere regarded them as aliens to the political

12. David H. Montgomery, *Beyond Equality: Labor and the Radical Republicans, 1862–1872* (New York, 1967), 230–31. The year 1879 also saw the publication of Darwin's *Descent of Man*, a popular version of his scientific work, in which "evolution" could have been substituted for "God" with very much the same effects.

13. Nathaniel W. Taylor, *Concio ad Clerum, A Sermon Delivered in the Chapel of Yale College* (New Haven, 1828); idem, *Lectures on the Moral Government of God*, 2 vols. (New York, 1859), 1:258–59, 2:162; Sweet, *Religion*, 199–200; Smith, *Religious Liberty*, 70–90; Hatch, *Sacred Cause*, 156.

14. The town meeting records on which this statement is based are in Massachusetts Archives in Boston, vols. 276 and 277; they have been edited by Oscar and Mary Handlin as *The Popular Sources of Political Authority* (Cambridge, Mass., 1966).

ideals of the republic. So far as the sources of faith were concerned, moreover, this stance was not a mere product of religious bigotry. When Pope Gregory XVI in 1832 issued an encyclical denouncing liberty of conscience as an "absurd and erroneous doctrine" flowing from the "polluted fountain of indifference," he did not make it easy for American Catholics to explain their dual attachment to the principles of the republic and the faith of Rome. "The pontiff," declared the Reverend J.F. Berg of Philadelphia, "is clearly committed against the first principles of American freedom and regards them as unmitigated abominations." [15] This highly representative expression of opinion helps to explain the sentiments out of which the nativist and anti-Catholic Know-Nothing movement arose in the 1850s.

The growth of a substantial body of American Catholic citizens exposed the doctrine of separation to questions that had not previously been asked. The truth was that Washington's quiet assurance as to the homogeneity of American religion had reflected the largely unquestioned assumption that political stability did indeed rest on certain religious foundations, which were the essential sources of republican virtue. The idea of separation of church and state was good Enlightenment doctrine, but all the same it was far more daring in 1791 than it has seemed in the light of subsequent history. No one could really be sure that a secular political system would have the moral resources to survive without the support of an officially recognized religious system. [16] Even those who believed in separation in a more systematic and doctrinal sense than most—and Jefferson and Madison, to name two, had thought their way through the problem—could still count on the overwhelming preponderance of Protestant sentiment as a fact of American life, which had the important function of taking up the ground left vacant by the absence of national political experience.

American religious experience, if only because of its irresistible plurality, increasingly with the passage of time tended to vindicate the intellectual basis which attributed ultimate autonomy to the individual conscience. This development was of the utmost importance for the principle of individual equality in the conceptual foundations of the modern state. For these autonomous individual consciences must, in

---

15. Smith, *Religious Liberty*, 103–04.
16. This point is persuasively argued by Sidney Mead, *Lively Experiment*, 59.

the nature of the case, be considered equal consciences—equal in both their ability and their right to judge for themselves.

This outcome had been anticipated long before in England. The fissiparous sectarianism of the Civil War led to an overt regard for what were often called "tender consciences." At one point, a century earlier, in European history, the peace between Protestants and Catholics was established (at the Peace of Augsburg, 1555) on the basis that the religion of the people followed the religion of their princes. But Protestantism could not stop there. When the meaning of the Bible was open to question, and people were free to ask questions, the morals of individualism were inseparable from the principles of equality.

Neither church nor state was in general particularly anxious to encourage these trends. But where the state lacked both religious conviction and coercive power, plurality was the mother of tolerance. This view was no more attractive to genuine Pietists than it had been to Puritans; it was at best a distasteful and theologically dubious consequence of the existing condition of religious politics. The members of a church covenant were bound by an extremely strong bond of spiritual community which effectively permitted very little independence to the individual. But individual choice was a fact of political and increasingly of Protestant religious life. The Roman Catholic church, on the other hand, rejected the first assumptions that lay deep in Protestant history. People after all had once chosen to be Protestants, but Catholics had merely continued to be Catholic. The training and indoctrination of Catholics was part of a complete program at home and school. For Catholic priests the idea of a secular education was a contradiction in terms; there could be no education without the teaching of religious truths. Yet American education, much of which was paid for by public funds, was based on the assumption of the religious neutrality of the state. The state might set aside land for churches or even exempt churches from taxation, but it could not enter into the process of education without taking sides with religion, and even if this could be achieved without giving preference to one religion over another, it could hardly be done without taking political actions "respecting an establishment of religion."

There were difficult problems here for Protestants as well as Catholics. The self-denying rigor of complete abstention had never been systematically practiced by the United States. Reposing in the security of the

Protestant aegis, Americans had not felt called on to think through the logical consequences of their own formal positions. The Ohio valley was settled in the early years of the nineteenth century under the Northwest Ordinance of 1787, which had explicitly linked "religion, morality, and knowledge" as "necessary to good government and the happiness of mankind" in providing for "schools and means of education." That, of course, was before the First Amendment, but it was re-enacted by the First Congress, and no one seems to have regarded that as a contradiction to the intentions of the Constitution. [17] American policy often protected religious interests and sometimes encouraged them; in any case it was only the federal government, not the states, that was restrained by the Constitution in religious matters. Moral precepts were normally given a religious basis, and Bible readings were often included in school hours—an inherently Protestant procedure.

In view of the vital importance of religious principle in the very nature of a Roman Catholic education, it is not surprising that the doctrine of "separation" was subjected to its most prolonged scrutiny by the sometimes fiery light of controversies over education. The heat became more intense after the separation enjoined on the federal government was held to apply to the states as well through the operation of the Fourteenth Amendment, adopted after the Civil War. The logic of this extension, known as "incorporation," did not reveal itself until the 1940s, and then only gradually. But by 1947 Mr. Justice Jackson could say without exaggeration that the whole historic controversy between Catholics and non-Catholics in temporal policy came into focus in their respective school policies. [18]

When Protestants living in Eastern cities began in the 1830s to comprehend that the Catholic presence was permanent and increasing, their hostility to Catholic communities sometimes made public schools into unpleasant places for Catholic children. The normal Catholic desire for parochial schools was accentuated by the attitudes prevailing in mixed communities. Bishop John Hughes, Roman Catholic diocesan of New York, brought the issue to a head in 1840 by applying for a share

17. The Northwest Ordinance will be found in several source books, among them J.R. Pole, ed., *The Revolution in America: Documents on the Internal Development of America in the Revolutionary Era, 1754–1788* (Stanford, 1970), 382–88.

18. *Everson v. Board of Education,* 330 U.S. 1 (1947).

of the public funds appropriated for education. The issue was inherently political. When liberal Protestants found their traditional respect for the system of free religious choice opposed by Catholics *on principle*, they found it hard to credit Catholics with any faith in free institutions—a discovery which only confirmed their previous suspicions. But the Catholic hierarchy did not believe that religion was acquired by free individual choice and knew that they needed parochial schools to maintain the body of their faith. To them the official view appeared actually hostile. On this ground they could meet and surprise the Protestants with the charge that the practice of separation was not neutral at all, but favored the prevailing Protestant majority.

After much wrangling, the state of New York resolved the problem of Bishop Hughes's challenge by imposing a more rigorous secularization of its educational system. A state commission reported in 1842 that the population of New York City was "by no means homogeneous." The attempt to provide a homogeneous system assumed that they all had an aim which the various communities did not in fact share. [19] The answer was to drive all religious teaching out of schools in receipt of public support, an outcome that gave Hughes no satisfaction beyond that of having forced the state to redefine its policy of neutrality and to recognize the truth that its population would never again be homogeneous in religion. [20] New York meanwhile moved very slowly towards a legal position which gave the Catholic hierarchy a satisfactory tenure of church property. An act of 1813 had vested trusteeship in the lay community—a procedure characteristic of the temper of the period but highly objectionable to a religious denomination whose structure was hierarchical rather than diffuse. Only in 1863 did New York mark out the lines along which American society at large might come to terms with its religious heterogeneity. The law of that year made each church and congregation a body corporate. Under these provisions, known as the "corporate aggregate" plan, the archbishop, bishop, vicar-general, and

19. Smith, *Religious Liberty*, 111–16.

20. Not that seventeenth and eighteenth century New York, with its Dutch, English, and French Protestant elements, could be said to be homogeneous, except in the sense of all being primarily Protestant; they do seem to have become significantly less mutually antagonistic with the advance of the commercial world of the eighteenth century. The Jews were another minority who seem to have benefited by an atmosphere of increasing mutual forbearance.

pastor of the diocese were to sign a certificate showing the title by which the corporation was to be known. This made it possible for the church to retain effective legal control in the hands of its superior officers.[21]

Many states, however, were less hospitable than New York to the Roman Catholic church and continued to place legal obstacles in the way of ecclesiastical concentrations of power.[22] The rise of a permanent and evidently increasing Catholic element in America's population had a toughening rather than an ameliorating effect on the Protestant majority's determination to keep formal religious teaching out of the domain of public education. President Ulysses S. Grant, in his seventh annual message in 1875, recommended to Congress a constitutional amendment providing for public education and including a provision to ban all teaching of "religious, atheistic, or pagan tenets," and went on to exclude any kind of aid or exemption, direct or indirect, for any religious sect or denomination.[23] If this amendment had been adopted it would have fallen equally on all religions, and Grant's intention may have been to prevent the schools from becoming the grounds of a new wave of public controversy—but the effect would have been to deprive Catholics of any prospect of public support for their own educational system. This, of course, was state neutrality; it bore on Protestants and Catholics alike. But the forms of neutrality had not prevented Protestants from flourishing in the past. Despite the failure of Grant's proposal, many states adopted constitutional provisions of their own, most of which forbade the use or appropriation of public funds or state property for the benefit of sectarian schools.[24]

American Catholics were obliged to maintain a delicate balance between their American and their Roman loyalties—a balance periodically upset by the Vatican's chronic difficulties in understanding the concept of religious neutrality in a republican state. European experience, of which there was plenty to be drawn on, taught it to believe that the state could not be neutral, and that a state which was not friendly must be

21. Stokes, *Church and State* 3:406–10.

22. Smith, *Religious Liberty*, gives a table at 118–19.

23. Richardson, *Messages and Papers* 7:334–35. Grant also proposed taxation of church property and suggested that people would soon lose patience with exemptions granted to ecclesiastical bodies while property taxes were rising. There is an anticlerical ring to his words.

24. Smith, *Religious Liberty*, 117–19.

hostile. The phase of American religious policy that took its inauguration from the adoption of the First Amendment in 1791 was based on the assumption that religious pluralism was safe for the American Republic because it was safe for American Protestants. That phase disintegrated gradually with the disappearance, not so much of the Protestant majority, as of the unchallenged nature of its ascendancy.

The rise of the Roman Catholic Church in America posed the question as to whether religious pluralism and competition might eventually undermine the assured ascendancy in which Protestants had indulged the liberties of other sects or creeds. Catholic leaders such as Bishop Hughes perceived the doctrine of separation as a disguised form of official hostility, and attacked it in the cause of gaining a Catholic foothold under public protection. This attempt failed, and the failure marked the limits of one form of Catholic compromise with American constitutional principles. A long time was to elapse—virtually another lifetime—before in the twentieth century the Catholic church was to perceive advantages in the American doctrine of separation. Strictly construed and enforced, separation could at least protect the church from hostile majorities and spare the children the indoctrination they might have suffered from hearing school assembly readings from the King James Bible. But toward the middle of the twentieth century, state governments began to provide benefits to the recipients of their school spending programs, not as a covert form of aid to religion but as part of the public contribution to education, and Catholics could hope to share in these advantages not as Catholics but as citizens. This subtle development helped to give them a friendlier view of the now much-disputed line traced by the serpentine wall of separation.

Did State Neutrality Mean State Ignorance?

While these difficulties exposed some of the deeper hostilities among different sectors of American society, the doctrine of separation also presented problems which required judicial solutions. Religious bodies are notoriously susceptible to disputes on points of doctrine, sometimes putting each other's members to death for their own good or the greater good of society. When doctrinal disputes, or even broad changes of sentiment, led to schism within a sect or congregation, the passions of faith in America were quickly translated into demands not for the deaths

of the dissidents but for the control of church property. With that control went power to appoint ministers.

Questions of this sort presented the religiously neutral state with moral and legal problems for which its formal training had given it little preparation. Ideally, state neutrality might have been conceived of as a condition of sublime ignorance; the state was an establishment of mechanisms of government; even if all of its members were religious, they were not supposed to carry their religion into the operation of government, nor was government supposed to operate on their religion. The essence of the matter was that the Constitution conferred on the government, operating through its several branches, no *formal knowledge* of religion, and no preferences among the religious opinions of its citizens, just as it had no formal knowledge of differences of race. [25]

This ideal state of affairs might have followed from a rigorous pursuit of Enlightenment doctrines. But we have already seen that the courts preferred to rest on the entirely different assumption that the whole complex mechanism was somehow interfused with and sustained by the Christian faith. [26] The constitutional warrant for this view could be expressed by saying that the Constitution was designed for the American people, and no other, and that the American people were by all their traditions a Christian people; a Constitution designed by and for them would by its nature embody Christian precepts and assumptions. This is the reading which sustains the pronouncements we have heard from the bench.

Disputes between members of a church about points of theology, when they turned into rival claims *to be* the church, and from there into rival claims to its property, invited the courts to enter into the disputed theological issues. The first case of this kind to require close judicial scrutiny arose in 1820 from the slow drift of the majority of the parishioners of Dedham, Massachusetts, into the newly fashionable doctrine of Unitarianism, while a majority of the actual members of the church remained with their old Congregational faith. The Massachusetts Supreme Court avoided the theological problems and adhered as best it

25. It may not be extravagant to suggest an analogy with the "veil of ignorance" proposed by John Rawls as a precondition for the assignment of goods (*A Theory of Justice*, [Cambridge, Mass., 1971]), except of course that Rawls's veil exists only to be torn away when the time for self-knowledge arrives.

26. See nn. 4, 5.

could to secular issues in deciding that a church had no legal existence except in connection with "some regularly constituted society," and that the whole parish was the legally constituted owner of its meeting house and other property. [27] Even this determination, of course, required the court to decide what was and what was not a church.

Fifty years later, and after a civil war fought on moral grounds, questions of religious doctrine could not be separated from sectional loyalties. The General Assembly of the Presbyterian Church had declared for the Constitution and the Union in opposition to the Church's southern members, who claimed that the Westminster Confession of Faith—to which they adhered—made it improper for the General Assembly to take sides on political issues. But the majority had not merely taken sides in a political division; they had held slavery to be impious and required persons seeking ordination to denounce it. The Supreme Court, deciding the question in *Watson v. Jones*, however, conscientiously averted its formal attention from the doctrinal issues and pronounced a ringing declaration of the American doctrine of separation. In drawing an exemplary contrast with an opinion in which Lord Eldon, when Lord Chancellor of England, had determined a case by entering into theological doctrine, Mr. Justice Samuel F. Miller declared, "In this country the full and free right to entertain any religious belief, to practice any religious principle, and to teach any religious doctrine which does not violate the laws of morality and property, and which does not infringe personal rights, is conceded to all. The law knows no heresy, and is committed to the support of no dogma, the establishment of no sect." The case was decided in favor of the General Assembly on grounds determined by the structure, not the doctrine, of the Presbyterian Church, and thus the southern charge about entering into political disputes was cast aside as irrelevant: "Where the local congregation"—in this case the southern inclined church in Louisville, Kentucky—"is a member of a larger and much more important religious organization, and is under its government and control and is bound by its orders and judgments, its decisions are final, and binding on legal tribunals." The Court's reasoning proceeded from the premise that courts, having no ecclesiastical jurisdiction, could not revise or question acts of church

27. Howe, *Garden and Wilderness*, 32–60; Stokes, *Church and State* 3:376–78.

discipline; the judicial power arose from the conflicting claims of the parties to church property and the use of it.[28]

The exceptions noted by Mr. Justice Miller might however prove more spacious than the sweep of his language suggested, since "the laws of morality and property" were those of Christian morality and capitalist property. The severest test of this definition was inevitably posed when a religious sect claiming allegiance to a different set of religious, moral, and economic principles established itself within the territorial bounds of the United States. The Mormons believed that polygamy was a religious duty; the United States charged their members with the criminal offense of bigamy, and in the resulting case of *Reynolds v. United States* in 1878, the justices gave short shrift to the defense that the concept of the free exercise of religion constituted a claim to exemption from the criminal law. It was in this case that Chief Justice Morrison Waite first introduced Jefferson's metaphor of the wall of separation into the language of the bench, which was clearly intended to give religion no liberty of exercise beyond the lawful limits of civil conduct.[29]

Whatever may be the merits of the case for a uniform law of marriage—and it is perhaps noteworthy that Poland and Edmunds, two of the senators who were responsible for legislation against Mormon practices, had also been strong proponents of civil rights in the era of Reconstruction—the government was not prepared to leave the Mormons alone. A series of laws strengthening federal authority in the territories culminated in the Tucker-Edmunds Act of 1887, which was not confined to the proprieties of matrimony; passing into law without President Cleveland's signature, this measure pursued the Mormons to the virtual destruction of their institutions. The Corporation of the Church of Christ of Latter-Day Saints was dissolved, all its property was declared forfeit, female suffrage (established in Utah), was abolished, and the children of plural marriages were disinherited. The Mormons had compounded their offenses against the laws of morality and property. For they had established a society whose church was its central institution of both political and economic life. The dissolution of the corporation meant the destruction of the most ambitious and successful of

28. *Watson v. Jones*, 13 Wallace 679–738 (1871).
29. *Reynolds v. United States*, 98 U.S. 145 (1878).

American attempts to establish a collective economy; the people of Utah were peremptorily returned to the morality of private business. These measures were upheld by the Supreme Court in 1890 over the dissents of Chief Justice Melville W. Fuller and Justices Stephen J. Field and L. Q. C. Lamar.[30]

Once the Mormons had agreed to conform to the majority view of American morals they were treated with tolerable leniency, and Utah was admitted to the Union as a state in 1896. But the legislation which destroyed the foundations of their economic order passed far beyond the considerations essential to a uniform morality while at the same time preserving an equality of respect for the individual, whether or not that morality was the result of religious conviction. In cases which touched the central nerves of majority morality less closely, the judiciary continued to observe the principle that its jurisdiction extended to matters of organization but not to doctrine, which meant that cases involving religion were resolved on secular and not theological points and that legal principles could not be interpreted through the lens of theology. The line could be a fine one, however. In the curious case of *Gonzalez v. Roman Catholic Archbishop of Manila*, decided in 1929, the Court had to adjudicate on the merits of the claims of a child to succeed to a chaplaincy which had been founded with provisions requiring a family succession. The Archbishop of Manila objected, raising canon law provisions that had not existed when the trust was founded. The Supreme Court, adhering to the principles of neutrality, denied the archbishop the satisfaction of a ruling under canon law, but awarded him the judgment on the secular ground that he was competent to decide the qualifications of a candidate for the chaplaincy under the will which founded that office.[31]

A more politically charged case came before the Court after the opening of the Cold War. The Russian Orthodox Cathedral Church of St. Nicholas had been incorporated by an act of New York in 1925, and continued, like the Church of Rome, to acknowledge a spiritual head abroad—in this case, however, in Moscow. Since the wartime rap-

---

30. *The Late Corporation of the Church of Christ of Latter-Day Saints v. United States*, 136 U.S. (1890); Leonard J. Arrington, *Great Basin Kingdom: An Economic History of the Latter-Day Saints, 1830–1960* (Cambridge, Mass., 1958), 353–75.

31. *Gonzalez v. Roman Catholic Archbishop of Manila*, 280 U.S. 10 (1929).

prochement between the Soviet government and the Russian church, a number of American adherents were unwilling to acknowledge Moscow as the third Rome, and prevailed on the State to convey to them the property of the church. But the Supreme Court could here find no issue over which the State could exercise lawful control. "There is no charge of subversive or hostile action by any ecclesiastic," observed Mr. Justice Stanly Reed for the Court. "Here there is a transfer by statute of control over churches. This violates our rule of separation between church and state." He cited *Watson v. Jones*, "The law knows no heresy," and pointed out that the record showed no schism of faith between the Russian church in America and the Russian Orthodox church.

But in the dissenting view of Mr. Justice Jackson the principle at issue pointed clearly the other way. New York, he argued, had done nothing to interfere with the free exercise of religion; the challenged law touched property, not liberty.[32] It certainly touched property, but with a view to affecting religious observance, since the Orthodox faithful would have been obliged to find somewhere else to worship—which makes it hard to differ from the majority's view that the state had invaded the free exercise of religion. If a religious schism had occurred, all precedent would have required the courts to adjudicate the difference on nonreligious grounds, which would almost certainly have meant a finding for the Russian patriarch in any case; other sections of the Constitution could have been found to prevent the state from making its own preferences a reason for transferring property from its lawful owners' hands; these considerations would have been further backed by the principle that where a state passed a law affecting religious practice for political reasons the Constitution commanded protection of religious liberty. The Court's finding was a notable vindication of the autonomy of religion at a moment of intense political hostility.

Such a determination, coming at such a time, maintained the viability of an American tradition. Religious neutrality at the individual level had been and could still be sustained when the courts refused to take sides in religious conflict along the lines marked out by the disputants themselves; and when it also refused to allow the organs of the state to interfere with religious practice, except where such practice broke the criminal law. The reason why we may say that this policy sustained

---

32. *Kedroff v. St. Nicholas Cathedral,* 344 U.S. 94 (1952).

individual equality may appear somewhat abstract but should nonetheless be clear from the nature of the argument that has been developed: it was by this means that the Court could maintain that it had *no constitutional knowledge* pertaining to the religious convictions of individuals and therefore could not intervene for or against them. This was a rational and fairly steady position and one which accorded with the responsibilities of the judiciary. But it can hardly be said to have been in harmony with that other line of opinions which held as a fundamental tenet that Americans were a Christian people. To make this affirmation of Christianity an element of one's constitutional creed was not the same as taking sides among Christians in dispute; but it at least amounted to saying that the judiciary was permitted to make use of the knowledge that Americans, as individuals, were expected to want to see religion maintained, suggesting that free exercise might gain the advantage over nonestablishment; and this suggested that the religious conscience would be preferred to the irreligious one. The inherent tension between the two clauses was to grow more acute with the complex animosities of the postwar years.

The crumbling of homogeneity had first raised at the political level some of the kinds of problem that would now begin to confront the courts. These developments had their principal source in the state policies of the New Deal era, which stimulated a new range of state activities aimed through interventionist methods to provide amenities for the people in their own localities but also in certain cases to secure conformity to social norms. As the relations between state policy and private conscience became more intricate, the problems of interpretation placed before the courts would grow more exacting, until wholly satisfactory and consistent conclusions seemed beyond the reach of logic.

Between Separation and Entanglement: The State and the Individual Conscience

There have been few periods in American history when the national state, often considered to have been conspicuous for its weakness compared with those of Europe, appeared in a more authoritarian guise than in the episode of the destruction of the original Mormon church. A disposition toward moral coercion had revealed itself under the armor of righteous propriety. This disposition recurred at different times and

places and with differing pretexts in the twentieth century. The Court found itself called on not only to protect society's moral order from the incursions of religion but to pick out and defend the line that marked the borders of the "free exercise" of religion.

This line was defined with some clarity in 1925, when the state of Oregon tried to banish parochial or sectarian schools and to bring all secondary education under the direct tutelage of the state. The well-known case of *Pierce v. Society of Sisters* in which this issue was tried resulted in the declaration that the child was not "a mere creature of the state"; those who nurtured him and directed his destiny had a high duty to prepare him for additional obligations. The Court was making an important statement about the kind and value of the equality that it perceived at the heart of the American system, whose significance reached beyond the issue of religious freedom raised in the case itself. That equality involved a fundamental respect—an *equal* respect—for the individuality of persons, which was confirmed as a matter of constitutional law; all the states of the Union rested on a theory of liberty which denied any power in the state "to standardize its children."[33] Equality was here once again a fundamental condition of individualism.

This recognition of the right to diversity in educational choice, and of the corresponding right of different religious bodies to the educational observances required by their very existence, was to reappear in much stronger form with the bitterly contested issue of concessions to parochial schools; the principles involved bore similarities to the equally intricate questions that would arise when obligations of religious conscience came into conflict with ceremonial observances ordained by public authorities. These observances, although civil, had about them an almost religious quality because they involved the flag of the United States. In 1940 the Supreme Court upheld the right of the state of West Virginia to compel children attending its schools to salute the flag and recite the oath of allegiance; Mr. Justice Frankfurter's opinion noted that the dissent of some children, if permitted, might undermine the conviction of others.[34] This remark suggested that the Court had subordinated the individual conscience to the social aims of the state, which seemed to contrast with the doctrine of *Pierce*

33. *Pierce v. Society of Sisters*, 268 U.S. 571 (1925), at 573.
34. *Minersville School District v. Gobitis*, 310 U.S. 1011 (1940), at 1015.

and raised a serious question as to how far individual conscience could depend on constitutional protection. Three years later, in the *Barnette* case in the same state, the Court reversed itself. As in the earlier case, the objectors were members of the sect of Jehovah's Witnesses, who took literally the biblical injunction against graven images.

By this time the justices may have been unfavorably impressed by the effects of government-compelled allegiance abroad. The year was 1943; four local groups had objected to the prescribed salute on the ground that it resembled Hitler's. The decision was notable for Mr. Justice Jackson's opinion, written in a style that in some respects recalled John Marshall. "It is not clear," he observed, "whether the regulation contemplates that pupils forego any contrary convictions of their own and become unwilling converts to the prescribed ceremony or whether it will be acceptable if they simulate assent by words without belief and by a gesture barren of meaning. It is now a commonplace that censorship or suppression of expression of opinion is tolerated by our Constitution only when the expression presents a clear and present danger of action of a kind the State is empowered to prevent and punish. It would seem that involuntary affirmation could be commanded only on even more immediate and urgent grounds than silence." Later he added, "There are village tyrants as well as village Hampdens, but none who acts under the color of law is beyond the reach of the Constitution."[35] The consequences of coercion were far more serious than those of permitting dissent. "Those who begin coercive elimination of dissent soon find themselves exterminating dissenters. Compulsory unification of opinion achieves only the unanimity of the graveyard." Jackson then added a reflection that distinctly echoed Madison's warning that "it is proper to take alarm at the first experiment on our liberties." Turning directly to the First Amendment, Jackson pointed out that "it was designed to avoid these ends by avoiding these beginnings. There is no mysticism in the American concept of the State or of the nature or origin of its authority. We set up government by the

35. The allusion is to Thomas Grey's "Elegy in a Country Churchyard," which is perhaps less widely read now than when Jackson was at school:

> Some village-Hampden, that with dauntless breast
> The little tyrant of his fields withstood;
> Some mute inglorious Milton here may rest,
> Some Cromwell guiltless of his country's blood.

consent of the governed, and the Bill of Rights denies those in power any legal opportunity to coerce that consent. Authority here is controlled by public opinion, not public opinion by authority."[36]

The modern state provides its citizens with many forms of protection and benefit in the course of its duty, including police protection, street lighting, libraries, schools, and public transport. The beneficiaries of these services are of all religions and no religion; their beliefs have nothing whatever to do with their rights as equal citizens to equal shares in the state's services. When, however, individual states began to respond to shifts in population, with their attendant voting powers, by including religious institutions in their benefits, they opened a new direction in American political practice. As early as 1930 the state of Louisiana was challenged to justify the provision of free school textbooks to children attending Catholic parochial schools—a policy as formally "neutral" in that part of the country as the provision of a King James Bible would have appeared in Virginia. The Court recognized that these demographic realities gave a claim on constitutionally protected rights and met the difficulty in the establishment clause by striking out along the line of citizenship rather than religion; the issue was defined as one of "child benefit"; it was not the schools but the children, and in due course the state, that gained the benefit from education.[37] But a far more divisive case came to a head soon after the Second World War in New Jersey. The state's laws authorized local school districts to arrange school trans-

---

36. *W. Virginia State Board of Education v. Barnette,* 319 U.S. 624 (1943). Frankfurter, in a powerful dissent, held that the aims of the ceremony were fully within the legitimate competence of the state authorities. "The constitutional protection of religious freedom terminated disabilities, it did not create new privileges," he said. "It gave religious equality, not civil immunity. Its essence is freedom from conformity to religious dogma, not freedom from conformity to law because of religious dogma. . . . Otherwise each individual could set up his own censor against obedience to laws conscientiously deemed for the public good by those whose business it is to make laws" (Ibid.). He anticipated correctly the complex of issues that would arise over such matters as textbooks, school lunches, and transport for children attending private schools. In this opinion he adverted to the thesis which occupied much of his judicial life, that "our constant preoccupation with the constitutionality of legislation rather than with its wisdom tends to preoccupation of the American mind with a false value"—a wise reflection, no doubt, since Frankfurter was referring to "the American mind" in contemplation of general policy, though surely the constitutionality of legislation was precisely the domain of the Supreme Court. Note the pejorative use of the word *dogma* to refer to religious convictions which he did not like. 646–71

37. *Cochran v. Board of Education,* 281 U.S. 370 (1930).

port, and one township authorized reimbursement to parents for money spent on their children's school transport. Some of this money was used to reimburse parents of children attending Catholic schools. To this procedure one local taxpayer objected, filed suit, and carried the matter to the Supreme Court.

It was in delivering the opinion of the court in this case that Mr. Justice Black rediscovered Jefferson's wall of separation, which he reduced to an archaeological specimen while satisfying himself that it had survived intact. The basic tenet of the judgment was that the Catholic beneficiaries of these funds were getting them in their capacity as citizens, not in their capacity as Catholics; the principle of equality was at stake here because all were equally entitled to the benefits of public welfare, and the court found nothing to prevent the authorities from offering these to individuals who then made a sectarian use of them so long as these benefits accrued to them as individuals and not to the sect.[38]

Although Black's opinion contained a strong reaffirmation of the establishment clause, the judgment marked a decisive step toward accommodating religious interests and away from a strict interpretation of that clause. It recognized two principles: that the Americans were a people sympathetically disposed toward religion, and that they were a people among whom religious pluralism was embedded. Given these conditions, the decision could be defended on the grounds that common sense then took priority over constitutional logic in tending to accommodate those religions. But this judgment, which was carried by five votes to four, provoked a series of cogent dissents, of which Mr. Justice Jackson's soon became famous. The First Amendment, he observed, "was intended not only to keep the states' hands out of religion, but to keep religion's hands off the state, and above all, to keep bitter religious controversy out of public life by denying to every denomination any advantage from getting control of public policy or the public purse. Those great ends I cannot but think are immeasurably compromised by today's decision."[39] The other dissenting justices took the historically interesting step of appending the full text of Madison's *Memorial and Remonstrance* of 1785 to their opinion. There could be no clearer state-

38. *Everson v. Board of Education*, 330 U.S. 1 (1947).
39. Ibid., 26–27.

ment of the basic principles of separation and no clearer demonstration that the Court's judgment represented a profound breach with those principles.

American governments at all levels had a long record of hospitality toward religion rather than the frigid neutrality which might seem to have been dictated by the language of the establishment clause of the First Amendment. It seemed pedantic to quarrel with the phrase "In God We Trust," which first appeared on the coinage in 1864,[40] to object to the use of the expression "So help me God" on solemn occasions, or—as soon came to be pointed out—to find religious establishment in the words with which the daily sessions of the Supreme Court were declared open: "God save the United States and this honorable Court!" As religions of different kinds revealed their permanence and voting power, it seemed much easier to accept their presence in a similar spirit to that in which the Protestant aegis had once been unquestioningly accepted than to insist on the logic of the Constitution. The very widespread practice of religious observance must also have eased the notion of hospitality. "We are a religious people whose institutions presuppose a Supreme Being," declared Mr. Justice Douglas when, speaking for the Court in 1952, he validated the practice of releasing school time for children to go elsewhere for religious attendance.[41] This remark, which seems to have been offered in a moment of intellectual relaxation, reflected an easy acceptance of ancient social habits of thought rather than the discomfort of analytical rigor.

The very weakness of Douglas's apology helps to clarify the relevant distinctions. It was true that American institutions owed much of their moral foundations to theories of natural rights, and that natural rights derived their force in the eighteenth century from a concept of deity, however vaguely conceived. But whig ideas of the justification of government did not really demand that such beliefs be pursued to their theological origins and could in fact have survived quite well without them; the practical force of the American Constitution was drawn from belief in the actual registration of political consent. This being the case, Douglas's dictum was irrelevant, and the remark that the Americans were "a religious people" was without constitutional interest.

40. Stokes, *Church and State* 3:602.
41. *Zorach v. Clauson*, 343 U.S. 306 (1952), at 313.

While the Cold War made people in American public life visibly anxious to affirm their godliness in face of the national enemy in the form of atheistic communism, the sectarian issue within America became increasingly bitter. Protestants objected with mounting vehemence to public support for parochial schools, but many adherents of other faiths, and unbelievers, objected to any form of state-sponsored religious observance, especially in schools, where the issue could not be kept down. The state of New York tried to find a nonsectarian form of prayer acceptable for all faiths attending its public schools, but when this method was challenged in *Engel v. Vitale* in 1962 it fell under the ax of the establishment clause. "When the power, prestige, and financial support of government is placed behind a particular religious belief, the indirect coercive pressure upon religious minorities to conform to the prevailing officially approved religion is plain," declared the Court; in this case, too, Douglas disposed of *Everson* as being "in retrospect . . . out of line with the First Amendment."[42] Oddly, however, although these opinions dealt with the susceptibilities of children, they failed to notice the difficulty for the nonconformist or irreligious teacher who might be assigned the duty of leading the class in prayer.

Pennsylvania tried to meet the problem by allowing dissenting children to be excused. A Unitarian family considered the offer and decided that it was not good enough because the request might prejudice their children in the eyes of their teachers and classmates. The Supreme Court agreed: "In the relationship between man and religion, the State is firmly committed to a position of neutrality." As Mr. Justice William Brennan commented, once it was found that the exercises were essentially religious, the availability of excusal or exemption had no relevance to the question of establishment. But if one turned to free exercise of religion, the authorities could not require people to profess disbelief, and children might be reluctant to be stigmatized as atheists or nonconformists.[43] It was not pedantry or a taste for antiquarian revivals that tempted some of the justices in these often divided judgments to quote Madison's *Memorial and Remonstrance* in these years. They were driven back to the doctrine of state neutrality by an inexorable logic without which the concept of separation would soon have lost its meaning.

On the other side, it was argued with considerable historical support

42. *Engel v. Vitale*, 370 U.S. 421 (1962), at 608, 615.
43. *School District of Abington Township v. Schempp*, 374 U.S. 844 (1963), at 862–905.

that religion was a medium through which the community defined and reaffirmed its moral character, but this could not be done—once it was challenged—without a violation of the establishment clause, and even under the conservative pressures of the Reagan era, the Court protected the equal sensibilities of minorities in the educational system by finding such a violation in every state-sanctioned expression of religion that it came to consider. [44] Outside the educational system, where non-Christians objected to such traditional Christmas observances as a nativity scene set up in a public place by a city corporation, the Court wavered in the direction of social custom, justifying the position with appeals to historical practice as the affirmation of community values. It was easier to explain the accommodation of traditional social values than of religion. The principle of equality of individual conscience, particularly in the case of minority consciences, seems to be discounted in these judgments, a conclusion which may say more for the Court's sense of social accountability than for its intellectual integrity. [45]

The problem of equality of individual conscience, of the meaning to the individual of his or her own experience, and whether the state had a right to interpret that experience, had been in the forefront of Jefferson's and Madison's thought, but they could hardly have anticipated the form in which it would come up, when a self-styled religious group calling themselves the "I AM" movement claimed to be able to cure diseases through the intervention of St. Germain. The state of Connecticut arrested them and charged them with fraud. But the Supreme Court struck down the conviction on the ground, essentially deriving from *Watson v. Jones*, that "the law knows no heresy and is committed to no dogma"; as earlier cases had shown, the First Amendment forestalled state compulsion to observe any creed and safeguarded the free exercise of any chosen form of religion. [46] There was sharp disagreement on the bench about this case. "The state of one's mind is a fact as capable of

---

44. "Developments in the Law: Religion and the State," *Harvard Law Review* 100 (1987), 1609–1781, at 1659. In *Wallace v. Jaffee*, 472 U.S. 38 (1985), the Court struck down a statute requiring a moment of silence for prayer.

45. The *Harvard Law Review* writers note in "Religion and the State," 1658–59, that in *Lynch v. Donnelly* (nativity scene in Pawtucket), 465 U.S. 668 (1984), and *Marsh v. Chambers* (appointment of a chaplain by a legislature, where the court adverted to the use of chaplains by the Continental Congress, seventeen of whose members had gone on to the Constitutional Convention!), 463 U.S. 783 (1983), the court's approach represents an inversion of the principle that the religion clauses protect unpopular minorities.

46. *Cantwell v. Connecticut*, 310 U.S. 296 (1940).

fraudulent misrepresentation as is one's physical condition or the state of his bodily health," observed Chief Justice Stone in a dissent strongly marked by the reasoning of common sense; but Jackson replied that truth or falsity could not be determined in religious beliefs, and the trial judge had been mistaken in telling the jury to make up their minds whether the beliefs were honestly held or not.[47]

Two issues of crucial significance for the enunciation of the constitutional basis of equality were involved in these and a variety of subsequent cases of similar import.[48] One was that, as we have seen, the prohibitions which the Bill of Rights set up against the Federal Government bore equally on the states; and this principle meant in turn that the *equality* of citizens was irresistibly established throughout the Union through the medium of the federal Bill of Rights. There was nothing intrinsically novel about this doctrine; it was wholly consistent with that of the Comity Clause, which protected the rights of the citizens when in other states than their own. It was in a deeper sense consistent, rather than being merely compatible, with the implications of the entire constitutional conception of citizenship, and it is a tribute to the allegiance of Americans to the idea of state sovereignty that it should have taken so long to establish.

The other principle was simply that the religious consciences of these American citizens were equal consciences. But if the government had no right or power to establish or favor religious beliefs of one sort or another, it followed that it had no right to determine nor power of determining whether a particular person's conscience was religious or not,

47. *U.S. v. Ballard*, 322 U.S. 78 (1944), 90, 92–95.

48. For debate on the incorporation doctrine in related cases, *Palko v. Connecticut*, 302 U.S. 319 (1937), a murder case involving the question of double jeopardy, forbidden by the Fifth Amendment; *Adamson v. California*, 332 U.S. 46 (1947), in which Mr. Justice Hugo Black put on record a dissenting opinion to the effect that the specific guarantees of the Bill of Rights were carried intact into the first section of the Fourteenth Amendment, 68–92; *Gideon v. Wainwright*, 372 U.S. 335 (1963), in which the Sixth Amendment guarantee of a right of accused to counsel is made obligatory on the states; *Pointer v. Texas*, 380 U.S. 400 (1965), which enforces an accused person's Sixth Amendment right to confront witnesses against him; *Griswold v. Connecticut*, 381 U.S. (1965), which enlarges the "penumbra" of constitutional rights inhering in the essential privacy of marital relations to enforce it on the states through the due process clause of the Fourteenth Amendment. The cases are not wholly consistent, and the Court takes some years to accept the doctrine in full, but the application of the Fourteenth Amendment has the ultimate effect of generalizing the Bill of Rights.

because it could not enter into the process of determining without touching on "establishment." But in reality the justices of the Court were themselves American citizens, sharing some of their prejudices and many of their preferences; these preferences had shifted the Court towards an accommodationist approach to the vaguely defined concept of religious establishment. But a further question remained: would the reasoning that seemed to be inherent in the state's religious neutrality permit a new kind of accommodation—which gave equal standing to the irreligious conscience?

The Religious Aegis Challenged

One legacy of the Protestant aegis was a fairly well-defined notion of religion. As the Supreme Court declared, when at length called for a definition in 1890, religion referred to a belief in and worship of a deity.[49] If legislative statutes were to deal with religion at all, the meaning of religion and the validity of the claim to act from religious motives posed questions that would one day have to be answered—for which reason the establishment clause would seem logically to preclude any statutes that even raised the question. But generations of precedent had steered the Court to the recognition of religion as an element of national life irreversibly intermingled with its social institutions and through them with its politics.

This mingling was revealed by the marked reluctance of American legislatures to give equal weight to the principled beliefs of irreligious persons, or of persons who made secular conscience rather than religion the determinant of duty. This legislative tendency would appear to call for the didactic intervention of the judiciary, whose reading of the establishment clause could be expected to be closer and more stringent than that of the lawmakers. If the Supreme Court leaned towards the protection of the irreligious and reached determinations which tended to help them, however, its reasoning was noncommittal and never conclusive. Maryland, for example, had a declaration of rights which by requiring all public officials to declare a belief in God might have seemed to contradict the American Bill of Rights. When this was challenged in the early 1960s, the Court (through Mr. Justice Black) said that neither state

49. *Davis v. Beason*, 133 U.S. 333 (1890).

nor federal government was permitted to aid those religions which depended on belief in the existence of God as against those which did not.[50] The judgment was a departure from the precept of 1890, but in principle it said nothing to invalidate religious qualifications for office and left the state free to require some religion as against none.

War is often the acid test of moral principles. The Military Selective Service Act contained a clause 6(j) which attempted to provide for the objections of religious conscience.[51] A draft registrant might object on the grounds that religion forbade him to take part in war in any circumstances, but it did not permit registrants to refuse service on grounds of political principles or to draw their own distinctions between just and unjust wars; the government would do that for them. This distinction might not have caused much difficulty during the Second World War, but the United States was embroiled in the 1960s in a war in Vietnam which an ever-increasing number of its citizens did regard as immoral and unjust.

The language of the act dealt in fine distinctions. For a draft registrant's conscientious objection to all war to be "religious" within the exempting provision it must stem from moral, ethical, or religious beliefs "held with the strength of traditional religious convictions." There was some comfort here for Elliott Ashton Welsh, who firmly declined to claim religious grounds of exemption but whose humanist grounds were as certain as those of any fundamentalist standing—as few have done— on the Sixth Commandment. Welsh's plea was accepted. But there was less comfort for his contemporary Guy Gillette, who objected for moral reasons to the war in Vietnam while declaring quite frankly that he would be prepared to fight for the United States in its own defense—or in a war sanctioned by the United Nations. Gillette's sincerity was not in doubt, but his plea for registration as a conscientious objector was denied on the grounds that he did not object on principle to all wars. The case was marked by a strong dissent by Mr. Justice Douglas, who put the rights of conscience at the center of the argument and asserted that an implied First Amendment right of conscience should stand at least as high as the right of association, which the court had upheld. The distinction drawn by the act between opponents of all wars and of particular

---

50. *Torcaso v. Watkins,* 367 U.S. 488 (1961), 495.
51. "Developments in the Law," *Harvard Law Review,* 1717.

wars seemed to Douglas misguided, and he added that "a classification of 'conscience' based on a 'religion' and a 'conscience' based on more generalized, philosophical grounds is equally invidious by reason of our First Amendment standards,"[52] an observation of wide significance.[53]

The Supreme Court has always denied giving preference to religious consciences, a claim that gained sustenance from a case in which a steel worker had objected to a transfer within his plant to a section manufacturing munitions. In this case the Court overruled the lower court to uphold what appeared to be a "personal philosophical choice"—a premise the lower court had rejected.[54] This judgment may perhaps be thought to complete a cycle of reasoning which had begun almost two centuries earlier with James Madison's reasoning in the *Memorial and Remonstrance* which had gained religious liberty in Virginia.

It would be easier to be sure about the principle if a comparable case had reached the Court involving exemption from the crucial test of military service on philosophical rather than religious grounds. Common law principles would suggest that the precedent of the munitions manu-

52. *U.S. v. Welsh*, 398 U.S. 333 (1971); *Gillette v. U.S.*, 401 U.S. 437 (28 L.Ed., 190–92).

53. The issue involves the problem of equality, but it can hardly be said that the principle of individual conscience, considered on the basis of personal equality, necessarily determines this kind of case. An individual may be mistaken about the facts. He or she may also be mistaken about their significance, a mistake that may be induced by personal apprehensions. A society which operated with complete subordination to this principle might run the risk of ceasing to exist as a society. It is not clear that equality would itself survive in the resulting state of either conquest or anarchy. The point is of some theoretical interest, since it demonstrates that cases in which equality is undoubtedly involved may have to be resolved on other grounds. I am indebted to Eric Barendt for comments.

54. *Thomas v. Review Board*, 450 U.S. 707 (1981). In the case of *U.S. v. Sisson*, 399 U.S. 267 (1970), the district court granted exemption from military service on the grounds that section 6 (j) of the Selective Service Act of 1967 offended the establishment clause because it "unconstitutionally discriminated against atheists, agnostics, and men, like Sisson, who, whether they be religious or not, are motivated in their objection to the draft by profound moral beliefs which constitute the central convictions of their beings" (278). Sisson had objected specifically to serving in Vietnam. His case eventually reached the Supreme Court, which found that it lacked jurisdiction on the technical grounds that the trial judge's decision amounted to an ordered acquittal. There has thus not to date been a definitive ruling on this question by the Supreme Court. It is not here being argued that any of the views noted is conclusive. As observed in n. 53, there are powerful arguments against selective conscientious objection, which is rather easily capable of abuse.

facturer should be followed, but precedent has been a remarkably unstable guide to the Court's reasoning in cases involving religious establishment and free exercise. The problem with the accommodationist approach is its reasonableness. Until the early 1960s the Court had held firmly that constitutional protection for free exercise of religion extended to religious belief—presumably involving worship—but not to conduct motivated by religion but otherwise socially excluded. The point had been established with some ferocity in the case of the Mormons. But in 1963 this line changed. A Seventh Day Adventist who refused on religious grounds to work on Saturdays was denied unemployment relief, took her case to the Supreme Court, and won. Mr. Justice Brennan in giving judgment shifted the burden of proving constitutional right from the religious objector to the state,[55] which on the face of the matter appeared to be a gain for the equality of individual conscience. Some ten years later a case of conscience with perhaps wider implications arose from the way of life of the Amish people. Wisconsin had imposed criminal penalties on Amish parents who refused to send their children to school. The Court overturned this outcome in a judgment rendered with some feeling by Chief Justice Warren Burger, who seemed to approve of Amish morality rather more strongly than he endorsed the central principle of religious freedom for the individual.[56] But the line thus marked was tenuous. When the Court was not moved by such feelings of protective identification, the state was upheld and the individual was deprived of protection. The point appeared in the case of Indian or Native American parents, who feared that a government-imposed Social Security number would rob their child of her spirit—surely a loss of some seriousness in any religious context.[57] The broadly accommodationist approach to the freest possible exercise of religion was a seemingly very democratic answer to the needs of the pluralistically religious people. But its interpretation by the Court tended strongly to the accommodation of broad majorities, and moreover,

55. *Sherbert v. Verner*, 374 U.S. 398 (1963), 402–10.

56. *Wisconsin v. Yoder*, 406 U.S. 205 (1972).

57. *Bowen v. Roy*, 106 S.C. 2147 (1986). The state would no doubt argue that a Social Security number conferred benefits more material than those accruing to the spirit. But there is Christian authority for a question as to the relative benefits of gaining the whole world and losing one's own soul, a question which does not appear to have detained the Court.

where it offered a protective tolerance to small minorities like the Seventh Day Adventist, it still tended to encroach seriously on the principle that precluded all or any establishment of religion. The irreligious conscience, if not discounted, was at a disadvantage in this atmosphere, where the establishment clause strictly construed might be held to give equality to all consciences.

After wrestling with a cluster of cases requiring some exceedingly fine distinctions, several of them arising from angry disputes over public education, the Supreme Court attempted in 1971 to resolve these difficulties by a set of tests known from the leading case as the *Lemon* tests.[58] To satisfy the requirements of the establishment clause, said the Court, any government action affecting religion must (1) have a secular purpose; must (2) neither advance nor inhibit religion as a primary effect; and must (3) not create "excessive governmental entanglement with religion." The word "excessive" would clearly bear a heavy future burden.

The effect, on the whole, was to put the establishment clause on the defensive. But no clear line of interpretation has emerged, a fair rule of neutrality has eluded the Court, and it has been rightly observed that the outcome of a case may depend on whether it is treated under the establishment clause or the free exercise clause.[59] When we find that the full weight and majesty of the Constitution decrees that school books may be provided at public expense to private schools but that other forms of educational equipment may not, we are drawn to some sympathy with the opinion that the judgments since *Lemon* have been not only inconsistent but incoherent.[60] The analytical mind does not

58. *Lemon v. Kurtzman*, 403 U.S. 602 (1971); and see *Robinson v. Di Censo*, 403 U.S. 672 (1971); *Tilton v. Richardson*, 403 U.S. 672 (1971); Donald A. Giannella, "Lemon and Tilton: The Bitter and the Sweet of Church-State Entanglement," *Supreme Court Review* (1971), 146–200; "Religion and the State," *Harvard Law Review*, 1633–34, 1644–46.

59. "Religion and the State," *Harvard Law Review*, 1634.

60. Ibid., 1676–81. This essay includes a useful summary of a variety of proposals for reducing the subject to order, to which the reader may refer for further enlightenment. Our own purposes here are limited to examining the bearing of the issue on the basic problems of defining and sustaining a commitment to equality. The first edition of this book (p. 111) adopted the proposal of Philip Kurland for a constitutional amendment to read: "The state may not use religion as a basis for classification for purposes of governmental action, whether the action be for conferring rights or privileges or the imposition of duties or obligations." Philip B. Kurland, *Religion and the Law of Church and State in the United States* (Chicago, 1962), 18. This intellectually rigorous approach would

relish such incoherence, which is the price paid for compromise rather than for either intellectual clarity or moral strength.

Compromise, of course, has its own benefits, not least to the lawyers themselves. The outcome of any particular case has been rendered more then ordinarily unpredictable. But the confusion is inherent in the language which it falls to the Court to interpret—a duty always undertaken in the light of a basic commitment to some principle of religious equality. When religious interests feel burdened by legislation that is on its face neutral, it becomes a duty of the Court to afford protection to the extent of permitting free exercise, but such protection often entails the danger of treating one religion with special consideration, at the cost of unequal treatment of others. A settled policy of accommodation or special sensibility toward religion in the nature of the case means toward *individuals* as members of religious sects; this has an innate tendency to afford higher consideration to such persons as individuals. In ways that are not explicit but are nonetheless pervasive, such a policy tends to confer on religion the advantages of status as well as formal protection. Translated into policy, this is difficult to reconcile either with strict neutrality in all matters affecting religion or with the equal treatment of individuals throughout the rest of the system covered by the Constitution. But, as we have argued, it is a system intended for individuals. In revealing inconsistencies in the applications of equality as a controlling principle, the analysis really reveals another fundamental truth, which tends to be concealed by the language in which decisions are formulated: that equality is not in fact the only consideration by which these decisions are determined.

The Bill of Rights had nothing to say on the claims or merits of different religions. In effect, it simply defined them as equal in the eyes of the government. It is logically impossible to separate this claim from that of the equality of the individuals who hold religious convictions. This principle forms a perfect harmony with the other categories, equality before the law and equality in political rights, sustained by and incor-

---

clarify the whole situation, but at a cost to accommodationism that would appear politically unacceptable, possibly even unattainable.

porating the equality of respect in which the government holds its citizens. It leaves the individual alone with his or her own conscience, a sovereign possessor of an autonomous moral being. But analysis and experience have reduced the concept of equality to component elements that have not always proved harmonious with each other. The concept of religious equality, so far from being an exception, has produced further refinements and inextricable entanglements. There is no need to conclude from this review of the history of the subject that some form of reduction is intellectually inconceivable. Free exercise might be assimilated to other established rights such as free assembly and the liberty of the press, leaving the establishment clause in possession of the rest of the field. It depends, perhaps, whether one wishes the life of the law to be dominated by logic or experience.

Chapter Six

Equal Rights, Unequal Conditions, and the Emergence of Equality of Opportunity

The men who led the colonial protest that turned into the American Revolution had little idea that they were inaugurating an intellectual upheaval. Yet by the time that its major achievements had been established—which may be reasonably set in the early 1790s—those who had lived through it or were newly emerging to claim responsibility for political policy could see clearly enough that they had experienced not only a profound social and political transformation but a period of extraordinarily concentrated thinking about the meaning and consequences of ideas that had originally seemed both familiar and simple. A rhetoric that had begun, in defense of colonial rights against British encroachments, as conservative, legalistic, and implicitly unified, had been splintered and diversified by the claims of newly emerging and in some cases conflicting interests. It had always been easier to employ the rhetoric of equality with a single voice than to define equality with a single purpose. As purposes multiplied, so did definitions. Yet equality, however deployed in social argument, retained a remarkably central place as the moral imperative around which American thinking turned— as much, given the difference of political systems, as in France, whose great revolution was dedicated to equality as one of a triumvirate of values, and much more so than in Britain, which had given America the first principle of equality before the law. With the exception of the category of sexual equality based on the thesis that men and women were capable of interchangeable roles, the more important analytical

categories of equality had emerged, or had begun to emerge, in the aftermath of the Revolution itself.

Primal Equality and the Concept of Interchangeability

Much republican thought, over many generations, incorporated a kind of remote moral primitivism. There had once been a time, or *ought* to have been, when the essentials of property were equally distributed, or arranged according to very simple needs. This principle did not need to be explained because it was in accordance with divine and natural law. It was departures from it that had to be explained and justified. Moreover, it had a place in the traditions from which the West drew its political and moral thought lying deeper than the concept of the privileged nature of private property. Lycurgus, the legendary founder of Sparta, who was familiar to all educated people in the eighteenth century through Plutarch's widely read *Lives of the Noble Grecians and Romans*, was reputed to have divided the land equally and to have virtually demonetized the economy by substituting an unportable iron currency for gold and silver. A basic equality of goods seemed to have been present in the Garden of Eden, although the brief history of that short-lived experiment had not tested the principle with the conflicts arising from demographic growth. The thought was traceable again in early Christianity and renewed from time to time, though not without divisive effects, in such movements as that of Saint Francis. In political morals, it was implicit in Locke's statement that God had given the world to men to be held in common.[1] One catches its inspiration in an early statement of Adam Smith about the benign effects of individual effort: "They are led," he told his students at Glasgow University, "by an invisible hand to make nearly the same distribution of the necessaries of life, which would have been made, had the earth been divided into equal portions

---

1. Locke, *Second Treatise*, s. 26. It is also worth noting, considering Locke's deep influence on American political thought, that he states unequivocally of the State of Nature that it is "A *State* also of *Equality*, wherein all the Power and Jurisdiction is reciprocal, no one having more power than another: there being nothing more evident, than that Creatures of the same species and rank promiscuously born to all the advantages of Nature, and the use of the same faculties, should also be equal one against another without Subordination or Subjection" (except in divinely appointed sovereignty). Ibid., s. 4.

among all its inhabitants, and thus without intending it, without knowing it, advance the interest of the society, and afford means to the multiplication of the species." [2] It was wholly compatible with the Scottish school of morals, as with Dugald Stewart, one of Smith's successors, to believe that progress from the present economic order could be justified on the grounds that it would eventually tend to produce *more equal* distribution of goods than already existed. [3]

This belief in the primary rightness of equal distribution was revealed clearly when American states seized the opportunity to abolish the principle of primogeniture in the immediate context of the Revolution. Zephaniah Swift, the first jurist to compose a treatise on the laws of a state, made the basic connections in his encomium on the laws of Connecticut: "The first rule of inheritance" was that where a proprietor died intestate, the estate should descend to his children in equal shares—in marked contrast to the laws of England; and in summarizing the system he declared not only that it was "the most liberal, and equitable system of hereditary succession, that ever was adopted," but moreover that it was "most consonant to the laws of nature." [4] In a world of increasingly complex and changing law, the jurist had not lost sight of the basic need of society for a legal order founded on the laws of nature, the source of primal equality. Swift also praised his state for putting the female sex on an equal footing in the law of inheritance. [5] North Carolina revised its inheritance laws in 1784 with the republican declaration that it would tend to promote "that equality of property which is of the spirit and principle of a genuine republic, that the real estates of all persons dying intestate should undergo a more general and equal distribution than has hitherto prevailed in this State." The legislators also rejected the

---

2. Adam Smith, *The Theory of Moral Sentiments*, ed. A.L. Macfie (Oxford, 1976), 184–85.

3. Thus, Stewart was said to have taken "for granted that the rise of commerce and the progress of society had led to the diffusion of wealth and the 'equal diffusion of freedom and happiness' than had ever existed before, and had none of Smith's reservations about the moral consequences of technological innovation which he associated with the rise of monopoly capitalism." Nicholas Phillipson, "The Scottish Enlightenment," in Roy Porter and Mikulasc Teich, eds., *The Enlightenment in National Context* (Cambridge, 1981), 39.

4. Zephaniah Swift, *A System of the Laws of the State of Connecticut*, 2 vols. (Windham, 1795), 281, 296.

5. Ibid., 296.

exclusion of children of the half-blood, terming it "feudal" and peculiar to Great Britain. The danger of undue power accruing to excessive property explained the abolition of entails, which "tend only to raise the wealth and importance of particular families and individuals, giving them an unequal and undue influence in a republic"—echoes, here, of the sentiments which moved the settlers of Kentucky to make moves to limit the amount of land on which a man might settle. Delaware, repealing a law which granted a double portion to the eldest son, declared that it was "the duty of every republican government to preserve equality among its citizens, by maintaining the balance of property as far as is consistent with the rights of individuals."[6]

Much the best known of these steps to abolish primogeniture and entail were those promoted in Virginia by Thomas Jefferson, whose aim was to eliminate the foundations of a possible future aristocracy and to lay foundations for a truly republican government based on a more nearly equal distribution of landed property. To a greater extent than seems to have been realized at the time, Jefferson was knocking at an open door; few landowners had a material interest in maintaining these archaic and uneconomic practices.[7] None of this really meant that a genuinely equitable distribution of goods would or could be a literally equal distribution. Few if any thinkers could have expected such extreme literalism to be taken seriously. But this instinctive undercurrent of elemental egalitarian sentiment was stimulated into more active protest by the sight of extreme contrasts in wealth which could never be honestly explained or rationalized as the result of the neutral operation of the laws of nature. Such sights may have been more glaring and

---

6. These statements are cited in Stanley N. Katz, "Republicanism and the Law of Inheritance in the American Revolutionary Era," *Michigan Law Review* 76:1 (1977–78), 15, 14. But North Carolina's reform has been criticized because, in the cause of simplifying the law, it forced widows with more than two children to share the inheritance equally, thus diminishing their traditional right to a one-third allotment. A North Carolina judge was able to declare within a decade that "dower at common law is abolished." Elaine F. Crane, "Dependence in the Era of Independence," in Jack P. Greene, ed., *The American Revolution: Its Character and Limits* (New York, 1987), 264; Linda Kerber, *Women of the Republic: Intellect and Ideology in Revolutionary America* (Chapel Hill, 1980), 147.

7. David J. Mays, *Edmund Pendleton, 1721–1803: A Biography* (Cambridge, Mass., 1952), 2, 137–38; Merrill Peterson, *Thomas Jefferson and the New Nation* (New York, 1970), 114–16.

offensive in Europe than in America; Jefferson was clearly offended by the extreme differences he saw in France,[8] but Americans had their eyes on their own home ground; as we have seen, they were often offended by inequalities less extreme than those of Europe, all the more so because their culture so earnestly asserted its republican morality.

At its most attractive, the highly personal feeling of moral equality which expressed itself as the basis of republican principles was capable of tolerating and respecting the same qualities in others, and it was this, no doubt, that touched the heart of the romantic French sojourner J. Hector St. Jean de Crèvecoeur, who in 1782 conveyed a vivid impression of a free, tolerant, prosperous society by dwelling mainly on those characteristics which appealed most forcibly to his own imagination. It was these impressions that he most wished to be true of the whole. In Crèvecoeur's opinion the mixture of peoples in America was producing a "new man," and among these new men there prevailed a high degree of economic and social equality. Enjoying their own freedom, they treated each other with amity and respect.[9] Some twenty years earlier in the neighboring province of Pennsylvania, the Reverend Jacob Duché (later to appear as chaplain to the Continental Congress) gave a telling indication of the social edge of this attitude when he remarked of the people of the province that they were "generally of the middling sort, and at present pretty much upon the level. They are industrious Farmers, Artificers, or Men of Trade; they enjoy and are fond of Freedom, and *the meanest among them* thinks he has a Right to Civility from the greatest."[10] Another Frenchman caught the same note when Andrew Jackson was president two generations later. "Equality," wrote Alexis de Tocqueville, "every day gives every man a multitude of little delights. The charms of equality are felt every hour and are within everyone's reach; the noblest hearts are not insensitive to them and the commonest souls delight in them. The passion to which equality gives birth must

8. Katz, "Republicanism and Inheritance," 17. Writing to Madison, Jefferson commented on the "enormous inequality" which caused so much misery to mankind; he ventured the interesting opinion that these excesses violated natural rights, echoing Locke with the statement that the earth had been given to men as "common stock" to labor and to live on.

9. Crèvecoeur, Michel Guillaume, called St. John de, *Letters from an American Farmer* (London, 1782).

10. Quoted in Theodore Thayer, *Pennsylvania Politics and the Growth of Democracy 1740–1776* (Harrisburg, 1953), citing *The Pennsylvania Journal*, March 25, 1756.

thus be at once energetic and general." [11] Tocqueville, though he would have resented the allegation, was in some ways as romantic as Crèvecoeur; but whatever the delights felt by Americans, it was the European eye that caught and *interpreted* characteristic qualities in American society. Benjamin Latrobe, architect and planner, was better qualified by residence than Tocqueville to observe—some twenty-five years earlier—that

> ever since the Revolution, the internal state of the United States has been undergoing a regular and gradual change. That deference of race which, without existing titles of nobility, grows out of the habits and prejudices of the people, was bequeathed to Americans by English manners and institutions which were established before the revolution. These manners could not be suddenly altered nor did the institutions of the country undergo any very great or sudden change. After the adoption of the federal Constitution, the extension of the right of suffrage in all the states to a majority of adult male citizens, planted a germ which has gradually evolved and spread actual and practical equality and political democracy over the whole union. . . . Every man is independent. [12]

Latrobe, an Englishman by birth, had resided ten years in the United States at the time of these remarks. His perspective was advantageous, but that did not give him the last word on the subject, and his observations were perhaps more accurate in portraying a characteristic that struck Europeans very forcibly: a certain *accessibility* that Americans expected of each other, more or less regardless of known and understood differentiations of class. It was this that James Fenimore Cooper ridiculed with some bitterness in his novels *Homeward Bound* and *Home as Found*, in which members of the aristocratic Effingham family (the name recalls Lord Howard of Effingham) return from twelve years in Europe to find their country very much changed for the worse. Socially uninstructed characters blunder through the story without apprehending the folly or the enormity of their mistakes. One of them characteristically accepts with joy an offer of introduction to a social superior because he "fancied he had the right, under the Constitution of the United States of America, to be introduced to every human being with whom he came in contact"[13] —no doubt one of the "delights" referred to by Tocqueville, but a

11. Alexis de Tocqueville, *De la démocratie en Amérique*, ed. J.-P. Mayer (Paris, 1961), 101–04.

12. Mathew Page Andrews, *History of Maryland* (Garden City, N.Y., 1929), 410. The word *race* was here used to mean a family or group connected by kinship.

13. *Home as Found*, 2 vols. (Philadelphia, 1838), 70 and throughout.

sensation that would lose its relish if the *concept* of social superiority were really to disappear. In a debate on a proposal to abolish pews in the rebuilding of the church, the editor Steadfast Dodge opines that "to my mind, gentlemen and ladies, God never intended an American to kneel." (Cooper lets him establish his social credentials by addressing the gentlemen before the ladies.)

Cooper's romance concludes with marriages that are appropriate to the proprieties of social class. (An English nobleman discloses his true identity before claiming the hand of the lovely Grace Effingham.) The scene of these events, which had a closely autobiographical element, was upstate New York. To the east, in Boston, the Unitarians found themselves locked in a not less complicated struggle, in which theology was called to the aid of class. Unitarian thinking revealed here a faint but significant line of descent from the historic Protestant doctrine of the calling, under which every individual was obliged to answer in his or her life to the call of providence. The call determined one's occupation and service to the community in this world, and service to the community was service to God. Since most of the trades and occupations available to man were already fixed and designated, the doctrine, with some exceptions, could hardly be said to have encouraged an enthusiasm for social mobility. Harvard-based Unitarians believed that there existed "a perceptible connexion between a man's character and condition in life," and that this connection was part of an established scheme of providence; God intended indolence to lead to poverty and want. Unitarian moralists certainly believed that honest toil should and would be rewarded, but in heaven rather than by a transfer of social rank. The elevation of the workers, explained William Ellery Channing, during the election year of 1840, was "not to be gained by efforts to force themselves into what are called the upper ranks of society." Although this was probably a warning against collective labor action rather than personal effort, Unitarian moralists were in the somewhat ambiguous position of finding it necessary to congratulate those who had risen in the world—which happened to apply to many of their own members—while tactfully dissuading others from too aggressively following their example. Their social emphasis differed from that of formal republican ideology by placing much greater emphasis on duties than on rights. [14]

14. Daniel W. Howe, *The Unitarian Conscience: Harvard Moral Philosophy, 1805–1861* (Cambridge, Mass., 1970), 145–46, 146–47 (n. 83), 127–28.

There is a distinctly defensive and uneasy note about some of these protestations. Western expansion well before the middle of the century was bringing marked implications of social as well as geographical mobility, with which Unitarian leaders in the east were not comfortable. [15] But not all western settlement had been a story of the burgeoning of equality of opportunity. None of the strenuous social jostling recorded by Cooper, for example, altered the fact that in the Southwest, men of the stature of William Blount and John Sevier dominated successive governments of Tennessee with an assurance that owed a good deal to the habit of command and very little to the exigencies of social equality of electoral politics. Thomas P. Abernethy, the first modern historian of Tennessee's early life, reached conclusions never superseded by more recent research when he demonstrated the immense political and economic power of the great land speculators and owners, who treated public office as their inheritance, secured the votes of the common people by their prestige, and felt no need to stoop to campaigning for election. [16] But in Tennessee as elsewhere, this order was assailed by the groundswell that, breaking out after the financial panic of 1819, brought James K. Polk to Congress in 1825 and was soon to be linked indissolubly with the name and image of Andrew Jackson. In face of this insurgency, Judge Emmerson, a retired justice of the state's supreme court, exclaimed with more passion than clarity, "Had I the power, no exertion of which I was capable would be wanting to arrest the progress of that wild and furious democracy which has long threatened to overwhelm our country at no distant date in the vortex of anarchy." [17]

Andrew Jackson, soldier, landowner and slave owner, a man who passed his youth in the aftermath of the revolutionary environment and was already a member of the Tennessee constitutional convention in 1796, may not have thought of himself as the embodiment of a wild and furious democracy, but he expressed the political aspect of these sentiments in his forthright way when as President of the United States, he had to defend the practice of supplanting his political opponents from offices in which they had served without failing their trust: "The duties of all public officers are, or at least admit of being made, so plain and

15. Ibid., 233–34.
16. Thomas P. Abernethy, *From Frontier to Plantation in Tennessee* (Chapel Hill, 1932), chs. 10 and 22.
17. Charles G. Sellers, *James K. Polk, Jacksonian, 1795–1843* (Princeton, 1957) 2:99.

simple that men of intelligence may readily qualify themselves for their performance."[18] This remark admittedly was addressed as much to the demystification of public office as to the qualifications of officers, and it did refer to "men of intelligence." But it evoked a gathering folk belief that one man, certainly any one American, was as good as another, and could probably (given adequate training and preparation) do another's job or fill his role with approximately equal results. Before the mid-twentieth century this claim was largely confined to the interchangeability of men.

Folk beliefs are difficult to prove. The evidence for them lives in fairy tales, oral traditions, anecdotes, and in certain habits of behavior, for most of which there may also be contradictory evidence. A folk belief in primal equality may be seen as much as a warning not to take false pride in social distinctions as an actual denial either of the existence of intrinsic qualitative differences between classes or of the necessity for some gradations of responsibility and honor in society. When the English peasantry rebelled under John Ball's leadership in 1381 it is said that they chanted the satirical verse,

> When Adam delv'd and Eve span
> Who was then the gentleman?

But the story of the princess who was bruised black and blue by a pea lodged under seven mattresses is also a folk story, which makes the opposite comment on the intrinsic qualities of the person so marked by nature or destiny. The peasants, no doubt, wished to say that exquisite sensitivity or high social rank did not necessarily fit a person to rule; both the American and French revolutions made much the same point, and it remained as part of their national consciousnesses. It was often clearer in the recently settled West than in the stable East, as suggested by a telling contribution to *The Western Review* in 1846:

We are but equals, if we would regard our condition with a philosophic eye. Our points of difference are all artificial—those of resemblance are all from nature. We are bound together by our common wants and our common frailties,—by our hopes, fears, aspirations, and aims,—by our lofty ambitions, our grovelling

18. Quoted in Leonard D. White, *The Jacksonians: A Study in Administrative History, 1829–1861* (New York, 1954), 318.

ERRATA

Two lines were accidentally dropped from the top of page 141. The complete quotation that begins on page 140 should read:

We are but equals, if we would regard our condition with a philosophic eye. Our points of difference are all artificial—those of resemblance are all from nature. We are bound together by our common wants and our common frailties,—by our hopes, fears, aspirations, and aims,—by our lofty ambitions, our grovelling desires, and our general pursuit of the vainest of vanities—by our manner of entering upon life, by our mode of spending it, by the way in which it ends.[19]

Two lines should have been deleted from the bottom of page 141, as they also appear at the top of the next page.

This consciousness manifested itself in Americans in a keenly felt resentment against demands for obsequious body language. (It was felt with particular force by black Americans over a lengthy period in which whites took it for granted.) The Civil War, by conscripting civilians into the disciplines of military life, brought out new signs of this abrasiveness in both northern and southern armies. The inspector-general of the Army of Northern Virginia reported unfavorably after three years of war on the difficulty of getting proper and prompt obedience to orders: "There is not that spirit of respect for and obedience to general orders which should pervade a military organization." A private from Georgia offered his superiors the same objections: "We have tite Rools over us, the order was Red out in dress parade the other day that we all have to pull off our hats when we go to the coln or genrel," he complained. "You know that is one thing I wont do. I would rather see him in hell before I will pull off my hat to any man and tha Jest as well shoot me at the start." A Massachusetts private echoed that "drill & saluting officers & guard duty is played out."[20] They were very American sentiments, not least because they so strongly reflected the individualist demand for equality of esteem.

The notion that Americans were exchangeable with each other, which we may call the Interchangeability Principle, is probably best viewed as a folk protest against social pretension and unearned privileges rather than as a systematic theory. But anyone who is familiar with the social subtleties and inflections of other nations (and particularly of England[21]) is likely to have noticed an almost conscious rejection of deference in American social style. As early as 1787 the physician and social publicist Dr. Benjamin Rush, writing on the educational needs of the republic, remarked that servants were less subordinate than in Britain.[22] Robert Coram—English by birth—also writing on education, addressed the question of birth with an agricultural analogy which must have made

19. April 1846, quoted by John Ashworth, *'Agrarians' and 'Aristocrats': Party Political Ideology in the United States, 1837–1846* (London, 1983), 25–26.

20. James M. MacPherson, *Battle Cry of Freedom: The Civil War Era* (New York, 1988), 329.

21. I say England because these distinctions are in some ways less evident in other realms of the United Kingdom, particularly in Wales and Northern Ireland.

22. Benjamin Rush, "Thoughts on Female Education," in Frederic Rudolph, ed., *Essays on Education in Early America* (Cambridge, Mass., 1965), 28.

Coram—English by birth—also writing on education, addressed the question of birth with an agricultural analogy which must have made sense to many contemporaries: "There may be a difference between the child of a nobleman and that of a peasant, but will there not also be an inequality between the produce of seeds collected from the same plant and sown in different soils? Yes, but the inequality is artificial, not natural."[23] In a sermon preached in the prison in Philadelphia, Thomas Dunn (lately from England) told the inmates that the rich did not possess more moral worth than the poor, who were "equal in their natural faculties." The differences were those of circumstance—vast differences made by education, habits of life, leisure; adverting to the recent epidemic of yellow fever, he comforted the prisoners with the reflection that rich and poor, saint and sinner, lay buried in the same heap of death.[24] Recent events and current argument were working to establish this view in the aftermath of the Revolution—the struggle was in a very strong sense a part of the Revolution itself; the lore into which it passed, transmuted into the faith that in America, what ought to be must be true, can still be observed in the strangely persistent folk belief that distinctions of social class *do not exist* in the United States. But if we were to try to give the idea some formal definition it would be enough to describe it as a widespread, and often rather optimistic conviction that the social, racial, educational and economic differences that divide people from one another are not the most significant indicators of their true qualities or abilities; that an interchange of circumstances, in other words, would produce an interchange of results.[25] This underlying faith was to reappear as a force of great political significance in the 1960s when President Lyndon Johnson called for the implementation of policies that would produce "equality of results."[26]

23. Robert Coram, "Political Enquiries: to which is added, a Plan for the General Establishment of Schools throughout the United States," ibid., 132.

24. Thomas Dunn, *Equality of Rich and Poor: A sermon preached in the prison of Philadelphia* (Philadelphia, 1793).

25. The Scottish folk poet Robert Burns had expressed it all characteristically enough:

> The rank is but the guinea stamp
> The man's the gowd for a' that; for a' that and a' that
> The man's the gowd for a' that.

Good radical sentiments.

26. *Public Papers of the Presidents: Lyndon B. Johnson* (Washington, D.C., 1966), item 301, pp. 635–40. The issue is discussed in Chapter 13.

At an earlier period, the most popular exponent of the interchangeability principle in American literary history was Mark Twain, who was particularly fond of using it to ridicule every kind of social pretension. In his children's tale, *The Prince and the Pauper*, two boys of those contrasting social positions, having met and changed clothes as a momentary prank, are accidentally separated. The prince, dressed in rags, finds himself shut outside the palace gates. Nothing he can do or say will convince anyone that he is the prince; meanwhile his friend the pauper, who is something of a dreamer and has earlier prepared himself for the role, is now taken for the true prince. The point about the succession is obvious: if the mistake had not been luckily corrected (the true prince having esoteric knowledge of the location of the great seal), the impostor's children would have been taken by all succeeding generations as being of royal blood, and, of course, vice versa. Mark Twain explored the idea more fully in his longer satire, *A Connecticut Yankee at King Arthur's Court*, one of the earlier fictions to depend on what is now called a time-warp, in which a man is thrown into prison for making the very subversive remark that "men were about all alikes, and one man as good as another, barring clothes. He said he believed that if you were to strip the nation naked and send a stranger through the crowd, he couldn't tell the king from a quack doctor, nor a duke from a hotel clerk." Mark Twain was influenced by social-scientific ideas about the determining effects of early training and environmental forces in the formation of character; but these were happily consistent with the underlying faith in the equality— which in effect meant the similarity—of human natures. He made one attempt, in *Pudd'nhead Wilson*, to explore the theme in the realm of race relations, but failed, in part because he undermined his own primary idea (which was based on a switch of infants in their cradles—in principle not unlike the *Prince and the Pauper* scenario) by taking the factor of color out of the picture. His "Negro" is to all intents and purposes white, the child of a serenely regal woman who is only one-sixteenth part African. The theme that survives from this highly didactic little story is that the two central characters, now switched back into their original racial roles, will be forever unfitted for them by their early training, speech, gait and, presumably, habits of mind. [27]

27. Mark Twain, *The Prince and the Pauper; A Connecticut Yankee at King Arthur's Court* (New York, 1917), 157; *Pudd'nhead Wilson* (New York: Signet Classic, 1964); Wright Morris, Foreword to *Pudd'nhead Wilson* in this edition.

In southern society the omnipresence of slavery—for it was a shadow even where it was not a presence—gave a peculiar twist to these assertions. Many southerners—white ones, that is—took comfort against an increasingly hostile world in the belief that Negro slavery not only unified the white race but endued all its members with a sort of primal equality. It was a difficult belief to maintain in view of the vast social differences between rich and poor in the South, but that only encouraged its assiduous cultivation. Congressman James F. Dowdwell expressed the political sense of this conviction in 1861 when he announced that he hoped the day would never come when the safety of slavery would require "social and political inequality to be established among white people. No, sir, never let it come.... Let us keep the white race as they are here and now and ever ought to be—free, equal and independent, socially and politically; recognize no subordinates but those whom God has made to be such—the children of Ham." The quality of "independence" which is the key to this claim linked freedom with equality and denied the right of any superiors to limit a man's autonomy; it was this ability to control one's own life that, however illusory, was so indispensable to a man's self-respect. All this made it imperative to defend one's equality constantly.[28] But independence so understood was essentially related to personal honor, which had taken the place of the old republican quality of virtue in the Southern vocabulary and was the very definition of self-esteem. To lack honor was to lack reputation.[29] Under these incessant pressures, the constant "delights" that Tocqueville detected in the experience of equality may have given way in the South—which he never visited—to the state of harrowing nervous tension that contributed to the frequent outbreaks of violence in the shadow of slavery.

Equality of Rights: Inequality of Conditions

The optimistic folk belief in the interchangeability of Americans, which never rested on very secure foundations and was perhaps never

28. Quotations and comment in J. Mills Thornton III, *Politics and Power in a Slave Society: Alabama 1800–1860* (Baton Rouge, 1978), 320–21, 443, 447–48; George M. Fredrickson, *The Black Image in the White Mind: The Debate on Afro-American Character and Destiny, 1817–1914* (New York, 1971), esp. ch. 5.

29. Bertram Wyatt-Brown, *Southern Honor: Ethics and Behavior in the Old South* (Oxford, 1982), xv, 34, 46, 103.

consistently entertained even by any one person, was subjected to severe buffeting by successive waves of immigration. The men and women who came trickling and then flooding into the country in the decades after the end of the Napoleonic wars in Europe were, after all, *not* Americans—at least not until they had arrived and, to some extent, acclimatized themselves if not assimilated. The rise of Protestant resistance to the increasing Catholic presence has been noted, but mid-century nativism had nationalistic undertones as well as religious ones. In the United States, more perhaps than in other industrial societies with mobile economies, the concept of equality of opportunity gained particular intensity from this underlying idea of interchangeability, but in the later nineteenth century the issues became more confused and complex. Interchangeability forced people to face the question of whether the brave language of the Declaration really applied to the whole human race.

Although Jefferson himself became aware that this aspect presented a problem, his generation did not have to face the complexities of mass immigration from countries that were not only non-English in speech, but alien in respect of politics, law and public morality. The essential task before the post-revolutionary generation was to work out the meaning of their formal commitment to equality among themselves. To Jefferson it was already clear that virtue and talent could lie concealed in existing social structures.

The founders of the new republics—for each newly independent state was a republic—had taken on a momentous responsibility. It was one thing to declare a republic; it was another thing to keep it. All readers of Montesquieu—which meant all men properly prepared for the role of leadership—knew that as despotism depended on fear, monarchies on the spirit of honor, and aristocracies on honor sustained by virtue, so republics depended above all else on virtue. Thomas Jefferson was quick, though not alone, to perceive that republican virtue must be cultivated by education.

Jefferson's bill for the more general diffusion of knowledge, which he prepared as a member of the state commission to revise the laws in 1778, declared two aims: "to illuminate, as far as practicable, the minds of the people at large"; and to ensure that "those persons, whom nature has endowed with genius and virtue, should be rendered by liberal education worthy to receive, and able to guard the sacred deposit of rights and liberties of their fellow citizens, and that they should be called to that

charge without regard to wealth, birth, or other accidental condition or circumstance."[30] Jefferson proposed a general system of education arranged in three grades, based on local communities and rising from three years of schooling for children of the masses, through a grammar-school grade for the select few, to the College of William and Mary for the genuine elite. The whole conception goes far to clarify Jefferson's views on equality, both natural and social.

By means of a system of selective examinations, Jefferson remarked in describing the scheme, "twenty of the best geniuses will be raked from the rubbish annually, and be instructed, at public expense, as far as grammar schools go."[31] Jefferson plainly had no illusions about equality of natural endowment, and the telling connection between virtue and genius betrayed his inner conviction that they were likely to be found together. But he did believe that the public interest required the state to use its powers to equalize opportunity. Virtue must be searched for and nourished; the republic could not afford to ignore its own people. Although Jefferson's bill was too expensive to appeal to the legislators of Virginia, not all of whom were the best representatives of virtue or genius, he persisted successfully later in life in his grand design for the University of Virginia. Facing rival plans for public funding, Jefferson supported a bill that left elementary education to local initiative while spending state money on the university.[32]

Even in his earlier period, Jefferson was convinced that most of the entrants to his grammar schools would be the sons of parents "in easy circumstances," with the advantage that they could lighten the expense by paying for tuition and board. (Possibly an unsuccessful attempt to make the bill more palatable.) His assumptions about the social distribution of intellectual ability were not far out of keeping with the existing distribution of social advantages. His public schools would have taught poor children to read, write, and figure, but would have given state support for the most part to the sons of planters. Whatever its limitations, and the felicity of style in which he described his constituency, Jefferson's scheme was the most comprehensive of its time. It combined

---

30. Merrill Peterson, *Thomas Jefferson and the New Nation* (New York, 1970), 146.
31. Ibid., 148.
32. Rush Welter, *Popular Education and Democratic Thought in America* (New York, 1962), 32.

opportunity for individuals with the interest of the state. Its rejection by the legislators shows how little they were inclined to convert the Declaration of Independence into public policy.

Jefferson's belief in the uneven distribution of natural talent was closely akin to that of John Adams or Alexander Hamilton, and also to that of his friend and associate Benjamin Rush, who denounced the Pennsylvania Constitution of 1776 for its false supposition of "perfect equality, and an equal distribution of property, wisdom and virtue, among the inhabitants of the state." Rush believed that commerce had introduced inequality of property, leading to what he called "natural distinctions of rank, as certain and general as the artificial distinctions of men in Europe."[33] Rush was one among a small cluster of republican thinkers who turned their attention to the need for public education after the formal revolution had been completed. Ranging from Delaware to Massachusetts, they all concentrated their emphasis on the need of the community for education and virtuous citizens.[34] Rush insisted that pupils be taught that they do not belong to themselves but are "public property"—not the most resoundingly individualist note of the era, but one which reflected a communitarian idea of equality that did not seem to look forward to the incentive-driven ethos of equality of opportunity. He insisted that individually acquired wealth must be made to serve "the wants and demands of the state." Samuel Harrison Smith, in an essay that won a joint prize from the American Philosophical Society, quoted Cambacères's dictum that "it is proper to remind parents that their children belong to the state and that in their education they ought to conform to the rules that it prescribes." Noah Webster pointed out that

33. Benjamin Rush, *Observations upon the Present Government of Pennsylvania in Four Letters to the People of Pennsylvania* (Philadelphia, 1777), 9, 4. Rush's views at this stage are almost identical to those of John Adams. Power would always follow wealth, the rich would always overmatch the poor, and "an aristocracy will be established" (8–9). Rush felt that the representatives of the common people would be overmatched by the rich in the unicameral legislature which had, in fact, been established to give a homogeneous representation; he pointed out that the dissensions of Athens and Rome had originated in single assemblies (7). These views, which reflect Harrington's dictum that "such . . . as is the proportion or balance of Dominion or Property in Land, such is the nature of the Empire," depart from Harrington in their emphasis on the changes brought about by commerce. Harrington was not much impressed by commercial wealth. John Toland, ed., James Harrington, *Works* (London, 1700), *Oceana*, 38–39.

34. These essays are collected in Rudolph, *Education*; page references that follow are to this volume.

American national character had not yet been formed and emphasized the vast importance of implanting in youth ideas of virtue, liberty, and attachment to country. But these writers agreed that the opportunity to receive a public education should be equal; and it may well be the case that their strong insistence on the community reflected a need to resist the fissiparous tendencies of a surging individualism in the social and economic atmosphere of the time.[35]

Of the early thinkers on public education, Jefferson most clearly anticipates the Whigs of the Jacksonian era in his belief that a few young people of exceptional talent can be drawn out ("from the rubbish") by a selective system and refined into an elite of leadership and responsibility. The later Whigs believed in acquired culture; Democrats frequently rejected this as representing the rebirth of artificial and aristocratic values.[36] But Jefferson would hardly have dissented from the importance attached by Coram and Smith to the development of the individual. Coram concluded that to make a man happy, "the first step is to make him independent. Dignity depends on independence." Smith argues that "he who thinks frequently imbibes a habit of independence and self-esteem which are perhaps the great and only preservatives of virtue."[37] The central value attaching to these sentiments could equally well have been called equality of esteem.

To interpret the meanings of equality in any particular past context, it is essential to appreciate not only the different interests which laid claim to its virtues but the limits to which equality of any sort was admitted to be a virtue. Conflicts of consciously defined economic class did not *determine* the outlines of American politics in this early, founding period because members of different interest groups had too many interests in common to make open antagonism worth the cost; but we have seen abundant evidence that they often viewed each other with suspicion and alarm. Federalists—and their immediate predecessors—

---

35. Benjamin Rush, *A Plan for the Establishment of Public Schools and the Diffusion of Knowledge in Pennsylvania* . . . (Philadelphia, 1788), 14; Rush set forth a comprehensive plan for state education not dissimilar to Jefferson's (3–4); Noah Webster, *Thoughts on the Education of Youth in America* (Boston, 1790), 45; Robert Coram, "Political Enquiries," 127; Samuel Harrison Smith, *Remarks on Education: Illustrating the Close Connection between Virtue and Wisdom* (Philadelphia, 1798), 190.

36. Daniel W. Howe, *Unitarian Conscience*, 36–37.

37. Coram, "Political Enquiries," 143; Smith, *Remarks on Education*, 188.

had a way of thinking of themselves as distinct from the common people—a style to which speakers on the Constitution adverted during the debates on ratification.[38] John Adams may have used phraseology about the "well born" to express his anxieties about the inherent tendency of "natural" aristocrats to assert their superiority in the political sphere;[39] but when associated with "the few" and "the rich," as well as the refined, leisured, and learned, the concept sat rather comfortably with many of society's traditional leaders.[40] Few participants in public debate would have wished to deny that society had its "natural" aristocrats, when the word was used in its original meaning of "the best." Anti-Federalists would certainly deny, however, that the ranks of the well born were filled with nature's aristocrats or that republican society should be so constructed that this class would move smoothly from one position of advantage to another, all the while subtly controlling the levers of power. Ideas of equality took a great deal of the strain in these contests because equality was a virtual synonym for the most fundamental principles of republican government.

Once these issues were in the open, Federalists were able to affirm their adherence to equal rights. For them, interchangeability was a false trail; government must *protect* property and status but promote true talent. That principle was indisputable; it was firmly lodged in the state declarations of rights, wherever these had been adopted; but that was not in every state, and Hamilton was able to exploit the weakness by

38. Cecelia M. Kenyon, *The Antifederalists* (Indianapolis, 1966), xlix–l; 384–85.

39. Adams was never in any doubt that aristocracies were a natural product of society and would tend to assert their natural advantages, but the extent to which he allowed himself to worry about these advantages and the need to contain them politically suggests a certain element of psychological ambiguity. "Every government," he once wrote to Benjamin Rush, "is an aristocracy in fact." Not only those of Europe, but even "the most leveling New England town meeting is an aristocracy." Safety was to be sought only in finding some means to control their passions, which caused them to form factions and tear the people to pieces. John A. Schutz and Douglass Adair, eds., *The Spur of Fame: Dialogues of John Adams and Benjamin Rush, 1805–1813* (San Marino, Calif., 1966), 173–75.

40. Dixon Ryan Fox, *The Decline of Aristocracy in the Politics of New York* (New York, 1918), 1–30 (chapter entitled "The Few, the Rich and the Well Born"); John R. Howe, Jr., *The Changing Political Thought of John Adams* (Princeton, 1966), 138–42; James M. Banner, *To the Hartford Convention: The Federalists and the Origins of Party Politics in Massachusetts, 1789–1815* (New York, 1970), ch. 4; Gordon S. Wood, *The Creation of the American Republic, 1776–1789* (Chapel Hill, 1969), ch. 8.

commenting pointedly that the federal Constitution with its itemized protections *without* a bill of rights afforded the people of New York more protection than their own constitution, which had none.[41]

Protection was a basically defensive concept. There was nothing in it that an honest Federalist could not defend, as John Jay, one of the original writers of *The Federalist* and now the first Chief Justice of the Supreme Court, clearly explained when he told a grand jury that civil liberty consisted in "an equal right to all citizens to have, enjoy, and do, in peace, security, and without molestation, whatever the equal and constitutional laws of the country admit to be consistent with the public good."[42] But equality of rights had more active, even aggressive, attributes for those who would put them to work. We have caught glimpses of the idea of a right to act, to gain a personal share in the good things of the world, to make the most of oneself—aims that looked beyond the quiet enjoyment of a settled farm or business.

Equality of Opportunity: Context and Concept

The dynamic concept of equality of opportunity, which by the mid-nineteenth century had become the ideological expression of a powerful convergence between the themes of national progress and personal self-advancement, was formulated slowly and tentatively out of the growing perception that rights could be made to match ambition. The concept of equality of opportunity has been accepted as belonging so naturally to the robust world of capitalist activity that its contextual significance has been easy to overlook. If the idea was slow to formulate, it is because opportunity has no intrinsic meaning without asking the question, "Opportunity for what?" The formula, when it emerged in the early middle period of the nineteenth century,[43] was not an accidental coinage of felicitous phraseology. It expressed two themes in threatened collision: buoyant hopes bred of expectations of both national and individual advancement—but the rise of obstacles to these hopes in the

41. *Federalist* 84.

42. *The Charge of Chief Justice Jay to the Grand Juries on the Eastern Circuit* (Portsmouth, N.H., [1790]), 13–14.

43. It is difficult to put one's finger on a specific "first use"; the Republican party made it into a sort of party-political logo, but it was obviously already in currency. See, in general, Foner, *Free Soil, Free Labor*, and for an indicative quotation, p. 16.

complex forms of a newly monopolistic economic order, and ultimately in the spread of slavery.

The answers to the critical question, "Opportunity for what?" changed momentously between the Revolution and the Jacksonian period. The Address which the Massachusetts constitutional convention of 1780 sent out to the towns explained the suffrage restrictions in the proposed constitution in a way that offers a partial answer to the question as it presented itself to the makers of the new republic. Only young men living on a paternal estate, or those whose idleness and profligacy would bar them from possessing property, would be excluded by these restrictions; the obvious inference was that any young man who was prepared to work for his living would soon qualify himself to vote.[44] Noah Webster, the lexicographer, reaffirmed this view of the prospects in an antislavery tract written in 1793. "Here," he said of the best in the United States (as opposed to Great Britain), "the equalizing genius of the laws distributes property to every citizen." There were no commercial or corporate monopolies and, he added, no religious tests (which might be true of Massachusetts but was not true everywhere else). But "here every man finds employment, and the road is open for the poorest citizen to amass wealth by labor and economy, and by his talent and virtue to raise himself to the highest offices of the State."[45] If Webster had scrutinized the records he would have had some difficulty in finding many examples of this kind of self-advancement, but the principle was certainly respected, and what ought to be true of the American Republic was easily transmuted into what was.

The idea of equality of opportunity was clearly present before the phrase reached—or was independently coined in—America. In the late eighteenth century it was already an insistent demand of the coterie of scientifically minded British radicals who were pressing for such reforms as the extension and democratization of the electoral system. The social and political interests of these religious Dissenters, of whom Joseph Priestley, William Godwin and Thomas Cooper were prominent exam-

44. Oscar and Mary Handlin, eds., *The Popular Sources of Political Authority: Documents on the Massachusetts Convention of 1780* (Cambridge, Mass., 1966), 437.
45. Noah Webster, Jr., Esq., *Effects of Slavery on Morals and Industry* (Hartford, 1793), 31–32.

ples, were restricted by the laws which conferred civil privileges on members of the Church of England. (Both Priestley and Cooper migrated to the United States; Cooper became a prominent figure in higher education and also a defender of slavery.)[46] Their close American contemporaries were not subject to civil disabilities on account of religion, but they felt the need to extol their country's God-given advantages as a stimulus to both patriotism and enterprise. Since all citizens were equal, declared Samuel Latham Mitchill in an oration to the Society of Black Friars in 1793, the only forms of inequality in America arose from office, talents, or wealth; as the road was "open to every one to aspire to these, it is by the exercise of one or more of his rights that a man acquires the means of influence." So the possession of equal political and legal rights opened the way to all men's legitimate aspirations; this was to prove a persistent view, which had the effect of narrowing the attention of reformers on the political field at times when the real road to personal independence (for which equality was often a synonym) was far more confusing and complex. It was this frame of mind that made it possible, half a century later, when the word *capitalist* was coming into vogue. for a prominent Massachusetts speaker to tell a society of mechanics that "the laborer of today is the capitalist of tomorrow. . . . Every man stands on his own merits. . . . The fact that he may become a capitalist, is a spur to exertion to the very newsboy in our streets." (But men could fall through their failings as well as rise by their merits; Lincoln also noted that a rich man's son might be forced to labor for his daily bread. This aspect added moral force to the argument, but sheer misfortune was seldom mentioned in this context, and the economic crisis that followed the panic of 1837 does not seem to have generated any systematic rethinking of the principles of American political economy.)[47] The controlling mood was one of economic and social optimism. This mood formed the context for the early formulations of the doctrine of equality of opportunity. But where anyone doubted whether these conditions existed as fully as they ought, there could be no doubt about the principle; and one of its strongest and most prominent statements came

46. Isaac Kramnick, *Republicanism and Bourgeois Radicalism: Political Ideology in Late Eighteenth Century England and America* (Ithaca, 1990), 62–63, 77–82. The author does not note Cooper's public defense of slavery.

47. Mary J. Kornblith, "Self-Made Men: The Development of Middling Consciousness in New England," *Massachusetts Review* 26 (1985), 469.

from the pen of Publius, propelled in this case by the hand of Alexander Hamilton:

There are strong minds in every walk of life that will rise superior to the disadvantages of situation, and will command the tribute due to their merit, not only from the classes to which they particularly belong, but from the society in general. The door ought to be equally open to all.[48]

Hamilton, of illegitimate birth in a remote West Indian island, had every reason to advocate this creed. He is too often treated as though he remained a sort of ideological outsider, but this statement places him in the mainstream of the American individualist tradition: the door ought to be *equally* open to all.

Later exponents of the interests of property had no difficulty in affirming this proposition as a basic element of the American credo of equal rights. The common law, said the Massachusetts Federalist Fisher Ames after Jefferson's presidential election, secured all the rights of citizens; his fear was that these securities would be swept away by majoritarian Jacobins. Under existing law, "All cannot be rich . . . [but] all have a right to make the attempt."[49] But James Sullivan, a leading politician of the same state had written a little tract a few years earlier which warned of some of the dangers facing a society of unequal wealth. Every member of society, he said, had as clear right to gain all the property which vigilance and industry, regulated by the laws of the state, could bestow on him—and these acquisitions advanced the interest of the public. So far, Adam Smith could not have said more. But he also noted that discontent arose when men saw their neighbors' property increase; unequal fortunes produced a spirit of envy and rendered unhappy those who had previously been content.[50] These percipient remarks were not offered as an argument against the acquisition, but

48. *Federalist* 36.

49. Fisher Ames, *Works*, ed. Seth Ames (Boston, 1854) 2:211, published in *The Palladium*, November 1801. John Adams, who described Ames as "that pretty little warbling canary bird," claimed that Ames had got all his best ideas from him—Adams—who was "twenty years before him." But his attack gathered more force when he accused Ames and his friends "The Aristocrats, or rather, The Oligarchs, who now rule the Federal Party" of imputing their own "sordid avarice" to the whole American people. Schutz and Adair, *Spur of Fame*, 174.

50. A Citizen of Massachusetts [J. Sullivan], *The Path to Riches: An Inquiry into the Origin and Use of Money* (Boston, 1792), 5–6, 7, 40.

they did anticipate some of the complexities that would beset the very idea of equality by indicating the ways in which envy of wealth gained through equality of opportunity would cut across that other vital category, equality of esteem.[51]

The argument that equal rights would rightly produce unequal results could be taken over by the less privileged, as was done in South Carolina by a committee demanding redistribution in the system of representation. The group, who represented the under-represented up-country of the state, was opposing the direct representation of property in the legislature. Equality, its members declared, was the natural condition of man, the basis of his moral excellence and political happiness. Although "equality of Conditions" could not be preserved in society, "equality of rights" was not only consistent with good government but formed its only firm and lasting foundation. To suffer property to be directly represented would destroy this equality by giving rich men different and more numerous political rights than their neighbors, "whose masters they would thus become."[52] If the writers of this address had been asked to state the category of equality into which it fell, they would undoubtedly have replied that it was political; the representation of property, as an end in itself, diminished the status of the political individual and amounted to saying that in some cases one man should have more than one vote. But it is clear that they were also saying that deprivation of political equality resulted in a curtailment of equality of opportunity (even if the expression had not yet been coined.) In some cases we have found different categories moving in different directions, but this was a

51. At an earlier period in the development of political philosophy, Jean Bodin, the founder of the modern concept of sovereignty, had made a related point: even genuine equality had its moral dangers for social stability, for there was no controlling envy. "There is nothing more dangerous to a Commonwealth," he observed, "than equality of goods. It can only be achieved by violating contracts, abolishing debts, &c; it ruins the poor widows who depend on interest." Hatred and jealousy were greatest between equals and were the spring and fountain of civil wars. Jean Bodin, *Six Books of the Commonwealthe* (London translation, 1606), 570–71.

52. "Appius," *An Address to the People of South Carolina by the General Committee of the Representative Reform Association at Columbia* (Charleston, June, 1794). Curiously for a pamphlet signed with a pseudonym, the committee also gave their names, including formidable ones in the future of the state: Wade Hampton, E. Ramsay, John Taylor, Robert G. Harper, Robert Stark, Daniel Brown, Wm. Montgomery, John Kershaw, Wm. Falconer.

definite case in which they converged toward unity. It was an argument that would have profound resonances in the very different context of American Reconstruction, when equality of political rights for the freedmen (together with equality before the law) became, for a time, the key to all others.

When economic setbacks began to scar the unsteady path of capitalist progress, beginning with the land crash and panic of 1819, they destroyed many individual hopes for self-advancement, but they did not provoke political leaders or economic thinkers to question the foundations on which Americans hoped to resume their progress in the future. It is, indeed, possible that one effect of these reverses was to keep the system more "open" than it would have been by shaking established businessmen from their hardened positions, thus promoting opportunity just when it seemed to be closing.[53] The economy recovered from these shocks as it continued to attract foreign as well as domestic investment and immigration, which offered a constant renewal of the labor force. But the economy was losing its earlier and simpler forms. Manufacturing industry advanced with the increasing concentration and division of labor in factories rather than small workshops, and with a deepening distance between owners and managers on one side and workers on the other.[54] Workers—still usually known as "mechanics"—also organized both industrially and politically in defense of their hours of work and demanded a lien law to protect their interest in work already completed.[55]

The changes that were affecting the economy promoted among the mechanics a wholly new sense of class, which began to take the place of the older sense of belonging to a specialist trade and skill. Workers were experiencing a disturbing sense of distance and alienation from their employers and customers, together with a felt loss of control over their livelihood and conditions of work. These conditions led both to union organization and to the formation of a Workingmen's party. Nothing

53. P.M.G. Harris, "The Social Origins of American Leaders: The Demographic Foundations," in *Perspectives in American History* (Cambridge, Mass., 1969), 3, 157–344.

54. Douglass C. North, *The Economic Growth of the United States, 1790–1860* (Englewood Cliffs, N.J., 1961), 146, 157–59.

55. Walter Hugins, *Jacksonian Democracy and the Working Class: A Study of the New York Workingmen's Movement, 1829–1837* (Stanford, 1960), ch. 4.

could have more forcibly stated the sense of loss that threatened the working men than the final resolutions of the convention of their National Trades' Union movement in 1834:[56]

And whereas the social, civil, and intellectual condition of the laboring classes of these United States, and the like classes in all countries [be it noted] exhibit the most unequal and unjustifiable distribution of the produce of labor, thus operating to produce a humiliating, servile dependency, incompatible with the inherent natural equality of man,

for these and many kindred reasons it was imperative that the every productive laborer should earn the gratitude of his descendants for having "barked the tree of Corruption, and nourished that of *Liberty* and *Equality*, without which life itself is a burden to its possessor." The first intimations of an international working-class consciousness were undoubtedly due to the leading influence exerted by the group of recent British arrivals. Robert Dale Owen was the son of Robert Owen, founder of the paternalistically organized co-operative factory in New Lanark, Scotland, and the New Harmony community in Indiana. George H. Evans was an anti-clerical English printer who later threw his energies into the movement for making land available to would-be farmers. Frances Wright, the brilliant Scot who dominated most of them by the force of her intellect and personality, became an early influence in the feminist movement and proved by example that women's contributions to public life need not be limited either by convention or by role models.[57]

The workers' organizations were at this period largely confined to eastern cities, notably New York and Philadelphia. But they have a significant place in the working out of ideas of equality, on which they dwelt with indignant emphasis, because they brought together two categories that were so often at variance: with the decline of that sense of having an element of personal freedom to determine one's livelihood, which would soon come to be called equality of opportunity, the trades unionists were keenly conscious of a commensurate loss of equality of

56. John R. Commons and associates, *A History of Labor in the United States* (New York, 1918) 1:12–18, 232–33, 459–62; Edwin C. Rozwenc, ed., *Ideology and Power in the Age of Jackson* (New York, 1964), 123–27; Hugins, *Jacksonian Democracy*, ch. 1, pp. 143–47.

57. Arthur M. Schlesinger, Jr., *The Age of Jackson* (Boston, 1950), 181–84.

esteem. Equality was living a complicated but certainly a vibrant emotional and intellectual life. It stood here as a synonym for dignity and status, self-esteem as influenced by social esteem; it stood also for the rectification of unfair distribution of the rewards of industry, meaning in that sense *proportion* rather than real equality; and it stood for the old value of independence, or personal control.

Abolitionists, who often had somewhat mixed feelings about the social implications of the program of emancipation to which they were dedicated,[58] did not perceive any general connection between their cause and the grievances of the workers. William Lloyd Garrison, founder and editor of *The Liberator*, attacked the labor critics of capitalism on the grounds that they were aiming at the wrong target. In a society where "the avenues to wealth, distinction and supremacy were open to all, society must in the nature of things be full of inequalities." Abolitionists had not subjected their society to the kind of scrutiny that would have revealed the hidden coercions of the supposedly free market, but Garrison was significantly aware of the problem of esteem, for he also observed that "Labour is not dishonourable. The industrious artisan, in a government like ours, will always be held in better estimation than the wealthy idler."[59] In the antebellum era, workers felt keenly susceptible to their loss of status in the society as a whole; the fully industrialized workers of later generations had other, and more desperate, concerns.

Economic life had always produced its failures as well as its successes. But the prevalent faith in the indefinite expansibility of the American future helped to keep open the frontier of the economic imagination. It is significant that the Cincinnati journeymen's newspaper chose to call itself *The Elevator*.[60] Americans of almost all denominations, with the obvious exception of the blacks and Indians, were anxious to maintain the belief system that was so neatly expressed in

58. Fredrickson, *The Black Image*, 33–42. Lydia Maria Child faced the social problem with a firm defense: "On the subject of equality," she wrote in 1834, "the abolitionists have been misrepresented. They have not the slightest wish to do violence to the distinctions of society by forcing the rude and illiterate into the presence of the learned and refined." But they did believe in equality of opportunity—equal for blacks as well as for whites (37).

59. Eric Foner, *Politics and Ideology in the Age of the Civil War* (New York, 1980), 61–76.

60. Steven J. Ross, *Workers on the Edge: Work, Leisure and Politics in Industrializing Cincinnati, 1788–1880* (New York, 1985), 59.

the preferred description of their economy as adopted later by the Republican party, as a "free labor system."[61] So long as this belief could be kept alive, so long could people also keep their distance from an ominous truth about the character of the economy—that it was, increasingly and for many operators oppressively, a *competitive* system. Thomas Cooper, now in America and becoming an influential figure in educational circles, could write a short book on political economy during Jackson's second presidential term, so fully devoted to emphasizing the harmony and interdependence of classes that he nowhere referred specifically to the existence of economic competition. He did, however, attack monopolies and corporations as subversive of republican equality of rights and privileges, and in this sense contributed to maintaining the tradition of the post-revolutionary generation and to opening the way for an explicit doctrine of equality of opportunity, whose time had nearly come.[62]

One of the difficulties facing those who honestly believed that equal laws would, and ought, to give the right opportunities to unequal talents, thus producing unequal results, was the impossibility of controlling the consequences. By the Jacksonian era the upper economic classes were already assuming much of the character and some of the social style of a hereditary caste, whose advantages were passed down from generation to generation.[63] In the same period, immigration grew more dense in quantity and more varied in character, with ethnicity playing an

61. Foner, *Free Soil, Free Labor*, 9, 11–13. This study is devoted to the beliefs of the Republicans, who were most explicit in their terminology; if Democrats and others were less addicted to the term, they do not seem to have had an alternative general description.

62. Thomas Cooper, *A Manual of Political Economy* (Washington, 1834), 48–49; but here is his central teaching: "The great maxims of political economy are, that people get rich by means of their own industry, in producing exchangeable value. . . . That the more wealthy, the more prosperous, the happier their customers are, the greater is their consumption, the more numerous their wants, the more extensive their dealings." It was the interest of each to promote the prosperity of all; all were mutually customers—and wars were folly (61–62). Joseph Dorfman, *The Economic Mind in American Civilization, 1606–1865*, 2 vols. (New York, 1946), finds no space for a discussion of competition as a theme, and lists only three writers specifically on "the competitive system" in his index.

63. Edward Pessen, *Riches, Class, and Power Before the Civil War* (Lexington, Mass., 1973), in general and p. 148.

almost unprecedented role in defining social attitudes and thus creating social issues.[64] All these forces put ideas of equality under stress. But they also imbued them with new urgency.

In one important sense, then, opportunities were multiplying with the diversification of the economy; but the implied question, "Opportunity for what?" could no longer be depended on to yield equally reassuring answers to all who would willingly seize whatever opportunity offered. The assumption behind the self-confidence of Hamilton and his contemporaries in the founding period of the republic was that honest work would always and necessarily produce a fair return. That assumption could no longer be made, not only because so much that was necessary to success lay beyond the individual's control, but because corporations were conspiring with legislators to narrow the field open to individual enterprise. It was these factors that gave rise to the Jacksonian spate of general incorporation laws, which opened the right to incorporate to any company fulfilling certain statutory requirements; it was also for these reasons that many Jacksonians were hostile to banks, and particularly to the second Bank of the United States. In the aim of keeping American resources, both natural and artificial, open to all, Whig and Democratic rhetoric tended to converge. Not many votes would have been attracted by opponents of equal opportunity; the meaning of the proposition therefore tended to depend on the prospects of the national economy. When the concept of equality of opportunity came to be identified, it was a program of action requiring political attention, not a comfortable expectation depending simply on the administration of equal laws.

William Seward, recently Whig governor of New York and now a senator, was aware of the need for positive policy when he spoke to these issues in the Senate in 1850 in support of a bill to grant homesteads to recently arrived refugees from Europe (where the revolutions of 1848 had caused a new and sudden outpouring):

I am in favor of the equality of men—of *all* men, whether they be born in one land or another. . . . There is no distinction in my respect or affection between men of one land and another; between men of one race and another; or between

64. The religious dimensions have been discussed in Chapter 5, which also goes far to explain the complex of antagonistic "ethnicities."

men of one color and another; no distinction but what is based, not on institutions of government, not upon the consent of society, but upon their *individual and personal merit.*[65]

These views did not commit Seward to a "melting pot" view of assimilation, as seemed to have been the case with Crèvecoeur, since Whigs in general tended to believe that the dominant Anglo-Saxon strain would absorb the rest;[66] but they spoke clearly for the equal rights of individuals to make their own way in the new American world. Whigs moreover were prepared to tolerate and approve of very unequal distributions of wealth resulting from advantages of position that could by now only be called competitive—if one looked around and chose to give it a name.[67] The economic side of the case had already been argued as early as 1835—the year after Thomas Cooper's plea for mutual harmony—by Henry Carey, in a statement of the need for the kind of diversity of skills that would absorb a variety of talents by creating a multiplicity of careers.[68] ("Career" is a nineteenth century word, probably first appearing in the French expression of "the career open to the talents.")

But one great social force was coming toward mid-century to dominate all others in American consciousness. The westward expansion of slavery, and its threatening propensity to expand into Central America and the Caribbean, erupting in the mid-fifties into the fearful struggle for the control first of Kansas and ultimately of the great Northwest—a symbolic struggle but nonetheless vital for that—cast a profound shadow over the prospects of freedom not only for blacks but for whites. Slavery, it was widely believed, could destroy the prospects for the settlement of free land by free men, and this threat turned many racially prejudiced farmers into violent opponents of slavery expansion.[69]

The ideology of the Republican party was inherited in large part from the Whig belief in equality of opportunity, which in the broadest sense was a doctrine of political economy. But it was refined in the light, or perhaps the shadow, cast by slavery. The Republican critique of slavery

---

65. Daniel Walker Howe, *The Political Culture of the American Whigs* (Chicago, 1979), 203.

66. Ibid., 202.

67. Ashworth, *Agrarians and Aristocrats*, 120, 137–38.

68. Daniel Walker Howe, *Political Culture*, 111–12.

69. An excellent account of the growth of northern opinion is in James M. MacPherson, *Battle Cry of Freedom: The Civil War Era* (New York, 1988), chs. 1–5.

involved a criticism of the whole society which it sustained, a society based on the indignity of labor. It was this that made the doctrine of "free labor" so meaningful a component of the entire Republican credo, whether the laborer was considered as a manual worker looking for advancement through hard work and personal economy, or a small, independent entrepreneur. Republicans believed ardently that America was, or could be, superior to Europe by the application of the principles that kept American society open, American opportunities equal for all. "What is it," asked an Iowa Republican in 1858 in pursuit of this theme,

> that makes the great mass of American citizens so much more enterprising and intelligent than the laboring classes in Europe? It is the stimulant held out to them by the character of our institutions. The door is thrown open to all, and even the poorest and humblest in the land, may, by industry and application, attain a position which will entitle him to the respect and confidence of his fellow-men. [70]

The door which Alexander Hamilton had proclaimed "ought to be open to all"[71] had indeed been thrown open: Republicans had great and sincere faith in the achievement as well as the potentiality of northern society. Equality of opportunity, they believed, had already been attained. Daniel Webster in 1838 declared that greater equality of condition existed in the United States than in any highly civilized society on earth, and gave as evidence that no man in the state—Massachusetts—drove a coach and four, while very few were unable to take their wives and daughters to church "in some decent conveyance."[72] Abraham Lincoln's ideas of equality were closely linked to both property and free employment; under equal laws, men should enjoy equal opportunities to choose their livelihood, work for a living, and retain the fruits of honest labor. [73]

The concept of equality of opportunity, then, was not an academic formula. Republicans, and most Democrats, for that matter, though they

70. Foner, *Free Soil, Free Labor*, 16.

71. *Federalist* 36.

72. Quoted by Ashworth, *Agrarians and Aristocrats*, 65. Compare, however, Webster's house on Summer Street in Boston, of which a photograph appears in Pessen, *Riches*, opp. p. 197. Counting by the chimneys, the house has at least fifteen rooms (and almost certainly more), and judging by the windows and general proportions, many of the rooms were very large.

73. Daniel Walker Howe, *Political Culture*, 290–91. I have, however, slightly expanded his words.

had other political preoccupations, believed in the American republic very largely because they believed these values had been attained and ought to be preserved. It was the threat to it all, multiple in origin, ominous in character, that forced them to forge so potent a definition of the ideal.

Where Equality of Rights Meant Equal Protection

A natural aristocracy formed of virtue and talents and based on an irreducible equality of rights was a tolerable character for the new Republic. Not many of the political and moral publicists we have been considering would at heart have contested that proposition. But the whole drift of the anti-bank, Anti-Federalist and eventually much of what became the Democratic-Republican stream resisted what they perceived as the tendency of the times, because they feared that a new, artificial aristocracy was being created by paper money, government funding of debts, governmentally supported banks, and the associated privileges of commerce. A line of connection runs from this resistance to the more radical wing of the Jacksonian Democrats. If these elements were less enthusiastic about equality of opportunity, it was not that they believed in inequality but that they had reservations about the consequences of encouraging American society to depart from what they held to be its republican foundations.

Ominously, Jefferson's victory in 1800 did little to check the processes that Hamilton had spurred onward in his brief but brilliant reign as secretary of the treasury and Washington's prime minister. John Taylor of Caroline County, Virginia, an early ally of Jefferson's, contemplated these developments with deepening dismay. It was not until long after Jefferson's retirement that Taylor published his first systematic treatise, which was also notable as the first large-scale attempt to examine the American system of government from the standpoint of a formal philosophy.

Taylor, persevering earnestly through laborious redundancies of style, was in one sense a purer Jeffersonian than Jefferson himself. His aim was to establish an alternative, non-Hamiltonian position on which he believed American society could still stand. His attempt was inspired by two somewhat different developments. One of these was what he called the system of paper and patronage; he witnessed with dismay the

rise of a new aristocracy, based on unworthy dealings in credit and paper money but lacking roots in the country's real agricultural wealth. This insidious process was the direct product of legislative policies which put legislatures in the hands of corporations and banks. Taylor's other inspiration was a retarded reaction to John Adams's *Defence of the Constitutions of the United States*, actually written as long previously as 1786 and first published before the federal Constitution had been adopted.

Taylor was deeply antagonized by Adams's insistence on the division of all societies, including America's, into social orders, and by his conviction that safety could be sought only by some arrangement that converted them into political institutions. In contrast to Adams, Taylor placed the whole weight of his own beliefs on the integrity of the individual. In this respect his position was akin politically to James Wilson's and was consistent with the school of thought and political practice which treated the equal representation of individuals as the only proper foundation of politics. "The sovereignty of the people arises, and representation flows, out of each man's right to govern himself," he laid down; and it followed that the true principle of government was representation of the majority in equal districts.[74] These views might seem almost conventional. But they still had to share the field with other views of earlier vintage whenever they threatened to upset entrenched privilege—a truth that emerged in the prolonged struggle for the reform of representation in Virginia itself.[75]

The case against Adams also had a moral dimension. "Mr. Adams's political system, deduces government from a natural fate; the policy of the United States deduces it from moral liberty," Taylor explained, making clear that a correct understanding of the principles which animated the American Constitution would go a long way to solving the problem. In his view the Constitution left property where it belonged, with those who had gained it "fairly . . . by talents and industry."[76] When, therefore, the legislature effected transfers of property through the agencies of paper and patronage, such measures were as unconstitutional as those for re-establishing king, lords, and commons—a sharp

74. John Taylor, of Caroline County, Virginia, *An Inquiry into the Principles and Practice of the Government of the United States* (1814; London, 1950), 35–57, 101, 365.

75. J.R. Pole, *Political Representation in England and the Origins of the American Republic* (New York, 1966; Berkeley, 1971), 304–38.

76. Ibid., 124.

thrust at Adams's belief in the inevitability of aristocracy and his reputation for monarchical principles.

Taylor's economics, however, were unequal to the demands made on them by his political preconceptions. He offered no theory of political economy, nor did he support his views with statistical information. His considerable reading in the literature of political economy had failed to disturb a rather elementary agrarianism, and he was perfectly satisfied to rest on the distribution of property before the poison of paper and credit had got to work. Agriculture was for him the source of all other wealth and the center of all interests. He was at his weakest when he discountenanced any danger from a landed aristocracy by arguing that "aristocracy is nowhere agrarian" and that a landed monopoly in England "was hardly felt as a political principle."[77] It seemed that an agrarian economy contained some self-correcting mechanism that would forestall the rise of a monopolistic aristocracy. Taylor's conviction that his principle of "moral liberty" was superior to Adams's belief in the value of historical experience did not serve him well, for the moral principles which Taylor regarded as fundamental to good government simply did not establish the actual superiority of his system, and his appeals to English and colonial experience did, in fact, constitute appeals to history rather than to moral intuition. He was not as inquisitive about the real distribution of land and goods as his opinions demanded, and failed to draw inferences from the real consequences of that distribution, even in his own state of Virginia. He rejected the idea that the free creation of property might tend to produce new forms of monopoly and sharply disapproved of any laws for equalizing either property or knowledge. "They pretend to keep property equal among evanescent beings, and to supersede mental inequalities," he declared; and later, "A Law has never been able to produce an equality of property, where industry exists; but it can produce its monopoly."[78]

Broadly, then, Taylor was not dissatisfied with the state of affairs that existed at the outbreak of the Revolution; if this was not an ideal equality of condition, it was an acceptable approximation; nor did subsequent changes infringe on his general principles, until the Hamiltonian engine began to work. Although he had criticisms of the Constitution, he

77. Ibid., 477.
78. Ibid., 472, 544.

thought it embodied right principles, which he wanted to impose as absolute rules of policy. Political equality played a vital part in these rules. The new aristocracy of wealth could gain power through a corrupt use of the natural desire for property, but it could never serve the interests of the majority. That was why it used patronage and favor. It was clear to Taylor that the country was sliding headlong from its own basic postulates. A sectional dimension is not difficult to see in his anxieties about the future. The landed interests which he had at heart were primarily southern and were losing ground to those of the bankers, the merchants, the monopolists, and the manipulators of credit, whose seats could be discerned in the cities of the North.

In the frenetic race for wealth, many were trampled underfoot; it was of small comfort for them that John Taylor faced resolutely in the opposite direction. In the very different, urban atmosphere of New York reformist politics early in Andrew Jackson's presidency, Thomas Skidmore made a still more radical attempt not only to set the country back on its foundations, but to correct the defects of those foundations. Skidmore based his political science on the absolute irreducibility of equal rights. "Rights are like truths, capable of being understood alike by all men;—as much so, as the demonstration of Euclid," he asserted.[79] This statement, an alternative formulation of the concept of the self-evident truth, would no doubt have been acceptable to Jefferson. But Skidmore was not satisfied with the credentials that Jefferson had bestowed on the young republic. He rebuked the author of the Declaration of Independence for losing the most valuable item in the vague rhetoric of "the pursuit of happiness." The item in question was property; for without property, happiness was impossible, and Jefferson was accused of evading the issue.

Skidmore thus differed from his agrarian predecessor Taylor in that he could never be satisfied with the position of 1776. Not only American governments, but all governments, had been wrong when they accepted the unequal division of property in the origins of society—for there was no society before government.[80]

Skidmore was more thorough and more radical than Taylor in cutting through to the logical foundations that his principles required. While the

79. Thomas Skidmore, *The Rights of Man to Property!* (New York, 1829), 31.
80. Ibid., 76, 126–27.

right to property was based on the produce of labor, he maintained that the materials of which goods were made still belonged to the community. He was scornfully irreverent about all claims to property as sanctified by law; the purpose of laws of property was in the main to sanction infractions of equal rights which resulted from the unequal division of property. These arguments led him to the question of inheritance, which he identified as crucial. Skidmore was not interested in half-measures or accommodations but was determined to advance a coherent plan, to be put in force in the first instance in the state of New York. The aim was to equalize all existing property while forestalling any possibility of the occurrence of new inequalities.

Although Skidmore's discussion was technically complex, his method was simple. It was to stop all transfers of property at death. All must revert to the state. Children—echoing Samuel Harrison Smith (not to mention Plato) belonged to the community, not to their parents.[81] He naturally demanded the abolition of slavery and added, with a vision that would reappear only among the more radical Republicans, that freed slaves should be given land and goods to earn their own living in freedom.[82] To bring about equality of property, Skidmore proposed that all existing property be surrendered to the state and then reapportioned in a "general division." Like many of the more radical thinkers about republican principles, Skidmore believed that education had to be made a public responsibility and proposed that the state treasury should pay for all schooling.[83] These views were far more radical than Taylor's, but Skidmore joined Taylor when he attacked every aspect of the system of legislative charters and privileges, quoting Paine in arguing that charters took away the rights of the people at large.[84]

Skidmore, whose political base collapsed after the development of a workingmen's political party and who died soon afterwards in a cholera epidemic, has been dismissed as a "fanatic," of whose "errant influence" the emerging workingmen's movement did well to purge itself.[85] That may be political wisdom. But men like Skidmore have their importance,

81. Ibid., 61–62.
82. Ibid., 270.
83. Ibid., 157–58.
84. Ibid., 160–68.
85. Schlesinger, *Age of Jackson*, 184.

because their logic clarifies the alternative choices. John Adams had once believed that there was "but one order" in American society (a view not held with great consistency); no one in Jackson's America still believed that, which itself is an important indication of the changes since the first generation of the republic; but Skidmore was quite clear in the view that there *ought* to be but one order. Nor was he satisfied with the moral completeness of the Founders' principles; he aimed to complete them. On the basis of real similarities among the people of the Republic, Skidmore aimed to *produce* the conditions which would encourage interchangeability.

Even in a workingmen's movement, Skidmore and his small coterie of followers were out of place and could never have secured a permanent footing. Ideals of equality in America could survive only in forms adapted to an age dominated by economic development—or by the prospects of economic development. Skidmore's contemporary, Langdon Byllesby, writing two or three years earlier, wanted to go the more practical way of promoting equality through labor associations for "securing Equal (or Mutual) Advantages (or Interests)" which would share the wealth derived from their activities.[86] It was growing increasingly clear to the labor radicals of this age, and to the leaders of political and economic labor organizations, that the workers as a class would never enjoy equality of economic opportunity with their capitalist masters, and few of them would escape from their class; but they insisted all the more passionately on equality not because they could hope for more equal rewards but because it was a metaphor for independence, control and self-respect. That was why the National Trades Union Convention, meeting in New York in 1836, resolved that co-operative trade associations be formed in order to secure for the mechanic "sole and absolute control over the disposal of his labor."[87]

Robert Rantoul, Jr., of Massachusetts, who worked for the Democratic party in his state, in allying it with the cause of labor, denied that it was a party of faction. The Democracy, he told an audience at Worcester on

---

86. L. Byllesby, *Observations on the Sources and Effects of Unequal Wealth, with Propositions towards Remedying the Disparity of Profit in Pursuing the Arts of Life and Establishing Security in Individual Prospects and Resources* (New York, 1826).

87. John R. Commons and associates, *A Documentary History of American Industrial Society*, 10 vols. (Cleveland, 1910), vi, 291–93.

4 July 1837, was the party of "equal rights, equal privileges, universal protection."[88] But four years earlier he had written an essay listing the claims that the workingman could make on society: (1) The right to his faculties, the right to the product of their use; (2) the right to choose the terms on which he will employ his time; (3) the right to steady wages at the highest going rate; (4) the right to education; (5) the right to respect; and (6) the right to advancement in life.[89] This list brought together two essential terms in which rights were universal and equal— the right to advancement, a synonym for equality of opportunity; and the right to respect, which was equality of esteem. Whatever their skills or fortunes, workingmen were entitled to the respect of society. As declared the next year by the call for a convention of trade unions, "to consult on such measures as shall be most conducive to the moral and intellectual dignity of the labouring classes, sustain their pecuniary interests, succour the oppressed. . . ."[90] Pecuniary interest was fairly in its place, but first came the dignity of the laboring classes.

It was a coincidence of date, but no mere coincidence of principle, that in 1834 the French rebel priest H.R.F. de Lamennais, whose work was known among American labor leaders, told the laboring masses of France that they must learn an eleventh commandment: "Respect yourselves."[91] Without that, nothing worth respecting could be achieved.

The moral and economic needs of the workers could never be satisfied by the compromises of party politics. Orestes Brownson, who threw himself into Jacksonian politics when he beheld the misery caused by the crisis of 1837, was under no illusion that America had achieved an equal society, and understood also that it had not achieved genuine freedom of competition. Facing away from collective views which derived from France and were gaining adherents in America, Brownson held that the true task was to restore a genuine state of laissez-faire. His diagnosis,

88. Marvin Meyers, *The Jacksonian Persuasion* (1957; New York, 1960), 222–23.
89. Ibid., 216.
90. Commons, *Documentary History*, vi, 194.
91. A.G. Lehmann, *Sainte-Beuve* (Oxford, 1962), 204; Arthur M. Schlesinger, Jr., *A Pilgrim's Progress: Orestes Brownson* (rprt., Boston, 1966), 320. H.R.F. de Lamennais, *Paroles d'un Croyant*, was translated as *The People's Own Book* by Nathaniel Greene, a friend of Brownson's, and appeared in Boston in 1839 (Schlesinger, *Brownson*, 303). It is not suggested that the Americans got the idea from the French, but rather that an international community of the working class under industrial capitalism was beginning to be conceivable.

however, required faith in two propositions. The first was the belief that the desired condition had really existed in the revolutionary era; the second was that the advance of the industrial economy could be reversed. These propositions may be considered dubious. Yet Brownson had a sense of social realities that alarmed his respectable Unitarian contemporaries in Boston. In a highly controversial article, "The Laboring Classes," published in 1840, Brownson declared that universal suffrage "is little better than a mocker, when the voters are not socially equal. No matter what party you support, no matter what man you elect, property is always the basis of your governmental action." Brushing aside free trade and universal education, he cut straight through to the center of the problem—the need to abolish inheritance. [92]

The timing of Brownson's revival of Skidmore's program was critical. The Whigs injected his ideas into the campaign of 1840 as typical of what was to be expected from a Democratic victory, causing resentful consternation among Democrats, and weakening their already damaged prospects of electoral success. The crushing Democratic defeat shook Brownson so badly that he lost faith in Democratic government; he would never again have so much confidence in the people. But his energetic thinking was one of the monuments of the heritage of the Revolution. Not only did he believe that the true principles lay there— he also believed that the Founders had practiced principles which Jacksonian America had lost, and that Jacksonian democracy had failed to recover. In this he differed from such historians as have considered Jacksonian democracy as a *fulfillment* of the promise of the Revolution. Still, a link with early republican principles survived; Skidmore and Brownson were in a sense, however remotely, descendants, in their aims if not in their specific remedies, of the agrarians of old. Reformers in the Progressive era or in the New Deal would not be found advocating the abolition of inheritance.

Brownson had never been an organizer. Skidmore attempted to found a movement. His and other early workingmen's movements did not begin by concerning themselves with any grand design. Their initial demands were beneficial and industrial; they overlapped into politics with a claim for a variety of laws protecting their immediate economic interests, including one for a law which, as we have seen, would give

92. Schlesinger, *Brownson*, 82–83, 88–111.

them a lien on the value of work completed before paid for, as well as a defense of their hours.[93]

The changes that were affecting the economy began to promote among mechanics a new sense of class, defined in contradistinction to the middle class of capital and individual enterprise. The effects were divisive, however, and were felt, even among the workers, to be contrary to the true spirit of the republic. A comparable trend in Cincinnati found the city's journeymen denouncing class conflict and embracing a philosophy of the harmony and mutual needs of all the "producing" classes.[94] If American society was, after all, to be a society of orders, the newly conscious workers were determined to define those orders by their economic functions—which meant their usefulness—and hence the respect to which their members were entitled.

Andrew Jackson, the Social Order, and Equal Protection

Not all of these problems had become fully apparent during Andrew Jackson's presidency. But many of them were anticipated. Jackson himself posed less of a threat to the social order than his political enemies feared—or professed to fear. He based his opposition to the recharter of the Bank of the United States not on any sort of *dirigiste* or centralizing doctrine but on the firm old ground of equal opportunity and opposition to any form of special privilege. On similar principles he turned against the creeping social conventions by which public service had acquired the character of unofficial property rights—in a manner that distinctly resembled customs which had not disappeared in Britain.[95] Jackson, however, ignored the question of how the "men of intelligence" who could be expected to perform the "plain and simple duties" of public office were to be recruited; the spoils system, operating in the service and under the control of political parties (or powerful individual politicians) supplied the answer. Whether or not this process

93. Hugins, *Jacksonian Democracy*, ch. 4; Sean Wilenz, *Chants Democratic: New York City and the Rise of the American Working Class, 1780–1850* (New York, 1984), ch. 4.

94. Steven J. Ross, *Workers on the Edge: Work, Leisure and Politics in Industrializing Cincinnati, 1788–1880* (New York, 1985), 56–59.

95. It was a historical irony that Britain, which Americans took as the archetype of corrupt aristocracy, began to introduce competitive examinations and an independent civil service soon after the spoils system had been established in the United States.

produced greater respect for equality of opportunity in the public service, it can hardly be said to have made public officers more accountable to the public than they had been as proteges of private privilege. It was no mere linguistic chance that incumbents of public office in the United States came to be called "office-holders" rather than civil servants.

Jacksonian theory was satisfied that government could maintain the basic conditions of what would soon be called equality of opportunity by such measures as the destruction of the Second Bank of the United States, and by legislation at the state level to require that corporation charters conformed to standard conditions, removed from the reach of pressure and privilege. Beyond this, Jackson and his party had little to offer but a sort of authoritative inactivity. His veto message on the bill to recharter the Bank stated the limits as much as the scope of his principles: "Distinctions in society will always exist under any just government. Equality of talents, or education, or wealth cannot be produced by human institutions." So much, then, for the reformers to his left. Political science had not yet began to analyze these distinctions conceptually, but a later generation would call Jackson's position one of "means-regarding" as opposed to "bloc-regarding" equality of opportunity.[96] His own aim for social policy rose no higher than making government neutral between competing interests; it was no part of his purpose to indulge in distributionist policies or to exercise paternalistic control. The economy (unrestrained by private charters), the professional and social worlds, agriculture, crafts and manufacturing, fisheries, finance, together with all systems of education, were to be open to all—meaning all male whites—provided only that they had the means to get into them. In affirming that everyone was entitled to the equal protection of the law, Jackson promulgated a phrase of resounding historical significance. This protection was to be enjoyed,

in the full enjoyment of the gifts of Heaven and the fruits of superior industry, economy and virtue; but when the laws undertake to add to these natural and just advantages artificial distinctions, to grant titles, gratuities, and exclusive privileges, to make the rich richer and the potent more powerful, the humbler members of society—the farmers, mechanics and laborers—have a right to complain of the injustice of the Government. There are no necessary evils in Government. Its evils exist only in its abuses. If it would confine itself to equal

96. Douglas Rae and others, *Equalities* (Cambridge, Mass., 1981), ch. 4.

protection, and, as Heaven does its rains shower its favors alike on high and low, the rich and the poor, it would be an unqualified blessing. In the act before me there appears to be a wide and unnecessary departure from these principles.

This can hardly be considered a complete exposition of the problems of social justice in the era of competitive capitalism.[97] Other good Jacksonians, such as the anti–paper money theorist William Gouge, were far better aware that the specious appearance of equality of opportunity concealed complex and growing disparities that could not be stopped in their tracks by high pronouncements accompanied by lofty restraint on the part of the government.[98]

No one interested in public life would have denied Jackson's tenet that the law ought to provide equal protection to all, with saving clauses for non-whites and females. The differences of opinion were political, not legal, and they turned, crucially, on the actual content of the laws that were to be equal to all. Jackson and his party maintained that such institutions as the national bank incorporated unwarranted inequalities into American life. Thus, in spite of himself, Jackson was involved if only in a limited way in affirming that social values must influence public policy: government could be neutral only to the extent that government set the rules. At the same time he believed, with Madison (who was still alive), that a just government would protect the consequences that would naturally flow from the free exercise of natural endowments.

But Jackson's language was fraught with unconscious irony. When he introduced the phrase "equal protection" he intended to *limit*, not to extend, the bounds of government action. It was a declaration of governmental nonintervention. Yet this was the expression that reappeared at a vital phase of American history when the Constitution itself was undergoing reconstruction by the addition of the Fourteenth Amendment—which guarantees to all persons under American jurisdiction the

97. The highest level of official recognition of the inherently competitive character of the system appeared soon afterward in the Supreme Court's judgment in *Charles River Bridge v. Warren Bridge*, 11 Peters 420 (1837). Recent legislation gave a new company, the Warren Bridge Company, the right to build a bridge over the Charles that would compete with the old Charles River Bridge Company, which operated under an original eighteenth-century charter for which it claimed exclusive rights. The Court in effect ruled that the public interest in innovation and competition overrode the rights of property vested in the charter.

98. Joseph L. Blau, ed., *Social Theories of Jacksonian Democracy* (Indianapolis, 1954), 183–98.

equal protection of the laws. But laws that bore unequally on different classes could not provide equal protection to individuals. It was to be found by a necessary logic that the *contents* of the laws would themselves be subject to the principle of equality. The equal protection of the laws would one day mean that the laws themselves must be equal laws.

At the time of the Reconstruction debates, the purpose of Congress was to extend the protection of the law to the colored race, as they were then formally called. This turn of events would have astounded Jackson, who would certainly have disapproved. But the truth was that this new application of equal protection was consistent with its original principle. Jackson, who never had the slightest concern for racial equality, might have failed to see the connection. But this difficulty arose from the limits of his—and his contemporaries'—social vision, not from the logic of the case. The life of the law, we might say, at some risk from higher authority, has been in the tension between logic and experience.

Chapter Seven

Race and Political Community

Inequality and the Constitution

On the scorching afternoon of 21 August 1858 in the northern Illinois town of Ottawa, in the presence of some twelve thousand people accompanied by banners, brass bands, and clouds of highway dust, Abraham Lincoln made his first speech in the series of debates between himself and Senator Stephen A. Douglas. The stake between them was the United States Senate seat, due for election, though by the state legislature, not by popular vote, in November. Despite the indirect nature of the electoral process, the public excitement was intense, and Lincoln's challenge and Douglas's acceptance expressed their recognition that national issues called for public debate. For these great matters concerned not only the electorate of Illinois but the people of the United States. The ultimate issue was the future of slavery. But for immediate political purposes the problem was whether slavery should be allowed to spread, indefinitely, into new areas of the Union according to the wish of local whites, or whether the national government possessed a constitutional power to stop it, and ought to exert that power.

A debate about slavery was also a debate about freedom. It was also, in the most fundamental sense, a debate about the ideals, possibilities, and limits of equality in America. The issue of race put the American dedication to equality to its most searching test because the racial issue was a *caste* issue; it raised the question of whether the offer of equal

opportunity, based on equal rights, was or ever could be open to all Americans. Free Negroes, in all states and sections, were subjected to crippling and humiliating discrimination, which effectively prevented them from participating in any of the advantages which white Americans universally regarded as their birthright. Blacks had every reason to be aware of this claim, and of the extent to which they were deprived of it.

These restrictions dated from the early years of the century, after the idealism associated with the Revolution had begun to fade into the ambitious and often furious competition for economic advancement and political power. By the later years of the old century, many southern whites were growing increasingly fearful and hostile in the presence of a multiplying population of free blacks, whose numbers owed a good deal to the emancipations that had accompanied the Revolution itself. The slave uprising which had begun in 1793 on the island of Santo Domingo, and which checked a threatened French deployment in Louisiana, and turned thousands of terrified white refugees onto the mainland, sent repercussive waves of fear through widening ranges of white society. Repression of free blacks, rather than sober analysis of the nature of the problem, tended to be the white reaction in those southern states where the black population was most numerous.

Through the passage of new laws specifically directed at the free black population, the white world of North America systematically denied to blacks the freedoms and opportunities which they themselves claimed by right.[1] In the southern states, it became almost impossible for black children to go to school, except under white control and supervision. In northern states, their best hope was to go to separate and inferior schools. (It was the New England state of Massachusetts which originated the doctrine of separate-but-equal in order to justify this school segregation.)[2] Everywhere, restrained in education and training, unable to enter the professions, with no access to the prospects of entrepreneurial opportunity through capital or loans, Americans of African descent lived on the margins of white civilization. Whites seem to have made little distinction in their own minds between free blacks and slaves;

---

1. Robert McColley, *Slavery in Jeffersonian Virginia* (Urbana, Ill., 1964); Eugene D. Genovese, *Roll, Jordan, Roll: The World the Slaves Made* (London, 1975), 31–32.
2. *Roberts v. The City of Boston*, 5 Cush. Mass. 198 (1849).

and since it was actually white policies that made it impossible for free blacks to enter into the fuller life of the community, white attitudes were responsible for the social problem that confronted white abolitionists. For immediately behind the project of emancipation there lurked the inevitable question of whether and how far blacks could or should be incorporated into the community and allowed to share its privileges. It was in every sense the starkest test of equality in all its aspects that Americans had ever had to contemplate. All these issues were caught up in the debates between Lincoln and Douglas.

Inequality, the Constitution, and the Struggle for Political Power

Douglas, standing a stout five feet four inches to Lincoln's great and craggy height, opened the debate with a confident and familiar assertion of the theme of Negro inferiority, which he coupled with the campaign argument that Lincoln and the Republican party believed in the full equality of the races. "I believe," Douglas declared, "this government was made on the white basis. I believe it was made by white men, for the benefit of white men and their posterity for ever, and I am in favor of confining citizenship to white men, men of European birth and descent, instead of conferring it upon negroes, Indians and other inferior races." He charged Lincoln with believing that the Negro was endowed with equality by the Almighty and that no human law could deprive him of rights conferred "by the Supreme Ruler of the universe." To these attributed opinions, Douglas replied that the Almighty never intended the Negro to be the equal of the white man. "If he did, he has been a long time demonstrating the fact," he added, and proceeded to call in evidence the history of Negro inferiority "in all latitudes and climes."[3] It was to these beliefs, and the vast mass of innate prejudice that sustained them, that Lincoln addressed his carefully guarded rejoinder. Lincoln, himself a product of the same white society, conceded that the physical differences between the races "will probably forever forbid their living together upon a footing of perfect equality" and expressed a preference for his own race occupying the superior position; in setting

---

3. Paul M. Angle, ed., *Created Equal? The Complete Lincoln-Douglas Debates of 1858* (Chicago, 1958), 111–12.

out to undermine Douglas's existing majority, even the "probably" in that sentence could be construed as a hostage to prejudice. "Perfect equality" could be postponed indefinitely, but it could at least be contemplated. "I have no purpose to introduce political and social equality between the white and black races," he declared, and elsewhere he denied that Negroes ought to be allowed to vote or to serve on juries. All this was a fairly safe distance from "perfect equality." Notwithstanding these reservations, he held that

> there is no reason in the world why the negro is not entitled to all the natural rights enumerated in the Declaration of Independence, to right to life, liberty and the pursuit of happiness. I hold that he is as much entitled to these as the white man. I agree with Judge Douglas that he is not my equal in many respects—certainly not in color, perhaps not in moral and intellectual endowment. But in the right to eat bread, without leave of anybody else, which his own hand earns, *he is my equal and the equal of Judge Douglas, and the equal of every living man.*[4]

The thunder of applause testified to a profound moral feeling. The ground was beginning to shift, and Lincoln, by giving form and force to these sentiments, was helping to shift it. But it was less easy to resolve the differences into political policies. Douglas, for all his display of moral indifference, did not approve of slavery and did not want to deprive Negroes of their ability to earn their own living, within limits and without offering them anything resembling equality of opportunity with whites; and neither of the antagonists proposed to place in the black man's hands those instruments of political or civil power that were actually needed to protect the right to economic independence.

The inconsistencies in Lincoln's position were at least as serious as those he exposed in Douglas during the further course of the debates. He was committed to maintaining that the equality of rights enumerated in the Declaration of Independence could be guaranteed without conferring the rights normally connected with citizenship. Douglas, if he had been a shade more subtle, could have made life very difficult for Lincoln on this point.[5] But Lincoln did not expect to change institutions; his aim

---

4. Ibid., 117.

5. Of course, there were members of the white community who did not enjoy all these rights—women, for example. And certain percipient women, notably those who had already begun by campaigning against slavery, had already observed a close analogy between their status and that of slaves. But the analogy was not an identity. Women

was to change attitudes. In his speeches and in replies to questions in these famous debates, Lincoln combined high principle with clear speech, a complete absence of theatrical rhetoric, and a supple wit that always included and never lost respect for his audience. His popular campaign was an immense success. Although he lost the Senate election in the legislature, he gained much more in a national prominence from which he was able to win the presidency only just over two years later. But all this should not obscure the fact that Lincoln was asserting formal principles which were incompatible with his advocated policies. That, indeed, was part of the reason for his success; the problem facing the numerous Republican supporters who wanted to see the Negroes free, who wanted them to support themselves in peace and safety, and who wanted the institutions of the country to ensure these things, but did not want to share those institutions with the African race, was inherently complex and had not yet been fully explored. The process of exploration was due to intensify with great rapidity during the next ten years. It was to entail a great civil war, accompanied by intense and bitter disputes about Negro participation in the normal life of white society. During all this the American creed of equality was to be catechized, its hidden assumptions, its moral assurances and rhetorical promises exposed to political conflict as never before in the nation's history.

But in 1858 all this was obscure, the forms to be taken though feared and anticipated were not yet known. For the time being it was clear that none of the critical categories of equality was to be extended to black Americans. Equality of opportunity, equality in politics, equality before the law were withheld from them even by most of their purported friends. Anything like equality of esteem, as Douglas's very characteristic language made plain, was totally out of the question. If in these circumstances Negroes were to enjoy the natural rights of the Declaration of Independence, it could only be by living out their entire lives on a different and lower plane, perhaps protected from molestation but without hope for better things even in the remote future. Neither Lincoln

---

could sue and give evidence in court, and were included in and to a large extent protected by the system of laws which excluded those of apparently African descent. White women and white men were members of the same families, both literally and in the more figurative sense.

nor anyone else would have tolerated such deprivations for the white race, or any subsection of it. No solution was possible within these terms of reference. If not full equality, then at least a very substantial degree of political participation and of legal rights were indispensable to the true enjoyment of happiness, to liberty, and often to life itself.

The Constitution of the United States, resting so lightly on the American multitudes, had permitted and protected the form of moral pluralism which Stephen Douglas held essential to its survival. Douglas could believe that the United States could endure—as it had in the past—half slave and half free, because he did not believe that the principles of the Constitution had any bearing on the morals of slavery. Lincoln, who understood the nationalizing character of the historical process of his time better than his rival, perceived that pluralism about fundamental moral values could not endure forever. In the past, that spacious and accommodating attitude to the reception of such diverse peoples into a single political system had been protected not only by the institutions of the country but by the land itself. The land could absorb and conceal incipient conflicts whose ideological character made them eventually inescapable. It was for this reason that abundant space gave so many Americans the sense of possessing infinite time. Wherever space ran out, as in many cities had already happened, conflicts between rival creeds and mutually hostile communities erupted alarmingly. The eastern cities experienced these eruptions earlier than the wide spaces of the West; but the quasi-war between slavery and free soil forces in Kansas in the mid-fifties, which lay in the immediate background of the Lincoln-Douglas debates, proved that space could not indefinitely conquer time. All this, manifesting itself at various levels and in diverse circumstances since the days of Jackson some twenty years earlier, seemed to have very little to do with anything the founders might have had in mind when they promised "a republican form of government."

Tocqueville had been impressed by "the delights of equality" which American society afforded. Not all foreign visitors were so favorably impressed. The tyranny of the majority, which Tocqueville himself so dreaded, was not one of political equality's more attractive attributes, and was not easily reconciled with an equality of rights, opportunity, or esteem. His contemporary Michel Chevalier, who also visited the United

States in the Jacksonian period, remarked sardonically how dead the word *equality* fell when a good citizen pronounced it.[6]

There were several white minorities, but most notably the Catholic Irish, for whom equality in America was at best a distant hope, at worst a contemptuous joke. Yet people of diverse origin, manners, and religions had shown that they could accommodate themselves to one another's presence and could work out forms of association in the political parties. The confederation of states which the Republic comprised always included a different confederation, that of communities with their own habits, and of regions with their own social and economic practices; and American republican government had always been hospitable to wide differences between communities, only notionally unified by a single system of law. Ideas of community worked more or less well according to the patterns of population left by the tides of ethnic, national, or religious migration, and were so frequently in flux as to defy exact meaning. But their outlines were most distinctly marked along the boundaries of race. The "delights" of experiencing social equality, whatever their limitations, were not normally available to blacks in their relations with whites. Whatever their ideological professions, it was all too clear that the visible facts of skin pigmentation marked the limit beyond which most white Americans were unwilling to carry their public opinions into civic, still less into private, life.

This republic contained two populations—those who were of the republic, and those who were merely in it. Differences between northern and Mediterranean Europeans, and between British and Irish, differences of sect or religion, could be sharp and cruel, but they did not hold with such stubbornness as the visible differences of skin pigmentation which the vast majority of European Americans regarded as marking an insurmountable contrast with those of African descent. In the sense that this contrast helped to define the community of whites, it may in some areas have strengthened the bonds of society—we have seen appeals to that sentiment in the South.[7] In the context of sectional tension, this heritage of racial distinctness had retrospective effects on the views held by rival

6. Michel Chevalier, *Society, Manners and Politics in the United States: Letters on North America* (1839), ed. John William Ward (New York, 1967), 371–74.

7. Cf. Congressman James Dowdwell, quoted in Chapter 6, p. 144, and the works there cited.

parties about the composition of the American community at the time the Constitution was made, and therefore on the question of *for whom* the Constitution was made. This retrospect assumed profound constitutional significance in a passage of Chief Justice Roger B. Taney's opinion in the famous case of *Dred Scott v. Sandford*, decided in 1857, after many years in lower courts. The judgment, which came just after the inauguration of President James Buchanan, but before the storm over Kansas and the preceding repeal of the Missouri Compromise had even begun to subside, was intended to put a stop to these agitations by giving a final judicial determination on the points in controversy.[8]

The case arose because Dred Scott, a black slave, had once been taken by his master from the slave state of Missouri into territories where, under the Congressional Ordinance of 1787 (first enacted by the Continental Congress, but re-passed under the Constitution), slavery was supposed to be forbidden. Subsequently, Scott's master, a Dr. Emerson, had returned to Missouri with Scott and his wife, thus restoring them to the jurisdiction of a slave state. The question that the Supreme Court had to decide was fraught with significance for southern owners of slave property. Had Scott and his wife become free by the mere act of setting foot on free soil in the Northwest—in a manner analogous to the way in which the slave Somerset had been declared free by Lord Mansfield in the English Court of King's Bench in 1772 by virtue of the fact that slavery had no lawful existence in Britain?[9] Southern courts were willing

---

8. Much the most thorough account of the case, giving both its prehistory and repercussions, is in Don E. Fehrenbacher, *The Dred Scott Case* (New York, 1978). In this edition I follow Fehrenbacher in spelling the defendant's name "Sandford," but the Supreme Court reports permit "Sanford," as in my edition of 1978.

9. T.B. Howell, *State Trials* (London, 1814), 82; David Brion Davis, *The Problem of Slavery in Western Culture* (Ithaca, N.Y., 1966), 485; Fehrenbacher, *Dred Scott*, 6; J.R. Pole, "Slavery and Revolution: the Conscience of the Rich," in *Paths to the American Past* (New York, 1979), 57–60, and n. 2. *Somerset* was a case of much concern to all sides in the American disputes about slavery—so much so that the Constitution of the Confederate States of America specifically overruled the Somerset doctrine. (Art. 4, sec. 2, para. 1), as noted by Robert M. Cover, *Justice Accused: Antislavery and the Judicial Process* (New Haven, 1975), 87–88, 167. Lord Chief Justice Mansfield had ruled in *Somerset* that in British jurisprudence, slavery could exist only when supported by positive law. It was clear that in the territories ruled by the Northwest Ordinance it did *not* exist by positive law. It was to clear up any doubt on this point that Chief Justice Taney had to find that the law in question lacked constitutional validity. The effect was not to stop the controversy but only to bring the Supreme Court into the center of it.

to agree that permanent residence in free territory made a person free, and some northern states had laws which permitted southern slave owners to bring their slave servants with them when visiting for limited periods. The distinction was between a *residence* and a *sojourn*. Southerners could not afford to admit the proposition that a slave became free merely by virtue of setting foot on free soil; but if not, the Northwest Ordinance and all other congressional enactments on slavery in the territories conferred only a qualified species of freedom. (This constituted a glaring breach of the fundamentals of equality before the law, which potentially threatened the liberties of innumerable free people.) If, on the other hand, Scott and his wife had been made free by touching free soil, how then could they have been re-enslaved by returning to Missouri? For a free person does not normally become a slave merely by entering a slave state. States had undoubted power to make their own laws protecting slavery, excluding it, or permitting it under the limitations of the master's "sojourn." If the states could do this, then it was hard to see why Congress could not do it in the territories over which it had jurisdiction.

The Supreme Court set about the problem by purporting to establish that Negroes were not citizens when the Constitution was made, from which it followed that even a free Negro could never be a citizen of the United States and had no power to sue in the courts. There was therefore no case to answer. But the Court also reached the conclusion, made technically superfluous by the disclaimer of jurisdiction just mentioned, that Congress had never possessed the constitutional power to exclude slavery from the territories, for which reason the Missouri Compromise of 1820 which had banned slavery forever from all territory north of the latitude 36 degrees 30 minutes was held to have been unconstitutional at the time and unconstitutional during the thirty-four years of its existence. (It had been replaced, and to all intents and purposes repealed, under the Kansas-Nebraska Act of 1854.) Chief Justice Taney and the six justices who concurred in this decision reached these conclusions by different routes, a fact which suggested to a skeptical public that their reasoning had been determined by the conclusions to be arrived at, rather than the other way round.

The chief justice would hardly have pleased adherents of the principle of strict construction. "The Constitution," he declared, "has conferred on Congress the right to establish an uniform rule of naturalization, and this

right is evidently exclusive, and has always been held by this court to be so. Consequently, no State, since the adoption of the Constitution, can, by naturalizing an alien, invest him with the rights and privileges secured to a citizen of a State under the federal government, although, so far as the State alone was concerned, he would undoubtedly be entitled to the rights of a citizen, and clothed with all the rights and immunities which the Constitution and the laws of the State attached to that character." And he continued, "It is very clear, therefore, that no State can, by any Act or law of its own, passed since the adoption of the Constitution, introduce a new member into the political community created by the Constitution of the United States. It cannot make him a member of this community by making him a member of its own. And for the same reason it cannot introduce any person, or description of persons, who were not intended to be embraced in this new political family, which the Constitution brought into existence, but were intended to be excluded from it." [10]

In this central passage the chief justice had in mind two different, but imperfectly distinguished, themes. The first was simple: only the Congress could make American citizens under the Constitution, so that persons who had been admitted as citizens by particular states did not thereby enjoy the protections of national citizenship. The Court was here reversing a general understanding that a state citizen automatically became a citizen of the United States. (States could do this by conforming to the "uniform rules" laid down by the Congress. [11]) His second theme arose from a purely subjective judgment about the kind of political community that existed in 1788, linked with an almost metaphysical doctrine that such a community *could not have intended* to make the Constitution adaptable to any later changes in that community—a view for which there was neither historical evidence nor logical support. In addition to his statement that a state could not make a citizen, Chief Justice Taney argued that a state could never make a citizen of someone who, by his definition, would have been excluded from the political community as it existed when the Constitution was formed—meaning, of course, a person of African descent. To make this argument convinc-

10. *Dred Scott v. Sandford*, 19 U.S. Howard 393 (1857), at 701.

11. James H. Kettner, *The Development of American Citizenship, 1608–1870* (Chapel Hill, 1978), 322–32.

ing, Taney would have had to hold that *all* persons who were not represented in the population in 1787–1788 would have been perpetually excluded, a ban which would have extended to eastern, central, and possibly Mediterranean Europeans. But in view of what had already been said, it was superfluous to declare that no state could introduce into "this new political family" any "description of persons who were not intended to be embraced" in it. That power rested with Congress because the Constitution confided it exclusively to Congress. The Chief Justice's theory had nothing to do with the law of the Constitution either at the time of its foundation or later; it was a *social* theory about the composition of the people—"the political family"—for whom the Constitution was made. Taney did not actually lay down that the Congress had no power to alter this position, though it is clear that he would have liked to have said so. Even so, he came perilously close to a usurpation of legislative power, for the Constitution is clear that the legislature, not the judiciary, determines questions of citizenship. He went as far as the case of *Dred Scott v. Sandford* would allow him toward defining the Constitution as a racial document, so that the admission of Negroes would violate its character and the intentions of its makers. That was the whole point of his homily, which is mere obiter dictum, about these limits of state powers, and it cannot be read in any other way. The opinion as a whole is a curious mixture of attributed "original intent" and highly strained construction of that intent.

The critical weakness in an opinion depending on these premises lay buried, but not buried very deep, in the use of historical evidence. Mr. Justice Curtis, in his dissenting opinion, showed conclusively that Negroes had actually enjoyed the privileges of citizenship in several states at the time of the Constitution. Under the Comity Clause, which here came back into the constitutional argument, the citizens of each state were to enjoy the privileges and immunities of citizens in the other states, but only the federal government could make citizens—from which it followed necessarily that all existing state citizens must have been taken up into United States citizenship when the Constitution came into force. Moreover, Negroes actually voted at the time in many states. Taney tried to deal with this difficulty by drawing a distinction between the right to vote and the rights of citizenship. This was unsafe ground, because noncitizens were allowed to vote only in the *expectation* of becoming citizens. But his specific difficulty, as Curtis pointed out, was

that Negroes could have voted for the ratification of the Constitution itself, in which case the Constitution owed its existence in part to black consent. [12] The lines which Taney and the majority tried to draw were soon to prove untenable. But they had made the fullest possible attempt to define the Constitution in terms not of the individual rights on which it had rested but of the social structure of the population—to create a system of caste under constitutional law.

The Anthropology of Inequality

Belief in equality of rights rested on a moral intuition. It did not require confirmation and could not in fact have been verified by observation. But the conduct of daily life is intimately connected with daily observations, which cumulatively contribute more than intuition to the way people behave to each other. Very few ordinary Americans felt any compelling incentive to divest themselves of beliefs which seemed to reflect the common sense of race relations. Observation revealed that blacks among them were everywhere in degraded and inferior conditions, defective in education and apparently wanting in ambition or ability. These views were self-protective; they did not require whites to alter their own practices and disturb their own attitudes. And if the moral intuition about equality of rights were extended to an assumption about equal abilities, the gradual advent of anthropological observations did little to promote the idea that the extraordinary variety of peoples making their way into the American continent were equally capable of the same achievements. The impact of immigration began fairly early to place heavy strain on the optimistically American idea of interchangeability. Even if the principle had been accepted, there was little reason to suppose that these different peoples entertained similar ambitions. The different nations of American Indians obviously differed from European Americans—as well as differing from one another—in their skills, interests, and ways of life. Meanwhile, immigrants from overseas had to struggle to establish their own claims to an equal place, supported by the

12. Ibid., 572–88. Curtis's argument is clearer and more cogent than that of McLean, who also dissented, and Curtis's logic overwhelmed Taney, who thereafter exhibited an extreme hostility to his younger colleague which Fehrenbacher attributes, very reasonably, to consciousness of his intellectual defeat. Fehrenbacher, *Dred Scott*, 414.

remote clauses of an austere Constitution, but with little assistance either from prevailing theory or from the evidence which presented itself to the senses of their contemporaries.

The intuition that men were equal and interchangeable, which corresponded to the hopes of many Americans with a force that probably exceeded the strength of their reasoned democratic principles, ran counter to the accumulating body of ethnic and religious prejudice, not to mention a great deal of social observation. Observation also began to assume a more orderly and scientific form with the cataloguing and comparison of physiological characteristics. But an older tradition, which gathered new force with the rise of evangelical religion, was that of biblical piety. So long as the Old Testament remained the point of departure for knowledge of the human race, mankind was believed to be descended from a single pair, and all differences of color, physiognomy, or aptitude must have been acquired subsequently—during our troubled sojourn beyond the Garden of Eden.

Thomas Jefferson was not inclined to be bound by biblical pieties. But he saw no reason to doubt the prevailing belief that God had created the world in a single, short burst, and that, since God could not have created anything in vain, all his creations must still, somewhere, survive. At different passages of his *Notes on the State of Virginia* he speculated about the presence in, and social consequences for, America of different peoples. He was beginning to worry about the prospective intake of peoples who were unfamiliar with republican government; these doubts did not spring from racial or national bias; where Jefferson saw advantages in a homogeneous population it was because of the dangers to the republic of admitting large numbers of people with no training in republican principles. When he turned to the Negro, however, the problem was racial. Given the constraints of the world-picture or paradigm within which he operated, it required a certain scientific skepticism to raise the possibility—and he put it no more strongly than that—that blacks might have been "originally a distinct race." "Originally." So Jefferson was prepared to contemplate the heresy of an originally separate creation. This was an early example of the paradox that the probing of the known boundaries of natural science did not necessarily lead to clearer solutions of the more pressing problems of social science. From this speculation, Jefferson passed easily to the next possibility, that blacks

might be inferior to whites in endowment of both body and mind.[13] Jefferson regarded it as a matter of reproach to his own people that the races of black and red men had never been made subjects of natural history.[14] Neither Jefferson's interest in fossils nor the other scientific researches of his time threw much additional light on these problems.

The philosophical Virginian patriarch was able to speculate in this way because he would have been more comfortable with scientific reasons for believing in Negro inferiority than in equally plausible reasons for believing that all these impressions were the subject of chance or circumstance. Jefferson's views conformed to those of a dominant intellectual climate, but they were not its necessary result; it is important to note that he had influential contemporaries, such as his associate in the American Philosophical Society, Dr. Benjamin Rush, and Samuel Stanhope Smith, who for many years was president of the College of New Jersey at Princeton, who held more optimistic views of Negro potential. White people seem to have had a general tendency to regard black skin as an abnormality which required explanation and which detracted from the possibilities of beauty. (Herodotus had speculated that the inhabitants of Africa had been scorched by the sun when it had once passed too near the earth.) Rush thought blackness might be due to disease, possibly a form of leprosy. Unappealing as this might seem, it gave rise to the prospect of cure (taking the form of whiteness), of which Rush thought he saw evidence; and these views were not strictly *racial* in that they did not attribute unalterable qualities of mind or character to inherited physiology. As an early member of the American Abolition Society, Rush, with several other American *philosophes*, signed a circular letter holding out the expectation of equal Negro achievement once the obstacles to equal opportunity had been removed. This was both an early and a very significant manifestation of the potentialities implicit in the doctrine of equality of opportunity, which was to emerge later as a cardinal American principle. Yet although Jefferson's social principles were wholly compatible with these views in a dynamic white society, his

13. Thomas Jefferson, *Notes on the State of Virginia*, ed. William Peden (Chapel Hill, 1954), 84–85, 142–43. Daniel J. Boorstin, *The Lost World of Thomas Jefferson* (New York, 1948).

14. He was apparently not aware of Cadwallader Colden's *History of the Five Indian Nations*, published earlier in the century and reprinted, Ithaca, 1958.

racial thinking seemed to move in the opposite direction. Smith, who with Rush believed that racial characteristics were produced by natural environment and could change with natural changes, also felt more comfortable than Jefferson in face of the possibility of Negro advance. For Smith, however, probably more than for Rush, this meant a progressive disappearance of "Negro" characteristics, and he found encouragement in the observation that black household servants were growing up with lighter skins. This was evidence that the races could grow together, the blacks amalgamating with the whites until all differences had disappeared. As sociological observation, it seems to have required, from a Presbyterian theologian, an engaging disposition to overlook the explanatory possibilities of sin. [15]

Theorists groping for a science of racial inequality encountered a stubborn obstacle in the limited time that man was believed to have inhabited the earth. According to the best information, deriving from the calculations of the seventeenth-century biblical scholar Archbishop Ussher, the world had been created in 4004 B.C., and this did not give mankind very long to have developed such marked differences, when one considered that no such differences could be traced to living memory. [16]

If on the other hand some non-heretical way could be found of circumventing the doctrine of a single creation, it would be much easier to believe that the visibly different human types had possessed their differing characteristics from the beginning. The urgency of finding such a solution was accentuated by information that Egyptian monuments had been found depicting Negro as well as more European figures. If these marked differences had somehow come about in the early years

15. Lyman H. Butterfield, ed., *The Letters of Benjamin Rush* (Princeton, 1951) 2:757–58, 785–86; Samuel Stanhope Smith, *Essay on the Causes and Variety of Complexion and Figure in the Human Species* (1787), ed. Winthrop D. Jordan (Cambridge, Mass., 1965), 11, 19, 28–30, 71–72, 103–05; Douglas Sloan, *The Scottish Enlightenment and the American College Ideal* (New York, 1971), 73–74; John P. Diggins, "Slavery, Race and Equality: Jefferson and the Pathos of the Enlightenment," *American Quarterly* 28:2 (Summer 1976), 206–08; Winthrop D. Jordan, *White Over Black: American Attitudes toward the Negro, 1550–1812* (Chapel Hill, 1968), ch. 12.

16. William Stanton, *The Leopard's Spots: Scientific Attitudes Towards Race in America, 1815–1959* (Chicago, 1960), 50.

after the origins of man, it was strange that no comparable process had been observed to take place over much longer subsequent periods.

These problems were the subject of speculation in eighteenth-century Europe. In Britain, Lord Kames and Erasmus Darwin (Charles Darwin's grandfather) proposed theories of human development, and notions of an evolutionary kind entered into popular thought and fancy in succeeding generations. In Europe these were mainly matters for scientific and popular curiosity. Even the writings of Count Gobineau, who in the mid-nineteenth century emerged as the first systematic exponent of theories of racial distinctiveness, had no immediate bearing on political policy. They did not, for example, modify the rise of European opposition to slavery.

In Britain a powerful emancipation movement could urge its cause in terms of humanity and religion without threatening the parliamentary classes with anything so unattractive as universal equality. This disclaimer was particularly important after the French Revolution had struck fear and horror into the hearts of the propertied classes. Thus, as David Brion Davis has observed, the British slave-trade abolitionists made a point of presenting themselves as "a force maintaining the existing political and constitutional structure"; and in 1799 the abolitionist bishop of Rochester replied to a charge of jacobinism that "the abolitionists had never talked of equality or the imprescriptible rights of man; they had strenuously upheld the existing gradations of society, objecting only to a power which no good king would claim." [17] The British system of parliamentary representation was itself gradually reformed during the nineteenth and early twentieth centuries to absorb the working people into what Gladstone once called "the pale of the Constitution," on the basis of a series of subtle redefinitions of the concept of the representation of interests. The process was extremely gradual, and could be turned to party advantage; but the great Emancipation Act of 1833, which freed the slaves in the British West Indies, did not confront the people of Britain with the problem of defining the political or social status of a large domestic population of freed blacks.

In this respect, American political theory, with its particular emphasis on equal rights, gave the American racial problem its own peculiar

17. David Brion Davis, *The Problem of Slavery in the Age of Revolution, 1770–1823* (Ithaca, 1975), 436–37.

character. There were certainly many American abolitionists who were moved by a sense of justice that did not extend to affection for blacks or to any desire to incorporate them into white society; the close connections between much early abolitionism and the movement for colonization of the slaves to be freed was enough to warn black Americans that they were not necessarily to regard themselves as being among friends.[18] We have noticed, also, that abolitionists had no sympathy for radically democratic interpretations of the social and economic problems of their times.[19] Abolitionists who did believe not only in universal equality of rights but in the equal potential of Negroes faced a double burden of argument. Abolitionists and their allies in the struggle for equal rights, although gaining strength with the advance of the movement in the mid-nineteenth century, encountered no more formidable obstacle to the extension of equal rights to free Negroes than the popular white belief in innate Negro inferiority.[20]

Neither American constitutional theory, nor the moral philosophy on which it was based, had any room for inequality of rights. The stark nature of the contradiction between racial slavery on the one hand and republican principles as professed in America was nowhere more apparent, or more difficult to deal with, than in confrontation with the equal principles of American law. For, unlike the forms of slavery known in the ancient world and in civilizations based on Roman law, American slavery was also a caste system. As such it tainted all persons of visibly African descent, whether slave or free. It is no exaggeration to say that the legal system was also reciprocally tainted, and in a manner that was detrimental to the interests of the whites. This was particularly apparent in the applications of the universal southern rule that the evidence of black people could not be admitted against whites. As slaves or free blacks were often the only witnesses to crimes committed by one white against another, the white administration of justice was immediately affected.[21]

The systematic restraints on the freedoms of free (or non-slave) black people, which had grown up rapidly around the turn of the century, were manifest denials of equality in politics, law, and opportunity. The logical

18. Fredrickson, *The Black Image*, 6–42.
19. As discussed in Chapter 6.
20. James M. McPherson, *The Struggle for Equality: Abolitionists and the Negro in the Civil War and Reconstruction* (Princeton, 1964), 134.
21. Genovese, *Roll, Jordan, Roll*, 40.

inconsistencies implicit in this position were most acute for southern courts, which though they found it difficult to develop a separate law of slavery from the traditions of the common law which they customarily administered to the white community, had no other standards for guidance. Southern judges moreover recognized that in dealing with slaves they were dealing with human beings, subject to human emotions; if slaves were to be *judged*, they must be held responsible for their actions, and it was irrational as well as inhumane to treat them as incapable of either rational judgment or moral principle.[22] Southern courts did not generally expect Negroes, whether slave or free, to be equal to the abilities of whites, but this might tend to make them less rather than more culpable for actions which white society held as crimes. Some southern judges went so far as to recognize that the observed limitations of Negro abilities might be considered as results of their circumstances rather than their nature. This, however, was taken to mean that since Negroes were in the habit of accepting humiliations which whites would find intolerable, they could be expected to have inferior sensibilities and to be less easily provoked. The courts did not dig very deep into black psychology. But they would not admit that either skin pigmentation or slavery had deprived blacks of all their rights: the murder of a slave was still murder—a crime of the utmost gravity, for which whites were occasionally punished and even hanged; and it was possible for a slave to kill a white man in self-defense and be acquitted of murder.[23]

If, however, as white society both North and South preferred to believe, the limits of Negro attainment were predetermined by racial endowment, equal *attainments* seemed impossible. It was not illogical for holders of these beliefs—which were questioned by many Abolitionists as time went on, but remained very largely unquestioned among most white Americans until after the middle of the twentieth century (and probably among Europeans, for that matter)—to conclude that people who were subject *by nature* to these limitations ought not to expect to share as equals in the life of the majority. This type of thinking resulted from the habit of treating individuals as members of preconceived groups or classes, and imagining that all aspects of individuality were

22. Ibid., 31–32; Mark Tushnet, *The American Law of Slavery, 1810–1860: Considerations of Humanity and Interest* (Princeton, 1981), 151.
23. Tushnet, *Law of Slavery*, 117–19; Genovese, *Roll, Jordan, Roll*, 28.

determined by that group membership. But blacks were not the only ones at risk when rights were controlled by race, ethnicity, or national origin. The abolitionists had exposed a problem which constitutional theory would not forever be able to ignore.

By the nature of their campaign, the abolitionists were to some extent responsible for stimulating a debate on the question of racial abilities and consequently for the emergence of early formulations of the idea of Negro inferiority. When abolitionists claimed that American society could absorb Africans as it had absorbed other peoples, books and pamphlets began to appear to confute these claims. The argument was encapsulated in the title of J.H. Van Evrie's publication, *Negroes and Negro "Slavery": The First an Inferior Race—the Latter its Normal Condition.* [24] These works drew heavily on biblical authority for slavery as an institution, on Aristotle for the view that some people are slaves by nature, on the record of African heathenism for the blessings brought to Negroes by Christianity, and on the history of Negro slavery for a circular proof that Negroes were fitted to be slaves. [25] Their general tone was theological, classical, and literary rather than scientific; they did not depend on natural or historical observations so much as on ancient rhetoric. Yet ever since Jefferson's musings on the possibility of Negro separateness, an unfurnished story had existed in the edifice of American thought, ready to be equipped with a more scientifically demonstrated theory of human inequality.

This vacancy was gradually filled during the first half of the nineteenth century by the development of an American school of anthropology. [26] The first substantial contribution was made by Dr. Samuel Morton of Philadelphia with laborious work in measuring human skulls, of which his shelves were lined with a formidable collection. Explanations that attributed physiological differences to differences of climate or circumstance could no longer be maintained in face of Morton's findings. The variations were impossible to reconcile to ideas of diverse developments from a unified creation within the biblical time span. Morton's findings were aid and comfort to racial theorists; but whatever his own

24. Quoted in McPherson, *Struggle for Equality;* I have not been able to consult the work there cited.

25. Eric L. McKitrick, ed., *Slavery Defended; the Views of the Old South* (Englewood Cliffs, N.J., 1963).

26. Stanton, *The Leopard's Spots,* 50.

motives, he hesitated before the risks of heresy incurred by these conclusions. It was left to Dr. Josiah Nott, a cheerful, bombastic physician and horse breeder practicing in Mobile, whose more blatant racial prejudices, blended with a breezy antipathy to the clergy, gave him the freedom to risk accusations of blasphemy by announcing to the American public that racial differences were attributable to the fact that the races of mankind had sprung from different original creations.[27]

Nott's polemical compilation incorporated much of the work of Morton and other investigators who had been carrying the search to the remains of ancient civilizations. Meanwhile, however, more dependable studies were in process of producing a more fundamental revision by altering the entire perspective within which Nott and his contemporaries had worked. The emergence of a science of geology in Britain, especially in the hands of Sir Charles Lyell, compelled people to contemplate the possibility that the Bible gave a misleading account of the origins of the earth. The process, it began to appear, had been gradual and continuous, not sudden and complete.[28] Then in 1858 Charles Darwin and Alfred Russel Wallace presented joint communications to the Linnaean Society in London expounding a theory of the evolution of species through natural selection. The effect of this revolution in science was to transform the whole time span of human development; there was no longer any need to find explanations for change within the short term of years that Nott and his predecessors had allotted to mankind since the creation. Their speculations became irrelevant.

The advance of the science of nature and man had ironic consequences for the more urgent problem of the art of human relations. It became easier to account scientifically for the perceived differences among the earth's peoples; the rigidities of older thought were gradually loosened in favor of general ideas of development in which primitive, savage, or backward races could be conveniently arranged at remote stages in the line of development which placed Europeans, and Americans of European descent, at the summit of progress. Yet this was itself an evolutionary development. These teachings could not be rapidly absorbed or easily digested, and for many Americans as for many British lay people

27. Josiah Nott, *Types of Mankind* (Philadelphia, 1854).

28. Roy Porter, *The Making of Geology: Earth Science in Britain, 1660–1815* (Cambridge, 1977).

and clergy, Darwin was heresy.[29] Louis Agassiz, a zoologist of considerable renown in Switzerland before he left in 1846 for the United States and settled as a professor at Harvard, made a much more acceptable contribution when he tried to contain his own belief in separate racial origins within the precepts of formal religion.

Agassiz had both higher academic standing and more influence on events than most of his contemporaries. His position at Harvard threw him into personal relations with many politically active Boston intellectuals, with whom he exchanged ideas. One of them was Samuel Gridley Howe, who served in 1863 and 1864 as a member of the American Freedmen's Inquiry Commission, which supplied information and proposals to the joint congressional committee planning for the postwar South. Howe sought Agassiz's views on practical problems, to which Agassiz responded that, while he welcomed emancipation, it would be dangerous to grant the newly freed blacks full equality in political and social rights. The history of the Negroes in Africa and the West revealed them, in Agassiz's opinion, as "indolent, playful, sensual, imitative, subservient, good-natured, versatile, unsteady in their purpose, devoted and affectionate." But in all this there was no evidence of qualifications for self-government. "I cannot think it just or safe," he observed, "to grant at once to the negro all the privileges which we ourselves have acquired by long struggles. . . . Let us beware of granting too much to the negro race at the beginning, lest it becomes necessary hereafter to deprive

---

29. Lyell's polemical *Principles of Geology* (1830) attacked the traditional association of science and theology; as late as 1830 he considered it his mission "to free science from Moses." Porter, *Making of Geology*, 2. The question of the antiquity of the human race, however, had a different dimension in both natural history and theology, from that of the antiquity of the earth. It would be a misreading of Porter's intentions to interpret this actually rather late expression of conflict on the latter issue as the theme of his book. Porter shows that among an increasingly widely read body of earth scientists, speculations about the age of the earth and the authenticity of Genesis had been going on even in the late seventeenth century. Geology in fact became an early form of "popular" science because anybody could pick up fossils or observe strata. The Geological Society of London, founded in 1807, made no mention of theology in its *Transactions*. Lyell himself had attended geology lectures as an undergraduate at Oxford (146–48). These intellectual and related utilitarian interests do not seem to have had much resonance in the United States, where much educated opinion was more heavily under the influence of fundamentalist theology. For the restraining effects of theology on scientific speculation in the United States, see Bruce Kuklick, *Churchmen and Philosophers from Jonathan Edwards to John Dewey* (New Haven, 1985).

them of some of the privileges which they may use to their and our detriment."[30] Remarks of this sort were often made, on prudential grounds such as the freedmen's lack of experience, without recourse to special scientific knowledge; and Agassiz did not rule out all possibility that Negroes might develop characteristics fitted to self-government; the only trouble was that this sort of advice tended to fulfill its own assumptions by ruling out all possibility of establishing conditions in which such development would have any hope of taking place.

Ideals of equality gained strength as the struggle with the South became more desperate and prolonged; they inspired much of the effort that won the Civil War for the Union.[31] But the failures of Reconstruction threw the hopes of both freedmen and northern abolitionists increasingly onto the defensive. And as the effort shrank and failed, views such as those of Louis Agassiz, and later of Darwin's successors, who adapted the idea of the struggle for survival into a national, racial, or economic process, made it increasingly acceptable to regard black Americans as lower down the evolutionary scale than whites. The word *primitive* expressed this idea by setting them closer to the human race's primal origins. In their aboriginal surroundings, such peoples, who were becoming better known through the European and American scramble for overseas territories, but less attractive since the disappearance of the romance of the noble savage, were increasingly perceived as human shoots that had somehow been arrested in the evolutionary stages of childhood or adolescence. In this light, it was temptingly easy to excuse the political failures of Reconstruction on grounds of Negro corruption and incompetence, deflecting from northern politicians both blame for the past and responsibility for the future.[32] One of the more pervasive intellectual consequences was an attitude to race that regarded the African American as an anomaly, a stranded representative of the backward peoples of Africa, in need of goodwill, care, and protection, of

---

30. McPherson, *Struggle for Equality*, 145–46.

31. McPherson, *Battle Cry of Freedom* (New York, 1988), 494–95; Eric Foner, *Reconstruction: America's Unfinished Revolution, 1863–1867* (New York, 1988), 254–55.

32. Foner, *Reconstruction*, 498–99. Foner demonstrates that as their nerves failed and their efforts shifted to other scenes, northern liberals rapidly turned to blaming the southern blacks for their own misfortunes.

course, but hopelessly incapable of aspiring to the heights of Western civilization.

Abraham Lincoln had made it clear that in his view Americans were not placed under any obligation to translate the ideals of the Declaration of Independence into institutional terms. In the South, however, the explicit language of the Declaration caused less moral conflict; as southern spokesmen affirmed both slavery and the racial basis of southern institutions as a positive benefit to both black and white in their different but complementary roles, the Declaration lost all meaning for southern thought, was rejected as a false doctrine devoid of all moral or constitutional force, and became a source of discord rather than harmony between the South and the rest of the nation.

Southern spokesmen turned from the defense of their own institutions to scathing and scornful attacks on the hypocrisy of the capitalist North. John Taylor of Caroline County, Virginia, had much earlier discerned something akin to slavery in the condition of industrial workers; but after the rise of abolitionism in the North, John C. Calhoun and later George Fitzhugh turned the critique of northern life and ideals into a systematic social theory.

Calhoun's insistence on the importance of progress as a condition of civilization was as positive as that of any northern businessman; his arguments retained the essence of a commitment to equality of opportunity among whites; and he agreed that the equality of citizens in the eyes of the law was essential to liberty in a popular government. But he denounced the doctrine that "liberty cannot be perfect without perfect equality"—a view that would have been found only among the most radical circles in the North, and certainly not among the bulk of the abolitionists—and argued that the highly unequal distribution of human abilities could only mean that liberty would in the normal course of events give rise to inequalities of condition. Inequality of condition, the natural result of liberty, was indispensable to progress. This last point represents a significant addition to the arguments about natural inequalities which were heard repeatedly in the debates about the nation's future both during and shortly after the founding of the Constitution. People at that time thought of improvement, and linked the improvement of individual fortunes with those of the community; the concept of "progress" was at best in process of formation.

But in these reflections, published posthumously in his *Disquisition on*

Government, Calhoun, for all his protestations, expressed himself in the language of bourgeois capitalism.[33] Some ten years before his death, in 1838, South Carolina's leading spokesman had offered the South a somewhat more attractive image of itself, and one which he neither abandoned nor ever fully reconciled to the idea of individualistic competition. Southern states, he said, were "an aggregate, in fact of communities, not of individuals. Every plantation is a little community, with a master at its head, who concentrates in himself the united interests of capital and labor, of which he is the common representative. The small communities aggregated make the State in all, whose action, labor, and capital is equally represented and perfectly harmonized."[34] It was an affecting picture, though it failed to provide room for competition even among members of the master race, which political and economic liberty were bound to permit. But whatever the inconsistencies of argument or imperfections in his evidence, Calhoun, with his picture of the harmony of the South, could claim to have presented an attractive alternative to the economic tyranny of the factory system and the abrasive individualism which ruled the social morality of the North.[35]

George Fitzhugh, the first American to use the word *sociology* in the title of a book, was more statistically informed if less systematically rigorous than Calhoun. Fitzhugh's most remarkable quality was his fearless pursuit of the consequences of his own reasoning. He accepted both the commonplace view that all high civilizations rested in some degree on the exploitation of labor, and the historical interpretation which derived laissez-faire capitalism from the liberation of the individual at the Reformation, whence had followed the doctrines of human equality, the sovereignty of the individual, and the right to private judgment, down to their logical consequences in the brutally competitive and acquisitive economy of the modern industrial era. Fitzhugh differed from most of his contemporaries by adopting opposite sentiments about these events.

33. *A Disquisition on Government,* in Richard K. Crallé, ed., *Works of John C. Calhoun,* 6 vols. (Columbia, 1851–57; rpr., New York, 1968), 56–57.

34. McKitrick, *Slavery Defended,* 6–11.

35. For this view there was powerful contemporary support in the North itself. Consider the reforming theologian Horace Bushnell: "The tendency of all our modern speculations is to an extreme individualism, and we carry our doctrines of free will so far as to make little or nothing of organic laws." *Views of Christian Nurture* (Hartford, 1847), 20, 21–22.

Apart from the Reformation, which he described as an act of a society shaking off the evils of its past, he denounced instead of praising the whole process. He was equally scornful of the softness of Locke and the superficiality of Jefferson, while he attacked Adam Smith's individualist economics and Blackstone's insistence on individual liberty under English law.

The American Revolution had nothing to do with personal equality. It was a social act, the act of an adult society gaining its independence from another society. In a powerful statement of protective paternalism, he declared, "Liberty and free competition invite and encourage the attempt of the strong to master the weak, and ensure their success." Men were not born entitled to equal rights, but only to rights appropriate to their condition; competition among men made each man the enemy of his fellow. Subordination and slavery, on the other hand, begat peace and goodwill.[36] Thus, although accepting the conventional view as earlier argued by Federalists that equality of rights would lead to inequality of conditions, Fitzhugh diverged sharply from its earlier and later proponents, including Calhoun, when he attacked that inequality as a cruel exploitation of the weak and vulnerable. The concept of equal rights was a pernicious trap through which the weak and vulnerable fell to their destruction in a world in which they lacked the power to compete. In a curious way, this theme was to be echoed more than a century later by the speakers for women who resisted a constitutional Equal Rights Amendment out of the very real fear that it would force women to compete, unequally, in a men's world.

Although Fitzhugh believed that Negroes were best suited to slavery, he does not seem to have been animated by the more obvious racial antipathies, and down to the Civil War, when he changed his mind, he regarded racial contempt as a bad reason for slavery because it led to debasement and abuse.[37] He differed from Calhoun and from many of his contemporary controversialists on both sides of the slavery issue in having a benign disposition, little real feeling of enmity for his ideological opponents, and a genuine compassion for the sufferings of the factory system. He drew much of his information about its worst abuses from

36. George Fitzhugh, *Sociology for the South* (Richmond, 1854), 179, 56–57, 183.

37. He severely criticized *Types of Mankind* for inculcating contempt and brutality instead of protective affection by masters to their slaves. Ibid., 95.

the same British sources as Marx and Engels, in which Fitzhugh saw a close resemblance to the development of wage-slavery in the American North. In a tone strikingly similar to that of the socialists and early communists of his time, he attacked the economic individualists for their irresponsible disregard for the consequences of their own doctrines in their pursuit of wealth. For Fitzhugh, who believed that doctrines of equality could not be derived from nature because they rested on a falsification of nature, the answer to modern trends lay in restoring paternalistic responsibility in the extreme form of slavery. He was severe on the consequences of equality that he supposed (wrongly) had operated in Ireland, asserting that half a million had died of hunger there in one year because "in the eye of the law they were equals, and liberty had made them enemies, of their landlords and employers. Had they been vassals or serfs," he added, presumably averting his gaze from Russia, "they would have been beloved, cherished and taken care of by those same landlords and employers. Slaves never die of hunger, scarcely ever feel want." Meanwhile in America, the blacks, being incapable of higher attainments, were fittingly employed in laying the foundations for the South's superior civilization.[38]

This school of thought was yet to receive its highest benediction. When Alexander H. Stephens of Georgia took his seat as vice-president of the Confederate States of America, he took his stand against the expressed beliefs of Jefferson and the founders of the Republic. "Our new Government," he declared, "is founded upon exactly the opposite ideas; its foundations are laid, its cornerstone rests upon the great truth that the negro is not the equal to the white man; that slavery, subordination to the superior race, is his natural and normal condition. This, our new

38. Fitzhugh developed his views in *Cannibals All! Or, Slaves without Masters* (Richmond, 1857), ed. C. Vann Woodward (Cambridge, Mass., 1960). See also Harvey Wish, *George Fitzhugh, Propagandist of the Old South* (Baton Rouge, 1943; rpr., Gloucester, Mass., 1962). This line of argument also had its roots; it had made its appearance when the slave trade came under attack in the 1770s. David Brion Davis has noted that "as early as 1772 *The Scots' Magazine* reprinted an essay from a London paper comparing the condition of the West Indian slaves to that of English common laborers, who were 'more real slaves to necessity, than to Egyptian taskmasters.' In some respects the slaves were better cared for; and the freedom of English laborers was 'the liberty of changing their masters for the same wages.' But they would 'still remain slaves to the necessity of constant and hard labour.' " This essay gained the endorsement of Anthony Benezet as an indictment of English conditions. Davis, *Slavery in the Age of Revolution*, 462.

Government, is the first in the history of the world, based upon this great physical, philosophical and moral truth."[39]

It did not follow from this theory that the same inequalities needed to exist in the white population. The system of white supremacy has in fact been credited with sustaining the morale of the whites in general—a sort of spurious sense of equality.[40] But four years after Stephens had spoken and the rubble had been cleared away, the cornerstone of the Confederacy appeared to have survived in remarkably good condition. It was soon afterward to be used as the base for a strikingly similar architectural structure. As the planting classes struggled to regain their old ascendancy over the economic and social structure of the region, sharecropping and tenancy and various forms of exploitation of the weak by the strong among the small white farmers as well as the blacks, became considerably more oppressive than—excluding slavery—they had before the war. Equality did not flourish in Southern soil.[41]

Racial harmony could have been achieved along the lines of white supremacy by establishing a state of intellectual as well as legal and physical black subordination. Blacks, however, were not so easily deceived as their masters chose to imagine. There is abundant evidence that slaves understood their situation and exploited weaknesses in their overlords' characters with a subtlety undreamed of by the whites.[42] Free Negroes were better informed and had more opportunity to express themselves. When they convened to petition legislatures or present their case to the public, they rejected the inevitability of their subordinate status, and frequently invoked the founding principles of the Republic.[43] For the most part they turned, not only against the degrading concept of caste, but against the inevitability of any form of racial pluralism under the Constitution.

39. Quoted by McPherson, *Struggle for Equality*, 61.

40. C. Vann Woodward, *American Counterpoint: Slavery and Racism in the North-South Dialogue* (Boston, 1971), ch. 4. Fitzhugh made the same point in *Sociology for the South*, 255, though it would not seem to have been central to his purpose.

41. Gavin Wright, *The Political Economy of the Cotton South* (New York, 1978), esp. ch. 6; Jonathan M. Wiener, *Social Origins of the New South: Alabama, 1860–1885* (Baton Rouge, 1978).

42. For extensive evidence and discussion, see Genovese, *Roll, Jordan, Roll*, esp. 431–41 and the story told on 611.

43. See in general the documents collected in Herbert A. Aptheker, ed., *A Documentary History of the Negro People in the United States* (New York, 1951) 1:17–459.

The Constitution, and the politics which made it work, gave little grounds for any sort of hope. Other remedies had to be sought. In 1852, Martin R. Delany, an outstanding black physician and editor, expressed his despair of improvement by proposing a movement for voluntary emigration. His first move was a book called *The Condition, Elevation, Emigration and Destiny of the Colored People of the United States Politically Considered.*[44] Two years later he followed this by organizing a convention which was well attended, despite the hostility of some of the abolitionists and of Frederick Douglass, with whom Delany had previously worked in close collaboration.[45]

From the black abolitionist point of view, emigration was acceptance of defeat. Douglass believed to the end of his life in the possibility of racial amalgamation—a faith he consummated by his second marriage, to a white woman. Delany by the time of his book had come to regard this as an illusion. Delany's defiant pronouncements contain some of the earliest declarations of black racial pride as well as national separatism; in this they suggest the origins of a movement that could have looked toward some form of protective pluralism. But Delany did not believe that any form of protection was to be had under the Constitution, and went into voluntary (though socially experimental) exile in Canada, to return only when the Civil War and Reconstruction seemed to open new hopes for the black people.

Delany dismissed those abolitionists who saw racial harmony within the Union as the only solution. To believe in harmony was not necessarily to be convinced of the basic similarity of the races, still less of the interchangeability of individuals. Yet it was one thing to observe obvious differences of appearance or aptitude; it was quite another thing to believe either that they reflected inherent, genetically fixed characteristics that could not change with training or circumstance, or that such qualities were in any case socially undesirable. White abolitionists who genuinely befriended the blacks, rather than merely wanting to get rid of them, often found themselves trying to put a friendly complexion on the observed differences between the races. In their hands these differences did not always appear to the advantage of Europeans. Theodore

44. Victor Ullman, *Martin R. Delany, the Beginnings of Black Nationalism* (Boston, 1971), 140–50.
45. Ibid., 153–60.

Tilton, a feminist as well as an abolitionist, explained racial variety through a romantic racialism which exalted the Negro character as being akin to the best of feminine virtues. "In all the intellectual activities which take their strange quickening from the moral faculties—which we call instincts, intuitions—the negro is superior to the white man, equal to the white woman," Tilton told a New York audience during the Civil War. What America needed was more of the Negro characteristics to modify the aggressiveness of the whites.[46] Moncure Daniel Conway, a Virginian patrician turned abolitionist, saw social advantage in the differences of racial qualities. European superiority in intellect and energy was balanced by black superiority in goodliness, kindliness, and "affectionateness"; a mixture of the races could be expected to produce a better character than either possessed by itself.[47] Others not unnaturally remarked on the instinctive Negro feeling for music and the Negro understanding of religion.

These views in all their variety reflected the attempts of serious minds to grapple with perplexing problems which certainly presented the gravest of social issues. From the black point of view, however, even the opinions of their white friends had an important disadvantage. They all tended to agree that blacks were defective in those hard, acquisitive, and competitive qualities which dominated the world of European and especially of American business. Equal rights might have a protective function; but they would still lead to unequal conditions, and unequal conditions as the outcome of the struggle for survival were used in turn to prove that Negroes were inferior in abilities.[48] There can have been few whites who really expected the Negroes to prove themselves capable of competing as equals, and still fewer who felt that it was part of the government's responsibility to compensate Negroes—or anyone else—for lack of qualities with which they had not been endowed. The competitive disadvantages that Negroes faced both North and South were overwhelming rather than merely unequal. Nothing in their history or training or in their political, economic, or social position gave them power to exert much control over this competition. But an increasingly

46. James M. McPherson, "A Brief for Equality: The Abolitionist Reply to the Racist Myth, 1860–65," in Martin Duberman, ed., *The Antislavery Vanguard* (Princeton, 1965), 166.

47. Ibid., 165–66.

48. Foner, *Reconstruction*, 496–99.

preoccupied and indifferent white world was easily able to reconcile itself to the difficulties experienced by American blacks in holding their own in the struggle; it was really no more than what one had expected.

Political Community Redefined

From the time of the Dred Scott decision of 1857, free Negroes were not citizens of the United States. This meant that American political society was so defined as to give legal sanction to a virtual caste system; a substantial portion of the population, who now stood under the law within but not of the republic, were declared to have no rights that a white man need respect. Even where Negroes did possess the rights of citizens, as in Massachusetts, a legal precedent had recently marked the outlines of a fundamental differentiation in rights. In 1849 Chief Justice Lemuel Shaw in the case of *Roberts v. The City of Boston* first announced the doctrine that was to become known as separate-but-equal—that the provision of separate facilities did not impair equality of rights if the facilities themselves were equal.[49] The Commonwealth of Massachusetts reversed this policy in 1855 when it introduced a law providing common schools without racial segregation.[50] But on a national scale, the Civil War would have been fought to little purpose if it had resulted in a hardening of a caste system sanctioned by the Constitution. Yet those who held these views found themselves confronted by a hostile president in Andrew Johnson, a recalcitrant South, and an unstable congressional and popular majority. While that majority lasted, its representatives lost little time in passing the Civil Rights Act of 1866 to confer citizenship on the freed slaves; under these provisions, citizens "of every race and color" were to enjoy equal status in all civil and legal transactions with equal protection for person and property.[51]

This was the first time in American history that Congress had consid-

49. 5 Cush. (Mass.) 198; Leonard W. Levy, "The Roberts Case: The Source for the 'Separate but Equal' Doctrine," *American Historical Review* 56 (1958), 510–18; David Donald, *Charles Sumner and the Coming of the Civil War* (New York, 1960), 180–81.

50. J. Morgan Kousser, " 'The Supremacy of Equal Rights': The Struggle Against Racial Discrimination in Antebellum Massachusetts and the Foundations of the Fourteenth Amendment," *Northwestern University Law Review* 82:4 (Summer 1988), 988–99.

51. 14 *Stat.* 27; W.R. Brock, *An American Crisis: Congress and Reconstruction, 1865–1867* (London, 1963), 111–15; Michael Les Benedict, *A Compromise of Principle: Congressional Republicans and Reconstruction, 1863–1869* (New York, 1974), 162–68.

ered it necessary to pass a civil rights act. For the most part, the field of civil rights both in definition and responsibility for enforcement had been left to the states; and the Supreme Court itself had held in 1833 that the Fifth Amendment to the Federal Constitution did not apply to the states,[52] thus at a stroke rendering the bulk of the Bill of Rights nugatory as far as the states were concerned. Equality before the law had always been a primary category of equality. Radical Republicans in the Reconstruction era attached more importance to this principle than to that of political equality exercised through the suffrage.[53] Yet the Civil Rights Act was the beginning of a process through which the concept of equality before the law was itself to be subtly but profoundly redefined.

The immediate problem, however, was to fix its existing definition. An act of Congress was a frail vessel for the protection of fundamental rights, which ought in principle to have constitutional status; the Republicans had good reason to fear that a future Democratic majority might simply repeal the statute. Citizenship had to be written into the Constitution, and for very substantial political reasons, the southern states had to be induced to allow their black populations to vote. In democratic theory, the problem of raising the blacks—whether or not formerly slaves—to the constitutional status of citizenship with all its privileges and immunities, was not dissimilar to that involved in extending the suffrage to wider classes of whites. The general principle of majority rule had by this time been almost universally adopted through the reform of state constitutions. But Negro suffrage encountered terrific resistance. To confer the suffrage on blacks was a more than formal political act: it meant taking them into the political community. Taney himself, when he used the expression "political community," had equated it with "this new political family."

The immediate political necessity of enabling blacks to vote arose less from an uncomplicated dedication to political equality than from a paradox in the electoral system. The danger to the Republican majorities in Congress arose from the fact that, once the freedmen were included in the numerical basis of representation, the representation of the southern states would actually *increase* as a direct result of the Civil War—which, unless remedied, would of course mean the representation of the

52. *Barron v. Baltimore*, 7 Peters 243.
53. Foner, *Reconstruction*, 60.

white South. When freedmen were counted in the basis of representation, but deprived of their own votes, their old masters would emerge stronger than before, even in the counsels of the union. The Fourteenth Amendment proposed to rectify this situation by the indirect means of depriving southern states of their share of representation if they failed to confer the suffrage on their whole eligible population—including the blacks. [54]

The debates on the Fourteenth Amendment when it first came up in 1866 made very clear that much influential white sentiment was extremely hostile to any idea of sharing this community with blacks on equal terms, or indeed on any terms. These resistances, combined with a certain caution and lack of emphatic commitment among many Republicans, help to explain why the Fourteenth Amendment was always intended as an act of persuasion rather than compulsion. To the extent that Radical Republicans were able to reconcile themselves to this incomplete measure it was because they hoped that it would prove more compulsive than in fact it did, and would consequently bring about a gradual but effective Negro suffrage by indirect means.

It was easy for opponents of the Fourteenth Amendment to point out that many northern states still refused to extend the suffrage to Negroes even after the Civil War. This was a constant source of weakness in the Radicals' position. It made them vulnerable both to the moderate and not intolerant conservatism of the elderly Democratic Senator Reverdy Johnson of Maryland, who said in the Senate that there was not a man within the sound of his voice who had any feeling against the black race, and the more vituperative Thomas Hendricks of Indiana, who though well within the sound of Johnson's voice denied any desire to make the Negroes into voters. "Without reference to the question of equality," he said, "I say we are not of the same race; we are so different that we ought not to compose one political community." He even rejected claims that the blacks had helped the North to win the war. That, perhaps, would have helped them to establish a claim to belong to the "political community" which had again appeared in Hendricks's vocabulary. [55]

---

54. These struggles have been chronicled in detail in several important works, among which reference may be made to Eric Foner's *Reconstruction* and Michael Les Bendict, *A Compromise of Principle.*

55. *Congressional Globe,* 39th Cong., 1st sess. (1866), 766, 860, 833–35.

Both sides clearly understood the issue; each knew what the other was contending for. The genuine racialists, whether apologetic like Johnson or outspoken like Hendricks, felt a deep repugnance at the idea of admitting Negroes into the circle whose circumference marked out the limits of political participation; and they maintained this hostility, not because Negroes were ignorant or inexperienced (in which connection Daniel Clark of New Hampshire remarked sarcastically that he had "never found one of those persons who oppose negro suffrage upon the ground of ignorance willing to exclude the white man for the same reason. . . . If the negro should learn to read and write before he votes, let the white man do the same"), but because political participation was itself a form of social activity.

Hendricks's remarks were drawn out in reply to an emotional speech by Clark two days earlier. The theoretical basis of Clark's views was a pure form of American republicanism. He hotly denied the power of Congress to confer the vote on the Negro as a gift or a boon: "The black man has just as much right to his vote as the white man has to his; and the white man has no more authority to confer or withhold it than the black man." The black man's rights had been equal from the beginning; the Declaration of Independence, which laid down that governments derived their just powers from the consent of the governed, implied that the governed could of right, not as a privilege, give or withhold consent—which they did with their vote.

Clark was moving along the recognized categories of equality. Equal political rights were the means by which the blacks could gain access to their other rights. "Man derives the right from his manhood and the quality of his manhood with his fellow-men," he explained. But this led him to the social question:

Does anyone say, Mr. President, that this is negro equality? So it is—political equality—not social. This last is not the creature of legislation, or political organization, but of taste, propriety, and fitness. In some of the States the negro has now, and has for a long time had, the same political rights as the white man. The law makes no distinction for or against him, but he is left to acquire that position in society to which his abilities and behavior entitle him.

There was here a quiet affirmation that the Negro was entitled to equality of opportunity, coupled with the belief, common at the time though sociologically somewhat optimistic, that political equality would gain access for him to his other social entitlements.

Clark's views of political rights came back again and again to the common humanity of men; it was in that common humanity that they were to be considered equal. "Here is the difficulty," he declared, "that the negro is a man! and however degraded, inferior, abject, or humble, it is our duty to elevate and improve him, and to give him the means of elevation and improvement; and the senator from Kentucky may prove that there are thirty-six, or fifty-six, or a hundred and six points of difference between him and the white man, but until he shows that he is not a man, the negro will be entitled to be treated as a man, and to demand and enjoy the same privileges as other men." Henry Wilson of Massachusetts and Thaddeus Stevens of Pennsylvania, neither of whom had earlier regarded the suffrage as the foremost issue, expected the Fourteenth Amendment to produce the desired results within five years, and regarded the suffrage as an instrument in the pursuit of wider ends.[56] Clark's position, which was pure in its republican principles, implied that a government not based on universal suffrage was illegitimate, and by inference lacking in lawful authority over those who were not allowed to vote.

As finally passed, the Fourteenth Amendment established American citizenship for all persons born or naturalized in the United States, forbade any state to deny to citizens of the United States the privileges and immunities of citizenship, and extended to all persons, whether citizens or not, the equal protection of the laws. That expression has been traced to Andrew Jackson—though we have noted that Jackson would never have extended it to blacks. The suffrage provisions were most intensively and fully debated. But the attempted persuasion failed to persuade, and the Fourteenth Amendment had to be followed by the Fifteenth, whose force (though limited) was compulsive. The essence of this remodeling of the Constitution was that it withdrew from the states a portion of the power they had constitutionally exercised over their own electoral systems. Even the Fifteenth Amendment, which represented the outcome of much tortuous compromise, was both negative in form and limited in content. It said simply, "The right of citizens of the United States to vote shall not be denied or abridged by the United states, or by any State, on account of race, color, or previous condition of servitude."

56. Ibid., 1254; H.R. 2459.

This simplicity concealed a wealth of meaning, most of it to the disadvantage of those persons of "color, or previous condition of servitude" whom the Amendment purported to protect. All attempts to include the right of nomination to public office, which at one point seemed to have a fair chance of adoption, had to be dropped in order to win enough conservative support to pass the amendment; and its negative form left the states free to impose other kinds of restriction. [57] The states lost control only of the items enumerated: another hundred years were to pass before the federal government took full possession of the field. As Oliver Morton of Indiana, who did as much as any member of the Senate to steer the amendment to its passage, remarked in exasperation near to despair: "This amendment leaves the whole power in the States just as it exists now, except that colored men shall not be disfranchised for the three reasons of race, color, or previous condition of slavery. They may be disfranchised for want of education or for want of intelligence. . . . They may, perhaps, require property or educational tests, and that would cut off the great majority of colored men from voting in those States, and thus this amendment would be practically defeated in all those States where the great body of colored people live." [58] By the early years of the twentieth century the former Confederate states had confirmed every detail of Morton's prognosis.

The debates on the Fifteenth Amendment reached deeper into the social context of constitutional problems than those on the Fourteenth. The Radicals now tried to make the great occasion of constitutional amendment into an opportunity for a real advance—or redirection—of American society in the sense that lay nearer to their conception of its ideological basis. Morton argued that exclusion from the suffrage on grounds of property or religion was a denial of democratic principles and republican sentiment, which he claimed was "rife throughout the whole nation." Henry Wilson spoke with feeling about the human quality of the relationship which ought to subsist among the people, white and black: "I recognize him not only as a countryman, a fellow citizen," he said of the black man, "but as a brother, given by his Creator the same rights that belong to me." The amendment was not an end; it was a step, an instrument of a greater program. Equality, Wilson declared, was an

57. Ibid., 40th Cong., 3rd sess. (1869), 1307, 1623, 1624.
58. Ibid., 863.

unfinished task: "If the black man in this country is made equal with the white man—and I hope he will be soon—I mean, by the blessing of God, while I live to hope on and to work on to make every white man the equal of every other white man. I believe in equality among citizens—equality in the broadest and most comprehensive democratic sense. No man should have rights depending on the accidents of life." [59]

The very exhaustiveness of the debates on the social values associated with the right to vote, as well as on its political significance, tends to conceal a still deeper change that these debates portended in American political ideology. No version of equality had been more fundamental than that of equality before the law, to which American political jurisprudence returned again and again as a touchstone for other values. This bedrock character tended to give the idea a sort of immovability, as though it were a solid base on which other values could be built. But the concept of equality before the law was itself experiencing subtle but profound changes.

This process began with the civil rights bill, passed as an act in 1866. To Radicals, as Eric Foner has observed, "equality before the law was an expansive doctrine embracing nearly every phase of public life." But while moderates envisaged a bill whose purpose would be served by securing to blacks the right to enter into contracts and compete equally with whites as free laborers, other congressmen saw the bill as giving additional leverage to poor and weak laborers in the struggle for employment and the means of holding and enjoying the proceeds of their toil. [60]

In the history of American political ideas, derived as they were from England, rights had originally been protective, defending the individual against abuse, cruelty, oppression; the concept of rights was an essentially defensive concept. But two aspects of the new situation had a possibly unexpected effect on the character of rights. One of these resulted directly from the nature of the federal system in the United States. Once it had become the office of the federal government to superintend the rights of its citizens, and to ensure the equal protection of the law to all *persons*, there began to develop a potentiality for a more active view of the nature of rights themselves. The federal power to

intervene became a federal power to ordain and determine, and it would be the function of federal officials to decide what conditions satisfied their concept of rights. In the Reconstruction period this function fell mainly to the officers of the Freedmen's Bureau, an agency set up primarily to administer relief in the immediate crisis, and whose life was terminated by Congress in 1869; these officers did not invariably perform it to the satisfaction of the people they were charged to protect. But it was a function which in principle could, and a century later would, pass to the Department of Justice in the federal government. By that time, the concept of rights as embodied in the Constitution had become an instrument of policy in a sense that was certainly not fully intended by more than a few of the makers of the Civil Rights Act of 1866 or the Fourteenth Amendment. But it had its origins there.

This second process, which did not depend on the federal structure, was part of that enlargement of the concept of law perceived and aimed at by Radicals. It was, in effect, to make the constitutional principle of equality before the law serve the purposes of another category, that of equality of opportunity. That is what speakers in Congress meant when they spoke of enabling blacks—and enabling all weak and poor workers—to enter into the workforce on terms of fair and equal competition. These were only beginnings. The opposing forces of corporate capital and racial prejudice were formidable; but the beginnings were significant, because they pointed to the possibilities of a social interventionism that had not been attributed to the law in previous generations—and, where it had operated unperceived, had certainly never pointed in the same direction.

Equality before the law had originated as an essentially *procedural* category; it ensured that the same processes would apply to all persons regardless of rank or position and it would by the same token make the law equally accessible to all. From these beginnings in the midst of Reconstruction, however, until its richer flowering in the civil rights revolution of the twentieth century, equality before the law became an active doctrine of interventionist social policy.[61]

61. Equality before the law was also a doctrine of social policy, as will be seen in Chapter 8, when the doctrine of separate-but-equal was promulgated by the Supreme Court in 1896 (*Plessy v. Ferguson*, 163 U.S. 537). But it was negative policy in both the senses of the above paragraph. The federal relation was used only to leave the making of social policy to the discretion of the state legislature, and the implications, for equality

The Individualist Basis of Equality of Rights

These debates brought forward into the conscience of legislators and their constituents a moral perception which some of them gladly proclaimed but from which others recoiled. That perception was that, where rights were concerned, equality was indivisible. To give equality to the black in political rights was an act, not a mere gesture; with that political equality, blacks might do what they could, but no principle in the moral law which sanctioned American democratic thought could stand between equality in legal and political rights and the full equality of individuals, *as individuals*, throughout American society. Black spokesmen were particularly articulate about this connection. "We claim," one of them asserted in a Montgomery newspaper in 1867,

exactly *the same rights, privileges and immunities as are enjoyed by white men*—we ask nothing more and will be content with nothing less. . . . The law [he went on, anticipating Justice Harlan's dissent in *Plessy v. Ferguson* nearly thirty years later] no longer knows white nor black, but simply men, and consequently we are entitled to ride in public conveyances, hold office, sit on juries and do everything else which we have in the past been prevented from doing solely on the ground of color.

How far this feeling had spread and how clearly it was understood was discovered by Martin Delany, back from his Canadian exile and active in South Carolina, when he "found it dangerous to go into the country and speak of color in any manner whatever, without the angry rejoinder, 'we don't want to hear that; we are all one color now.' "[62]

The American concept of equality had become, by the necessity of the case, a subject of enlarged public consciousness and intense refinement. But persons of the most racially radical views did not find their ways to the same conclusions in other aspects of social conscience. Charles Sumner, who had always been a Manchester liberal in economics, told the Senate in 1871 that he would prohibit separate cars for white and black travelers but would not interfere with the provision of first, second,

---

of opportunity, of the entire situation that gave rise to the action, were not even considered.

62. Montgomery *Alabama State Sentinel*, 21 May 1867; Robert G. Fitzgerald Diary, 22 April 1868, Robert G. Fitzgerald Papers, Schomburg Center for Research in Black Culture; as quoted by Foner, *Reconstruction*, 288, n. 15.

and third class accommodations: "That is simply a matter of price."[63] The problems of class relations were not on the agenda of Radical Republican policy. Sumner in this situation was really concerned, though he did not say so, with equality of esteem, as between persons perceived to be of different races. In a political economy which still hoped to offer opportunity on an equal basis, the problem of esteem as between the wealthy and the less wealthy was not a political question.

With the debate taking this turn, however, and with labor organizations mobilizing their forces while Reconstruction was still the primary problem, there is no occasion for surprise that social conservatives began to feel that much more was threatened than the structure of race relations. There was less apparent danger of a racial upheaval than of a new wave of labor unrest against the economic inequalities that the war itself had done much to accentuate. All the more comprehensive provisions that could have made the Fifteenth Amendment into an instrument of radical politics were struck down in the debates. The form in which it emerged was the least positive, and the least powerful, that it could have taken.

It should also be no occasion for surprise that the rights of women appeared in these debates. For some they were a mere instrument of mild ridicule serving to illustrate the practical impossibility of the demands the radicals were making for Negro suffrage on grounds of general principle. "If you wrong the African," said James Dixon, a conservative Republican senator from Connecticut, "you wrong the woman. She has the same natural right to vote as the African has." The whole idea was clearly intended to appear ridiculous. But other speakers fearlessly proceeded from the principle of equality of individuals regardless of property or race, to equality regardless of sex. Joseph Fowler of Tennessee could not see why descendants of China or Africa or India should give laws to the women of America; the moral was that the women of America should have equal rights with the men. Willard Warner, an Ohio Republican representing Alabama, believed that female suffrage was not yet attainable but would come when women were united in action.[64]

The question of female suffrage was beginning to encroach on the definition of republicanism. Women would soon take the cause to the

63. Foner, *Reconstruction*, 237.
64. *Congressional Globe*, 40th Cong., 3rd sess. (1869), 670, 860, 862.

point where they forced men to redefine the political community. By the time the Fourteenth and Fifteenth Amendments had been debated, amended (many times), and adopted, the problems of equality within the context of republican theory had been exposed to their most searching analysis since the formation of the Constitution.

This was a crucial period of examination and redefinition in the history of the American political mind. When conservatives took it upon themselves to remind their opponents that equality was indivisible, they forced radicals to face the consequences of their own theories. If majorities in Congress and in state legislatures had fully believed that American blacks were likely to climb to positions of social and economic equality through the instrument of political and legal rights, they might have had some hesitation about accepting the risks. But the almost innate white assumption of the inferiority of Negro abilities had the ironical effect of appearing to diminish the danger of the social consequences. People could believe quite honestly that it was right that blacks should have the powers that Americans needed to look after their own interests while believing at the same time that these powers would never enable blacks to equal whites in achievement or status. Some whites reconciled themselves satisfactorily to Negro suffrage with the reflection that it was right in principle, but that once conceded, it would be little used. [65]

In the slow course of these debates, ideas of equality underwent analysis and refinement. But they could never be discarded as irrelevant. In the United States, to an extent unheard of in any other country, including France, the most fundamental political principles were discussed and measured in the light of the idea that equality was the touchstone of justice. Where racial or economic conservatives could sometimes trap their radical opponents into inconsistency, they themselves were speaking the language of equality of rights. They accepted a right to egalitarian participation among whites, while differentiating between the right to vote and to hold office; as between the races, they rested on the assumption of white superiority, which they believed would assert itself once the excitement had died down. On all sides it was recognized that American constitutional politics could not be conducted without regard to an egalitarian theory.

65. William Gillette, *The Right to Vote: Politics and the Passage of the Fifteenth Amendment* (Baltimore, 1965), 87–88.

Chapter Eight

Social and Constitutional Foundations
of Racial Separatism

What Black Americans Meant by Equality

When the American Civil War broke out in April 1861, the Federal government neither intended nor expected it to lead to the abolition of slavery. If the war had been short—as both sides expected at first—there would have been no abolition, and slavery might well have survived into the twentieth century. Abolition was only a first step towards substantive, individual equality as a national responsibility. Abolition, moreover, did not in itself create rights or confer them on the freed men and women of the black race. The first major step in that direction was the Civil Rights Act of 1866, which was itself only an indirect outcome of the Union victory. In their turn, the Reconstruction amendments, which set the framework for future debates on equality, were even more indirect and unintended when considered as results of the Civil War.

The South, already divided by its racial heritage, was now further divided politically, socially, and morally by the Constitution under which it was required to live. Neither the Fourteenth Amendment with its guarantee of equal protection, nor the Fifteenth with its qualified guarantee of the equal right to vote, could conceivably have arisen spontaneously out of the historic sociology of the South. They had to be imposed; and they could hope to survive in the long run only if their operation succeeded in bringing a transformation in Southern society.

The effort eventually failed, but only in retrospect does the failure appear to have been inevitable. For several years the outcome was in doubt. In the long struggle to reclaim the South in the cause of white supremacy, violence and fraud were often tempered with caution and compromise. A great deal was at risk for the white leaders who styled themselves Redeemers. And they could seldom be sure that they had adequate control of those political and judicial processes in Washington or the nation that might still decide the contours of political responsibility in the South.

Black people were now also citizens of the Southern states, and essential elements in the new South's complex sociology. During the war, black people in the Southern states demonstrated their feelings mostly by deserting the plantations when Federal troops were in the vicinity and by acting as guides and runners to the Union armies.[1] It was easier for such a political leader as Frederick Douglass in the North to expound wider political aims. Until the election of 1864, Douglass was apprehensive that a Democratic administration might re-enact Taney's Dred Scott doctrines. Nor was he certain of the Republicans' commitment to abolition. Douglass believed and Lincoln himself feared that the Emancipation Proclamation would lose its validity after the war. While Douglass planted his principles firmly in the Declaration of Independence, he pressed most intensively for the ballot, which he saw as the best protection against white racism, as a means of black education, and—perhaps above all—as a source of self-esteem.[2] Here was a powerful convergence of categories of equality which white spokesmen had often preferred to keep apart. But the truth was that in a democracy, to be deprived of the ballot was to be deprived of the means of securing one's interests, even one's safety; and without these things, equality of esteem was impossible. It was, once again, the question of political community, or what Chief Justice Taney had so rightly styled "political family." Black spokesmen concentrated their public attention on political and civil aims. But this does not mean they were unmindful of

1. Vivid accounts of the consternation of the masters as their slaves deserted while Federal forces drew near appear in Robert C. Meyers, ed., *The Children of Pride: A True Story of Georgia and the Civil War* (New Haven, 1972), 925, 929–30.

2. David W. Blight, *Frederick Douglass' Civil War: Keeping Faith in Jubilee* (Baton Rouge, 1989), 176, 179, 184; Philip S. Foner, ed., *The Life and Writings of Frederick Douglass* (New York, 1950), 3:411–12, 418.

their peoples' deep desire for an end to all the dispiriting meanness of racial discrimination and prejudice. We have already seen how Martin Delany discovered hostility to the very idea of racial distinction deep in the countryside of South Carolina;[3] Douglass had long been a proponent of free public schools and a fierce opponent of educational segregation. It was grudgingly and, he hoped, temporarily that he accepted the political necessity of segregated schools as part of the price for northern support. At least he could hope that black schools could develop a spirit of self-reliance.[4] Where blacks were able to contribute to making the public policies of the reconstructed states, they supported social aims that went far beyond their own immediate interests, including free public education for all children, full civic equality for all people, and humane treatment of the insane, the sick, and the criminal.[5]

All these policies were basically egalitarian because they were based on the belief that all people had equal claims on the resources of the community; this was an assumption deriving from a strong sense of moral community rather than an examined and thought-out political idea. It cannot be said to have had its roots in classical American principles of the liberal state. But the fact that black people everywhere wanted to be respected as equals and endowed with the full rights of citizens should not be taken to mean that a desire for individual integration into white society played a prominent part in the ambitions of the black masses. The vast majority of them were countrymen and women of the southern states, living among their own sort, and wanting above all to support themselves and their families on their own farms.[6] The stigma of racial contempt actually bit more deeply in northern cities such as Philadelphia, where many public facilities, including transport were segregated.

In a world whose rules were made by whites, blacks were degraded by the very fact that their own aspirations and aims had to be cast in the language of the white world. One acutely personal case was that of Charles Waddell Chesnutt, a man of exceptional ability who was socially identified as black although, it seems, he was only one-eighth African by

---

3. See above, Chapter 7.
4. Blight, *Douglass' Civil War*, 199.
5. Joel Williamson, *The Crucible of Race: Black-White Relations in the American South Since Emancipation* (New York, 1984), 49.
6. Ibid., 45–47.

descent. Chesnutt, a linguist and teacher, encountered rejection and hostility from the upper class of whites with whom, on intellectual grounds, he would naturally have mixed; the culture he imbibed and taught was largely a product of Europe, yet he encountered obstacles to gaining ordinary access to the better educated white circle of his own neighborhood. Chesnutt resented this bitterly but did not let it affect his self-esteem. "I have no white friends," he wrote in his diary. "I could not degrade the sacred name of 'Friendship' by associating with any man who feels himself too good to sit at table with me, or to sleep in the same hotel. To me, friendship can only exist between men who have something in common, between equals in something, if not everything; and where there is respect as well as admiration." [7] Denial of equality of esteem caused Chesnutt psychological pain and anger, but he was too sure of his own worth to let it demoralize him. It is a mistake to suppose that equality of esteem is invariably essential to self-respect.

Both Frederick Douglass and Booker T. Washington, born and bred into slavery, found their way up by the hardest of hard ways. Douglass—who had fought his owner for his own physical survival and later escaped from slavery—wanted to create conditions for the entry of blacks into the normal processes of economic life, in which he seems to have been prepared to accept the normal risks of economic competition; he lectured frequently on the theme of the self-made man. Douglass was a rare case of a black man who had won equality of esteem in the white world; his massive influence and powerful presence must have made up for much earlier pain, but the equality he really sought for black people, once the fundamentals had been gained in politics and law, was equality of opportunity. [8] Without that, equality of esteem was an impossibility, though with it, esteem was far from assured. When the black lawyer John Rock of Boston, who had long been a prominent spokesman for equal rights, was admitted to practice before the Supreme Court, the real possibilities of the concept of equality of opportunity were beginning to gain concrete meaning. [9] But he was still a black lawyer in a white man's profession, a rare phenomenon and an unlikely example.

Where Douglass wanted to *change* the rules of white society, it was

7. Ibid., 65, quoting Chesnutt's diary for 7 March 1882.
8. Blight, *Douglass' Civil War*, 195.
9. Ibid., 187.

only to alter their governing principles so as to make them include black people. Since so much of the Southern labor force was black, even in the best of times this was never going to be a trivial undertaking. Beyond this, however, he had little by way of general political theory. Booker T. Washington belonged to a younger generation; his emancipation had come to him in boyhood with the Union victory. By contrast with Douglass, the subtle accommodationism practiced by Washington (at whatever cost experienced in the depths of his own complex personality) represented a formal acceptance of the white order: black Americans had an acknowledged place within the scheme of things, but that place was inferior, fixed, and unalterable. The Tuskegee Institute, which Washington built up and controlled for most of his life, trained black boys and girls for the service of a social order which would in essence have been much the same even if it had not been divided along lines of race. But Tuskegee was premised on the acceptance of the black place within the service departments of that order, and in such an order, equality of esteem was a dangerous thought even to think, and equality of opportunity, to the extent that it could exist at all, could be developed only *within* the sphere assigned to black Americans. Tuskegee, which was established as a Normal School by the state of Alabama with public funding, deserved all the support it received from the white world, to which it made an important and stabilizing offer; it not only provided a stream of trained servants, artisans, and technicians but it also taught them to keep their aspirations under control.[10]

It might have been expected that the challenge to Booker Washington's ascendancy would spring from a new drive to subvert the racial order in the interests of equality through assimilation. But the young W. E. B. Du Bois, brought up in western Massachusetts and educated at Fisk University and Harvard (where he became, in 1895, the first black graduate student to take a Ph.D. degree), was too complicated a man for predictable responses to the white world. Du Bois had much in common spiritually with Alexander Crummell, an Episcopal clergyman who had spent the middle years of the century in Liberia and had come back to

10. Booker T. Washington, *Up From Slavery* (many eds; New York, 1963); Louis R. Harlan, ed., *The Papers of Booker T. Washington* (Urbana, 1972) 2:107–09; for Washington's views on the value of industrial training both for economic reasons and as "moral training," 260–61, 310. Louis R. Harlan, "Booker T. Washington in Biographical Perspective," in *Booker T. Washington in Perspective* (Jackson, Miss., 1988), 3–22.

Washington in the 1870s, where he became the minister at St. Luke's Church. "We are living in this country," Crummell told his parishioners, "a part of its population, and yet, in diverse respects, we are as far from its inhabitants as though we were living in the Sandwich Islands. It is our actual separation from the real life of the nation, that constitutes us 'a nation within a nation.' " He saw this enforced separateness as the root cause of a demoralization which afflicted the self-confidence, the business, and the politics of the black people.[11] The young Du Bois got to know Crummell in the last years of the latter's life, and wrote an extraordinarily moving, if somewhat romantic, account of him in his first collection of essays; in his own life, Du Bois pursued the theme of dual identity, which he popularized in his most famous essay, until it led him back to a full assertion of black consciousness by way of black separateness.[12] The Niagara Movement, which Du Bois launched with a conference at Niagara Falls in 1905, broke fiercely from Washington's accommodation to the dictates of the white world and attacked almost everything the older man had so painstakingly labored to construct.

In aiming at full political, civil, and economic equality Du Bois did appear at first to be leading toward a program of assimilation. And when the Niagara Movement merged with a group of white racial liberals to form the National Association for the Advancement of Colored People in 1910—which by 1914 had 6,000 members and an agency in almost every southern city—they gave no encouragement to the idea of matching white racial exclusiveness with a similar attitude on the part of blacks.[13] That was not their idea of progress. Thus, on the basis of his early record and pronouncements, Du Bois, a proud man who was not unconscious of his own intellectual superiority, could have been the NAACP's most influential spokesman. But he never found it easy to work with others; this was complicated by his very personal search for a path to his own psychological independence through an intense identi-

11. Alexander Crummell, "The Social Principle Among a People," in *The Greatness of Christ and Other Sermons* (New York, 1882), 290–91.

12. W.E.B. Du Bois, *The Souls of Black Folk* (Boston, 1902), ch. 12 and ch. 1.

13. The formal founding followed a National Negro Conference in New York in 1909, from which the NAACP is sometimes dated. The Association's newspaper, *The Crisis*, had a circulation of 10,0000 within a year, 100,000 in ten years. Richard Kluger, *Simple Justice: The History of Brown v. Board of Education and Black America's Struggle for Equality* (New York, 1977), 97–98.

fication as a Negro. To achieve this to his own satisfaction, he seems to have needed to repudiate the white element in his own mixed heritage. From this he projected the conviction that black salvation could be attained only along the road of a recovery of racial consciousness, a commitment that for him seemed to exclude the possible aim of eventually submerging all ideas of race in a new, amalgamated American identity. By the 1930s he had split from the NAACP and had earned the opposition of almost every black leader in America.[14] But he was far from being alone in his belief that a full recovery of black self-respect would depend on a passionate affirmation of racially conscious self-awareness.

The flamboyant Marcus Garvey, who founded an Africanist movement which ramified into multifarious mercantile and educational enterprises and attracted the savings of numerous black people before its collapse, demanded for black people complete control of their own schools and institutions "without interference by any alien race or races."[15] Garvey, if only for a few years in the 1920s, undoubtedly involved more black Americans in his schemes than did Du Bois in his movement. And Garvey was more widely and much more affectionately remembered in other parts of the black world.[16] He also left a legacy of passionate commitment to the idea of blackness, which he associated with racial purity to the extent of condoning the white racism of groups such as the Ku Klux Klan and displaying open contempt for light-skinned Negroes—who included such rival leaders as Du Bois.[17] In Du Bois's last years (which he passed in Ghana: there is a Du Bois Avenue in Legon), the theme of black pride was proclaimed by James Baldwin[18] and was afterward taken up by the Black Power movement of the late 1960s. The moral force of these alternatives to assimilation may have become obvious after the emergence of the rhetoric of Black Power and the visible presence of the Black Panthers, but their earlier value should not be overlooked. As observed in the very personal case of Charles

14. Williamson, *Crucible of Race*, 75–77. The present author met Du Bois about 1951 and has talked with others who knew him. These remarks depend to some extent on personal impressions.

15. *Philosophy and Opinions of Marcus Garvey* (1933; New York, 1967) 1:140.

16. The author made this discovery in Jamaica.

17. Harold R. Isaacs, *The New World of Negro Americans* (New York, 1963), 135–45.

18. James Baldwin, *The Fire Next Time* (New York, 1963).

Waddell Chesnutt, they offered another route to self-respect. Equality of esteem would never cease to be a value of the highest importance, but it was no longer to be valued as a favor conferred by whites on blacks. Blacks might form their own opinions as to who deserved esteem, and act accordingly.

Equality But Not Identity: The Road to Segregation
Under the Awning of Equal Protection

In 1896, thirty years after the enactment of America's first Civil Rights Act, the Supreme Court formally laid down the doctrine of "separate but equal," which meant that the Fourteenth Amendment would tolerate racial segregation provided that the facilities for the two races were in some notional sense equal or similar facilities. In taking this position, the Court spared itself the difficulties that might have followed from an investigation of the substantive effects of the policy of separation, but the position could nevertheless be taken to imply that if such an investigation were made, and if substantive inequalities were then discovered, it could become a matter for constitutional concern. The Court, although clearly satisfied that it had disposed of the issues, had in fact looked a little beyond the questions of procedure and jurisdiction by which it had very substantially allowed itself to be guided in the past.

On the subject of race, the Fourteenth Amendment is silent. [19] It is a general declaration of the constitutional category of United States citizenship, which safeguards the "privileges and immunities" of that condition against encroachments by state laws. To all persons under American jurisdiction it extends the equal protection of the laws—which by necessary inference means *all* laws, not merely those imposed by one or another form of government. The amendment makes no distinction between classes of citizens. It is, of course, true that it was evolved by the Joint Committee on Reconstruction after hearing masses of evidence about conditions in the South, most of which indicated the existence of

19. Section 1: "All persons born and naturalized in the United states, and subject to the jurisdiction thereof, are citizens of the United states and of the state wherein they reside. No State shall make or enforce any law which shall abridge the privileges or immunities of citizens of the United States; nor shall any State deprive any person of life, liberty or property without due process of law; nor deny to any person within its jurisdiction the equal protection of the laws."

a crisis in race relations; but the constitutional solution to that crisis was not to create new protected categories of citizen, but to reinforce and extend old and established principles. Like the Civil Rights Act which had preceded it and to whose content it gave constitutional status, the amendment looked to the creation of legal equality of all American citizens, state and federal, on the individual basis that lay at the existing foundations of American constitutional law.[20] A second clause of the amendment conferred on Congress the power of enforcement by appropriate legislation.

When, near the end of the century, the Supreme Court arrived at the conclusion that for the purposes of the amendment, citizens of the United States *could* be designated by race, it imposed on the amendment's language a construction which had not been evident to its makers. The distinction is fundamental. What the Court did in 1896 was to give constitutional sanction to a policy which regarded the rights of individuals as determined by their status as members of designated blocs, as opposed to regarding their rights as determined by their status as equal individuals under American jurisdiction. The rule was explained on the principle that the separate *blocs* were to be equally treated. The route by which the Court arrived at this construction had been neither direct nor originally intended. But the idea was far from being new, for within a few years of the amendment's passage, the first oblique indications had begun to appear of the view that would later become the law of the land.

The history of the Fourteenth Amendment through this crucial period was the history of a paradox. A measure designed to eliminate substantive violations of rights by insisting that all rights were to be enjoyed equally was subjected to interpretations that turned much more heavily on matters of procedure than matters of substance. The amendment lent itself to this treatment because it nowhere actually defined rights. It only said that the privileges and immunities of citizens of the United States— which were not themselves identified—were to be immune against encroachments by the states, and, without defining the content of the laws, that their protection was to extend equally to all. These omissions were not significant of some sinister or self-defeating intent; constitutions do not exist to define the content of laws but to determine the

20. Laurent B. Frantz, "Congressional Power to Enforce the Fourteenth Amendment Against Private Acts," *Yale Law Journal* 73:2 (1964), 1353–84, 1354, 1383.

framework of jurisdictions and rights in which they will work. When state and federal courts began to consider claims arising out of the first clause of the amendment, they consistently emphasized that the leading principle was "an impartial equality of rights." But in order to understand the course of the courts, it is necessary to appreciate that this did not necessarily mean, nor did the courts admit, that the amendment had *granted* any rights to anyone at all; at the same time, it could not mean anything less than that whatever rights were granted or recognized by federal government or by the individual states should be equal to all.[21]

It might mean more than that, however. For the second clause, which granted to Congress a power of enforcement, might also be thought to give Congress the power to judge what rights should be enforced. The makers of the amendment could be forgiven for considering it in that light. But the amendment's language could also be interpreted as leaving the judiciary with the burden of deciding two further questions, whose answers were not explicit in the language of the amendment: first, Where did civil rights come from—from the federal government, or from the states? (If not from nature.) And secondly, Who was responsible for enforcing them?

During the Civil War, the Supreme Court gave fairly consistent support for the emergency extensions of the powers of the central government.[22] But the justification for this exercise was to save the Union, not to rebuild it on new, consolidated principles. So long as it remained in principle a federal Union, a Union of states retaining many attributes of self-government, judges who were entrusted with the duty of preserving the Union would generally be inclined to seek ways of preserving such state prerogatives as were compatible with the essentials of national sovereignty. The effect of this preoccupation with constitutional purity was that all questions of substantive, individual equality were subject to the previous determination of the authority under which it was to be established. To say this is not to say that the Court was indifferent to seeing justice done; it is to say that, as *federal* justices, its members considered it their duty to see that justice was done by those with the proper constitutional authority to do it. But the long-term effect

---

21. William E. Nelson, *The Fourteenth Amendment: From Political Principle to Judicial Doctrine* (Cambridge, Mass., 1988), 151.
22. Stanley I. Kutler, *Judicial Power and Reconstruction Politics* (Chicago, 1968).

of the series of decisions that effectively buffered the implementation of the substantive intent of the Fourteenth Amendment was fateful to the future of any sort or category of equality, because the effect of these decisions was to remove the enforcement of civil rights from the agenda of national policy.

By a fateful chance of litigation, the Fourteenth Amendment first reached the Supreme Court in a case which did *not* involve the interests of black Americans. The legislature of Louisiana had granted a monopoly over the butchering business in New Orleans, to which the plaintiffs, as unprivileged operators, objected, giving as their grounds that the monopoly deprived them of their privileges and immunities as citizens of the United States.[23] Given this opportunity to define the issue of jurisdiction, the Court, through Mr. Justice Samuel Miller, took the occasion to embark on two lines of reasoning, both of which were to have profound constitutional consequences. In the first place, Miller rejected the plaintiffs' claim that their case lay under the Fourteenth Amendment, holding that the amendment was intended to apply only to the rights of blacks. "We doubt very much whether any action of a State not directed by way of discrimination against the negroes as a class, or on account of their race, will ever be held to come within the purview of the provision. It is so clearly a provision for that race and that emergency, that a strong case would be necessary for its application to any other."[24]

As we have seen, however, the Fourteenth Amendment establishes general rules for all persons to whom it applies. That is why we have noted that it says nothing about black people "as a class," or about any other class. To anyone disposed to criticize Miller's argument, the conventions of common law reasoning might have suggested that a strong case would be required to *depart* from this rule for any reason. But this was not all. Miller's second departure lay in the significant realm of

23. The law did not drive them out of business but required all other operators to rent premises from the beneficiaries of the monopoly. The dubious internal politics of this issue need not concern us here.

24. The Slaughterhouse Cases, 83 Wall. 16 (1873), 81. For the interpretation of the cases considered in this section I am deeply indebted to the comments of Michael Les Benedict and William Nelson. They have influenced my thought but should by no account be held responsible for my conclusions. Much of what follows represents a considerable modification of the interpretation offered in this book's first edition.

jurisdiction. The question concerned the meaning and reach of the "privileges and immunities" clause. These, he concluded, applied only to such rights as owed "their existence to the Federal Government, its National character, its Constitution, or its laws." There could hardly have been very many of these, but examples included the transacting of any business the citizen might have with the federal government. The distinction that emerged was between the rights of citizens of the United states as expressly protected by the Fourteenth Amendment against infringement by the states, and the vastly greater field of the rights of state citizens remaining wholly under state jurisdiction.

These views, which satisfied a narrow majority, five to four, of the Court, went a long way in the direction of restoring the exposed boundaries of state jurisdiction. The Court was prepared to forgive the cost of a strained construction of the amendment's language, notwithstanding the historical fact, easily ascertained and familiar to all who had lived through those years, that this construction was wholly inconsistent with the record of the amendment's passage and ratification. The decision was a major act of judicial law-making, a trend which was to have an increasing role in the determination of civil rights.[25] The effect on the interests of black Americans was indirect but severe. By weakening the protective immunities of federal citizenship, the Court impaired the defenses of black people whenever it could be argued that the discrimination in question applied to the characteristics of state rather than American citizenship. This was no mere abstract possibility, as would appear in many subsequent cases involving civil rights.

At whatever cost to the value of the Fourteenth Amendment, the Court's decision was consistent with the body of sentiment which wished to reinforce the damaged principle of state autonomy. The fact that the Court now included five justices who had been appointed by Lincoln, all of them opponents of slavery and all, except Stephen Field, Republicans, suggests the strength of this feeling. But Miller's approach did not arise from the logic of the situation out of which the Fourteenth Amendment had arisen or which the amendment created. The vulnerability of his thesis was exposed by Mr. Justice Field in a strongly written dissent, which began by conceding that the states might regulate feder-

---

25. Nelson, *Fourteenth Amendment*, 156–59, states that Miller was engaged in "conscious judicial lawmaking"; also, Frantz, "Power to Enforce," 1381–82.

ally protected rights, providing that when they did so their actions applied equally to all concerned—which was far from being the case with the New Orleans monopoly. He then went on to his positive argument: the meaning of the amendment was that the privileges and immunities of United States citizens, which were already coextensive with the United States itself, were not henceforth to be abridged by any form of state legislation. If the amendment meant anything less than that "it was a vain and idle enactment, which accomplished nothing, and most unnecessarily excited Congress and the people on its passage." Congress had earlier enacted the Civil Rights Act of 1866 as an earnest of its determination to extend the rights of American citizens throughout every state in the Union; but, not satisfied with that, after the passage of the Fourteenth Amendment it had passed that act again, with some alterations, in 1870, in the belief that any remaining doubts about its validity had been removed by that amendment.[26] Field's dissent is the more notable because of his own commitment to the preservation of state autonomy; that commitment, rather than his argument against the *Slaughter-House* judgment, proved to be more consistent with the trend of the Court's subsequent thinking.

Congress Proposes: The Supreme Court Disposes

The theme of equality in its many manifestations had been at the center of public debate throughout the years of Reconstruction. But the single-minded pursuit of a single theme could never hold the interest of a complex political system for more than a brief period. Northern politicians were beset by manifold problems, among which racial justice in the ex-Confederate states began to assume smaller dimensions. But the Republicans were unwilling to abandon the struggle. After the mid-term election of 1874, in which their party lost control of the House of Representatives, the lame-duck majority made a final but far-reaching effort. The Civil Rights Act of 1875 was the fullest statutory assertion of equal civil rights ever yet placed on the statute book—and was to be the last until 1957. Even so, and despite their own convictions, the act's sponsors took the precaution of omitting its provisions for mixed education, partly because of the strenuous opposition of the Peabody Fund,

26. 83 Wall. 16 (1873), 96.

a charitable foundation which had financed much educational enterprise in the South. [27]

The principles declared in the preamble were of considerable theoretical interest. The act's declared object was to secure equality before the law. But the law itself was then made to extend to equal access to all public services and facilities. In other words, the old principle of equality *at* law was now expressly defined in terms of the *content* of the law. Seeking to implement the Fourteenth Amendment in the field of equality before the law, and perhaps fearing the restrictive tendencies already appearing in the Supreme Court, the bill's framers also included a provision guaranteeing the equal rights of citizens to sit on juries. The Democratic opposition sought to deprive the amendment of this content. Senator Allen Thurman, Democrat of Ohio, countered that the amendment did not confer the right. A profound difference—which was basically a party difference—was beginning to reveal itself on the content of equal protection. The idea that it did not extend to equality in the courts themselves may well have been the most extreme form of the negative view of rights ever proposed. On the other side, the Republican Senator Matthew Carpenter saw the need to establish a legal right in view of the implications of the *Slaughter-House Cases*. [28]

The central issue was joined when Thurman interrupted the Republican George Boutwell of Massachusetts, who supported the bill, to observe that the Fourteenth Amendment made no mention of "race, color, or previous condition of servitude." To this, Boutwell answered that equality was an individual attribute; it had no connection with class or race; since the amendment extended the same rights to all, there could be no need to mention race or color. Oliver Morton, also Republican, asked whether the colored man enjoyed the equal protection of the law when he was not allowed to sit on juries. In the circumstances of South Carolina, he obviously did not. And in a state such as South Carolina, where there was a black majority, whites would certainly claim their rights under the Fourteenth Amendment if local processes of selection prevented white men from sitting on juries! The right to trial by one's

---

27. Forrest G. Wood, *Black Scare: The Racist Response to Emancipation and Reconstruction* (Berkeley and Los Angeles, 1970), 139; Alfred H. Kelly, "The Congressional Controversy Over School Segregation, 1865–75," *American Historical Review* 64 (1959), 553–54.

28. *Congressional Record*, 43d Cong., 2nd sess. (1875), 1792, 1863.

peers, he insisted, was a common law right. (It would have been superfluous to add that in existing circumstances, blacks were not the peers of whites in southern states.)[29]

A debate of considerable intellectual interest explored issues that would come to the surface when equality again became the principal theme of politics a century later. Thurman pointed out that property requirements, which Morton accepted, were also unequal; Morton answered that states could not impose property qualifications on one race but not on another. But Thurman attacked the Republicans along a line which tested their liberal assumptions. The bill, he said, forbade discrimination on grounds of race while permitting it on other grounds.[30] The key to the Republican position was that rights adhered to the essence of individuality. The principles of the laws remained constant when cases changed; a man might change such attributes as his residence, his economic position, even his literacy, but not his race. The Republican Senator George Edmunds of Vermont took firm grasp of these issues when he replied to the Democrats late in the debate. A national Constitution created a national citizenship, and a citizen could not be deprived of whatever belonged to his character as a citizen. If laws could distinguish between black and white, why not between French and Germans, or between different religions? This was an argument which the Democrats chose not to meet, although it was developed at several points by opponents of racial discrimination. It, too, was to have resonances, both in the arguments in *Plessy v. Ferguson* in 1896 and a century later.

If the discussion had turned on the principles of American law, the racial conservatives might well have conceded these points. They had no permanent interest in concepts of group identification, still less of group privilege. Certainly the Democrats did not have a record of general hostility to the equalities that formed part of the American canon; on the contrary, they would have claimed much of the credit for them. But they regarded men and women of African, or partly African, descent as falling into an entirely different category. In this they were still fighting on the line marked out by Chief Justice Taney when he excluded persons of African descent from the "political family" which formed the Constitution. Where black people were concerned, race supremacy determined the contours of

29. Ibid., 1793–94.
30. Ibid., 1794, 1866.

constitutional law. What the racial conservatives really wanted was a Constitution that reflected the structure of a caste society.[31] At the practical level, Edmunds gave a clue to the need for a civil rights bill when he warned the Congress that the Democrats intended to inaugurate a period of reaction. Reaction also threatened in the southern states, in the form of laws to bind Negro labor. In the legislation now pending, if a man broke his engagement, all the damages were to be a lien on all his future earnings, "a mortgage on that man forever." This was a renewal of involuntary servitude, another name for slavery.

The passage of the Civil Rights Act in 1875 was to prove only a temporary failure for the Democrats in their struggle to prevent the legal codification of rules for civil equality. Behind the theoretical reasoning of this opposition lay the deep anxiety aroused by the fear that whenever black people gained access to judicial processes on an equal footing, whenever they entered into the trafficking of offers and services that formed the food and drink of everyday political life, the barriers of caste began to crumble. White supremacists in the North no less than in the South felt instinctively that the country's political life was inseparable from its social life. The customs and mores of a community were almost indistinguishable from its laws, since they translated immediately into such civic arrangements as segregated schooling, higher levels of education for white children, or the exclusion of black men from juries—and, needless to say, from public office. These white tribal instincts were consistent with and went far to explain the policies pursued in the southern states after the Redeemers had taken possession of their governments in the mid-1870s.

So long as the black vote could be of service to Redeemer or Democratic Party interests in the South, it was permitted, though hardly enforced as a right. But toward the end of the century, when changing political formations threatened to confront these parties with a new alliance of rebellious white Populists and black farmers, the old southern rulers were not without their share of responsibility for inflaming a politics of race in the cause of political dominance. Black Americans for their part could never count on constant allies among the Populists, most of whom had in any case only a limited appetite for genuine racial alliance and had often seen black masses enrolled to vote for their class

31. Ibid., 1870.

enemies. Although conditions differed from state to state, there was a remarkable consistency in the manner in which blacks were eventually driven out of political life in the later years of the century.[32]

While from the mid-1870s the white supremacists were confidently in command of the high ground in the South, the national political parties, losing heart for relentless struggles over the rulership of the South, withdrew from the field. An important if negative feature of the period was the almost complete silence of Congress. It was true that the South could not count on this situation with complacency; from time to time, Republicans in Congress threatened to reawaken the North to its responsibilities, particularly in education. The election of Benjamin Harrison as Republican President in 1888 was a new moment of alarm. But the South was able to head off these dangers, not least because Northern politicians were now much more concerned with reconciliation than with renewing the enmities of the Civil War. In the event there proved to be no further Congressional intervention; and in the absence of presidential leadership, the interpretation of national responsibilities for policies on equality was left almost entirely to the judiciary.[33]

The Supreme Court, as we have noticed, was generally guided by its sense of a primary duty to preserve the proper boundaries between state and federal authority so as, in effect, to leave the state system intact. But the Court was also concerned to interpret the divisions of power so as to preserve the legitimate authority of Congress over interstate commerce. This concern had a paradoxical, but in this period not uncharacteristic, effect in the case of *Hall v. DeCuir*, which had resulted from an incident of racial segregation on a Mississippi steamer. Louisiana's Reconstruction legislature had passed in 1869 a statute requiring carriers to provide similar accommodations for all passengers and expressly forbidding discrimination on grounds of color. Mrs. DeCuir, who was travelling upriver, having been denied a cabin in the accommodations reserved for whites, sued the master of the vessel over her "mental and physical

32. For this development in general, see J. Morgan Kousser, *The Shaping of Southern Politics: Suffrage Restriction and the Establishment of the One-Party South, 1880–1910* (New Haven, 1974), and the more recent and somewhat differently organized work of Joel Williamson, *Crucible of Race*, esp. ch. 2.

33. Nelson, *Fourteenth Amendment*, 151.

suffering on that account." Although her own voyage had begun and ended in Louisiana, the vessel continued its voyage across the river to Mississippi. This meant that *all* phases of the vessel's voyage were subject to the principles affecting interstate commerce. On this issue the precedents were strong. In the case of *Gibbons v. Ogden* in 1824 Chief Justice Marshall had laid down that a state could not intrude into the domain reserved for Congress under the Interstate Commerce clause, even when Congress had omitted to act. This time, Chief Justice Morrison R. Waite, in writing for the Court, admitted the difficulties involved in drawing clear lines to separate the powers of Congress from those of the states but observed that ten states bordered the Mississippi, and that it would impose an intolerable burden if operators had to conform to ten different sets of regulations in a single voyage. "If the public good requires such legislation," he declared, "it must come from Congress and not from the State." [34]

This decision was consistent with a strong assertion of congressional powers over all aspects of interstate commerce, even when part of the operation was conducted by an agent wholly within a state, decided by the Court in a recent case in which questions of race were not involved; [35] even if Mrs. DeCuir's grievance had not involved race, the case might well have been settled by the powerful precedent of *Gibbons*. The case is a cogent example of the Court's primary concern with questions of jurisdiction, rather than with the enforcement of substantive equality, but it passed no adverse judgment on the merits of such legislation if Congress chose to enact it. [36]

The language of Chief Justice Waite's opinion was racially neutral.

34. 95 U.S. 485 (1877), at 490.
35. *The Daniel Ball*, 10 Wall. 557 (1870).
36. This remark, which concluded the Chief Justice's opinion, was timely. It is impossible to determine from the Report at what exact date the incident affecting Mrs. DeCuir occurred. By the time the case came to the Court, Congress *had* passed the Civil Rights Act of 1875. This certainly clarified the full extent of transactions in which civil rights were equally protected, but it did not specifically apply to interstate commerce. This, possibly, may have been thought superfluous since the act applied to all the states of the Union. The Court abstained from reference to this aspect of the problem and may have been confining itself strictly to the state of affairs in 1869, when Louisiana passed its own anti-segregation law. But even if the Court had been inclined to do so, it would probably have held that it had no power to make Congressional legislation retroactively validate previous state legislation, even when the provisions of state and Congressional legislation were similar.

More significant for the future was the concurring opinion of Mr. Justice Nathan Clifford. In defining the limits of equal protection, Clifford pronounced that "equality is not identity." Two people, whatever their race, could not both occupy the same seat. The Court had simply respected the master's right to make his own disposition for maintaining order on his own vessel, but Clifford's sympathy with that order was undisguised. It was, he said, "not an unreasonable regulation to seat passengers so as to preserve order and decorum, and to prevent contacts and collisions arising from natural or well-known customary repugnances which are likely to breed disturbances, where white and colored persons are huddled together without their consent."[37]

It was of course well known that these "natural or well-known customary repugnances" (the phraseology allowed for the possibility of their *not* being natural) were more strongly entertained by whites against blacks than by blacks against whites. (In fact there was remarkably little record in American history of black expressions of *racial* repugnance against whites, in spite of the record of white treatment of blacks.) It was not an unreasonable inference that in Clifford's opinion, where it was difficult to be sure of the law (a condition Waite had admitted), white preferences were superior to those of blacks. But was it still possible, in Clifford's view, for these repugnances to justify separation without violating the requirement of equal protection. The interesting point about this question is that Clifford was willing to be led beyond the Court's concern with jurisdiction to pronounce on the substantive issue and to deny Mrs. DeCuir's plea on his view of its merits.

It was here that Clifford pronounced the dictum that equality was not identity, for which he looked back to the prewar Massachusetts case of *Roberts v. The City of Boston*. This connection was revealing. For the *Roberts* case had been decided before the abolition of slavery and, of course, before the Fourteenth Amendment. In Clifford's view, so far as race relations were concerned, the Civil War and the Reconstruction amendments had changed nothing of substance. But Clifford took his attack into enemy territory, in a manner reminiscent of Thurman's argument in the Senate, by pointing out certain more general difficulties raised by the theory of equal protection. The "colored race" was not the only class of persons who might claim to be involved. It was not insisted,

37. *Hall v. DeCuir*, 503.

for example, that children of different sexes must be educated in the same schools; he went on to raise the interestingly modern suggestion that if equal protection were rigidly enforced it might raise problems of equal opportunity for schoolchildren of differing intellectual abilities.

Clifford's racial views, and their explicit injection into his interpretation of the obligations imposed by the Constitution, may well have been unacceptable to some of his brethren on the bench, who should certainly not be made answerable for them. But Clifford clearly knew what he was about. He went to the question of substantive equality in order to block future appeals from procedure to substance. If equality was *not* identity, then separation need not be a denial of equal protection. Thus in 1877 he anticipated the doctrines that would prevail in 1896.

There was a sense in which those who cleaved to the issue of jurisdictional priority and those who went to the substance of equal protection were talking past each other. As late as 1890, when the boot was on the other foot, and the Court upheld the right of Mississippi to segregate passengers on its railroads, it did so in language which left *Hall v. DeCuir* intact. The Court found that Mississippi's requirement of separate compartments applied only to commerce within the state—whereas DeCuir's claim had been that Louisiana's arrangements extended beyond the state's borders. The implication was that Mississippi would also be out of bounds if it tried to apply its laws to interstate commerce. Moreover, the Court did its best to avoid a direct confrontation with the problems of conflict of laws raised by both segregation and its opposite, so far as they were involved by interstate commerce; even at this date, the case still left open a theoretical possibility—soon to be closed—that racial separation imposed by a state on interstate commerce might be found unconstitutional on the same grounds that had been applied in *Hall*.[38]

None of this reasoning impressed Mr. Justice Harlan, who also took note of *Hall*, and was unable to understand how a state enactment requiring the separation of the white and black races on interstate carriers was a regulation of commerce within the states, while a similar regulation forbidding such separation was not.[39] But Harlan, it must be sup-

---

38. *Louisiana, New Orleans and Texas Railway Company v. Mississippi*, 133 U.S. 587 (1890).

39. Ibid., 592–95.

posed, like Clifford before him, was looking to results. The difference was that Harlan wanted to use the Constitution to enforce racial equality where Clifford wanted to deprive the Constitution of any power to affect the substance of relations between the races.

The tenor of the Court's rulings in cases arising directly from violations of civil rights was reasonably consistent. All Americans enjoyed the same civil rights, though this was not to say precisely what those rights contained, which was in the first instance a matter for the states: rights might vary, on this view, from one state to another, so long as they were consistently protected as equal rights within each state. It was consistent with this view to hold that the states themselves had a positive obligation to afford their citizens the equal protection of the Fourteenth Amendment. None of the cases of this period rejects that view. What a state could not do was to offer different levels or types of protection to different groups of citizens. If that happened, or if a state through one of its official agencies violated the equal protection clause, then, but only then, would the Supreme Court intervene.[40] It would

---

40. 83 Wall. 16 (1873), 81. In *U.S. v. Reese*, 92 U.S. 214 (1876), a case of denial of suffrage, the Court found the statute under which the case was brought unconstitutional because the statute extended *beyond* the issue of suffrage—which, on its own, would have been within its purview. The option of choosing to invalidate the legitimate part of the statute along with the illegitimate part, rather than to enforce the substance of equal voting rights, was possibly not the only choice before the Court in such a case. Chief Justice Morrison R. Waite was concerned that a penal statute must be so construed that a citizen knew whether he was violating the law or not. It would certainly have been *possible* to design a valid statute within the precepts of *Reese*—but, of course, political power in the South had changed hands; this was simply not going to happen, a fact of which the justices could not have been unaware. See Frantz, "Power to Enforce," 1360–61, who comments that the decision on the Civil Rights Act followed the pattern set in *Reese*. Previous commentators had observed that, "the Court refused to limit the sections to discrimination because of race, although such limitations were contained in other provisions of the Act." Will Maslow and Joseph B. Robinson, "Civil Rights Legislation and the Fight for Equality, 1862–1952," *University of Chicago Law Review* 20:3 (Spring 1953), 372 n. 28. Other cases in which the minimalist interpretation of powers conferred by the Fourteenth Amendment effectively deprived aggrieved blacks of any substantive remedy at law include: *U.S. v. Harris*, 106 U.S. 629 (1883), in which a vital section of the Ku Klux Act of 1871 was rendered void on the grounds that the Fourteenth Amendment could not be used to sustain a proscription of private action (e.g., lynching). Also *Baldwin v. Franks*, 120 U.S. 678 (1887); and *Hodges v. U.S.*, 203 U.S. 1 (1906), where Section 16 of the Act of 1870 was held void on the now-established grounds that the Fourteenth Amendment could not reach "private actions"—in this case the right of Negroes to make contracts.

have been difficult to find a more stringent application of this doctrine than occurred in the circumstances of the *Cruickshank* case.[41] A massacre of Negroes had taken place after an election whose results displeased prevalent white opinion. It was here that the Supreme Court decided that the Fourteenth Amendment did not, on its own and without congressional legislation, impose constitutional obligations on private individuals, thus leaving the states alone with their autonomy in the administration of justice. Mr. Justice Joseph P. Bradley ruled for the Court that the indictments were unconstitutional because they denied the state the opportunity of affording its own remedy, but he also determined that the right to peaceable assembly was not an attribute of national citizenship unless the assembly was related to a function of the federal government, for example, to petition Congress. The judicial law-making of the *Slaughter-House Cases* was now developing into a seasoned practice.

The luminosity of these principles appeared somewhat more clearly when refracted from the yellow rather than the black race. On the West Coast there was much more animosity against Orientals than against Negroes. But when the city of San Francisco passed ordinances aiming to deprive Chinese launderers of their livelihood, the Supreme Court stood ready to intervene. The issue, said the Court, was one of arbitrary power, which could not be compatible with equal protection, notwithstanding the plausible impartiality of the wording of the ordinance. The Court rejected the defense contention that the state was the final judge of its own legislation and denounced "class" legislation.[42] Certain somewhat similar precedents affecting the Chinese did not escape the notice of the lawyers who presented the case against racial segregation in state-controlled schools some seventy years later.[43] In a crucial sense, the cases were not strictly analogous. To deprive people of their livelihoods is virtually an attack on their existence; to subject them to segregation is to permit them to exist under different conditions. In theory, indeed, the conditions affecting whites and blacks were still held to be equal, though separate. But another aspect of the comparison survives inspection: the Court objected to legislation addressed to a "class," but it had no such objection to the separate treatment, as a *class*,

41. *U.S. v. Cruickshank*, 92 U.S. 542 (1876).
42. *Yick Wo v. Hopkins* and *Wo Lee v. Hopkins*, 118 U.S. 356.
43. Kluger, *Simple Justice*, 120–22.

of black Americans, even though the nature of the treatment was different.

From the cases of the 1870s, these principles had already emerged clearly enough to suggest the lines on which the Supreme Court would in due course review the cluster of cases arising out of the Civil Rights Act of 1875. All these cases arose from incidents in which facilities such as places of entertainment, hotel accommodations, or first-class railroad seats were denied to black people.[44] A momentum had developed, an inner logic to the Court's style of thought, which that particular group of men had no compelling incentive to reverse. And their preoccupation with the logic's internal consistency saved them from avowing a constitutional responsibility for the substantive consequences of each decision.

Mr. Justice Bradley, writing the opinion of the Court in the collective Civil Rights cases of 1883, agreed that positive rights and immunities were "undoubtedly secured by the Fourteenth Amendment"—he did not say "created," but the effect was the same. He went further, basing his discussion on the assumption that the right to enjoy equal accommodation and privileges was one of the essential rights of a citizen which no state could abridge or interfere with. In contrast, Harlan, in his dissenting opinion in the Civil Rights cases, declared that the Fourteenth Amendment had created a new constitutional right "secured by the grant of State citizenship to colored citizens of the United States" of freedom from racial discrimination.[45] Both these opinions looked beyond jurisdictional questions into the content of the rights of citizenship; for Bradley, however, the statement was hypothetical, since he claimed that the question of whether such a right actually existed was irrelevant to the case.

The act, said Bradley, applied to *persons* guilty of violating civil liberties. In other words, it entered directly into the province of personal behavior. The question for the Court, then, was not whether racially prejudiced personal behavior was right or wrong, but whether Congress had power to make such a law as the Civil Rights Act of 1875, with its substantive enforcement of equal rights in public places? Bradley was retracting his gaze from the question of content and redirecting it firmly in the old and limiting direction of jurisdiction. The power conferred on

44. *The Civil Rights Cases*, 109 U.S. 3 (1883).
45. Ibid., 19, 36–37.

Congress (by the second clause of the Fourteenth Amendment) was to adopt appropriate legislation for correcting the effects of prohibited state laws and acts by state agents: "This is the legislative power conferred on Congress, and this is the whole of it. It does not invest Congress with power to legislate upon subjects which are within the domain of State legislation, or State action; but to provide relief against State legislation, or State action, of the kind referred to. It does not authorize Congress to create a code of municipal law for the regulation of private rights."[46] After taking this narrow construction of Section One, the opinion objected to the law on the grounds that it made no mention of any supposed or apprehended violation of the amendment; it gave the states no time to formulate their own policies but applied equally to "States which have the justest laws respecting the personal rights of citizens."

The Court had to take note both of the Civil Rights Act of 1866 and of its own recent decisions under the Fourteenth Amendment. It was not necessary to inquire whether the whole of the earlier act had been authorized by the Thirteenth Amendment, which had just abolished slavery and the badges of servitude; it was sufficient to note that Congress did not then seek to adjust men's social rights. But there were important recent cases affecting equality before the law. When the official agent of the *state*—a judge, in this case—had infringed the equal protection clause, as had happened in a case of the selection of an all-white jury to try a black prisoner, then even the fundamental principle of the independence of the judiciary could not stand against the Constitution.[47] (Field joined Clifford in dissenting on the ground that the decision posed a grave threat to the independence of the states.) But in that case, according to the Court, the amendment was correctly applied as a *corrective* to improper state action. The act before them, on the contrary, claimed to take possession of the field, regardless of whether or not a state had enacted its own civil rights policies. This had the effect of depriving a state of a function which, in the view the Court had previously held, the Fourteenth Amendment actually commanded the states to perform.

This insistence on maintaining the maximum degree of autonomy for

---

46. Ibid., 9–11.

47. *Ex Parte Virginia*, 118 U.S. 356 (1880). Similarly, *Strauder v. West Virginia*, 100 U.S. 303 (1880).

state law reflected the dual citizenship which in turn reflected the idea of a federal republic. It had been used recently to permit states to regulate the operations of business, where that business affected the public interest.[48] To have undermined the authority of the states in any one of these various and unrelated cases might have set a precedent for impairing that authority across the whole field. But this reflection cannot have brought much comfort to the victims of racial persecution, whose grievances ranged from the discomfort and social humiliation of segregation in public places, through the provision of inferior services, to murder and even massacre.[49] The judgment omitted to address the issues raised by the fact that many of the injuries complained of, involving theaters or railways, were caused by individuals who operated under some form of public license. Conducted under the authority of state (or local) law, these activities were arguably subject to the provision that their amenities should conform to the principle of equal protection.

The Court had also to deal with the argument of counsel that racial discrimination was a relic of slavery and therefore a violation of the Thirteenth Amendment, but this problem did not long detain the justices. "It would be running the slavery argument into the ground," the judgment explained, "to make it apply to every private act of discrimination in which individuals might see fit to indulge."[50] In language that must have read differently to whites and blacks, Bradley opined that when a man had emerged from slavery, a stage must be reached at which "he ceases to be a special favorite of the laws, and when his rights as a citizen, or a man, are to be protected in the ordinary modes by which other men's rights are protected."[51] These remarks were capable of being construed as devoid of racial content, but a moment later, Bradley let slip a revealing aside. Under slavery, he observed, many free Negroes were subjected to discrimination, "yet no one, at that time, thought it an

---

48. *Slaughter-House Cases*, 83 Wall. 16 (1873), and *Munn v. Illinois*, 94 U.S. 113 (1877); cf. Nelson, *Fourteenth Amendment*, 193–95. In the *Trade-Mark Cases*, 100 U.S. 82 (1880), the defendants were indicted for counterfeiting trademarks which appear to have been in use in interstate or foreign commerce. Nonetheless, the Court accepted the defense that the statute was beyond congressional power because the language of the act was not limited and could not be so limited by construction. Henry Paul Monaghan, "Overbreadth," *The Supreme Court Review* (1981), 10 n. 36.

49. As recorded in *U.S. v. Cruickshank*, 92 U.S. 542 (1876).

50. 109 U.S. 3, 838–44.

51. Ibid at 25.

invasion of his personal status as a freeman." How Mr. Justice Bradley came by his intimate knowledge of the psychology of free blacks before the Civil War was left unexplained, but a Court, one of whose members had recently drawn on the record of *Roberts v. The City of Boston* for an argument of doctrinal continuity, might also have noticed the social context from which that case arose. Roberts was only trying to get an equal education for his own daughter. It is not necessary to attribute to racial prejudice the Court's constitutional sensitivity to the problems of a federal jurisprudence; but it is not unreasonable to discern, in the preference given to one set of priorities over another, a subtle but pervasive insensitivity to the psychological consequences and moral implications of racial prejudice.

The opinion of Mr. Justice Harlan, the only dissentient (he had once, incidentally, been a Kentucky slave owner), rejected the central contentions of the Court. On the substantive question of rights, as we have noticed, he asserted that the Fourteenth Amendment established a new constitutional right to be free from racial discrimination. This view was not quite as remote from Bradley's as the language might at first suggest, but Bradley effectively checked the power to protect that right. Once that right was acknowledged, Harlan sought out constitutional precedents for the power of enforcement which Bradley denied. As early as *Prigg v. Pennsylvania*, in 1842, the Supreme Court had decided that Congress possessed powers enough to implement the intentions of Congress with regard to the recapture of runaway slaves.[52] The decisive passage was from Mr. Justice Joseph Story's opinion in that case: "The fundamental principle, applicable to all cases of this sort, would seem to be that when the end is required the means are given, and when the duty is enjoined the ability to perform it is contemplated to exist on the part of the functionary to whom it is entrusted."[53] Harlan even rejected the majority's reasoning on the Thirteenth Amendment, abolishing not only slavery but the marks it left behind. The peculiar character of American slavery was that it rested wholly on racial inferiority, which in his opinion meant that the amendment did entail immunity from racial discrimination.[54] He also drew the Comity Clause into evidence for the

52. 16 Pet. 539.
53. 109 U.S. 3, 28, 29, 30.
54. Ibid., 36–37.

uniformity of treatment to which all citizens were entitled, a departure from the restricted interpretation usually accorded to that provision of the Constitution.[55]

The Court had recognized a duty to protect those rights which were "of the essence of citizenship"; and Bradley in fact said that life, liberty, and property were "all the rights that men have."[56] Against this, Harlan's assertion of a *new* constitutional right must be considered in two lights: as an addition to the rights "essential to citizenship," and as coming from the Constitution and not from the states. This would deprive the states of the last vestiges of power to stand between citizens and their rights in the name of a surviving federalism. From here he went on to sweep aside any restriction introduced by the Court in the *Slaughter-House Cases:* the states, in his opinion, had never had any power to abridge the privileges and immunities of citizens of the United States; the Fourteenth Amendment's prohibition on state laws was an express limitation on the power of a state but was never intended to diminish the nation's authority in protecting rights secured by the Constitution.[57]

Harlan argued from the recent case of *Ex parte Virginia* that any denial by a state of equality of civil rights was a denial of equal protection of the laws. But in the rhetorical structure of his argument, the most devastating blow was struck with a weapon from the Court's own armory, for *Hall v. DeCuir* had found the Court arguing (as we have seen) that if in the context of interstate commerce the public good required such legislation, "it must come from the Congress and not from the States." There was a gap in the argument here, for the Congress had not in fact thought it necessary to define the issues within the context of interstate commerce. This may well have been because it had gone further and done more, very clearly defining the terms of reference for the general interpretation of individual civil rights in *all* the states—in which sense it was from Congress that the legislation had come. Drawing with some acerbity on the long history of congressional and judicial actions to uphold the rights of slave owners, all of which furnished decisive evidence of the adequacy of existing constitutional powers,

55. Ibid., 47–48.
56. Ibid., 22, 13.
57. Ibid., 54–55.

Harlan pointedly observed that, "with all respect for the opinions of others, I insist that the national legislature may, without transcending the limits of the Constitution, do for human liberty, what it did, with the sanction of this Court, for the protection of slavery and the rights of masters of fugitive slaves." [58] Negroes, he warned, might not be the only victims of race discrimination, which he identified somewhat prophetically as a new form of class tyranny.

Harlan's long opinion, whatever the merits of his constitutional arguments, was one of the earlier warnings—and almost certainly the first to have come from the Supreme Court—of the deeper implications of restricting the effect of the Fourteenth Amendment as a protection for equal and individual rights. The United States had always consisted of a variety of regions, societies, and even of differing social orders, held together rather lightly by a limited number of shared beliefs, ideals, and laws. Throughout almost all of the Western world, the tendency of the nineteenth century lay in the direction of nationalism—a truth that there is reason to believe that Abraham Lincoln had understood and toward which the Civil War had steered the United States of America. In adjudicating the civil rights issues, the Supreme Court had its reasons, implicit in a still largely centrifugal dispersal of power. But the Court was, nevertheless, choosing the arguments that systematically restrained the nationalizing implications of the Reconstruction amendments.

The great difficulty lay in a central conflict of American values that lay far beyond the reach of ideas of equality. Everything that Americans learned about both British and American history taught them to believe that when central governments were empowered to intrude into the lives of local communities, liberty was threatened; liberty was intensely identified with local autonomy. Yet local autonomy did not necessarily guarantee the rights of local people. The Supreme Court was within the mainstream of American traditions when it resolved this very real dilemma in favor of the ancestral tradition of local liberty in the form of the states. It is arguable that this policy was made attractive by the geopolitics of America's virtual isolation from external world forces in the nineteenth century; one effect was to give the American government

58. Ibid., 53.

less power over its own domestic sphere than that of any other major industrial nation as it entered the dangerous world of international relations in the twentieth century.

In domestic relations, if the trend which permitted bloc designations to take shape under the auspices of equal protection were to continue until the separate social structures within the Union grew harder and more engrained in the customs and laws of their localities, then Americans of the future might have to adapt themselves to certain limits of their social mobility. Such limits might be designated not only by race and color but by religion and national origin, conceivably even by region and class. Such considerations as these, although speculative at the time of the *Civil Rights Cases*, were well within the logical order of possibilities mentioned in Harlan's warning; the Court's version of the Fourteenth amendment offered precarious protection against them, which could be disputed from the Court's own language. During the generation already beginning as Harlan spoke, they were to evolve into much more concrete and visible forms, affecting a great variety of other minorities. [59]

The jury cases had proved that the Court could come down on the national side of the fine line that distinguished federal from state powers. Even here, however, the issue for the Court was not that of the substantive category of equality before the law, but whether these were cases in which states had failed in their constitutional duties. Undeniably, the effect was contradictory. Failures of substantive equal protection in the southern states were not rare aberrations calling for special notice; they were the normal course of events, and it would hardly be an exaggeration to say that, after Redemption had established itself, they reflected southern *policy*. The Fourteenth Amendment was held in these cases to deny the illegal consequences of white social prejudices while tolerating, within the states, the practices which represented the normal and consistent expression of those prejudices. The eminent respectability of the carefully chosen language through which the Court expressed its views does not altogether overcome a doubt which may be expressed in the

59. This prognosis was not mere speculation, nor did it derive from irrational fears. The restrictive property covenant that was eventually struck down by the Supreme Court in 1948, in a very different social climate, applied, in addition to Negroes, to Indians, Jews, Chinese, Japanese, Mexicans, Hawaiians, Puerto Ricans, Filipinos, and others. *Shelly v. Kraemer*, 334 U.S. 1 (1948).

form of an unanswerable question: whether a bench of white justices would have found themselves intellectually compelled by the same jurisdictional priorities and the same procedural reasons if the circumstances in the South had been such that predominantly black legislatures, black judges, and black officers of local government were treating white people as white people were actually treating black people. Unanswerable questions are not necessarily trivial questions.

The problem was admittedly intractable. The Court was committed to administering the Constitution in a manner that preserved some sort of social order; without wishing to impose a racial solution, it found order in the postwar regime of white supremacy. In Harlan's opinion—he sarcastically described his colleagues' arguments a "subtle and ingenious verbal reasoning"—the Court was denying to government the power to perform its proper protective duty. Since the Civil Rights Act of 1875 was held unconstitutional, for pre-empting the powers of the states, it was not clear from Bradley's reasoning whether the Congress was expected to intervene with new legislation on every occasion on which a state failed to afford equal protection. Such a course was politically impracticable. The result was a curious anomaly, in which the United States may have been the only country in the world: a gap had been created between the national government's obligations under law and its lawful powers to fulfill those obligations.

Even the limited gains already registered were undermined by the Court in the same year as the *Civil Rights Cases*. When the decennial census of 1850 first introduced the word *Mulatto* into the records, it recognized a phenomenon of wide occurrence to which, during the Civil War, a Negrophobic anti-Republican satirist gave the name "miscegenation." [60] One of the social results of Reconstruction was that the races seem to have mixed more freely in the formal sphere but less freely in private; at any rate, this tendency turned into deeper alienation between whites and blacks during the early phases of "redemption." [61] The case of *Pace v. Alabama* came up to the Supreme Court in 1883 upon an appeal

---

60. [David Croly, George Wakeman and E.C. Howell], *Miscegenation: The Theory of the Blending of the Races Applied to the American White Man and Negro* (New York, 1864).
61. Williamson, *Crucible of Race*, 40, 51–52.

against conviction for felony where a white man and a black woman had been found guilty of fornication, which was treated for legal purposes as a case of intermarriage, presumably because they were living together.

The law had been applied similarly to a member of each race. On this basis, the Supreme Court satisfied itself that neither race could complain of unequal treatment, and the requirements of equal protection had not been infringed. It may be regarded as evidence of the potency of the emotions connected with human sexuality that even in the mind of Harlan, who concurred in the judgment, racial identity overcame the more fundamental principle of individual equality.

For the Fourteenth Amendment, as Harlan well knew, said nothing about *race*. It simply referred to citizens and to persons—in other words, to individuals. The question to be decided could therefore have been differently defined. The state law in question denied to these individuals, a man and a woman, the right to make their own emotional choices in an intimate area of private life. It may be doubted whether a law would have been upheld which prescribed that individuals might not marry outside their residential area, religious affiliation, or economic class. The Court found reasons for sustaining this limitation on equal treatment of these supposedly equal individuals because it was thinking in terms of racial blocs. The judgment recognized "Negroes" as a class, available for legislative action just as women, children, aliens, or lunatics could be distinguished for legislative purposes. ("Whites," by the same token, might be considered a class, though were not so considered because they were the norm from which, in matters of race, the other classes differed.) It seems fair to suggest that no racial group other than the African Americans could have been singled out for this kind of treatment— particularly in the light of the strong denunciation of "class" legislation when it affected the Chinese in California only three years later. If a state could forbid sexual relations or intermarriage between blacks and whites, it becomes hard to see by what logical reasoning it could be inhibited from forbidding such relations between Jews and Gentiles, or Catholics and Protestants. *Pace v. Alabama* suggested that the time would come when the gap between obligation and enforcement would be closed; Clifford's dictum that "equality is not identity" pointed the way it would come. When, in *Plessy v. Ferguson*,[62] the Supreme Court dissolved the

62. 163 U.S. 537 (1896).

remaining ambiguities by proclaiming the doctrine of separate-but-equal, it was really doing very little more than completing a testament that already existed in draft.

Separate-But-Equal: Consolidating the Foundations of Constitutional Pluralism

Plessy's case did not arise by chance. If the new wave of Jim Crow laws were not to become the settled custom of the southern states, a challenge was called for at the highest level. An anti-segregationist committee chose Homer A. Plessy partly because, being seven-eighths "Caucasian," he claimed the rights and privileges of a white man. The case came up from Louisiana, which had recently reversed its Reconstruction policies by passing a statute requiring racial segregation in railroad cars. Albion Tourgee, a former northerner who spent several years as a Reconstruction judge in North Carolina and who had written a popular novel, *A Fool's Errand*, was engaged as counsel. As Tourgee anxiously appreciated, much was at stake in the case, the timing did not seem propitious, and defeat would have lasting and profound effects.[63]

Plessy's claim that he was being deprived of the reputation of being white did not impress the Court, which did not think him entitled to it, and did not impress a considerable number of blacks, who suspected that a judgment along these lines would tend to relegate more conspicuous skin pigmentation to the realms of constitutional darkness. The Court rejected out of hand the claims arising from the Thirteenth Amendment. That segregation could no longer be considered a mark of slavery was "too clear for argument." In fact, if this claim had been upheld, black Americans would have enjoyed an unusual constitutional status of double protection, since most forms of discrimination or bias are not derivatives of racial slavery; anti-Semitism is presumably not to be traced exclusively to the period of Egyptian servitude. But these considerations did not concern the Court. In 1883 the questions under the Thirteenth Amendment were considered worthy of serious discussion; by 1896, though Harlan still considered that discrimination on grounds of color

63. Charles F. Lofgren, *The Plessy Case: A Legal-Historical Interpretation* (New York, 1987), esp. ch. 8; Jack Greenberg, *Litigation for Social Change; Methods, Limits and Role in Democracy* (New York, 1974), 12–15.

was a badge of slavery, the rest of the Court dismissed the point as trivial.

The Court's opinion, given by Mr. Justice Henry Billings Brown,[64] a native of Massachusetts, represented the culmination of the idea, already seen twenty-three years earlier in the *Slaughter-House Cases*, that the Constitution could be legitimately applied to socially defined blocs rather than to independent and equal individuals. Given that perspective, it is not without longer significance that the decision dealt with the substance of equality and not merely, as had many of its predecessors, with questions of jurisdiction. If separate treatment could be equal treatment, then by saying so the Court could appear to close the argument.

Brown recognized that the object of the Fourteenth Amendment "was undoubtedly to enforce the absolute equality of the two races before the law, but in the nature of things it could not have been intended to abolish distinctions based on color, or to enforce social, as distinct from political equality, or a commingling of the two races upon terms unsatisfactory to either."[65] Brown held that the plaintiff's argument was flawed by an underlying fallacy, consisting "in the assumption that the enforced separation of the two races stamps the colored race with a badge of inferiority." In language which from a different perspective could easily have been supposed to be satirical, he went on, "If this be so, it is not by reason of anything found in the act, but solely because the colored race chooses to put that construction upon it."[66] Yet in dismissing Plessy's claim for reputation as a white, the opinion did recognize that a claim might be entertained to belong to "the dominant race." [67] But if one race was dominant, the other must be subordinate; the colored race's choice of "construction" appeared to correspond exactly with the Court's view of the actual state of affairs.

The Court's opinion, however, should be considered as a whole. The difficulty would no doubt have been met by the view that the admitted dominance of the white race did not constitute a social grievance because it lay "in the nature of things." Consequently there was no remedy at law. This being the case it is relevant to bear in mind Brown's acknowl-

64. Of whom there is a well-executed portrait in the lobby of the New York University Law School.
65. 163 U.S. 537, 544.
66. Ibid., 551.
67. Ibid., 549.

edgment that the government was, indeed, required to secure "to each of its citizens equal rights before the law and equal opportunities for improvement and progress."[68] The link between equal rights and "opportunities for progress" was significant; Brown's judgment actually constituted a fairly full recognition that equality of opportunity derived from equality of rights. Here Brown's language passed from the bloc designations that dominated the main content of the judgment to an apparent recognition of citizens as individuals. On its face, the judgment thus reflected an internal conflict of principles, but the Court was satisfied that the requirements of equality of opportunity had been met. This satisfaction might be explained by the belief that, under the provisions of the doctrine of separate-but-equal, Negroes had adequate opportunities of individual advancement within the sphere of their allotted existence, and that this sphere represented all that they were naturally capable of. The "nature of things" was thus an expression for natural law. *Plessy v. Ferguson* belongs to the intellectual climate of its time, and in the past generation, the meaning of natural law had been heavily influenced by racial adaptations of Darwinian evolutionism. Africans and their descendants were now perceived as lower than Europeans on the evolutionary scale.[69]

By this time it had become a commonplace for opponents of this line of reasoning to point out the dangerous implications of group legislation, and the Court had to reply to counsel's warning that the state's reasoning could justify distinctions being drawn not only between white and colored people, but people of different nationalities, or hair colors, if it came to that. To all this Brown replied that the exercise of the state's police power must be "reasonable."[70] The majority of the Court showed no sign of anticipating that within a very few years the white southern conception of reasonableness would have imposed just such differentiations on the minutiae of daily life, with the result that whites and blacks sat in different waiting rooms, bought tickets at different booths, used different entrances to the same buildings, and settled to a pattern of segregation more profound and rigid than anything seen since the end of slavery. In 1935 a distinguished constitutional historian could con-

---

68. Ibid., 551.
69. Lofgren, *Plessy*, 101–02; 110–11.
70. Ibid., 549–50.

clude—not without apparent relief—that "for the main purpose in the minds of its originators, the [Fourteenth] Amendment has been a complete failure." He was satisfied, however, that the essentials of civil liberty were not interfered with by state enactments.[1] But at the time of the judgment, Mr. Justice Harlan, once again, had not shared the satisfaction.

Harlan had expounded his views clearly and at great length thirteen years earlier in the *Civil Rights Cases*. In principle he had not much to add, and the earlier opinion was probably superior in its reasoning. Although his dissent in *Plessy* has become one of the most celebrated of American constitutional documents, it is not free from logical imperfections. He dismissed the irrational fears of the whites by remarking that sixty millions of them were in no danger from eight million blacks.[72] This remark was intended to alleviate white hysteria, but his argument would have had little effect in southern districts where the blacks were in fact a majority. Proportions of population, however, in no way affected the constitutional position, which of course would have been exactly the same if the blacks had been in a majority throughout the nation. That, indeed, was the core of Harlan's argument. Linking the Constitution with the structure of the society which it ruled, he famously said, "There is no caste here. Our Constitution is color-blind."[73] The Constitution did not know, and could not sanction, distinctions of class or color, and therefore could not permit officials to enforce distinctions based on them.[74] Harlan was keenly aware of the damage the decision would do in the South; he correctly anticipated the advent of new forms of segregation. As to the arguments to which the majority of his brethren subscribed, he was not deficient in the candor which their reasoning seemed to invite: "The thin disguise of 'equal' accommodations for passengers in railroad coaches will not mislead anyone, nor atone for the wrong this day done."[75]

71. Andrew C. McLaughlin, *A Constitutional History of the United States* (New York, 1935), 727.

72. 163 U.S. 537, 560. Lofgren's analysis in *Plessy* also reveals structural defects in Harlan's opinion (191–95). See also J. Morgan Kousser, *Dead End: The Development of Nineteenth-Century Litigation on Racial Discrimination in Schools* (Oxford, 1986).

73. 163 U.S. 559.

74. Ibid., 554.

75. Ibid., 562. An excoriating critique of Brown's opinion is found in Robert J. Harris, *The Quest for Equality:The Constitution, Congress and the Supreme Court* (Baton Rouge,

Although this decision was recognized as critical by blacks and their friends, it did not arouse significant protests in the North, where in fact it passed generally without comment. Other minorities, such as Jews and Catholics, who might in principle have felt threatened by the underlying separatist thrust of the *Plessy* doctrine, kept their distance. The full significance of the case, however, was not as straightforward as it appeared on the surface, or as it has seemed in most historical treatments. *Plessy v. Ferguson* legitimized a social caste system under American constitutional law, without at the same time authorizing a corresponding legal or political system—and this left open the gap through which doctrines of substantive equality could eventually lever their way back.

Even these tenuous lines were threatened only two years later, when, in *Mississippi v. Williams*, the Supreme Court agreed that a state had a right to impose voting tests that did not specifically exclude citizens on grounds of "race, color, or previous condition of servitude." This development, as we have seen, had been precisely anticipated during the debate on the Fifteenth Amendment. It was only on their face that Mississippi's laws did not enact racial discrimination in voting; the Court admitted that "evil" in their administration might make them an instrument of discrimination, and in that case it still seemed possible that they would fail the test of the amendment. Oklahoma's "grandfather clause" fell in this way in 1915. But at this period the Supreme Court did not make a practice of inquiring how a statute was actually being applied. It left such matters to the good faith of the states—to Mississippi in voting, to Louisiana in the provision of "equal" accommodation on the railroads.

It was only so long as the judiciary refrained from inquiring into the actual state of affairs that the Supreme Court could hold some sort of balance between "separate but equal" and "equal opportunities for improvement and progress"; the effect was achieved by implicitly denying that *equal protection* implied equality of opportunity associated with full and equal participation in the wider world of white America—in other

---

1960), 101, where he describes it as "a compound of bad logic, bad history, bad sociology, and bad constitutional law." These views strongly reflect the frame of reference established by the Supreme Court's decision in *Brown v. Board of Education*, 347 U.S. 483 (1954), which declared that separate facilities (in public schools) were "inherently unequal."

words, by denying the substantive content of the Fourteenth Amendment. But it was the actual state of affairs in the southern states that had produced the segregation laws. If, as individuals, the members of the two races had really been equals, in "opportunities for improvement and progress," in political rights, and above all in respect for one another as individuals, it is scarcely conceivable that segregation laws would ever have come into existence, in which case the Court would have had none of these problems to resolve. It was also inherently unlikely (though perhaps not technically impossible) that black people might receive equal protection, at least in due process, from laws which in other ways treated them as inferiors.

The Court's reasoning clearly reflected the instincts of the vast mass of white Americans, but the tensions and inconsistencies that have been found in it demonstrated the intellectual difficulties of maintaining a functional division between the categories of equality of esteem and equality in those rights which pertained to "the essence of citizenship" and gave rise to equalities in law, politics, and opportunity. But of course, the Fourteenth Amendment, which upheld equality in law, and the Fifteenth, which upheld a limited equality in politics, said nothing about the intangible category of esteem. A recognition of a right to equality of opportunity, a derivative of equality of rights in general, was more or less acknowledged in Brown's opinion. Intellectual difficulties and inconsistencies may for certain periods seem rather remote from everyday life, but they have a way of working their way back into the substance of politics, even if the process takes generations to come about. The process took about half a century.

The white masters of the southern states had never offered to confer equality of esteem on black people, whether citizens or not. They were by this time engaged in redesigning their constitutions to erect impassable barriers against black participation in politics. The development, which began in Mississippi in 1890, was gradual, complicated, and piecemeal, each state taking its own time and giving its own reasons. In retrospect, however, the results were uniform, if somewhat rough around the edges. But it was not only the black citizens who were swept so unceremoniously into political oblivion; restrictions based on poll taxes and literacy, and the complexity of the operation of voting tended to disfranchise poor and uneducated white southerners as well, which made elections safer and easier for the prevailing party managers.

It would, moreover, be a mistake to imagine that American political ideas have proceeded from an assumption that all acceptable republican principles must represent one or another variant of equality. We have seen the positive rejection of socially egalitarian ideas among Whigs of the Jackson era—and, indeed, among Jacksonians, for James Fenimore Cooper identified himself as a supporter of President Jackson—and these thoughts were revived by some of the reformers whose main concern was to clean up American politics after the unsavory episodes that followed the Civil War. Opponents of American expansion asserted that inferior peoples (such as those of the Dominican Republic) could not be incorporated into the United States because they were "too degraded" for citizenship. Such reformers as Charles Francis Adams regarded egalitarian ideas as sentimental and unscientific. There was no disposition here to regard the Constitution as an instrument for social amalgamation either of race or class.[76] With the upsurge of racist legislation of the 1890s came further claims from speakers and writers in several southern states, who reverted to the views of earlier periods and urged that political power be restored to competent and socially responsible hands.[77]

The American Constitution was always in important respects a pluralistic document. Stephen Douglas's case against Lincoln was that its pluralism was the essential condition for accommodating under one political roof the variety of customs and moralities that made up the United States. With the acquiescence of American leaders in politics, law, and religion to the doctrine of separate-but-equal, the bulk of the people, through their national institutions, seemed to recognize that the cause of domestic tranquility demanded that the nation tolerate separateness in its regional arrangements as well as in the relations between races. This principle, as Harlan had shown in his dissent in the *Civil Rights Cases*, as Plessy's counsel argued, and as Harlan said again in that case, could without logical difficulty be extended to other minorities or to institutionalize other social or religious differences. As we have already seen more than once in the course of the argument, Catholics and Protestants, aliens and native Americans, Jews and Gentiles, might find themselves

76. Eric Foner, *Reconstruction: America's Unfinished Revolution* (New York, 1988), 496–98.

77. Kousser, *Dead End*, 144, 151, 160, 164, 169.

arranged by law in separate stations—which, with regard to residential and sometimes educational arrangements, very soon began to happen. There can be little room for doubt that the overwhelming mass of white Americans accepted the sociology of the *Plessy* judgment (without, in most cases, having heard of the judgment itself) that the perceived distinction between the races lay "in the nature of things," from which certain material consequences followed. In saying so, Brown only echoed many previous dicta to similar effect.

In order to understand the general acceptance of the doctrine of separate-but-equal, it is essential to grasp this deep sense of its consonance with the natural order. A certain stretching of intellectual consistencies seemed a tolerable price to pay for making the Constitution accommodate conflicting principles. Separate-but-equal, itself reaching back before the Civil War, was an ingenious solution to the problem. But customary social arrangements, whatever their origins, easily acquire the character of a natural order, especially to those who benefit by them. This same principle was not by any means inconsistent with the ethnic separatism which also began to acquire some of the appearances of conforming to the natural order when it appeared in the late 1960s as a radical development of the civil rights movement under the impetus of the doctrine of "equality of result." Natural rights themselves would also seem to claim their authenticity from natural order.

When this mode of interpretation was introduced to justify separation between ethnic or religious groups, it could not be ultimately reconciled with the individualist postulates of the Constitution, nor, indeed, with the way the Court preferred to consider the Constitution when other types of "class" consideration were involved. One year before *Plessy*, the Supreme Court had for the first time considered the constitutionality of a federal income tax. Most of the judgment was concerned with the nature of direct taxation and similar matters, but Mr. Justice Field gave an interesting concurring opinion which did more to explain the philosophical background. The income tax law, he said, "discriminates between those who receive an income of four thousand a year and those who do not." This discrimination he considered to be arbitrary and therefore vicious. [78] A strong, even anachronistic strand of individualism controlled the Court's thinking about political economy; it revealed itself

78. *Pollack v. Farmers' Loan and Trust Company*, 146 U.S. 429 (1895), 596–97.

again ten years later, in *Lochner v. New York*, when a state law regulating the hours of work in bakeries was declared to be unconstitutional because it interfered with freedom of contract.[79] But in racial sociology the same Court was willing to subordinate the rights of the individual to those of the group to which he, or she, was held to belong. Both these typologies were perceived as conforming to the order of nature. The contradiction was deeply rooted in American history.

79. *Lochner v. New York*, 198 U.S. 45 (1905).

Chapter Nine

Corporate Power and Social Pluralism

The Emergence of a Triangular Paradox:
Individualist Ideology, Economic Monopoly, Social Pluralism

From the time in the 1870s when John D. Rockefeller consolidated the grip of Standard Oil on the oilfields of Pennsylvania, the owners of America's leading industries drove relentlessly toward monopoly of power over the full range of their operations. Many efforts failed; there was a significant element of risk. Those that survived provided a convincing analogy in the world of business economics to the Darwinian picture of the survival of the fittest which was rapidly penetrating from biological into social thought. The rapid rise of trusts—essentially a legal device to permit unified management of multiple enterprises—and of large-scale corporations exerted a transforming effect on the balance of economic power throughout the nation. When small businesses were overwhelmed by the annihilating competition of big ones, and the big ones grew relentlessly bigger, the ideology of equal opportunity seemed to be losing its force. Equality of condition, Tocqueville's favorite American discovery, was little more than a ghost from the Jacksonian past. The equal rights of the individual remained at the core of the Constitution. But when individuals were overpowered by corporations, it was only by forming new aggregations, of which labor unions were the most prominent, that they could reassert the old value of individual worth. The struggle for the empowerment of the legally equal individual would, henceforth, be very largely fought by the delegates of collective bodies.

During the same period, however, by another notable historical paradox, massive waves of immigration brought multifarious and largely new groups into the American population. These peoples, who originated in the Mediterranean, the Balkans, and Eastern Europe, were largely unfamiliar to existing Americans; there were extraordinary varieties in national and local origin, religion, physical appearance, and languages. They had in common one negative attribute: they were not native speakers of English. We have noted the Supreme Court giving formal cover to the doctrine of separate-but-equal, which could in principle be interpreted as extending to an elastic form of constitutional pluralism. The intake of population at much the same time was creating the conditions of a new, rich, and extremely diverse state of social plurality. In principle, this condition was not new to American experience; social plurality was one of the essential conditions of American history. But the scale and rapidity of the new intake, with consequent pressures on the existing population's powers of absorption, were without precedent.

Principles of equality would not on the surface have seemed to be much involved in these developments. But they were never far from the surface. While separate-but-equal itself represented one interpretation of the Fourteenth Amendment's requirement of equality, the increasing social, religious, and ethnic pluralism created reinforced grounds for regarding the individualist basis of the Constitution as giving an inadequate account of the people over whom the Constitution presided. An individualist Constitution ruled a pluralist people. The paradox was that in the field of economics, the individualist doctrine of equality would have to face the test set by business consolidation; in that of group relations, it would have to face the test of ethnic pluralism. In the first case, the defenses of traditional equality were rallied once again under the doctrine of equality of opportunity. In the second, the basic question of whether the individualist principle at the heart of equal protection could find adequate cover by defining individuals as members of ethnically defined groups, gave rise to prolonged and inconclusive debates in which different parties discerned rival principles. Simple ideas of equality had no power to dictate the outcome of these issues; the best that could be said for the egalitarian principle in American politics in this period— and it was not entirely trivial—was that the issues and their outcomes tended to be expressed in terms of equality.

Black Americans, whether liberated slaves and their descendants, or former free Negroes, were only some among a heterogeneous assortment of racial, religious, and ethnic groups with overlapping memberships but dissimilar interests, disunited by their common interest in economic survival. From the early days of Reconstruction, economic issues dominated the aims of many of these groups, with a new urgency which contributed to the revival of organized labor. Political equality became an issue of the first importance; it presented itself as an instrument in the hardening struggle for economic survival.

During Reconstruction, radical leaders such as Charles Sumner in the Senate and Thaddeus Stevens in the House, who fought wholeheartedly to give meaning to racial equality in America, could differ widely over economic issues, and government economic policies would inevitably affect the prospects for other aspects of equality. Sumner was a firm adherent of unregulated competition as taught by the Manchester school of economics. In his view, government had no authority to assume responsibility for the economic activities of the people in the name of general policy; it existed to serve the people, not to control or define them, and its duty was discharged by leaving them alone—with the strict proviso that it should leave them fairly alone. Stevens, on the other hand, combined his passionate belief in racial equality with a potent brand of economic nationalism.[1] Both could recognize the need to confiscate the estates of former rebels. The class whose greed and intransigence they blamed for both slavery and the war was thus to be prevented from regaining power over the South—or in the counsels of the Union. Their lands were to go to the freed slaves, as earned compensation for their past labors and as the minimum requirement for securing their economic and political liberty in the future.

The southern question aside, the egalitarian in Sumner was satisfied with the economics of fair competition, and in denouncing racial oppression he was fully consistent with these principles. His aim was to use whatever government action was required to set the victims in a position of equality with other competitors. When Sumner died in 1874, the full consequences of these doctrines had not come to fruition. Stevens had

---

1. David H. Montgomery, *Beyond Equality: Labor and the Radical Republicans, 1862–1872* (New York, 1967), ch. 2 and pp. 84–85; Kenneth M. Stampp, *The Era of Reconstruction, 1865–1877* (London, 1965), 106.

died six years earlier, but his brand of utilitarian nationalism could ultimately have proved a more effective instrument for holding the disparate elements of egalitarian principle together in a single spectrum. Stevens had much more confidence in government as the proper agency for shaping the character of the republic and was ready to use it for economic policy as well as for racial justice. When the Radical plan to distribute land to the freedmen failed, however, the failure left a heavy burden on the efficacy of the political weapon, the right to vote, which remained in black hands after the Fifteenth Amendment. The right of equal suffrage satisfied the demands of other Republicans, who stood on the basis of political individualism without looking too closely into the social context in which it had to be exercised. Most of the freedmen's allies, in fact, were quite satisfied that the suffrage alone would bring their other needs within reach. Such a determined campaigner as Wendell Phillips could take a remarkable degree of comfort in the power of the suffrage. "A man with a ballot in his hands," he said in supporting the Fifteenth Amendment, "is the master of the situation. He defines all his other rights. What is not already given him, he takes. . . . The Ballot is opportunity, education, fair play, right to office, and elbow room." [2]

The ballot, however, had given American labor precious little power to resolve its problems in the struggle with capital, and most Northern states showed no particular relish for genuinely universal suffrage until the Fifteenth Amendment forced it on them as it did on the South. In its organized form, moreover, labor shared this distaste for the full participation of black people in the institutions of civic life. The first postwar labor convention, held in 1866, adopted an unusually broad declaration of racial and religious solidarity, concluding with the words, "If these principles be correct, we must seek the co-operation of the African race in America." [3] But within a year this language had proved too strong, and in 1867 the new National Labor Union, meeting in congress in Chicago, decided to lay the whole Negro question over until the following year on the grounds that "while we feel the importance of the subject, and realize the danger in the future competition of mechanical

2. In *The National Anti-Slavery Standard*, 20 March 1869, quoted in William Gillette, *The Right to Vote: Politics and the Passing of the Fifteenth Amendment* (Baltimore, 1969), 87.

3. John R. Commons and associates, *A Documentary History of American Industrial Society*, 10 vols. (Cleveland, 1910) 9:158–59.

negro labor, yet we find the subject involved in so much mystery, and upon it so wide a diversity of opinion among our members, we believe it is inexpedient to take any action on the subject in this National Labor Congress."[4]

A spirited debate followed the introduction of this resolution. One member, who asked whether any union could be induced to admit "colored men," pointed out that "respectable colored mechanics" were persistently excluded. Another member, on the other hand, was sorry to see the words "colored" and "white" being used; labor owed a duty to the colored worker in common brotherhood, and colored men were proving themselves industrious and susceptible to improvement and advancement. These remarks seem to provide some sort of echo to the desire we have found on the part of black people in the South to forgo all talk of color. Another member took up the theme by expressing his understanding that the intention was "to legislate for the good of the entire laboring community of the United States" but went on to reject the premise of unity by arguing that the blacks would combine together on their own part, without assistance from the whites, who ought not to try to carry the blacks on their shoulders. "God speed them," he blandly remarked, without clearly indicating the direction in which he hoped they would proceed. To all these and similar speeches, William H. Sylvis, America's first great labor leader, replied. In the South, he said, the question had already arisen, the whites striking against the blacks and creating an antagonism which would kill off the trades unions unless the two were consolidated. "There is no concealing the fact," he pointed out, "that the time will come when the negro will take possession of the shops if we have not taken possession of the negro. If the working men of the white race do not conciliate the blacks, the black vote will be cast against them."[5] But Sylvis's contemporaries were unprepared to face the consequences of this reasoning and took refuge in the view that the interests of labor could be equally well served by separate racial organizations. In times of hardship, when employers brought in black labor to undercut white strikers, this reasoning was to be disproved, but instead of teaching trade unionists to reverse their error, such conflict between working men of the two races brought more antagonism.

4. Ibid., 185.
5. Ibid., 185–88.

The unions were not much more sympathetic to the claims of women—though one or two expressions of sympathy escaped. From the constitutional standpoint, white women, who did not enjoy the benefit of the suffrage, were even more excluded from the political process than black men. The demands of women—exclusively white ones, it is to be presumed—caused a heated debate at the labor convention of 1868, where members refused to commit themselves on the broader political question of suffrage but willingly supported the principle of equal treatment for women as fellow workers. Similar motions were adopted in 1869.[6]

The blacks understood this situation only too well; they had the advantage of experience. In 1869 they held a National Colored Labor Convention in Washington, where the resolution adopted made an addition to the list of natural rights—that of laboring in the field of one's abilities. This was essentially to say that equality of opportunity was a natural right. It was, of course, capable of almost indefinite extension in the direction of a right to discover, through education, just where the field of one's abilities lay. The convention adopted a "harmony of interests" view of the relations between capital and labor, thus firmly rejecting the socialist doctrine of class antagonism; it deplored intemperance and advocated a universal free school system to be instituted "without regard to race, creed, or sex." The convention also favored the development of co-operative workshops and building and loan associations.[7] But the resolution which most poignantly expressed the feelings of African Americans declared that the country was the common property of the whole people and bitterly denounced the white trade union practice of excluding blacks.

While organized labor divided itself along lines of race, the labor force was itself a product of a newly industrial economy. Two-thirds of all productively employed Americans were now employees. The basic issues of equality had been established, but their applications would have in future to be addressed to a changed industrial and social order. Labor was asking for equality of condition, and also, as its Jacksonian forebears had done, for equality of esteem. But liberal ideologists of the older school did not necessarily welcome these intrusions, in which the liberal

6. Ibid., 198, 233.
7. Commons, *Documentary History* 9:243–52.

intellectual E.L. Godkin, editor of *The Nation,* perceived a new threat both to American values and to the refinements of civilized life that had been built on them. Taking note of concessions that Massachusetts Republicans had made to labor demands in the elections of 1872, Godkin commented that the labor question "contains the seeds from which this Christian civilization of ours is to perish." Why? Because of the very pursuit of "equality of conditions on which the multitude seems now entering, and the elevation of equality of conditions into the rank of the highest political good"—a process which would "prove fatal to art, to science, to literature, and to law." The point of view was consistent with that of Charles Francis Adams, who, we have seen, regarded egalitarian ideas as a sentimental anachronism. [8] The difference between them was small in outcome, since neither of them wanted to see the working class exerting its collective power to gain what Godkin called an "equality of conditions." But Godkin, at least, placed his own faith in a more traditional American equality of rights. It was this that he thought was threatened by the new manifestation of class activity. Godkin's position, in other words, was rooted in the individualism of equal rights. Along with a group of intellectually well equipped contemporaries such as David A. Wells, who had worked for the Treasury, the Boston textile manufacturer and philanthropist Edward Atkinson, and a number of sociologists and economists who included William Graham Sumner of Yale, Godkin opposed all "special" or (as it was called) "class" legislation. Such policies were anathema, not simply because they favored labor or agriculture or manufacturers, but because they favored selected groups at the expense of the public interest. This was a laissez-faire position which claimed its own authority on both equality of rights and the laws of classical economics. [9]

A very great distance had been traveled since an earlier European had perceived equality of conditions as the very foundation of American social life and the end to which not only America, but in the long run Europe, was tending. The entire point of view had now changed. Godkin was right in observing that equality of conditions did not exist in his

8. Eric Foner, *Reconstruction: America's Unfinished Revolution, 1863–1867* (New York, 1984), 497–98.

9. Michael Les Benedict, "Laissez-Faire and Liberty: A Re-Evaluation of the Meaning and Origins of Laissez-Faire Constitutionalism," *Law and History Review* 3:2 (Fall 1985), 293–331, 305–06.

own time. But the class relationships which had been latent in the Jacksonian economy were now far more menacingly defined. It was *organized* labor—and, indeed, organized farmers—who now threatened the libertarian, laissez-faire order of Godkin's world of liberty. It was in that order that men like him could conceive of equality as an individual attribute in a free market. The "equality of conditions" that Godkin so greatly feared was the perceived advance of a general equality of classes, in which unions would force the equality of labor on an already differentiated society. In such a society he could see no future for the refinements that American civilization had already attained. It was this that threatened the foundations of social stability; his fears for the future of the American social order were expressed when he asserted that the gathering movement he detected in the direction of equality of conditions would be nothing short of disastrous to the intellectual and moral fiber of the Republic.

This band of laissez-faire ideologists showed no sign of feeling that they were in command of the situation. On the contrary, special interest legislation, particularly in the form of tariffs, had a substantial history of attainments. The use of legislative power to favor special interests seemed to Godkin and his associates to be virtually identical with socialism or even communism. [10] Godkin's carefully chosen evocation of the idea of equality of conditions set the central issues in the clearest light for his generation: the ideal of equality of conditions was not (as some imagined) the desirable outcome of an equality of rights but was to be seen as the most insidious enemy of equality of rights. The one idea was collective, the other, individualist. These ideas were to have distant resonances in the conflict between group and individually conceived equalities more than a century later.

Laissez-faire liberals like Godkin did not understand or sympathize with the individual costs to laboring men and their families of the struggle for subsistence, still less for education and the advancement of their children, in this industrial order. They were not ready to consider the possibility that inequalities reaching into the very foundations of society affected the meaning and value of the formal equalities to which they adhered. Labor and agrarian reformers, for their part, do not seem to have used the language—which, as we have suggested, already

10. Ibid., 309.

sounded anachronistic—of equality of condition, but they certainly did not regard their struggles with their employers as leading toward social disorder. The laissez-faire liberals attributed to them a set of aims which they did not recognize in themselves. Even while they fought collectively—for it was all they could do—they continued to employ the language of the spirit of individual equality. The same was true of the farmers, whose conventions in the 1870s invoked the ideals of equal justice and equal division of the profits arising from work,[11] and when the Knights of Labor declared their aims they reverted to a theme that recalled the defensive class consciousness of labor's earlier struggle for identity. "We mean to uphold the dignity of labor, to affirm the nobility of all who live in accordance with the ordinance of God, 'in the sweat of thy brow shalt thou eat bread,' " they declared; but this poignant appeal for equality of esteem concluded by advocating the harmony of interests between capital and labor.[12] This was a long way from the class war that Godkin seemed to envisage as the motivation and outcome of labor activity.

The truth was that the now venerable idea of American equality had affected the thinking of labor leaders. The exemplary successes of capitalist enterprise and the academically respectable doctrines of free competition provided the system with a highly articulate theory. The intellectual consequences of this situation were translated into economic consequences, and the reformist analysis was penetrated by the assumptions of its opponents in what Marxists, socialists, and many of the spokesmen of organized labor in Europe would have designated as the class struggle. Again and again, American labor's public pronouncements harped on the mutual interests of capital and labor, in language surprisingly redolent of the more unctuous statements of the same theme from the capitalist side of the argument. American workers were brought together from extremely heterogeneous sources and included a high proportion of immigrants of more or less recent standing in the country. Such people could not lightly disregard the commitments, emotional as well as economic, that they had made in emigration to America, and immigrant attitudes could easily be reconciled to uses of equality now adopted to serve the purpose of the industrial order.

11. Commons, *Documentary History* 10:47–48, 61.
12. Ibid., 24.

These values, however, did not escape criticism from the North American Federation of the International Workingmen's Association—the First International—when it addressed a message to the General Council in London in August, 1871. The workers, particularly the immigrants, were dupes of an ideology which hired them into a captivity that they celebrated as freedom. "We are sorry," the American committee observed,

to state that the workingmen in general, even in spite of the industrial development—are quite unconscious of their own position toward capital and slow to show battle against their oppressors for the following reason:
I. The great majority of the workingmen in the Northern States are immigrants from Ireland, Germany, England, etc. (in California, coolies imported under contract), having left their native countries for the purpose of seeking here that wealth they could not obtain at home. This delusion forms itself into a sort of creed, and employers and capitalists, parvenus having gained their wealth in the former period, take great care in preserving this self-deception among their employees.

The capitalists rendered the goal ever more impossible to realize. Yet the trades unions, founded in the vision of that idea—wealth through capitalist enterprise—now found it to be the stumbling block over which they fell and perished. The address continued with a scathing denunciation of the "so-called Reform Parties" which were growing up and disappearing overnight, advocating "glittering educational measures, benevolent and homestead societies," and other schemes. Wrong guidance within the labor movement itself was also chosen for criticism; labor activities were directed to reforms that ended by taking their abode "in one of the political parties of the ruling class, the bourgeois." [13]

These expressions are conspicuously different from the usual conventions of American rhetoric. They ignore the nation's founding ideals, show no interest in the harmony of capital and labor, and neglect the ideal of individual equality. From this Marxist standpoint, the ideal had proved a snare and a delusion, misleading the workers into a belief that they had a share, or the prospect of a share, in a social system whose whole tendency in reality was to deprive them of the fruits of their toil. It is significant of the extent to which the prevalent ideology had permeated the minds of labor spokesmen that they generally subscribed

13. Ibid. 9:361–66.

to the nomenclature in which the economic system was called not the "capitalist" system but one of "free labor." [14] It is also significant that American labor spokesmen did employ the historic American rhetoric of equality, not as a tactical weapon, but because it was the language they spoke in common with other Americans.

The Economics of the Survival of the Fittest

Quite soon after the Civil War it began to appear that economic growth was acquiring new forms as well as new dimensions. Massive accumulations of corporate but private property were bringing into existence the most conspicuous inequalities (barring slavery and the continuing structure of racial caste) in the nation's history—as was, if not self-evident, certainly evident to the senses, once it had received documentation from social critics such as Henry George, Ida Tarbell, Henry Demarest Lloyd, and other forerunners of the Progressive Movement. "Capital is piled on capital, to the exclusion of men of lesser means and the utter prostration of personal independence and enterprise on the part of the less successful masses," Henry George declared as early as 1868; by that year he had perceived the paradox of increasing misery amidst growing affluence. [15] Lloyd, one of the earlier American political publicists to exalt the state, as against the traditional preferences of American political thought for local powers, was less occupied by ideas of equality than most contemporary reformers, though he did attack Standard Oil for destroying the independent operators, a view that derived moral force from the ideal of equality of opportunity. He did not associate his own analysis with that of George, whom he believed guilty of perpetuating a myth of natural equality that had served its historical purpose and ought to be discarded. [16] But all these publicists were at one in promoting a public concern about new concentrations of economic power, which produced such public inquiries as the Senate investigation of the Sugar Trust in the early 1880s.

These vast accumulations, and the power they wielded throughout

14. Montgomery, *Beyond Equality*, 14.

15. John L. Thomas, *Alternative America: Henry George, Edward Bellamy, Henry Demarest Lloyd and the Adversary Tradition* (Cambridge, Mass., 1983), 49.

16. Ibid., 144–45.

the nation, represented challenges to the old republican principles. But at least one of the new giants, Andrew Carnegie, soon equipped his class with a naturalistic justification from the social applications of Darwinian evolutionism. The ethics associated with the theory of the survival of the fittest by adaptation to the environment through natural selection did not have much in common with earlier theories about natural rights, but its leading beneficiaries demonstrated a remarkable facility, if not in adapting themselves to their environment, then in remaking the environment in their own interests. This at least was not an uncharitable interpretation to place on their manner of creating new forms of corporate business organization to achieve monopolistic control of the sources, means of creating, and outlets of wealth, while the Fourteenth Amendment was taken over by constitutional lawyers in the defense of these organizations.

The unfit did not accept defeat gracefully. Out of the conditions of rapid population growth, of competitive and mechanized agriculture or rapid but unplanned urban development, of massive immigration from mainly non—English speaking countries, there sprang the grievances and resentments which followed the experience of failure and disappointed hope. When the Populist party raised its colors in 1892 it returned once more, and not merely in a passing flourish of rhetoric, to the American theme of equal rights and equal power. Populists declared "that the forces of reform this day organized will never cease to move forward until every wrong is remedied, with equal rights and equal privileges securely established for all the men and women of this country." They sought "to restore the government of the Republic to the hands of 'the plain people,' with whose class it originated." [17] And they asserted that their purposes were identical with those proclaimed in the national Constitution. Among their specific economic and political policies, the graduated income tax would ultimately have the most power to restore the equality of goods which they felt had been lost. This statement depended on a folk belief of great importance to the self-esteem of people who felt themselves to be victims of a new industrial and financial tyranny. The populists were passionately convinced that America had been made by its "plain people"—the yeomen of America, who came

17. The Omaha Platform, 1892. Norman Pollack, ed., *The Populist Mind* (Indianapolis, 1967), 59—66.

from the same stock and had similar moral qualities to the yeomen of England. This belief was associated with another historical concept, that the Revolution was made by a people among whom the country's resources had been more or less equally distributed.

The National Farmers Alliance, which was closely associated with populism in mood and political orientation, also emphasized these themes. In order "to restore and preserve these rights under a republican form of government, private monopoly of public necessities for speculative purposes, whether of the means of production, distribution, or exchange, should be prohibited." When such utilities fell into monopolistic hands, they should be appropriated by eminent domain (paying a just value therefor) and operated in the interest of "the whole people." This pronouncement was added to the original Omaha declaration of populist principles in 1896. It reminds us forcibly of the communal aspect of the egalitarian thrust of the populist protest. [18]

The populist manifesto thus brought together two egalitarian themes of fundamental importance. It drew on American history for the authenticity of the demand for equality, applying the moral meaning of the Republic to the crisis of the hour. And it looked to the future by advocating the introduction of a federal graduated income tax as an instrument for the redistribution of wealth. The aim was to redress the imbalance brought about by industrial and corporate economics and the re-affirm the *moral* as well as the material foundations of the Republic. Individual rights lay at the base of all this, for monopoly power and special privilege threatened the very foundations of equality of opportunity. But the egalitarianism of individuality was not the most urgent issue for the populists. Both their moral force and what hopes they had of political strength lay in their profound sense of community, a sentiment that also had some of its sources in the Revolution.

The civil rights movement of the Reconstruction era had been concerned with the extension of existing rights to deprived sectors of the population, but had never addressed itself to general social policy. The populist program has a claim to be considered the most ambitious and far-reaching egalitarian political program, certainly since the days of

18. Lawrence Goodwyn, *Democratic Promise: The Populist Moment in America* (New York, 1976), 467.

Andrew Jackson, arguably since the American Revolution. It also, however, revived the concept of equality as an idea of protest. Politically, however, populism was a losing cause.

The idea of restoration, of a return to past, almost primitive values, was particularly important in the thinking of Henry George, for whom natural justice was associated with fair distribution of land. This proved to be the last period in which the French physiocratic tradition could be applied to American conditions. George, who advanced his own specific remedies for the country's gathering ills in *Progress and Poverty*, published in 1879, was impelled by the need to secure in the existing more complex state of society "the same equality of rights that in a ruder state was secured by equal partition of the soil, and by giving the use of the land to whoever could procure the most from it." [19] Whether or not this "equal partition of the soil" had ever actually existed would have made little difference to the moral basis of George's proposals for the confiscation by the state through a "single tax" of all rents from land; but the conviction that Americans had once lived under a more equitable order undoubtedly helped to make the plan seem more legitimate. It was thus more consistent with American traditions, and it tended to rectify an injustice that had come about since the Revolution.

George's book is transfused with the language of equal rights, though he did not confuse equality of rights with similarity of attainments. He also believed, however, that progress was kindled by cooperative action, which he called "association"; inequality perverted it into "retrogression." He called "association of equality" the "law of progress"—but then, in a significant parenthesis, defined equality almost out of existence by offering as equivalents "justice or freedom, for the terms here signify the same things, the recognition of the moral law." [20] This casual remark warns us not to take too seriously George's concept of equality as the moral basis of the state. George was here exemplifying the argument that equality has often been used as a sort of synonym to represent the values of independence and self-respect, but whatever view one may hold of the categories of equality or of their relationship to such concepts

19. Henry George, *Progress and Poverty* (1879; London, 1931), 286; Thomas, *Alternative America*, ch. 3.
20. Thomas, *Alternative America*, 359.

as liberty or justice, they are certainly not interchangeable, and to treat them as mere equivalents diminishes the prospects of any one social objective as seen in the light of any specific item of equality.

George earned support from the recently formed Knights of Labor, who believed that his land reforms would help to make every man his own employer—a thoroughly individualistic aim which had nothing in common with Marxism or socialism. George argued, against the socialists, that labor's quarrel should not be with the capitalists but with monopoly; and he also took on Malthus with the argument that "the greater the population, the greater the comfort which an equitable distribution of wealth would give to each individual." But his vision was flawed by its elemental simplicity. Academic economists declined to take him seriously, and after a skirmish in Berkeley, he visited Britain, where he came to grief in Oxford at the hands of Alfred Marshall, who had no difficulty in showing (though not to George's satisfaction) that the economy operated through the interaction of much more complex relationships than could be allowed for in George's single-minded dependence on land values. Back in the United States, the Columbia economist E.R.A. Seligman confronted him with similar difficulties. Essentially, George was a moralist; he was—and perhaps remains—far better known than the major economists who have influenced the development of the subject; but single ideas often have greater impact on the public than complex accounts of complex reality.[21] The idea of a single tax had prominent supporters in American public life, including Louis F. Post, founder of the magazine *The Public*, who later became assistant secretary of labor; and Frederic C. Howe, one of the most prominent of the Progressives and at one time commissioner of immigration in New York.[22] But none of these positions gave them an influence on federal policy, which is perhaps the more important point.

George's single tax was the sovereign remedy intended to claw back for the people all the profits accruing from the rise of land values. His notion that land had been evenly distributed at the time of the Revolution was widely shared among reformers of the later nineteenth century, an American myth which somewhat resembled myths of medieval agrar-

---

21. Ibid., 184, 109, 201, 326.
22. John A. Thompson, *Reformers and War: American Progressive Publicists and the First World War* (Cambridge, 1987), 42.

ian felicity sometimes to be found in Europe. Among these reformers was Edward Bellamy, who had spent years reflecting on the perplexing injustices of modern society and had filled many notebooks with moral and political reflections before he published his most famous novel *Looking Backward* in 1888. At some date apparently a few years after the Civil War, he rejected the ethics of competition with the comment, "What difference does it make if you or your oppressor is a self-made man risen from the ranks? His rod is even heavier than the born rich man's." [23] This was Bellamy's reply to the attempts of so many reformers to come to terms with the capitalist system in both economics and ethics by demanding merely that equal opportunities should be restored. But an agrarian social order was not going to dominate the future, and instead of it Bellamy conceived of a society that was to be wholly mechanized; the methods would one day be known as "automation." In a manner closely akin to that soon to be adopted by H. G. Wells, Bellamy used the novel to combine science fiction with political science. When his sleeping protagonist awakes in A.D. 2000, he finds himself in a world refined and depersonalized by technology. Private rewards are still admitted to the incentive system for the workers, because Bellamy was aware of the role of personal ambition even in a fully collective social system. But the country is run by a small group of nobler citizens who are liberated from the profit motive and respond to an inner directive. The universal free education which forms an important element in his society consists mainly in training in industrial and professional skills. Since all the fundamental problems of society have been resolved by agreement, there is no further need to make laws; government has become the most routine form of management.

Edward Bellamy aimed to create a system in which economic equality would be as normal for all citizens as the political equality which he seems to have believed already existed. He agreed with such contemporary reformers as Henry George and Henry Demarest Lloyd that private property ought to correspond to natural inequalities, and he was not troubled by the fact that his system was not fully cooperative and that the need for a central class of managers, moved by morally finer sentiments than the masses, had about it a strong flavor of the kind of moral

23. John L. Thomas, Introduction to Edward Bellamy, *Looking Backward* (Cambridge, Mass., 1967), 19.

hierarchy that had once characterized the Puritan magistrates; a later generation would call it elitism. It was not inconsistent with the views of middle-class reformers, viewing with apprehension the new masses of illiterate immigrants, that in an autobiographical novel he had just set aside, he described the workers as they left the factory gates as "mere human oxen," some of whom exchanged "coarse jests, voluble with vulgarity." The protagonist, looking on, reflects that each of these narrow foreheads was a prison to the dark soul within it—"and what a prison, what a dungeon dark!" These attitudes might not have won him many votes in elections but failed to deter his admirers. *Looking Backward* sold some 60,000 copies in its first year of publication, rising to 100,000 the next year, with editions in Britain, France, and Germany.[24]

In America Bellamy proceeded to found the "Nationalist" movement, which was to bring in the promised age without social upheaval. In a series of articles and in editorials for his movement's paper, *The New Nation*, he explained that Nationalism—a name that referred to the national scale of the organization, without implying the competition with other nations which it later acquired—was a purely American program rooted in the political egalitarianism of the American Revolution. For him as for so many others, this claim of consistency with American traditions was of the utmost importance; Bellamy claimed that his party were true conservatives, seeking to maintain and conserve the true purposes of the republic.[25] In restoring the nation to its own true ideals, equality was a moral imperative. Then, for two years, Bellamy threw himself into the populist movement, which at first seemed capable of achieving his aims, or at least of taking steps toward them. Politics failed him, however, and in 1897 he turned back to publishing his last book, simply called *Equality*. Bellamy had spent much of his time in religious musings and now made it his purpose to bring the American egalitarian tradition into union with the country's potent capacity for religious revivals; Christian evangelism would continue the tradition begun by the Declaration of Independence.[26]

Bellamy's Nationalist movement faded rather quickly into obscurity. Its western elements were absorbed into the more politically promising

24. Ibid., 50; Thomas, *Alternative America*, 169, 234.
25. Thomas, Introduction, 76.
26. Ibid., 82–83.

populist movement; in the East it simply lost its relevance. [27] Nationalist clubs had sprung up on every side and no doubt contributed some springs of political awareness and vitality to other movements, but they had never been co-ordinated into a political force, and Bellamy was not the man to give them leadership. But the unified vision he gave Americans was inspired by the ethics of equality. It may well have been the last of its kind. Except for sex, where he discerned a functional distinction, Bellamy did not break equality into categories or try to draw lines between equality before the law, equality of opportunity, and other varieties; he saw no need for such distinctions, which would have spoiled the purity of his theme. Deviations from the central theme there might be, but they would be required to justify themselves as deviations from the dominant ethic. A sharper analysis would have obscured his vision, though it might have given a keener cutting edge to his program.

The Threat to Economic Democracy

It is not surprising that the principal egalitarian theme to be emphasized in the early years of the twentieth century was that of equality of opportunity. In law and in politics—where individual equality is defined as access to power through the vote—the principles had long been settled. Yet none of this had any direct effect on the major transformations that were overtaking the economy of the nation. These transformations may be described as three in one: industrialization, nationalization, and monopoly. Only very large corporations could have created a national economy, made possible, of course, by the advance of the continental railroads, and the development of a national market provided ample economic justification for the scale of the operations. But this immense scale appeared to raise completely new dangers for the cherished American values of individual independence secured through economic equality. Successive waves of crisis afflicted the closing decade of the old century. The announcement of the census report in 1891 that the historic frontier of free land no longer existed undoubtedly set in motion psychological repercussions beyond its practical significance; a severe industrial downturn, beginning in 1893, caused new alarms because it raised the question as to whether an economy so massively converted

27. Robert H. Wiebe, *The Search for Order, 1877–1920* (New York, 1967), 70–71.

to industry possessed the means for resolving its own internal problems. Meanwhile, the rising scale of immigration, though it certainly demonstrated that the great American experiment offered a prospect of hope to the outside world, presented Americans with problems of social absorption which appeared to many of them to be unprecedented in kind and were certainly unprecedented in scale and rapidity. In these circumstances the state of the republic became a matter of the most active moral concern, and many of the ablest minds of the period, particularly among the younger generation of journalists, politicians, and other publicists, felt impelled to give their best efforts to diagnosing the complaints of their generation.

The ideas associated with equality were broad and flexible enough to contain differing points of view and different remedies. But not all the more prominent thinkers of the time wished the country to continue to justify itself in the egalitarian language of the past. William Graham Sumner, who dominated the teaching of sociology at Yale, had no time for egalitarian sentiments. Observing that the best men of the seventeenth century believed that witches ought to be burnt, he compared these beliefs with "the dogma that all men are equal and that one ought to have as much power in the state as another"—which was in turn the culmination of nineteenth-century political dogmas and social philosophy.[28] Reformers who were much less comfortable than Sumner with the consequences of the economic struggle found it difficult to agree about the exact requirements called for by equality of opportunity and still more difficult to translate that doctrine into social policy enforced by law.

Some of the dominant trends of recent years could hardly fail to cause alarm. American agriculture, as Frederick C. Howe pointed out, had witnessed the two related phenomena of tenancy and the increasing size of the larger farms. By 1900, one-fourth of all farms under cultivation were over 1,000 acres, and 25 percent of farm acreage was owned by 0.006 percent of the people, reflecting a steep hierarchy of owners and laborers, landlords and tenants. In a truly Jeffersonian vein he argued that from ten to twenty million persons might have been housed on farms of 50 acres each. Howe's strictures were not confined to agriculture, however; he also noticed the increasing rise of tenancy in cities, where

28. William Graham Sumner, *Folkways* (1906; rpr., New York, 1940), 66.

he reported that the homeowner was rapidly disappearing, with only 29 percent of homes owned free of encumbrances. Howe feared that America would soon be comparable with Ireland.[29]

Although many of the Progressives were concerned with the social consequences of economic inequalities, Howe was unusual in his insistence that the unequal distribution of wealth, accompanied by the growth of steep hierarchies of power, themselves required public attention. "We know practically nothing of the distribution of wealth," he remarked; the universities were silent on the subject, and it was neglected by political science.[30] The difficulty in formulating a political policy was in reconciling this kind of anxiety with the aspirations for self-advancement which led Howe's contemporary, Charles Horton Cooley, to comment on the "almost inevitable dualism which makes it natural that a man should strive to aggrandize himself, his family and his class even though he truly wishes for a greater equality of privilege." This curious notion of an "equality of privilege" is revealing; privilege is by definition a form of inequality. Perhaps Americans expected a natural superiority of privilege over less favored peoples; or perhaps it was a synonym for or an approximation to equality of opportunity. Cooley, however, was prepared to defend class sentiment. In America, he contended, class did not mean hereditary caste—which would be objectionable, it seems, because it was uncongenial to commerce. The main aim—and here he returned to the older American theme—was freedom of opportunity. By this, he does not seem to have meant quite the same thing as *equality* of opportunity, but in such an intensely competitive society, his version, as an expression of practical aspirations, may have been nearer the mark.[31] Progressives were deeply concerned with the inequitable distribution of wealth; Howe spoke for them when he calculated on the basis of the census returns that there would be enough for all if it were justly distributed. But their diagnosis of what had gone wrong in the economic system did not clearly indicate the remedy of redistribution. Control or restraint of the trusts was a less directly interventionist policy. Socialists like Spargo and Walling had a

29. Frederick C. Howe, *Privilege and Democracy in America* (New York, 1910), 75–87.
30. Ibid., 185.
31. Charles Horton Cooley, *Social Organization* (1909; rpr., New York, 1962), 265–67.

somewhat easier time of it, since they had no doubt that economic inequality lay in the nature of capitalism.[32] Where equality recurred as a theme in Progressive rhetoric, its meaning and applications tended to emphasize opportunity and the individual; this marked a departure, or at least a difference of primary emphasis, from the deep populist preoccupation with the values of the community.

The trend toward an industrialized economy on a national scale, however, would not be reversed. In 1870, some seventy percent of the working population were still employed on their own farms or businesses; a century later, the figure was five percent.[33] Anti-trust laws did not alter the basic character of the institutions of industrial control and economic management. But these difficulties did not mean that equality of any sort was a lost cause. The real need of the time was to redefine the issues in terms of an industrial society. Large-scale industry has multiplier effects which are better understood now than they were in the early years of the process and may well stimulate the growth of small suppliers and parallel industries; they also, when operating successfully, create new kinds of employment on a scale commensurate with their size. The period of heavy industrialization produced no clear trend toward a more rigid, constricted social structure, and a clear majority of working-class youths succeeded in climbing to positions higher than those of their fathers.[34]

All the same, poverty was frequently transmitted by generation, immigrants were almost invariably at a disadvantage, and middle-class immigrants had much greater difficulties than middle-class natives in passing their own gains on to their children. An always substantial

32. Thompson, *Reformers and War*, 42.

33. Richard Sennett and Jonathan Cobb, *The Hidden Injuries of Class* (Cambridge, 1972), 57.

34. Stefan F. Thernstrom, *The Other Bostonians* (Cambridge, Mass., 1976), 92, 249. These observations are not confined to Boston. The author specifically generalizes them, and finds considerable stability in patterns of mobility (221, 239). The working-class parents studied by Thernstrom seem to have preferred present gains to making sacrifices for the benefit of their children. A century later, this attitude had completely changed. Working-class fathers of the post–Second World War era—a generation which had experienced the Depression—would use their own lives not as a model for their children but as a warning, and demonstrated an intense desire and willingness to make sacrifices to give their children an occupational mobility which, they felt, had been denied to themselves. Sennett and Cobb, *Hidden Injuries*, 127–28, 166.

proportion of the labor force perpetually failed to elevate itself from conditions of recognized poverty. There were few grounds for believing that industrial society held any internal key to the alleviation of the associated distresses. There was virtually no improvement in the conditions of blacks until the 1940s.[35]

Whatever the indications of relative prosperity or deprivation, there could be no doubt that the problem of power was itself acquiring new dimensions. Among the new barons of industry, even a president of the United States sometimes found himself in a position rather resembling that of those feudal kings who were expected "to live off their own" and were obliged to contend for authority among their barons. The American Progressives, in their turn, could look only to the power of national institutions to dominate that of the great private corporations. It is a notable fact that men as varied in their views as, in politics and political science, Theodore Roosevelt and Woodrow Wilson, or as Herbert Croly, whose *Promise of American Life* promoted him to an influential position in Roosevelt's counsels, and his somewhat more radical contemporary Walter Weyl, or again, the socialist John Spargo, who became famous as the author of *The Bitter Cry of the Children*, and the young Walter Lippmann, all recognized the necessity for national power.

When the French philosophes were moved by the desire for greater equality as a mode of protest against the injustices of the ancien regime, they sought to strengthen the monarchy while convincing it of its duty to the nation as a whole. If the strategy was ultimately to fail, it was the only one which, until almost the last moment, seemed to have any hope of success. Progressives understood their nation's problems in a comparable light. Much must depend on the nature of the presidency and the conduct of executive policies, and a great deal of the political excitement and controversy of the era turned on presidential elections and politics. But the United States had also a constitution which enshrined certain egalitarian precepts, and unlike any earlier or other nation, it had a more permanent guardian of its values in a Supreme Court.

The appearance of certain significant inconsistencies which revealed themselves in the Court's collective thinking suggests that the period of business consolidation, mass immigration, and widespread social protest that ran from roughly the end of Reconstruction to the outbreak of the

---

35. Thernstrom, *Other Bostonians*, 45–46, 73, 77, 84, 119–24, 194.

Great War in Europe in 1914 was a period calling for redefinition of national priorities. It suggests at the same time that justices of the Supreme Court recognized their own responsibilities in that process. In racial matters the Court was prepared to countenance bloc designations as constitutionally valid. In economic relations, it swung from a position strongly in support of the exercise of public powers in the public interest toward a more protective attitude toward private, or corporate, interests. Down to about 1890, in political economy, if not in civil rights, the Court was willing to sustain the powers of government, whether state of federal, where those powers were indispensably called for to serve larger public interests. But much would depend on how the powers of government were deployed, and Mr. Justice Stephen Field, writing in 1890, offered an explanation of a judicial posture that was designed to hold the pass of laissez-faire principles against the oncoming columns of corporate powers: "As population and wealth increase—as the inequalities in the conditions of men become more and more marked and disturbing—as the enormous aggregations of wealth possessed by some corporations excite uneasiness lest their power should become dominating in the legislation of this country. . . it becomes more and more the imperative duty of the court to enforce with a firm hand every guarantee of the constitution."[36] The point here, which is easily misunderstood, was not to oppose the aggregated powers of the corporations as such, but to recognize them, alongside other forms of aggregated power— labor, the farmers—all striving to bend government to their wills, as a threat to laissez-faire values; hence the redoubled need to protect the existing constitutional prohibitions on the use of government power to redistribute wealth. This was a view based, if somewhat remotely by this time, on the equality of individual rights which those constitutional prohibitions were supposed to protect. There had been a more socially oriented promise of equality in the message of *Munn v. Illinois* in 1877, when the Court upheld state legislation fixing the price for the storage of grain; when a person devoted his property to a use that affected the

---

36. "The Centenary of the Supreme Court of the United States," *American Law Review* 24 (1890), as quoted by Morton Keller, *Affairs of State: Public Life in Late Nineteenth Century America* (Cambridge, Mass., 1977), 367. Keller views this as an example of judicial activism in face of rising corporate power.

public at large he had to "submit to be controlled by the public for the common good, to the extent of the interest he has created."[37] In seeking to rectify gross disparities of economic power, the state had used legislative power to keep open the channels of equality of opportunity, and at that time the Court saw nothing unconstitutional in the policy.

It is thus a mistake to regard laissez-faire economics as a doctrine that controlled the ethos which determined legislation, or through which the Constitution was interpreted by the judiciary. For some ten or more years the Court consistently upheld state powers to regulate private economic activities which affected the public; in one such case, Pennsylvania had prohibited the manufacture of oleomargarine as a substitute for butter; in many others, the interests affected were those of railroads; and hundreds of state cases followed the same pattern.[38] In a significant criminal case, *Hurtado v. California*, the Court accepted jurisdiction over the question of whether due process of law had been observed in a trial for murder but determined that indictment by a grand jury was not in itself an indispensable element of due process; in a similar case, it declared that no state had the right to deprive any person or class of persons of "equal and impartial justice under law."[39] But although Chief Justice Melville W. Fuller pronounced these words, it was under his aegis that the Court's mood underwent a change. The decision against the federal income tax in 1895 was much more characteristic of the more individualistic conservatism of the Court under Fuller. That point of view was revealed in full flower in the celebrated case of *Lochner v. New York*, in which the Supreme Court struck down a state statute regulating the hours of work in bakeries on the grounds that it interfered with individual freedom of private contract, without the mitigating justification of regulating public health.[40] Nevertheless, the Court continued to sustain

37. 94 U.S. 113.

38. *Powell v. Pennsylvania*, 127 U.S. 678 (1888); *Missouri Pacific Railroad v. Mackey*, 127 U.S. 205 (1888); *Stone v. Farmers' Loan and Trust Company*, 116 U.S. 307 (1886); *Wabash, St. Louis and Pacific Railroad v. Illinois*, 118 U.S. 557 (1886); William E. Nelson, *The Fourteenth Amendment: From Political Principle to Judicial Doctrine* (Cambridge, Mass., 1988), 171, 192–93.

39. 110 U.S. 516 (1884) (California's constitution provided for indictment on information, after commitment by a magistrate); *Caldwell v. Texas*, 137 U.S. 692, 697; Nelson, *Fourteenth Amendment*, 193.

40. 198 U.S. 45 (1905).

the state legislatures in some three-quarters of the cases in which state laws were challenged by private interests.[41] A Court which countenanced such extensive use of legislative power might do so again when a social philosophy of public interest came to dominate that of private rights.

From the point of view of the somewhat diffuse strands that made up a Progressive political philosophy, as for more radical successors in later generations, the theme of equality was never far from the surface; of greater immediate significance, however, was the possibility that national power might enter into the enforcement of whatever policies were held to be in the major public interest. The Supreme Court was to be the instrument of that process. If the process of redefinition was extremely slow, that was hardly a matter for surprise; the elements running through American history were both complex and conflicting. In the midst of these conflicts, demands for one or another sort of equality had by no means disappeared from the agenda of reform. But it would have henceforth to be reform rather than restoration.

New Departures and the Loss of the Ideological Past

For the reformers of the new century, again as for their French philosophic predecessors, equality was not a concrete aim but, as we have suggested, a mode of protest. This comparison goes some way to explain why the idea of equality, though pervasively accepted in some form or other, was so limited an instrument of substantive policy. American political thought was undergoing a profound shift in its basic orientation. The concepts of bloc identity which persuaded the Supreme Court in racial issues seemed to be reflected in close analogies applying both to the social order and to political economy. As floods of immigrants settled into neighborhoods which came to bear their social, religious, and often linguistic identities, Americans tended increasingly to think of their society in terms of bloc designations.[42] Israel Zangwill's concept of the "melting pot" might be pitted bravely against this trend,

41. Keller, *Affairs of State*, 368–69.
42. John Higham, *Strangers in the Land: Patterns of American Nativism* (New Brunswick, N.J., 1955); Higham, *Send These to Me: Jews and Other Immigrants in Urban America* (New York, 1975); Michael Novak, *The Rise of the Unmeltable Ethnics* (New York, 1972).

but it was by no means sure that it had the power to fight a winning battle (and Zangwill was British: he returned to live in his home country).

Certain egalitarian principles had been firmly established as precepts of the Constitution. This was true both of political equality—equal access to political power as secured by the right (of men) to vote—and of equal access to and treatment in the courts—equality before the law. But the constitutional basis of these claims now lay in the Fourteenth and Fifteenth Amendments, and appeals to the political ethics of the Declaration of Independence or the original Constitution played little part in the argument. Obstructions to the realization of these principles lay in the nature of the federal system; while the states remained their guardians, and while the Supreme Court protected the independence of state jurisdictions with keener jealousy than it protected individual rights, the experience of the victims of racial intolerance made a mockery of these professions of principle. But that is not to say that these equalities had been discarded from the American canon of rights. The equality of women was an issue already on a minority agenda, but the case would gain its leverage when future circumstances could engage with the moral force derived from the philosophies of the past.

The most active egalitarian theme of the age was that of equality of opportunity. Traces of this idea have indeed been picked up before the end of the eighteenth century, and it may be held to be implicit in the individualist basis of the Constitution. But equality of opportunity, as we have seen, was an idea which, although based in equality of rights, drew much of its motive force from the rise of entrepreneurial capitalism. The right to it may have been a constitutionally protected right, but the force comes from the development of the economy. What had really happened in American political ideology since around the turn of the nineteenth century was that profound changes in economic and social structure, unforeseen at the making of the Constitution, had called for new and unforeseen responses. Rights, as individual attributes, were grounded in the Constitution and the Bill of Rights; but the constitutional basis of these responses has been sought primarily in the Reconstruction amendments. All this is manifested in both the social analysis and the rhetoric of early twentieth century Progressives, who showed little interest in reviving the kind of popular egalitarian formula that had appealed to past generations. Croly recognized that "all Americans, whether they are professional politicians or reformers, 'predatory' millionaires or common

people, political philosophers or schoolboys, accept the principle of 'equal rights for all and special privileges for none' as the absolutely sufficient rule of an American democratic political system. The platforms of both parties testify on its behalf."[43] In keeping with this standpoint, Theodore Roosevelt was able to declare without fear of contradiction when he accepted his party's nomination for the presidency in 1904, that "this government is based on the fundamental idea that each man, no matter what his occupation, his race, or his religious belief, is entitled to be treated on his worth as a man, and neither favored nor discriminated against because of any accident in his position."[44]

Successful candidates tend to be satisfied with the system. Before leaving office Roosevelt observed, "Politically we can be said to have worked out our democratic ideals, and the same is true, thanks to our common schools, in educational matters."[45] In the first of these statements Roosevelt had referred to the important category of equality of esteem. But not all Americans shared his satisfaction. That only served to make the ideal of equality in all its aspects the more popular, while giving it the status not of a thoroughly worked out ideology but of an unfinished agenda. Political equality would have had little point if it could not be used to improve economic policies in the same direction; and effective power itself commands esteem. In spite of the very prominent fact that Progressives regarded America's historic values as being under threat, equality remained an active organizing principle for political and social action; but it seems a decided paradox of the political situation that Theodore Roosevelt could at the same time pronounce himself satisfied that the nation's principal egalitarian aims had been fulfilled.

Yet it was at the link between politics and policy that Croly turned from party politics to develop a remarkably scathing attack on the popular addiction to the idea of equality; in Croly's treatment it becomes a little difficult to distinguish the faults due to popular misconceptions from those to be attributed to the principle itself. The weakness of the equal rights principle, according to Croly, was that it concealed a contra-

43. Herbert Croly, *The Promise of American Life* (New York, 1909), 151.
44. A.B. Hart and H.R. Ferleger, eds., *Theodore Roosevelt Cyclopedia* (New York, 1914), 167.
45. Ibid., 167–68.

diction—the elementary contradiction between the right to an equal start and the right to equal fulfillment. The contradiction, he observed, was concealed so long as the economic opportunities of the country had not been developed or appropriated, but "continued loyalty to a contradictory principle is destructive of a wholesome public sentiment and opinion." The principle itself, not merely ill-considered faith in it, was to blame. "The principle of equal rights encourages mutual suspicion and disloyalty. It tends to attribute individual and social ills, for which general moral, economic and social causes are usually in large measure responsible, to individual wrong-doing; and in this way it arouses and intensifies that personal and class hatred, which never in any society lies far below the surface."[46]

Yet Croly strongly affirmed his faith in social equality, and in terms not altogether consistent with the foregoing critique he attributed "the fluid and elastic substance of American life" and the accessibility of economic opportunities to the "democratic dislike of any suggestion of authentic social inferiority." If the flexibility of American institutions had permitted the present concentrations of wealth in the hands "of a few irresponsible men," the task for the future was to gather up into national institutions the power to confront them and assume the responsibility "for a morally and socially desirable distribution of wealth." In this program he discerned "the beginnings of a revolution."[47]

The penetration of the American acquisitive ethos into reformist thought is demonstrated in two books by John Spargo on the principles and the applications of socialism. Primitive notions of human equality were disavowed. "Not human equality, but equality of opportunity to prevent the creation of artificial inequalities by privilege is the essence of Socialism," he explained.[48] Whatever the merits of this view, it could hardly be considered the *essence* of socialism in any sense understood by the movement's European adherents; it was an unself-consciously American variant. In his later book, Spargo made clear that he recognized inequalities of talent and denied that socialism would mean equality of remuneration; equality should not be confused with uniformity. He quoted with approval Lester Frank Ward's assertion that "all men are

---

46. Croly, *Promise*, 183–85.
47. Ibid., 14, 23–24.
48. John Spargo, *Socialism* (New York, 1906), 236.

intellectually equal in the sense that, in persons taken at random from different social classes the chances for talent and ability are the same for each class." This amounted to a reminder, if not a resurgence, of the idea of interchangeability. Spargo objected to the present social system because its unequal opportunities repressed much latent ability; the removal of these inequalities would result in much greater equality of intellectual equipment than actually existed.[49] What was missing from this vision was the profound socialist faith in the human potential for co-operation and collective achievement. Spargo's ideals might not seem to have much in common with Croly's, yet in their different ways they both wanted to return to the individual some of the control over his own life, some of the power of self-realization, that they believed had been lost to the corporations; and both recognized the state as the agency of the process. The more Jeffersonian Gifford Pinchot, leader of the first major American struggle for conservation of natural resources and amenities, shared this commitment to the idea of equality of opportunity, which he declared was "the real object of our laws and institutions." It was also their moral justification; by turning away from equality of opportunity, the economic order inflicted "a bitter moral wrong."[50] Walter Weyl, also a campaigner for conservation, which he extended to the general principles of social organization, saw some grounds for hope in the "socialization of consumption." Weyl was willing to reduce the comparative rewards of the successful in the cause of raising the standards of the lowest; much like Spargo, he held that "what a socialized democracy demands is an equalization, not of men, but of opportunities."[51]

Like Herbert Croly, Walter Lippmann—writing a little later, under Woodrow Wilson's administration—wanted to establish mastery over the drift of the times. Like his contemporaries, he assumed a general right to something like equality of opportunity, though he was too shrewd to define it. He had before him, however, the example of a muddled administration with incoherent social aims. "I am for big business," Lippmann quoted Wilson as saying, "and I am against the trusts."

49. Spargo, *Applied Socialism* (London, 1912), 171–74. The title of this book recalled Lester Frank Ward's *Applied Sociology*; Spargo was an English immigrant, concerned to represent socialism as compatible with American ideals.
50. Gifford Pinchot, *The Fight for Conservation* (London, 1910), 24, 69.
51. Walter Weyl, *The New Democracy* (New York, 1912), 352.

"That," Lippmann commented, "is a very subtle distinction, so subtle, I suspect, that no human legislation will ever be able to make it. The distinction is this: big business is a business that has survived competition; a trust is an arrangement to do away with competition."[52] Wilson's desire to restore the conditions of free competition rather served to recall Andrew Jackson than to anticipate the modern state. However his policies might have developed, they were interrupted by American entry into the Great War.

The war led the federal government to assume powers for economic mobilization which it might one day have been obliged to acquire for social legislation. From the point of view of all those who, at least until that moment, had been primarily concerned to adapt the powers of government to control economic institutions, it was a bitter irony that an overseas war could call forth unity of purpose and effectiveness in action greater than those called forth by the unresolved crisis at home. Since, from this position, the war was the wrong crisis, it could not be surprising that it led to the wrong consequences, under which ideas of equality were submerged for another political generation, and another war.

52. Walter Lippmann, *Drift and Mastery* (New York, 1917), 138–39.

Chapter Ten

Individual Equality and Ethnic Identity

Immigration and the Concept of Race

With the exception of the constitutional principles associated with states' rights, the vague doctrines pertaining to one or another form of pluralism had seldom if ever been given explicit form. A pluralism of regions and economic interests could overlap with or be defined separately from those of religion and national origin. But however the components of these pluralities might be defined, any one group was inevitably composed of individuals. In the United States no less than in more traditional societies, one inescapable truth about individual identity was that people were socially defined and received much of their sense of identity from the group they belonged to. These social groups are talked about, and take shape in people's minds, as though they were embodied, concrete forms, but they need to be understood as *concepts*, and concepts of a very porous and indeterminate nature. A southerner might feel a sense of communal identity with other southerners when faced with that other collective identity, the North; but, if Virginian, might feel quite differently vis-à-vis Mississippi; if the southerner were a man, he would in certain respects feel a different identity from a woman's, and if a black, would certainly feel a different identity from a white's—and vice versa. These varying, shifting, and undefinable collective identities had no fixed status in constitutional law; the Constitution, as we have observed, when it was not contemplating the states, knew only individuals.

In matters of equality, two major developments introduced a new tension into the relations between individuals and groups. One of these, as we have seen, was the Supreme Court's willingness to tolerate bloc designations as having formal status under the Constitution. The other was the new scale and character both of immigration and, equally important, of internal settlement. In residence and employment patterns, the irresistible realities of immigration and social grouping seemed to make pluralism a fact before it had a theory. But, as the Supreme Court had been warned in *Plessy v. Ferguson*, specifically racist policies of segregation in one area had the effect, incidental but not trivial, of bringing other types and other objects of segregation into view. As white social thinkers and publicists turned away from the seemingly insoluble distractions of "the Negro problem," it was to the implications of mass immigration from various and new sources that they increasingly turned their attention.

The responses of native and settled white Americans to the new scale of immigration were more varied and confused than their general prejudice against blacks. The distinction between white and black was the clearest case of what people meant by race; in popular parlance, race meant color. [1] The other races of which the mass of Americans had any clear notion were American Indians and Orientals, and both these were special cases, nearly always located in distinct geographical areas. Gradually, however, as individuals who had originally seemed indistinguishable from one another stepped forward from the huddled masses to identify themselves by differences of appearance, language, food, and social behavior, new concepts of race began to take shape in the minds of uneasy nativists. In these perceptions only the broadest outlines were at all clear; the more subtle personal details about immigrant character remained blurred and obscure, the gaps being filled in by rumor and explained by preconceived ideas.

It would be quite misleading to characterize American reactions as nothing more than undiluted dismay and hostility. Americans would have been required to repudiate immense tracts of their nation's past if

1. John Higham, *Send These to Me: Jews and Other Immigrants in Urban America* (New York, 1975), 45. It may be added, however, that race was a normal category for purposes of bureaucratic classification. Until long after the Second World War, applicants for United States immigration visas were required to declare their "race," even if this was only defined as "Dutch" or "French."

they were to accept the gloomy thesis that American society was incapable of absorbing foreign peoples. Even so restrictionist a newspaper as *The Press* of Philadelphia had observed in 1883, "The strong stomach of American civilization may, and doubtless will, digest and assimilate ultimately this unsavoury and repellent throng. . . . In time they catch the spirit of the country and form an element of decided worth." [2] The "repellent throng" consisted of stocks still largely unfamiliar in the United States. Yet until the middle of the 1890s, some 80 per cent of all immigrants continued to come from the more traditional sources in Northwest Europe. [3] It was only for a period of nine years beginning in 1899 that the notion of the "new immigration" corresponded with the statistical facts. But during that period a staggering rise in the intake from eastern Europe and Russia's European provinces, from the Balkans, Italy, and Sicily, altered all previous perspectives of the problems involved in the reception of immigrants. Impressions long preceded facts, and the effect of these crowded years was to quicken older anxieties about the problem of assimilation. [4]

These anxieties were made more acute toward the end of the old century because they coincided with a series of shocks to America's older and more confident nationalism. The ending of the frontier of free land, the business panic and depression of 1893, recurring violence between labor and employers seemed to be bringing the New World closer to the character of the Old. As early as 1883 Henry George, only in some respects a reformer or humanist, perceived a dangerous connection between the anticipated closing of the frontier and the continuance of immigration: "Will it make our difficulty the less that our human garbage can vote?" he asked. Five years later the American Economic Association, whose patrons were associated with measures for economic reform, offered a prize for an essay on "The Evil Effects of Unrestricted Immigration." In 1891 Samuel Gompers requested the convention of the newly formed American Federation of Labor to place the issue of immigration on its agenda. After the panic of 1893, a mood of restriction began to attain new strength in the stricken areas of the South and West. [5]

2. John Higham, *Strangers in the Land: Patterns of American Nativism* (New Brunswick, N.J., 1953), 62–63.
3. Ibid., 88.
4. Ibid., 158–59.
5. Ibid., 35–43, 71, 73–74.

It was idle to deny that these problems had assumed unprecedented proportions, and had done so in an extraordinarily short time. The fact that a certain spectrum of people ranging from reformist intellectuals to labor leaders, who were genuinely concerned about the future of American democracy with special emphasis on class structure and the concentration of economic power, should have been those who were most anxious about unlimited immigration does not prove that their reform commitment was shallow or hypocritical or that their humanity was flawed. It rather reveals the fact that their basic beliefs about the nature and prospects of American democracy were based on certain undisclosed assumptions. The most basic of these was that of a pervasive homogeneity of national character. Among others was a faint residue of the old notion of the interchangeability of Americans, which helped to legitimate the faith that equality of opportunity could be sustained in a competitive society.

These assumptions, deriving from the conventional historical accounts of the founding of the republic, were clearly revealed in the opinions of the dominant political rivals, Theodore Roosevelt and Woodrow Wilson. Both these men believed that the character of American nationality was fixed in the period from 1776 to 1787—a character already determined by the history of British North America before independence. All subsequent mingling was a process of continued assimilation into the original type; the numbers were enlarged, the type might even be enriched, but it retained its basic qualities in such fundamentals as law, education, and religion, in the sense of political obligation and responsibility, and in certain aspects of social and personal style.[6] Similar views were held by Progressive publicists. They deserve attention here because of their implications for the possibilities of equality as perceived by those who were already dissatisfied with the system and apprehensive about its development. John R. Commons, a Progressive of the Wisconsin school and the leading early historian of the labor movement, explained the problem by reference to the fact that Americans had always possessed a common language, an instrument at hand

---

6. I have elaborated this comment from Milton M. Gordon, *Assimilation in American Life: The Role of Race, Religion and National Origins* (New York, 1964), 122. Compare Henry James's characterization of "the American type" in *The American* (Boston, 1877), 1.

"for conscious improvement through education and social environment." Not physical amalgamation but mental community united mankind: "To be great a nation need not be of one blood, but must be of one mind," he declared. Commons went from this to emphasize that everyone should have "equal opportunity to make the most of himself, to come forward and achieve high standing in any calling to which he is inclined"—an assertion of the standard doctrine of equality of opportunity. It had its corollary: it was equally important not only that laws and institutions should generate these opportunities, but that all citizens should be equally capable of participating, especially in making and enforcing the laws.[7]

Three categories of equality converged in a now conventional pattern: equality of opportunity was a right which America owed to all its people but which could be assured only by other, still more fundamental equalities, those of law and access to political power. The existence of virtual consensus on these points establishes the significance of equality as the criterion of the American sense of justice; for it was by reference to these criteria that the performance of the American system would be judged—would indeed judge itself.

But in the new and alarming circumstances, these convictions faced a new question: whether alien candidates for admission to the status of Americans could or should themselves be judged by their prospect of assimilability. It was in this atmosphere and with regard to these questions that American concepts of race began to assume newly diversified and newly political forms. But assimilation was not a self-defining process. To some, both immigrants and residents, it came to mean absorption into the more or less separate social, residential, and economic structures already formed by their racial, national, or religious predecessors. This process, of course, was of the highest value to those who desired to retain and preserve the customs and sometimes the religion of their original group. But it ran counter to an older tradition, that of Crèvecoeur, reinforced by generations of social mixing, in which earlier identities were confused and merged together; and there were other Americans, priding themselves on the superiority of older stock, who feared that the more traditional kind of assimilation into the homogeneous whole would result in a loss of the finer qualities of their national identity.

7. John R. Commons, *Races and Immigrants in America* (New York, 1907), 20.

After a group of patrician nativists led by Henry Cabot Lodge and Charles Warren, both of Massachusetts—the former a politician and author of a life of Alexander Hamilton, the latter a founder of the study of American constitutional law—had begun about 1905 to develop an ideology based on the distinction they drew between the "new" and the "old" immigration, it began to become increasingly clear that two further concepts of assimilation were under discussion. The first of these was cultural and political: foreigners could be said to be assimilated when they adopted and governed themselves by prescribed rules of procedure, style, and manners; conservative patricians shared with Progressive reformers the belief that something like this had happened continuously throughout the American past, and that the safety of the Republic required that this concept should determine the extent and character of all future immigration. The second concept was racial or genetic. Logically, however, the racial problem preceded the cultural, because it supposed some doubt as to whether certain physical or genetic types were capable of adapting themselves in the manner prescribed.

Whatever view American social analysts took of the questions of policy, they were on familiar ground when they addressed themselves to the connection between physical type and cultural achievement. Nineteenth-century popular as well as scientific thought was brought up in the knowledge that different civilizations, whatever their levels of attainment, had existed in the past and had crumbled to dust.[8] It was a commonplace that civilizations could be identified by the appearance and character of their peoples. Neither was there anything especially new in the idea that evolutionary processes could be social as well as biological; during the formative years of the American Republic, European social evolutionists generally assumed that all people had innate abilities that would enable them eventually to ascend the heights attained by Europeans and Euro-Americans—it was with reference to this proposition that Jefferson had harbored doubts about the African race.

Since then, physical anthropology had garnered immense amounts of detailed information about physiological differences, not least in the weighing of brains. The English anthropologist E.B. Tylor, who origi-

---

8. Consider Thomas Cole's epic series of paintings, "The Course of Empire," which depicts the passage of civilization from hunting, through agriculture, to civic grandeur, followed by invasion and devastation and ending with desolate ruins. The originals are in the New-York Historical Society.

nated the anthropological study of culture, regarded European brains as more fully developed organisms than African ones, but he seems also to have thought that primitive stages of development remained like older deposits in an advanced civilization, and he compared savages and barbarians to "what our ancestors were and our peasants still are." The idea that European *peasants* were arrested at a primitive stage of the progress of civilization comparable to that of "savages," a remark made in the 1870s, throws suggestive light on the fluidity of the concept of race in that period. American Progressives who received and shared these views were decidedly not cultural relativists in the sense that was to develop later. They fully accepted the evidence for the standard European view that Western history had established the cultural superiority of Western man.[9] And it was temptingly easy to adapt physical and cultural anthropology to the Lamarckian principle that characteristics acquired during encounters with the environment could be transmitted to succeeding generations. If racial characteristics were malleable and racial type not immutable, improvement might be hoped for in the future. Both foreign savages and domestic peasants could become civilized. But geological science had not stood still either, and much more was now known about the true antiquity of life on earth; the effect, perhaps paradoxically, was to depress the prospects of progress in any imaginable lifetime, and the makers of American policy could hardly be expected to wait until foreign races had adapted their genes to the requirements of republican forms of government.

In the very period when these questions were opening to the exploration of the comparability of cultures, the advance of physical anthropology took a form which produced a paradoxical setback for advocates of open social policies based on cultural adaptiveness. During the twenty years after 1890, laws of heredity propounded by the Austrian monk Gregor Mendel in 1865 but since neglected were rediscovered by a new

9. George Stocking, *Race, Culture, and Evolution* (New York, 1971), 129–30, who makes this remark about the Reform Darwinists, that is, social reformers who accepted Darwin's application of evolutionist views to society but believed in working to change men's social environment for the better. It applied to political Progressives more generally, whether or not they concerned themselves with the social adaptation of Darwin's theories. In this connection, consider Commons's distinction between "superior" and "inferior" races, where he believed that the Chinese, whom he regarded as superior in innate abilities, were in a backward state of civilization. Commons, *Races and Immigrants*, 211.

generation of geneticists. Their publications rapidly superseded the views of Lamarck.[10] The discovery that genetic characteristics followed interior rules of transmission that owed nothing to the organism's experience in the world tended to harden the notion that physical, or "racial," characteristics were immutable. This development gave encouragement to the concept of eugenics.

The eugenics movement had about it an attractive air of benign reformism. Its sponsors had the advantage of representing precisely that level of genetically endowed and historically authorized Anglo-Saxon superiority that gave them the presumptive right to pass judgment on other races; and if they wanted to breed out the poorer stocks and raise the population to their own standards, they seemed at worst to be combining self-esteem with science. The movement could hardly have expected to prove attractive to the representatives of racial inferiority, but it also suffered from the internal weakness of its failure to supply any credible racial typology. It did, however, propose a core of doctrine around which racial purists could gather, and a platform from which they could address the public. In this cause eugenicists founded the Galton Society in New York in 1918, confining its membership to native Americans who were held to be anthropologically, socially, and politically sound.[11] Their ideas, which were widely disseminated by Madison Grant and *The Saturday Evening Post* in the 1920s, rested on the belief that racial mixture was always racial debasement: "The cross between a white man and an Indian is an Indian; the cross between a white man and a negro is a negro; the cross between any of the three races of Europe and a Jew is a Jew." America, from an addiction to muddled sentimentalism, was being swept "toward a racial abyss."[12]

The relatively new science of applied psychology tended to encour-

---

10. Though not universally. Under Stalin, Soviet official biology sponsored Lamarckian views in Lysenko's researches on cereals and ruthlessly persecuted geneticists who rejected official doctrine. *International Encyclopedia* 14:403. Sigmund Freud, it seems, remained a convinced Lamarckian all his life. Joseph Frank in *The Times Literary Supplement*, 18 July 1975.

11. Higham, *Strangers*, 149–52; Stocking, *Race, Culture*, 289.

12. Oscar Handlin, *Race and Nationality in American Life* (Boston, 1957), 176–77; Higham, *Strangers*, 201, 265; Madison Grant, *The Passing of the Great Race* (London, 1917), xv, 11–12, 15–16, 77, 228. Grant's book was not a particular success when it appeared in 1916; his popularity owed much to the publicity afforded in the 1920s by *The Saturday Evening Post*.

age beliefs that race determined character. The Great War gave psychologists the opportunity to apply newly devised intelligence tests to soldiers on a large scale, and William McDougall, one of the leading applied psychologists of the period, went so far as to advance a racial interpretation of history based on results of "intelligence quotient" tests. The effects of army intelligence tests were particularly damaging to black Americans who, through their long history of economic, nutritional, and educational deprivation, and what may be called deprivation of legitimate hopes, were least equipped to meet the challenge. But the findings of the testers only confirmed the conventional white suspicions of black racial disability. [13]

From the point of view that regarded equality, in any form, as a cardinal moral principle, the danger inherent in these trends was apparent. If members of supposedly inferior races were genetically *incapable* of achieving the heights open to Americans of the superior European stock, then the whole concept of equality of opportunity was pointless. And serious questions might be raised about the validity of the principles of equality in law and politics. John R. Commons, in many ways a typical Progressive, believed that black Americans should not vote until they had proved themselves capable of democratic qualities. Commons recognized that they were the victims of slavery and believed them capable of elevation, but he did not explain how people were to go about proving themselves capable without actually taking responsible part in political life. However, he sharply reproved the southern states for depriving them of educational opportunities, pointing out that southern school systems spent $2.21 cents for every black child, $4.92 for every white child. [14] Commons evidently retained the more optimistic strand of American faith in education as offering a positive prospect of advancement for the disadvantaged.

Even the socialists, who were making much more progress in Ameri-

---

13. The accuracy of intelligence tests as indicators of performance may also be thought to suffer from the reading given to the abilities of new immigrants at Ellis Island, where, in 1912, it was found that eighty-five percent of the Jews, eighty percent of the Hungarians, and seventy-nine percent of the Italians were "feeble-minded." Philip Green, *The Pursuit of Inequality* (New York, 1981), 72.

14. Higham, *Strangers*, 275–76; Stocking, *Race, Culture*, 267; Commons, *Races and Immigrants*, 44–45. Commons emphasized environmental hostility as a cause of Negro backwardness (39–62).

can urban society than they were able to maintain in their subsequent history in America, offered very little comfort to black Americans. In a manner characteristic of white reformers, they took a generally patronizing view of people who had the misfortune not to be Anglo-Saxons; Victor L. Berger, the Milwaukee socialist leader, viewed the peoples of the world as naturally unequal, and blacks as biologically inferior.[15] The Socialist party was inclined to be skeptical of the blacks' potential for equality and, with the exception of a few energetic dissentients, took no active part in putting the issue on its political agenda. The few exceptions were not insignificant, however. Charles Edward Russell and William English Walling (member of a wealthy Kentucky family) were among the founders of the NAACP. Nor was the party idle in the South. In Oklahoma, a leading socialist state, the party fought consistently for full black enfranchisement, while socialists also showed strength in Texas, Louisiana, and Florida. In 1917, aspiring black leaders such as A. Philip Randolph and Chandler Owen joined the Socialist Party and advised black voters to vote socialist. Randolph used *The Messenger*, which he founded in 1917, to urge black New Yorkers to vote for Hilquit as mayor because he represented the working people, and "99 per cent of the negroes are working people." He added that the Socialist party, which Hilquit represented, did not hold race prejudice even in the South. In 1920 Randolph stood in New York as socialist candidate for state comptroller—the first black candidate for statewide office in the twentieth century. Their membership no doubt assisted in the racial education of white socialists; but African Americans never showed much collective interest in abolishing capitalism.[16]

Alternatives to Racial Determinism

Among all the deprivations that damaged the prospects of black Americans, that of equality of esteem was ultimately the most injurious, both to their psychology and to their social aspirations. This damage

15. Paul Buhle, *Marxism in the U.S.A. from 1870 to the Present Day* (London, 1987), 95. This is not to propose Berger as representative of socialist views on race. But positive expressions of racial egalitarianism were inconspicuous.

16. James Weinstein, "The Problems of the Socialist Party: A. Before World War One," in John M. Laslett and Seymour Martin Lipset, eds., *Failure of a Dream? Essays in the History of American Socialism* (New York, 1974), 308–10.

was inflicted from without so consistently as to become incorporated within the individual's psychology; this external damage, moreover, had an innate tendency to reproduce the external circumstances which sustained it, since white people who disesteemed blacks ceased to regard it as a duty to offer them opportunities for improvement. And the blacks seemed always positioned to be the victims of external circumstance. In the late nineteenth century, explorations of interior Africa, Australia, and Tasmania had the gratuitously damaging effect of connecting African-descended Americans with what the Euro-American mind perceived as primitive origins and barbaric customs.[17] It is no exaggeration to say, in more general terms, that the rise of industrial civilization in Europe and North America had the effect of widening the visible gap between Western civilization and the civilizations of aboriginal peoples who had not yet conceived of the Idea of Progress.

There was in principle no obvious reason why concepts of natural inequality should be confined to the differences between races of European and African origin. If the formative forces in national character were racial, then the direction of research must be to discover the history of races. When American social thinkers addressed themselves to these problems, they had first to confront the body of European writings, which claimed to have established the three dominant European races—the Nordic, the Alpine, and the Mediterranean. The American sociologist and economist William Z. Ripley confirmed as much in his book, *The Races of Europe*. But he did not take the same route as the extreme Caucasiophile Madison Grant was soon to do. Ripley's skepticism was aroused by the inextricable racial mixtures that had taken place, by the utter uncertainty and inconclusiveness of the historical records which applied to the very concept of race, and by the absence of any precise correlations between physical type and social behavior on which the conventional inferences rested. After investigating matters as diverse as divorce, artistic genius, and suicide (said to be high among Teutons), he concluded, "It is not race but physical and social environment that must be taken into account."[18]

---

17. Joseph Conrad, *Heart of Darkness*, almost the literary archetype of these views, was first published in 1902; but note also the way it begins, with the reflection of a sailor on shipboard in the Thames Estuary that Britain, too, had once been a remote region on the edges of the civilization of Rome. Although Conrad's thought is not free of racial typology (e.g., *Under Western Eyes*), his philosophy has marked elements of relativism.

18. William Z. Ripley, *The Races of Europe* (New York, 1899), 527.

It is a mistake to suppose that social scientists of this school, who concerned themselves with the long-term implications of immigration, were trapped in a narrow racial determinism. The orientation of their views was cultural rather than racial, but in their firm conviction of the superiority of the values that America had maintained throughout its history, through education and the Constitution, they saw no grounds for doubting that their own duty lay in finding means to maintain those values for the indefinite future. But in their opinion that duty did not lead in the direction of making America into a replica of the racial, religious, and social complexities of the rest of the world.

Edward A. Ross, a member of the contentious Wisconsin school of Progressives and an outspoken opponent of big business, put the whole question into a phrase when, after observing the continuance of population pressures in countries from which immigration was originating, he challenged "the equal right of all races to American opportunities."[19] Ross used racial designations to sustain his objections to unlimited immigration, but his argument was political and cultural, not racial. "Race" was at most a weak descriptive designation for groups who were difficult to define in terms of nationality. Although Ross can be quoted as making remarks that sound anti-Semitic, an attentive reading shows quite clearly that his hostility to the recent waves of Russian Jewish immigrants was based on economic methods and social attitudes which Ross, in common with many others, disliked; his views may be compared with those of another "older" American, W.E.B. Du Bois, who complained that in some southern states, Russian Jews had seized much land on which Negroes had worked all their lives.[20] But Ross believed that Jews included both the finest and the worst among foreign contributions to American culture; the first wave of Russian Jewish migrants of the 1880s he placed with "our British, Scandinavian, Teutonic . . . naturalized citizens who have benefited American politics."[21] So far was Ross from wanting to be racially exclusive that he described America as "probably the strongest solvent Jewish separatism has ever encountered" and welcomed mixed marriages as ending the distinct ethnic strain and absorbing the Jewish qualities for the benefit of the community.[22] He

---

19. Edward A. Ross, *The Old World in the New* (New York, 1914), 227.
20. W.E.B. Du Bois, *The Souls of Black Folk* (Chicago, 1903), 126–33.
21. Ross, *Old World*, 263.
22. Ibid., 166.

was much more concerned about the apparent inability of the Irish to adapt themselves to the American idea of law. "What is the Constitution between friends?" was not an attitude which he found compatible with popular government, and he condemned "the principles of the Celtic clan" as being responsible for heavy casualties from bad water, bad housing, poor sanitation, and rampant vice in the running of American municipalities. [23] Among Slavs he found evidence of ill-treatment of women, and evidence of weak educational attainments among a variety of immigrants. [24] It is, of course, wholly in keeping that he had no critical comment to make on the manners and morals of white Americans of northern European descent and in general of Protestant religion. But the problems as discerned by Ross were not confined to the early nineteenth century. After two world wars, and with New York's first anti-discrimination law on the statute book, the sociologist Henry Pratt Fairchild could still in 1947 ask whether democracy extended to people of widely different social habits, customs, ideals, standards, and values. These remarks, which were in fact directed against Jews, were once more conceived of, according to their author, as social, not racial; but on the other hand he did distinguish the Negro problem as based on racial characteristics. [25]

From this standpoint, which had a social and intellectual influence out of proportion to the numbers it represented, Americans were not expected to doubt that the Anglo-American type was the standard of excellence by which all the rest of the world would be judged. Yet there were alternative ways of looking at the world. About 1870, as we have seen, Edward Tylor had begun to work toward a virtually new concept—that of "culture" in its modern anthropological sense. When Tylor wrote of "primitive culture," he was making a novel and original use of language. Franz Boas, an immigrant German of Jewish descent who settled in the United States in 1882 and who, through his intellectual power and dominant if abrasive personality, came to influence successive generations of anthropologists, appears to have been the first scholar before 1900 to have used the word "culture" in the plural. [26] In

23. Ibid., 260–63.
24. Ibid., 138–39, 167.
25. Henry Pratt Fairchild, *Race and Nationality* (New York, 1947), 148–49.
26. Stocking, *Race, Culture,* 69.

Boas's hands, the study of *cultures* became the study of each ethnologically separable group in its entirety and in its integrity; his life's work assumed a fundamental respect for the values of other cultures and a profound recognition of the truth that each ethnological group possesses techniques, beliefs, and language reflecting its own perceptions and experience.

Boas set forth his basic position in 1894 when he delivered an address as vice-chairman of the American Association for the Advancement of Science, and chairman of its section on anthropology. His views were much more fully stated with the appearance in 1911 of his most influential book, *The Mind of Primitive Man*, and despite various revisions remained the principal theme of his teaching. "There is no fundamental difference in the ways of thinking between primitive and civilized men," Boas argued. "A close connection between race and personality has not been established. The concept of racial type as commonly used even in scientific literature is misleading and requires a logical as well as a biological definition."[27] In 1910 Boas contributed a large section to the Report of the Congressional Committee on Immigration (known as the Dillingham Commission), in which he reported the application of biometrics to the study of man and argued for the plasticity of the human organism; by these methods, Boas found surprisingly recent changes in head forms, arguing that his findings suggested the emergence of an "American type" with a uniformly "American" face.

This discovery, which does not appear to have been borne out by experience, no doubt represented a case of a scientist finding what he was looking for. But Boas's reported findings had serious implications; head form was generally believed to be one of the most stable indices of race.[28] The threatening prospect of the disappearance of the older form in favor of a new homogeneity caused immediate consternation among Anglo-Saxon purists.[29] But while Boas was educating the public away from ideas of racial fixity and determinism, his methods did not contribute much toward liberating the popular mind from the notion that head forms and physical structure had something to do with what was inside the head. Boas was educated in a generation dominated by ideas

27. Franz Boas, *The Mind of Primitive Man* (1911; rev. ed., New York, 1963), 8.
28. Higham, *Strangers*, 125.
29. Grant, *Passing of the Great Race*, 15.

of physical determinism, and in contributing to the new concept of cultural anthropology he drew on materials which owed their authority to the old methods he was trying to supersede. Boas's work was susceptible to attack by arguments based on his own continued respect for measurements of the cephalic index.[30]

The educational task before the cultural anthropologists was fraught with immense significance for the future of ideas of equality in America. For it was nothing less than that of dispelling the popular belief that different races and peoples of the world owed to inherited natural endowments the positions they occupied, their intellectual and technological attainments and political systems, whether more or less "advanced," that these were unalterable within any politically realistic time span, and that social policies should follow directly from these principles. Since a surprisingly large proportion of the world's races were now represented in the United States, it was certain that domestic attitudes would be affected by the opinions that Americans held of each other.

Yet there was an alternative and more fundamental tradition on which they could draw. Certain aspects of American individualism, and American rejection of ideas of class and caste, ran back to the origins of the republic and provided a historic American base from which to confront evolutionary doctrines which led to separatism and exclusion. But the prospect of a resurgence of individualistic principles did not have to depend on the republic's first principles. As Boas was demonstrating—and he can hardly have owed much to Jefferson's and Madison's generation—new scientific research could undermine old racial assumptions. Lester Frank Ward, the extraordinary, largely self-taught social anthropologist who gradually compelled the academic world to listen to his views with respect, was an immediate contemporary who, from the 1880s, brought to his arguments a strand of American experience that was absent from the arguments of Boas. Like Boas, Ward rejected the idea that the great differences observable among individuals and classes arose from differences of race, or color, or nationality; like Boas he maintained that there were no inborn inequalities of any kind that could of themselves prevent the equalization of opportunity.[31] Existing inequalities among men—and between men and women—were due to

30. Fairchild, *Race and Nationality*, 97–103.
31. Lester Frank Ward, *Applied Sociology* (Boston, 1906), 95.

circumstance, not to class or race or blood. "There is no better or nobler blood," he said; "there are no inferior peoples, only undeveloped or stunted ones. The same is true of individuals." Ward thus brought the strongest and most venerable of American ideological convictions to the support of the belief that equalization of opportunity would bring equalization of intelligence.[32] Boas in his turn developed the same theme in relation to the most stubborn of domestic problems when he argued that, whatever differences bodily build might tend to give to the direction of black people's activities—a somewhat uncertain question—there was no obstacle to black participation in American social organization, and no evidence of racial inferiority. "We do not know of any demand made on the human body or mind in modern life," he said, "that anatomical or ethnological evidence would prove to be beyond his [the Negro's] powers." In keeping with the spirit of comparative cultural thinking, he added that the traits of the Negro were adequately explained on the basis of history and social status.[33]

When Ward died in 1913, Boas had not yet reached the height of his influence, and it remained far from certain that the arguments even in scientific circles against physical and racial determinism would prevail. Boas lived to see that battle substantially won, at least in university departments of anthropology throughout the country, where by the 1920s and 1930s his students occupied many of the leading positions. But it would have been a flight of implausible optimism to have equated university departments with public opinion. In the hard world of the struggle for economic survival, ethnic resentments were bearing a different kind of fruit.

By the end of the war, organized labor had been fighting for restrictions on immigration for some thirty years, against the opposition of employers who wanted cheap labor, of Progressives who believed in the nation's assimilative powers, and of President Woodrow Wilson, who was not prepared to commit the nation to a denial of the optimistic idealism of its past. Mass immigration of very cheap laborers constituted a particular threat to skilled workers. Employers found immigrant labor cheaper than expensive new machinery; but the presence of immigrant

---

32. Samuel Chugerman, *Lester Frank Ward, the American Aristotle* (Durham, N.C., 1939), 431, 433, 436–38.
33. Boas, *Mind of Primitive Man*, 240.

workers freed the manufacturers to install machinery at the expense of their skilled workers. The hostility of organized labor was stimulated not by xenophobia but by the economics of survival.[34] After the war, no doubt assisted by a tide of isolationist revulsion against international obligations, Congress passed successive immigration restriction laws which tied the quotas available to individual countries to the proportions of the American population which their nationals represented at earlier dates. The measure taken by the act of 1921 was indicated by the census of 1910, but after further struggles, the representative date was pushed back to 1890, a year which was held to give a fairer representation to older American stock without discriminating against the new.

The immigration law, which was designed to come into gradual operation and to take full effect in 1929, gave an immense advantage to northwest Europe, and served implicit notice on all newer immigrants that they were less desirable candidates for American nationality.[35] Well before 1929, with the congressional debate over, the issue had fallen from its prominent place in public debate. But it would be a mistake to imagine that it had failed to leave its mark on the minds of the very large numbers of the extremely diverse but mainly Roman Catholic populations, as well as smaller numbers of Jews, mostly from southern and eastern Europe, or on their descendants. The consequences were charged with deep significance for the structure of American social history, with political implications that were yet to be calculated. The deep sense of being possessed of an imperfect claim to American nationality left Theodore Roosevelt's "hyphenated" Americans with an alternative course toward the fulfillment of their need for national identity. Identification with national origin became a source of pride through collective grievance. Foundations were laid for a form of pluralism that would run counter to the old aspirations of the melting pot and would later join the civil rights movement to give the new politics of plurality an unprecedented claim to consideration on the basis of equality of rights.[36] Behind

34. Richard Sennett and Jonathan Cobb, *The Hidden Injuries of Class* (Cambridge, 1972), 12.

35. Maldwyn A. Jones, *American Immigration* (Chicago, 1960), 247–77; Higham, *Strangers*, 317–24.

36. This is the thrust behind Michael Novak, *The Rise of the Unmeltable Ethnics* (New York, 1972), which seeks to establish a place for America's Catholic minorities of central, eastern, and southern European origin within the ambit claimed in the late 1960s by the minorities that were more conspicuous by virtue of "race" or language.

this claim, and giving it power, it is not difficult to discern the driving force of the demand for equality of esteem.

One area in which Americans felt no need to hesitate or apologize for openly racialist feelings lay on the West Coast, America's face toward the Far East. The violent clamor against Chinese immigration, to which the federal government yielded by passing the Chinese Exclusion Act as early as 1882, had no original connection with other aspects of nativism; it was presented as a defense of white civilization against an alien and inferior form. In 1904 the Chinese were completely excluded, a ban not repealed until 1943.[37] Early in the twentieth century, the West Coast discovered another enemy in the Japanese, who soon made matters worse by their success as farmers. The Japanese were the chief victims of the limited Immigration Act of 1907, but a new frenzy against them arose after the Great War. On the European side, restrictionists had long felt that the "new" immigration represented types that America could not digest. But anti–Japanese Americans, who began to make their feelings seriously felt in the East and South only after 1918, regarded the Japanese as something far worse—an alternative civilization, wholly un-American rather than merely unassimilable. This violent antipathy was reflected in the total exclusion built into the Act of 1924, which clearly marked the Japanese with the Chinese as belonging to a different category from the restricted, but not excluded, Europeans. Asians in America experienced no refreshment from new intakes of their own kind, which in turn weakened their political position by contrast to those of European descent. The hostility against them grew more ominous with the rise of the Japanese military empire in the 1930s. Anti-Japanese sentiment was to subject American doctrines of constitutional equality to their most severe test when the United States found itself at war with Japan in 1941.

Restrictionists of all sorts had to fight hard and long to get their views translated into law; their policy, and their social attitudes, could from one point of view be considered a denial of the meaning of American history, and by the end of the 1920s they could reflect that the struggle had taken nearly half a century. They knew well that they had to contend not only with the fact that Henry George's "human garbage" was armed with the ballot—equality of political access—but that they had to contend with an alternative sociology.

37. R.M. MacIver, *The More Perfect Union* (New York, 1948), 34.

This sociology was not, in principle, new. But circumstances gave it new applications. It had in effect to be claimed that the interchangeability principle applied to all the world, that anyone could *become* an American. This was a proposition that rested on faith. The task of applying the interchangeability doctrine to those already present in the United States may have seemed formidable enough in all conscience; yet it was the universal validity of this doctrine that was the conviction expressed by the sociologist A.L. Kroeber when he affirmed in 1915 that cultural anthropology must assume the "absolute equality and identity of all races and strains."[38] This was the faith of Lester Frank Ward, which came close to Kroeber's universalism. To win the argument, it was necessary to supplant the common belief that race was expressed in physical type in ways that determined the mold of character and the limits of potential.

Even to win this argument did not resolve all the problems or satisfy the requirements of equality as interchangeability. About race, the argument had always been vague; in the hands of sophisticated analysts such as Commons or Ross the concept of "race" was little more than a convenient shorthand. And the difficulty remained that when specific groups—the Swedes, the Poles, the Jews, the Irish, the mainland Italians, and the Sicilians were prominent examples—adhered among themselves through strong cohesive forces which continued to dominate their language, their economic behavior, their religious observances, and their relations to other ethnic groups, nativists could still object that these group characteristics made them unsuitable for assimilation into American life. The argument was not really, in the last analysis, about natural abilities; it was about group psychology and its effects on group behavior. At any level, the convictions people held in these matters affected the prospects for both equality of opportunity and equality of esteem, even when the struggles for political and legal equality were effectively decided.

As immigration and its demographic consequences formed more or less settled patterns, the ensuing realities of local life showed very little sign of conforming to ideas of interchangeability. They settled instead

38. But Kroeber's confidence was shaken soon afterward by the results of the army intelligence tests and his own collaboration with Lewis Terman in trying to develop a culture-free intelligence test at Stanford. Stocking, *Race, Culture,* 298.

into complex patterns of cultural and structural pluralism, which in turn claimed their rights under constitutional law.

Pluralism as a Positive Principle

The Anglo-Saxonist racialists left no one in any doubt that they regarded any form of assimilation as degenerative in terms of inheritance and undesirable on grounds of social behavior.[39] But they did not belong to the only group to hold somewhat exclusive views of its cultural, possibly its racial, inheritance.

The school of cultural anthropology that had grown to authority in recent years had a corollary in the development of cultural pluralism. As an academic theory, this school took a benign view of all cultures and advocated their harmonious acceptance of each other. The Anglo-Saxon stock took its place in this spectrum. But pluralism had its own potential as a school of cultural separatism, whose leading early exponent was the Jewish social philosopher and early Zionist Horace Kallen, who began to expound his views in *The Nation* in 1915. Kallen, who was as anxious to preserve Jewish culture from the corrosive influences of the American environment as Madison Grant was to preserve the American environment from Jewish culture, had clearly been alarmed by the popularity of Israel Zangwill's famous play, *The Melting Pot*, which had a successful run in New York in 1908.[40]

Zangwill—who dedicated his play to Theodore Roosevelt—used the dramatic form to propound a fusionist theory of the American social future. The idea was as old as Crèvecoeur's, but despite the undercurrent of faith in "interchangeability," it had played only an intermittent part in American social philosophy since his day. The implications of the melting pot were naturally destructive to strong group identities. Kallen, in opposition, maintained that the special duty of a government in a free society, dedicated to emancipating human capacities, was to permit free development of the ethnic group. This thesis rested on the belief that the individual's happiness was "implied in ancestral endowment," a view

39. Whether as a matter of high principle, or from physical repugnance, Mr. Justice James C. McReynolds of the Supreme Court would not shake hands with his Jewish colleagues Brandeis and Cardozo.

40. Israel Zangwill, *The Melting Pot: A Drama in Four Acts* (rev. ed., New York, 1914).

reflecting the fact that Kallen's own feelings were deeply imbued with his sense of ancestry. "Men may change their clothes, their politics, their wives, their philosophies to a greater or lesser extent," he observed, but added, as though closing the argument, "they cannot change their grand-fathers." [41]

Kallen was at one with the Anglo-Saxon racialists in the conviction that race was central to character. Moreover, he used the concept in the physiological rather than the looser ethnical sense. The basic difference between those who held Kallen's views of Jewish identity and the racial anti-Semites was that they belonged to different races, and each of them liked his own race best. By the time Kallen had collected his views into a book, published in 1924, another Jewish writer had subjected his views to a searching critique.

Isaac B. Berkson argued from a standpoint which, without departing from its deep roots in Jewish consciousness and tradition, placed much fuller emphasis on free individual choice. Taking up the theme of equality of opportunity, he emphasized that it called for a multiplicity of actual choices for the individual. Society must recognize the uniqueness of the individual; it must open multiple choices; and at the same time, individu-als must recognize their interdependence. These were the criteria for democracy. He went on to examine four possible theories of the process of assimilation into American life. The first was "Americanization"—a total absorption into the previously existing Anglo-Saxon core; the second was the melting pot, which in time produced a new norm. Both of these he found objectionable on the ground that they called for the destruction of previous identity. He then came to Kallen's "Federation of Nationalities"—which he might have called "indestructible nationali-ties." This view, because it made ethnic groups basic and permanent, offended Berkson's feeling for individual freedom of choice. He dis-missed as a mere sophism Kallen's assertion that men could not change their grandfathers. Grandfathers were psychological, not physical, he replied; people's attitudes, even their memories of their forebears could change, and in any case, by marrying outside his group, a man could change the ancestry of his children. Berkson preferred a fourth concept,

---

41. Quoted by Isaac Berkson, *Theories of Americanization, A Critical Study with Special Reference to the Jewish Group* (New York, 1920), 79. See also Higham, *Send These to Me*, 198–208.

that of community, a principle which gave people a kind of prior interest in their own groups and gave these groups a limited social and educational interest in individuals born into them, while rejecting claims to either racial or moral determinism. The duty of democratic government was to provide favorable conditions for the continued existence of groups with different cultural heritages and different contributions to offer to the wider American community.[42]

By the time Kallen's views on pluralism were collected into a symposium some forty years after his original publications, very little remained of the early structure, although he retained his intense interest in the preservation of Jewish cultural identity.[43] By that time, in the mid-1950s, newer studies had more realistic information as to the meaning for individuals of economic and cultural "pluralism" as they actually affected freedom of choice in the United States. R.M. MacIver, writing shortly after the Second World War, remarked on the consequences of anti-Semitism that the economic and educational concentrations to be found were evidence not so much of aptitudes and interests characteristic of the Jewish group as of "the deep fissure line that separates the group from the community." He did not stop with the Jews, but proceeded to analyze the effects of poverty and permanent exclusion from opportunities of economic advancement of the Chinese, the Mexicans, and the Negroes; he also described the advance of the restrictive covenant in closing large areas of desirable land and property against residence by undesired minorities and suggested that the recent trend was toward an increase in segregation, which had accentuated group tensions and disturbances. The only redeeming feature of this ominous situation was a growing public concern over racial prejudice and an increasing resistance to it by victimized minorities.[44]

The obvious difficulty about pluralism, from the point of view of individual liberty or equality of opportunity, was that the voluntary separateness of one group translated into the involuntary exclusion of another. According to MacIver, various forms of exclusion placed some forty to fifty million Americans where they might feel that they were not

---

42. Berkson, *Americanization*, 32–39, 54–65, 73–79, 88.

43. Horace M. Kallen, *Cultural Pluralism and the American Idea: Studies in Human Relations* (Philadelphia, 1956).

44. MacIver, *More Perfect Union*, 33–35, 41–42, 43.

wholly incorporated into the community; some quarter of a century later, this sense of exclusion, with all its damaging effects, was expressed as a bitterly felt grievance by the political sociologist Michael Novak.[45] When Daniel Patrick Moynihan and Nathan Glazer analyzed the social structure of New York City in the early 1960s, some fifteen years after MacIver had written, they found a society of well-formed and clearly identified groups, known by national origin, religion, and ethnic designation. "Time alone," they concluded, "does not dissolve groups if they are not close to the Anglo-Saxon center."[46]

Assimilation still seemed to be defined as a disappearance of differences that divided the minorities from the Anglo-Saxon center, and it would follow that equality in America would be measured by the success of these minorities in absorbing themselves into that venerable core. But an alternative, at least in theory, had made its appearance. Under some form of acceptable pluralism, parallel ethnic columns might rise to considerable heights without mutual interference and, indeed, with a minimum of mutual contact. In this situation, individuals belonging to one or another group could reasonably expect to have opportunities within the business, education, professional, and social structures maintained by that group.

This form of pluralism, structural rather than genuinely cultural, was one way of analyzing the society that had emerged by the end of the Second World War, if not earlier. But the outlines of this picture had a deceptive clarity, and a more rigorous concept of pluralism would have been hopelessly at odds with the shifting shapes to which this picture was appropriate. Instead of one melting pot, three had been identified, corresponding not so much to plural ethnicities as to the three leading faiths about which only the dominant enthnicities were believed to cluster—these being Protestant, Catholic, and Jewish. But there was evidence of a fourth group—a category of marginal men and women, largely to be found among the newly independent class of intellectuals and artists and in the various media of news, entertainment, and communication, who were consciously emancipated from the constraints and exclusions of ethnic background.[47] Between members of the major

45. Ibid., 26; Novak, Unmeltable, passim.
46. Daniel Patrick Moynihan and Nathan Glazer, Beyond the Melting Pot: The Negroes, Puerto Ricans. Jews, Italians, and Irish of New York City (Cambridge, Mass., 1963), 20.
47. Milton M. Gordon, Assimilation in American Life: The Role of Race, Religion and National Origins (New York, 1964), 67, 80–81, 105–14, 157–59, 172–73, 194–216.

ethnic-religious groups, it appeared that intermarriage, one of the principal indicators of lateral mobility, remained rare. But a closer analysis suggested that men and women of the indicated religions tended to identify themselves with national groups rather than by religious faith; a Catholic of Slavic family marrying a Catholic of Italian or Irish family would fall within the broad category of marriages within a single faith, but the intermarriage of members of such distinctively different national groups might well be a more significant index of freedom of individual choice.[48]

In these complex, shifting, and imprecise conditions, whatever form of pluralism might survive would hardly seem to be a strong candidate for the protection of constitutional law. Yet such a source of support could be found in an older version of pluralist doctrine. Under the principles of *Plessy v. Ferguson*, it was legitimate to conceive of equality of individuals upheld within separate vertical structures, each of which could in theory give to each of its members both the equal protection of the laws common to all Americans and equal opportunity for personal advancement. That, in fact, became the official aim of many southern states when, soon after the Second World War, they caught the scent of equality borne down on the breezes from Washington.

When President Harry S. Truman's Commission on Civil Rights published its report in 1947, it declared that separateness was incompatible with equality, a doctrine that was to reappear in the Supreme Court's judgment, seven years later, in *Brown v. Board of Education*.[49] But that pronouncement did not seem to end all possibility of a sophisticated pluralist alternative. The Report laid the large share of its emphasis on existing inequalities of conditions, listing the massive differences of tax money spent by southern states on white and black education and gross inequity of material conditions of every sort. The obvious fact was that the doctrine of "separate but equal" had never been carried into effect, a conclusion that in itself was enough to expose the falsity of the historical doctrine. But its history was not conclusive evidence as to its logic: Harlan had warned the Court in 1896 that *Plessy* was opening the way to new forms of legally sanctioned separateness; many such forms had grown up to pervade American life in the ensuing half-century. It

48. Ceri Peach, ed., *Urban Social Segregation* (London, 1975).

49. *To Secure These Rights: The Report of the President's Committee on Civil Rights* (Washington, D.C., 1947).

is at least arguable that constitutional law could have been adapted to those circumstances. Cultural and structural pluralism had some historical claim to have established their credentials as a genuine theoretical alternative to the path of individualistic equality. At least until the Second World War and in some respects for several years after, it could claim as much right to the Supreme Court's authority under the Fourteenth Amendment as could the doctrine of interchangeable individual rights.

As late as 1951, four years after the publication of the Truman Committee's influential report, after the reception of Gunnar Myrdal's famous two-volume study of America's racial problems in *An American Dilemma*,[50] after the setting up of Truman's Fair Employment Practices Commission in 1948, and after the Democratic party had committed itself as the party of civil rights over the bitter opposition of its southern wing, Congress still included in a bill for the support of education in federal establishments a provision to respect the laws of the states in which those establishments were sited. This meant simply that federal installations in the South would operate racially segregated schools. President Truman, whose convictions on racial equality had shown some signs of following rather than preceding his party's policies, stopped the bill with a veto in which he twice linked "equal rights" with "opportunity." But it was not yet possible to foresee what course the Republicans might take. A Republican Congress had given some encouragement to segregationists, and it remained possible that some development along the lines of separate-but-equal might be the course of the American future.

For racial or ethnic separationists or cultural pluralists, the problem posed by this situation was to demonstrate that the doctrine could operate in practice without violating the meaning of equal protection. The tide of the times might be running against them, but in principle they still had a portion of constitutional law on their side. They also had the advantage that so much of the structure of American society reflected their preferences and prejudices that an unusual combination of forces might be required to bring fundamental change. Such forces existed, however, and were running strong; and they were assisted by the infinite and indefinite social, geographical, and economic mobility that was incessantly at work in corroding formal and restrictive institu-

50. Gunnar Myrdal, *An American Dilemma* (New York, 1944).

tions. How these forces combined in a program of legal and political action dating from earlier in the century is a theme to be taken up in the next chapter.

But the opposite problem faced the individualist egalitarians. They had yet to convince many ordinary Americans that arbitrary group exclusion or segregation in any form was a violation of the very essence of equal protection. The concept of "arbitrary" exclusion was here pinned to the practice of designating individuals by race, religion, or national origin. At this stage of the proceedings all this seemed a rather simpler matter than it was later to appear; the search for "neutral" principles of public policy, under which fairness to individuals was defined in terms of fairness to groups, was soon to emerge as a major issue of public contention.[51]

Under the prevalent version of constitutional law, the line was wavering, but equal protection had not yet clearly broken through its narrower legal bounds. As MacIver insisted, in two works of advocacy written in the immediate postwar period, what was needed was to expand the outlook of public policy beyond legal equality to equality of opportunity.[52] This argument began with recognition that although equality in politics and at law were indispensable foundations, they were in themselves mere pieces of machinery in the struggle for equal attainments. Ethnic discrimination was a denial of equal access to what MacIver called "public opportunity," meaning opportunity in those affairs and callings which it was the province of public policy to protect.

In what seemed a distant generation, distant by two world wars fought for democracy, the publicists of American ideals had never doubted that America was committed to equality of opportunity. Even before the Fourteenth Amendment, Mr. Justice Field had taken the occasion of a test oath (which was intended to prevent ex-Confederates from entering certain professions) to give a strikingly firm statement that the Constitution protected equality of opportunity: "The theory upon which our political institutions rest is, that all men have certain inalienable rights—that among these are life, liberty and the pursuit of happi-

51. Herbert Wechsler, "Toward Neutral Principles of Consitutional Law," *Harvard Law Review* 71 (1959).

52. In these works, MacIver was to some extent anticipating the analytical method used in this book.

ness; and that in the pursuit of happiness all avocations, all honors, all positions, are alike open to everyone, and that in the protection of these rights all are equal before the law."[53] The question after the Second World War was whether equality of opportunity could take its place as a right entitled to claim the equal protection of the laws. An answer to this crucial question had been developing, with some encouragement from all branches of government, over a period of at least twenty years. Yet there was no point in Truman's presidency when the outcome could have been predicted with certainty.

53. *Cummings v. Missouri*, 4 Wall. 277, quoted by Thomas R. Adam, *"Isotes; or, Equality Before the Law,"* in Lyman Bryson et al., eds., *Aspects of Human Equality* (New York, 1956), 172.

Chapter Eleven

Reconstructing the Constitutional Environment

The Social Geology of Change

Oppression, says the Preacher, maketh a wise man mad. And, as Ralph Bunche once remarked, for those who are suffering from the alienation of their inalienable rights, gradualism can never be a sufficient remedy, because inalienable rights cannot be enjoyed posthumously.[1] Yet any strategy for restoring egalitarian principles to positions of priority in the national political agenda was realistic to the extent that it accepted the inevitability of gradualism. The ground had to be very carefully and patiently prepared. But habitual prudence has its own perils; those who prudently pursue gradualist methods are likely to lose the fruits of their patience if they fail to seize immediate opportunities: timing is everything.

The timing was an immediate precipitate of American participation in the Second World War. But the circumstances which made this timing possible had accumulated through generational shifts in the racial structure and distribution of the American population. At the time when the Supreme Court sanctioned racial segregation at the end of the nineteenth century, ninety percent of American blacks lived in the South. Two great developments in national affairs effected a decisive shift in this disposition. The first was internal Negro migration, which was a consequence,

1. In a lecture at Princeton University attended by the author in 1952.

in the first instance, of American entry into the Great War in 1917. Although taking place when the war was already three years old, this step called for a more massive mobilization of resources than any effort the nation had been called on to make since the Civil War. For military reasons, immigration came almost to a stop, and southern blacks began their great drift into the border states, the Northeast and the Midwest, where their labor was now needed as never before. Soon after the war, by an unrelated development, immigration laws closed the gates of American opportunity on the European masses, and the continued growth of industry drew more and more southern blacks into the cities of the North. The process was interrupted by the Depression, to be renewed with the renewal of prosperity and spurred on by the industrial demands of the Second World War. The introduction of tractors and other items of machinery in the early 1940s and mechanical cotton-pickers in the 1960s caused a deepening reduction in the market for field labor in the South's traditional cotton states. These industrial developments, which had nothing to do with the war, weakened the old bonds to the soil and released a gradual but huge migration to the labor market that was believed to beckon in the northern cities.[2] (They also, if indirectly, strengthened the potential for civil rights activity by weakening the bonds which had ancestrally tied black southerners to their landlords.)

Over the span of half a century, the effects were overwhelming. By 1960, more black people lived in New York state than in any other state in the Union; Illinois's black population outnumbered that of all but four southern states, while Pennsylvania and California each had larger black populations than either South Carolina or Virginia.[3] The black presence had fulfilled the fears of the North in the years of Reconstruction by becoming a national presence, and the problem presented by race relations, which whites usually described as "the Negro problem," had become national in its dimensions.

The second great event was the collapse of the old, unregulated capitalist order in 1929, which brutally exposed the system's basic

2. C. Vann Woodward, review of Nicholas Lemann, *The Promised Land: The Great Black Migration and How It Changed America* (New York, 1991), in *New York Times Book Review*, February 24, 1991.

3. Alan P. Grimes, *Equality in America: Religion, Race, and the Urban Majority* (New York, 1964), 67.

inequities. The crisis created a need first for relief and then for the rebuilding of the machinery of production, on a scale that had never before been seen and had never before been conceived of as the province of the national government. In its early phases, the Depression was generally regarded as an emergency rather than an opportunity. Franklin Roosevelt, in his second nomination acceptance speech in 1936, made an emotive reference to "the royalists of the economic order," and six months earlier, in a message to Congress, he had denounced "our resplendent economic autocracy." But he was sparing of egalitarian rhetoric and never committed the New Deal to a program of economic equality.[4] However, the famous coalition of interests which drew the second generation of immigrants, now armed with the vote, together with an increasingly organized and militant labor force, into the columns of the Democratic party under the aegis of the New Deal, did in important respects prepare those elements for future co-operation in the cause of a renewed struggle for greater economic equality, with implicit social dimensions. What was equally important for the future was that the national government met the crisis with national powers. It was going to be increasingly difficult to think of the United States as a federation of sovereign, self-regarding states.

In the Republic's early years, a very powerful school of thought maintained that republican government could be made to endure only if the people were infused with republican principles, and republican principles could not survive massive inequalities of wealth. American economic thought and social reform had very largely lost sight of those ideals. The debates of the Progressive era seldom adverted to anything as remote as classical republican ideology. The rhetoric of Wilson and Theodore Roosevelt resonated to the ideal of equality of opportunity, essentially a nineteenth-century principle, and it is significant that although both these party leaders wanted to curb the operations of monopolistic business, they did nothing to suggest an interest in redistribution of wealth or progressive taxation. Roosevelt, as we have seen, was content to believe that the principal objectives had been achieved;

4. John Major, ed., *The New Deal* (London, 1968), 98; Samuel H. Beer, "Two Models of Public Opinion: Bacon's 'New Logic' and Diotima's 'Tale of Love,' " *Transactions of the Royal Historical Society*, 5th ser., vol. 24 (1974), 94–96. Beer makes clear that Roosevelt adopted this phrase for his renomination acceptance speech after catching the militant mood of the convention. I am grateful to John Rowett for drawing this to my attention.

Wilson felt that American achievements and ideals were facing their gravest danger. Shortly after the war Herbert Hoover, himself in many ways an old Progressive, expressed concern about the eclipse of the American ideal of individualism, but he had no remedy more effective than some form of self-regulation on the part of big business.[5]

Among Franklin Roosevelt's closest advisers, however, Felix Frankfurter and Josephus Daniels had criticized earlier Republican party tax policies as socially unjust as well as economically ineffective, and had urged on Roosevelt the need to take the occasion to introduce a more progressive tax system.[6] Between 1935 and 1938, they prevailed on the president to call on Congress for major changes in tax codes. Frankfurter's thinking, however, did not recall the simplicities of the early republic; his prescriptions were based on an analysis of the world of modern economics.[7] "Wealth in the modern world," he insisted, "does not come merely from individual effort; it

results from a combination of individual effort and the manifold uses to which the community puts that effort. The individual does not create the product of his industry with his own hands; he utilizes the many processes and forces of mass production to meet the demands of a national and international market. Therefore, in spite of the great importance in our national life of the efforts and ingenuity of individuals, the people in the mass have inevitably helped to make large fortunes possible.

These proposals probably came closer than any other aspect of the New Deal to writing the theme of economic equality into the political agenda. But Frankfurter and Daniels encountered intense opposition, not only from enemies in Congress but from within Roosevelt's own camp. Bernard Baruch, probably Roosevelt's wealthiest as well as one of his closest advisers, attacked the equality question head-on. It was not, he said, that he necessarily objected to increased taxation where it could achieve "just and fair things." But the taxing power should not be used

5. Herbert Hoover, *Individualism* (New York, 1922).

6. Larry G. Gerber *The Limits of Liberalism: Josephus Daniels, Henry Stimson, Donald Richberg, Felix Frankfurter and the Development of Modern American Political Economy* (New York, 1983), 315–24; the remarks on the following passage depend on this work.

7. Frankfurter served as Eastman Professor at Balliol College, Oxford, in 1933–34, where he took advantage of the location to confer with John Maynard Keynes, who at that time was a Fellow of King's College, Cambridge. A rail link between the two ancient university cities existed in that unreformed era.

"to punish or to equalize that which neither Nature nor God intended should be equal." People could no more be made equal in the results of their efforts than they could be made equals "as athletes, hunters, lawyers, singers, or what not." Baruch's deepest fear seems to have been that redistributive taxation would destroy incentives, drying up investment and enterprise; and the influential Henry Stimson, whose views on economics were innocent of Keynes's distinction between savings for investment and uninvested savings, joined Baruch in opposition to any form of redistributive taxation. The Revenue Act of 1935 sharply raised personal income tax levels for the rich and graduated income tax to penalize big corporations, as well as raising estate duties, and Congress then passed an undistributed profits tax; but these measures made very little long-term impression on either personal or corporate concentrations of wealth, and the distribution of personal income remained largely static throughout the 1930s. All told, the tax reforms which formed part of the New Deal achievement, though not negligible, were both limited and in some cases short-lived. Progressive tax rates on capital gains were repealed by Congress in 1938. It cannot be said that by the time of the Republican mid-term successes of 1938, the New Deal stood committed to ambitious redistributionist principles or that it looked forward to further reforms in the direction of economic equality. Its late burst of anti-trust activities, undertaken with impressive fervor by Thurman Arnold, made little long-term impression on the structure or power of corporate business.[8]

The Roosevelt administration's contributions to economic equality were both indistinct and indirect. Thurman Arnold's anti-trust campaign—highly successful in the courts, where he won many suits—aroused a higher degree of national consciousness to the idea that monopolistic concentrations of economic power were inherently undemocratic and contrary to the national ethos as well as to the national interest. But Roosevelt also presided over the wartime recovery of economic growth. The legacy of the New Deal was a legacy of compensatory government, endowed with a heavy political responsibility for economic performance. And since the New Deal left American govern-

---

8. Anthony J. Badger, *The New Deal: The Depression Years, 1933–1940* (London, 1989), 102–04; Mark Leff, *The Limits of Symbolic Reform: The New Deal and Taxation, 1933–1939* (Cambridge, 1984).

ment much more powerful than before, and more heavily attributed with accountability for the economy, the indirect effect was to make the government of the day, of whichever party, more aware of perceived injustices in the distribution of wealth. An injection of Keynesian thinking fused the idea of the welfare state to an enlarged vision of sustained economic growth that could return to the benefit of the community.[9]

The Democratic party garnered the support of the greater part of the varied forces in the country that were looking for salvation through economic reform. But it was better at gathering hopeful support than at satisfying its constituents' aspirations, and its leadership did not possess the advantage of a coherent analysis of the causes of the continuing Depression. In the circumstances of these failures, it is less surprising than it came to seem later that, among the social reformers who were committed to improving the general condition of the people, some of the ablest thinkers turned with hope and more than a touch of faith to Marxism. The old order appeared to have failed; attempts to make it both fairer and more prosperous through the existing mechanisms of government had achieved only partial successes; had it not been for the revival of the economy immediately caused by the Second World War, it is not at all unrealistic to suppose that America might in fact have had to settle down for the indefinite future to regarding a second-class level of productivity and distribution as the normal performance of a capitalist economy. The traditional fusion of an individualist ethos with a monopolistic economy had lost its earlier power to distribute goods to the masses or even to treat their needs as its primary concern; yet a prospective world war—which all Americans hoped to avoid—could hardly be viewed as the nation's best hope of economic salvation. The versions of Marxism then being put into practice by Stalin in Soviet Russia, or offered by Trotsky in exile, could never appeal to numerically significant support among the American people; but they did appeal, for a few years, to some of those who wanted a more concrete program for economic and social equality, and who in intelligence and moral commitment were not inferior to the nation's political leaders.

The Second World War brought fundamental changes to the domestic situation. Aggrieved minorities had long perceived themselves as

9. Alan Brinkley, "The New Deal and the Idea of the State," in Steve Fraser and Gary Gerstle, eds., *The Rise and Fall of the New Deal Order, 1930–1980* (Princeton, 1989), 105–10.

having unfulfilled claims on the moral responsibilities of the nation; now, for the first time, they could bring the leverage of moral and political influence to bear on the processes of law and legislation. In this sense, the war achieved more for the moral and ideological identification of American society than the New Deal had been able to do. The nation's external enemies might almost be said to have done as much as its leaders to emphasize the commitments of American ideology. Americans were coerced by their enemies into re-examining their own society. The Nazi ideology of racial supremacy, combined with tyranny over the spiritual, intellectual, and physical liberties of all individuals and associations that failed to conform to the state's prescriptions were fairly clear opposites to any traditions that Americans were anxious to claim as their own heritage. There were, of course, extensive and numerous exceptions, but it was increasingly the case that the exceptions had to be half-apologetically explained away: as historical deviations—as in the South—or special cultural peculiarities, as with anti-Semitism or other ethnic prejudices in the North. In the immediate aftermath of the war, the Rockefeller Foundation commissioned the Swedish economist Gunnar Myrdal to undertake the study of race relations that appeared in 1948 as *An American Dilemma*, a work which detected an element of spiritual malaise in the fault line between promise and achievement in America's egalitarian ideals. This was an external as well as a liberal view; southern white opinion almost universally regarded the existing solution to the racial problem as both right and natural and furiously resisted reform when it eventually descended on them from the centers of national power.

But victimized minorities were provoked to a newly urgent sense of both the need and opportunity for remedy. In every direction, grievances were felt as inequalities—in political access, especially in the South; in law, again especially in the South; in economic opportunity, throughout the nation and among innumerable minorities; and perhaps above all, and everywhere, in esteem. But in both politics and law, the ground was being carefully prepared for a reassertion of equality as practical policy. The possibilities inherent in the new configuration of forces and the new climate of sentiment rendered a more comprehensive definition of equality probable in terms of the Fourteenth Amendment, but they did not determine any particular outcome nor the forms that such a redefinition would take.

The wartime upsurge of egalitarian sentiment was forcefully stirred

by minority interests, notably by Jews and blacks, the latter of whom had well-grounded reasons to be skeptical of their country's war aims. Those black Americans who regarded the whole conflict as a white man's war were among the most committed isolationists. [10] Blacks were quick, however, to recognize the tactical openings that the war created for them. "This is no fight merely to wear a uniform," declared *The Crisis*, a leading organ of militant black opinion, in December, 1940. "This is a struggle for status, a struggle to take democracy off parchment and give it life." [11] Yet when America entered the war a year later, the armed services maintained the same kind of racial separation to which blacks were drearily accustomed in civil life; on the home front, however, they were now better positioned than at any time since Reconstruction to exert their own leverage on the springs of political power. War created a different kind of crisis and called for a different kind of commitment than had economic disaster a few years earlier. The leadership of the National Association for the Advancement of Colored People, spurred by A. Philip Randolph, threatened a Negro march on Washington, which Roosevelt narrowly averted in June 1941 by announcing the establishment, for the first time, of a Federal Fair Employment Practices Commission, [12] which operated throughout the war. Its life was terminated by the Eightieth Congress elected in 1946—one of the few acts in the record of what Truman was in the habit of calling "the do-nothing Eightieth."

Making Equality of Opportunity an Object of Law

Nothing could have been more significant of the currents now stirring in American society than the difference between the prospects of domestic reform after the First World War and those after the Second. Reformers now had behind them a history of gradual but cumulative

10. Address by John Hope Franklin to the convention of the Organization of American Historians, St. Louis, 1989.

11. Richard M. Dalfiume, "The 'Forgotten Years' of the Negro Revolution," *Journal of American History* 55 (1968), 92.

12. Richard Polenberg, *One Nation Divisible: Class, Race, and Ethnicity in the United States Since 1938* (New York, 1980), 33–34. But the newly created Fair Employment Practices Commission was given no power to enforce its own orders. The armed forces remained segregated until the war in Korea, thus unintentionally illustrating the folk saying that it's an ill wind that blows nobody any good.

constitutional cases to sustain their hopes; moreover, they represented an alliance of minority interests whose commitment, resources, and voting power were more impressive than ever before.

Targets presented themselves across the whole face of American life. For a long phase of the campaign, running from the mid-1910s to the civil and voting rights legislation of the mid-1960s, the main target area was found in the South. The problem was to establish that equality involved national principles—usually under the Fourteenth Amendment—and to bring those national principles to bear on some local regulation. Southern states, pursuing the ultimate logic of white supremacy, enforced in the early twentieth century a separation more detailed and rigorous than had ever been practiced before and extending to residential separation. But when such principles were not only sanctioned by practice but enforced by law, they necessarily curtailed the individual's freedom to dispose of his or her property. The issue came to a head before the First World War in Louisville, Kentucky, where local whites formed an association to secure a city ordinance for the segregation of Negro housing. Significantly, the alarm spread rapidly beyond the intended victims. Mr. Justice Harlan had observed some twenty years earlier that if whites and blacks could be lawfully separated, so too could other classes; and it is not altogether surprising that local Jews began to suspect the longer-term consequences of the precedents being established. In 1916 the chief of the Louisville residential association went to the trouble of assuring Jewish leaders in the neighborhood that no extension against their people was contemplated. [13] But if the principle were accepted, it is hard to see how Jews or any other minority could have maintained a constitutional defense of their residential freedom. It was the blacks, however—the immediate victims—who fought the issue through to the Supreme Court, which found it significantly easy to decide in their favor, under the Fourteenth Amendment. The city ordinance clearly deprived persons affected of the power to acquire, use, and dispose freely of property, a violation of the rights of both property and equal protection which could not be defended as a legitimate exercise of police power. Mr. Justice Charles Evans Hughes, giving the opinion,

---

13. Winston L. McIntosh, "The American Negro Faces European Competition, 1830–1924," Ph.D. thesis, Cambridge University, 1970, 199–200, citing *The Crisis*, April 1916, May 1916.

emphasized the disparity between group classification and individual rights with a significant quotation from a recent case involving train passengers, in which the railroad company had argued that the volume of traffic did not merit the expense of outlay on equal accommodations: "This argument with respect to volume of traffic seems to us to be without merit. It makes the constitutional right depend on the number of persons who may be discriminated against, whereas the essence of the constitutional right is that it is a personal one." [14] Although most of the judgment dealt with the absolute nature of property rights, this emphasis on the *personal* nature of a constitutional right was fraught with a meaning that would resound through the future of the civil rights movement and ought to have sounded like a distant gong throughout the South.

Campaigns are not so easily won. The Supreme Court had refused to protect what counsel for Louisville called "the purity of the race," but lawyers soon devised the restrictive covenant, by which purchasers of residential property undertook a contractual obligation not to dispose of it to persons of designated classes, or even to offer them such civilities as overnight accommodation, in some instances. The apprehensions of the Jewish community proved to have been well founded, for restrictive covenants frequently operated to reserve whole neighborhoods not only for whites but for "Caucasians." [15] The question as to whether the state ought to permit itself to be involved, at any level, in arrangements which bore unequally on different, designated classes, but in ways to which the designation bore no functional relationship, raised obvious difficulties for the most elementary principles of equality. It is one thing to quarantine infectious diseases; quite another, to quarantine people by race or religion. Such people might well ask whether they enjoyed the equal protection of the laws.

The problem was not without complexities. Contracts, after all, are normally purely private arrangements, and the law which upholds their administration may be quite neutral as to their content; the machinery of law is technically involved in the administration of wills, through

14. *Buchanan v. Warley,* 245 U.S. 50 (1917); the citation is from *McCabe v. Atchison,* 235 U.S. 151.

15. As indicated by the Supreme Court in *Shelly v. Kraemer,* 334 U.S. 1 (1948), 21 n. 26.

which it is normally believed that private persons have an almost sacred right to make their own dispositions; in such cases the law may be called to protect the most idiosyncratic prejudice. But the Second World War, unlike the First, had transforming effects on attitudes to racial prejudice, which in turn prompted the Supreme Court to reconsider the constitutional implications of restrictive covenants, in the landmark case of *Shelly v. Kraemer*. The Shellys, who were black, were contesting for the ownership of property covered by a racially restrictive covenant. But the Court was told that such agreements also excluded Indians, Jews, Chinese, Japanese, Mexicans, Hawaiians, Puerto Ricans, Filipinos, and others. The variety of minority interests affected by the case was not without ulterior political significance, and the government's concern for the outcome was made unequivocally clear, the solicitor general taking part in the case. The United States was now officially host to the United Nations. Its international reputation was becoming, as never before, deeply involved in its civility to representatives of the peoples of the world.

It is a highly significant aspect of this case that the Court drew on the record of numerous earlier civil rights and property cases going back to the *Slaughter House Cases*. One principle affirmed in that case was that the Fourteenth Amendment was specifically—the Court then thought, exclusively—designed to protect the Negro race. The historical context of the amendment was drawn into the argument; it had been intended to establish the equality of basic civil and political rights against discriminatory action on the part of the states based on considerations of race or color. The *Civil Rights Cases* of 1883 had determined that "State action of every kind" was covered by the amendment.[16] Mr. Justice Bradley had excluded the possibility that the mere validation of private acts would come under the heading of state action, yet his language supported the interpretation now given by the Court. The state—as had been declared in *Ex Parte Virginia* in 1880—could act only through its agencies, a fact which covered the present situation;[17] *Buchanan v. Warley* was clearly in evidence on individual property rights;[18] and in 1927, a unanimous Supreme Court had invalidated an ordinance which

16. 109 U.S. 3 (1883).
17. 100 U.S. 303 (1880).
18. 245 U.S. 50 (1917).

forbade purchase by black people of property in a certain estate without the written consent of the majority of the residents.[19] The Court's conclusion, by Chief Justice Fred M. Vinson, was double-edged: there was nothing to offend the Fourteenth Amendment in a private agreement to exclude designated groups, but the equal protection clause would prohibit the state from using any of its agencies to enforce such a provision. Restrictive covenants were not illegal; they were merely unenforceable at law. As private agreements, they continued to be widely practiced.[20]

Where aggrieved minorities could concentrate their collected forces, legislation offered the attraction of quicker and more positive results than the courts. New York, with its ethnic diversity and political vitality, provided the scene and opportunity for the first act of state legislation to establish a permanent commission to oversee and enforce fair employment—which meant the elimination of racial and religious discrimination in hiring, promotion, and job allocation. The Ives-Quinn bill had an exciting passage, often competing with the allied invasion of Europe for space in the newspapers. It was opposed by a dignified array of public bodies, including the New York Chamber of Commerce, the Railroad Brotherhoods, the West Side Association of Commerce, and City Park Commissioner Robert Moses. But a profound shift had taken place in the demography of the state. Even Republican strategists began to perceive the need to regain their standing among minority groups whom they had previously felt free to ignore. Governor Thomas E. Dewey, soon to be a presidential candidate, read the political signs and intervened in the bill's support. The Congress of Industrial Organizations made the bill its own; representatives of Protestants, Catholics, Jews, and blacks all gave evidence at a hearing in Albany which had been planned by the bill's opponents but backfired against them and virtually ensured its triumph. Eventually, as *The New York Times* reported, in an expression charged with profound social significance, opposition had "crumbled today under the weight of one of the most formidable political combinations ever to appear in support of a single legislative proposal." The Ives-Quinn bill became an act by overwhelming majorities in both houses.[21]

19. *Harmon v. Taylor*, 273 U.S. 660 (1927).

20. J. Harvie Wilkinson III, *From Brown to Bakke: The Supreme Court and School Integration, 1954–1978* (New York, 1979), 143–44.

21. *New York Times*, February 7, 8, 12, 13, 14, 15, 16, 17, 18, 19, 21, 22, 28, March 1, 5, 1945.

The bill's supporters had laid emphasis on the fundamentally American character of the right to make one's own living. Formal invocations of equal justice and the Declaration of Independence were called in support of the argument on employment and earning power. But the debates make clear that supporters, who were far from sure of success, deeply feared that if the impetus given by the war were lost, and if an expected postwar recession caused unemployment, the aggrieved minorities would not only have lost the struggle but would be in a weakened position for the future. This was the danger that made the matter of timing so important. The passage of the act was a signal of encouragement to minority interests throughout the northern states.

In the annals of equality, moreover, it may be said to have established a new principle. For the claim could now be made that equality of opportunity had taken its place as an object of legislative protection; the claim to be employed according to one's abilities without regard to race, or color, or religion, or national origin, but on one's credentials or potential as an individual, had been transformed into a legal right. But it was a right that so far extended in law only to the male sex. Nor did the racist antipathies that were deeply embedded in the ranks of organized labor yield lightly or gracefully to the enacted program of liberal ideals. Racism was endemic in the labor movement. [22]

The New York commission, which formed a prototype for similar agencies in other states during the next few years, was periodically given increased powers, reflected in its changes of name from the Commission Against Discrimination to the Human Rights Commission. In the next twenty years, the commission realized few of its enemies' worst fears but also failed to achieve its sponsors' highest hopes; it chose to rely heavily on conciliation and fought very few cases through the courts or even through its own ultimate powers of enforcement. One of the commission's more significant achievements was that its investigations and reports brought to the light of public notice the extraordinary depth and complexity of the network of discriminatory and exclusive practices that had come into existence and which determined the limits of the opportunities available to racial and religious minorities in economic, residential, social, and recreational life. Many of these practices remained comparatively little disturbed, particularly in limiting choices of residence.

22. Paul Buhle, *Marxism in the U.S.A. from 1870 to the Present Day* (London, 1987), 63–64.

Much prejudice had been cut down but had not been torn up by the roots.[23]

But new and fundamental principles had been established. Extensions of state power, which progressively involved agencies of government in responsibility for trying to maintain equality of access not only to employment and training but to housing, public accommodation, and entertainment, implied a profound transformation in the American concept of the obligations owed by society to its individual members. It was an old doctrine that the government had an obligation to maintain equality of access to opportunity; the Supreme Court of *Plessy v. Ferguson* had accepted that principle, without offering a remedy for abuses of it in practice. There was now a difference. In the old view of the matter, the most the government would ever be expected to do was to check individual abuses when they were brought to the courts. It was a new discovery, amounting to a new principle in American government, when this responsibility required a continuous process of intervention, supervision, and enforcement.

Civil Rights: Combining Strategy with Circumstance

In most democratic countries, reforms in the law are undertaken through the legislature. That was certainly the general expectation at the founding of the American Constitution.[24] But the unusual, tripartite structure of the Constitution offered another possibility. In the years that followed the passage of the Reconstruction amendments, interests that were threatened by regulatory legislation passed by the states began to discover that they could protect themselves in the courts. The most familiar aspect of this process concerned the challenge of corporations and other business interests to such measures as grain storage and railroad regulation, but when black people and their allies challenged laws imposing racial discrimination, as they did most signally in *Plessy v. Ferguson*, they were making use of essentially the same procedure.

23. Morroe Berger, *Equality by Statute* (New York, 1968), 169–215; New York Executive Department, *Annual Report of the State Commission Against Discrimination* (1956); Jay Anders Higsbee, *Development and Administration of the New York State Law against Discrimination* (University, Ala., 1966).

24. Consider Madison, "In republican government, the legislative authority, necessarily, predominates." *Federalist* 51.

It was only a slight, though subtle shift of emphasis to turn this process to the uses of a positive campaign. Where, as in all the southern states, there could be no hope of progress through legislation, the principle of equal protection and the prohibition on racial discrimination in voting rights could be taken to the courts. Early in the 1930s the judicial campaign began to play a part in American life quite unlike any judicial process in other countries. The American Liberty League and its National Lawyers Committee took to the courts very early in the history of the New Deal to oppose its economic reforms, but as early as 1929, a foundation called the American Fund for Public Service gave a grant to the National Association for the Advancement of Colored People with a view to testing the unequal allocations of school funds between different races. The initial policy memorandum in which this strategy was proposed was based on the assumption that America was a racially divided country and that separate but equal was destined to remain the rule; NAACP strategists continued, right into the *Brown* litigation, to fear that a settlement on the enforcement of the separate but equal principle might be the best outcome they could get from the Court.[25]

Early in the 1930s, however, a group of lawyers for the NAACP, after making a close study of the problem, came to the conclusion that equality could never be achieved under a system of separation, if only because school administrators could not be relied on to allocate resources equally. But the issue went deeper. Nathan Margold, who wrote the group's report, argued that segregation itself was "the very heart of the evils in education against which our campaign should be directed." Margold's argument was based on constitutional cases which showed that segregation had always been a synonym for inequality. A precedent for Margold's strategy was provided by the reasoning of the Supreme Court in 1886, when Chinese launderers and not southern blacks had

25. Jack Greenberg, *Litigation for Social Change: Methods, Limits and Role in Democracy*, Benjamin N. Cardozo lecture before the Association of the Bar of the City of New York (New York, 1974), 9–11. Richard Kluger, *Simple Justice: The History of Brown v. Board of Education and Black America's Struggle for Equality* (New York, 1977), ch. 24, pp. 290–91, 520–21. On precedent, there would have been no constitutional obstacle to separate-but-equal practices in northern states; but the object was very substantially provided for by the de facto segregation effected by differences in residence. If such a move had been made in the North, politicians would have had to reckon with the fact that their black constituents had votes.

been the victims of racial discrimination.[26] Three leading NAACP lawyers, Charles Houston, William Hastie, and Thurgood Marshall soon afterward brought another shift in direction.[27] The new strategy was to strike at the weakest point in their enemies' defenses by challenging racial discrimination in admissions to southern law schools—institutions closest to the experience and interests of the justices themselves, and institutions in which the denial of equal admissions or equal facilities most obviously represented a basic denial of equal treatment for persons of similar merits. Equality before the law itself could hardly be a product of unequal legal training. It was only after gaining decisive victories in these law school cases that the NAACP strategists turned their attention to the much more delicate area of admission to the public schools of the South.

The law works slowly, though it sometimes has a sense of direction. Equality was at the heart of these cases. There was a gathering certainty that the Supreme Court would insist on a more realistic definition of that evasive concept than it had ever done before, and there were at least a few glimmering indications, though they could not be considered certainties, that the inner logic of the argument would carry the Court through to the ultimate vindication of the individualistic basis of the Constitution. The central point, as Chief Justice Charles Evans Hughes emphasized in a strongly worded opinion as early as 1938 in *Missouri ex. rel. Gaines v. Canada*, was that the right to a law school education was a personal right, which was quite unaffected by the fact, as claimed by the state of Missouri, that few people of Gaines's race had so far sought to claim it.[28] Nor was the Court any longer to be taken in by outward appearances. When Texas tried to anticipate trouble by building a black law school, which the state courts held to be equal to the existing law school of the University of Texas, the concept of equality in education came under close scrutiny. Chief Justice Vinson could now speak for a unanimous Court in holding that the new law school was inferior in its faculty, in its variety of courses, and, most significantly, in "those qualities which are incapable of objective measurement but which make for greatness in a law school."[29] The justices knew whereof they spoke; such

26. *Yick Wo v. Hopkins*, 118 U.S. 356 (1886), discussed above, p. 235.
27. Greenberg, *Litigation*, 17.
28. 305 U.S. 337 (1938), 634.
29. *Sweatt v. Painter*, 339 U.S. 629 (1950), at 634.

qualities included intangibles such as the reputation of the faculty, the tradition and prestige of the school itself, and, of course, the influence of the alumni. The underlying meaning of this and other decisions, not yet fully disclosed, was the Court's objection to the policy of assigning students on inadmissible grounds—grounds of race rather than legitimate academic qualifications and potential. The theme now entering into the Court's thinking was that it was not only the quality of the school that counted for constitutional purposes, but the grounds of the assignment. From the point of view of the white South's iron guard, the most ominous aspect of these cases was that the fact of separateness was emerging as a substantive issue in identifying inferiority. The point was made perhaps even more firmly on the same day as *Gaines*, when the Court ordered the state of Oklahoma to cease discriminating against a black student who was being subjected to separate treatment *after* being admitted to the state law school, in ways that clearly interfered with his education.[30] The *effect* of segregation was an unconstitutional denial of equal treatment—and unequal treatment was incompatible with equal protection.

The Court had treated these cases on the merits of the evidence presented, but it had not yet gone behind the doctrine that separate could, in principle, be equal. That finding was implicitly present in the assertion of a personal right. But as Southern states poured their resources into building new, bright, well-equipped schools for black children, the outcome could still be in doubt. If the resources offered were effectively equal in all tangible points, if by the criteria of books, laboratories, buildings, gymnasia, and the training of teachers, the separate schools were demonstrably equal, would the fact of separation alone constitute an inadmissible failure of equal protection? Might not the principle of equality of opportunity be maintained within a pluralist structure of institutions?

This question was at the heart of the celebrated decision in *Brown v. Board of Education of Topeka, Kansas,* handed down on 17 May 1954, a collection of cases which had originated several years earlier in the schools of South Carolina. It had not been difficult to prove that the facilities offered to black children were inferior, but the NAACP team, led by Thurgood Marshall, also brought forward testimony from child

---

30. *McLaurin v. Oklahoma State Regents,* 339 U.S. 637 (1950); Greenberg, *Litigation,* 18–19.

psychologists to show that segregated facilities were unequal in practice and psychologically damaging in their effects; it was further argued that racial classification followed no rule of reason. As the case advanced, the emphasis fell increasingly on the argument that segregation was unlawful because it was in the very nature of the case a product of inequality. This argument manifested itself in Chief Justice Warren's pronouncement for a unanimous Court that "in the field of public education the doctrine of 'separate but equal' has no place. Separate education facilities are inherently unequal."[31] If, as Nathan Margold had argued more than twenty years earlier, segregation was a synonym for inequality, that situation had now been decisively reversed, and integration had become a synonym for equality.

This reversal was of the most profound significance for American constitutional history. But in Warren's construction of the argument, a heavy burden fell on the meaning of the word "inherently." Before the "deliberate speed" called for in the Court's order had advanced southern schools more than a few paces along the road to integration, a revival of black separatism had raised, at least in some quarters, the question as to whether separateness must in all circumstances be a reflection of inequality.[32] A crucial question was at stake here. Kenneth Clark, the prominent black psychologist, had presented the results of research showing that segregation damaged the morale of black children. But counsel for the board of education argued, with some of Clark's publications in his hands, that Negro children in southern schools showed more signs of stability than Negro children in mixed Northern schools. While Chief Justice Fred M. Vinson was still on the bench—and the case began under him—Thurgood Marshall himself had doubts about the strategy of attempting to unseat *Plessy* and feared that a modified doctrine of separate but equal might be the best they could hope for.[33] There were two crucial points, however, which would have strengthened Warren's argument. The first was that sepa-

31. 347 U.S. 483 (1954), at 495; Kluger, *Simple Justice*, ch. 26.

32. *The Autobiography of Malcolm X*, with the assistance of Alex Haley (London, 1966), esp. ch. 14; Abigail M. Thernstrom, "Language: Issues and Legislation," in Stephan Thernstrom, ed., *Harvard Encyclopedia of American Ethnic Groups* (Cambridge, Mass., 1980), 619–28, who states that black spokesmen were unanimous in rejecting the values of integration by the late 1960s (621).

33. Kluger, *Simple Justice*, 290–91.

ration must be a sign, indeed the very hallmark, of inequality when it is imposed by one race upon another without consultation or consent. But this position would have theoretically left room for a modified *Plessy* because it implied that black citizens formed a collective entity which could somehow be consulted and could give its consent. The second, and more important unspoken point, which overrides the first, was that race could not be a rational criterion for assignment of school places because race is a concept incapable of yielding educationally valid meaning. Whatever may be the correlations in specified places or periods of history between race and other social considerations, race cannot on its own account be a decisive indication of an *individual* child's educational potential or needs.

The judgment in these cases, despite the sweep of the Chief Justice's language, was curiously limited. It did not order the immediate admission of any one child to any one school. States were enjoined to end school segregation "with all deliberate speed," a mode of progress which was found to take a great many years. But racial segregation, and therefore by implication racial *selection*, were now under the ban of constitutional law, and there followed almost immediately a series of cases in which the Court, giving judgment *per curiam* (and therefore without giving its reasons) extended the principle to virtually the whole range of places requiring public access.[34] Reasoning which extends from public education to golf courses, swimming pools, hotels, buses, and amusement parks could not be based exclusively on educational criteria. But the logic that controlled the extension beyond school and beyond childhood is equally close to the principles of the Fourteenth Amendment in protecting individuals against painful and humiliating treatment through invidious classification. The point had appeared in Warren's comments on the effects of school segregation. Kenneth Clark had written that "human beings who are forced to live under ghetto conditions and whose daily experience tells them that almost nowhere in society are they respected . . . will, as a matter of course, begin to doubt their own self worth."[35] The Fourteenth Amendment was gradually

34. *Baltimore v. Dawson*, 350 U.S. 877 (1955); *Holmes v. Atlanta*, 350 U.S. 879 (1955); *Gayle v. Browder*, 352 U.S. 903 (1956); *New Orleans Park Association v. Delige*, 358 U.S. 54 (1958). Herbert Wechsler, "Toward Neutral Principles of Constitutional Law," *Harvard Law Review* 73 (1959).

35. Abigail Thernstrom, "Language," 621.

emerging as a guardian of the most elusive of equality's categories, equality of esteem.

By a quirk of the Constitution, the Court was obliged to look elsewhere for similar principles in the District of Columbia, because the Fourteenth Amendment applies only to the states. The Court took the opportunity for a slightly fuller statement of its own principles. Segregation, the Chief Justice declared, was not directed to any legitimate governmental objective, but deprived Negro children of their liberties without due process of law. In dispatching the case under the Fifth Amendment as a deprivation of due process, the Court now almost incidentally recognized that an equal exercise of individual liberty was protected by right under the Fourteenth Amendment.[36] This lacuna in the Constitution thus revealed a convergence between liberty and equality.

Brown was an undisputed watershed in American history. Laws, it is often said, reflect a society's values; but it is equally true that society draws its values from the laws. When the Supreme Court declared in Chief Justice Warren's words that separate facilities were "inherently unequal," it condemned the principle of separation, *no matter how that separation might have come about,* and endowed on American society a constitutional obligation to put an end to the manifold practices which had made separation a institutionalized ingredient of American life.

The *Brown* case was initially about education. It found a denial of a constitutionally protected right when a small black girl was excluded from a school which afforded better educational opportunities to white children. The decision evoked the principle of equality of opportunity and reasoned from it to equality of esteem—both now confirmed, in effect, as rights enjoying constitutional protection. But the second round of the *Brown* case showed that what was at stake in the school system was nothing less than the racial structure of American society as a whole—and this in due course would mean in the North and West as well as the South.

The chief justice's language had not fully satisfied all opponents of segregation.[37] As the passage of time brought changes in the circum-

---

36. *Bolling v. Sharpe,* 347 U.S. 497 (1955).

37. Louis H. Pollack, "Racial Discrimination and Judicial Integrity: A Reply to Professor Wechsler," *University of Pennsylvania Law Review* 103 (1959–60), 24.

stances of legal challenges to conditions of inequality, the use of the adjective "inherently" proved to have been a crucial flaw. When separation was imposed on one group by another, in a manner that stigmatized the other, then certainly the inequality was an inherent inequality, since it arose from discrepancies of power and perpetuated inequalities of free choice. Even the *Plessy* Court had implicitly recognized this objection. When the Court was discussing equality in law schools, it was relatively easy to confine the issues to educational opportunity. But when it entered into the education of schoolchildren, it necessarily entered into the more complex realm of historically derived patterns of residence. Many of these patterns had also resulted from imposed separation. Restrictive covenants were still, though unofficially, in force on a very wide scale—affecting Jews and other minorities as well as blacks; real estate agents and property developers carefully observed racial and ethnic divisions, in the conviction that it was their duty to protect the values of property, while public policies at the local government level sanctioned and encouraged ethnic separateness.[38] Ethnic and immigration-derived patterns of residence were far from consistent, coherent, or stable; it is possible that they played a larger part in conceptual designations of neighborhood than in the realities. But they existed as a fact of life in many cities, in many cases were deeply ingrained, affecting people's real choices in a society whose overall ethos emphasized freedom. They certainly and massively kept black Americans out of the more desirable residential locations. These restrictive patterns naturally also reflected class structure. The poor lived in poor districts, and although many poor people were white, the majority of blacks were poor.

The aim of achieving racial balance within the schools was originally justified on educational grounds. Not only were white schools better equipped and taught, but segregation, which damaged self-esteem and damaged self-respect, impaired the likelihood of achievement. But racial balance *within* schools was soon revealed to be practically inseparable from the wider aim of social desegregation. When the Supreme Court returned, nearly fifteen years later, to review the consequences of *Brown*, it found that all too little had changed—certainly not enough to satisfy the cautious prescription of "all deliberate speed." It was at this point

38. Wilkinson, *Brown to Bakke*, 143, 222–23.

that the Court took its major step towards intervention. Technically speaking, when it found a constitutional violation, it required a specific remedy. But in *Green v. County School Board*,[39] arising in 1968 from New Kent County in rural Virginia, the Court introduced the use of statistics to satisfy itself as to the extent of achieved integration. Further, it began to make suggestions about ways of advancing the process. Once statistics have been introduced into an argument, it becomes impossible to avoid using them for reference. In New Kent County there were two schools, one black and the other white, with children conveyed by bus to their racially designated schools if they did not live near enough to walk. There was nothing unusual here about the use of the school bus to achieve a preconceived racial distribution. Following *Brown*, the school board permitted but did not require racial cross-registration, and inquiry revealed that only fifteen percent of the black parents had taken advantage of the *Brown* principle to register their children for the white school. (There were none the other way round.) This left eighty-five percent of the black children attending the black school. This was the situation into which the Court intervened, not to permit racial cross-registration by choice, as was already done, but to *require* cross-registration to achieve a distribution reflecting the proportions of the two races throughout the county. The process was made more systematic in Charlotte–Mecklenburg County in North Carolina, where the federal judge imposed a detailed and extensive plan to produce racial integration throughout a large county. The opposition was widespread and fierce, not least because the county had already gone some way to implement the *Brown* principles. The Supreme Court, however, upheld the dispositions made by the federal judge in the case of *Swann v. Charlotte-Mecklenburg Board of Education*.[40] The enforcement of the same principles in Richmond, Virginia, achieved the desired statistical results but at considerable cost to the quality of education available to children of both races.[41]

But the clear outlines of the early decisions were giving way to new complexities of fact and principle. After Earl Warren's retirement, and twenty years after *Brown*, the Court under Chief Justice Warren Burger

39. 391 U.S. 430 (1968).
40. 402 U.S. 1 (1971).
41. Wilkinson, *Brown to Bakke*, ch. 6.

began to retrench the active interventionism that had marked its recent policies. Segregated housing had very largely kept the races apart in northern cities and for many generations had spared the people of northern states the social tensions and moral dilemmas associated with integration. In Detroit, where white removal and resettlement in the suburbs had left the inner city almost entirely to the blacks, the old problems of residential separation had reappeared, to create a new but very effective separation of the races in the city's schools. Federal district court judge Roth found that the school board had connived at this separation by providing transport to carry black children to prescribed black schools, away from white schools that were closer to their homes; he concluded that the board's policy amounted to deliberate creation and perpetuation of school segregation. Pursuing the logic of *Brown v. Board of Education*, he consequently redrew the boundaries of Detroit's school districts to include the whole suburban area in a single system with that of the city. The basis was consistent with the Supreme Court's own recent policy: racial segregation in the public schools was an evil to be corrected by constitutional intervention. But now the Supreme Court overruled. It emerged that racial mixture was no longer an end in itself; separate facilities were no longer "inherently unequal." It could depend, presumably, on how they came to be separate.[42] One new ingredient of an increasingly turbid situation for the courts was that this view was now shared in principle, though probably not with reference to Detroit, by many black organizations.

The Right to Vote: An Equality of Ineffectiveness

Republican theory has not always regarded the right to vote as a corollary of citizenship. Apart from the requirement that the ballot should be exercised by adults of sound mind, qualifications of property, sex, and residence have been normal attributes of the right of suffrage; until the transforming events of the 1960s, American states had in reality depended for the legitimation of consent on a residue of the discredited British doctrine of virtual representation. The Reconstruction debates had reopened the whole question of the meaning of citizenship and revealed that men in highly responsible and representative positions

---

42. *Milliken v. Bradley*, 338 F.Supp. 583 (1971); 418 U.S. 717 (1974).

differed widely on the question as to whether the right to vote was a right inherent in the political system, or a privilege conferred by the system on persons of suitable quality. These debates produced the Fourteenth Amendment, which introduced the concept of citizenship into the actual language of the Constitution, and the Fifteenth, which was intended to complete the work of enfranchising the black people of the South, which the Fourteenth had failed to bring about. Since the various sophistries by which the southern states effectively denied the suffrage to black citizens were obviously intended as race barriers, the Fifteenth Amendment provided the ammunition in the opening rounds of the NAACP's long campaign.

The state of Oklahoma had adopted an amendment to its constitution by which intending voters were required to show that they could read or write any section of that constitution; loopholes were provided for those who, though they might fail the literacy test, had been entitled to vote on or before 1 January 1866, or had lived in a foreign country before that date, or were lineal descendants of such persons. The members of these subtly designated classes were, of course, white; all those threatened with exclusion were black. It rested with the election officers to decide whether an applicant had proved his literacy. When the first challenge reached the Supreme Court, in 1915, the justices still agreed that a state was competent to require a literacy test for voting, but the exclusionary provisions were so obviously directed against Negroes that the Court declared the act a violation of the Fifteenth Amendment without seeing any need to look into the question of equal protection.[43]

The aftermath of counter-Reconstruction left the South to all intents and purposes as a series of one-party states. Since no contest occurred at the formal elections, all effective political choices were made in the primaries of the Democratic party. By excluding black people from membership of the party, and thus from voting in its primaries, southern politicians could avoid the effects of the blow that had fallen in Oklahoma. The NAACP's next step was therefore to challenge the validity of the all-white primary. The fundamental distinction, toward which the Court groped uneasily through a succession of cases which took from 1927 to 1944 to resolve, was between the official propriety of the formal procedures of southern state Democratic parties and the intent behind

43. *Quinn v. U.S.*, 238 U.S. 347 (1915).

those procedures. The actual disfranchisement of a large section of the citizenry was an obviously unsatisfactory state of affairs in a country that called itself a democracy, and when it was patently obvious that the procedures had been devised specifically in order to effect that disfranchisement, it could hardly have been expected that the system would survive judicial scrutiny. The issue was finally disposed nearly at the end of the Second World War, when in *Smith v. Allwright* the Court addressed itself to this distinction. The conclusion was that where the consequences of a procedure were totally at variance with constitutional principles, the consequences must be held to invalidate the procedure. Primary elections were conducted by the party under state statutory authority, and no name could appear on the ballot without having been certified by either the party committee or the state party convention. The opinion, given by Mr. Justice Reed, then adverted to fundamentals: "The United States is a constitutional democracy. Its organic law grants to all citizens a right to participate in the choice of elected officials without restriction by any state because of race.... Constitutional rights would be of little value if they could be thus indirectly denied." [44]

This judgment deprived white supremacists of important legal supports, but did not in itself provide the means of opening the southern political system to black participation. The Court, as Andrew Jackson had once grimly observed when it was trying to protect the rights of Cherokee Indians, had no powers of enforcement. Nine years later, the *Brown* decision provoked a fierce storm of protest and sabotage in the white South, accompanied by numerous demands for the impeachment of Earl Warren. Southern legislatures revealed a sustained ingenuity in devising methods for frustrating the law of the land, and while southern blacks were persistently excluded from elections, black children were still

---

44. *Smith v. Allwright*, 321 U.S. 649 (1944), at 664; the previous cases being: *Nixon v. Herndon*, 273 U.S. 536 (1927), when the Court stated that the exclusion by class of a designated group of citizens was a violation of the equal protection clause of the Fourteenth Amendment; *Grovey v. Townsend*, 295 U.S. 45 (1935), in which the Court *permitted* Texas Democrats to exclude non-whites from party membership—an aberration from the course of reasoning that had appeared to prevail; *U.S. v. Classic*, 313 U.S. 299 (1941), a case that arose from an election fraud which, as it happened, had nothing to do with Negroes; but it was here that the Court revealed a new interest in the intentions behind the law, and the NAACP read the lesson correctly, proceeding to challenge the exclusion of Negroes from primary elections. *Smith v. Allwright* dismissed appeal to past determinations: "*Grovey v. Townsend* is overruled."

contained in segregated schools. The results could have been anticipated with a modicum of political intelligence: inevitably, if only gradually and reluctantly, the federal government was drawn back into the field of providing direct protection for the rights of citizens who could not obtain relief from their states.

The issues turned centrally on the meaning of equality and confronted the American people, for the first time since the end of Reconstruction, with the question of finding an intelligible, morally consistent meaning to their proclaimed national ideology. It had long been settled that equality before the law and equality of political access were fundamental and indispensable to the American political system. And it was abundantly clear that without these, nothing else would follow. But for a large part of the population of at least eleven states, these fundamentals *did not exist*. To the extent that white Americans in the North had insulated themselves from these disagreeable truths and preferred to leave them to the care of the states, events in the South were tearing away a veil of voluntary ignorance and forcing the issues into their consciences. But the Second World War had given the whole, tangled, immense historic problem new and unheard-of dimensions. Not only had the United States based its moral stance on democratic principles, but the development of the Cold War had set those principles under the unaccustomed glare of international scrutiny.

At the lowest level, the propaganda implications of racial segregation were disquieting. The nation was now the host to innumerable foreign diplomats, a large and increasing proportion of whom represented non-white populations, and the State Department found itself subject to a buzzing of indignant complaints from members of foreign diplomatic missions who had been snubbed and rejected by American restaurants and American hotels. This was no problem of mere diplomatic courtesy. Insults often inflict more penetrating and more permanent damage than do altercations over conflicts of interest. The African and Asian diplomats, not to mention increasing numbers of university students who would exercise future influence in their own countries, who found themselves subjected to the consequences of an inequality of esteem may have been sharing the experience of American blacks and, indeed, Indians; but they had by a curious paradox more resources at their backs than Americans who could neither vote nor get their children an equal chance

in life.[45] The United States appeared to hold a sort of world hegemony, but that hegemony depended, in the long run, on opinion more than on force. And opinion was susceptible to experience.

It was becoming increasingly clear to American administrations and legislatures—though with the very reluctant agreement of President Eisenhower, who showed distaste for the issues—that they must accept the lapsed responsibility for the two linked fundamentals of legal rights and voting rights.[46] Eisenhower's attorney general, Herbert Brownell, insisted against his chief's reluctance that federal force must be used to ensure the admission of black children at Little Rock, Arkansas, where the governor had tried to interpose state powers to prevent integration of the schools. During Eisenhower's second administration, Congress took the first steps since Reconstruction to make the federal government itself responsible for the right to vote. The Civil Rights Act of 1957 established a federal Civil Rights Commission, entrusted with limited powers of investigation and intervention, but produced disappointing results; a further stiffening was injected by an act of 1960 which empowered the federal government to enjoin a state and established a federal voting referee to whom aggrieved persons might appeal.[47]

Continued southern white resistance was not blunted by the arrival of a new Democratic administration, but the extreme and now nationally televised violence of southern hostility to black citizens exercising a constitutional right to demonstrate peacefully in the streets brought a

45. Harold R. Isaacs, *The New World of Negro Americans* (New York, 1963), 16–21. Secretary of State Dean Rusk is quoted as saying in August 1961, "The biggest single burden that we carry on our backs in our foreign relations in the 1960's is the problem of racial discrimination here at home. There is just no question about it."

46. Kluger, *Simple Justice*, 664–65; Stephen A. Ambrose, *Eisenhower the President* (London, 1984), 304–05. Eisenhower always maintained that integration was a problem for the courts; the judges should exercise leadership, which was not an executive responsibility. This was an unusual view of the balance of responsibilities in the American government, which would have greatly surprised the Founders of the Constitution. Eisenhower refused to speak on the lynching in Mississippi of a fourteen-year-old Chicago boy named Emmett Till; he also declined to express himself on the Montgomery bus boycott in 1955. (Ambrose, *Eisenhower*, 307). He did not fail to recognize that a serious problem existed but was anxious to avoid letting it become a party issue and preferred the idea of a bipartisan commission.

47. Berger, *Equality by Statute*, 103–05; Noel T. Dowling and Gerald T. Gunther, *Cases and Materials on Constitutional Law* (Brooklyn, 1965), 436, 472–78.

crisis of conscience throughout the rest of the nation. Television did for the civil rights movement what Harriet Beecher Stowe had done for anti-slavery only just over a hundred years earlier. A climax occurred with a national march from Selma to Montgomery, Alabama, in the spring of 1964.

Civil Rights, Voting Rights, and the Climax of Individualism

The rapid rise of the new civil rights movement as a popular campaign—it built, of course, on years and generations of specialized preparation—created a situation that in certain instances came close to local outbreaks of civil conflict. With the martyrdom of three young civil rights workers in Mississippi in the summer of 1963, a mood of emergency spread throughout the nation. In the autumn the crisis was internationalized when a bomb killed four black children attending Sunday School in their church in Birmingham, Alabama. The shock was felt around the world. A new civil rights bill was introduced into the House of Representatives on 20 November 1963; the Kennedy administration, which had hitherto placed a cautious pragmatism so far above principle as to leave some doubts as to how far its principles extended, began to respond to the politics of protest. Two days later President John Kennedy was assassinated.

The young president's death produced a mood of national horror and contrition which conduced to the exceptionally rapid passage of a bill that might otherwise have encountered much more formidable obstacles; there can be no doubt of the importance of the newly inaugurated President Lyndon Johnson's leadership in aiding its congressional passage. The bill, which became law on 2 July 1964, brought the federal government back into the field of individual rights on a scale not seen since 1875. Its effect was to make a national responsibility of those fundamentals without which anything remotely resembling equality of opportunity was manifestly impossible—responsibilities which many northern state governments had already built into the fabric of their policies.[48] Yet the legislative impetus proved hard to sustain. Only two years later, a bill to add a provision for open housing to the range of

48. House of Representatives 7152, *Congressional Quarterly Almanac*, 1964, 338.

federal responsibilities proved too indigestible for the Senate, the recent coalition of northern Democrats and Republicans dissolved, and it seemed that the inspiration of the almost revolutionary movement of the previous generation had already begun to fade.[49]

But these reverses, complicated by fissures in the civil rights alliances and by the development of conflicting views of the movement's ultimate aims and philosophical principles, followed on an advance whose momentous scale should first be recognized. What had happened through executive initiatives—dating back as far as Franklin Roosevelt's executive order of 1941—and through federal legislation was a fundamental extension of responsibility for the categories of equality. The American doctrine of equality of opportunity had once belonged to the free play of economic forces, leaving to the government the limited and residual role of an umpire or at the most a caretaker to ensure that the play was fair as well as free. All that had now profoundly changed. Equality of opportunity, at least in principle, was now established as an object of national policy, a charge laid upon the government by the nation.

Equality of opportunity in this sense became an attribute of the possession of individual civil rights, grounded in the other equalities of law and voting, and aspiring, no doubt, to equality of esteem. No theme stood out more clearly in the debates on the civil rights bill than that of the individual basis of the rights in question. The whole avowed aim was to establish the principle once declared by the older Mr. Justice Harlan: the Constitution was to be color-blind; it could have no knowledge of and could therefore offer no protection for arrangements based on distinctions of race. The concept of bloc designations, which had dominated a significant sector of constitutional thought under the sturdy aegis of *Plessy*, had given way to the more fundamentally individualistic principles embodied in the original concept of rights.

This principle was not left to mere inference. On the contrary, it was vital to the passage of the bill in a Senate where northern Republicans had to be drawn into an alliance to overcome the resistance of southern Democrats. Hubert Humphrey, the senior Democratic Senator from Minnesota and the bill's leading sponsor, gave repeated assurances that all racial discrimination would be forbidden, including discrimination to achieve racial balance. "In effect, it says that race, religion and national

---

49. *Congressional Qu. Almanac*, 1966, 450–51.

origin are not to be used as a basis for hiring and firing. Title VII is designed to encourage hiring on a basis of ability and qualifications, not race or religion." To which Senator Thomas Kuchel, a Republican from California, added that "employees and labor organizations could not discriminate in favor of or against a person because of his race, his religion, or his national origin. In such matters . . . the bill now before us . . . is color-blind." [50] On no other terms could the bill have been assured of success.

The obduracy of southern white resistance had also very clearly demonstrated that legal claims were of little avail without an equal right to participate in the political process. President Johnson was determined not to let the initiative slip, and his leadership helped to secure the passage of a new Voting Rights Act in 1965. [51] This act did not abolish literacy tests or similar methods of selection, but it did establish machinery for placing in the attorney general's hands the power to determine whether such tests were being used as a means of racial discrimination, and to appoint federal examiners to supervise elections if this took place. Every phase of the electoral process was covered. The federal examiners, appointed by the Civil Service Commission, were empowered to determine an individual's qualifications to vote not only in federal, state, and local elections but in selection of delegates to party caucuses and state political conventions.

South Carolina duly objected. When, in *South Carolina v. Katzenbach*, and in other kindred cases, the Supreme Court validated the power of Congress, what in effect it did was to clear the way for congressional intervention wherever the states themselves failed to afford equal protection to the rights of United States citizens; the process amounted to a reversal of the *Civil Rights Cases* of 1883, which had curtailed the powers of Congress to operate "directly" in the states. This change in the scope of government power corresponded to the change in the intentions of government policy. Events of commensurate significance have sometimes been given the name of revolution.

Yet these developments were not in themselves the culmination of the re-establishment of equal rights. Even in the crucial matter of voting,

---

50. 110 *Congressional Record* (1964), 6549, 6564, quoted by Justice Rehnquist in his dissenting opinion in *United Steelworkers v. Weber*, 443 U.S. 193 (1979), 220–21, 238.
51. Senate 1564; HR 6400, *Congressional Qu. Almanac*, 1965, 533.

it was only by the middle of the 1960s that constitutional lawyers were grasping the fact that equality itself, as an individual matter, had emerged as the guiding principle in the dominant areas of public policy. In this same period, the Supreme Court was called on to consider the right to vote within the broader context of political representation.

There appears to be an elemental common sense to the assumption that when an elector casts a vote in a free election, he or she casts *one* vote: not five votes, not one-fifth of a vote. This assumption, however, has seldom corresponded to the facts as established by the actual numerical relation of voters to their elected representatives. When Thomas Jefferson wrote his *Notes on the State of Virginia* in the mid-1780s, he complained of the unequal representation of the counties, which gave the Tidewater a superiority of voting power in the assembly.[52] But no Virginia assembly took serious note of this grievance for almost another fifty years. Jefferson took for granted the assumption that fair representation was equal representation—equal as to individual voters, not by some other and more abstract principle of interests or superior rights.

The principle of equality of political individuals, which translated into one man, one vote—and in due course, one person, one vote—in approximately equal electoral divisions, was implicit in the Constitution, though not there clearly declared. Suffrage arrangements were left to the states, which might work out their own variations (often involving property qualifications). But the evidence both of the debates in the Constitutional Convention and of the political context in which they took place implies that electoral districts were in fact expected to represent roughly equal numbers.[53] It was to these principles that the Supreme Court adverted when confronted with the same issue more than one hundred and seventy years later.

The first question to confront the Court, which it grasped firmly in the leading case of *Baker v. Carr* in 1962, was that of justiciability.[54] Legislators, who had an interest in the matter, had always kept electoral

52. William Peden, ed., Thomas Jefferson, *Notes on the State of Virginia*, "Query VIII: Constitution" (Chapel Hill, 1955), 119–29.

53. For this argument, see Chapter 3.

54. 369 U.S. 186 (1962).

districting (now coming to be called apportionment) in their own hands. Two justices of the Court, Harlan—a descendant of the famous dissenter of an earlier generation—and Frankfurter, felt deeply that the issue of representation were essentially political and lay outside the competence of the judiciary. The balance of divergent interests was the essence of political life. Frankfurter, in a famous phrase, argued that these were "political thickets" which the judiciary should avoid. It would be easy to enter them, but not to emerge, and the Court would find itself acting as a party rather than a judge in a tangle of conflicting interests and local circumstances. Frankfurter also attacked the view that the doctrine of equal protection defined the character of American representative government and maintained that the proposition that the proportional principle established a link between the American system and "the standard of equality between man and man . . . preserved by the Fourteenth Amendment" as "bluntly, not true."

Mr. Justice Harlan's dissent testified to the survival of a style of whig thought which had survived in the Revolution and was not without its place in the republican tradition. It occurred to him that "the location within a county of some major industry may be thought to call for a dilution of voting strength." But thought by whom? Not, presumably, by the workers whose votes were to be diluted. Yet James Madison, who had made a similar point about prospective cities when writing to Jefferson, might well have agreed with Harlan.[55]

Baker v. Carr arose because the legislature of Tennessee had consistently failed to comply with the requirement of that state's constitution to redraw the electoral boundaries every ten years in correspondence with the decennial census. The result was that rural areas were very heavily over-represented at the expense of the cities. The Court sent the case back to the state courts for adjudication. In the ensuing case of *Reynolds v. Sims*, which arose from discriminatory districting in Alabama, the chief justice dispatched arguments about "political thickets and mathematical quagmires" by saying, "Our answer is this: a denial of a constitutionally protected right requires a judicial protection."[56] On the sub-

---

55. "Observations on the Draft of a Constitution for Virginia," in Gaillard Hunt, ed., *Writings of Madison* (New York, 1910) 5:284–94. It may be noticed that these views are inconsistent with his expressions of support for the proportional principle in the Convention.

56. 377 U.S. 533 (1964), at 565.

stance of the issues, he indulged in similarly straight speech. "Legislators represent people, not trees or acres," he said; "legislators are elected by voters, not farms or cities or economic interests." As for the argument that certain interests deserved additional weight, it was "inconceivable that a State law to the effect that, in counting votes for legislators, the votes for citizens in one part of the State would be multiplied by two, five, or 10, while the votes of the persons in another area would be counted only at face value, could be constitutionally sustainable." The Constitution forbade "sophisticated as well as simple-minded modes of discrimination."

Through a series of cases involving both state government and congressional districting, the Court moved with great firmness of purpose to establish the principle of one person, one vote. The clear simplicity of the rule had much to commend it; it was not subject to perplexing local exceptions and variations, it conferred no privileges, had no favorites. The other side of the coin was the specific weakness of the position defended by Harlan and Frankfurter: no uniform rule could be offered in defense of the numerous cases of imbalance which blotted the political map. Malapportionment was not the adventitious result of a series of unhappy historical accidents; it reflected conscious decisions in matters for which legislators were responsible. They should hardly have been surprised when the judiciary at last took the whole matter out of their hands. [57]

But Frankfurter had been right in his warning that the Court would be drawn deeper into the details of the political process. Within a few years it was beginning to vary the principles that applied to Congress from those that determined the limits of representation in state assemblies. United States citizens, it seemed, must be more equal than state citizens; congressional districts, observed Mr. Justice Byron White, were not so freighted with local interests as state ones, and where "minimal" deviations from the law of equality occurred, they did not require state justification; the burden now was on the plaintiff to show that the deviation was invidious. [58] By 1973, the Court seemed willing to tolerate a variation of ten percent between one district and another. When

57. See in general for this discussion the essays in Nelson W. Polsby, ed., *Reapportionment in the 1970s* (Berkeley and Los Angeles, 1971).
58. *Abate v. Mundt*, 403 U.S. 182 (1971); *White v. Regester*, 412 U.S. 755 (1973).

congressional districts were drawn so as to exclude or minimize the voting power of special minority interests, as happened in Texas, such interests could claim special protection. The interests in question were those of African and Mexican Americans, which were impaired by the device of multi-member districts whose effect was to dilute the minority's voting strength. With single-member districts, a much wider margin of error was acceptable—a move away from the mathematical purities of some important cases of recent years. Justices Powell and Rehnquist and Chief Justice Burger observed that legitimate state interests could actually be violated by the use of mathematical precision.

The recent decisions which had most firmly applied the law of precision had given no indication of the right standards for creating districts.[59] This disclosed a deeply disturbing if not altogether surprising paradox, for these decisions were widely interpreted as a license to party managers to gerrymander their districts. The opportunity was plain: with no rule to guide them other than that districts should be equal, managers were free to resume the form of craftsmanship which had so often cordoned off special groups to give them minimal representation, or had divided them so as to give none. In Connecticut, political leaders took the view that political parties were themselves interests entitled to representation, and in order to allow the public a fair opportunity to change its preferences, they devised a plan which created a certain number of "swing" districts. The District Court held all this to be a denial of equal protection. But the Supreme Court reversed, disagreeing with the view that this principle of "political fairness" was a "gigantic political gerrymander." Precedent showed, they agreed, that an otherwise acceptable statute could be invalid if it fenced out a racial group so as to deprive its members of a previously existing vote, but the Court was now disenchanted with ideas of complete political neutrality. In the majority opinion there was no such thing as politically neutral districting, because all districting was bound to produce certain groupings, whose effects must inevitably be political. "The reality," the Court now declared, "is that districting inevitably has and is intended to have substantial political consequences."[60]

A sharp disagreement now existed on the bench as to the possibility, or desirability, of neutral districting. Mr. Justice Brennan, dissenting in

59. *Wells v. Rockefeller*, 376 U.S. 52 (1964); *Kirkpatrick v. Preisler*, 394 U.S. 526 (1969).
60. *Gaffney v. Cummings*, 412 U.S. 735 (1973), 311–12.

the related case of *White v. Regester*, maintained that *Reynolds v. Sims* had set the "as nearly as practicable" standard for districting, which demanded that "the State make a good-faith effort to achieve precise mathematical equality." Brennan was here cleaving to the individualist principle, that "our paramount concern has remained an individual and personal right—the right to an equal vote." The weight of a person's vote ought not to depend on the district in which he lived.[61] But in *Gaffney v. Cummings* the majority had just taken a radically different view, not only of the practical possibilities of neutral representation but of the desirability of making the attempt. According to this view, political considerations were "inseparable from districting and apportionment." It was not only obvious, but "absolutely unavoidable, that the location and shape of districts [might] well determine the political complexion of the area. . . . The reality is that districting inevitably has and is intended to have substantial political consequences." The majority regarded the concept of neutral districting as "politically mindless."[62]

The issue, as ever, was equality, and the problem was to define it. Neutrality was one way of approaching strict political equality. Yet it was a way that put the initiative firmly in the hands of managers who knew the lie of their own political land and the means by which to produce desired results without violating the numerical equality of districts. To check this kind of abuse, it was necessary to depend on local knowledge—which meant knowing the identity of the affected interests—but could the use of this knowledge ever be a "neutral" act? The Court had entered Frankfurter's political thickets, and it would never be free of the problem of determining the actual meaning of permissible standards. The best that could be said for political equality was that those standards would always have to take the assumed equality of individuals as a starting point; the burden of explanation would fall on whomever chose to depart—or depart more than a few percentage points—into the forbidden territory of numerical inequality.

An Inconsistent Neutrality

Equality, we have earlier argued, is a metaphor. But once the Supreme Court had become possessed of the idea that equality was the central

61. Ibid.
62. Ibid.

constitutional value of the age, it moved with some determination to make the values of equality more concrete in particular categories. In the new civil rights era the national legislature assumed the power to determine and to enforce uniform national standards; equality became a synonym for uniformity, not among people but in the rights guaranteed to them by the state. The Supreme Court, which had anticipated congressional action by redefining the Constitution to outline the basic principles of uniformity, gave the necessary blessing to congressional action and confirmed that the branches of national government were in effective harmony as to the right ends of government, and also of the appropriateness of the means employed to those ends.

It is not surprising that observers discerned a threat to the federal character of the system. [63] It should not be concluded, however, that the judiciary was arrogating excessive powers to itself; what it did, in the first place, was to determine that certain types of discriminatory practice were themselves unconstitutional; beyond that, it restored to the legislature the powers intended for it by those clauses of the Fourteenth and Fifteenth Amendments which specifically empowered the Congress to pass the necessary legislation.

The Constitution is neutral as to persons and confers no authority for the preferential treatment of designated classes. But legislation in its nature constantly differentiates between groups, frequently doing so in order to respond to special needs. The characteristic drive of the era was toward the elimination of invidious inequalities resulting from racial and religious prejudice—which are states of mind—and from poverty and social disadvantage. Whether the latter are or are not a person's own fault, they clearly do not affect his or her constitutional rights.

Poverty could affect the quality of justice. Were poor people afforded due process of law when, as appeared early in the Warren era, state laws required convicted prisoners to pay for trial transcripts needed for their appeals? This, said the Supreme Court, violated both due process and equal protection. [64] Mr. Justice Douglas quoted both Leviticus and Magna Carta, but notwithstanding these formidable precedents, Mr.

---

63. Philip B. Kurland, "Foreword: Equal in Origin and Equal in Title to the Legislative and Executive Branches of the Government," *Harvard Law Review* 78 (1964–65), 143–76.

64. *Griffin v. Illinois*, 352 U.S. 12 (1955).

Justice Frankfurter, though concurring, rather deflatingly insisted that the Court was establishing a new rule of law for the United States.[65] A few years later another and far more salient case revealed that in Florida only defendants charged with capital offenses were entitled by law to free counsel. The Supreme Court here held that the Sixth Amendment— which does guarantee the right to counsel in all criminal prosecutions— was obligatory on the states through the Fourteenth Amendment. These cases did much to redeem the promise of equality before the law as an individual right, a right enforceable regardless of the victim's social or economic circumstances.

The Bill of Rights was changing in character. In all previous history it had been a defensive instrument, protecting the individual against encroachments by the powers of government; now it had become an instrument of action, commanding governments to intervene against the institutional forms taken by private or social prejudice. It had become the state's duty to eliminate inequalities which violated the basic categories of equality, as they had emerged and been identified in American history, even when the state had no responsibility for imposing them.

The individualist principle was the core of the issue. This makes it all the more surprising that the Warren court inflicted a startling defeat on the general character of its own policies in the crucial matter of interracial marriage, which, for certain classes, the laws of Virginia forbade. Two years after the *Brown* decision, the Court upheld this rule by dismissing an appeal from the Virginia courts.[66] This decision can only be considered an aberration from the Court's own central line of reasoning, even if that line was still in its early stages and had not yet been fully thought out. It was no more true in 1956 than in 1883 that members of different races were treated equally when a prohibition affected them both alike, *as races;* individuals, not races, were the proper subjects of constitutional protection, and when individuals, on account of their race, were so defined as to prevent them from exercising a free personal choice, those

---

65. "Ye shall do no unrighteousness in judgment: thou shalt not respect the person of the poor, nor honour the presence of the mighty: but in righteousness shalt thou judge thy neighbour" (Leviticus). "To no man will we sell, or deny, or delay, right or justice" (Magna Carta).

66. *Naim v. Ham Say Naim,* 197 Va. 80; 350 U.S. 985 (1956).

individuals were not equally treated. The real problem before the Court was to discover permissible standards of legislative categorization and to strike down the use of irrational or arbitrary standards. The Court was not generally inclined during this era to recognize race as a permissible standard, except where special help was needed to rectify past wrongs, and a few years later it reversed itself when it invalidated Virginia's anti-miscegenation law as a violation of both equal protection and due process. The right to be married was now held to be a basic civil right. [67]

If hard cases are law's supreme test, the concept of civil rights is often under greatest stress in times of war. The wartime experience of Japanese Americans revealed the limitations of such liberal thinking as had so far taken place. For the United States, the Second World War began with Japan's attack on Pearl Harbor, and the large Japanese-American population on the West Coast, long the object of bitter economic rivalry and racial resentment, was at once suspected of disloyalty. The commanding officer of the region, General DeWitt, issued orders to exclude them from certain areas. These orders prevented a Mr. Korematsu from living in his own home, and after declining to comply with them, he was arrested. He took his case to the Supreme Court. [68] As a United States citizen, he could not be classified as an enemy alien; the case tested the civil rights of American citizens.

Mr. Justice Hugo Black began the Court's opinion with a firm tone covering an ambiguous position: "Pressing public necessity may sometimes justify such restrictions; racial antagonism never can." Real military dangers were discerned, and the majority had no doubt of the general's right to take whatever steps he deemed necessary to protect the territorial integrity of the country. The difficulty, however, was that the "pressing public necessity" was perceived in the light cast by "racial antagonism." General DeWitt's own final report on the evacuation of the Pacific Coast spoke of the Japanese as an "enemy race" and of all persons of Japanese descent as "subversive." No reliable evidence was offered to support these views, but much light was thrown on the subject by Austin E. Phelps, managing secretary of the Salinas Valley Grower-Shipper Association: "We're charged with wanting to get rid of the Japs for selfish reasons," he said, candidly adding: "We do. It's a question of

67. *Loving v. Virginia*, 388 U.S. 1 (1967).
68. *Korematsu v. U.S.*, 323 U.S. 214 (1944).

whether the white man lives on the Pacific Coast or the brown man. They came into this valley to work, and they have stayed to take over. . . . They undersell the white man in the markets. . . . We don't want them back when the war ends, either."[69]

The dissenting opinions of Justices Roberts, Murphy, and Jackson made quite clear that military necessity was not the only question that the Court ought to be considering. Roberts denied that any emergency had existed, though he admitted that he might have agreed with the exclusion order if the facts had justified it; he found, however, that the government had distorted the facts disclosed, which were among others that Korematsu had been required to leave his home. Murphy perceived an obvious case of racial discrimination and quoted the evidence just cited. Jackson drew attention to the constitutional rule against attainder of treason working "corruption of blood, or forfeiture during the life of the person attainted." It was an uncomfortable fact that in a previous case the Court had permitted a curfew on racial grounds, which in principle was certainly an act of racial discrimination, even if its effects were comparatively light. If, however, they had stood their ground at that point, the subsequent much more serious case would have been much clearer. The outcome was that in the definitive case of its kind the United States was left with a ruling that did not, in all possible circumstances, eliminate race as a "permissible" subject of discriminatory action.

War certainly makes hard cases. The Court's ruling was more consistent with those emergency circumstances in which the rule of law is temporarily suspended—to be resumed and the injustices redressed after the emergency has passed—than with the requirements of equal protection. The Court, however, did endeavor to cover its flank by rejecting the notion that racial prejudice could be a legitimate cause of discriminatory action in itself, and chose the view that the restrictions were justified on other grounds.

The treatment of the Japanese Americans was out of character with both surrounding and ensuing cases involving American minorities. Once the idea of equality was out of its box again, it multiplied and divided like the sorcerer's apprentice's broom. The period between, approximately, the concluding phases of the Second World War and the election of Ronald Reagan in 1980 as President of the United States was

---

69. These remarks appear in the Court record, ibid., 236, 239.

marked by a succession of events that were epoch-making but not wholly consistent. The era of a unified civil rights movement included the Ives-Quinn Anti-Discrimination Act in New York, its many successors elsewhere, the school segregation cases, federal legislation on civil rights and voting, and the Supreme Court's decisions on representation. These were not isolated events. They were elements in a great and, for the time being, unified historical process. But that process was made by the efforts of men and women, and the unity was an artifact. Each of these events gave rise to new problems and new divisions of purpose. If the pursuit of equality appeared at times to be the pursuit of an illusion, it was because equality was a complex concept which, even at the most philosophical level of abstraction, could not envisage or aim at a single goal. The mere fact of winning new and higher ground in the pursuit changed the perspective of the viewer. But the victories often yielded ambiguous and deceitful gains, for not all the new ground appeared to correspond with the original objectives. What had been lost in the victory was unity of purpose.

Chapter Twelve

Sex and Gender:
Where Equality Is Not Identity

Sex, Gender, and Power

In the second century of the Christian era, young men of the privileged classes of the Roman Empire were brought up to consider themselves the fairest part of the earth and the most civilized portion of mankind. They had the satisfaction of knowing themselves to be in every way superior to women, slaves, and barbarians; their dominance over women was unchallengeable because it was in the order of nature. Women were scientifically considered to be derived from fetuses which had failed to develop the full male potential in the womb. But according to no less an authority than Galen, this imperfection which resulted in the creation of the female sex was a result of a broader design, being necessary to enable them to produce children, as he explained with considerable physiological detail; if this were not so, he added, men might think that "the Creator had purposely made one half of the whole race imperfect, and, as it were, mutilated." [1]

The idea that women were mutilated men, however, appears to have persisted in the male imagination; some seventeen hundred years later, the founder of psychoanalysis attributed to women a basic envy of male physiology. It was equally natural that both sexes should have characters

1. Peter Brown, *The Body and Society: Men, Women and Sexual Renunciation in Early Christianity* (New York, 1988), 9–10. Edward Gibbon, *The Decline and Fall of the Roman Empire* (1776), I, 1.

in keeping with their functions, and the related conception of female character as a construct of physiology also persisted in medical thought. The urge to motherhood, explained an American textbook on gynecology published in 1943, was the fundamental biological factor in women, balanced by a merely secondary interest or even an absence of pleasure in sex. As late as 1971, another medical textbook declared that "the traits that compose the core of the female personality are feminine narcissism, masochism and passivity." These statements are clearly not mere formal accounts of the psychological consequences of female physiology; they reflect their authors' notions of the natural relationship between the sexes, and are explanations, not to say justifications, of the masculine exercise of social power.[2]

The sexual aspects of relationships between individuals, within families, and among circles of friends, are extremely subtle, and their subtleties are threatened by broad generalizations. But a certain level of generalization becomes valid and indeed necessary, when they shade off into gender relationships; although still capable of intricate and delicate nuances, the concept of gender has had a historical tendency to reflect ultimate inequalities of power. At different historical periods, and in widely differing economic and social conditions, such relations have been stabilized under paradigms that function as ideal statements of the roles and mutual obligations of the sexes. One of the most familiar—to take a prominent example by way of illustration—is the Victorian ideal of domesticity, paralleled in the Southern United States by the ideal of the plantation mistress. This paradigm was based on the ancient conception of woman as being weaker than man, but this defect was now seen to enhance the need for male protection and was nicely compensated by her superior beauty. Women were in fact traditionally characterized, if not personally flattered, as "the fair sex." But this ascription hardly compensated for the male conviction that the weaknesses of females were intellectual and moral as well as physical. Woman was inherently more spiritual though less intellectual than man, closer to the divine yet, paradoxically perhaps, more subject to her animal instincts, more moral yet less in control of her morality.[3]

2. Helen Callaway, " 'The Most Essentially Female Function of All': Giving Birth," in Shirley Ardener, ed., *Defining Females: The Nature of Women in Society* (London, 1978), 169.
3. Carroll Smith-Rosenberg and Charles Rosenberg, "The Female Animal: Medical and Biological Views of Woman and Her Role in Nineteenth-Century America," *Journal*

For a long period, and for significant sections of society, this ideal appeared to be right and proper because it was held to be a social reflection of the natural order. If in places it imposed restraints, these were called for to repair the weaknesses with which natural impulses threatened social propriety, and through it social order. In these ways the Victorian upper and middle classes of the Anglo-Saxon social culture incorporated and rationalized a set of relationships which still, at its base, subjected women to the power of men. The system seemed to those who expounded it to be natural, solid, enduring, and yet constantly threatened by the manifest passions and weaknesses of human nature itself. Yet this elaborate conceptual framework was in truth only an artifact of historical struggles, reconciliations, and compromises, in some ways perhaps a sort of triumph over nature, but not a manifestation of it. And it reflected only the outcome of those issues in a particular class. Moral and social nuances associated with ideas of domesticity were influenced by the question of whether or not the household employed domestic servants. Working-class women, both white and black, might go out to work in factories or other people's homes, but they still for the most part had to do a lot of their own work at home; there is little reason to suppose that Victorian ideas of domesticity were reflected in their style of life, and still less in relations between black women and their menfolk. Indeed it was for black men a particularly damaging aspect of the situation both under slavery and in free black communities that they were frequently disabled from the protective and supportive role ascribed to their sex by the prevailing ideology of gender relations. On the other hand, the situation gave rise to a greater measure of equality between the sexes among blacks than was usually available to white women.[4]

Men's domination over women has assumed many forms and been sustained by various explanations. But such explanations have seldom appeared in formal political theory, which has generally had nothing to

---

of American History 9:2 (1973); Catherine Clinton, *The Plantation Mistress* (New York, 1982); Joan W. Scott, "Gender: A Useful Category of Historical Analysis," *American Historical Review* 91:5 (December 1986), 1068.

4. Suzanne Lebsock, *The Free Women of Petersburg: Status and Culture in a Southern Town, 1784–1860* (New York, 1984), 109–10. The author observes that the fact that black men had less moral or economic purchase on black women, giving the latter less reason for deference than existed among their white sisters, may also have led to higher levels of domestic conflict among blacks.

say about the female sex, either in the formation of the state or in theories of representation and consent.[5] Plato's advocacy, in *The Republic*, of equal education and political responsibility for suitable women (though based on observation and though resumed, if somewhat equivocally, in his late work *The Laws*) left few traces in its own or later times. Locke, it is true, said that "the *first Society* was between Man and Wife"; but society for Locke was not government. A "voluntary Compact between Man and Woman" in turn created "conjugal society," but that again was not *political* society; and Locke was firm about paternal authority in the family. As between husband and wife, "the last Determination, i.e. the Rule, should be placed somewhere," and it naturally fell to the man "as the abler and the stronger."[6] But these passages, which pay more attention to women than most works of theory, do not allocate a *political* role to women, even in the formation of the state. And it may be noted that all formal writing about the state before the emergence of modern scholarship was by men.[7]

The lines of authority at all levels of the social order reflected those of patriarchy. Kings were *fathers* of their people. James I had argued that a king could be compared with the father of a family, "for a king is truly *Parens patriae*, the politique father of his people"; this image was carried

5. Quentin Skinner, *The Foundations of Modern Political Thought*, 2 vols. (Cambridge, 1978), finds no need for a discussion of the place of women in the concept of the state; the civic humanist tradition as traced by J.G.A. Pocock, *The Machiavellian Moment* (Princeton, 1975), finds room for women only in symbolic connections. In a much earlier work, now often considered to be superseded, George H. Sabine, *A History of Political Theory* (London, 1937), 34–35, pointed out that when Aristophanes lampoons women's rights in his play *Ecclesiazusae*, performed circa 390 B.C., he may well have been commenting on Plato's communistic society in *The Republic* (though the chronology is unclear); whether or not this was the case, the ideas were clearly in the air.

6. John Locke, *Two Treatises of Government*, ed. Peter Laslett (Cambridge, 1964) II, ss. 77, 78, 81, 82, pp. 336–39. Discussed in Linda Kerber, *Women of the Republic: Intellect and Ideology in Revolutionary America* (Chapel Hill, 1980), 17–19. There is a possibly unsuspected degree of consistency in these views with those of Aristotle, whose organic concept of social origins had in fact much more to say about the role of women in the family and household. Aristotle, who respected the goodness of women in their role, had no doubt about masculine superiority in reasoning (Plato's observations notwithstanding) and in consequent authority in the fn the family, and quoted with approval Sophocles's line: "A modest silence is a woman's crown." *Politics*, I, xiii, para. 10.

7. Women appeared as historians in the era of the American Revolution, on the English side in the person of Catherine Macaulay, and with Mercy Otis Warren in America. Both these writers had strong views on politics and used their historical writings in, essentially, the whig cause.

to and formally accepted in the colonies, where, eventually, George III was bitterly reproached for turning from a father to a murderer.[8]

The relationships which can be so clearly traced in the vocabulary of gender were not confined to mere power. Qualities and personified ideals also had sexual identities. Liberty was always feminine, virtuous but weak, threatened by masculine aggression and tyranny, and therefore in abject need of protection by the countervailing masculine quality of republican virtue. The superior attributes of America were by no means exclusively male. When newspapers and magazines began to represent them in graphic form, Columbia and Minerva—goddess of wisdom—were always female.[9] But the same could hardly be said of the bald eagle, which seemed to be a formidably masculine bird.

In general, language had historically expressed power relationships through the symbolism of gender and had thus perpetuated the impressions which this symbolism conveyed. Unmanly or womanish conduct, an effeminate demeanor, was always unbecoming in a man, while mannish or boyish manners or style were out of order in a woman—out of order, but nevertheless subtly less damaging to her reputation. A man who wore woman's clothes would in most societies be subject to different and more critical comment than a woman who wore men's. (And the fact that in the Elizabethan theater women's parts were played by boys invested English drama with a tolerance for the transvestite which may have blurred the outlines of social criticism. Shakespeare's heroines are often at their most attractive, to *both* sexes, when dressed as boys.) The values expressed in these linguistic shadings and behavioral trends were often more subtle and significant than the more obvious power relationships. Hamlet, in a moment of conspicuous psychological instability,

8. Ruth H. Bloch, "The Construction of Gender in the Republican World" in Jack P. Greene and J.R. Pole, eds., *The Blackwell Encyclopedia of the American Revolution* (Oxford, 1991). The last Romanov czar of Russia was loved by a possibly misguided people as "the little father." It hardly overextends this image to add that Josef Stalin was projected to the people in the same light, if under the designation of "Comrade."

Jacob Burckhardt stated that the Renaissance placed women "on a footing of perfect equality with men." *The Civilization of the Renaissance in Italy* (1860). But a more recent study has reversed this view, arguing that upper-class women of the middle ages were real beneficiaries of the tradition of chivalry and courtly love, all of which disappeared in the state-dominated cultures of the Renaissance. Joan Kelly, "Did Women Have a Renaissance?" in *Women, History and Theory* (Chicago, 1984).

9. Bloch, "Construction of Gender."

reproaches the steadfast Ophelia with, "Frailty, thy name is woman." The reproach reflects on Hamlet, not on the deeply wounded Ophelia, but such expressions are often repeated, as we now say, out of context. Shakespeare's men often deride the feebleness of women's reasoning, but a close observer will note that Shakespeare's women often have the better of the argument. Gender values were also subject to considerable changes of emphasis in different times and circumstances. Shakespeare's men reproach themselves for feminine behavior when they weep; but in the eighteenth century, Fielding's Tom Jones repeatedly bursts into floods of tears without incurring reproach either from his author or from other characters. (Odysseus spends most of his time on Kalypso's island in tears, in circumstances that lesser men might have found enviable.) But male tears were unmanly once again in the nineteenth century. Sexuality and social power were intimately reflected in the question of dress throughout a long period that seems to have faded only with the Second World War. The wearing of trousers by women was considered sexually provocative and socially improper. But when women were recruited in large numbers to serve as bus conductors in Britain, convenience began to prevail over convention and they were issued with trouser suits; the British armed forces, however, dressed women in uniform skirts. Factory work and military duties seem to have eroded these barriers in the United States in roughly the same period.

These modifications in the *style* with which the sexes presented themselves made little impression on language. It was only when the reborn women's movement of the 1960s onward took the question of language deliberately in hand that the gender implications of linguistic usage were revealed as having been anything more than neutrally descriptive. The new movement not only introduced the *Ms.* designation but neutralized, if not actually neutering, the gender implications of such formally designated officers as chairmen, and challenged the claim that the masculine pronoun could serve for both sexes. The aim of this program was to introduce a revolution in consciousness, and through it nothing less than a revolution in the sexually based distribution of power.

The political thought of colonial resistance took shape in an already changing moral environment, marked by the expression of a broader

attack on the idea of patriarchy and on the legitimacy of all claims to inherited political privilege.[10] But these views of the proper relations of human beings were not in any particular sense the product of the American situation, nor were they distinctively American. The American situation lay along the circumference of the Enlightenment, in which Americans shared and to which they made their own varied contributions.[11] Americans had for generations been reading Locke's works on education and epistemology, which supplemented his attack on Sir Robert Filmer's treatise on patriarchy by teaching a new respect for the independence of the individual's will and judgment. The parents of America's revolutionaries had read and brought their children up on Robinson Crusoe, the greatest of all works on the survival of the lone individual. Oliver Goldsmith's immensely popular novel, *The Vicar of Wakefield*, became available only in 1772, but its ideal of the responsible and affectionate Lockeian parent fell in with what was by now a popular faith. Much of the Scottish Enlightenment, in the teachings of Francis Hutcheson (Adam Smith's teacher), James Burgh (who was also widely read as a compiler of whig tracts and history), and English contemporaries, absorbed and Christianized Locke's views on education, placing a new emphasis on the obligations of parents to their children, and these teachings were reaching into American homes during the years which saw the stirring of protest against British parliamentary policies.

These ideas did not cause the Revolution, which might have come about without them. But they profoundly affected the frame of mind of those who made it, and therefore affected the kind of revolution that it turned into. It was partly through the influence of a general, post-Lockeian concept of a benevolent universe, partly through the diffusion of Hutcheson's doctrine of a common moral sense through the more thoughtful circles of British, French, and American society, that this was

---

10. Pauline Maier, "The Beginnings of American Republicanism, 1765–1776," in *The Development of a Revolutionary Mentality* (Library of Congress, Washington, D.C., 1972); Jay F. Fliegelman, *Prodigals and Pilgrims: The American Revolt Against Patriarchal Authority, 1750–1800* (Cambridge, 1982). The following paragraph draws on Fliegelman, 20–64.

11. Henry F. May, *The Enlightenment in America* (New York, 1976); Donald H. Meyer, *The Democratic Enlightenment* (New York, 1976); J.R. Pole, "Enlightenment and the Politics of American Nature," in Roy Porter and Mikulas Teich, eds., *The Enlightenment in National Context* (Cambridge, 1981). Henry Steele Commager, *The Empire of Reason* (New York, 1977), offers a robust version of the American Enlightenment as a product of the American genius working on American circumstances.

also a period in which the mutual obligations and affections of members of families were growing more prominent in the sensibilities of the adult world. It has been noticed, for example that after about 1780 the composition of American family portraits began to arrange all members on the same level, instead of following earlier practices which placed the father in the highest or most prominent position, the women of the family below him, and the children below their mother. [12]

Americans shared in these trends, which diminished the sense of formal hierarchy in the family as in the adult world. One of the consequences of an enhanced sense of the status of the individual, accentuated by the competitive nature of urban life and the closeness and informality of much of American society, was a psychology that was almost abnormally sensitive to threats of oppression. Eruptions of protest and disorder were frequent enough in both cities and countryside without any British provocation. And it is hardly surprising that the women who made up half the population and were integral to any family no matter what its social position or economic style should have begun to sense and share these impressions.

Women, however, lacked any forum for the formation of group consciousness, let alone of protest. Only those who were well educated or well placed, of whom one of the most notable was Abigail Adams, could at all freely articulate their feelings, or perhaps, even, formulate their thoughts. Abigail Adams was much influenced by reading the English historian and political publicist Catherine Macaulay, to whom as early as 1774 she wrote a remarkable letter offering to correspond with her on American affairs. Mrs. Adams's celebrated request to her husband John that the men when making a new code of laws should "remember the ladies" and refrain from putting unlimited power into the hands of husbands—a remark she repeated soon afterwards—was an appeal for restraint; it did not reach as far as a demand for any form of political power. But her language makes very clear that she understood and, for her sex if not for herself, resented the tyrannical authority which the laws committed to men over their wives. [13] It was only too clear that she knew it was often abused. Abigail Adams was not beyond drawing the analogy between royal tyranny and male tyranny.

12. David Hackett Fischer, *Growing Old in America* (New York, 1977), 94–95.
13. L.H. Butterfield, ed., *Adams Family Correspondence: Volume I, December 1761–May 1776* (Cambridge, Mass., 1963), 177–79, 369–71, 402–03.

War precipitated women into a new range of responsibilities. Wives had very rarely been invited to share in estate or business management, of which they had little or no experience; separated from their husbands for the first time, many of them made painful discoveries of their own disabilities and limitations, but as they grew more used to the experience of running the family's business affairs and to making decisions without a husband in sight, their self-confidence seems to have improved. [14] Colonial women, where their views can be found, generally deprecated their own abilities and worth. The fact, indeed, that only some half of the white female population could sign their names to a will must have had a deeply depressive effect both on their competence and on their self-esteem. [15] The war drew innumerable women from their homes, many of them following the armies in indispensable roles as nurses, laundresses, cooks, and dispensers of comfort—in some of which capacities they had difficulty in securing General Washington's unqualified approval. And as the war bit more deeply into American life, women gave important support in the war effort, spurred and dominated by the socially prominent wives of male leaders. Esther Deberdt Reed, whose husband Joseph Reed was one of Pennsylvania's leading politicians, and Sarah Franklin Bache, daughter of Benjamin Franklin, led a fund-raising drive which collected 300,000 continental dollars, an amount worth some $7,500 in specie. The Philadelphia Ladies Association, which officially undertook this task, also performed important services in providing clothing for the army; women in New Jersey also devoted their efforts to raising substantial sums. [16]

The American woman's experience of the war was entirely different from that of her British counterpart. American women were *involved* as British women were not—either in the War of American Independence or in the later and far closer French Revolutionary and Napoleonic wars. [17] As a direct result of the war, American women became aware of

14. Mary Beth Norton, *Liberty's Daughters: The Revolutionary Experience of American Women, 1750–1800* (Boston, 1980), ch. 7.

15. Ibid., xv.

16. Ibid., 177–87.

17. Jane Austen's novels are often cited as evidence. In *Persuasion*, for example, Captain Wentworth, a relatively poor naval officer, makes his fortune by capturing enemy shipping, which in turn conduces both to his marriageability and to the domestic comfort of his future wife. Her contribution is pathetically passive. It is not to be supposed that Jane Austen altogether approved of this state of affairs. For a more explicit view, see *Northanger Abbey*.

their own significance in a collective struggle that reached far beyond their own households. "Was not every fireside, indeed, a theater of politics?" John Adams later rhetorically asked his friend Mercy Warren. The household economy itself was not only intensified, but in a sense made part of the public domain, by participation in the war. [18]

There was, however, no forum in which this sense of female relevance could take its hold. Nor, in fact, were there more than a few glimmerings—which, as with Abigail Adams, were privately expressed—of an inclination to challenge the general order of gender relations. If some women had begun to think themselves capable of entering politics or the law, they seem to have kept the thought to themselves. The successful achievement of American independence brought an end to the era of emergency which had called forth so many unused resources and restored women to their normal dependency on the political and economic hegemony of men.

With one exception, the new state constitutions offered no more openings in women's direction than the colonial charters had done. The exception was New Jersey, where a hastily drafted constitution appeared to permit women to vote through language which endowed the suffrage on free "inhabitants" without reference to sex. [19] There is no evidence of a feminist movement behind this clause, which only used the pronoun "he," not "he or she," as would have been appropriate if women had been intentionally included. It was not until 1790 that this alternative was introduced into the election laws, probably due to Quaker influence. [20] After an excited contest a few years later, the lawyer William Griffith, writing in the press, expressed his disgust at this abuse of the sacred right of suffrage by persons "who do not even pretend to any judgement of the subject." But he added that it was important to clear up the rights of some ten thousand widows and adult spinsters. [21] This point is of some interest because it implies a connection with common

18. Kerber, *Women of the Republic*, 41–42; I have, however, extended her interpretation.

19. L.Q.C. Elmer, *The Constitution and Government of the Province and State of New Jersey . . . with Reminiscences of Bench and Bar* (Newark, 1872), 32; E.R. Turner, *Women's Suffrage in New Jersey, 1790–1807*, Smith College Studies in History, vol. 1, 1915–16, p. 169.

20. New Jersey session laws, 19th sess., 1st sit., 925–26; Turner, *Women's Suffrage*, 168.

21. William Griffith, *Eumenes* (Trenton, 1799), 33–34.

law property rights, although in fact the right to vote was exercised under the state constitution and statute laws. The active phase of female suffrage in New Jersey lasted for some seventeen years, and whatever may have been the intent of the constitution, its introduction in 1790 was not an accident. At that time the meanings of republican principles were being tested. But voting by women does not appear to have affected the generally acknowledged principle that women had no place in politics, and it was probably permitted to continue because it increased the prospects of victory in keenly contested elections, both between Republicans and Federalists and between cities competing over such questions as the location of courthouses. Griffith promoted an abolition movement which seized its opportunity after a scandalous election over the Essex County courthouse in 1807. Nearly 14,000 votes were recorded out of a total of some 22,000 inhabitants (about half of whom probably were under age); with voting by aliens, Negroes, women, and children, some of them several times over, at the discretion of corrupt or indifferent election officers, the electoral system seemed to be breaking down, and the misogynist reformists had little difficulty in passing an election law which confined the suffrage to adult males, and white ones at that.[22]

Although the New Jersey episode cannot be ignored, it remains difficult to incorporate. It seems to have retained its local character. There was very little public discussion of the issues, nor did it influence other states. The very fact that the revision passed with little comment suggests that the whole business was admitted to be something of an anomaly.

Women and the Idea of a Republic

The broader consequences of the Revolution can best be described by saying that the men, and the small number of women, who worked to formulate principles appropriate to a republican order of government began to recognize an important principle which had received inadequate attention from most of the previous thinkers who had built the western traditions of political philosophy. Forms of government may be

22. New Jersey Session Laws, 32d sess., 1st sit., 14. Newark *Centinel*, Feb. 24, 1807; *New Jersey Journal*, Feb. 24, March 3, 1807.

considered as varieties of ideal types, but every form relates to an order of society. By including women in that order, the social thinkers of the new American republic were getting closer to a realistic description of society in all its essential functions. But they were not content with description; their aim was to apply republican principles to the fashioning of a new society. Realistic description—it would soon come to be called sociology—was fused with ideal aims. Much was at stake, for they were convinced that the republic could not survive without incorporating the values associated with the female sex. And, as the economic struggle became more intense, the significance of this insight would become more urgent. If this did not mean political participation, it did at least mean that the political order had an obligation to recognize the role of women in maintaining the very foundations of a republican society.

The most basic of these was in motherhood. It was generally agreed that republican government could survive only with virtuous citizens, and those who took upon themselves to instruct the public began to argue that mothers rather than fathers had the responsibility for molding their children's characters and educating their minds. Dr. Benjamin Rush, the Philadelphia physician and philosophe, placed great emphasis on the concept of public interest. "Let our pupil be taught," he said in 1782, "that he does not belong to himself, but that he is public property. Let him be taught to love his family, but let him be taught at the same time that he must forsake and even forget them, when the welfare of his country requires it." The pupil in this sentence is masculine, but it soon appeared that the teacher of these grave truths was to be his mother. "The instruction of children naturally devolves on woman," he explained in another pamphlet the next year; since women were also the stewards and guardians of their husbands' property, their education must teach them to discharge these duties.

Rush was writing for a middle class. He wanted American ladies to devote more attention to their families than happened in Britain, not in the first instance for reasons of affection but out of necessity; for he observed that in America servants were less subordinate than in Britain. The proper subjects of female education, apart from English language and writing a fair hand, should include geography, astronomy, and natural philosophy (which would later be called science)—the use of the latter being to combat superstition. They should also learn to sing;

dancing was "by no means improper"; and they could profitably read history, travels, poetry, and moral essays. [23] Rush strove to impress these views on the governors of Philadelphia's newly opened Young Ladies Academy, which took in one hundred pupils in its first year. Rush's concern was not addressed only to the mental welfare of the daughters of the Republic; he shared with Franklin the belief that female influence had the capability to mold the manners and morals prevalent among men. And this was an essentially republican responsibility. [24] Samuel Harrison Smith, publishing in Philadelphia some ten years later, insisted that society must acknowledge a duty to educate all its children—but admitted that he had made no provisions for female education, because, he explained, the improvement of women was marked by rapid progress and "a prospect opens equal to their most ambitious desires." [25] It is possible, however, that the learned author did not know what the full extent of those desires might prove to be.

These had been recently suggested in the most forthright and original contributions of the period, which happened to be the work of women. Much the best known was that of the Englishwoman Mary Wollstonecraft, whose *Vindication of the Rights of Woman* was reprinted in Philadelphia soon after its publication in London in 1792. Wollstonecraft, who was well aware of her own superior intellectual abilities, was deeply affronted by the constant trivialization of women's minds, manners, and morals, which not only kept them in subjection to men but rendered them accomplices in their own debasement. She called for nothing less than a REVOLUTION—her capitals—in female manners. She had much to say about education, holding that if boys and girls went to school together they would acquire a respect for each other without regard to sex. Women would prove themselves better companions of men if they were first given full recognition as rational creatures and free citizens.

In the single volume of the three she had planned, Wollstonecraft did not proceed—perhaps she had meant to—to demand equal rights in

23. Benjamin Rush, *A Plan for the Establishment of Public Schools and the Diffusion of Knowledge in Pennsylvania* . . . (Philadelphia, 1786), 14–15; idem, *Thoughts on Female Education* (Boston, 1787), 27–30, in Frederic Rudolph, ed., *Essays on Education in Early America* (Cambridge, Mass., 1965).

24. Kerber, *Women of the Republic*, 211.

25. *Remarks on Education: Illustrating the Close Connection Between Virtue and Wisdom* (Philadelphia, 1798), in Rudolph, *Essays on Education*, 190, 217.

property and political participation; it comes as something of a declension to find her concluding that the aim is to make women into good wives and mothers. But the persistent thrust and animus of her argument is based on the demand for equality of esteem. She did not like being patronized by men, and she did not like seeing other women accepting patronage.[26] Middle-class and well-read American women quickly recognized their own hitherto unspoken thoughts.[27] Both Wollstonecraft and, a few years later, the American Judith Sargeant Murray (writing under the pseudonym "Constantia") insisted that women be treated as men's intellectual equals. *"The idea of the incapability* of women, is, we conceive, in this *enlightened age,* totally *inadmissible"*; a "share of equality" would remove every obstacle to women's advancement. But in what direction? Murray mixed vigorous criticism of male patronage with a curious willingness to reconcile men to her aims by promising that the outcome of her reforms would be the cultivation of such feminine virtues as "mild benignity" and "retiring sweetness" in wives and mothers. But in the end she went further than Wollstonecraft—whose influence she acknowledged—in demanding political empowerment for women and citing historical instances of women's capability in government. She did not, however, hesitate to adopt masculine imagery, as when she gave instances of women who had exhibited "masculine understanding."[28] With these publications, assisted by the earlier works of Rush, the first public steps had been taken toward the articulation of an egalitarian feminist position.[29]

There may, of course, have been a tactical element in these powerful feminists' decision not to intrude so far into prevalent male sensibilities as to demand full political rights for women. Murray, for example, said nothing specific about women's suffrage; with her, as with her contemporary Susannah Rowson and with Benjamin Rush, the model republican

26. Mary Wollstonecraft, *A Vindication of the Rights of Woman* (London, 1792), 324, 370–90, 412, 447–49.

27. Kerber, *Women of the Republic,* 222–24.

28. Judith Sargeant Murray ("Constantia"), *The Gleaner, or Miscellaneous Production in Three Volumes* (Boston, 1798), 189, 191, 206, 211–12. Murray filled many pages with instances of women who had shone in many supposedly masculine accomplishments, including courage, patriotism, eloquence, philosophy, and literature. The volume is dedicated to John Adams, L.L.D.

29. Nancy F. Cott, *The Bonds of Womanhood: Women's "Sphere" in New England, 1780–1835* (New Haven, 1977), 201–02; Kerber. *Women of the Republic,* 227–28.

woman was still a mother, and no attempt was being made to repudiate a woman's natural connection to her home and family; the education and reading prescribed for girls was designed for its appropriateness to the teaching and nurturing role of the female sex in a republic whose public life would continue to be dominated by men. Murray was even anxious that it would not seem *"unsexual"* for women to be taught the rudiments of Latin![30] The prospect, such as it might have been, of a feminist position in the public domain was in any case overtaken by the onset of the Second Great Awakening, a powerful Protestant impulse which had no use for the public role of women.[31]

It should not be supposed that these intellectual constructions, even when supported by the emergence of some thousands of young women with republican educations, made much difference to the ways in which the vast majority of American women actually lived their lives. To slave women, of course, they made no difference at all; to free black women, most of whom were systematically denied the opportunity of elementary education, they were probably for the most part unknown. But changes were taking place at least among the white middle and upper classes in the relationships of families to the wider society; and in humbler homes, both urban and rural, the demands made by the rapidly growing economy had disruptive—or in some cases, liberating—effects on family cohesion, affecting both men and women. Life was fraught with uncertainties, husbands frequently died young and without providing for their wives, and the need to give young women some preparation for the world beyond their parental homes increased the obvious need of female education. Nor had Rush and his contemporaries worked in vain. Their arguments were taken up by the sponsors of the growing number of girls' schools, who emphasized the influence of women over men in a manner that might well have begun to raise some questions as to the independence of the male character. But female academies and their sponsors always insisted that female education should be adapted to female character.[32] There is an important difference to be observed between this position and that of Wollstonecraft, whose standpoint did not admit that the sexes had different characters and who recognized the

---

30. Murray, *Gleaner*, 6.
31. Cott, *Bonds of Womanhood*, 203.
32. Ibid., 115–21.

extent to which the observed differences were the products of the existing educational structure, of sexually differentiated manners, and of the morals that the system inculcated in both sexes. The difference she did recognize was socially differentiated roles; but these were at least to be based on complete mutual respect. If she had lived long enough she could well have worked from here to the other claims that women would eventually make in the feminist cause. [33]

The educational exercises developed by the growing institutions for female education had important long-term effects. Women were at last stepping out of doors to take their places as teachers, their first step in the direction of a professional identification. [34] Literacy among white women greatly advanced, and by 1840 it was reported, perhaps optimistically, to be almost universal. Debate about the proper role of women had subtly shifted to new ground. The idea that women were intellectually inferior to men, which few people seem to have questioned in the seventeenth century and which was sustained by an almost universal deprivation of educational opportunity or practical experience until— and generally long after—the War of Independence, was gradually giving way before the evidence of effective female enterprise and activity. But people who exercise authority over others' lives seldom yield it merely because their original reasons have failed them; men still needed women to perform what was essentially a service operation in a masculine society. And most men, as appeared when women began to take their stand in public life, were unwilling to change their habitual convictions. The struggle was still in progress, and gaining ground slowly against tenacious resistance, nearly two hundred years later.

The Revolution was only in a very indirect sense the cause of changes in the position of women. Even the gradual though deep changes in the social environment in which women lived, which eventually created both new opportunities and new problems, could only be attributed in the indirect and sometimes dubious ways to the Revolution itself. It did

33. Wollstonecraft's comment on schoolmasters and dons bears quotation: "There is not, perhaps, in the kingdom, a more dogmatical, or luxurious set of men, than the pedantic tyrants who reside in colleges and preside in public schools" (*Vindication*, 370).

34. Lebsock, *Free Women of Petersburg*, 172–75; Richard H. Chused, "Married Women's Property Law, 1800–1850," *Georgetown Law Review* 71 (1983), 1417.

provide them, when their more audacious leaders chose to seize it, with a vocabulary of natural rights, which was available to turn against the traditions of the common law. But on the other hand, much of the justification of female education, and many of the circumstances which conduced to the development of a collective feminine consciousness, were still based on the old assumption that the biological differences between men and women could be described as the deviation of *women* from the male norm, a distinction which took its force from the principle by which men remained the norm for the human race; it was this conception of the differences that justified and explained the natural foundations of wholly different and separate social roles, the fulfillment of which conformed to the purposes of God and nature. This was the position that drew the attacks of Wollstonecraft and Murray and some of their peers, but they had no power to move mountains of inertia, and to have criticized the position of women in language that was soon to be used of race, as separate but unequal, would have appeared to most men—and probably to most women—as totally beside the point. That which was *naturally* different could not be made artificially the same; equality could apply only to those things which would be equal in a natural world. There was room for an analogy with the mythology of race, which ascribed biological characteristics to different races. That nexus was in due course to be explored by women.

Justice could never be separated from the moral order. The redefinition of women's role in society that was gradually making itself known in approximately the first third of the nineteenth century—or was at least making itself available to be known—still generally, though with some outstanding exceptions, accepted the natural separateness of women and demanded justice for them on a level that did not challenge the primacy of men in the public domain. When equity courts found in favor of married women's claims to their own property, as they increasingly did, the decisions were not based on claims to or admissions of equal rights. By the end of the century, daughters were inheriting greater shares of their deceased parents' property than before, but they never achieved parity with their brothers.[35] Equity concepts applied the principles of *fairness* to the best of the judges' ability within a paradigm of

---

35. Joan Hoff, *Law, Gender, and Injustice: A Legal History of U.S. Women* (New York, 1991), 85.

fundamental gender difference. No concession was being offered in any direction that might be expected to lead toward political equality based on individual rights.[36]

If women were to aspire to equality on the principle of interchangeability, which we have discerned as emerging as the post-revolutionary masculine ethos and was a principle commensurate with that of individual rights in law and politics, the basic requirement of their situation could now at least be stated. Their advocates—of both sexes—would have to break down the concept of woman as a separate case. Each individual woman would have to appear not only before the law, but in the familial, social, and eventually the economic order as a differentiated individual, unprotected except by the law which was supposed to protect every individual alike.[37] In the fiercely competitive conditions of American entrepreneurial capitalism, the prospect might be invigorating to some, but it was certainly daunting to others. In such a stormy world, a great many women were alarmed at the prospect of being endowed for their protection with nothing more weather-worthy than the individual "rights" about which men so loudly protested. The rumblings of a distinction, both emotional and ideological, between advocates of equal rights for women and advocates of a concept of rights that would protect women, would grow louder and more distinctive as the objectives seemed to come within reach.[38]

Female aspirations have generally been subjected to the test of a norm defined by the masculine gender. We have seen evidence of recognition by men concerned with the ethics and virtue of the republic that men were influenced, their characters shaped, by women. It is salutary, in this emphasis on masculine domination, not to overlook the ways in which the concept of the feminine shaped the definition of masculinity. Men were disparaged when they exhibited feminine types of frailty, emotion, or dependence. It was true that the dominant prospects in life were open

36. Norma Basch, *In the Eyes of the Law: Women, Marriage, and Property in Nineteenth Century New York* (Ithaca, 1982), 135–38.

37. Although the phrase "equal protection" came into the Constitution only with the Fourteenth Amendment in 1868, the principle was largely present in the common law and was also implied in many of the states' bills or declarations of rights.

38. This theme is developed in great depth by Hoff, *Law, Gender*, throughout.

to men and not to women, and the concept of male character and the virtues of manliness were shaped around the ideals and images of those prospects. In any competition, the trump cards were held in the men's hands. But all this placed a terrible burden on men to maintain the masculinity ascribed to them, which often involved violent demonstrations of virility and physical courage without recourse to either prudence or intelligence. Men had to be constantly on guard against letting their cards slip; although a male of poetic disposition might be complimented for his "almost feminine" sensitivity, and women could still be thought of as mutilated males, it was generally of much greater importance to American males not to appear as mutated females.[39]

Equality has been reduced in this inquiry to certain basic categories. One of these is sexual equality. If the equality of women had been historically accepted on an individualist basis, there would have been no need to treat sex, or gender, as a category like, for example, equality before the law. And this study deliberately refrains from making race or ethnicity the subject of separate categories because it is based on the assumption that the individualist concept of equality demands that the individuals who comprise these groups be *treated* as individuals. Adopting the individualist principle, five of these categories now can be turned inwards to test the sixth, constituting an inquiry into the historical condition of women, the social, psychological, and ideological conditions of change, and the aspirations and frustrations of the movement for full, individuated equality.

Women and Religion

Religious equality, as we have seen, emerged from the conflicts of a multiplicity of sects. It was a condition of legal and political liberty claimed *by* the sect rather than *for* the individual. But the very existence of these sects vindicated a certain freedom of individual choice. Anne Hutchinson, herself one of the earliest of the Puritan migrants, scandalized her male

39. All this was especially vivid in the nineteenth-century southern states, as most revealingly described by Bertram Wyatt-Brown, *Southern Honor: Ethics and Behavior in the Old South* (New York, 1982).

contemporaries in the mid-1630s, not only by her religious teachings but by her flagrant disregard for sexual roles; driven into exile, she suffered a pathetic miscarriage, in which male Christians divined just retribution, perhaps exhibiting less charity than had been recommended to them. Hutchinson's antinomian teachings would have caused disquiet even if she had been a man; as a woman, she threatened social order. It was after all another puritan, John Milton, who would later set these relationships in perspective when he assigned to Adam and Eve their relative theological standings: "Hee for God only, shee for God in him."[40]

But when torpid theocratic air was stirred by the breath of revival, as happened in the 1730s, women were conspicuous not only for their presence but often for their initiatives. "It must be owned," admitted a puzzled George Whitefield, "that some of the crying or roaring Women among us have brought forth something that may be both seen and felt."[41] A psychological release was sometimes effected through which women were able to vent a pent-up bitterness which took men by surprise and disturbed their complacency; although women gave much spiritual strength to the Awakening, they also sometimes spoke to their ministers, both in private and in public, with unaccustomed acerbity.[42]

New Light sects gave women the opportunity for a much more prominent part in religious activity than was permitted to them in the older congregations. Women observed the prescribed limits, however;

---

40. *Paradise Lost*, IV, 299. Mary Wollstonecraft faulted Milton for giving Eve the lines: "God is *thy law*, thou mine; to know no more / Is Woman's happiest knowledge and her praise"—remarking that she had often used these arguments to children. Adam, on the other hand, understood the virtue of equality: "Among *unequals* what society/Can sort, what harmony or true delight?" *Vindication*, 35–36. Milton, it may be added, was keenly aware of the force of the category of equality of esteem in revolutionary politics:

> Is this the Region, this the Soil, the Clime,
> Said then the lost Arch Angel, this the seat
> That we must change for Heav'n, this mournful gloom
> For that celestial light? Be it so, since hee
> Who now is Sovran can dispose and bid
> What shall be right: fardest from him is best
> Whom reason hath equald, force hath made supream
> Above his equals.
>
> *Paradise Lost*, I, 242–49.

41. Alan Heimert and Perry Miller, eds., *The Great Awakening: Documents illustrating the Crisis and its Consequences* (Indianapolis, 1967), xxviii.

42. Philip Greven, *The Protestant Temperament: Patterns of Child-Rearing, Religious Experience and the Self in Early America* (New York, 1977), 129.

they do not appear to have written any of the literature of the Great Awakening, which is not surprising in that most of it took the form of sermons, and no sect admitted women to the ministry. But their activities did not fade out with the first impulse of the Awakening. Among Virginia Baptists, women were often in a majority, voted on church matters, and sometimes served as exhorters; several women took prominent parts in leading local revivals and in maintaining them against male opposition.[43] It was only among Quakers, however, that the equality of women seems to have been fully recognized as inherent in the core of Christian doctrine.

In the sense that freedom to make one's own moral choice, or to answer in one's own conscience to the voice of God, was a mark of equality, it was in religion more than in any other walk of life that American women came close to some sort of equality with men in the long era before the onset of legally recognized women's rights. But this freedom, which often had to be exercised over the objections of men, was exercised within limits that reflected the general order of male dominance. Women could stimulate, organize, and minister, but not by entering into the official ministry; nor do they seem to have entered into the public realm of theological discourse. The openness of American society, however, was attractive to new sects to an extent that might almost be described a tending towards an equality of religious opportunity—though certainly not the sense in which that phrase was familiarly used in the nineteenth century. These circumstances were propitious for the emergence of a new group of women as spiritual and organizational leaders. Among these were Ann Lee, an English blacksmith's daughter who, having formed the belief that the Second Coming would be in female form, and that form her own, migrated just before the Revolution with her band of followers to plant the so-called Shaking Quakers near Albany in upper New York. Jemima Wilkinson, daughter of a prosperous Quaker farmer, founded a sect based on her own declared role as Public Universal Friend. It survived, rather than flourished, during her lifetime, despite internal dissensions and land problems, and some adherents continued to meet after her death in 1819.[44]

There was a valid sense in which equality of religious choice was

43. Norton, *Liberty's Daughters*, 126–32.
44. Sydney E. Ahlstrom, *A Religious History of the American People* (New Haven, 1972), 492–96.

actually open to and achieved by the adherents of these sects. Innumerable sects flourished in the new United States, enjoying a spacious freedom that owed very little to the constitutionally declared right to the free exercise of religion. A great many of the charitable activities which women organized, as they searched for extramural roles in the early nineteenth century, were related to churches, though the English author Harriet Martineau, observing these activities with a skeptical but discerning eye, unkindly noted that American women filled their vacant time, and minds, with religion.[45] When women bumped their heads against male obduracy within any of the conventional churches, they had no institutional recourse; the need, and the opportunity, came together when religious convictions took them along the public road of antislavery. At that point the issues became political, to merge, in due course, with the category of political equality.

Equality and Law: Procedure and Protection

England's American colonies were not the product of political or legal theory, and not much theorizing went into their legal foundations. They were subject from the beginning to the simple dictum that they were to make no laws repugnant to the laws of England, but they were given considerable freedom to make their own laws as the need arose. Early in the eighteenth century the counsel to the Board of Trade declared that the crown's subjects overseas carried with them the protection of English common law.[46] But the common law, which had principally accrued from judicial precedents since receiving royal authority in the reign of Henry II, was very much what the English judges said it was.[47] The transmission of English judicial doctrines, mainly in the form of recent decisions, began to occur before the middle of the eighteenth century; at no time do colonial courts appear to have had any difficulty in

45. Lebsock, *Free Women of Petersburg*, 224–26; Cott, *Bonds of Womanhood*, 137–38.

46. Elizabeth Gaspar Brown, *British Statutes in American Law* (Ann Arbor, University of Michigan Law School, 1964), 11.

47. Sir John Fortescue answered an inquiry from Henry VI in language that would have done credit to Chief Justice Charles Evans Hughes of the American Supreme Court: "Sir, the law is what I say it is, and so it has been laid down ever since the law began, and we have several set forms which are held as law, and held and used for good reason, though we cannot remember the reason." Shannon C. Stimson, *The American Revolution in the Law* (Princeton, 1990), 17.

receiving common law principles as they related to the status of women.

Women's problems at law—though not perhaps only at law—began with marriage, a condition which society agreed to regard as the normal state for an adult woman. The governing common law principle was that marriage merged the two souls into one, and that one, as Sir William Blackstone was to state the matter, was the husband.[48] On marriage a woman surrendered all her property to her husband, to whom she became in every sense a legal dependent and subordinate. She could neither sue nor, significantly, could she be sued in her own name, which placed on the husband a very real burden of responsibility for his wife's economic conduct, and on the law a responsibility for ensuring that her power to undertake legal obligations was correspondingly limited.

The crowded advertisement pages of the newspapers, right through the mid-century into the early republic, reveal a large number of women in business. Most of them were selling small goods such as millinery, presumably from their own homes. Thirty different trades and crafts, including those of silversmith, gunsmith, tanner, brewer, baker, harness-maker, and mortician, were practiced by women.[49] There were a few more prominent examples of females in command. Clementina Rind, widow of the original printer, owned and printed Virginia's only newspaper, *The Virginia Gazette*, for some years before the Revolution; Eliza Lucas Pinckney ran no fewer than three South Carolina plantations as a young girl for her absent father, before getting married and thankfully relieving herself of some of these burdens. She is generally credited with enterprise as well as competence for the introduction of indigo. Some of the small businesswomen of the towns were undoubtedly spinsters, and others were widows. But married women could only operate under the legal cover of their husbands' ownership; if they got into debt, the husband was liable under law. A wife could not be imprisoned for debt, not least because her husband was entitled to the companionship of her person. (A husband could, however; his wife's need for *his* companion-

---

48. Sir William Blackstone, *Commentaries on the Laws of England* (London, 1765), I, 430–33, in which the learned author also comments that the female sex are the favorites of the laws of England; and ibid., II, 433: "Husband and wife are one in law, so that the very being and existence of the woman is suspended during the coverture, or entirely merged and incorporated into that of her husband." Basch, *In the Eyes of the Law*, 17, 22–23.

49. Hoff, *Law, Gender*, 88.

ship did not have the force of a legal entitlement; the distinction is revealingly characteristic of the masculine bias of the law.)

The adoption of republican governments did nothing directly to alter this situation. While the courts of London, under the leadership of Lord Chief Justice Mansfield, at the center of the world's commerce and of much of its growing industry, were quietly fashioning the common law to make married women responsible for their own business debts, American state courts assumed no such responsibility. Nothing had happened to disturb the assumption that a wife could not act as an independent individual, which was the corollary to and explanation of her inability in law to own and control property. This was wholly consistent with the old whig principle that a person with a stake in society must be presumed to have an independent will; the characteristics of the politically defined "individual" which played such a prominent part in American ideology *presupposed* these conditions of personal independence. There was a certain inherent tension between the facts and the suppositions, with a strong legal propensity to bend the facts rather than the theory. But it is a mistake to look to the republican principles which Americans (of both sexes) proclaimed as their own in the Revolution as though they *ought* to have been a source of a new wave of liberation for women. As late as 1824, a married women in Massachusetts could not obtain credit on property held in trust for her. [50]

The changes that affected the status of women in the long and ill-defined period that began even before independence and carried through to the beginnings of a self-declared women's movement in the mid-nineteenth century, are none the easier to plot because they were devoid of public drama. Much of the economic diversification, the multiplication of commercial and eventually of industrial enterprise, along with upheavals in population, waves of religious revivals and the growth of free choice of marriage partners and freer relationships within the family, affected or were products of the activities of women; very little of all this had changes in women's status as a primary objective. But these changes did not occur by chance or mere drift; they were the results of decisions, large and small, and important contributions to a changing social order resulted from decisions made in specific cases by

50. Marylynn Salmon, *Women and the Law of Property in Early America* (Chapel Hill, 1986), 15, 42, 45, 137–38.

the courts. Equity rather than common law was the main source of legal assistance to women who found themselves in need of relief;[51] but the aim of such relief was in no sense to bring about a higher measure of general equality in women's social position. By the end of the eighteenth century, such changes as had taken place did sometimes afford a greater measure of financial independence to a wife who could make out a case on the specific terms of her settlement, but this gain might be at the expense of assurance of support from her husband's real estate after his death. As women often outlived their husbands, this was an ambiguous gain, and illustrates the uncertainties attending women's causes.[52]

It was not women's rights but women's needs that often attracted the sympathetic intervention of the courts. In the competitive, unsafe world of entrepreneurial capitalism, women increasingly needed the security of separate estates, which could be touched neither by the husband nor— still more important—by his creditors. The aim was security; equality might be a kind of fall-out from greater legal independence, but it was an effect, not a motive.[53] The inability of married women either to control or protect the property they had brought into a marriage, and their lack of rights in the family's means of subsistence, exposed not only wives but children in case of the husband's bankruptcy. The common law of coverture came to appear as an anomaly before it appeared as an injustice. When laws giving married women control of their property began to make their appearance, the first being introduced in Arkansas in 1835, to be followed by the better known case of Mississippi in 1839, their immediate aim was to protect wives and children from the husband's creditors.[54] But there was another, more subtle motive, arising from the fluctuating state of the economy, which frequently created needs for investment capital or for cash to pay for immediate debts. The common law procedures for getting a married woman's consent to the release of her property were an obstacle in these situations, and by

51. John D. Johnston, "Sex and Property: The Common Law Tradition, The Law School Curriculum, and Developments Toward Equality," *New York University Law Review* 47:6 (December, 1972), 1052, notes that equity was eventually responsible for (1) full enforcement of prematrimonial contracts; (2) a wife's entitlement to separate estate, and (3) her equity to a settlement. These, however, were not distinctively American developments, and the origins of (1) are traced to English courts in 1581.

52. Ibid., 1057.

53. Lebsock, *Free Women of Petersburg*, 69, 79.

54. Salmon, *Women and Property*, 185; Johnston, "Sex and Property," 1052.

entrusting such women with control, the law reforms could release capital where it was required.[55] Moves for protection and codification, which had the advantage of clarifying the position as well as clearing up inequities, were not motivated by sexual equality, though they may have had such effects indirectly.[56]

Women, however, were becoming increasingly active and articulate in their own cause; and male legislators had wives and daughters. New York in 1848 went as far as to recognize a wife's property in her estate without any form of agreement made before the marriage, though it was not until 1860 that New York gave a wife the right to sue in her own name. The same year saw a Married Women's Earnings Act. The legislation that followed in the several states, though piecemeal and unsystematic, had taken fairly full effect by the end of the nineteenth century.[57] At least in matters of property rights, women were approaching a condition of equality by law, rather than merely before the law.

In the post-patriarchal world, men found it increasingly difficult to defend arrangements that hurt or threatened their wives. But male dominance was not surrendered lightly. Neither affection nor enlightenment was a strong enough lever to prize open the doors of power. The situation became increasingly confused and difficult to define as the needs of families for their own economic security, which dictated that wives should be given some power to protect their property, conflicted with the idea that the authority of the father—and its justification—was sustained by his own obligation to protect his family. The confusion resulting from occasional and partial reforms left difficult choices, none of which could satisfy all the interests involved.

As in the colonial period, the courts of the Republic did not deny to women the procedural elements of equality before the law. Women had equal access to the courts, equal standing as litigants and witnesses; the male notion of protection did, however, exclude women from juries, which were thought to subject their members to experiences to which females should not be exposed. But when one passed from procedure to matters of substance, the law which the courts dispensed to women was

55. Basch, *In the Eyes of the Law*, 112.

56. Ibid., 115–19.

57. Johnston, "Sex and Property," 1061–62, 1066; Basch, *In the Eyes of the Law*, 73–114.

not the law they dispensed to men. Judges and legislators might flatter themselves, as Blackstone had flattered the common law of England, that American law afforded special protection to women as a members of a collective gender, but when an individual woman found herself in a civil court, while she could always reasonably expect due process, even the passage of the Fourteenth Amendment gave her no assurance of effective comfort from the doctrine of equal protection.

This position was established when an Illinois woman who was in every other respect well qualified—she edited a law journal—applied for admission to the state bar. Although she was a citizen of the United States, and could not in principle be denied any of the privileges of that status, the Supreme Court decided the case on the same grounds as the *Slaughter House Cases*, which had been decided in the same term. The question at issue was held to pertain to state citizens only; the Court would not project the Fourteenth Amendment between the state and its citizens. In a separate concurrence, Mr. Justice Bradley—later to speak for the Court in the *Civil Rights Cases*—disclosed the sociology which the majority were perhaps concerned to protect. "The constitution of the family organization, which is founded in the divine ordinance, as well as in the nature of things, indicates the domestic sphere as that which properly belongs to the domain and functions of womanhood. The harmony, not to say identity, of interests and views which belong or should belong to the family institution, is repugnant to the idea of a woman adopting a distinct and independent career from that of her husband," he explained.[58] Quite apart from the consideration that women do not always have husbands—although this one did—the Court clearly shared Bradley's conception of a natural order which prevailed over individual rights; the expression "in the nature of things" would reappear in Mr. Justice Brown's opinion in *Plessy v. Ferguson*. Sex was thus officially analogous to race as a legitimate ground for discriminatory legislation.

Political Equality: A Closed Door

During the War of Independence, a Massachusetts Loyalist named William Martin emigrated from the state and was deprived of his prop-

---

58. *Bradwell v. Illinois*, 83 U.S. 130 (1872), 445–46.

erty by confiscation. His wife Anna, whether out of conviction or obedience, left with him. After the war, their son, William Martin, Jr., sued for restoration of the property on the ground that he had inherited through his mother, arguing that her property ought not to have been liable to condemnation. The case raised in a complex form some of the political implications of the doctrine of feme covert. Martin's attorney, Theophilus Parsons, a prominent lawyer later to be chief justice of the state, argued that as feme covert Anna had "no *political* relation to the *state* any more than an alien," a view that saved his client's property at the cost of making married women into political aliens. The essence of the argument was that she did not share in her husband's treason because she had no political will of her own; the Massachusetts court agreed, and returned Anna's estate to her son; for the state could no more demand that a wife should rebel against her husband than it could tolerate rebellion against the state.[59]

In common law parlance, Anna Martin was a feme covert, and that concept governed her son's plea. In political life, it would be no exaggeration to say that the concept of feme covert governed the whole female sex, married, unmarried, or widowed. So it could not be a case of dependent women having no wills of their own; they had wills, but their wills were *incompetent* to deal with politics. This debility was generally associated with their propensity to hysterics and a deficiency in that steadiness and fortitude of character, and ability to think in clear, analytical, and dispassionate ways that so happily qualified the male sex for the solemn responsibilities of government.

Well-bred American women of the eighteenth century were not even expected to discuss political questions or to think political thoughts. Women as well educated and eloquent as Abigail Adams and Mercy Warren were aware, when writing to each other, that they confronted a problem when they entered into political discussion, and the problem included the risk of incurring the disapproval of their menfolk. Judith Sargeant Murray attempted to deflect this sort of criticism by offering her reasons for "assuming the masculine character," implying a diffidence

---

59. The case is retrieved and the issues expounded by Kerber, *Women of the Republic*, 132–36. A fuller discussion is in Kerber, "The Paradox of Women's Citizenship in the Early Republic: The Case of Martin vs. Massachusetts, 1805," *American Historical Review* 97:2 (April 1992), 349–78.

in writing about political issues which in all probability she did not feel.[60] But most women did, and this formal diffidence undoubtedly bears a large share of responsibility for the timidity of women in face of the self-confident facade erected by men. In the man-made public arena, women simply lacked the most elementary experience of presenting themselves or controlling procedures. Yet they were essential to male operations when that arena converged with the domestic, a point nicely admitted by Christopher Gadsden, the South Carolina merchant and revolutionary leader, when he commented that it would be essential to get their wives to agree to operating non-importation: "I allow the impossibility of succeeding without their concurrence."[61] The very evident and energetic contributions of women to many aspects of the War of Independence have already been noted; but from the larger perspective of the republic, it is at least equally noteworthy that these activities were never translated into a new concept of the political role of women. The New Jersey exception remains extraordinary in a strict sense of the word; nothing followed from it, no other states allowed themselves to be influenced, and in New Jersey itself, it seems never to have been hinted that women might be elected to serve in public office.

By the 1820s and 1830s, so loosely and undeservedly designated the Jacksonian period, the effects of reform movements in the male world had begun to shake the ethos that governed the restraints of gender. Such exceptional women as Margaret Fuller and Frances Wright were lecturing on political and social questions and contributing to debates on educational and labor policies. The fact that their conspicuous abilities were directed toward more general problems than those of women and their place in American society was a warning to the male sex of what to expect, or fear, if women were politically empowered. One could not begin to imagine such activities in the comparatively recent periods when Washington or Adams or Jefferson presided over the nation. But even these were still exceptions, which excited much curious and hostile comment; the predominant masculine view was very little affected by the increase in public affairs activities on the part of women in the early years of the new century. So long as women were busying themselves with charities and religion, and with a limited (but increasing) amount of

60. Ibid., 82–84; Murray, *Gleaner*, ix.
61. Kerber, *Women of the Republic*, 37.

teaching, they did not seem to impinge improperly on politics. But these activities should not be minimized. They absorbed the energies of increasing numbers of educated women while in their nature they produced still larger numbers, and these were not people who would indefinitely remain as political deaf mutes in face of public issues which touched their consciences. The rise of an organized anti-slavery movement in the 1830s would inevitably excite the feelings and provoke the activity of women, not least of those whose fathers were ministers of religion.

When, toward the end of the 1830s, Sarah and Angelina Grimké, daughters of a South Carolina slaveholder, abandoned their home to move North and speak in public against slavery, they ran up against the resistance of a male-dominated society. The Council of the General Association of Orthodox Churches of Massachusetts—the Congregationalists—defined the position of women as it had been and as they meant that it should remain. "The power of woman is her dependence," they explained, "flowing from that weakness which God has given her for her protection. . . . When she assumes the place and tone of man as a public reformer . . . she yields the power which God has given her . . . and her character becomes unnatural."[62] Women's dependence is here seen as a social reflection of the order of nature; it is nothing less than the law of God. Woman, of course, could depend on her weakness for her protection only in a world in which men unfailingly offered that protection. What the council's language unwittingly betrays is the psychological dependence of the men themselves, a dependence on the female sex to need and desire their protection.[63]

While views like these prevailed, there could be no more possibility of political equality for women than there had been through the ages of history. Men, passionately bent on eradicating evil from American society, reacted with severity to the incursion of women into their domain, and ridicule of female abolitionists was sometimes followed by physical assault. But the women who, like William Lloyd Garrison, insisted on being heard, soon perceived a disagreeable similarity between the Negro

62. Elizabeth Cady Stanton, Susan B. Anthony, and Matilda Joslyn Gage, eds., *History of Woman Suffrage* (New York, 1881) 1:81–82.

63. Slave women were of course not presumed to need protection—a fact poignantly expressed by Sojourner Truth at the women's convention in Akron, Ohio, in 1851 in a speech whose fragmentary record suggests that it may be considered beside those of Abraham Lincoln. Ibid. 1:115–16.

slavery that both they and the male abolitionists attacked, and their own relationship to the masculine world. So many anti-slavery societies excluded women from membership that they began to form their own; in 1837 Sarah Grimké wrote the president of the Boston Female Anti-Slavery Society a letter which directly addressed the question of women's status. "All history," she maintained, "attests that man has subjugated woman to his will, used her as a means to promote his selfish gratification, to minister to his sensual pleasures, to be instrumental in promoting his comfort; but never has he desired to elevate her to that rank which she was created to fill. He has done all he could to debase and enslave her mind; and now he looks triumphantly on the ruin he has wrought, and says, the being he has thus deeply injured is his inferior." [64] Only slight alterations would have been necessary to convert this indictment into an explanation of the white sense of superiority to blacks. In women's writings there began to appear analysis of the social and psychological processes of the moral as well as the material aspects of subjugation. [65] The increasingly evident need for political action in the cause of anti-slavery could only tend to turn these perceptions in the direction of politics. But women were better placed than men to perceive the connection.

The Horizons of Opportunity and Esteem

Eliza Southgate of Maine had never expressed a desire "to deviate from the laws of female delicacy and propriety," nor did she doubt that women and men were designed to occupy separate spheres of action. Yet in 1802 Southgate admitted that she "had often thought what profession I should choose were I a man." She anticipated many of later generations by expressing a preference for the law. [66] Her inclination could never, as she recognized, be dignified as an ambition; there was no

---

64. Judith Hole and Ellen Levine, *Rebirth of Feminism* (New York, 1971), 3–4.

65. Consider also the opinion of the English visitor, Barbara Bodichon, who compared the injustices of slavery she observed in New Orleans with injustice to women. Negro slavery was the worse, but "it is allied to the injustice to women so closely that I cannot see one without thinking of the other and feeling how soon slavery would be destroyed if right opinions were entertained on the other question." Barbara Leigh Smith Bodichon, *An American Diary, 1857–8*, ed. Joseph W. Reed, Jr. (London, 1972), 62–63. Bodichon was a woman of considerable private fortune, which she used to help in founding Girton College, Cambridge.

66. Norton, *Liberty's Daughters*, 112–13, 250–52, 296.

possibility that a woman could either qualify or be admitted to practice law. But the mere reflection was unusual. In surveying from her enclosed tower the wide landscape that was forbidden to women, she had glimpsed the world of urgent, ambitious striving for success and fame which drove men forward in their lives; and with some self-perception of more than private interest she added that she "did not feel that great desire for fame I think I should if I was a man."[67]

So long as the vast majority of women did not feel impelled by the spur of fame (which Milton had called "That last infirmity of Noble mind"[68]), they would not be likely to test to its limits the concept of equality of opportunity, which became increasingly prevalent until it had come to dominate American ideas of economic and social justice by the middle of the century. For most American women, the limits were plainly drawn by the Reverend John Ogden of Portsmouth, who observed in 1793 that "every man, by the Constitution, is born with an equal right to be elected to the highest office, and every woman, is born with an equal right to be the wife of the most eminent man."[69]

There is much evidence, as we have seen, that by roughly the 1820s, middle-class white women in various parts of the United States were entering into a greater variety of activities that had the effect of taking them outside the limiting sphere of their own homes. Some of these were charitable and unpaid, but others were livelihoods, and teaching bordered on a profession.[70] As women entered into the market in one way or another, they increasingly needed the kind of protection offered by the law rather than by mere masculine paternalism. The effect of these experiences was not to introduce a greater degree of equality of opportunity but to bring many more women up against the fact that they did not have it. It is generally fair to say that the concept of equality of opportunity was thought of as applying exclusively to the world of men; it is equally to the point, since women's aims are the central issue, that most of the activities in question did not cause serious conflict with the priority of the home as the center of woman's world.

Many of the doubts expressed by such women as Abigail Adams and

67. Ibid., 296.
68. Lycidas.
69. Cott, *Bonds of Womanhood*, 109.
70. Lebsock, *Free Women of Petersburg*, 172–75, emphasizes the increasing opportunities for women as teachers in the early nineteenth century.

Mercy Warren, Judith Murray and Eliza Southgate—to mention a handful whose comments we have already noted—turn critically on the question of esteem. However affectionate their family lives might be, it was difficult for women to esteem themselves, as a sex, in a men's world when they could not even begin to acquire the educational weapons that men habitually possessed. But the emerging recognition that men and women could fulfill their aims in spheres marked out for them by God, nature, and social convention offered women the opportunity for whatever degree of esteem seemed fitting to the circumference of their allotted sphere. And the scope, purpose, and limits of that sphere were, of course, determined by men.

Marriage was the aim and center of this world. But one of the social emollients associated with the women's sphere was the idea that marriage ought to be a companionship based on affection, mutual respect, and complementary roles. Affection was not merely an agreeable prelude to married life; it was an entitlement, and it has been noted that within ten years of 1776, ten percent of women seeking divorce in Massachusetts alleged loss of affection as a cause—grounds which had never been heard of before 1765.[71] This concept of companionate marriage was far from being a novelty of the republican ethos.[72] Love, companionship, and mutual support were ancient ideals in marriage in the Western world, and in America, puritans had given much care and attention to making the ideal into a living reality.[73] What the early republican state of mind seems to have articulated was a much higher level of equality of esteem than had ever been formally recognized in earlier years; marriage was said in new republican circles to be an exalted form of friendship, in which words like "equal," "mutual," and "reciprocal" were freely exchanged. Republican marriage at its best was supposed to be a friendship of equals.[74] This did not, of course, imply that ideas of

71. Carl N. Degler, *At Odds: Women and the Family in America from the Revolution to the Present* (New York, 1980), 15–17.

72. Aristotle, *Nicomachean Ethics*, Book Eight, discusses various kinds of love and says, "The love between husband and Wife is considered to be naturally inherent in them." Trans. J.A.K. Thompson (Harmondsworth, 1955), 280.

73. David Hackett Fischer, *Albion's Seed: Four British Folkways in America* (New York, 1989), 83–85.

74. Jan Lewis, "The Republican Wife: Virtue and Seduction in the Early Republic," *William and Mary Quarterly* 44:4 (1987), 707. The idea of "separate spheres," with its corollary of "companionate marriage," is not a discovery of recent scholarship. It was

equality should apply in the public arena. But the trouble with the women's sphere was that its circumference was porous, and that with the advance of the entrepreneurial society of the early Jacksonian era, its periphery was increasingly perforated by pressures from within, which increasingly responded to pressures from without.

The Emergence of Feminist Consciousness

Individualism, which was to gain a rapid ascendancy in the values of the increasingly commercial American Republic, as it also gained a more gradual legitimacy of status in the industrial societies of Britain and France, was a masculine ideal. The concept is complex, and has been applied to many and various historical manifestations of the human spirit. [75] Its American manifestation, however, forms an essential corollary to the "equality of conditions" which Alexis de Tocqueville traced as the central theme of American development in his time. [76] But Tocqueville said nothing about individualism in American women—and he might have found much more to say about that subject if he had been

---

observed by that most acute of observers Alexis de Tocqueville: "The Americans have applied to the two sexes the grand principle of political economy which in our times dominates industry. They have carefully divided the functions of man and woman, in order that the great work of society shall be better done." The "grand principle" is, of course, the division of labor. Tocqueville was convinced that American women accepted this order of society more whole-heartedly than our more recent evidence suggests, but he was also aware of social trends which were subtly moving women toward a greater equality with men, and that the lives of men were subject to extreme vicissitudes of fortune. J.-P. Mayer, ed., *De La Démocratie en Amérique* (Paris, 1961) 1:209–11, 219–22. As noted above (n. 72), an early but clearly articulated account of separate spheres based on different functions and abilities was given by Aristotle, *The Nicomachean Ethics*, Book Eight, 280. This natural affection between the sexes was completely compatible with inequality of abilities and power.

75. The locus classicus for the modern study of the subject is probably Jacob Burckhardt, *The Civilization of the Renaissance in Italy* (1860); but as individualism enters into the whole fabric of post-medieval life—and arguably into much that went before—and the project of giving a bibliography would fill several pages of footnotes, it must be hoped that the above statement will be allowed to stand without the pillars of pedantic support. There is some introductory discussion in J.R. Pole, *American Individualism and the Promise of Progress: An Inaugural Lecture Delivered Before the University of Oxford* (Oxford, 1980).

76. To all intents and purposes, it is correct to say that the word *individualism* entered the English language by way of Henry Reeve's translation of Tocqueville in 1840. He apologized for its unfamiliarity but explained that he could find no English equivalent.

writing primarily about Europe. Yet the bonds of sympathy and sister-hood which women in very different parts of the United States were quietly and unobtrusively forging through their shared experiences and commiserations, when combined with their emergence into various kinds of market activity, formed the conditions of a feminist alternative to male individualism. This ideology, however, could not claim less than the basic individual rights on which the American Republic was founded. Women searched for their own identities on the basis of values which only awaited some public collision to become an individualism of rights. [77]

The presidency of Andrew Jackson, during which Tocqueville visited the United States, was marked by manifestations of social turbulence which, as we have seen in earlier chapters, threw many old values into doubt and many men of different walks of life into apprehension and perplexity about the future. American women would have needed to be exceptionally well protected in their separate sphere to have failed to notice what was going on in the male world; and in a world which frequently exposed them to the consequences of a highly individualistic market economy, they could not have failed to discover their own vulnerability. The formulation of concrete political aims in the suffrage movement was not a result of any one influence; it was a natural response to the upheaval in political and economic activities that went back before Jackson. But when middle-class women, many of them allied with Garrison in a passionate egalitarian faith, threw themselves into the anti-slavery movement, they soon discovered for themselves the logic of applying to their own sex the democratic political individualism which was dominating the world of white male politics. Garrisonian abolition-ists themselves shared and stimulated a faith in common humanity which they willingly applied to women. [78]

The leading women members of the new anti-slavery movement were

77. Lebsock, *Free Women of Petersburg*, xix; Cott, *Bonds of Womanhood*, passim. Al-though the theme runs through much of these books, both writers are equally aware of the often overwhelming resistances. The fact, noted by Lebsock, pp. 26–27, that Peters-burg widows who were left in relatively comfortable circumstances were unlikely to marry again, preferring independence and control of their own property to the solace of marital union, seems to be evidence of a feminine individualism of a very personal sort.

78. Ellen Carol DuBois, *Feminism and Suffrage: The Emergence of an Independent Women's Movement in America, 1848–1869* (Ithaca, 1978), 32–37.

given an unwelcome opportunity to make the connections between their own condition and that of the oppressed class they aspired to help. At the World Anti-Slavery Convention held in London in 1840, Lucretia Mott and Elizabeth Cady Stanton were refused seats in the hall and were relegated to the gallery. On their way home they determined to embark on a campaign for women's education as a first step toward a political program of women's rights. It was not until eight years later that they succeeded in organizing the first Woman's Rights Convention, which met in the New York town of Seneca Falls.

This convention adopted a Declaration of Sentiments which launched the American women's movement on its course. Carefully paraphrasing the Declaration of Independence, and holding it "self-evident that all men and women are created equal," the declaration alleged a series of "injuries and usurpations on the part of man toward women, having in direct object the establishment of an absolute tyranny over her." Facts were then "duly submitted to a candid world." The parallel was sustained in a series of items of oppression. Men had certainly compelled women to submit to laws in the formation of which they had no voice; had made them, "if married, civilly dead"; had monopolized profitable employments, had allowed them but a subordinate position in church and state; and had "created a false sentiment by giving the world a different code of morals for men and for women." The items showed significant variation on their original, and the drafters showed that they had grasped the vital importance of self-esteem: "He has endeavored, in every way that he could, to destroy her confidence in her own powers, to lessen her self-respect, and to make her willing to lead a dependent and abject life." 79

It was in the nature of the case, as with all movements in which minorities or subsets claimed equality of civil rights from a powerful majority, that the founders of the women's rights movement treated women as a social unity. But the thrust of this subtly worded pronouncement was twofold. The first target was the consciences and consciousness of the women of America, and in this sense the declaration was a collectivist document; the use of the word "sentiments" may perhaps be considered feminine in tone. But this in no way detracted from the fact

79. Stanton et al., *History of Woman Suffrage* 1:69–71; Hole and Levine, *Rebirth of Feminism*, 5–7.

that the claim now staked was an individualist claim in law and politics. It set women, as individuals, on the same footing as men, as individuals. The intellectual foundations had been laid for the modern women's rights movements, and these were foundations which would support the application of the interchangeability principle to women as individuals. By implication it therefore disclaimed the benefit of favors or protection for the female sex. This was the boldest claim yet made in women's history. But as its fuller implications were unraveled, it was also to prove the most divisive.

Women's Rights: Women's Interests?

When people find their interests at risk from some public policy or private grievance, they are tempted to express their grievances in the language of rights, and there is probably no country in which this temptation encounters less resistance than the United States. Rights and interests frequently appear to be interchangeable, at least to the antagonists in a dispute. The legal profession is consequently well rewarded. The founders of America's organized women's movement had no doubts on this question. Women's interests extended far beyond formal rights, and their full meaning had yet to be explored; but politically they could only be served by extending to women all the civil rights enjoyed by the male sex. The crucial paradox of the women's movement, particularly as it approached its original goals, was exposed by a dichotomy that no militant feminists had previously observed: that real and effective equality of rights, translated into corresponding changes in economic and social relations, might actually threaten the interests of large numbers of women. But this issue lay in the future, lying in wait for the advancing guards of the women's columns. In the political world of the mid-nineteenth century, where the suffrage was being extended almost without qualification to white men, there was also no doubt in their minds that the first and most important right in a democracy was the right to vote.

Much of this political consciousness had arisen in the campaign against slavery, and the leaders of the women's suffrage movement agreed to subordinate their cause to that of emancipation during the Civil War. The National Loyal Women's League, organized by Elizabeth Cady Stanton and Susan B. Anthony, raised 400,000 signatures in favor

of the Thirteenth Amendment, which abolished slavery in the United States.[80] But women then found their own demands for political recognition treated with derision. In the debates on civil rights and Negro suffrage during the Reconstruction era, opponents of extension used the demand for female suffrage as though it were evidence against Negro suffrage. The essence of their position was simple: the vote was not a right; it was a privilege conferred by society on certain classes of persons possessing the requisite qualifications. Women, children, convicts, the insane did not vote—yet they enjoyed all the rights of citizenship that were appropriate to their position in society. The state, as Senator James Dixon of Connecticut observed in the debates on the Fifteenth Amendment, had the right to make the distinction.[81]

In these arguments it was the debating role of the conservatives to invoke the abstract claim that equality was in principle indivisible; the rhetorical intention was ironical, because this was also the claim of the most committed egalitarians. If equal rights were to be extended to blacks, then no logical ground remained on which to resist their extension to women or to other groups who had remained below the line of political visibility. In 1869 Senator Willard Saulsbury of Delaware raised merriment in the Senate by offering an amendment to abolish all distinctions of color or sex.[82] When similar tactics were used in the debate on the civil rights bill of 1875 Oliver Morton, a Republican supporter of the bill, accused his opponents of "getting behind the ladies."[83] But most Republicans were anxious to avoid entangling the cause of the Fifteenth Amendment with female suffrage or women's rights. Senator Willard Warner of Alabama assured women that they would get the suffrage as soon as they acted with unanimity—an expression which, notwithstanding his professed sympathy for the cause, might have been taken to mean "not in our lifetime"—which would have been true enough.[84]

The concentration of radical Republicans and former abolitionists on securing the civil and political rights of blacks irremediably damaged their alliance with the women's movement. A Women's Rights Convention held in New York in May 1866 resolved to form the American

---

80. DuBois, *Feminism and Suffrage*, 53.
81. *Congressional Globe*, 40th Cong., 3d sess., 858–61.
82. Ibid., 1310.
83. *Congressional Record*, 42d Cong., 1st sess. (1875), 1795.
84. *Cong. Globe*, 40th Cong., 3d sess., 862.

Equal Rights Association, with equal rights for blacks *and* women as its aim; but soon afterwards, Stanton and Anthony denounced the Fifteenth Amendment for its exclusion of women and actually began to seek support among the Democrats—who did not prove much more sympathetic than the radicals. In the very year of the Civil Rights Act, the Supreme Court reaffirmed the general masculine view of the constitutional rights of women by laying down that the Fourteenth Amendment did not give them the right to vote—which a state government therefore had power to deny.[85]

Sharp and painful differences appeared among women's movement ranks in face of these disappointments. Stanton and Anthony founded a feminist weekly paper with the uncompromising title *The Revolution* and determined to campaign for women's rights across the whole spectrum under the motto: "Men, their rights and nothing more; women, their rights and nothing less." Their purpose was to examine the whole range of institutions by which women were adversely affected and unfairly judged. The dominance of men in the property laws affecting marriage, the difficulties besetting women ill-treated by their husbands, the conventionally accepted double standard of sexual morality—all came under their scrutiny.

The centenary of the Declaration of Independence in 1876, an occasion of official national celebration, gave the women's leaders another opportunity for public attention, which they seized by publishing a Declaration of Rights. In this they declared their faith in self-government and "our full equality with man in natural rights." The independence in question was independence from men—from the man-made world of morals and prescriptions. "Woman," they declared, "was made first for her own happiness, with an absolute right to herself—to all the opportunities and advantages that life affords for her complete development." They denied the dogma that woman was made for man—a dogma, needless to say, that had biblical authority.[86]

Stanton soon became conscious of the antagonism of organized religion to any change in the sexual structure of social or political relationships; the clergy seemed especially susceptible to the fear that women who assumed masculine roles would exert a disruptive influence on their

85. *Minor v. Happerset*, 21 Wallace 162 (1875).
86. Quoted in Hoff, *Law, Gender*, 180.

authority, or that which divine providence transmitted through their agency. Anthony, for her part, and with the assistance of twenty-three women (three of whom were ministers of religion) attacked this clerical influence by producing a volume called *The Women's Bible*, which exposed the original to a searching feminist critique. The story of Eve's creation was dismissed as "a petty surgical operation," and the subjugation of women was traced to the story of the temptation in Genesis.

Stanton, first president of the National American Women's Suffrage Association, which she and Anthony had founded, became increasingly preoccupied with the need to combat the influence of organized religion, but *The Women's Bible*, widely considered to be sacrilegious, threatened to bring the movement into disrepute. The more strictly political wing of the movement was represented by Lucy Stone, who founded the American Woman Suffrage Association soon after the Civil War, about the same time as Stanton and Anthony's association. Stone's purpose was to win the suffrage by confining attention to clearly respectable and political issues and avoiding the wider problems of women in society— which could be tackled when women had won the voting power to influence events through the normal processes of politics. The two organizations ran their parallel courses for some twenty years, but only in the twentieth century did the NAWSA, under a new generation's leadership, gather the wider body of women's resources into a dominant movement.[87]

The women's suffrage movement was not based on any revolutionary critique of the economic system or of the class relationships which upheld it. In one sense, *The Revolution* was a title that claimed more than it deserved. A strain of racial animosity entered into Stanton's style as she expressed the resentment of white, Anglo-Saxon women of high social standing at being deprived of a ballot which was extended to recently freed black slaves, followed by hordes of ignorant immigrants, most of whom could not even read or speak English when casting their votes. The spokeswomen of the Reconstruction period, facing the sudden enfranchisement of the freedmen, were not beyond using language which exploited the white woman's fear of the Negro.[88] This social and

87. Judith Hole and Ellen Levine, "The First Feminists," in Anne Koedt, Ellen Levine, and Anita Rapone, eds., *Radical Feminism* (New York, 1973), 9–13.
88. DuBois, *Feminism and Suffrage*, 178.

ethnic resentment was widespread and became more extensive with the relentless advance of immigration. Florence Kelley, addressing a suffrage convention in 1906, said that she had "rarely heard a ringing suffrage speech which did not refer to the 'ignorant and degraded men,' or 'ignorant immigrants' as our masters. This is habitually spoken with more or less bitterness."[89] In 1902 an aged Elizabeth Stanton expressed herself willing to accept more general restrictions on the suffrage itself and was prepared to suppress the votes of the ignorant both among men and women, provided that properly educated women were allowed to vote.[90] This position was strikingly similar to the "impartial suffrage" that Booker Washington favored for Negroes qualified by education or property along with similarly qualified whites; in both cases, those without sufficient qualification would be denied the right to participate in the political process.[91]

Conservatives who had resorted to the argument that equality was indivisible, an ideal always proclaimed by Garrisonian abolitionists as an article of faith and still in effect maintained at the founding of the American Equal Rights Association, must have felt entitled to smiles of ironic satisfaction when they had the occasion to witness this fragmentation of the very principle of equality of rights in favor of a socially selective distribution of privileges. The need to protect new western states from immigrant influence may well have helped to advance the cause of women's suffrage where it made most progress in the Progressive era. After the older generation had passed from the scene with only a glimpse, here and there, of the promised land, Carrie Chapman Catt and a more militant leadership injected new life into the National American Woman Suffrage Association. The suffrage issue won its place in national politics with the support of Theodore Roosevelt and the Progressive party which he represented in the campaign of 1912; Woodrow Wilson's conversion followed in 1915 and 1916.[92]

The actual winning of the suffrage followed from a leadership deci-

89. Degler, *At Odds*, 335.

90. Andrew Sinclair, *The Better Half: The Emancipation of American Woman* (London, 1965), 299.

91. Louis R. Harlan, *Booker T. Washington: The Making of a Black Leader, 1856–1901* (New York, 1972), 302–03.

92. John Milton Cooper, *The Warrior and the Priest: Woodrow Wilson and Theodore Roosevelt* (Cambridge, Mass., 1983), 208–09.

sion to go for a constitutional amendment rather than waiting for a state-by-state series of reforms. Soon afterward, Alice Paul founded the small but more intense and dynamic Congressional Union—later the National Woman's party—to concentrate all attention on the central objective of an amendment. It was as a direct result of American participation in the First World War that women were enabled to make the greatest contribution to their own cause. As had happened in the Civil War, women released men for military service, working in factories and on farms in jobs that had been men's. The argument for their indispensability merged with that of indebtedness for their contribution to the war effort; there was now no prior cause such as Negro suffrage to stand in the way. As in Great Britain, where it was introduced by act of Parliament, women's suffrage followed from and was a consequence of the Great War. Whether or not Wilson had this in mind when he spoke of making the world "safe for democracy," he could not quarrel with the result.

The sequel showed how little there had been to fear. America's newly empowered womanhood showed no disposition to disturb the social order; they arranged themselves instead along lines already marked out by the social habits and economic interests of a society dominated by men. What was more surprising, and disappointing to those who had hoped that political equality would lead to equality of opportunity, was the limping and limited manner in which women themselves attempted to move into positions occupied by men throughout industry and the professions. Leaders of the old suffrage movement did not see their duty now as that of inspiring a diffused and dispersed multitude of followers to seize the strongholds of business and education. Carrie Catt, perhaps the most prominent of them, turned her energies to the peace movement and may have felt that her efforts had been rewarded when in 1928 the United States signed the Kellogg-Briand Pact, whose signatories renounced war as an instrument of international policy. The failure of women to build educational, economic, and political strength on the foundations of suffrage bore a curious comparability to the earlier failure of blacks to build similar gains on their own liberation and enfranchisement. The sociology of power was proving to be far too dense, subtle, and complex to be determined by the political simplicities of the ballot. Political equality, it appeared, could not work alone. This discovery should have been an important contribution to political science, and it is perhaps not too late to make it so.

The First Equal Rights Amendment: A Conflict of Aims

"Men and women shall have equal rights throughout the United States and in every place subject to its jurisdiction. Congress shall have power to enforce this article by appropriate legislation." With these words, adopted in 1923, Alice Paul and her National Woman's party announced the aim of passing a constitutional amendment to secure for women the rights already theoretically assured to men. The language is significant of the extraordinary influence of the rhetoric of equality in the American mind. There is nothing in the choice of the phrase "equal rights" that would not have been served by speaking of "the same rights"; and it is arguable that the latter usage would have been less susceptible to subtle variations of construction; the words "equal protection," after all, had not saved black Americans from the violation of every conceivable right that the Constitution was intended to protect. This language also signaled the individualist policy, posited on the basis of interchangeability, that was intended to unite women about the social character of their gender and the best means of securing their own interests. It did not have that effect.

The problem of protecting women's interests in the world of the factory system had appeared as one of the themes of the Progressive era. Women of great ability and dedication were already emerging in roles of authority. Like the leaders of the suffrage movement, most of them were people of middle-class family and education, and even the poorest, Charlotte Perkins Gilman, who sometimes had to struggle to make ends meet, had been brought up to middle-class expectations. Gilman, who like Ida Tarbell exerted analytical faculties fully equal to those attributed to men in her generation, became an influential critic of economic institutions. Probably the highest level of administrative authority achieved by a woman fell to Florence Kelley, whom Governor John Peter Altgeld appointed chief factory inspector of Illinois. Kelley was a social critic who perceived the connections between the industrial system and the social morals which it generated, drawing a further lesson from the moral heritage of slavery: "Our industrial epoch," she wrote "has corroded our morals and hardened our hearts as surely as slavery injured its contemporaries, and far more subtly. There is grave reason to fear that it may have unfitted us for the oncoming state of civilization, as slave-owning

unfitted the white race for freedom and democracy, while it left its blight of race hatred from which the Republic still suffers."[93]

Far from gaining in personal freedom, women were increasingly victims of factories and workshops. Employers under the pressure of fierce competition exploited their defenseless position in the labor market just as the need for subsistence, lack of special qualifications and the absence of alternatives drove innumerable young women into the factories and garment-making shops. In 1909 a great strike of New York women garment workers under the authority of the New York Women's Trade Union League dramatized the power that organized labor could exert, even in the cause of the weakest of its members. It did more, for middle-class women identified themselves to a previously unknown degree with their working-class sisters, joined their pickets and demonstrations, and spread the message of their cause in circles where it would not ordinarily have been heard.[94]

Alice Paul's program of equal rights had no appeal for the women who had led these struggles and whose cause was identified with that of the working class. When political leaders and the men who formulated the political rhetoric of the republic spoke about "equality of opportunity," they always meant opportunity for men, but equality of opportunity had no relevance to the desperate strivings of working-class women, of whatever race or status in the tides of immigration. Women who had fought for the protection of women in the factories, who had campaigned, with ultimate success in the Eighteenth Amendment, adopted in 1919, for the prohibition of alcohol in the interests of battered wives and children, saw nothing but danger in the program of equal rights. To them it meant only unequal threats.

The paradox which was to confront the future of the women's movement was summarized in the salient Supreme Court case of *Muller v. Oregon*, in which an employer challenged a state law limiting the work of female employees to ten hours a day. If the Court had been content to follow its own recent judgment in *Lochner v. New York*,[95] it would have been obliged to hold that this law represented

93. Florence Kelley, *Modern Industry in Relation to the Family, Health, Education, Morality* (New York, 1914), quoted in William L. O'Neill, *Everyone was Brave: The Rise and Fall of Feminism in America* (Chicago, 1969), 149.

94. O'Neill, ibid., 130–33, 141.

95. Ibid., 130–33.

an unwarranted interference with freedom of contract; but the fact that the object of the legislation was to protect the interests of women altered the character of the case. Upholding the act, the Court through Mr. Justice Brewer applied different standards to the female sex. "The two sexes differ in structure of body, in the functions to be performed by each, in the amount of physical strength, in the capacity for long-continued labor, particularly when done standing, the influence of vigorous health upon the future well-being of the race, the self-reliance which enables one to assert full rights, and [a Darwinian touch] in the capacity to maintain the struggle for subsistence. This difference justifies a difference in legislation, and upholds that which is designed to compensate for some of the burdens which rest upon her."[96] Apart from the perceptive comment about self-reliance, this judgment, with its obviously benign intentions, was based on the fundamental inferiority and dependence of women, which was considered the permanent and natural condition that alone could justify a departure from constitutional precedent. But the justice failed to follow his own perception; if women lacked self-reliance, it was not because of their physiognomy but as a consequence of their social subordination. Brewer specifically placed woman "in a class by herself." These views were of a single fabric with those which his predecessor, Bradley, had expressed when rejecting a woman's claim to practice at the Illinois bar. It was precisely this sort of legal separation, which defined woman by law as belonging to a special category, that Alice Paul, in succession to Stanton and Anthony, had set out to fight.

Paul's Equal Rights Amendment attracted powerful enemies from the ranks of the most prominent women of the Progressive causes, including Carrie Catt, Jane Addams of the Hull House settlement program in Chicago, and Florence Kelley.[97] Their generation was passing, but not their generation's views of the problems. Their most prominent successor to hold public office in the New Deal was Frances Perkins, Secretary of Labor under Franklin Roosevelt and the first woman ever to hold cabinet office. Although she was an obvious beacon to the aspirations of younger women, Frances Perkins often endorsed the traditional view that the woman's normal place is the home; married women should not

---

96. *Muller v. Oregon*, 208 U.S. 412 (1908), at 422–23.
97. Degler, *At Odds*, 359–60.

abandon their homes for the sake of making money.[98] This is what a great many married women were in fact doing for the first time during the Depression, though their motive was not so much ambition as economic survival.

The surge in the economy that accompanied the Second World War and was sustained by later events, did not float any corresponding surge in women's liberation. One significant effect of the great expansion of the market for domestic appliances, however, was a genuine depreciation of the value of the woman as homemaker. Well-educated and well-off women were vaguely aware of a growing discontent with their domestic subordination, a state of mind that easily spread to women of less substantial families with the rapid distribution of consumer goods. The opportunities available to them, and more especially to their daughters in the 1960s, included a new level of sexual liberty. Equality of opportunity is generally thought of in connection with the economy. But contraceptive pills immediately found a mass market for the obvious reason that there already existed a massive demand for them; the enhanced freedom (it cannot be said that it was new) to control their own bodies and make their own sexual choices added to women's sense of power, a psychological as well as a physical liberation which represented a significant development in the direction of equality of opportunity in the most intimate aspects of their lives. Men, after all, had exercised this privilege of sexual choice from times immemorial. It hardly exaggerates the sociology of the age to say that women's liberation was bringing new dimensions to the old concepts of opportunity and individualism. But such newly felt freedom in turn generated still further resentment against social and economic restraints. Early publicists of the new feminism, such as Betty Friedan and Kate Millett, writing of women's experience of the subtle repressiveness of the social ethos under which they had been brought up, supplied fuel to a long-smoldering fire.

At the center of the problem of the need for separate identification lay the unexpressed and not yet fully understood need for equality of esteem. But this was a psychological problem, complicated for women as for other repressed groups by the history and consequences of psychological domination. The women who made up the first wave of the

98. William H. Chafe, *Women and Equality: Changing Patterns in American Culture* (New York, 1977), 104.

new feminist movement still belonged to a generation who, under controlled tests, tended to place a higher value on works ascribed to men than to women. [99] As lately as 1947 a poll had shown that no fewer than twenty-five percent of all women would have preferred to have been men. [100] This mentality has been aptly called "women's version of the self-disdain of the colonized." [101] The concrete outcome of the new movement, and one of its few points of unity and unification, was a new version of the Equal Rights Amendment. The first clause read simply, "Equality of rights under the law shall not be denied or abridged by the United States or by any State on account of sex." This was not in fact a strong statement; its scope was confined to whatever the courts decided to interpret as the action of governments, either federal or state, and it had no immediate reach into such areas as employment; it might well have been objected to as promising much but offering little. In the liberating climate of the time, it was passed by the Senate in March 1972 by the overwhelming majority of eighty-four to eight. To become part of the Constitution it then required ratification by thirty-eight states. By 30 June 1982, ratified after numerous vicissitudes by thirty-five states, it had failed. [102]

The advocates of this reform had in their dialectical weaponry several generations of the rhetoric of equality. Not all, by the end, was lost. Most of the substance of what would have been gained by a constitutional amendment was in fact conceded by the Supreme Court, acting in the knowledge that an amendment was before the states. What the defeat of the ERA really meant was the loss of a symbol; if that is true, it is a signal of the argument of this book that equality has to be understood as much for its metaphorical value as for its substantive meaning.

Failure of a Metaphor

The promoters, at whatever level, of the new wave of the women's movement had to transform the consciousness of the female sex in the

99. Jo Freeman, "The Building of the Gilded Cage," in Koedt et al., *Radical Feminism*, 142; Jane J. Mansbridge, *Why We Lost the ERA* (Chicago, 1986), 38–39.

100. Chafe, *Women and Equality*, 83.

101. Kelly, "Did Women Have a Renaissance?" 80.

102. Mansbridge, *Why We Lost the ERA*, 1.

process of transforming the consciousness of the nation. The scale of the task was suggested by a Gallup poll which in 1962 showed that a majority of *female* respondents did not think that women were discriminated against; the scale and rapidity of the transformation is suggested by the answers to a similar question in 1974, which found more than two to one endorsing efforts toward more equality for women. Another survey conducted in the early 1970s, this one on college campuses, where young people might be expected to respond to recent social impulses, found a doubling in the space of two years of those who regarded women as an oppressed group. The notion that a woman's place is in the home, still surprisingly widespread in 1970, was in a state of rapid collapse, and a survey also done in the early 1970s revealed a large majority for the view that men and women were born with the same talents. With all this, only one-third of women in college would now claim that having children was an important personal value. [103]

The civil rights movement and the war in Vietnam, which between them convulsed the nation from the early 1960s, were responsible for immense changes in social consciousness. Yet when women moved into such bodies as the Southern Non-violent Coordinating Committee—known by its initials "SNCC," pronounced "snick"—they often found themselves subjected to sexual discrimination even as they joined the fight for racial equality. This was a state of affairs which women, especially black women, were not prepared to tolerate, and there can be no doubt that the experience greatly intensified their commitment to women's rights. Nor, once the ERA was on the agenda, were these activities confined to a self-assured middle class. Among the working classes, blacks were at least as likely as whites to support the ERA, while support proved stronger among Catholics than among Protestants. [104]

Behind the Equal Rights Amendment lay several years of prominent activity at the levels of Federal government. President John Kennedy, perhaps to relieve the pressure on his administration, appointed a Commission on the Status of Women in 1963. The commission's study groups produced masses of evidence of the disadvantages of being a woman in the United States. Many state laws still discriminated against women in matters affecting the control of conjugal property, contractual

103. Chafe, *Women and Equality*, 139.
104. Ibid., 110; Mansbridge, *Why We Lost the ERA*, 15.

rights and the jobs women were allowed to do. The report of the full commission, which was more temperate than that of some of its study groups, proposed an executive order on equal opportunity in employment but did not think it would be expedient to add "sex" to the language of existing proposals for equal opportunities in matters of race. The report seemed to hanker after the separate-spheres concept when it favored a view of marriage by which "each spouse makes a different but equally important contribution." But the commission remained at this stage unimpressed by the idea of a new equal rights amendment. It was due to the pressure of the feminist lawyer Marguerite Rewalt that the word "now" was added in the conclusion that "a constitutional amendment need not now be sought." [105] The president's political obligations to women were met in part by the passage of an Equal Pay Act in 1963, but the exceptions to this act's provisions, which included executive, professional, and administrative employees, rendered it ineffective where women's contributions were likely to be outstanding. Some of its provisions were extended in 1966.

The next step was to establish clearly that sex should rank with race, economic status, and religion as an impermissible ground for discrimination. The opportunity arose, if unexpectedly, with the Civil Rights bill of 1964, which was designed to deal with racial discrimination. By a remarkable legislative tour de force, sex was added to race, color, religion, and national origin as prohibited ground, making equality of opportunity between the sexes into official national policy. Women's interests seem to have owed this success principally to the tactics of their opponent, Representative Howard Smith of Virginia, who moved the clause as an amendment with implausible professions of sincerity but with the object of making the whole clause objectionable.

Title VII, the operative section of the act, did not go as far as to enact the interchangeability principle. Latitude for discretion was left in a class of jobs for which sex might be considered a "bona fide occupational qualification," jobs which included attendants at women's lavatories, models for women's clothes, and actresses. There would have been little hope for a law that did not recognize such classes as these. The commission hesitated for some years to define its views or even to enforce its authority, preferring to leave these details to the states. But by 1970, the

105. Hole and Levine, *Rebirth of Feminism*, 17–28.

Equal Opportunities Commission and the federal courts between them had interpreted Title VII as making protective legislation invalid. The Department of Labor was by this time putting its weight behind a new Equal Rights Amendment.[106] The professed conservatism of the Nixon administration concealed a considerable expansion of civil rights. The "Philadelphia Plan" of 1969 required firms working under Federal government contracts to hire a set proportion of workers from listed minority groups; and these gradually evolved into so-called "set-asides" for minority businesses, creating the beginnings of the situation that was to lead to the much-publicized Supreme Court cases of Weber and Fullilove. In 1971 Nixon broadened the Civil Rights Commission's mandate to extend to sexual discrimination.[107] Republican government was a declared partisan in the civil rights movement.

The new amendment, launched on this rising flood of feminist sentiment, did much to excite more general political consciousness of the issues and to mobilize opinion among both sexes. At the least, women had votes which predominantly male legislators would be unlikely to ignore. These votes were equal votes; they reflected the category of political equality. But although political equality was vitally important, other groups had never found it capable, on its own, of winning control of the social and economic circumstances of their lives; it was, as we have seen, a significantly demonstrated truth of the history of equality that political equality did not furnish all the leverage for winning equality of opportunity, equality at law, or equality of esteem. (In fact it was a curiosity of the history of women that a large measure of equality in the law had been gained without exercising political equality). Success would be measured by the measure of equality achieved in these other categories. The practical aims of the proposed amendment would have been very substantially achieved if the Supreme Court had accepted the principle that, under its own way of proceeding in matters of racial or similar types of discrimination, gender was to be considered a "suspect class." This would not mean more than that all legislation treating the sexes differently would have to be examined with exceptional rigor, and permitted to stand only if it were deemed to promote some compelling

106. Ibid., 28–37; Anna Hobson, pseud., *The Equal Rights Amendment: How Do I Love It, Let Me Count the Ways* (Pittsburgh, 1976); Mansbridge, *Why We Lost the ERA*, 10.
107. Hoff, *Law, Gender*, 235, 245.

general interest essentially affecting both sexes—and presumably, affecting them both equally.

A convincing case can certainly be based on common law and constitutional principles of legal reasoning that the Fifth and Fourteenth Amendments could do for sexual equality what they had done for racial equality—from which it would follow that the expensive struggle for the Equal Rights Amendment was a diversion of energy from specific issues on which valuable constitutional progress could be attained without it. [108] If the Court, on the other hand, was not wholly prepared for this step, as proved to be the case in *Frontiero v. Richardson*, precisely on the grounds that the question was then before the states for political decision, it at least implied that the Constitution was as yet unclear. [109] By 1976 the Court very nearly jumped the vital hurdle, though dragging at the uppermost crossbar, when it ruled in *Craig v. Boren* that states could classify persons on the basis of sex only when it could be shown that the classification bore a "substantial" relationship to an "important" governmental objective. These adjectives were not lightly chosen. Important objectives were so designated because they were more important than "legitimate" ones, but less important than "compelling" ones; and "substantial" relationships were more than "rational" but less than "necessary."

The ERA could hardly have done less than make sex a "suspect" classification (a class recently and rather ingeniously invented by the Court for treating of these arcane distinctions), but it is significant that its advocates could not claim that it would have done more than

108. The issue is discussed in Leo Kanowitz, *Women and the Law: The Unfinished Revolution* (Albuquerque, 1969), 197.

109. 411 U.S. 677 (1975). Four justices, the "liberals" Brennan, Douglas, White, and Marshall, wanted to declare "that classifications based on sex, like classifications based on race, religion and national origin" were "inherently suspect and must therefore be subjected to strict judicial scrutiny." But the majority were not ready to make sex a suspect classification yet, and Justice Powell, who was not against consigning sex to that category, made the above position clear by declining "to preempt by judicial action a major political decision." Mansbridge, *Why We Lost the ERA*, 50. The adjective "inherently" perhaps echoed *Brown v. Board of Education;* but to be inherently *suspect* is less damning than to be inherently unequal, and there was no getting away from the conclusion that even the minority's formula would have left hard cases in the hands of the courts rather than drawing clear and determinate lines. Whether the amendment would have actually made those lines clearer was a doubt which left room for skepticism—and which the loss of the Amendment left unresolved.

that.[110] The outcome, in each case, as with cases touching religion and race, would be in the hands of the judges. That outcome would involve the question of how to define "state action"—a problem which had arisen earlier in the protracted efforts to grapple with the Fourteenth Amendment's power to protect the civil rights of freed persons after the Civil War. The similarity of the constitutional problem was no matter of chance, but arose from the similarity of principles. Activities originating in the private sector are very often subject to state licensing and regulation; is that state action? The answer depends to some extent on the political climate, and in certain cases the Court actually drew narrower lines round the concept of what amounted to action by a state after 1972. On the other hand, a Court which had already held that gender-based classifications were unlawfully discriminatory in pensions had plainly advanced deep into ERA territory.[111]

The effect of the Court's advance into that territory was to deprive the ERA of some of its raison d'être. People who were generally sympathetic to its aims could see less compelling reasons for a prolonged and embittered struggle against rising opposition. By the end of the 1970s, a battery of family laws which had distinguished between the roles and rights of parents solely on the basis of sex had been struck down under the Fourteenth Amendment. But this was one of the areas in which the opposition gathered and recruited its forces. So long as the demands of the ERA were expressed as claims to abstract rights, they gained much wider popular support than they retained when these rights could be seen in terms of really substantial changes in the ways people lived, and of their responsibilities to each other, moral and, more important, financial. The Supreme Court had appeared to enter the political arena when converting abstract rights to equality in education into edicts on the transportation of schoolchildren by bus. It was not possible to know what another set of abstractions might bring. The most potent fears, orchestrated by the well-funded organization and information service of Phyllis Schlafly, concerned single-sex toilets, the abolition of sex distinctions in sport, and above all the fear that women soldiers would be sent

110. This remark is based on the opinions expressed in Mansbridge, *Why We Lost the ERA*, 80, where the above details are given.
111. Ibid., 40, with cases cited in n. 16, pp. 242–43.

into armed combat. The opposition gathered more potent forces when aroused biblical fundamentalists resorted to scriptural texts as authority for the separation of the sexes.[112]

A residual, measureless fear lay like lees at the bottom of the glass of equal rights and, when the glass was stirred, rose to the surface. It was especially pronounced among women who had never left their homes, had never ceased to depend on their husbands, or to depend on being depended on by them, and were sick at heart when they thought of being exposed to the deeper consequences of equal rights. These were psychological as well as material. "I am a widow, have three children, and work to make ends meet," declared one woman for whom the status quo had hardly worked well; but "I am still against the ERA. I am a woman—and I want to be treated as a woman—not a man!"[113] For if equal rights meant exactly *the same* rights, then equal responsibilities meant the same responsibilities, the same burdens, perhaps the same experience of life. When the abstract gain of rhetoric was converted into hard fact, separation, job-hunting in middle age, and loneliness in later life might prove to be the reality. Not that all these things did not already happen: the difference was that the equal rights of these strong, independent, career-minded younger women were making a Constitution that would seem to condone a way of life which the more cloistered and protected classes feared and resented. For this latter class, whose numbers were difficult to assess but were not trivial, even the symbolism of equality of esteem was a mixed and dubious blessing. For, associated with legally enforced equality of opportunity, proclaimed now as constitutional law, it represented a modern world in which they saw their husbands sharing offices and other places of work with ambitious women of the newly liberated order. These temptations might arouse anxieties about the attractions of the domestic spouse. The psychology of this kind of consideration might not yield much to the statistician, but cannot be dismissed in a struggle of symbolic values.

Defeating the Equal Rights Amendment could not really make much

112. All very clearly summarized in ibid., 20, 28, 173–77, on which this passage mainly depends.

113. Hoff, *Law, Gender*, 327.

difference to all this; all of it was already happening. But defeating the Amendment could at least be a moral protest, all the more striking because it was a symbolic statement rather than a substantive change in the course of events. And the force of these objections appeared all the stronger because so much of substance had already been won. It was not very likely that the passionate opponents of the ERA would be much worse off if the amendment passed; nor that they would be much better off, either. By the end of the 1970s, as proponents admit, it was becoming difficult to explain the meaning of the ERA in terms of concrete aims.[114]

The most concrete of these aims was to be found in the category of equality of opportunity. The practical meaning of this class was much easier to express in terms of equal pay, which had not been achieved by the Act of 1963. Analysis had revealed that women, on average, were paid only fifty-nine cents for every dollar received by men, and one of the campaign's strongest arguments was simply to pin the ERA to the claim to close that gap.[115] But the principle of equality of opportunity had wider horizons, and by the early 1970s, affirmative action was an almost universally accepted keynote of recruitment. Governments both state and federal, the press, television, radio, businesses, universities and other institutions were giving increasing prominence to female labor, offering promotions on the basis of ability, and sometimes even short-cutting the usual requirements in order to demonstrate their goodwill. At the professional level, entry into law schools was one of the most salient indicators, and only hardened skepticism would depreciate the consequences when, between 1969 and 1974, female admission to law schools increased by three hundred percent, while from 1970 to 1975, the proportion of women gaining the degree of Ph.D. increased from eleven to twenty-one percent.[116] All this, of course, without the benefit of an Equal Rights Amendment.

●　　●　　●

114. Mansbridge, *Why We Lost the ERA*, 45. This is an extremely fair-minded review of the episode by a committed advocate.

115. Ibid., ch. 5.

116. Chafe, *Women and Equality*, 140.

The study of equality in modern history has generally been based on an assumption that the natural condition of man, and of woman by extension, is to desire equality wherever it does not exist, and to desire more of it where it is imperfect. It is partly by reason of this assumption that the category of sexual equality has presented so many difficulties in analysis; equality, for women, has often had an actually different content from the historic norms of men. This was the basis of a wing of radical feminism, which gained renewed strength after the defeat of the Equal Rights Amendment, and which regarded that proposal as an implicit threat to the peculiar binding of female consciousness and sentiment. [117] The apparent antagonism of the ERA and the radical feminist positions is at least partly based on false assumptions. The radical claims for respect of feminine interests as inherently different from those of men in no way deprives women of the *rights* to those equalities which men have claimed and striven for, but it is clear that substantial numbers of women, without special reference to class, race or religion, had interpreted those equalities as having different social meanings, and had looked on them in the light of the bearing of those meanings on their own lives.

Another difficulty arises from a still more fundamental condition of the subject. Law, political philosophy and science, and the structure of institutions, have historically assumed that as between the sexes there was a single norm, and that norm, to paraphrase Blackstone, was the man. Some of the fissures and stresses experienced by the women's movement have arisen from differences, often passionately felt, as to whether women ought to want to define themselves in relation to the male norm or to seek other definitions which did not depend on male values. [118] But if women were both to live with men, make the best of them, and hope to raise children, they had another task—to persuade men to share similar aims. Whatever accommodations and compromises were to be worked through, a considerable measure of reconstruction of the norms of family life was inevitable; for those norms had not been friendly to the idea of extending to the female sex the atomizing individ-

---

117. Hoff, *Law, Gender, and Injustice*, which appeared when the present work was thought to have been completed, is a cogent presentation of this view.

118. These differences did not take long to become apparent. Varieties of view are manifested in Koedt et al., *Radical Feminism.*

ualism of modern economic life.[119] The outcome would depend on innumerable private decisions. But freedom to make those decisions was itself the outcome of a series of historic struggles to win political recognition, and also of private struggles to win points at law.

To the extent that women and men were physiologically, perhaps psychologically, different from each other as genders as well as being different as individuals, all women's movements had to dedicate themselves to the proposition that all were equal in rights, and that equality in rights took from men nothing to which they were entitled to withhold from women, and gave to women nothing more than they were entitled to have. The old idea of interchangeability, however shaken by the claims of the old "protective" feminism or the newer radical variety, could draw some comfort from at least two considerations. One was the necessity for equality in the rights that have been enumerated, whatever use individual women might wish to put them to; and the other was that in fact—a commonplace of biological science—male and female are not opposites, but merely the far ends of a continuous spectrum.

For the female end of this spectrum it was claimed that women possessed, by nature, certain nurturing qualities, certain gifts for cooperation, and also certain vulnerabilities, which required respectful consideration in the policy of a civilized society. The depreciation of women by mass-circulated pornography was perceived from this viewpoint as a *physical* threat, seriously accentuated by its implicit denial of equality of esteem.[120] On the other hand, the principles of the Equal Rights Amendment were based on a categorical denial that women were a special case, so defined by their differentness from men.

Susan B. Anthony had seen it all, clearly and in perspective, toward the end of her life. "Woman will never have equality of rights anywhere," she said in 1902, "she never will hold those she now has by an absolute tenure, until she possesses the fundamental right of self-representation. This is so obvious as to need no argument." This was directed at the time toward the suffrage—political equality. But: "Had this right been conceded from the start, the others would speedily have

---

119. That an irreducible antagonism has characterized the relations between feminism in the public sphere and the family as a private sphere is the core of Carl Degler's argument in *At Odds*.

120. Hoff, *Law, Gender*, 332–49.

followed; and the leaders among women, instead of spending the last half-century in a constant struggle to obtain their civil and political rights, might have contributed their splendid services to the general upbuilding and strengthening of the government." [121] When all these points had been effectively won by the extension of the basic American principle of individual rights, it was an unnoticed irony of this commitment to the interchangeability principle that it occurred at about the time that a new sectarianism was unexpectedly emerging to challenge the individualistic precepts which had dominated the field of ethnic equality.

121. Ibid., 191.

Chapter Thirteen

A Fissiparous Revolution

A Transformation of Consciousness

Revolutions are always incomplete. When a great social movement achieves its initial aims with a wide measure of public support, it not only raises expectations which it cannot satisfy but also tends to create new expectations, to which its official ideology gives imperfect guidance. The participants and allies of such movements, instead of distributing the fruits of victory, find themselves skeptical, resentful, and often divided. One result is a natural tendency to depreciate what has been achieved. Yet a historical perspective offers the advantages as well as the risks of far-reaching comparisons. The ideal of equality may not have acted as an independent force in American society, but it symbolized and inspired the moral, social, and political forces which had transformed the American political landscape. When that landscape, as viewed from the mid-1960s, is compared to that of any previous era, the difference to be observed in the power and salience of the principles of equality amounts to a far greater transformation in the social distribution of opportunity, and of the obligations of government, than had occurred at any time since the American Revolution. For the first time in the nation's history, equality became a major object of government policy. Also for the first time, with the exception of the Freedmen's Bureau of the Reconstruction era, the federal government not only made laws but established institutions for carrying egalitarian policies into effect.[1]

---

1. State governments had begun earlier, with the successful passage of the Ives-Quinn Act in New York in 1945, followed by the establishment of equal opportunities or human rights commissions in other cities and states. Recounted in Chapter 11.

These political achievements were products of, and in turn contributed to, a transformation of national consciousness. National consciousness of an issue did not amount to national agreement, however. The combination of the civil rights movements (there were more than one) and the war in Vietnam divided the nation's conscience more deeply than at any time in most people's memory. But on all sides, divided opinions reflected aroused consciences, and in this newly tense situation, the leaders and spokespersons of America's principal minorities began to sense that they had gained a tactical advantage.

Arguments for redress of the effects of past injustices were difficult to resist. In 1965 only 1.5 percent of the country's law students were black, and California, with a Hispanic population of more than two million, had as late as 1969 only three Hispanic graduates from the state's law schools. At the same time, the universities of Utah, New Mexico, and Arizona, states with large Indian populations, had never graduated an Indian.[2] Nor was the rate of improvement encouraging. Between 1969 and 1974 the total number of African Americans, Mexican Americans, and mainland Puerto Ricans enrolled in medical schools was 8 percent.[3] Facts and figures of this scale and import in an increasingly aroused and resentful population stood behind the policies known as affirmative action, through which federal and state governments, businesses of many sorts, and colleges and universities sought means to increase the proportions of their minority intake—and very soon of their minority staff members. The pressure emanating from the Department of Health, Education and Welfare for increased admissions and employment opportunities for women were part of the same policy, based primarily on the same principles. Indeed, since women were not a numerical minority in the American population, the word itself came to be redefined to include all people who suffered a minority status with respect to their rights.

The growing public awareness of these questions had many sources. It was a diffuse phenomenon, kindled by the transmission of scenes of resistance and repression. But it gained much concrete advantage from the leadership of President Lyndon Johnson, who, with the possible exception of Martin Luther King, contributed more powerfully than any

2. Nina Totenberg, "Discriminating to End Discrimination," *The New York Times Magazine*, April 14, 1974.

3. *Bakke v. Regents of the University of California*, SF 23311, 1976, Superior Court no. 31287, p. 27.

other individual to this new sense of national responsibility. Speaking at Howard University in the summer of 1965, Johnson gave a new name to the aims of his civil rights legislation. "This," he then said, "is the next and more profound stage of the battle for civil rights. We seek not just freedom but opportunity. We seek not just legal equity but human ability, not just equality as a right and a theory but equality as a fact and equality as a result."[4]

Nothing in Johnson's language appeared to conflict with the individualistic premises of the civil rights legislation over which he presided. The aim was equality of opportunity, and equality of opportunity was essentially individualistic; its appearance in the civil rights agenda was the modern way with an old American ideal. So clearly was this the explicit meaning of the Civil Rights Act of 1964 that when, some fifteen years later, a case arising from a racially preferential training program in the steel industry was before the Supreme Court, Mr. Justice Rehnquist, in his dissenting opinion, was able to argue his objections to the principles of that program by quoting extensively from speeches by Hubert Humphrey and other congressional supporters of the measure during the debates on its passage: a qualified white candidate could no more be displaced in favor of a black *on grounds of race* than could a black be displaced for a white.

"The truth is that this title forbids discriminating against anyone on grounds of race," Humphrey, the senior Democratic senator from Minnesota, and later to be the party's presidential candidate, assured the Senate in 1964. "This is the simple and complete truth about Title VII." He dismissed the idea of requirements intended to achieve racial balance as a "bugaboo" which had been brought up a dozen times but was "nonexistent." The very opposite was true: "In effect, it says that race, religion and national origin are not to be used as a basis for hiring and firing. Title VII is designed to encourage hiring on a basis of ability and qualifications, not race or religion." The Republican Senator Thomas Kuchel of California, speaking on the same point argued that "employers and labor organizations could not discriminate in favor of or against a person because of his race, religion or his national origin. In such matters . . . the bill now before us . . . is color-blind." He denied that minorities

4. *Public Papers of the Presidents: Lyndon B. Johnson* (Washington, D.C., 1966), item. 301, pp. 635–40.

would be eligible for preferential treatment. Senator Williams, in what was perhaps the most philosophically resonant of these speeches, declared that "equality can have only one meaning, and that meaning is self-evident to reasonable men. Those who say that equality means favoritism do violence to common sense."[5] Not for the first time, the self-evidence of a truth was in the eye of the beholder, and some truths appeared to be more self-evident to some than to others. The types of problem that were likely to arise under the bill were so clearly foreseen that Weber's case (in which Rehnquist cited the passage just quoted) was anticipated with considerable accuracy, and an assurance was given that people in his position would not suffer from adverse favoritism. These assurances were important to securing the bill's passage over deep-seated mistrust and antagonism, which were not confined to the South.

Equal Opportunity and Affirmative Action: The Crucial Dilemma

The rhetorical power of Johnson's language, in the charged atmosphere of the time, clearly committed his administration to achieving results that could be appreciated by all concerned. The revolution in progress was encouraged to become a revolution of enhanced expectations. Subjected to analysis, Johnson's language might be considered forceful rather than distinct.[6] The fact that Johnson emphasized and the result that he intended were already embedded in his legislation. But

5. *United Steelworkers v. Weber*, 443 U.S. 193 (1979), 220–21, 238–40, 244. 110 *Congressional Record* 6549, 6564, 8921 (1964). The majority of the Court held that the larger purposes of the Act would have been defeated if these considerations had prevailed, and these larger aims included the setting right of inequalities in the present resulting from racial prejudice in the past. It is, as usual, difficult to separate the principles involved in this case from the more general historical background which left black workers less skilled and less well paid than their white fellow-workers. Racial discrimination imposed by labor unions took several forms, including exclusion of blacks from training and apprenticeship for skilled trades, admission to which had been controlled by the unions. Management had generally acquiesced in these policies. Robert L. Carter, in Robert L. Carter, Dorothy Kenyon, Peter Marcuse, and Loren Miller, *Equality* (New York, 1965), 117–26.

6. It might seem rather odd to draw a distinction between *freedom* and *opportunity*; real freedom would presumably be real opportunity. The distinction between *legal equity* and *human ability* also presumably referred to the liberation of human ability by the application of legal rights.

neither Johnson's nor subsequent administrations could control the future course of the results of which he had spoken and which would, within the next few years, be transformed by a new conception of the aim and meaning of civil rights. Under newly emerging ideas of the meaning of equality in America, those who spoke for ethnic minorities began to assert a claim to equal *group* representation in such varied fields of public life as employment, education, and politics itself.

It was just at this point, and for this reason, that the classic principle of equality of individual opportunity lost its direction. The concept of affirmative action for the rectification of existing disproportions in these fields looked in its nature to the identity of social groups; its aims were satisfied when increases in the *proportions* of those employed or admitted corresponded approximately to their proportions in the population. This aim came to be known as "equality of result," or, in other formulations, "proportional representation," "statistical parity," or, perhaps more appropriately, "proportional pluralism."[7] By whatever name, the system raised moral and constitutional problems hardly less serious and perplexing than those it sought to solve. By concentrating on group proportions rather than on individual merits, it not only played off the rights of one individual of one group against those of another individual of another group, but in many subtle ways it played the present against the past.[8] This, proponents of the program might reply, was no new thing; the weapon was simply pointed at a different target. No honest person could doubt that, in the past, innumerable members of the privileged groups, though of mediocre ability, had often gained benefits from the indulgence of a system that was unquestionably biased in favor of whites, of

---

7. There are legitimate objections to each of these expressions. *Equality of result* or *results* fails to convey the fact that a transition has subtly taken place from the individualistic basis to the collective basis of enumeration, and implies by a sort of sleight of hand that the results in question would satisfy the original demands of equality of opportunity. *Proportional representation* is already a well-established usage for certain types of electoral system, and might lead to confusion. *Statistical parity* appears to refer, not to parity but to a specified type of disparity. Although *proportional pluralism* compresses seven syllables into two words and is open to objection on grounds of euphony, its advantage as a designation is simple: it hits the point. It does this by employing the idea of proportion while referring directly to the pluralistic character of the population.

8. The language employed in these discussions is part of the argument itself. The concept of individual *merit* is also open to challenge, since it evolved with the value systems of modern society. The definition of *merit* may be held to depend on who writes the rules (Philip Green, *The Pursuit of Inequality* [New York, 1981], 175–76).

Protestants, and also of the urban middle classes. The case for redress of collective grievances gathered its force from very deep historical sources and from very abstract principles of justice. But this did little to alleviate the pain of newly threatened men and women, boys and girls. The egalitarian critique of the manifest inequities of the past provided no obvious answer to the sense of grievance that arose when individual members of socially privileged groups were displaced in favor of minority claimants who might in some cases be of more doubtful ability or qualifications.

Affirmative action programs as adopted by universities, and particularly by professional schools, were liable to displace candidates coming from more traditional backgrounds. Worse still, they sometimes displaced applicants holding conventionally adequate academic qualifications for persons holding less adequate qualifications by those same standards. It was to be expected that these policies would be contested in court.

The most celebrated cases of the period concerned admission to professional schools.[9] The suit of Allan Bakke, a white man of Norwegian descent, already in his mid-thirties, soon superseded earlier claims to public attention.[10] Bakke's case became the archetypal test for the issue of affirmative action, and it was generally recognized while the case was being fought out not only in the courts but in the press, radio, and television, as well as in unnumbered intense public and private discussions, that an unequivocal judgment for Bakke would be a serious setback for the entire concept and program in universities across the country.

The School of Medicine at Davis, California, had set aside sixteen places for minority applicants whose claims could be considered to rest in part on non-academic grounds. Bakke's sense of grievance was understandable; he had scored far higher in examination results than any of the

---

9. *DeFunis v. Odegaard*, 416 U.S. 312 (1974); Ronald Dworkin. "The DeFunis Case: The Right to Go To Law School," *The New York Review of Books*, February 5, 1976. Marco DeFunis, the first plaintiff to go to the Supreme Court, had achieved higher test scores than thirty-six minority applicants who were given preference over him by the University of Washington School of Law. He was admitted by a court injunction, but the case remained moot because he was close to graduation before the Supreme Court could reach any decision.

10. *Regents of the University of California v. Bakke*, 438 U.S. 265 (1978).

members of minority groups who had got in before him.[11] If examination grades were to be considered the sole criterion for admission, Bakke's exclusion would seem to have been a violation of equal protection, as well as being inconsistent with the professed aims and principles of the Civil Rights Act. But there was a weakness in this position, for nothing in either the act or the Fourteenth Amendment, or in the conventions governing university admissions, could be held to establish that test scores were expected to be the exclusive determinants. No such claim had been normally entertained in the past, and the long history of privileged admissions to higher education of the sons and daughters of alumni, of the children of the wealthy in general, of Gentiles over Jews, of whites over blacks, suggested that non-academic considerations had frequently—in some institutions, normally—prevailed.

The same was true of the workplace and the labor unions. Every manner of restriction, from racial exclusion and ethnic recruitment to family networks, had historically dominated the opportunities of entry into the workforce. This applied with particular exclusiveness and persistence in such specialist crafts as plumbing. That phase of history might be coming to an end—brought about indeed by the consciousness of the criteria of personal merit implicit in the civil rights legislation—but it seemed rather hard that it should be coming to an end just when the children of the historically underprivileged stood to benefit by the adoption of social as well as academic criteria. These restrictive practices may not have been the subject of legislative or judicial approval, but they were well known to all concerned. This reflection in turn suggests that the entire program of affirmative action was more ambitious than it was officially proclaimed to be; its efforts could not rest until the merit principle, linked to equality of individual opportunity, had been established throughout the land.

The principle faced further difficulties when the Supreme Court gave its protection to an alternative view of public policy. A recent case of a different order but involving a similar problem of principle, had shown that, in the Court's opinion, the claims of the qualified individual need not necessarily determine the policy of an institution. Where a state

---

11. J. Harvie Wilkinson III, *From Brown to Bakke: The Supreme Court and School Integration, 1954–1978* (New York, 1979), 254.

wished to award privileged status to veterans of military service, public policy could lawfully prevail over the claims of individual equality.[12]

A troubled as well as a deeply divided Court was saved from paralysis by the subtle ambivalence of Mr. Justice Powell. Powell's opinion, which came to be known as the "swing vote" between the evenly divided parties on either side, rejected the view that educational institutions were entitled to act on their estimate of a need to compensate individuals for the past wrongs done to their race; the concept of "societal discrimination" opened uncharted possibilities of subjective judgment about the vexed question of group suffering. But in its place he introduced a notion of positive social benefit in diversity—a consideration which won his approval in the influential example of Harvard (which happened to be Powell's alma mater). Unavoidably, this diversity was that of an ethnically mixed society, and the concept of race or ethnicity smuggled itself into the judgment. In this mixed society, it was conceivably a part of the legitimate educational experience of young men and women to encounter members of other ethnic groups than their own. The four justices who firmly endorsed affirmative action, and wanted to uphold the Davis medical school's program in categorical terms—Brennan, White, Marshall, and Blackmun—went further than this in declaring as a constitutional principle that administrators might take race into consideration as a means of overcoming the results of past discrimination. Affirmative action, though without ringing endorsement, survived the judgment; but this was done without dismantling the criterion of individual qualifications, on which basis Bakke's personal claim was upheld. (By 1978, when the case was decided, he was thirty-eight years old.) Mr. Justice Marshall, who was particularly displeased, felt that the Court had failed in its duty to support the just claims of classes whom American history had injured.[13] But the concept of diversity, which gained exceptional prominence if only because it defined the outcome of Powell's opinion, did not close the door to further claims based on group identity rather than on individual ability.

Industry also felt the wave of egalitarian reform. The *Weber* case arose from a training program at Kaiser Aluminum works which aimed to make

---

12. *Personnel Administrator of Massachusetts v. Feeney*, 442 U.S. 256 (1979).
13. Wilkinson, *Brown to Bakke*, 298–99.

up for the effects of past discrimination by offering privileged admittance to black workers already employed by the firm. The claim for justice here involved a speculative, but reasonable, determination that the firm's black workers had been prevented by past racial discrimination from reaching the higher positions attained by their white contemporaries. Brian Weber, a white worker who had been deprived of the place he sought (though he had good objective qualifications) was thus not entitled to compete on an objective footing with the black man who got the place, but he had not suffered a denial of equal treatment if it could be sustained that his black rival would already have been promoted but for the malign effects of past racial discrimination. In this case, the redress of past inequalities appeared to survive as the determining principle. [14]

Congress, which had been given considerable opportunity to think in terms of group representation in its many deliberations on various aspects of civil rights, took charge of the question in an act dealing with government loans to small businesses. Hitherto, the concept of the quota had long had a bad name; it revived disagreeable memories of Jewish quotas at prominent eastern universities. It was also open to the obvious objection that, as a matter of experience, a quota as a minimum proportion for a particular group very quickly turned into a ceiling, blocking further increases without regard to individual merits. This violated all individualistic principles by operating unfairly against individual members of groups that the system was meant to favor. But it was not easy to dissociate the quota principle from the measure which set aside ten percent of small business loans in Southern California for firms run by minorities. One interesting aspect of this policy, perhaps deserving of notice, was that the traditional American principle of contract determined by the market was bypassed in favor of proportional pluralism. [15] When the Supreme Court sustained this act it recognized the claim that

14. *United Steelworkers v. Weber*, 443 U.S. 193 (1979); Green, *Pursuit of Inequality*, 168, 172; Burstein, *Discrimination, Jobs and Politics: The Struggle for Equal Employment Opportunity in the United States since the New Deal* (Chicago, 1985), 169–70.

15. This would appear to be the case in principle. But the Court was now interested in matters of substance; it was looking beyond rules to the substantive effects of rules. And in the present type of case it could be argued that the established firms enjoyed "unfair" market advantages over small, new, or struggling enterprises. Established firms, for example, normally expected to have better access to credit with local banks and with suppliers who had served them well in the past. Thomas Byrne Edsall, *The New Politics of Inequality* (New York, 1984), 48. Thus, an additional injection of assistance to weaker firms might be justified on grounds of equality of opportunity. This act of Congress

Congress had a right to establish programs of so-called reverse discrimination wherever it found justified grounds for believing that the minority in question, as a group, had suffered from damage inflicted by past discrimination. [16]

But, as appeared in the debates over civil rights and the emerging problems of language policy, this did not constitute grounds for a claim that ethnic, linguistic, or religious groups, by virtue of their mere existence, were entitled to a representative presence in proportion to their numbers in the general population. This was not a necessary conclusion to the philosophy of affirmative action. That program could, in principle, go so far as to ensure that candidates from all the unprivileged groups had a fair hearing, without going so far as to determine what the outcome of the hearing would be.

The choices open to the affirmative action policy were either to be "soft" or permissive, in the sense suggested above, or to be "hard" or determinative, to ensure that each particular outcome conformed statistically to the original intentions, and expectations, of the interests which had promoted the legislation. Many government agencies, colleges, and universities which were either subjected to official pressure, or took that pressure into their own consciences, embarked on extensive policies of making far-reaching searches for minority admissions and appointments. Even in institutions where expertise was by definition a requirement of the work to be done, unofficial quotas were adopted and minority candidates were sought with less than the standard regard for their qualifications. [17]

---

conflated the need for economic help with minority status. The real active principle at work here seemed to be the concept of the United States as a multivariate republic of ethnicities and businesses—a pluralism of economic activities—while subscribing to the doctrine of the need to redress injuries or deprivations deriving from past discrimination. Without minute investigation of local circumstances, the distinction might prove rather difficult to establish.

16. *Fullilove v. Klutznick*, 448 U.S. 448 (1980). Judith Baer, *Equality Under the Constitution* (Ithaca, 1983), 134–35.

17. Nathan Glazer, *Affirmative Discrimination* (New York, 1975), esp. ch. 2. A letter to *The New York Times* from certain members of the Cornell University faculty quoted a letter from the president of that university to deans and departmental chairmen telling them that his policy was to hire "additional minority persons and females" even if "in many instances, it may be necessary to hire unqualified or marginally qualified persons." *The New York Times*, 6 January 1972, quoted in Glazer, *Affirmative Discrimination*, 60. An

The policy certainly succeeded in its primary aims. The effect was to induct a great many persons from minority sources into branches of public service, business, and the professions. In many cases, these policies had the advantage of bringing a visible, even a conspicuous, alteration in the personnel who staffed such institutions as banks, public agencies, law offices, and college faculties. But the policy gave rise to new difficulties quite early in its progress, which its sponsors had either underestimated or had regarded as trivial by comparison with their wider social aims.

The politics of proportional pluralism did not owe either its inception or its successes to any unified or comprehensive theory. Some social thinkers could openly defend the idea of a quota system on the claim that it was as likely as any other method to find the deserving or talented persons within each group, and had the manifest advantage of making sure that all of America's ethnic groups would be consulted in the process. [18] Other theorists sketched the outlines of a less competitive and basically more fraternal—or perhaps, sisterly—society, less bent on the very mode of life that seemed to glorify individual differentiation; but for this ethic, it was difficult to find much support in American history or the modern society it had produced. [19] The fact that the social order *as a whole* reflected the prevailing values of liberal individualism, and that its constitutional rules stood on an individual basis, did not mean that these free individuals in their constitutionally guaranteed equality of rights were in any way deterred from forming themselves into small fraternal or sisterly clusters. [20]

Ivy League university was told by its regional Health, Education, and Welfare officials to get rid of "old fashioned programs that require irrelevant languages [Greek and Hebrew in this case]. And to start up programs on relevant things which minority groups students can study without learning languages." Ibid., 61.

18. Philip Green, *The Pursuit of Inequality* (New York, 1981), 191.

19. Amy Gutman, *Liberal Equality* (Cambridge, 1980), 220–30; Gregory Vlastos, "Justice and Equality," in Richard B. Brandt, ed., *Social Justice* (Englewood Cliffs, N.J., 1962).

20. The great West Indian cricketer Vivian Richards played for some years for the English county of Somerset. One evening, Richards invited a group of West Indian friends to join him. An observant English member of the team noticed that although they all regarded Richards as a very superior batsman, in every other way, they were equals—an example, one may think, of the equality of esteem that prevailed in such fraternal clusters. Peter Roebuck, *A Cricketer's Day* (London, 1986), 46.

These views of the meaning of equality neither derived from nor converged on any one theoretical position. The advances of proportional pluralism were best understood as derivatives of the unusual politics of the period, working on deep, underlying strata of discontent in American social experience. The objections they had to encounter were both theoretical and practical, in some cases to the extent of being politically explosive, and of inciting new outbursts of racial hostility. The first and most obvious type of problem arose when underqualified or unmotivated persons were appointed to responsible tasks, tending to diminish the efficiency of the service in question. The public, which incidentally included *all* minorities, was the sufferer from deteriorating services. In the academic world, where intellectual performance tends to be regarded from the inside, sometimes with a certain rigor, the effect on students was bound to be noticed. Not only did underqualified or insufficiently motivated students fail their courses in large proportions, but the inferences drawn by their classmates could only be deleterious.[21] This led directly to the psychological stress of what was called "reverse stigma." In the hard-working and competitive atmosphere of academic, professional, and business institutions, the merest suspicion that a minority member was there in order that he or she should be seen to be there, that his or her presence was representative rather than functional, could be more demoralizing to the individual than to the institution. This, however, could hardly be a conclusive argument against the principle of equalization involved in at least the milder forms of affirmative action. The stress that individuals suffer when breaking new ground in their societies is part of the price that has to be paid, if new ground is to be broken. The problem would hardly seem to be grounds for abandoning the effort.

Another objection was that the policy of making appointments to meet a required level of ethnic or gender visibility did not in itself necessarily call for further scrutiny into the needs, merits, or deserts of individuals. A candidate whose mother might be a white lawyer and whose father might be a black professor was defined as a black candidate;

---

21. Shelby Steele, *The Content of Our Characters* (New York, 1990). The author, a black professor teaching in San Jose, states that he knows, at the beginning of the academic year, that three-quarters of his black students will have dropped out before the end.

his (or her) status as a candidate was deemed to deserve privileged treatment on grounds of redress and racial balance; a candidate for the same position whose father was an unemployed Pittsburgh steelworker of Polish descent was designated a white. Under the hard version of the policy, it seemed likely that the blackness of the middle-class candidate would prevail over the whiteness of the working-class candidate. In economic affairs, it was objected that a policy of enhancing the corporate presence of a more or less well defined group did little to ensure that the neediest or worthiest members of that group would be the ones to benefit. As between individuals, inequalities were likely to remain as deep as before, and to the victims hardly less demoralizing. Affirmative action of the hard variety was charged by its critics with seeking ethnic representation not only without regard to, but at the expense of, the original civil rights aim of seeking individuals on their own needs or merits. But it should in fairness be observed that objections on these lines did not propose a better way of achieving that aim.

Beyond these objections, however, lay another, with its foundations in the very nature of the composition of the society that called for such remedies: that the ethnic group itself, with its porous boundaries, its fluctuating and uncertain social character, and also with the very great differences of intensity with which its different members, as individuals, either wished to or in any practical sense did adhere to it, was an inherently weak and unstable basis on which to establish a social policy that was to be viable, systematic, and lasting. Ethnicity afforded a very problematic and insecure basis for any sort of general theory.[22]

One of the causes of the economic weakness in the bargaining position of American workers lay in the historic weakness of labor organization. It would hardly be necessary to take a Marxist standpoint to observe that, if the working classes were to draw any advantage from identifying themselves in class terms, the politics of ethnicity repre-

---

22. Alan Goldman, *Justice and Reverse Discrimination* (Princeton, 1979), 230–33; Douglas Rae and associates, *Equalities* (Cambridge, Mass., 1981), 80; Glazer, *Affirmative Discrimination*, passim.; Steele, *Characters*, passim.; J.R. Zvesper, "Ethnic Pluralism and Affirmative Discrimination in America," paper presented to the University of East Anglia Political Thought seminar, 17 November 1987. I am grateful to John Zvesper for letting me see this unpublished paper. This subject has generated a large literature, to which members of a variety of racial or ethnic groups have contributed, and of which it is no part of the purpose of the present footnote to offer a bibliography.

sented a serious distraction.[23] If the economic individualism of the old, entrepreneurial ethic was one enemy of working-class organization, surely no further hope of progress would lie along the road of a newly politicized ethnicity. As for the old American ideal of interchangeability, it could survive only as a folk memory.

Constitutional Adjudication and the Refinements of Principle

When equality became an organizing principle for a national agenda of action, government agencies and above all the courts soon found themselves obliged to examine constitutional principles in the light of the new pressures. These in turn opened up unexpected conflicts that had lain buried, but which we have already seen emerging, in the ideal of equality itself. There followed a proliferation of commentaries and analyses by social and political scientists, by economists and historians, by moral and jurisprudential philosophers, directed to the social, economic, and philosophical implications of equality; to these were added a series of judicial decisions which normally involved (or implied) a component of similar analysis. Although different lessons were drawn and divergent arguments were propounded, certain truths could be inferred by those who were willing to stand back from the mêlée and observe the implications with reasonable clarity of mind. It appeared as an inescapable truth that not all inequalities could ever be rectified within the framework of a single system; it was equally certain that some could be rectified only by creating new inequalities and new and bitter grievances. This paradox lay concealed in the historical interstices of the case. Its exposure revealed conflicting aims and made old allies into enemies. But this did not mean that from the point of view of previous or present generations of reformers, nothing had been achieved, that the effort had been futile or the energy wasted.

In the American political system it falls to the Supreme Court to mediate these conflicts back to the larger society through the prism of constitutional interpretation. The Constitution seen in this light is the nation's moral law, and the justices are society's moral arbiters. This may seem a heavy burden for lawyers to assume. Levels of awareness have

23. Much material in Edsall, *New Politics of Inequality*, and Green, *The Pursuit of Inequality*, supports this view.

stimulated corresponding grievances at different periods of American history, sometimes tending to differentiate among the categories that we have analyzed in this study, rather than unifying them. Inequalities of opportunity, seen in terms of economic class, of race, religion, and sex have presented themselves under different conditions as primary grievances. The remarkable aspect of the period in which Chief Justice Earl Warren presided over the Supreme Court was the historically unprecedented convergence of these issues. Lyndon Johnson's civil rights policies and political rhetoric both reflected and concentrated this convergence. The whole intelligence of the country was made conscious of the demand for equality as arising from the nation's founding principles, from the needs of the hour, from long-delayed moral obligations. But these principles neither adequately defined the obligations nor fully satisfied the demands. The methods of remedy differed as the aims themselves diverged. But despite the increasingly fissiparous character of the movement, this nationalization of consciousness had no precedent in American history.

Constitutional rules or rulings could not dictate specific policies, but they did call for one fundamental change of attitude: the obligations of government could no longer be discharged by mere restraint. Government intervention became a positive duty for the protection of the civil rights and interests of citizens. By 1967, Archibald Cox, reviewing the cases decided in the Supreme Court's previous term, had no difficulty in pronouncing equality their principal theme. [24] It was highly significant that in the case of *Katzenbach v. Morgan*—dealing with the application of the Voting Rights Act in South Carolina—the Court had deferred to Congress's opinion in overruling a state; within broad limits, Congress now had power to decide how the equal protection clause was to apply to local conditions. [25] The case, Cox said, "cleared the way for a vast expansion of congressional legislation promoting human rights," yet it was "soundly rooted in established constitutional principles." The general consequence of these decisions was that Congress resumed the power it had taken in 1875 to deal with "the whole domain of rights appertaining to life, liberty and property, defining them and providing

24. Archibald Cox, "Foreword: Constitutional Adjudication and the Promotion of Human Rights," *Harvard Law Review* 80 (1966–67), 91–272.
25. 384 U.S. 641 (1966).

for their vindication." When Mr. Justice Bradley spoke for the Court on the Civil Rights Act of 1875, he checked the extension of Federal power into the domain of state legislatures; now, more than eighty years later, the fundamental principles underlying that act were reaffirmed. What the Supreme Court had now done, in Cox's conclusion, was to overturn the *Civil Rights Cases* of 1883.[26]

The cumulative direction of the recent cases was to establish that when either legislatures or other agencies such as public or private corporations exercised choice or discrimination in selecting individuals, it must be done on grounds that were relevant to their proper function, not on grounds of caprice or prejudice. This policy was advanced an important step further when in 1971 the Supreme Court, in *Griggs v. Duke Power Company*, held that the use of test scores and other credentials to select employees was a violation of Title VII of the Civil Rights Act of 1964 when, first, the process of selection resulted in underrepresentation of minorities, and, secondly, the employer could show no relation between test scores or similar criteria and the qualities required for performing the job in question.[27] This left a gap in the area between intention and result: what if there were no intention to discriminate on illegitimate grounds but the outcome of the selection process did in fact reveal a numerical underrepresentation of one group? In *Washington v. Davis*, decided in 1976, which arose from the selection processes of the Washington, D.C., police department, the Court closed this gap by deciding that although a general, not specifically job-related, test might produce racially unequal recruitment, it did not deny equal protection if there were no intention to discriminate racially. "Respondents, as Negroes," said the Court, "could no more claim that the test denied them equal protection than could white applicants who failed." The test which the petitioners had failed to pass was in general use throughout the civil service and was designed to test verbal ability, vocabulary, reading, and comprehension. The Court denied that it had ever accepted the rule that a law or other official act could be unconstitutional *solely* because it had a racially disproportionate impact. Mr. Justice Brennan disagreed. The outcome, in his opinion, plainly conflicted with *Griggs*. "Today's decision," he said, "has the potential of significantly weakening statutory

26. Cox, "Constitutional Adjudication," 107, 118.
27. *Griggs v. Duke Power Company*, 401 U.S. 424, also cited as 91 S.C. 849 (1971).

safeguards against discrimination in employment."[28] The important point about the decision, however, was that unconstitutionality was to depend not on the test of unintended result in racial imbalance but on the test of an intent to create a racial imbalance.[29]

The formula which distinguished between "intent to discriminate" and unequal *impact* on different communities had obvious advantages. It was, in the first place, reasonably manageable. Moreover, within its own terms of reference, which implied that applicants for jobs or promotions were to be considered as individuals and not as group representatives, it was also consistent. But it overlooked one socially significant aspect of the whole problem, and that was the profound inequality—or disparity—of the way in which unequal impacts were perceived and felt among different groups, or between majorities and minorities. In a society historically permeated with racial assumptions, these disparities looked very different depending which side of the fence the observer was on; and because of this disparity, an adverse impact was liable to have disproportionate implications for different individuals within such groups. Conscious and deliberate racial discrimination of the sort which had once motivated southern states in restricting civil and political rights may have almost disappeared from the American scene, but an element of unconscious or of *unintended* racial disparagement survived in circumstances where white people quietly assumed that when neutrally designed tests produced racially unbalanced results, it was simply because individuals, not the racial character of the society, had fallen short of the demands made by individual aspirations.

Soon after the affair of the Washington police had been settled, a predominantly white and upper-middle-class suburb in Chicago received an application for a proposed housing development for persons of much lower incomes. The local authority stopped the proposals by rejecting the necessary application for rezoning the district to permit the building

28. 426 U.S. 229 (1976); 109 U.S. 6 (1976); 11 EPD, no. 10,958.

29. 329 U.S. 629 (1950). However, the question of whether it is fair to judge by this distinction as a matter of principle, or whether the linguistic tests in application in the particular case were appropriate for the duties of policing black neighborhoods, was far from having been resolved and has given rise to a considerable literature. The following paragraph reflects Charles R. Lawrence III, "The Id, the Ego, and Equal Protection: Reckoning with Unconscious Racism." *Stanford Law Review* 39 (1986–87), 317–88; for further discussion, see also Neal Devins, "The Rhetoric of Equality," *Vanderbilt Law Review* 44:1 (January 1991), 15–44.

of units designed for more than one family. Since most of the beneficiaries would have been black, the Supreme Court acknowledged that the effects would be discriminatory in terms of race. But the black tenants' equal protection claim was rejected on the grounds that they had failed to prove racially discriminatory *intent*. The issue, in other words, was consistent with *Washington v. Davis*. And there was indeed no overt evidence of a consciously racial intention; the local policy might (and probably would) have been exactly the same if the poorer people had all been whites. But the black tenants inevitably perceived the policy, and the Court's decision, as reflecting the racism which appeared to permeate their society. (Where *else*, one might ask, were they to find better homes?)[30] A neutrally conceived equality of rights appeared in these situations to conflict with ideas of equality of esteem that arose from cultural experience. This issue, charged with conflicts of ideology, political ambitions, and group interests, was to undergo further and highly controversial vicissitudes because it remained endemic in American society.[31]

The philosophy of equality of opportunity was not only essentially individualistic. It also reflected a deep strand of American historical optimism, a faith that the desired results would flow from the right institutions exercizing the right intentions. The social philosophy of the school of equality of results, on the other hand, was skeptical. The desired results could not be expected unless they were engineered. Government agencies would have to intervene to produce the new, distributive equalities and could not rest until they had achieved their aims. It was somewhat pre-emptively assumed in both schools that those results would be a random distribution approximating closely to the proportions of the general population represented by its different ethnically defined groups. No doubt, whatever the outcomes, a fair propor-

---

30. *Village of Arlington Heights v. Metropolitan Housing Development Corp.*, 429 U.S. 252 (1977); Lawrence, "Id, Ego," 347.

31. *The New York Times*, 22, 23 October 1990. Lawrence's essay, cited above in note 29, need not be taken as calling for a specific determination in cases where unconscious racism, however evaluated, may be suspected; it does call for a higher level of judicial scrutiny. In a case comparable to that of Arlington Heights, one may still ask whether a rezoning rejection would be unconstitutional where it affected blacks but constitutional where it affected poor whites? And whether, indeed, the perception that poverty deprives its victims of equal opportunities might not be made an issue on the same principle of equal protection?

tion of the individual results would overlap, whichever school prevailed; but their underlying principles were profoundly different, and both claimed the mantle of equality. Conspicuous inequalities of wealth were themselves forms of "results" which would continue to arouse the criticism and disturb the consciences of both schools of equality. From the group-centered point of view, the outcome was intolerable; unfair discrimination remained to poison the system's bloodstream. From the individualist point of view, the outcome was merely disappointing; the reforms had not produced the results that had been desired and expected.

The Distribution of Wealth

Ever since James Madison's analysis of the causes of inequalities in the distribution of property, which formed an integral part of the complex argument of *Federalist* 10, Americans had been in possession of a strong theoretical justification for the very observable fact that the principles of equality to which they subscribed did not imply equality in the distribution of material resources.[32] No theory, however benign, could produce equality of distribution out of an open, mobile economy. As we have also seen, the egalitarian in Andrew Jackson was satisfied with the unequal results that flowed from the free exercise of unequal efforts and abilities. In the economic sphere, which, after all, occupied most of the people through most of their lives, equality of opportunity could never produce the equivalent of a literal equality of results.[33] If such an outcome had been possible, it would in fact have conflicted with the motivation behind equality of opportunity.

These relatively simple truths have prevailed for the simple reason that they sat comfortably with the powerful aspirations to self-advancement that provided one of the motive forces of American history. But they tended also to forestall the more troublesome implications of the profoundly unequal distribution of wealth that continued to prevail under Lyndon Johnson. In round figures, it was still true that one-fifth of the nation received 46 percent of its income and owned 77

32. However, return to Chapter 3, pp. 58–60, for our own analysis of the reasoning on which Madison relied for this argument.

33. This fact has a specific significance in the context of the controversy over so-called equality of results. It makes clear that that concept was developed with specific application to the politics of ethnicity, not to that of other—often more traditional—types of recognized interests. We shall return to this theme later in this chapter.

percent of its wealth; at the top of this scale, one-twentieth of the population received 20 percent of the nation's income and 53 percent of its wealth. By contrast, 3 percent of the national income, and less than 0.5 percent of its wealth, was spread among the lowest-paid sector, amounting to approximately one-fifth of the people. Comparable inequalities dominated the distribution of income and ownership of corporate assets in the business world, among whose total of almost two million corporations, 55 percent of corporate assets were controlled by one-tenth of one percent.[34] These inequalities might or might nor be considered inequities, depending, presumably, on the services rendered, and the comparability of the distribution of public burdens through taxation, but the Internal Revenue Code systematically extracted higher proportions from the poor than from the rich. Although welfare programs which distributed public money among the needy attracted much attention (and no little criticism), it could in the circumstances be no great flight of fancy to describe the preferences and exemptions offered to recipients of high incomes, to holders of public securities and owners or purchasers of property, as "a welfare program that reverses the usual pattern and gives huge welfare payments to the super-rich but only pennies to the poor."[35]

Whatever might be the attractions of financial incentive, these disparities could not be defended on grounds of economic utility. Disparities would exist, as we have seen, under any open system, no matter how carefully the market might be regulated, but disparities on this scale bore absolutely no correlation to the functional needs of the economy. If the aim were to maximize the production and fair distribution of wealth, certain protections and certain incentives could be justified, and certain apparent disparities might prove to be beneficial to the economic whole. But these theoretical principles had no bearing on the realities of the American case. The reported levels of economic inequality could not be adequately explained on the grounds that they were serving the public by producing prosperity.[36]

America was far from being the only industrial economy which

34. Herbert J. Gans, *More Equality* (New York, 1974), 13–14.

35. Philip Stern, *The Rape of the Taxpayer* (New York, 1973), quoted by Gans, ibid., 15.

36. Sidney Verba and Gary R. Orren, *Equality in America: The View from the Top* (Cambridge, Mass., 1985), 150–51; Jeffrey G. Williamson and Peter H. Lindert, *American Inequality: A Macroeconomic History* (New York, 1980), 280.

produced and perpetuated large-scale disparities of wealth and income. But American disparities had roots in special aspects of American labor and economic history. Lower-income groups had very poor access to the political process, while the low level of unionization, when compared with the major industrial economies in Europe, was a factor making for inequalities of distribution of the products of industry. America's more influential craft unions had little general interest in social policy.[37] This conclusion in its negative way reinforces the observation that the immense inequalities generated by the system were in no way needed to make that system an overall success.

These disparities occupied only the most limited space in the public consciousness during the sustained prosperity of the postwar years, which induced a tolerant complacency over the merits of the economy, as received from the hands of the New Deal and its successors.[38] But this complacency received a rude shock when in 1962 Michael Harrington published his analysis of poverty in *The Other America*, from which the country learned the humiliating news that the poor had always been with them, and still were. They had not disappeared from existence, only from public view.[39] Between forty and fifty million Americans, about the one-fifth of the population which had been mentioned as receiving three percent of its income, lived in poverty and hunger. The American economy had failed, it seemed, to feed, clothe, house, or minister to them, but it did succeed in concealing them from sight.[40]

These stinging revelations worked their way through to the administrative conscience in Johnson's presidency and were not without their influence on his program of War on Poverty, whose aim was to extend

37. J. Rogers Hollingsworth, "The Political Structural Basis for Economic Performance," *Annals of the American Academy of Political and Social Science* 459 (January 1982), 28–45.

38. Richard Hofstadter remarked in the mid-1950s, "The New Deal may have been a failure in the thirties, but it sure is a success in the fifties."

39. This omission was duly corrected by the conspicuous rise of homelessness in the 1980s.

40. Michael Harrington, *The Other America* (New York, 1962; Harmondsworth, 1963), 19. The only aspect of this situation that could be called new was the apparent unawareness of the existence and amount of serious poverty on the part of the better informed classes. In the nineteenth century the poor were known to exist, and certain elements of them were referred to as a "dangerous class." Eric H. Monkkonen, *The Dangerous Class: Columbus . . . 1860–1920* (Cambridge, Mass., 1975).

the benefits of the existing American economy to the sector whose needs had been neglected.[41] This campaign included specific programs such as Head Start, which aimed to bring intellectual stimulation to young children of families in very depressed circumstances, and Aid to Families with Dependent Children—in both cases approaching the poor and the black populations and finding many who belonged to both. The Head Start initiative succeeded in promoting a measure of recorded intellectual improvement. But the campaign as a whole could not be said to have brought about either an educational or an economic transformation before the political will began to fail, a domestic casualty of the war in Southeast Asia.[42] It is right, however, to record a governmental initiative of the period which was to no small extent inspired by the current preoccupation with equality. The impulse was sustained in 1966 with a major reform of the immigration laws. Again under Johnson's aegis, the old designations, which gave carefully graded preferences to the peoples of Northwest Europe and established the hierarchy of social preferences of an earlier era, were swept away; the idea of the quota collapsed under the onrush of equality for all the world, enacting the most exuberant confidence in America's capacity to make anyone, from anywhere, into an American. At no time since Reconstruction had the central tenet of American ideology attained the power to move governments to this extent.[43]

A stronger Civil Rights Act, aimed at eliminating racial discrimination in the employment market, was passed under Nixon in 1972.[44] But the Democrats, though in general much more disposed than the Republicans to spending on social amelioration, had little taste for taxation as a general means of redistribution. When they put it on the agenda of George McGovern's campaign in 1972, they seem to have convinced large numbers of voters that their ideas were dangerously radical.[45]

Policies of piecemeal relief always offered relief even where they

41. Verba and Orren, *Equality in America*, 44–51, 63; Green, *Pursuit of Inequality*, 38.

42. For a personal account of this failure, see Eric H. Goldman, *The Tragedy of Lyndon Johnson* (London, 1968).

43. Philip Gleason, "American Identity and Americanization," in Stephan Thernstrom, ed., *Harvard Encyclopedia of American Ethnic Groups* (Cambridge, Mass., 1980), 52.

44. Godfrey Hodgson, *In Our Time: America from World War II to Nixon* (London, 1976), 454.

45. Gans, *More Equality*, 53.

could not solve larger problems, and they had the advantage of appealing to specific groups who might either be influential in themselves or have access to influential spokesmen. (Farmers had a long record of political influence beyond their numbers.) But with initiatives like Head Start, such remedies resulted from administrative intervention rather than arising from the conscious and concerted demands of the afflicted communities. Urban riots and burning buildings, not organized political processes, aroused the anxieties and stirred the consciences of the political public. When relief was then voted, the aim of the remedies proposed tended to be local alleviation rather than economic reconstruction. In any case, the structure of political power made the prospect of more extensive programs implausible. The poor may, though many of them do not, vote at elections. But they never finance candidates or maintain continuous pressure on members of Congress. It was a significant aspect of the political crisis, which led directly into the newest round of the struggles to define the meaning of equality, that such limited pressure as the poor were able to exert sprang more from the power of *racial and ethnic* identification than from the condition of poverty itself. Many of the urban poor were blacks, many of the urban blacks were among the poor. Consciousness of racial inequality stimulated the political demonstrations of the period, and it was to this consciousness that American society responded, rather than to the stimulus to conscience arising from the deprivations and injuries of economic class.[46]

If maps were designed to identify districts by their economic character, inequalities of opportunity would be easy to trace. The colors used to show poor districts would appear with striking similarity in the districts with poorly endowed schools. Racial inequalities very often ran along the same lines as those of the distribution of wealth. Schools and their segregation had been at the center of the modern phase of the struggle for equality; but race was not the only line along which schools

---

46. Gans, ibid., has a large bibliography of this subject, of which it is significant that the great majority of works cited date from the late 1960s and early 1970s. The issues were gaining a new purchase on the attention of the public; see also Edward C. Budd, ed., *Inequality and Poverty* (New York, 1967); William L. Taylor, *Hanging Together: Equality in an Urban Nation* (New York, 1971). These and many other titles testify to the thesis of this chapter that a wholly new level of consciousness of the issue of equality came to the surface of politics in this period.

had been effective institutions of social segregation. If the Constitution forbade racial segregation, on what grounds did it permit other forms, equally damning to their victims? In San Antonio, Texas, the state-sponsored school finance system gave great resources to the rich Alamo Heights district while depriving the poor Edgehill neighborhood of any comparable advantage. A suit was initiated under the Fourteenth Amendment. The district court held that the system's discrimination on the basis of wealth amounted to an inadmissible denial of equal protection; wealth was deemed to be a suspect ground for classification, the state having failed to explain that it had a reasonable basis for making these distinctions.

The implications were portentous. If unequal systems of school finance were held to be unconstitutional, reorganizations of vast scale and infinite complexity might be expected to follow. The outcome of this case depended on how one defined "class." The whole weight of the political definition of equality had borne down on the principle that, to isolate certain individuals as a class, and to deprive that class of equal opportunities, violated the protective cover of the Fourteenth Amendment. But if inherited membership of a race, or chosen membership of a religion, constituted membership of such a class, it could be argued that inherited poverty or unchosen location in a neighborhood of poor resources was a condition that deserved similar protection. Children, in any case, were no more at liberty to choose their social class than their race or the religion in which they were brought up.

Whether the suburban upper and middle classes owed their advantages to inheritance or to merit, they certainly owed them in no small part to the institution of private property and the laws which sustained it. The power to transmit these advantages to their children might from a traditional point of view be considered a fundamental right. But the institutions of public education were by definition answerable to principles of public policy, and the power, through the funding of those institutions, to transmit commensurate disadvantages to the children of the poor could as well be considered as a fundamental wrong. Education was undoubtedly one of the most fundamental determinants of further opportunities in life. The Supreme Court now faced the problem of whether the egalitarian principles of the Constitution demanded that the educational consequences of American economic history were to be

undone, to be replaced, so far as the public sector was concerned, with a system of equal educational opportunity. It was not an impossible demand; generations of racial history had been set in reverse by *Brown v. Board of Education* less than twenty years earlier. But the Court did not venture into this dangerous territory. Mr. Justice Powell, for the majority, took carefully chosen narrow ground in holding that the school district system did not operate against any class fairly defined as indigent or as "composed of persons whose incomes are beneath any designated poverty level." The Texas system did not operate to the disadvantage of a "suspect class" in the Court's own usage—by which was meant a classification requiring special scrutiny. A child might have a right to a public education, but he did not find that a child's right to any particular *standard* of education was a "fundamental" right in a sense that called for its provision by government; a deprivation of equal education, even if proved (which was not admitted) would therefore presumably not amount to a constitutionally inadmissible deprivation—unless the denial was itself based on inadmissible grounds such as race.[47]

A minority of four justices held that the case came within the purview of the recognized principles of equality of rights established by previous decisions. Mr. Justice Marshall, representing the dissent, replied that the Court was now engaged in a retreat from "our historic commitment to equality of educational opportunity." The equal protection clause was not addressed to the question of whether the state supplied a minimal sufficiency, but to the unjustifiable inequalities of state action. "It mandates nothing less than that 'all persons similarly circumstanced shall be treated alike.' " He added that it was inequality—not some notion of gross inadequacy, as the majority seemed to think—that raised the question of denial of equal protection of the law. Mr. Justice White, also dissenting, observed that the Texas system provided a meaningful option for the rich Alamo Heights district but almost none to those districts with a low basis of real estate taxes for each pupil; where the property raised no funds, no real choice of spending was possible, so that the scheme of local participation, desirable in principle, worked exclusively to the advantage of those who could afford it. Essentially, the majority's position rested on the assumption that the issue was political. The people of Texas were free to change their system through their representa-

47. *San Antonio Independent School District v. Rodriguez*, 411 U.S. 1 (1973), 22–23.

tives—a course which Marshall regarded as too unlikely for serious consideration.[48]

The Court seemed to be withdrawing the extended and intrusive hand of the Constitution. It was certainly withdrawing from the use of the Constitution as an instrument of social change. Felix Frankfurter, who had recognized that political decisions could be wrong without being unconstitutional, would undoubtedly have approved this retreat from the Court's more interventionist commitments at the time of his recent death.

This was not to be the last word on the subject, since certain states later began to initiate equalizing educational policies within their own jurisdictions. They could not, however, do much to check the danger of middle-class flight into private schools, provided always that the middle classes could continue to afford the considerable costs. The issue was closely parallel to the previous phenomenon of "white flight" which had produced the suburban ring of predominantly white schools in many areas, and which had led to the case of *Milliken v. Bradley* in Detroit.[49]

The Texas case did nothing to diminish the reasons for thinking that political policies designed to promote greater levels of racial, religious or ethnic equality had achieved more than those designed to redistribute wealth—a conclusion which has very broad significance for the interpretation of American society. The more general trends of wealth distribution in the history of the United States have responded only minimally to public policy. Allowing for a few ups and downs, the distribution of wealth remained fairly constant from 1800 to about 1940, and inequalities then began to decrease slightly. Even the plutocrats of the fin-de-siècle era whose ostentations provoked Thorstein Veblen to coin the phrase "conspicuous consumption" and to devote an essay to *The Theory of the Leisure Class* (which appeared in 1899) made little difference to the statistics of the share held by the top ten percent. Between twenty and forty percent of working men seem to have been unable to accumulate

48. Ibid., 71, 89. Whether the matter were essentially political or not, the point of the plaintiffs' case was that *whatever* system was adopted would have to conform to the principle of equal protection.

49. 338 F.Supp. 583 (1971); 418 U.S. 717 (1974).

wealth during their lifetimes. Political parties came and, in some cases—the Jacksonian Workingmen, the Populists, the Socialists—went; but the question of the distribution of wealth seldom figured for long, or for large numbers, as a national problem. One explanation of the tolerance for these seemingly unsatisfactory conditions was no doubt that the hope of individual improvements, though not often attained, did often seem (however delusively) to lie within the realm of the possible.[50] These private aspirations may often have blunted the edge of protest; but protest, however well directed, normally tended to have local objectives; more profound and diffuse explanations would extend to the structure of politics and the wide diffusion of an individualistic economic ideology.

To become a political issue, inequality must be felt not only as a grievance but as a grievance that can be remedied through some form of political or politically conspicuous action. (Riots, such as those of the mid- to late 1960s, do not rank as formal politics, but they were often politically conspicuous. They do not demonstrate power, but are manifestations of powerlessness.) Americans had lifetimes of experience of inequalities of all sorts, and much experience of nudging here and there at the edges of the problem. It would be a mistake to trivialize these efforts or the ideals which sustained them. But when that has been said, there remained an impressive measure of acquiescence in the huge disparities of fortune.

Americans wanted a society run on equal principles without wanting a society of equals. In this aspiration they were similar to other modern societies, but one feature that distinguished the Americans was the strong and public rhetorical commitment to an unspecified egalitarian ideal, which constantly brought arguments about social policies round to its own terms. The tension between rules and substance could never be resolved, however, and the most ardent proponents of substance had to be content with responding to the preferences of a wide range of otherwise differentiated people, with enhanced but never adequate welfare and social security policies. The limits of redistributive policies had shown only too clearly that only impractical visionaries could entertain ideas of a more structurally egalitarian society.

---

50. Lee Soltow, *Men and Wealth in the United States, 1850–1870* (New Haven, 1975), 122–23, 174, 183.

These welfare policies were themselves sustained and stimulated by a great nationalizing of public consciousness brought about initially by the Depression and then, principally, by American participation in the Second World War. Between the crash of 1929 and the Republican regime of Dwight Eisenhower, popular thinking effected a large-scale transition. Ideas of dynamic and highly individualistic opportunism gradually gave place to ideas associated with personal security. Much as the corporation had often proved itself better insulated against economic shocks than the private firm, so the individual became increasingly identified with corporate aims and with institutional safeguards. These developments set the tone and context of public policy, but neither in the case of business nor in that of local government did ideals of equality play any important role. One effect of the achievements of the ideas, and some of the practices, of the New Deal, was that the ideal of equality as it affected the American masses was subtly infiltrated and altered by the advance of the concept of welfare as a major obligation owed by government to the people. Welfare, like other goods at the disposal of government, became a resource; equality, at the level of achievable political action, became for most people a demand for equal access to the resources of welfare. Competition for these resources grew more fierce at any time when they threatened to be scarce—as happened with reasonable frequency in the uncertainties of trade cycles, especially when linked to the uncertainties of international economics. This element entered later into the resistance of blue-collar workers to the new policies of affirmative action, whose aim, in effect, was to distribute the resources of the economy on a broader basis of race or ethnicity. In spirit, this resistance sprang from much the same sort of feeling that had earlier dominated organized labor's resistance to immigration—and was consistent with organized labor's long record of resistance to racial integration in the workshop.

At a different level, and also blunting working-class dispositions to seek egalitarian solutions to social problems, the idealization of success (which did not become less prominent through the media's emphasis on great private fortunes) and the residual glow of the diminished fires of individual enrichment, continued to exercise a sort of dull enchantment; working people were reluctant to renounce them completely. This may have been one reason why, particularly among the skilled working classes, ideas of equality imposed on individuals a burden of responsibil-

ity which few of them were eager to bear. Under deep investigation, skilled workers did not express their aims, either for themselves or their country, in egalitarian rhetoric. Opportunity remained important, and an individual worker's skill, energy, and ambition were seen to create a legitimate claim on society's capacity to maintain opportunities. But the fulfillment of earned aspirations was not all. Skilled male workers tended to think that an individual ought to be allowed to keep the goods of fortune, and that one who had made a million dollars had deserved his reward; they were perhaps reluctant to exclude all thought of such possibilities for themselves or their children, however illusory such aspirations might be. No evidence or sign appeared of any general vision of a different social order, nor any clear picture of how a more equally ordered society would distribute its goods.[51]

People who were unwilling to attach blame or responsibility to the system as a whole for their own personal place in it, for their frustrations and disappointments as well as their satisfactions, were by the same token unlikely to be interested in analyzing it—even, indeed, to identifying such a thing as a "system" within whose compass they worked. One exception to this diagnosis was beginning to emerge in the case of women. The new wave of feminists did discern a "system," organized by and in the interests of the male sex and operating with extraordinary

---

51. Robert E. Lane, *Political Ideology: Why the American Common Man Believes What He Does* (New York, 1962), 57–81; idem, "The Fear of Equality," *American Political Science Review* 53 (1959), 35–51; W. G. Runciman, *Relative Deprivation and Social Justice: A Study of Attitudes to Social Equality in Twentieth Century England* (Harmondsworth, 1972). The focus of American labor unions on pragmatic issues, a policy which has limited organized labor to being essentially one among a variety of pressure groups operating within an accepted system, has, of course, played a vital role in this entire scheme. Most Americans will feel that any sort of larger social vision would be inappropriate in such a context. The argument proposed here is historical, not ideological. There was nothing inevitable or in the nature of things about the American way of perceiving social needs. One need only contrast the immense part played by organized labor in the *politics* of Britain or France or Sweden to appreciate that broader social vision was a possible alternative. But there was an irony here. If British and French workers were subject to fewer illusions about the prospects for individualist advancement, they were, for that reason and the history of their own forms of social bonding, also much more content with the limitations imposed by collective sorts of labor consciousness. While most British and French workers have historically been willing to improve the conditions of the working class, there is not much evidence of a desire to cease being members of the working class or to renounce a class-bound identity. Although class is almost as socially definitive in America as in Europe, the *idea* of class sits uneasily and is often rejected.

effectiveness through the whole range of politics, law, employment, finance, public service, education, and through most of private life. The movement for equality in what was soon to be called "gender" not only challenged the existing distribution of power in almost every respect; it also had a transverse effect on existing movements for racial equality, challenging the male-dominated power structures that operated within those movements. But this willingness to see the social system as a totality was limited by its aims. In principle these could have been satisfied by a redistribution of power between the sexes; American ideology was under criticism for being a masculine ideology; this particular criticism did not, in principle, object to its tolerance of other social injustices and economic inequalities.

Ethnicity and Language:
The Resurrection of the Hyphen in American Ideology

The new movements of the mid-1960s were thus driven by somewhat inconsistent and confusing impulses. But they all contributed to a great stimulation of consciousness. Out of the confusion, two powerful drives emerged, one generated from above, the other from below. The first, Johnson's War on Poverty, was led, as we have seen, by the administration. The second egalitarian drive of the period had social and cultural sources in America's variegated ethnicities. Since most of the intended beneficiaries of Johnson's reform programs in fact belonged to ethnically (or racially) identified minorities, these constituencies of the economically deprived and the ethnically deprived substantially overlapped each other. There is no reason to believe that the administration had aimed or expected to arouse a new political consciousness in these minorities, to convert minority consciousness into a new and dynamic political force. Yet this development and its longer consequences were as potent as they had been unexpected. In the recent past, under both Kennedy and Johnson, the basic relationship was still one in which the government gave, the deprived minority received; relieved to some extent of its deprivation, the minority responded by ceasing in any politically meaningful sense to be a minority. The winning of the initiative by the minorities within a very few years mounted a challenge to the rules under which the game of equality was being played.

It was the blacks who first seized that initiative, symbolized in 1966

by Stokeley Carmichael's coinage of the phrase "Black Power." And it was an unintended irony that this assertion of separateness should follow immediately on the implied offer of the American form of oneness, of assimilation into the American whole, which had historic roots in the entire liberal program. [52] The prospect of a new wave of self-segregation, however, was not entirely unforeseen; it had already been observed in 1962 that America's brand of pluralism was leading in that direction, the examples to hand being those of white Protestants, Catholics, and Jews. [53] The crumbling of the walls of legal segregation soon disclosed the existence of forms of segregation erected by the communities themselves, to the sound of the protests of a new breed of radicals who rejected the idea of "integration." In the rapidly changing group and personal relationships of the time, it was sometimes difficult to discern the boundaries between one community and another or between what was old in social custom and what was new in self-defense. Perhaps the crumbling of the legal walls was simply revealing the existence of older, self-constructed walls. But a peculiarity of the American situation was also beginning to reveal itself: black Americans—the designation *black* was itself now asserted in place of *Negro*—were less than willing to admit that they were merely one minority among others; for profound historic reasons, perhaps the black case was different: "Do I really *want* to be integrated into a burning house?," James Baldwin had searchingly demanded in his essay, *The Fire Next Time*. [54]

Black people were finding new, and much needed strength in racial pride and ethnic solidarity. Advocates of Black Power did not accept the old, essentially liberal notion that integration would bring either benefit or self-esteem to their people. Drawing on—or renewing—themes that had roots in the thought of Du Bois and Garvey, they now argued that white culture, under whose power, laws, and social morality the blacks

52. Gleason, "American Identity," 52.

53. Harold R. Isaacs, *The New World of Negro Americans* (Cambridge, Mass., 1963; London, 1964), 328, 335–39. Another class of self-identified "alienates" was also associated with radical protest, but this author called them "pseudoradicals" and suggested that these young people might be fleeing from personal rather than social or political failures. But there was very little connection between these generally middle-class young people, often based in universities, and the alienated classes of the inner cities or the South, and the two should probably not be compressed into a single movement.

54. James Baldwin, *The Fire Next Time* (London, 1963), 108.

had suffered endless oppression, was an "alien" culture; to urge or force them to assimilate themselves and their children into it was a further act of humiliation and oppression. In a profound reversal of the precepts that had governed the civil rights movement through all the phases that had led to *Brown v. Board of Education*, advocates of Black Power and racial self-esteem now revived Marcus Garvey's demand for separate black schools with a teaching emphasis on black culture and history. Congressional representatives such as Shirley Chisholm denounced the out-moded theory of the melting pot. We must, she declared in 1974, "get rid of this melting pot theory and realize this country is really a salad bowl of all types of groups who have a contribution to make."[55]

The crisis of race relations in the South, the urban disorders in the North, and the increasingly hopeless war in Vietnam did not constitute a favorable background for the propagation of the traditional American values for the enlightenment of the peoples whom those very values had so persistently excluded from the beneficent effects of American history. The new phase of the struggle for equality in America was taking place during a crisis of moral confidence.[56] The situation was not made any the better by the fact that it was the traditional liberals, the sons and heirs of the New Deal, led first by John Kennedy and then by Lyndon Johnson, who committed the nation to its longest and most disastrous overseas war—a war which some well-placed black Americans perceived as having a racial dimension.[57]

Other ethnic minorities began to take notice of these initiatives. If, as Chief Justice Warren had laid down, separate facilities were "inherently unequal," then there were other ingredients of Shirley Chisholm's salad bowl who might claim in some sense to have suffered from the effects of unequal treatment. The most conspicuous and largest in numbers were the various orders of Americans of Spanish descent. The very large numbers who lived in the Southwest were increasing by immigration from Mexico, much of it clandestine; huge numbers had also gained

55. Abigail Thernstrom, "Language: Issues and Legislation," in S. Thernstrom, ed., *Harvard Encyclopedia*, 619–21.

56. This is the argument of Gleason, "American Identity," 52–53; My interpretation adopts its outlines and takes it a little further.

57. The view that the United States was engaged in a racial war in Vietnam was very forcibly put to the author by Kenneth Clark at some unrecorded date about 1970.

ground in eastern cities. Public announcements and advertisements now frequently appeared in the Spanish language. During the same comparatively brief period of the mid- to late 1960s and early 1970s, other groups of more or less distant immigrant status found spokespersons ready to make claims for some sort of compensation for past grievances. A sociologist writing from the self-declared point of view of the minorities of Catholic religion and Balkan, central, or eastern European descent, identified a new form of ethnic politics, which he described as essentially a cultural politics.[58] These peoples could not claim to have been enslaved, and if they had been economically exploited it was only in the same sense as the working classes at large; but the moral damage they had experienced was more subtle and hardly less pervasive. For (it was now argued) their traditional family, religious, and community-centered relationships had suffered grievously, if silently, from the individualistic ethic attributed to the nation's historic rulers and law-givers of Protestant, Anglo-Saxon descent. The prevailing American value system, with its dominant myth of self-help, had in this view divided America more deeply even than the issues of war and race.[59]

The underlying theme of this plea was inspired by a feeling of psychic damage. The demand was for equality of *esteem.*[60] But inequalities of esteem, especially when derived from differing social values, were unfortunately the least susceptible to political remedies. Many of the identified victims were working-class men (the women were not prominent in this depiction) of generally conservative social and political disposition. Apart from blacks and, within limits, the Hispanics, ethnic minorities had not seemed eager to precipitate themselves into political action; which should not be too surprising, since they were already effectively represented, as voters, in traditional political constituencies. The record seemed to be somewhat mixed. Blacks, Jews, Italians, and Slavs generally tended to support candidates of their own image, while Irish and Mexican Americans were less politically motivated. But there were indications here for the future. Positive leadership and the inculcation of pride in

58. Michael Novak, *The Rise of the Unmeltable Ethnics* (New York, 1972), 289.
59. Ibid., 97.
60. Ibid., 12, 19, 55, 69. But the remedy was less certain, and the argument itself was not free from objections. For it was not wholly clear whether the "unmeltable" ethnics of Novak's title had always been there—as the title suggests and the author argues—or whether they had recently risen—as the title also suggests.

ethnic identity were beginning to show that minorities could exert definite if local influences on the outcome of elections.[61]

A marked indication of congressional sensitivity to the new force of ethnicity in politics was the passage in 1972 of the Ethnic Heritage Studies Act, described by its sponsors as "a new federal effort to legitimize ethnicity and pluralism in America"; grants were to be allocated to promote ethnic studies. The emphasis on ethnicity as "a positive constructive force in our society today" was a response to the appeal for equality of esteem—a response whose own force came from its capacity to promote ethnic self-esteem.[62]

It was easier to identify the cultural aspects of ethnic life, which involved such staples as food, church, and family relations, than to discover grievances or interests calling for political intervention. The sheer size, not to mention the very great diversities, of the Spanish-speaking minorities and their linguistic problems brought language itself forward as the principal issue of ethnic politics. Under its prevailing English aegis, the United States had always, throughout its history, been very tolerant of linguistic variety. Martin Van Buren, President of the United States from 1837 to 1841, had been raised in a Dutch-speaking community in Kinderhook, New York;[63] one hundred years after his presidency, no fewer than 237 foreign-language periodicals were published in New York City and ninety-six in Chicago.[64] While English remained the official language of the republic and the states, this proliferation of tongues had never previously been thought to impair the social or economic opportunities of the rising generations. But now it began to appear that the children of Spanish-speaking families were at a serious disadvantage, which was likely to be prolonged throughout their lives.

In a political culture with one recognized language, children of linguistic minorities had an obvious claim to be given enhanced opportunities to acquire that language. Anything less was a denial of equality of opportunity—in a field for which government was plainly responsible.

61. Mark R. Levy and Michael S. Kramer, *The Ethnic Factor: How America's Minorities Decide Elections* (New York, 1972), 19, 24.

62. Richard Polenberg, *One Nation Divisible: Class, Race, and Ethnicity in the United States Since 1938* (New York, 1980), 246.

63. John Niven, *Martin Van Buren: The Romantic Age of American Politics* (New York, 1983), 5.

64. Polenberg, *One Nation Divisible*, 36.

Programs designed for this objective, while maintaining the original language for a period of transition, which were no new thing, gained attention with respect to the increasing needs of the Hispanics. The true meaning of equality in these programs was far from clear. But the makers of public policy were seeking guidance along lines that would be compatible with the rising demands for group satisfaction; and events then turned on a Supreme Court decision arising from the demands, not of Hispanics, but of non-English-speaking Chinese students in San Francisco, who claimed that they had been denied equality of educational opportunity. In *Lau v. Nichols*, decided in 1974, the Court chose between two different views of equality. Instead of relying on the plaintiffs' claims under the equal protection clause of the Fourteenth Amendment, the Court preferred to depend on statute. The guidelines issued by the Department of Health, Education and Welfare under the Civil Rights Act of 1964 banned discrimination on grounds of race, color, or national origin but said nothing about language. The Court countered this omission by assimilating language into the concept of national origin and ordered "affirmative steps to rectify the language deficiency."[65] There was nothing in this judgment that did more than meet the Chinese students' desire to be given the opportunity to learn English, but the department, responding to the almost atmospheric pressure for equality in all things pertaining to group relations, interpreted it as requiring bilingual and even bicultural instruction.

By 1974, under the leadership of senators Edward Kennedy and Alan Cranston, Congress approved legislation that looked towards the positive maintenance of a second language, a move reflecting a gradual departure from the earlier principle that the original language should be retained and supported only during a period of transition. Bilingual instruction now became a statutory requirement.[66] Under the original aegis of the Voting Rights Act of 1965, Congress was incorporating the principles of ethnic protection on the basis of ethnic identification by language. But the principles of equality which dominated the debate only raised further problems; for there were many millions of Americans who had an "original" language in their domestic background. The

---

65. A. Thernstrom, "Language," 626–27; *Lau v. Nichols*, 414 U.S. 563 (1974).
66. A. Thernstrom, "Language," 623–24.

problem for educational policy was to discern linguistic situations that resulted in some ascertainable disadvantage in entering the competitive struggles of an Anglophone culture. The long history of immigration had surely registered a number of successes by earlier generations, so many of whom had come to American shores without any knowledge of the English language. In 1975, Congress simplified the problem by defining four major groups as "linguistic minorities"—these being Alaskan natives, American Indians, Asian Americans, and those of Spanish heritage. By the adoption of the classification of "linguistic disadvantage," Congress had solved the constitutional problem that would undoubtedly have arisen if a specified minority—in this case the objective was the Mexican-American population—had been singled out for protection. For that would have been special, not equal, protection.[67]

As constantly happened in the pursuit of equality, a deeper problem had been revealed. One of the sustaining ideals behind the movement to maintain minority languages was a fundamental respect for the idea of persistent ethnic identity. It was the long-distance retort of America's innumerable minorities, of ever-increasingly diverse origins, to Theodore Roosevelt's reference to "hyphenated Americans"; this was no trivial element in the transformation of consciousness with which this chapter began.

Such a retort was a powerful gesture of ethnic self-respect. Translated into a policy, however, it raised acute problems of choice and even of identity for the individuals who comprised these minorities—for minorities, like majorities, are made up of individuals. The archetypal American ethic of equality of opportunity, which implied an individualistic and ambitious mobility, was not wholly compatible with that of ethnic solidarity, which encouraged individuals to remain within the social and psychological confines of the group. Conscious ethnic movements have been described as "weak systems" when contrasted with the rival incentive of gains in wealth and status—to which, it is here by no means irrelevant to note, competence in the English language is normally indispensable. The retaining power of the group may be strengthened when its language is built into the educational structure, and the attractions of English may be weakened—or weakened during crucially for-

67. Ibid., 627–28.

mative years. But group equality might seem to conflict with that individual equality which builds esteem on personal achievement.[68]

The policy of keeping immigrants' languages in being, when multiplied by a considerable variety of languages, presented immense practical difficulties in resources and organization; it also raised serious questions as to whether this generation of ethnically sensitive reformers was necessarily best equipped to judge the long-term interests of a new generation of American children. It was hard to be sure that the intended beneficiaries of the language program would thank their benefactors for cutting them off from their nation's cultural mainstream. Beyond all this loomed the deeper, unavoidable question of whether these policies envisaged an ultimate, officially recognized, multilingual nation, and what that would mean for law, politics, education, and business. The question gained leverage as an item on the political agenda by its association with the related issue of ethnicity as a principle of political representation.

Ethnicity and Representation

Political representation was the foundation stone in the structure of the republic. American constitutional principles, as articulated by the Supreme Court in the 1960s, required equal representation, meaning equal access to the political process, of all mature citizens. The sole aim of the Voting Rights Act of 1965 was to implement that principle by securing unrestrained access to the political process for black citizens in the southern states. When, within a few years, southern officials introduced new obstacles (such as county-wide voting aimed at reducing the impact of black voting strength), the Supreme Court made use of one of the act's clauses to enforce the right to vote. The essence of the case was that every vote was entitled to equal effect; there could be no justification for "diluted" votes.[69]

The first observation to be made about this combination of legislative and judicial policy was that, for the aims immediately in view, it was a

68. Joshua A. Fishman, "Language Maintenance," in S. Thernstrom, ed., *Harvard Encyclopedia,* 629–37.

69. Abigail M. Thernstrom, *Whose Votes Count? Affirmative Action and Minority Voting Rights* (Cambridge, Mass., 1987), 3–4, 20–21; *Allen v. State Board of Elections,* 393 U.S. 544 (1969).

very striking and visible success. By the very early 1970s, blacks and whites were registering to vote in almost equal proportions in southern states where Negro voting had been almost unheard of for generations. But civil rights workers, white and black, had become convinced that black voting would never reflect the needs of the black communities of the South until it resulted in the election of black men and women to public office. The difference between the *right* to engage in public activities such as entering a restaurant or registering to vote, and the *result* in terms of opportunity or effective representation, was all the difference between formal equality and substantive equality—which is the distinction that President Johnson had in mind in his speech at Howard University. But this distinction might be refined into three possible further categories of action: first, making formal rules, second, bringing about circumstantial conditions which would foster and encourage equal participation, and third, an extension of the second, enforcing this type of "substantive" equality by creating conditions in which the desired outcome would be an almost inevitable consequence of the rules themselves.[70] The example of this third kind which was to emerge as official policy was that of creating electoral districts in which candidates from only one ethnic group could hope to be elected. (It did not, of course, prescribe the individual candidates).

This development could not be attributed to the failure of the Voting Rights Act. After ten years of increasingly effective operation, the act had secured a very large measure of its original aims. But the results still disappointed the more active members of the civil rights movement, who wanted to ensure that the new rules would result in the election of black officials. The distinction to be made here is between what the rules would *permit*, and what the motives and interests of the voting community would actually bring about. More interventionist measures seemed to be required to overcome the southern blacks' generational acquiescence in some or another form of white rule.

---

70. A. Thernstrom, *Whose Votes Count?* ch. 3; Terry Eastland and William J. Bennett, *Counting By Race* (New York, 1979), esp. 118–19; Edwin Dorn, *Rules and Racial Equality* (New Haven, 1979), 4–11. Although Thernstrom and Dorn argue opposite conclusions, Thernstrom's distinction between "formal" and "substantive" equality is close to Dorn's insistence on the need to distinguish between formal rules and actual results. He insists on the importance of focusing on the latter. The third category suggested above reflects my own attempt to refine the possibilities.

The time had arrived for a new act of Congress. The tactics involved a link between the black interest and that of the Mexican Americans, who were also, on these premises, under-represented. Since Mexican-descended Americans could only doubtfully be described as a "race," and not at all by color or religion, the linguistic designation was here introduced, with the concept of linguistic disadvantage as described above.

In the strongly reinforced act of 1975, undoubtedly the most interventionist measure since Reconstruction, the concept of "dilution" as previously explained by Chief Justice Warren was converted into a principle of interpretation justifying federal action. This would not in itself seem to have been a controversial procedure; the doctrine was fully consistent with the principles of the apportionment decisions, and if it was good constitutional law, then it was not merely the right but the duty of the federal power to enforce it. But a significant transmutation then took place in the substantive meaning attributed to "dilution," which was henceforth to be judged by the outcome of elections. The language frequently used by advocates was that voters should have an equal opportunity to elect "representatives of their choice," thus assimilating the cause to that of equality of opportunity.[71] And it soon appeared that when they spoke of "representatives of their choice," the proponents of the new legislation meant representatives of their (that is, the specified ethnic group's) own race or group. Black people, in other words, were to be represented by blacks, Hispanics by Hispanics, and so forth, as far as group designations could be carried. This thesis had not, indeed, been fully established, but it had emerged as a force to be contended with in the debate on equality. After prolonged debates and negotiations in the Senate, the bill passed with a somewhat modified reading of the meaning of "results"; the proportion of minorities elected was reduced to being one consideration, among others, which might be taken into account. But the major proposal was defeated; and the act rejected the proposition that minorities had a right to representatives in strict proportion to their numbers.[72]

This act, nevertheless, was a strong one both in the rights it formulated and in the powers it conferred on the government. Combined with

71. A. Thernstrom, *Whose Votes Count?* 6–7.
72. Ibid., 135–36.

the principle by which, essentially, the test of *intent* behind electoral rules was supplanted by the test of the *results* of those rules, the new legislation took its character from some portion of both the second and the third cases that we have just noticed: it disclaimed the principle of proportional voting, but at the same time it created conditions which would greatly enhance the likelihood that black candidates would be elected. Both the majority of Congress and the new administration of Gerald Ford, who had succeeded Nixon after the latter's resignation in August 1974, were satisfied that the historic conditions under which the South labored, and which its white supremacists had so assiduously maintained until the last ditch of resistance, justified this unprecedented level of Federal intervention. [73]

It is important, in seeking to trace the history of America's pursuit of social justice through ever-increasing elaborations of equality, to recognize that there was nothing inevitable about this particular outcome. It was an immediate result, not of high historic principles bearing their ordained and rightful fruits, but of the complexities of congressional politics and of ethnic alliances generated in the heat of a fluid political situation. And in the context of southern politics, if it was in one sense the consequence of a new sense of urgency in black American leadership, it was also no less a consequence of the strategies of their enemies. If white southern leaders had used their influence to modify white resistance and lead the South into an era of interracial co-operation, instead of inflaming a populist opposition to the very principles of republican democracy, the entire legislative and judicial history of equality in the South would have had the opportunity of taking a different course. It does not fall to the historian to judge what that course would have been.

The idea that equal opportunity to elect representatives of the voters' choice was a means of ensuring that they would choose members of their own race had not been the initial driving force of the act of 1975. But

73. Unprecedented? In terms of predetermining the *racial* composition of a legislature, yes. (Reconstruction legislation was not designed to yield a preconceived representation of freedmen by freedmen or of whites by whites.) But if one steps back from the racial issue and looks at the history of party struggles, it may be argued that every act by which party advantage is secured through a gerrymander of electoral districts, a long if not wholly honorable American tradition, partakes of the same principle. Every gerrymander is by definition a way of designing the electoral rules so as to predetermine electoral outcomes. It remains true, of course, that this level of federal intervention was unprecedented.

it entered into the debates and appeared to gain force from the act itself. In the context of a long history of the suppression of minority interests by majority legislators, and more specifically of black interests by white legislators, it is easy to understand how minority representation almost automatically translated into minority office-holding. An essential element of this assumption, rather less openly recognized, was that people of different races occupied clearly defined areas of residence, as was to a certain extent true of African Americans and also, in important areas, of Hispanics. The principle at issue was that if these considerations were observed, each community would be represented by one of its own members and like would represent like; this principle was sanctioned from the federal bench in Indianapolis in 1969, in a decision by Judge Otto Kerner, who had recently chaired the commission which produced a report on urban violence. But the Supreme Court had other thoughts on the case. It was not the blacks in their capacity as blacks, but the Democrats as a political party, who had lost the election under scrutiny; there were ways of losing elections other than being black.[74] But the Court was less willing to tolerate devices which fell foul of the "dilution" principle, and in *White v. Regester* it held that multi-member districts, in which minority candidates were outvoted throughout the county, failed the Fourteenth Amendment's test of equal protection.[75]

The Voting Rights Act was somewhat modified on its renewal in 1982, when the Senate took the opportunity to insist on denying any claim that members of "protected classes" were entitled to elect members in proportion to their numbers in the population. But the basic test of a discriminatory result was still there. For practical purposes, result remained the key to intent.[76]

Except for those who were set in advance on a particular result and were therefore prepared to shape the rules to achieve it, the issue presented genuine and perplexing difficulties. It had always been difficult to diagnose the symptoms of discriminatory intent; as the Court had implied in *Whitcomb v. Chavis*, any candidate was entitled to win or lose an election on his or her merits and defects, or those of his or her party.

---

74. A. Thernstrom, *Whose Votes Count?* 67–69; *Whitcomb v. Chavis*, 403 U.S. 124 (1971).

75. A. Thernstrom, ibid., 70. The principle recognized by the Court here was that of equal access. Dorn, *Rules*, 88–89; *White v. Regester*, 412 U.S. 755.

76. A. Thernstrom, *Whose Votes Count?* chs. 5 and 6, describe the passage of the act in great detail. I have relied on her account but have added my own comments.

It was not safe to assume that when white candidates lost elections it was on account of the political issues, but when blacks—or Hispanic Americans—lost them it was always on account of "race." (Such a view, indeed, would have very curious consequences for democratic theory.) The test of "result" applied a very broad and often crude brush stroke to the political canvas. But at that level, it had the obvious advantage of appearing with the election returns.

Still further complexities unraveled as electoral districts changed shape. When Petersburg, Virginia, enlarged itself by annexing a neighboring district (incidentally, at the instigation of black business interests), the black constituency was effectively diluted—though plainly not by the "intent" or in the interests of hostile whites. In response to the weakening of black voting strength, the federal court ordered the city to redraw its electoral lines. The object was to re-create a district in which black voters would be as effective, as a bloc, as they had been previously.[77] This judgment appeared to reflect the doctrine that dilution of minority votes was to be avoided, though the language of the Court left room for doubts as to the legal implications. But these doubts were cleared up a few years later when, in 1980, in a case involving the City of Rome, in Georgia, the criterion which determined the Court's opinion was exclusively confined to race: only blacks, in effect, could represent blacks in situations where there was any reason to believe that the races voted as blocs. The courts were not in the habit of doubting that this tendency was the rule in southern politics.[78]

This proposition was open to question. Innumerable cases could by this time be cited of black officers elected with the help of white citizens' votes and of white candidates elected with the help of black votes. There was also room for doubt on two other points. Was it the role of the judiciary to decide how voters should vote, in blocs or otherwise? And was it consistent with the democratic principles of individual equality to maintain, as a matter of policy, a situation which encouraged that—or any other—habit of voting? One of the obvious (if indirect and unintended) effects of creating and maintaining safe "black" seats was to isolate the black community, as well as to diminish electoral competition. Where African American voters were confined to one constituency, they might well be certain of electing *one* African American candidate, but he

77. Ibid., 138–39.
78. Ibid., 154.

or she might also be the only one—or a member of a small, heavily outnumbered and consequently ineffective band. Meanwhile, the African American electorate suffered a diminished capacity to influence white representatives who might have taken their concerns into account if they themselves had needed to rely on black votes. Black citizens who were interested in economic, educational, or other local issues such as public service provision were in danger of forfeiting the opportunity of voting for their primary interests; since most black voters supported the Democrats, and most black voters were corralled into a limited number of districts—sometimes into only one—another effect—not, perhaps, wholly unintended, at least where the Republicans were an electoral force—was to add to the legislative strength of the Republican party.

The idea that minority status, *in an ethnic group*, constituted a particular form of deprivation, demanding redress through the electoral system, was not new when applied to the African American population. There had been a strong element of this consideration to support the political measures of Reconstruction after the Civil War. But it presented a wholly new complex of problems when it reappeared a hundred years later. These problems assumed a new constitutional dimension when the idea of minority representation began to migrate from the circle of African America to those of other minorities.

The Court had sent out signals, where blacks were concerned, that it was willing to recognize the principle of proportional racial representation. But the objects in view could still be defined as specific to the peculiar experience of the African Americans as an oppressed group in American history. The most salient of these was to redress the effects of past inequalities. But another object had appeared, in electoral matters as it had in employment and education, and it had been discovered in the struggle to make equality work in practice, rather than confining it to formal rules. The equality in question resolved itself ultimately as equality of opportunity; and in order to breathe life into the formal rule and translate that ideal into living practice it was necessary to inject an element of social psychology into the situation; members of the oppressed minority had somehow to be made to *believe* in themselves—to believe that their efforts were worthwhile, and that if they made those efforts, the system would work for them as it had done for others. Not merely black electors, but, as we have seen, black legislators, commissioners, mayors and councillors were the visible signs that the system did work. But if blacks were truly a special case, could the arguments that

applied to them be adopted by other minorities? Should the "cultural politics" of the descendants of eastern and central Europe undergo a translation into forms requiring the same kind of political representation?

It was the black leadership, clearly, who set the example. But the example was infectious, and the theory of justified compensation for past deprivations did not stay indoors. In 1979 the Department of Justice required the city of Houston to draw its electoral lines so as to provide for the specific, linguistically defined interests of inner-city minorities, who in this case were predominantly Mexican Americans.[79] The ethnic thesis was making two powerful claims: to be generalized into American culture, and to be translated into American electoral politics.

The sense of belonging to a distinctive culture, which retained its own style and integrity while being included in the pluralistic American whole, may well have had exceptional values deriving from the history of American immigration and settlement. In a world where ethnicity was taken for granted, the mere absence of any defining ethnic identity might be considered a stigma.[80] Many advocates of some form of pluralism had expressed their desire to retain what they believed to be a quintessential strain of ethnicity; Jewish identity had been a strong case in point, as witnessed earlier in the century by Horace Kallen. But ethnic identity was inherently unstable. It tended to disappear, to change shape and character, or to manifest itself chiefly in holiday parades and celebrations, while many of the individual members of these communities, in the course of their daily lives, mixed freely with others in the workplace, in schools and colleges, in entertainments, neighborhoods, laundry basements, and (sometimes consequently) weddings.

These instabilities, however deplorable to the core of ethnic retentionists, seemed to follow inevitably from the frailties of a volatile human nature in a relatively free society. But the reformers of the voting laws were not daunted by these tendencies. They argued both that ethnicity ought to be protected because it tended to erode, and that it ought to be respected because of its power of survival.[81] The United States was

---

79. A. Thernstrom, "Language," 628.

80. Harold J. Abramson, "Assimilation and Pluralism," in S. Thernstrom, ed., *Harvard Encyclopedia*, 159.

81. Both these contingencies seem to be present in Novak's statement that many persons do not think of themselves as belonging to any one ethnic group after three or four generations of intermarriage. "All sorts of material in their psyche are suppressed." (This raises some question as to how their existence is known.) But on what basis is one

not, like the Soviet Union, a republic of nations; but the new wave of reformers seemed willing to contemplate with equanimity the prospect of a republic of political ethnicities.

The proposed reforms of 1982 did nothing to assuage the fears of those critics who perceived a distinct trend towards the politicization of ethnic identity. The two points of view were plainly seen and frankly stated. In 1977, J.F. Paulucci, the national chairman of the Italian American Foundation (the hyphen had been dropped) hinted broadly at the opportunities that would be open once compensatory racial preferences entered into public policy. He wanted to extend the preferences to include white ethnics from southern and eastern Europe, who also suffered from under-representation in higher education and the professions. "To do anything less," he asserted "is to promote racism, not to eradicate it." Colleges and universities should adapt their admissions procedures to the ethnic composition of the populations they served. [82] It was in answer to this principle that Professor Henry Abraham warned the Senate committee, "This is not India; there is no right to be represented on the basis of group membership." The United States, in other words, was a republic of equal citizens, not a republic of ethnic or religious groups. Another critic, after pointing out that the Constitution spoke only of individuals, asked whether individuals were elected to office to represent individual citizens or to represent ethnic or racial blocs of voters? [83] The difficulties were compounded by disputes over the question of who had the right to determine the kind of group characteristics which constituted an ethnic identity entitled to political rights. In a bitterly fought case arising from a redrawn electoral boundary which split a Hasidic Jewish community in New York in order to accommodate the interests of blacks, it appeared that the Hasidics attached much more importance to their religious identity than to their more general characterization as "whites." The Court decided, however—the year was 1977—that the petitioners had no constitutional right to representation

---

rather than another of these intermingled ethnicities deemed to have survived the others? (32–33). The same problem presented itself to Horace Kallen, as discussed above in Chapter 10, pp. 303–4.

82. Allan P. Sindler, *Equal Opportunity: On the Policy and Politics of Compensatory Minority Preferences*, American Enterprise Institute (Washington, 1983), 14.

83. A. Thernstrom, *Whose Votes Count?* 132. It is not quite clear on what basis Abraham thought that the citizens of India were represented politically as members of ethnic or religious groups.

in their character as Hasidic Jews.[84] It seemed that in the Court's view, either one of two views could be taken: that ethnicity had no claim on the politics of representation, or that black ethnicity had such a claim, Hispanics might have one, but others did not. This judgment, not surprisingly, did nothing to check the dynamics of the issue; when the time came some ten years later to revise the charter of New York City, the solons of that metropolis made it a principle of the electoral system that the ethnic groups who formed the City's population were entitled so far as possible to be represented by their own kind.[85]

Two variant theories of representation, drawing their inspiration from the same roots, now bore mature fruit in American constitutional soil. Both claimed the authority of equal rights. One vested those rights in equal individuals; the other agreed that these individuals were politically equal but identified the political choices available to them with the fortunes of the ethnic groups to which they were, voluntarily or involuntarily, assigned. This development had remote antecedents in the idea that such groups as Massachusetts towns were the true measures of equality in the eighteenth century;[86] but its true historical sources lay in the history of immigration and the limited success of the concept of assimilation. It might be considered as the latest and most mature form of American federalism, but it was not a federalism to which the founders of the republic had subscribed, or that, in the circumstances of 1787, they could have envisaged.[87]

84. *United Jewish Organizations v. Carey*, 45 L.W. 422 (1979); Dorn, *Rules*, 93–96.

85. Charter of New York City, 1988, chapter 2-A, sec. 50, b. 1: "The commission shall have among its members (a) at least one resident of each borough, and (b) members of the racial and minority groups in New York City which are protected by the United States Voting Rights Act of nineteen hundred sixty-five, as amended, in proportion, as close as practicable, to their population in the city."

86. This principle was stated as a protest against the Constitution of 1780; it did not prevail and has no apparent continuity with the principle of group identity asserted later.

87. This statement is based on the historical memories and republican concepts available in 1787. Its claim to historical authenticity does not give it any additional validity as a criticism of the new "ethnic federalism" suggested above. The Constitution is an organism, adaptable to changes in the fundamental structures of the republic.

Chapter Fourteen

Equality and Justice

The Categories of Equality in the Trial of History

Equality had proved to be an infinitely more complex subject than it had seemed to most of its exponents and devotees of earlier generations, including the Founders of the republic. That at least was clear to anyone who stood back and viewed in their historical perspectives the plethora of legislation, court decisions, and social comment, together with more formal works of philosophy and political science.

It is true that even in the early period, in which American principles of republican government were first codified, equality was already capable of presenting complex problems to the philosophers and law-givers of the Enlightenment. But in essence they believed that to the relatively limited extent that equality came within the compass of political aspiration, it could be secured by essentially political rules. When the right rules had been made and those rules conformed to the principles of equality, then the consequences that flowed from them would satisfy the moral requirements of the philosophy of equality. In this light, political equality could mean nothing less than equal access (for those individuals to whom it applied) to the political process, through equality of votes in equal districts. The importance of this fundamental principle was demonstrated more than a century and a half later by the dramatic changes in the structure of power throughout the southern states in the wake of the Voting Rights Act and the apportionment decisions of the Supreme Court.

American society in 1787 was more deferential than two hundred years later, but to those who enjoyed the advantages of citizenship, its politics afforded more direct and equal access. Substantive change, occurring with the creation and development of political parties, took the form of greatly enlarging the class of citizens rather than of advancing or refining the concept of political equality. But experience proved that equality of access to the externals of the system tended to leave the individual dissatisfied, even disillusioned. Political participation gave only a limited smack of the sensation of political power, and experience was to prove, if only gradually, that political access did not give control over many other aspects of economic, educational, and social opportunity that were equally vital to the goal of controlling one's own life. In politics alone, moreover, the individual was liable to feel dwarfed rather than empowered by the huge numbers of voters among whom he (and later, she) was only one. But voting was, nevertheless, an act of power, of participation, an assertion of the political self. It was a social as well as a strictly political act. As the politics of the republic grew more sophisticated, there seemed paradoxically to be much more reason for concern about the very small numbers who thought the exertion was worthwhile. But this was due at least partly to the recondite complexity of the political process itself, which was giving rise to other reasons for concern. In the intricacies of lobbies, of committee appointments which owed little to representative principles, of public hearings but private deals, the idea of political equality seemed a blunt weapon with neither weight nor edge. More particularly after the advent of television as the principal means of publicity and campaigning, the enormous funds raised by campaigners for public office seemed increasingly to exclude or diminish the weight and significance of the individual. More subtle problems unfolded when experience probed the limits of the elementary formal rules which set up equality as a mode of procedure. In the search for formal equality, men and women also discovered deeper aspirations within themselves and consequently made stronger demands on the system.

The concept of equality as a set of rules was no less prominent in the field of law. Due process of law was what it claimed to be—process, equally fair and accessible to all, but saying nothing of any constitutional requirement that the laws be equal in substance. The idea of "substantive" due process began to widen an opening gap in the social dimen-

sions of law even before the Civil War; a law which deprived a man of his property—slave property in this case—was bad and invalid law because it deprived him without going through a legal process against his claim to that property.[1] Chief Justice Taney may not have intended to use the Dred Scott case to introduce a new jurisprudence, but the principle was open to extension. The concept of equal protection, once introduced into the Constitution by the Fourteenth Amendment in 1868, was more creative. A person who was deprived of certain other equalities might reasonably claim that a law which permitted or sanctioned such deprivations was failing in its duty to afford him, or her, equal protection. This rule was fraught with enormous potentialities for substantive social change under the cover of law. The political path was to prove tortuous, but the law moved from rules to substance when the political situation permitted. In many ways indeed, the law led and showed the way to the legislator.

If the First Amendment's elliptical pronouncements forbidding establishment of religion but enshrining the right of free exercise were to be considered the guiding rule of the federal government, the imbalance between them was certain to make the rule bend under the weight of substance. It could not be said here that the rule laid down by the amendment enforced recognizably equal principles. It was more indicative of the organic character of the Constitution, rather than the consequence of its inner logic, that a rule of equality which had been formulated from the experience of sectarian rivalries proved eventually to be arguable as a protection for the conscience of the individual. Equality was in this sense a very individual matter.

The problem in the case of sex might be stated as a matter of effecting a transition in nomenclature: from sex to gender. The problem was inherently one of substance, and rules restricting the legal, economic, and political powers and liberties of women reflected a widely held view of their natural capacities. It is this that has justified the treatment of sex as a separate category of equality in this study. In none of these cases could it be safely said that the rules led directly to forms of equality that were either satisfying to all concerned, or ultimately stable. And this dissatisfaction and instability arose from the ferment in the other categories, equality of opportunity and equality of esteem.

1. The leading case is *Dred Scott v. Sandford*, 19 Howard 393 (1857), discussed above, pp. 181–85.

In the most influential philosophical work of the era, John Rawls described self-respect as "perhaps the most important primary good."[2] He defined self-respect as an ability, within one's powers, to fulfill one's intentions. This definition was in tune with the concept of ability to control one's environment, which the sociologist James S. Coleman had recently used when introducing his celebrated report, commissioned by Congress, on school conditions in the South.[3]

The problem of self-respect was inextricably connected to that of equal respect. We have argued in earlier chapters that the American Revolution contributed to increasingly articulate demands for the individualization of equality of esteem. This process was more subversive—and more creative—in the socially inflected historical context within which it occurred than it has tended to appear in later generations, and not least since the upheaval of the French Revolution. American ideals mixed with American events to liberate the individual from the trammels of rank, class, or "order," while of course leaving a very large proportion of individuals subject to the impositions of race or caste, as well as those of gender.

The political results were often turbulent, sometimes confused, at least colorful. But the ideologies associated with the republic did not place the problems of social esteem, or the protection of self-esteem, within the immediate orbit of political authority. The Constitution and the laws did not speak to the issue of esteem; it was not in their province. Even if political agendas had extended to such matters in the eighteenth century,

2. John Rawls, *A Theory of Justice* (Oxford, 1972), 433, 440.

3. James S. Coleman et al., *Equality of Educational Opportunity* (Washington, D.C., 1966); listed as *Coleman Report*. There is no internal evidence, however, that Rawls was influenced by the Coleman Report, which is not mentioned in his book. This view of self-respect is consistent with that of Bernard Williams, who defines it as "a certain human desire to be identified with what one is doing, to be able to realise purposes of one's own, and not to be the instrument of another's will unless one has voluntarily accepted such a role." Bernard Williams, *Problems of the Self* (Cambridge, 1973), 322–24. Respect was also identified as a vital category by Christopher Jencks and his associates, who reviewed a vast bulk of evidence about schooling and the family in *Inequality: A Reassessment of the Effect of Family and Schooling in America* (New York, 1972). In place of self-respect they used the term "prestige" and noted that American society was committed by its professed values to attaching different measures of prestige to different occupations. The type of respect of which they speak is related to what people do rather than to what they are by birth or inheritance. Jencks was in agreement with Coleman that the effects of schooling were socially trivial but went on to argue that socialism was the only system that could produce the equality to which Americans were committed.

they would not have been easily reconciled with the strong strand of American whig ideology that constituted the Revolution's other specific contribution—which was precisely to reduce the government's bearing on individual lives. Of the categories of equality defined through the study of this subject in American history, that of equality of esteem has always been the most elusive, the most difficult to define, and the least amenable to specific or political interventionism.

Our conceptual formulation, however, has been made possible, and eventually necessary, by the ways in which the issue was politicized. That was a historical process, and emerges through the turbulent phases of many periods in American history. A brief return to the historical development of the consciousness of esteem as a force in social life will explain its significance as a political force—or better, perhaps, as a somewhat diffuse scatter of political forces.

African America put this issue to its most extreme test, because no element of the American population experienced the meaning of the deprivation of social esteem, with concomitant economic, legal, and political disempowerment, more intensely than its African Americans. Physical and economic oppression produced their obvious consequences in psychological oppression. A brief review of the reflections of African American social thinkers on their own experience of the problem will therefore serve to illuminate the whole issue as a critical test of the meaning of equality in its American dimensions. These dimensions of the racial problem had long been known and understood in the more reflective quarters of the black community. In the mid-1870s, the Reverend Alexander Crummell, an Episcopal clergyman recently settled in Washington after a long period of service in Liberia, set out to reclaim a sense of racial solidarity and pride for his people. Although his own mission, and his aspirations to leadership, were not altogether successful, his theme gained strength as southern oppression deepened. Crummell was one of the earlier black leaders to draw attention to the fundamental problem of the alienation of black Americans from, or rather *within*, American society—which was also their own society.[4] This theme was later to be propounded with greater eloquence by his young disciple, W.E.B. Du Bois: the veil through which the Negro perceived America

---

4. Alexander Crummell, "The Social Principle Among a People," in *The Greatness of Christ and Other Sermons* (New York, 1882), 290–91.

was also a veil through which he saw himself, yielding "a peculiar sensation, this double-consciousness, this sense of always looking at oneself through the eyes of others, of measuring one's soul by the tape of a world which looks on in amused contempt and pity. One ever feels his two-ness,—an American, a Negro; two souls, two thoughts, two unreconciled strivings; two warring ideals in one dark body, whose dogged strength alone keeps it from being torn asunder."[5] These words were written early in a career that was to lead Du Bois, as we have seen, in the direction of strong racial affirmation, for reasons which affected so many talented and aspiring black people. Twenty years earlier, in 1883, the Bethel Literary and Historical Association in Washington had held a lively debate on racial pride and unity. One speaker put a finger on the recurring question—it was to become salient again a century later—when he argued that the trouble with making it a policy to stress individual rather than racial achievements was that "the white people will not let you get rid of the idea of race." As the debate continued in the pages of the Negro press, contributors urged the importance to Negro self-advancement of the theme that the race must supply its own standards of behavior. The Kansas lawyer and editor C.J.H. Taylor pointed out that Negroes were weakened by their own habit of self-depreciation. "We have no reason to complain until we take more pride in our own," he observed, a state of affairs which was not improved while Negroes hated themselves, despised their own folk songs, bleached their skins, and straightened their hair.[6]

This essential spirit of self-esteem, and the need to inspire it when it was weak and enfeebled, was never absent from the motive force of black protest. It emerged in moments of great crisis and endurance such as bus boycotts and struggles for admission to schools reaching back before the Civil War, and forward to the famous Montgomery bus boycott of 1955.[7] Just as surely it was present in a minor matter of etiquette that found its way to the Supreme Court in 1964. The Alabama state prosecutor had insisted on addressing a black woman, Mary Hamil-

5. W.E.B. Du Bois, *The Souls of Black Folk* (Chicago, 1903), 3.

6. August Meier, *Negro Thought in America, 1880–1915* (Ann Arbor, Michigan, 1968), 50–51.

7. J. Morgan Kousser, " 'The Supremacy of Equal Rights': The Struggle Against Racial Discrimination in Antebellum Massachusetts and the Foundations of the Fourteenth Amendment," *Northwestern University Law Review* 82:4 (Summer 1988), 941–1010.

ton, as "Mary." She refused to answer his questions until he addressed her as "Miss Hamilton." The state supreme court, finding the name Mary "an appropriate appellation," convicted her of contempt of court. But the appeal carried to the Supreme Court of the United States, which held that it was the prosecutor who was in contempt of the proprieties of judicial procedure.[8] This minuscule episode encapsulated a charge of enormous moral significance. On a seemingly trivial question of forms of address there turned the fundamental issue of equality of esteem. But this was not a mere matter of procedure; it is arguable that the depreciation of Miss Hamilton's status as a person could be expected to entail her depreciation as a witness. Before the abolition of slavery, southern courts could not hear evidence by black people against whites.

Mary Hamilton was not lacking in self-respect. Supported by anger and impatience, self-respect carried the blacks through the Montgomery bus boycott and into the dangerous sit-ins and demonstrations of subsequent years. But no one could seriously doubt that being perpetually subjected to contemptuous or supercilious treatment had a damaging effect on the self-estimation of many of the victims, especially when these attitudes supported a complex social structure which effectively deprived them of just that ability to control their own circumstances which has been identified as essential to—even to be the defining feature of—self-respect. The evidence given, notably by Kenneth Clark, at *Brown v. Board of Education*, had introduced to a wider audience the information that children in school respond to diminished expectations with diminished performances. This—along with its opposite—have since become a commonplace of educational theory.

When the white political philosophers of the mid-twentieth century, supported by the amenities of the university and the reports of research, discovered the category of self-respect, and when they related it to equality, they were thus not saying anything that their black fellow citizens had not discovered long before. But there were important differences. One was that the white academics were able to reach a much wider and far more influential audience; henceforth, the issue could never be completely ignored. Another was that they both refined the concept of respect and produced new evidence from research into the character

8. Morroe Berger, *Equality By Statute: The Revolution in Civil Rights* (Garden City, N.Y., 1968), 116–17.

and consequences of its denial; and these resources enabled them to weave the theme of equality of respect, both as a social and a personal category, into intricate arguments about the obligations of society as a whole. Political philosophy was enlarged in the process.

Political philosophy was itself a product of social experience. The experiences of African Americans were different in intensity from those of other ethnic, religious, linguistic, or economically disadvantaged groups; for European Americans, especially, Americanization could often be a positive discovery of self-esteem. This view, which sharply differentiates white from black America, derives support from historical observation from a very early period of America's independent existence. Its importance lay not only in the ability of American society to validate the claims of the individual but, more subtly, in its power to explain the kind of social bonding which had served to keep the order of American society. Observant visitors had for several generations noticed a certain immediacy in American social relations, a personal, one-to-one familiarity which impressed them as differing from comparable relations in Europe. "The rich man shakes hands with the worker and talks with him," wrote the duke de la Rochefoucauld-Liancourt when the republic was barely twenty years old, "not as elsewhere in order to honour him, but as one who may need his help one day—and further, without calculation, by habit, by education." The contrast between honest informality and artificial manners was obviously a contrast with France, where citizenship had lately come into vogue; but the wholesome straightforwardness between people as individuals struck him as "very satisfying to the free soul." Many comparable remarks may be found until Alexis de Tocqueville made equality of conditions the central theme of his own book—a state of affairs that afforded daily "delights" to the free citizen.[9] The English visitor Barbara Bodichon was impressed some twenty years later by the pride in being American that she found in German and French immigrants to America. "It makes them feel at home, gives them an importance which they probably never had before, makes them respect themselves, gives them a standing which creates a new motive for self-improvement," she observed—which led to caustic comments

---

9. La Rochefoucault-Liancourt, *Voyage dans les États-Unis, fai en 1795, 1796 et 1797,* 5 vols. (Paris, L'An VII de la République), 253–56; Alexis de Tocqueville, *De la Démocratie en Amérique,* ed. J.-P. Mayer (Paris, 1961). For "Delights," see above, pp. 136–37.

on the humbug people talked in England about all people being equal before God. [10]

Some thirty years later a far more famous Briton, James Bryce, devoted a section to "Equality" in his book *The American Commonwealth*. [11] His definition of the subject included "estimation," which was essential to the popular meaning of equality. Bryce, who was not favorably impressed with Tocqueville's abstract treatment and wanted to put the study of the United States on a firmer footing, was bound to observe the great changes that had taken place. Inequality of wealth had grown greatly in the past sixty years and would continue to grow; he saw no prospect of a return to primitive simplicities, and American ideals accepted these developments because the gifts and attainments of men who had won great wealth by the exercise of remarkable talents were felt to be a credit to the nation. Bryce was too observant to miss the grades and distinctions of society which, without tangible expression, were as sharply drawn as in Europe; the exclusiveness of the "best sets" was spreading, he noticed, from the East into the western cities. Yet there remained with him profound impression that seemed to outweigh these refinements, an "equality of estimation" based on the simple fact that "in America men hold others to be at bottom exactly the same as themselves." He obviously liked the earthy realism with which Americans looked on men of high achievement. "Respect for attainment excites interest, even reverence," he observed, but it did not lead a man to treat the object of his respect "as if he were made of porcelain and you only of earthenware." [12] The attitude was noticed even among servants. He remarked that on the West Coast, colored people often sat down to table with whites, although he noted the ill-treatment of the Chinese there. On the whole Bryce averted his attention from the more serious aspects of race relations; the American Commonwealth that formed the subject of his observations, in his earlier editions, was an almost entirely white commonwealth.

Two years earlier, the great steelmaster Andrew Carnegie, a child of impoverished Scottish weavers, had extolled the different but intercon-

10. Barbara Leigh Smith Bodichon, *An American Diary 1857–8*, ed. Joseph W. Reed, Jr. (London, 1972), 72–73.

11. James Bryce, *The American Commonwealth*, 2 vols. (Chicago, 1891) 2:615–27.

12. Ibid., 622.

nected categories of equality in a fanfare of praise that began with the dedication of his book, *Triumphant Democracy:* "To the BELOVED REPUBLIC under whose equal laws I am made the peer of any man, although denied political equality by my native land, I DEDICATE THIS BOOK with an intensity of gratitude and admiration which the native-born citizen can neither feel nor understand." And in his preface he explained that the republic had "removed the stigma of inferiority which his native land saw proper to impress on him at birth, and has made him, in the estimation of its great laws as well as in his own estimation (much the more important consideration), the peer of any human being who draws the breath of life, be he pope, kaiser, priest or King—henceforth the subject of no man, but a free man, a citizen!" [13] Equal laws here did much to *confer* equality of esteem, as with the other European immigrants commented on by Barbara Bodichon. But this was, perhaps, as Carnegie hinted, a first-generation phenomenon. Nor do we have here the witness of the steel workers who fought out their cause in the great Pittsburgh strike of 1892, while their master remained at his Scottish castle in Skibo.

Rights and Social Respect

The political significance of the issue of esteem had emerged again and again in periods of stress and crisis. But it was wholly characteristic of the American experience—and, we may perhaps add, of the American contribution to the more general aspects of the subject—that these formulations were provoked by *denials* of respect. The nationalized consciousness of the issue in the mid-nineteenth century produced something more than specified demands for rectification of abuses: it produced, as we have seen, a formal philosophy.

John Rawls's pronouncement that self-respect was the most important primary good, however, had been preceded by the qualification "perhaps." The caution was prudent. For on further inquiry, as conducted by Robert Lane, self-respect might prove to be a less than primary good, and in some cases to be not a good at all. At its best, it was to be considered as a means to other goods, such as the right to work, which offered the opportunity to achieve. Where self-respect—here used inter-

13. Andrew Carnegie, *Triumphant Democracy, or The Fifty Years' March of the Republic* (New York, 1886), dedication and pp. v–vi.

changeably with self-esteem—was based on achievement rather than ascription, the right to work was the right to *achieve* self-esteem. Self-esteem based on achievement, Lane argued, was more satisfactory both for the individual and for society than self-esteem based on ascription. For the one, it yielded a higher satisfaction; for the other, it served as a source of energy for society. [14] But self-esteem might do more harm than good in cases where an individual derived his or her own self-esteem from making invidious or injurious comparisons with others—which human nature and the competitive ethos of modern times ensured would not be an uncommon phenomenon. [15]

Modern American society claimed, in a general sort of way, to award esteem on the basis of what people did, or how much they had earned, rather than what they ascriptively *were* (whether Texas millionaires, old southern black families, or immigrant Nigerian taxi-drivers). It would be no great exaggeration to say that American society's own claims to self-esteem depended in no small measure on the ability to make this claim about itself with some credibility.

But this thesis revealed a fundamental flaw in any plausible attempt to establish a unified theory of equality. Modern society was extremely complex. It was also in a normal state of internal fluctuation. And the argument for achievement derived its social justification from the equally fundamental American principle of equality of opportunity. Where men and women had equal opportunities to work, it was inevitable that they would begin with different interests and aims in life and find themselves attaining to a widely differentiated variety of occupations, from doctor and lawyer to postman (or woman), janitor, or teacher, all of which attracted widely different levels of social esteem.

14. This observation is no doubt generally valid for modern America, but it is not a universal truth. European landowners had traditionally attached far greater value to the status deriving from the leisure based on rents from their tenants than on the status of their tenants drawn from their toil in the fields.

15. Robert E. Lane, "Government and Self-Esteem," *Political Theory* 10:1 (February 1982), 5–29. The controlling assumption is that a society which sustains economic growth is better off as a whole than a society whose economy is static. The middle ages did not produce theoretical economists, but that was perhaps because the concept of growth was unknown. Where self-esteem is carefully measured in terms of the personal or family consumption of highly advertised consumer goods, and is monitored through the eyes of watchful neighbors, the power to consume becomes a primary interest of all classes, and organized labor is much engaged in protecting or enlarging it. Rawls notes that the pursuit of self-respect may set people at odds with each other. *Justice*, 545–46.

Lane had anticipated this difficulty by an empirical finding with important theoretical consequences. Careful investigation revealed that people cared less about *equality* of opportunity than about having *some* opportunity. The skilled worker compared his lot with that of his immediate circle, of those a little above and a little below in the hierarchy of positions that were in principle, attainable by all the workforce. He (or, increasingly, she) might be aggrieved by some local, visible inequality but was unlikely to resent the inequalities that shone from unattainable stars in the corporate hierarchy.[16]

This insight was capable of extension. If people cared more for practical opportunity within their own grasp than for some abstract notion of equality of it, then they could be expected to care more for the quantum of esteem proper to their occupation and afforded to—and among—their social circles, than to yearn for the esteem attaching to the great. Unattainable heights were not normally objects of envy. The effect was to soften the hard edges of social resentment. It should be noticed, however, that this argument makes equality of opportunity into a cardinal principle of American ideology, while permitting esteem to follow as it may in the wake of opportunity.

Equality and the Obligations of Society: The Quest for a Theory

The words *respect* and *esteem*, though they have different derivations, are used almost interchangeably, and dictionaries tend to use them to define each other. They are frequently interchangeable in the writings of modern thinkers. But Michael Walzer, in his argument for the possibility of an egalitarian value system in a complex society, distinguishes self-esteem from self-respect. It is the latter that involves *socially purposeful role or occupation*, and therefore approximates to the kind of respect that forms the main object of Lane's discussion of *esteem*.[17] A physician is respected by others for his social value, but we may hope that a self-

16. Robert E. Lane, "The Fear of Equality," *American Political Science Review* 53:1 (March 1959). This perception is closely allied to the theme of "relative deprivation," as developed by W.G. Runciman, *Relative Deprivation and Social Justice: A Study of Attitudes to Social Inequality in Twentieth Century England* (Harmondsworth, 1972).

17. Michael Walzer, *Spheres of Justice: A Defense of Pluralism and Equality* (New York, 1983), 274.

respecting physician will treat patients according to their needs, not their fees; [18] a carpenter may be less socially honored, but a self-respecting carpenter will take pride in the perfection of his or her work. Walzer places the concept of esteem in the slightly less estimable light which attaches more closely to unearned distinctions.

For Walzer, the concept of respect (as distinct from esteem) belongs to *acquired* roles in life. John Rawls's point of departure, by contrast, was a position of primary equality in which individuals, shrouded by a veil of ignorance, do not know what their position in life will be. At the point where their moral values are formed, they have no acquired roles. Subsequent departures from equality may occur, but are justifiable only if they are to everyone's advantage, not least to the advantage of the least well-off. [19] From the moral consequences of the "original position," Rawls was able to develop the view, which earlier philosophers had held for other reasons, that all persons ought to treat each other with respect due to their human character, an attitude which assumes a basic regard for the equality of persons in some moral capacity. This fundamental requirement of mutual respect is the basis of Kant's command, discussed by Rawls in some detail, that people are always to be treated as ends in themselves, never as mere instruments of others' purposes.

Rawls's moral person is assumed to have a conception of his own good and is also assumed to have a sense of justice. Moral personality may not always be fully present, but it exists in normal persons as a potentiality capable of being realized. This statement seems to express a principle of fundamental moral importance, but nevertheless of somewhat limited application. For the statement that people owe each other *equal* esteem in their capacity as moral beings had earlier been criticized on the grounds that respect alone does the required work: the idea of equality has nothing to add to it. What is required of people is simply that they treat each other as complete human beings, each of whom is, for him or herself, an end and not a means. [20]

18. That at least is the principle. It has often been noted, however, that brain surgeons are rated higher than those who operate on lower parts of the body, though their work is not more difficult or necessary, which suggests that there is some sort of irrational allocation of esteem at work in society.

19. Rawls, *Theory of Justice*, 19, 60–62. There is of course more than one sense in which one may be more or less well off; the world of folklore, not to say fairy tale, tells us that the poor may be more honest and therefore happier than their social superiors.

20. Stanley I. Benn, "Egalitarianism and the Equal Consideration of Interests," in J.R. Pennock and J.W. Chapman, eds., *Nomos IX: Equality* (New York, 1967), 66–67. The

Egalitarian theory would impose an impossible burden on judgment if it required each person to ask whether the respect t people are held to owe to each other, simply because they are p was to be *all* the respect they owed to each other for any reason Stated like this, the demand for equality of respect becomes unk and not worth holding.

Societies live by meeting the needs of their members. The qu tions required to meet these needs will always bear some relat the esteem in which the persons bearing those qualificatio held—varying with supply and demand, changes in fashion, a merous ephemeral criteria. It need not follow that such persons be accorded more respect than is due to them for the exercise of functions. But societies do not work with such rational simplicit perhaps an excess of rationality tends to dehumanize humar tions.[21]

Personal esteem has always been a variable item in the free p human relations. In the relations of individuals, it cannot be dicta determined by governments. But one of the most massive chan American history had nevertheless taken shape in this elusive but sive arena of social esteem. To an extent and depth unheard of in generations, American governments in the years after the Second War found themselves ineluctably drawn into responsibility f

argument raises to a theoretical level the question of whether the idea of equa bear the weight of any concrete meaning, since all the interests that make cla equality can express them in other terms without much loss of persuasion. The ar is developed by Peter Westen, "The Empty Idea of Equality," *Harvard Law Ret* 3 (January 1982), 537–96. This does nothing to diminish the force of the fact that have historically believed, often with passion and sometimes with subtlety, that e however understood, was the soul of social justice. We have noticed that n Aristotle was immune to this notion. Such beliefs have power to move events, an events can be understood in the light of such beliefs; to this extent, they deser treated with respect by the historian, if not by the philosopher. They *are* treat respect by philosophers, notably Bernard Williams (*Problems of the Self*) and Nagel who, in "Equality," suggests that formal equality should be considered value among two principal others—utilitarianism and individual rights. See *Mortal Questions* (Cambridge, 1979).

21. "He is a good scholar but a terrible chairman"; "she is a great sin impossible as a member of the cast"; "he is a skilful carpenter but a bad father." I may add their own examples. In each case, a distinction is made pertaining to the function, and these distinctions are constantly made in practice. But a certain res respect usually attaches to the person on account of his or her talent or achievem the moral difficulties, however, consider George Bernard Shaw, *The Doctor's D*

ndefinable field, if not of personal esteem, then of

ne political as a protest rather than as a demand.
igious, and other ethnic groups, notably African
the first instance, wanted to free themselves from
teem of their fellow citizens. Equality of esteem
: of negative demand—an entitlement not to be
or arbitrary and irrational reasons. It appeared
to link the individual with the group by identify-
lividuals in their group capacity; this fact of social
y that individual problems would be solved en-
m of group recognition. But the American ideol-
s distracted the attention of political scientists
ted by social and economic rather than ethnic
s of class are not less damaging for being better
e in fact both more openly acknowledged and
e organized working men of the Jackson era.)
less or unsuccessful individuals—often taking
h them—was not alleviated by the harshness
f competitive values condemned failure. To fail
ings but social esteem. There was not much that
d do to help.

although "respect" and "esteem" are frequently
e used by some writers in different ways. A
lly useful refinement may help to clarify this
ns. "Respect" may be thought of as a political
e concern owed by government equally to all
station of equal *respect* that governments are
y in political access, equality before the law,
lom, equality of opportunity, equality as be-
one without distinction of race or religion,
iomic class. In this sense, we can now say that
ic, though without having subscribed to it as
r all, believe in the political sense of equality
llow that the government can confer equal

athan Cobb, *The Hidden Injuries of Class* (Cambridge,

[468]

esteem on individuals, or that it can or ought to intrude so far as to try. What it evidently can do is to use its power over respect to influence esteem by removing the economic and institutional obstacles which cast deep shadows on the esteem in which otherwise promising people are held, frequently blighting their prospects and drying up their hopes.

Ronald Dworkin has argued that government can treat people as equals in the scheme of property it designs; this proposal concerns our concept of respect. But to treat them as equals will not necessarily mean maintaining them as equals; he adds that people are not therefore obliged to treat *each other* as equals, whatever the scheme assigns to them. Society has at its collective disposal a vast range of resources, in material goods, nature, and the variety of human talents. In adjudicating equal concern, in Dworkin's view, equality in the distribution of resources is the foundation. Where resources are understood to include rights, this principle assigns to government its proper role in a complex society. Since the objects of this equal concern are individuals, Dworkin's analysis respects the individualistic basis of equality which underlies the mainstream of the Western tradition since, at least, the Enlightenment, as well as the American Constitution. [23]

Modern government exercises great powers over the allocation of the nation's resources—so much so that it can neither act nor refrain from acting without effectively making a difference. [24] This accretion of governmental power has been the principal feature of political development over more than two centuries. It cannot be undone, and no amount of rhetoric can unwind it. In measures such as the act of Congress which allocated certain resources to minority firms in Southern California (and gave rise to the *Fullilove* case) public policy was actuated by a desire to show the flag of equality of respect through its distribution of resources among a cluster of minority interest groups. Two points of caution need attention. The first is that this procedure had regard or, to use Dworkin's preferred language, "concern," for groups, or for individuals when identified in their primary capacity as members of groups; but secondly, it is important not to make the mistake of regarding every conflict of interest

---

23. Dworkin, *Law's Empire* (Cambridge, Mass., 1986), 297–312. He notes that individual talents are among people's resources, and that these are unequally distributed; this natural inequality demands some effort to compensate the less talented.

24. Lane, "Government and Self-Esteem," 5.

over resource allocations as a conflict involving the problem of respect or esteem. Rival tribes or nations, or ethnic or religious groups may fight for control of the same resources without despising each other (though it is true that in the process of summoning up an efficient degree of antagonism they usually manage a measure of mutual disparagement). It has often been the case in American history that members of disesteemed minorities (the blacks, the Irish, the Chinese, in certain cases the Jews) have been deprived of fair opportunities for employment and have consequently lost grip on the opportunity for earning the respect appropriate to that employment. Where government intervenes to ensure these opportunities, it opens to them the possibility of gaining esteem; and these gains are enjoyed by individuals. In offering a fixed share of the market to specified groups, government may be actuated by this motive. But where firms run by minorities work in the same market, and compete for the same resources, a policy of allocating those resources among the competing groups may well stop short just where the interests of individuals begin to count. The motive, in other and bleaker words, may be more related to the need for keeping some sort of political peace than to securing equal opportunities for individuals. On the other hand, fairer allocations of resources in terms of individual opportunity did appear to yield fairer results in the language of social esteem—a conclusion which confirmed the link between government and sentiment. Government policies had initiated the principle and practice of "fair employment"—which originated with the aim of approximating to the ideal of equality of opportunity. Law, adequately enforced, is one of the strongest educators known to society. And law was increasingly backed by formal education. As late as the closing period of the Second World War, only forty-two percent of white Americans were reported as believing that their black fellow citizens *ought* to be given equal job opportunities; by 1972, this proportion had risen to ninety-five percent. Title VII, the operative clause of the Civil Rights Act of 1964, did not pass through Congress until eighty-five percent of the American public could be shown to favor equal economic opportunity for blacks, while ninety percent favored equal pay for women doing the same work as men. There can be little doubt that the authority of the federal courts had influenced this deep shift of opinion. White attitudes changed too slowly to satisfy black demands, but they nevertheless changed more rapidly than at any previous period. The ancestral myth of Negro

inferiority was also yielding to the evidence of the senses. As late as 1963, the year of Kennedy's death, thirty-nine percent of whites could be found to believe that blacks had inferior natural intelligence; but this figure had dropped to twenty-five percent fifteen years later.[25] White Americans had been convinced, it seemed, by the demonstrated powers of their own latent faith in equality of opportunity, and almost universally agreed (if they did not proclaim) that people of whatever background were entitled to rewards in accord with their deserts.[26]

These changes of view were by their very nature transformations in the *esteem* in which one group held another—and the enhanced esteem in turn yielded enhanced expectations and corresponding improvements in real opportunity. The paradox should not be overlooked. For what this meant was that improvements that operated for the group, and through the group, were the best course to the elevation of the individual, who could not have made these advances on his or her own. Enhancement of group esteem could and obviously did enhance the self-esteem of countless individuals; the political significance of equality of esteem thus emerged as a group phenomenon. This very real social fact created expectations and allegiances from which it would often be difficult to disentangle the individual when the appropriate time for disentanglement had arrived.

James S. Coleman, reflecting on his report on educational inequalities in the South, had reached a conclusion which will now come as no surprise. His commission disclaimed the role of defining equality for

25. Burstein, *Discrimination, Jobs, and Politics: The Struggle for Equal Employment Opportunity in the United States since the New Deal* (Chicago, 1985), 40–41; Edwin Dorn, *Rules and Racial Equality* (New Haven, 1979), 50–54. There is considerably more detail here than has been introduced into the text above. All the evidence points toward a gradual but very marked equalizing of *expectations*. Men and women, with less and less regard to their ethnic backgrounds, were expected to perform according to their own abilities rather than within limits ascribed to those backgrounds. On the other hand, an eruption of what may be styled *geneticism*, taking the form of inferences drawn from performances on I.Q. tests, caused a sharp though (it seems) a short-lived controversy in the late 1960s and early 1970s. I.Q. tests may not be entirely nugatory as evidence of ability (particularly, of course, the ability to do I.Q. tests) but tell little or nothing about the vital factor of motivation. I have not included a discussion of this episode, but there is a full account of it, admittedly hostile, in Philip Green, *The Pursuit of Inequality* (New York, 1981), 38–75.

26. Sidney Verba and Gary R. Orren, *Equality in America: The View from the Top* (Cambridge, Mass., 1985), 82.

policy-making purposes: "Such a definition will be the outcome of the interplay of a variety of interests, and will certainly differ from time to time as these interests differ. It should be our role to cast light on the state of inequality defined in the variety of ways which appear reasonable at this time."[27]

In the course of its prolonged and often turbulent history, the concept of equality had yielded a variety of meanings.[28] Not all of them could even have been found in earlier periods; the ancient world, which gave birth to ideas of moral equality, did not project the claims of the individual on society in terms of rights, yet equality of rights was the key to the thought of the Enlightenment, American as well as European, and was incorporated into American political principles. Equality of opportunity emerged as a rallying cry in an expanding economy. Whether expanding or periodically contracting, that economy could never seriously contemplate a stable system of equal distribution of goods. The idea of "simple" equality as it might apply to a simple and static society, might be the plaything of philosophers or the ideal of moralists but was unlikely to take its place on the agenda of reform.

Fundamental Law and Political Circumstance

It may seem ungrateful, after more than two hundred years which began with the principle of equality perceived as a moral truth given by fundamental law, to conclude that the concept should be considered as a beginning, or a means, rather then an end. Yet this long period, during whose course the idea of equality had been reinterpreted to meet many different needs and contingencies, had yielded the perception that the brand of equality favored in given circumstances would always be the result of social choice. The demands of social morality have been seen to vary with time and circumstance. This conclusion represents a profound transformation from the moral ideas on which the republic was based. When Americans subscribed to the Declaration of Independence,

27. James S. Coleman, "The Concept of Equality of Educational Opportunity," *Harvard Educational Review* 38:1 (Winter 1968), 17.

28. See, in general, Douglas Rae and associates, *Equalities* (Cambridge, Mass., 1981), whose title makes this point. This work, by political scientists, confirmed the historical analysis adopted in *The Pursuit of Equality in American History*, which had appeared three years earlier.

they subscribed by that act to the concept of an equality that was rooted in unalienable and immutable rights; though policies might change, these rights were indestructible, incapable of varying with different societies or periods.

The founders of the republic, whatever their differences, could in general agree about the permanence of the laws of nature; the gifts of God were not thought to be susceptible to either deterioration or improvement. But the inconsistencies and limitations observable in their own practices, where equality and liberty were concerned, did not escape criticism in their own time; and the passage of two centuries has instructed us to view with cautious skepticism the truths revealed in the blinding faith of the Enlightenment.[29] It has been found that the rights that citizens could claim in their own society must at least be mediated to them by the rules and needs of that society rather than received directly from the hand of nature. In an ultimate philosophical sense the source of individual rights might indeed be the same—nature, or in Rawls's modern analogy, the moral imperatives of the "original position." In the earlier periods, however, government had at the most a limited, protective part to play, and the rights in which people were equals were more likely to require protection against government than by it. This situation was entirely reversed when government, often through its judicial branch, became the central agency for deciding what interpretation to place on equality in conflicting cases, and for enforcing their protection through policies constantly supervised and periodically reassessed. Government itself must decide how far it should promote equality of opportunity for individuals or equality through proportional pluralism. Profound differences of social and political philosophy turned on these different views of the contemporary meaning of equality.

Questions of this order were not answerable from criteria of equality alone since they arose, as has been seen, from imperfect or conflicting definitions of equality itself. They could be answered only by turning to the higher concept of equity, or, in more common parlance, fairness. The Supreme Court turned in this direction when it asked whether certain

29. I confess here to a resonance from Gibbon's famous chapter on the causes of the spread of Christianity: "The revolution of seventeen centuries has instructed us not to press too closely the mysterious language of prophecy and revelation." *The Decline and Fall of the Roman Empire*, ch. xv, s. II.

forms of discrimination were rational or arbitrary, whether they would stand the test of objective standards. Fairness belongs to a higher order in ethics than equality, and one way of understanding equality is as a method of applying the mandate of fairness to specific circumstances. But fairness demands that departures from manifest equality be justified by considerations that are not antipathetic to the individualist basis of equality itself. And it is on this basis that inequalities cannot be created or sustained for their own sake, or for the sake of their immediate beneficiaries, but only as part of a consistent ethical system.

Successive renewals of the debate on equality have revealed the movement toward social equality as a movement toward a vision, but with a constantly changing destination. To appear to have arrived at the answer proves to be only to have reached the point at which the problem has changed its character. But that is not the last word. For to recognize this as historical truth is not to admit that the ideals were illusions or that the struggle was fruitless. There is after all only one common destination in human affairs, and that one involuntary.

The United States, through its own proclaimed ideals, became a troubled, but in some ways privileged testing ground for the issue of equality. Its public commitment has conferred a conspicuous and exemplary role of responsibility. This role could no more be disclaimed in the opinions of the modern world than in the opinion of mankind to which the Declaration of Independence was formally addressed. The special character given to the American example by the federal Constitution adds some complexities but in no way diminishes its general significance.

The problems presented by the varieties of equality have been more prominent in America because America's commitment was itself so prominent; but it was without specific reference to the United States that Giovanni Sartori made essentially the same point in observing, "We must now cease to speak of equality in the singular and proceed to deal with equalities in the plural. . . . Just as liberty actually comes down to the struggle to achieve particular liberties, so equality is defined, historically speaking, as the repudiation of certain differences instead of others. And the discourse on equality must bring us to reply to a precise question: What is the specific equality that has precedence in democracy?"[30] But American democracy, which was not only earliest in the

30. Giovanni Sartori, *Democratic Theory* (New York, 1967), 334.

field but most specifically committed to an equality of rights, has never yielded a specific answer to this "precise question." That the answers changed with time and circumstance was one inference at least to be drawn from the first two hundred years of American history.

The idea of fairness draws the guiding principles of political justice back towards the Aristotelian concept of proportion.[31] But that does not mean that Aristotle, or the eighteenth century's concepts of common or natural law, or the language of the American Constitution, or the French Revolution's Declaration of the Rights of Man and Citizen—or, for that matter, the European Community's Charter of Human Rights—can be expected to have the last word on the proportions proper to the needs of a changing society. In the last analysis, the reason why equality eludes a general theory is that, as an end in itself, it ceases to be a unified concept; its various aspects, while they all partake of some of the essential ingredients of a central ideal, cannot all be held in constant and stable balance with each other. But in public life the last analysis is never arrived at, and there is always more to be done than has been achieved.

The first generally agreed rule of equality in the Anglo-Saxon jurisprudence inherited by Americans was equality before the law. The idea that justice required similarity of procedure, however, was never merely a procedural rule. It represented as a principle even of a stratified society that whenever people from different ranks found themselves on common or on neutral ground, as they do when justice is sought among them, the condition of humanity required that the same procedures must apply to all. In short, to give preference to rank or wealth or sex or race or religion could give no guidance in seeking the truth, and it is the essence of justice to seek the truth.

By an extension of this principle, it may be maintained that the principle of equality can never be less than a rule of procedure, a method of assessing the proportions that actually exist, in relation to the proportions that would satisfy so far as is ever humanly possible the combined needs of individual aspirations and social aims. This, however, was the crux of the problem, not its solution. Equality, as we have seen in this study, was capable of being a metaphor, or a synonym for social conditions achieved or aspired to; it was the language men and women used when they wanted to narrow a perceived gap between their own condi-

31. For discussion of Aristotle, see Chapter 1.

tions and those of others who had gained undeserved advantages over them. As such it was the most emotive and powerful metaphor in American political discourse.

But individual aspirations, which have a rightful claim to be protected by society's rules, have not always been in harmony and have sometimes been in conflict with the same society's broad interest in achieving some sort of racial or group balance, to put the problem only in its most familiar terms. The problems posed for American legislators and judges during the years of the incomplete revolution after 1954 dramatized one unavoidably paradoxical demand: that of searching in each instance for a general principle on which to resolve microcosmic cases in a mass society. Equal rules of procedure remain the indispensable point of departure and the essential method. It is possible that they may eventually yield an approximate equality of results throughout the population as a whole. But in the America of the civil rights era, that aspiration rested on a hypothesis, not on a demonstrated syllogism in social science (if such a thing were possible). If a changed society were to result from these procedures, that society would in turn have different requirements, and very possibly a different intuition of the demands of social justice with which to assess those requirements. In previous periods of American history, there had been elements to challenge the prevailing consensus (if it existed) in the hope of creating a new consensus in their own image; whether or not a consensus could be said to exist at any one time, there could be no reason to expect this process to cease.

The policy that pointed towards proportional pluralism, formerly known as equality of results, as the actual determinant of the meaning of equal justice in social, economic and educational policy, represented a substantial departure from earlier methods of assessment, and from the individualist basis of the historic American concept of equality of opportunity. It proposed a new path for a formally protected concept of American pluralism. At the time of the struggle over desegregation in the South, the problem of race absorbed everything else, dramatizing and simplifying the issue into a choice between equality and inequality. The outcome of that struggle left future generations of Americans, in a newly mixed population, to determine their preferences no longer between equality and inequality, but between one concept of equality and another.

The debates which have produced these significant refinements of

meaning have done much to clarify the character of the choices that have had to be made. Such clarifications, of course, cannot determine the outcome of particular cases. The controlling principles adduced from American history and republican government had in the past justified policies which aimed to obtain the substance of results through the application of equal rules. But that was not the last word. To understand this reasoning it is crucially necessary to recognize that in *any* given historical period the distribution of goods, which include education, domestic background, and the evidence of measured intelligence, itself represents a profound inequality of the results of past allocations. For this reason, wherever these conditions have called for a program of action, the primary aim has been to redress a gross inherited imbalance rather than to create an ideal, preconceived plateau of attainments.

Departures from the principle of equal rules could never be constitutionally justified. Departures from equality of conditions might often have been justified and necessary. What the Constitution requires is simply that the burden of justification falls on those who demand such departures. It is not too heavy a burden to place on the Constitution to say that its normal gravitation may be expected to pull in the direction of equalization, where it has the power to act. This burden, however, contains several imperfectly reconciled ingredients, of which the most important is that the Constitution extends its protection equally and impartially to all—to every individual on American soil—in his or her capacity as an independent and irreducible individual. It was the individual whose rights were made the object of the special solicitude of the Constitution, and for whose protection the republic had been called into existence.

Index

Abate v. Mundt (1971), 343n
Abernethy, Thomas P., historian of Tennessee, 139
Abington School District v. Schempp (1963), 122n
Abolitionists: American, 51–52, 103, 157, 187, 190–92, 195–96, 201–2, 391; British, 189; and women's rights, 380–81, 386
Abraham, Henry, on ethnic pluralism, 452
Adams, Abigail, 358, 360, 378
Adams, Charles Francis, reformer, 251, 260
Adams, John: and claims of Baptists, 85–86; *Defence of the Constitutions* by, 43, 163–64; and hereditary privilege, 43, 147, 149; perplexed by Guarantee clause, 64; *Thoughts on Government* by, 34; on women, 360
Adams, Samuel, on religion in Massachusetts, 85
Adamson v. California (1947), 124n
Addams, Jane, 395
African Americans: civil rights legislation and, 203–4, 227–28; Coleman Report on, 457, 471; in debates between Lincoln and Douglas, 174, 176–79; debates on suffrage, 194–95, 204–6, 211, 293,

334–35, 444–45; difficulties faced by, in business competition, 202; equal protection and, 232; equality of esteem and, 293–94, 458–60; increasing knowledge of "primitive" peoples and white attitude to, 290; organized labor and, 257–59; other minorities and, 420; Rush on character of, 187–88; and sexual equality, 353; and *Slaughter House Cases*, 224–27; support Ives-Quinn bill, 322; Tilton on character of, 201–2; Ward and Boas see no natural obstacle to advancement of, 299; white belief in inferiority of, 39, 185–88, 190–92, 194–95, 198–99, 213, 246, 471; women's position compared to that of, 39, 198, 381; World War II and position of, 318. *See also* Race; Segregation; Slavery
Agassiz, Louis, on race, 194–95
Alabama: apportionment in, 342–43; equality of esteem in, 460
Allen, William, chief justice, against writ of assistance, 32
Allen v. State Board of Elections (1969), 444
Allison, Francis, Presbyterian leader, 21
Altgeld, J. P., governor of Illinois, 393

American Association for the Advancement of Science, addressed by Boas, 297

American Economic Association, on unrestricted immigration, 286

American Federation of Labor, and immigration, 286

American Fund for Public Service, aids NAACP, 325

American Liberty League, fights New Deal in courts, 325

American Woman Suffrage Association, 390

Ames, Fisher, Massachusetts Federalist, 153

Amish sect, 128

Anabaptists, name used also for Baptists, 78

Anglicans: Anglo-Saxon racialists, 291, 303; in Virginia, 89–91

Anglo-Saxons: and prevailing value system, 440; supposed superiority of, 391

Anthony, Susan B., leader of women's movement, 387–90, 406

Anthropology: American school of, emerges, 192; cultural, 297–98, 302–3

Anti-Semitism, 295, 305. See also Jews

Apportionment (of electoral districts), 341–45

Aquinas, Thomas, 1, 2n

Aristotle, 6–8, 192, 354n, 383n, 384n, 467n, 475

Arizona, Indians in, 409

Arnold, Thurman, anti-trust campaign, 315

Asbury, Francis, abolitionist, 51

Assimilation of immigrants, 286–88, 301–2, 306, 453; alternatives to (Berkson), 304; (Kallen), 304; groups resistant to, 303, 439; two concepts of, 289

Atkinson, Edward, philanthropist, 260

Awakening, religious. See Great Awakening

Bache, Sarah Franklin, wife of Benjamin Franklin, 359

Backus, Isaac, Baptist spokesman, 78, 82, 84–88

Baker v. Carr (1962), 341–42

Bakke v. Regents of University of California (1978), 409, 413

Baldwin, James, on black self-esteem, 220, 438

Baldwin v. Franks (1887), 234n

Balkans, immigration from (after 1899), 286, 440

Baltimore v. Dawson (1955), 329n

Bank of the United States, opposition to re-charter of, 170–71

Banking, opposition to, 54–57

Baptists: and equality of religious conscience, 69–73, 85, 87–90; and resistance to British policies, 80; Separate Baptists, 78, 80; and taxation, 77–88, 82–86; in Virginia, 29, 88–89, 371

Baruch, Bernard, adviser to Franklin Roosevelt, 314–15

Beecher, Rev. Henry Ward, on social order, 104

Beecher, Rev. Lyman, Evangelist preacher, 101–2

Bellamy, Edward, *Looking Backward* by, 269–71

Benevolence, philosophy of, and theory of equality, 13

Berg, Rev. J. F. of Philadelphia, on the Pope, 105

Berger, V. L., socialist leader, 293

Berkson, Isaac B., social philosophy of, 304

Bible: on position of women, 380, 390, 403; reading of, in schools, 107; on slavery, 192; views derived from, 193

Bill of Rights, 65, 119, 124, 130; change in character of, 204, 347

Biometrics, 297

Black, H. L., justice: dissents in *Adamson v. California*, 124n; in *Japanese-American Case*, 348; and Jefferson's wall, 120; and Maryland Declaration of Rights, 125–26

Black power revivalists, 220, 438–39

Blacks. See African Americans

Blackstone, Sir William, on women and law, 373, 377

Blount, William, in government of Tennessee, 139

Boas, Franz, develops cultural anthropology, 296–99

Bodichon, Barbara, *An American Diary* by, 381, 461, 463

Bodin, Jean, on equality of goods, 154n

Bolling v. Sharpe (1955), 330n

Boston, 40; merchants of, oppose writs of assistance, 29; Unitarians and Universalists in, 76, 80, 168

Boston Female Anti-Slavery Society, 381

Boston Tea Party, 84

Boutwell, George (senator from Massachusetts), on equality, 227

Bowen v. Roy (1986), 128n

Bradley, Joseph P., justice: on civil rights, 235–36, 238, 240, 243, 321, 423; on social assumptions affecting women, 377, 395

Bradwell v. Illinois (1872), 377

Brennan, W. F., justice: and discrimination, 423–24; dissents in *White v. Regester*, 344–45; on religious establishment, 122; on religious liberty, 128

Brewer, David J., justice, on sex differences, 395

Brown, Henry B., justice, in *Plessy v. Ferguson*, 246–47, 250, 252, 377

Brown v. Board of Education (1954), 249n, 307, 325, 327, 330–33, 335, 347, 432, 439, 460

Brownson, Orestes, political views of, 168–69

Bryce, James, *The American Commonwealth* by, 101, 462

Buchanan v. Warley (1917), 320n, 321

Bunche, Ralph, on gradualism, 311

Burger, Warren, chief justice: and Amish, 128; on apportionment, 344; and interventionism, 322–23

Burgh, James, Scottish philosopher, 357

Burns, Robert, quoted, 142n

Bushnell, Horace, on Protestantism and Republicanism, 102, 197n

Byllesby, Langdon, *Observations on Sources and Effects of Unequal Wealth* by, 167

Caldwell v. Texas, 277n

Calhoun, John C., *Disquisition of Government* by, 196–98

California, minorities in universities of, 413

Calvinism, and Declaration of Independence, 36

Calvinists, 71, 74, 83, 103–4

Cannon, James, Philadelphia radical, 27

Capitalism: as American creed, 152, 155, 157–58, 256; collapse of (1929), 312–13; inequalities due to success of, 159, 254; and labor, 262–63; Southern critics of, 196–97; and women, 375

Capitalists, equality of opportunity for, 161, 279

Carey, Henry, 160

Carmichael, Stokeley, 438

Carnegie, Andrew, 265, 462–63

Carpenter, Senator, of Wisconsin, on civil rights, 227

Caste: attempts to create legal system of, 203, 249; class not equivalent to (Cooley), 273; rejection of idea of, 104–5

Catholics, Roman: as Americans, 109; and education, 106–9, 119–20; Irish, 180; parochial schools, 68, 117, 119, 122; question of interchangeability of, 440; and religious pluralism, 70, 99, 102, 106; support Ives-Quinn bill, 322

Catt, Carrie Chapman, leader of woman's movement, 391, 395

Census (1910), 300

Charles River Bridge v. Warren Bridge (1837), 171

Chauncy, Charles, on religious establishments, 86

Chesnutt, Charles Waddell, on equality of esteem amongst blacks, 216–17, 220–21

Chevalier, Michel, on equality, 179

Chicano population of California, 409

Chinese, discrimination against, 235, 301, 325, 442

Chinese Exclusion Act (1882), 301

Chisholm, Shirley, congresswoman, 439

Christianity: assumed to be American national religion, 87, 91, 94, 100, 111, 115, 121, 125; and equality, 10–11, 16–18, 27, 75; and women, 390, 403

262–63; end of flow of, during World War I, 312; and labor, 299–300
Immigration Acts: (1907), 301; (1921), 300; (1924), 301; reformed (1966), 429
Income tax, federal: exemptions for churches, 106; graduated tax advocated by Populists, 265–66; in Republican policy, 314–15; single tax on land rents only, advocated by H. George, 267; systematically extracts higher proportion from poor than from rich, 427; vetoed by Supreme Court (1895), 252, 277
Indians (American), 285, 443; selective legislation for, 128–29; universities and, 409
Individualism: appearance of word in France (1826), 14; as characteristic of American life, xiii; and Declaration of Independence, 1; in early Republic, 148; economic, 252; in prevailing value system, 153, 163, 440; and women, 384–85
Individuality, egalitarian principles based on respect for, 117, 130, 228
Inheritance, proposals to abolish, 169
Intelligence tests, on American soldiers, 292
Interchangeability of individuals, xv, 140–42, 145, 149, 186, 282, 287; not necessary to racial harmony, 201, 302–3; principle of equality assumes, 37; Skidmore and, 166; women and, 368, 387, 406
Internal Revenue Code, extracts higher proportions of tax from the poor, 427
Ireland: Fitzhugh on famine in, 199; immigrants from, 296
Ireton, General, 13
Irreligious conscience, 125–26, 129
Italian immigrants, 286
Ives-Quinn Act, New York State (1945), 322, 350, 408n

Jackson, Andrew, president, 426; America in period of, 3, 50, 54, 158, 165, 169–72, 379, 385; and

doctrine of equal protection, 171–72, 207; economic policy of, 56, 159; and hereditary principle, 43; and public officers, 139–40
Jackson, Jonathan, Constitutionalist pamphleteer, 43, 47
Jackson, Robert, justice: dissents in various cases, 115, 120, 349; on flag salute, 118; on religion in education, 107; on religious beliefs, 124
James I, on patriarchy, 354
Japanese Americans, during World War II, 348–49
Japanese immigrants, 301
Jay, John, first chief justice of Supreme Court, 150
Jefferson, Thomas, 17, 92n, 100, 162, 165, 198; drafts Declaration of Independence, 33–34, 36; and education, 145–46; and Locke, 15–16; *Notes on the State of Virginia* by, 186–88, 341; as president, 96; and racial equality, 186–87, 289; and religious liberty, 89–92, 98, 105, 123; and republican principles, 43; and social equality, 59, 135–36; and "wall of separation" between church and state, 68, 97
Jehovah's Witnesses, object to flag salute, 118
Jews: and cultural separatism, 303; as group in social order, 303–5; hostility to, *see* Anti-Semitism; immigration of, 295; as minority suffering disabilities, 108n, 317–19; segregation of children of, attempted in Detroit, 333; support Ives-Quinn bill, 322
"Jim Crow" segregation, in Mississippi, 245. *See also* Segregation, racial
Johnson, Andrew, president, 203
Johnson, Lyndon B., president: and civil rights, 338, 340, 409–10, 422; distribution of wealth under, 426, 428; movements under administration of, 142, 437
Johnson, Reverdy (senator from Maryland), opposes Fourteenth Amendment, 205–6
Juries: right to sit on, 227, 377; right to trial by, 227–28

Kallen, Horace, exponent of cultural pluralism, 303–5, 451

Kames, Lord, speculates on evolution, 189

Kant, Immanuel, 466

Katzenbach v. Morgan (1966), 422

Kedroff v. St. Nicholas Cathedral (1952), 115n

Kelley, Florence: against Equal Rights Amendment, 395; on heritage of slavery, 391, 393

Kellogg-Briand Pact (1928), 392

Kennedy, John F., president: assassination of, 338; and status of women, 398

Kent, James, chief justice of New York, on Christianity in United States, 100

Kerner, Otto, 448

Keynes, John Maynard (Lord), 316

King, Martin Luther, 409

Kirkpatrick v. Preisler (1969), 344n

Knights of Labor, 262, 268

Korematsu v. United States (1944), 348–49

Kroeber, A. L., sociologist, on racial equality, 302

Kuchel, Thomas, Republican senator, 340, 410

Labor, organized, 167–69, 212, 256, 420–21, 436n; and African Americans, 199, 257–59, 323; concessions to demands of (Massachusetts, 1872), 260; and restrictive practices, 414; in struggle with capital, 257, 262; supports Ives-Quinn bill, 322; and women, 394

Laissez-faire economics, 14, 62, 101, 168, 197, 260–62, 276–77

Lamar, L. Q. C., justice, dissents in case of Mormon church, 114

Lamarck, 290–91

Lamennais, H. R. F. de, on self-respect, 168

Lane, Robert E., on self-esteem, 463–65

Language, attack on assumptions affecting sex and race in, 356; proliferation of, 441; second

language a statutory requirement, 442

Latrobe, Benjamin, on social change (1806), 137

Latter-Day Saints (Late Corporation of Church of Christ of) v. United States (1890), 114n

Lau v. Nichols (1974), 442

Law: common, *see* Common law; natural, *see* Nature, law of

Law, principle of equality before, 171–72, 210, 227, 231–33, 240, 242–44, 247, 310, 326, 347; not for African Americans, 190–91, 250; Calhoun on, 196; erosion of, 204, 209; needs expansion towards equality of opportunity (MacIver), 309; and women, 377

Lee, Ann, Quaker, 371

Leland, John, argues from politics to Pietist religion, 88

Lemon v. Kurtzman (1971), 129

Leonard, Daniel, 40

Levellers, in English Civil Wars, 12, 13

Leviticus, quoted by Douglas, 346, 347n

Liberty: Lincoln on, 53; viewed as feminine quality, 355

Lilburne, John, English Puritan, 12

Lincoln, Abraham, xi, 152, 161, 215, 241; debates between Douglas and, 174, 176–79, 251; and Declaration of Independence, 196; on liberty, 53

Lippman, Walter, *Drift and Mastery* by, 282–83

Lloyd, Henry Demarest, social critic, 264, 269

Lochner v. New York (1905), 252–53, 277, 394

Locke, John, 13–16, 198, 357; *Letter on Toleration* by, 89–90; on Man and Wife, 354; *Second Treatise* by, 41–42, 133

Lodge, Henry Cabot, and immigration, 289

Louisiana: and Catholic parochial schools, 119; monopoly privilege case from, 224; segregation cases from, 230–31, 245

Louisiana, New Orleans and Texas Railroad Corp. v. Mississipi (1890), 233n

analogous to, 198, 381. *See also* Abolitionists

Slavs, as immigrants, 296

Smith, Adam, 133–34, 153; attacked by Fitzhugh, 198

Smith, Howard (congressman from Virginia), and women's rights, 399

Smith, Samuel Harrison, social publicist, 148, 166, 187–88; on education of women, 363

Smith v. Allwright (1944), 335

Socialism: and racial equality, 293; rejected by National Colored Labor Convention (1869), 259; Spargo on, 281

Society of Friends. *See* Quakers

Sophists, on equality of men in sharing faculty of reason, 6

South, of United States: all-white primaries in, 334; apportionment in, 341–45; Calhoun speaks to and for, 196–98; confiscation of rebel estates in, 256; Fitzhugh on "superior civilization" of, 196; Negro population shifts away from, 312; Negro suffrage in, 204; school finance in, 292, 307; school standards in, 457; segregation in, 203, 247, 250; "separate but equal" in, 203; trades unions in, 258

South Carolina: application of Voting Rights Act in, 340, 422; school segregation crises in, 327; Writs of Assistance in, 29

Southgate, Eliza, early feminist, 381–82

Southern Non-Violent Coordinating Committee, 398

Spargo, John, socialist, 273, 275, 281–82

Stamp Act (Britain, 1765), 28

Stanton, Elizabeth Cady, leader of women's movement, 386, 387–91, 395; on qualified suffrage, 391

State, and church. *See* Church and state

Stephens, Alexander H., vice-president of Confederate States, on racial inequality, 199–200

Stevens, Thaddeus, of Pennsylvania: on Negro suffrage, 207; social and economic views of, 256–57

Stewart, Dugald, Scottish school of morals, 134

Stimson, Henry, economist, 315

Stoics, and equality, 7

Stone, H. F., chief justice, dissents in *Cantwell v. Connecticut*, 124

Stone, Lucy, founds American Women Suffrage Association, 390

Stone v. Farmers' Loan and Trust Company (1886), 277n

Story, Joseph, justice, cited on congressional powers, 239

Strauder v. West Virginia (1880), 237n

Suffrage, 257, 333, 341, 444; African American, 204–6, 212–13; under Fifteenth Amendment, 334; under Fourteenth Amendment, 205, 334; qualifications for (property) 44, 47, 151, 168, 391; tests for, 249. *See also* Women's suffrage

Sugar Trust, investigated by Senate, 264

Sullivan, James, Massachusetts politician, 153

Sumner, Charles, radical leader: favors unregulated competition, 256; on Guarantee Clause, 64; and racial equality, 211

Sumner, W. G., sociologist, satisfied with unlimited competition, 260, 272

Supreme Court of United States: and all-white primaries, 334; and apportionment, 344, 454; in Chinese laundry cases, 235, 325; and civil rights, 241, 423; and Comity Clause, 239–40; in *Dred Scott* case, 181–83; and equality before the law, 227, 240, 243–44, 404; and equality of opportunity, 247, 277; and federal income tax, 252; and Fifth Amendment, 204; and flag salute, 117; and Fourteenth Amendment, 221–24, 235, 237, 241, 246, 308, 319–20, 330; and Guarantee Clause, 64; in *Japanese-American Cases*, 348–49; jurisdiction of, extends over church organization but not doctrine, 114; and law school segregation, 326–27; and Mormons, 114; and political representation, 444; and

Wilson, James, Philadelphia lawyer, on political representation, 163

Wilson, Woodrow, president: and American nationality, 287; committed to reform, 299; quoted by Lippman, 282–83; and women's suffrage, 391

Winthrop, John: on separation of church and state, 71; on social order, 74

Wisconsin school of Progressives, 287, 295

Wisconsin v. Yoder (1972), 128n

Wollstonecraft, Mary, *Vindication of the Rights of Women* by, 363–65

Woman's Party, 392

Woman's Rights Convention, Seneca Falls (1848), 386

Women: Aristotle on, 354n; assumed inferiority of, 39, 352, 395; assumed personality traits of, 352, 378, 406; dress of, 356; in economic system, 394–97; education of, 362–63, 365; and equality of esteem, 359, 364, 383–84; and Equal Rights Amendment, 401–5; and the law, 373–74; and linguistic usage, 356; literacy among, 359, 366; and property, 367, 373–74, 376, 378, 399; regarded as men's equals by Quakers, 360, 371; rights of, 37, 177n, 212; role to instruct children, 362; social and psychological difficulties of, 397–98; suffrage for, *see* Women's suffrage; and trade unions, 259; and war, 359

Women's Bible, The, feminist satire, 390

Women's suffrage: abolished in Utah, 113; adoption of, 392–93, 400; early claims to, 212, 259; female opposition to, 396, 388; movement for, 388, 390–91, 395; permitted in New Jersey (1776), 360–61, 379; World War I causes adoption of, 392

Working men's movement, of Jacksonian era, 166–67

World Anti-Slavery Convention (1840), treatment of women wishing to attend, 386

World War I: and army intelligence tests, 292; industrial demands of, 283; and women's rights, 392

World War II: and economic revival, 316; Japanese-Americans during, 348; and racial prejudice, 317, 321, 336; and religious pluralism, 70; and social reform, 5, 318, 435; and women's movement, xv, 396

Wright, Frances, social thinker, 156; in public life, 379

Writs of Assistance: issued by Massachusetts Superior Court, 29–30; in South Carolina, 29

Yick Wo v. Hopkins (1886), 235n, 326n

Zangwill, Israel: on melting pot, 278; popularity of *The Melting Pot* by, 303

Zorach v. Clauson (1952), 121n

Design:	Al Burkhardt
Composition:	Com-Com
Text:	10/13 Palatino
Display:	Palatino
Printer and Binder:	Haddon Craftsmen, Inc.

The Pursuit of Equality
in American History